The New Immigration

The New Immigration

An Interdisciplinary Reader

Edited by

Marcelo M. Suárez-Orozco,
Carola Suárez-Orozco, and
Desirée Baolian Qin

Routledge New York and London

Published in 2005 by
Brunner-Routledge
Taylor & Francis Group
270 Madison Avenue
New York, NY 10016

Published in Great Britain by
Brunner-Routledge
Taylor & Francis Group
27 Church Road
Hove, East Sussex BN3 2FA

Printed in the United States of America on acid-free paper
10 9 8 7 6 5 4 3 2 1

International Standard Book Number-10: 0-415-94916-5 (Softcover)
International Standard Book Number-13: 978-0-0000-0000-0 (Softcover)

Library of Congress Cataloging-In-Publication data:

The new immigration : an interdisciplinary reader/edited by Marcelo Suárez-Orozco, Carola Suárez-Orozco, and Desirée Baolian Qin.
p. cm.
Includes bibliographical references and index.
ISBN 0-415-94915-7 (hb : alk. paper)—ISBN 0-415-94916-5 (pb : alk. paper)
1. Immigrants—United States. 2. United States—Emigration and immigration. I. Suárez-Orozco, Marcelo M., 1956- II. Suárez-Orozco, Carola, 1957- III. Qin-Hilliard, Desirée.
JV6465.N49 2004
304.8'73—dc22 2004015921

Taylor & Francis Group
is the Academic Division of T&F Informa plc.

Visit the Taylor & Francis Web site at
http://www.taylorandfrancis.com

and the routledge Web site at
http://www.routledge-ny.com

For John U. Ogbu and Henry T. Trueba
In Memoriam

Contents

Introduction

The New Immigration: Interdisciplinary Perspectives[1]

MARCELO M. SUÁREZ-OROZCO, CAROLA SUÁREZ-OROZCO, AND DESIRÉE BAOLIAN QIN

At the turn of the millennium, the United States had the largest number of immigrants in its history. As a consequence, immigration has emerged once again as a subject of scholarly inquiry and policy debates. This volume brings together the dominant conceptual and theoretical work on the "New Immigration" from such disparate disciplines as anthropology, demography, psychology, and sociology. Immigration today is a global and transnational phenomenon that affects every region of the world with unprecedented force. Although this volume is devoted to scholarly work on the new immigration in the U.S. setting, many of the broader conceptual issues covered here also apply to other postindustrial countries such as France, Germany, and Japan.

Immigration in the United States is both history and destiny. The current wave of immigration has many similarities to the transoceanic experiences of large-scale immigration of one hundred years ago, and, yet, several significant features seem to distinguish it as unique to the present era. Prior to 1965, immigration to the United States was an overwhelmingly European phenomenon, with countries such as Germany, the United Kingdom, and Ireland leading the way. Today's immigrants are a highly diverse population originating in such varied settings as Latin America, Asia, and the Caribbean. Majorities of new immigrants who are phenotypically not white are subject to a process of racialization that transforms them in the new context from immigrant outsiders to "people of color." In the aftermath of the great struggles of the civil rights movement, race, color, and ethnicity continue to be essential to social processes shaping the opportunities and life experiences of these new arrivals.

In earlier eras, immigration was structured in time-delineated, discrete, and bounded waves. There was a clear beginning and end date to the various European migrations to the United States. The current pattern of U.S. immigration, which had begun to intensify in 1965 and gained extraordinary momentum in the last two decades, can best be characterized as an ongoing flow that ever replenishes the immigrant stock of the nation. This flow seems to be the consequence of several distinct factors. First, the postindustrial economy has developed a voracious appetite for immigrant workers. Also, under the 1965 Hart-Cellar Immigration Act, family reunification has become a powerful force that generates and strengthens immigrant chains, as those left behind are given the opportunity to join relatives and loved ones living in the United States. Further, a host of social formations—including the ease of mass transportation, instant access to information about job opportunities, and the dream for a better standard of living—have made migration an increasingly attractive option for many. Armed conflicts, ethnic and religious tensions, and political repression are also significantly implicated in population displacements—witness the million-plus Southeast Asians and million-plus Central Americans now living in the United States.

Globalization is yet another basic characteristic separating the new immigration from the old. In Chapter 1, Marcelo M. Suárez-Orozco presents a conceptual framework for the study of immigration in the context of global changes in economy, society, and culture. He claims that globalization is the general backdrop for any understanding of the new immigration. At the turn of the millennium there were an estimated 175 million translational immigrants and refugees worldwide.

Earlier waves of immigration took place in the context of nation-building efforts where immigrant workers, consumers, and would-be citizens played a significant role. Immigration today is at the heart of globalization. The three main pillars of globalization include post-national economies, new information and communication technologies that instantaneously connect peoples across vast spaces, and large-scale immigration. These three phenomena, though discrete, are intertwined. The globalization of capital and the increasingly internationalized production of goods and services are predicated on new communication technologies, and on capital's ability to mobilize human labor with stunning speed and force.

Over the course of the last century, immigration to the United States has become thoroughly dominated by the Latin American experience. More than half of all immigrants originate in Latin America, the vast majority from Mexico. Nearly a third of the foreign-born population in the United States today is of Mexican origin. Debates over Mexican immigration to the United States have sharply focused on policy considerations, including undocumented immigration, border controls, and the causes and consequences of large-scale immigration to the United States. In Chapter 2, Massey, Duran, and Malone examine recent policies aimed to control Mexican immigration to the United States. They point out that "American attempts to raise the costs and lower the benefits of living and working in the United States have had little effect on the likelihood of undocumented migration, on increasing the odds of migrants returning home, on decreasing the odds of unauthorized employments, or on reducing the probability that migrants will undertake a successful border crossing." The unanticipated consequences and indeed the general failure of these recent policies stem from an erroneous and simpleminded conceptualization of the forces and dynamics that structure migratory flows today. This chapter offers a sober reflection on the complex economic, political, and social calculus that need to be a part of any effective binational migration management initiative.

Large-scale immigration generates important societal transformations. As Harvard historian John Coatsworth recently noted, today in the United States we eat differently, dress differently, dance differently, and talk differently because of immigration. In this volume, we examine both how new immigrants are reshaping American society and how they are being transformed by the forces that they encounter in the new setting. In Chapter 3, Alba and Nee examine the idea of assimilation and trace the history of this classic sociological concept to earlier patterns of large-scale immigration from Europe to the United States. They find that the main tenets of assimilation theory emerging from the earlier work on European immigration remain quite viable to explain the adaptations of the new wave of post-1965 immigrants. They focus on the evidence regarding the socioeconomic and residential assimilation of recent immigrant groups. They claim these and other data are quite consistent with the predictions of assimilation theory, "albeit unevenly."

In Chapter 4, Marcelo M. Suárez-Orozco is somewhat more skeptical of the application of earlier assimilation thinking to explain the emerging adaptations among new immigrants. A number of recent studies suggest that the tenets of straight-line assimilation—the notion that all groups undergo a single path of assimilation into American society—need reexamination. He explores three assumptions that compose the essence of earlier thinking on assimilation: the "clean break," the "homogeneity," and the "progress" assumption. He argues that rather than following the slow but steady transgenerational progress over time predicted by straight-line assimilation, many immigrants today seem to be moving into the well-remunerated sector of the U.S. economy at an unprecedented rate or finding themselves locked into highly segregated, deep-poverty social spaces that hold no promise for social mobility. This suggests that instead of following a single path, immigration today reveals a highly dimorphic pattern in which some immigrants thrive (nearly 40 percent of all businesses in California's famed Silicon Valley are immigrant-owned) and others struggle to survive.

In Chapter 5, Portes and Zhou wisely suggest that theories of immigrant assimilation ought to be tested against the long-term fortunes of the children of immigrants, not of the immigrants themselves. They have articulated the most coherent and thorough alternative to straight-line assimilation theory. Their influential work on "segmented assimilation" suggests that there are diverse possible outcomes in the trajectories followed by various immigrant groups. Immigrants' modes of incorporation are mediated by the various resources and vulnerabilities they bring with them as well as by the context of reception they encounter in the host society. Although some immigrants are indeed replicating earlier patterns of immigrant assimilation, others are undergoing very different pathways of adaptation.

Immigration deeply affects the family. Family roles need to be renegotiated, and new scripts concerning gender relations, child rearing, values, and social attitudes come to the fore. In the next section of this volume, we examine from a variety of disciplinary perspectives—anthropological, sociological, psychological—the impact of immigration on the family. In Chapter 6, Garcia-Coll and Magnuson provide a comprehensive overview of basic scholarship on the impact of immigration on child development. They rightly emphasize that much of the research has focused on the negative aspects of immigration and argue for a more balanced research agenda that would also consider its benefits. They underscore the importance of understanding how developmental stages mediate adjustment.

In Chapter 7, psychologist Carola Suárez-Orozco examines how the stresses of immigration influence identity development. She focuses on the impact of immigration on children with a particular emphasis on the stresses induced by psychological violence and exclusionary practices directed towards many immigrants and their children. She develops the concept of "social mirroring" to examine how hostility towards immigrants influence identity formation among immigrant youth.

Anthropologist Nancy Foner, in Chapter 8, explores changes in family and kinship patterns as a function of immigration. She examines the plasticity of immigrant families and kinship patterns. As families synthesize old and new roles, they create fresh forms of family life and new kinship relations. As a result, gender relations often shift in significant ways. In Chapter 9, sociologist Hondagneu-Sotelo approaches the topic of immigrant families in a gendered and transnational framework. She discusses how the emergence of a new pattern of social reproduction—the activities that are necessary to maintain human life, daily, and intergenerationally—has led to a voracious appetite for immigrant domestic workers in Southern California and beyond. Drawn to plentiful work as live-in domestics, housekeepers, and child-care workers, these new "braceras" are forced to leave behind their own children and other family members. Hondagneu-Sotelo estimates that between 40–50 percent of Mexican and Central American immigrant women in her survey left their children behind in their countries of origin. She claims that these transnational family forms have brought about new meanings in family and motherhood. Hondagneu-Sotelo also observes that after mothers are reunited with their children, generational conflict tends to be prominent in the family.

Family reunification is at the heart of the new immigration. Since 1965, in the United States, family reunification has been a fundamental principle behind immigration policy. Ironically, immigrant families often undergo extended periods of separation between loved ones—not only from extended family members, but also from the nuclear family. In Chapter 10, Suárez-Orozco, Todorova, and Louie study of adolescents originating from China, Central America, the Dominican Republic, Haiti, and Mexico reveal that fully 85 percent of the participants had been separated from one or both parents for extended periods. While family separations are common to all country of origin groups, there are clear between-group differences in lengths of separations as well as from whom the youth are separated. They conclude with a discussion of attenuating and complicating factors in immigrant family adjustment.

In Chapters 11 and 12, psychologists Celia Jaes Falicov and Ricardo Ainslie integrate concepts from family systems and psychoanalytic theories, as well as race and ethnicity, and acculturation theories to explore the psychosocial processes of family upheaval and change over time and across generations. Jaes Falicov argues that ambiguous losses of languages, loved ones, and native culture and rituals create unique challenges to immigrant families, often resulting in "incomplete, postponed, [and] ambiguous" mourning that reverberates across generations. Ainslie extends the notion of mourning to the realm of chronic longing for "familiar" cultural rituals. He argues that in dealing with cultural mourning, immigrants have created "transitional areas of experiencing," using linking objects and processes to help sustain the sense of connection to the world left behind.

For immigrant youth today, after the family, school is the single most important institution in their lives. School functioning is a powerful indicator of children's ongoing and future well-being. This is even more the case for immigrant children, as schools are their primary point of contact with the mainstream society. Among immigrant youth learning English the process of language acquisition plays a significant role in mediating school outcomes. English-language learning is indeed at the heart of the immigrant experience in the United States. Immigrants today are more likely than ever before to arrive in this country speaking a number of extraordinarily diverse languages. In New York City alone, more than 100 different languages are represented in the student body. Language signifies identity and social relations. It is structured by power relations. It is not surprising, therefore, that language matters are central to many debates over immigration, especially in the United States. Although some see immigrant languages as a resource that adds to the total cultural stock of the nation, others see linguistic diversity as a threat to unity and as a source of potential Balkanization and further ethnic divisions. The next four chapters focus on language and the immigrant with a special emphasis on the issues facing immigrant children.

In Chapter 13, educational researcher Patricia Gándara reviews the politics and policies governing the education of English learners in California. She examines both the short-term and likely long-term impacts of the various recent battles over the education of immigrant students with limited English proficiency. Gándara argues that Proposition 227, which dismantled bilingual education, has significantly affected the schooling experiences of immigrant children receiving instruction from bilingual teachers. Gándara cites sobering evidence suggesting that in the aftermath of the new proposition, gaps between native-English speakers and English learners remain significant. Rather than continue to focus narrowly on efforts that seem to feed politicized interventions, Gándara argues that a new research and policy agenda ought to consider multilingualism as a possible and positive outcome for all English learners.

In Chapter 14, eminent linguistic psychologist Kenji Hakuta and his colleague Diane August provide an overview of research findings on bilingualism and second-language learning. The authors observe that much of the early research in this area suggested that bilingualism would lead to negative cognitive outcomes in children. These earlier studies largely have been discredited because of poorly selected samples and the failure to control for socioeconomic status. The authors argue that once proper controls are put into effect, the data suggest a different and more positive story. More recent studies have found a positive relationship between bilingualism and a host of cognitive outcomes. The authors also highlight the importance of examining individual differences such as age, intelligence, social attitudes, and personality traits in the development of bilingualism and second-language learning. Finally, August and Hakuta remind us of the importance of the social environment in the linguistic settings that serve as the primary base for second-language acquisition: schools.

How does bilingualism affect academic outcomes? In Chapter 15, Ann C. Willig conducts a meta-analysis of a number of studies examining the efficacy of bilingual education. She asserts that when strict statistical controls are employed for socioeconomic background, the preponderance of evidence demonstrates that participation in bilingual education programs consistently produce small to moderate differences. Students enrolled in bilingual education programs tended to perform slightly better than their counterparts in non-bilingual classes on tests of reading, language skills, mathematics, and total achievement.

In Chapter 16, Lily Wong Fillmore discusses findings from a nationwide study of language shift among language-minority children. Immigrant and other families were surveyed to determine the extent to which family language patterns were affected by their children's early learning of English in preschool programs. Wong Fillmore compares children who had attended English and bilingual preschools. She finds that immigrant children lose their primary languages as they learn English and that this effect is greater for children who start learning English at a younger age. Wong Fillmore points out that there is a cost to be paid in this pattern of language shift, particularly in how it affects parental authority and familial intimacy. She also points to the potential negative cognitive and educational consequences of primary-language loss.

Alejandro Portes has contributed much to our theoretical understanding of the sociology of immigration and the role of schooling in immigrant mobility. In Chapter 17, Portes and MacLeod examine the findings of a bicoastal survey of more than 5,000 second-generation students attending high schools in California and Florida. Their highly diverse sample includes second-generation youth of Cuban, Vietnamese, Haitian, and Mexican origin. Perhaps not surprisingly, their data suggest that parental socioeconomic status and education, length of residence in the United States, and the number of hours children spend doing homework are significantly related to their academic performance. More surprising however, is the finding that national background plays a significant independent role in the schooling adaptation and outcomes of today's immigrant youth. For example, controlling for all other factors, Vietnamese-origin children tend to do better than Mexican-origin children in a variety of schooling-adaptation indicators.

In Chapter 18, sociologists Grace Kao and Marta Tienda analyze data from the 1988 National Educational Longitudinal Study to explore the role of generational status on three indicators of educational achievement: grades, test scores, and college aspirations among eighth graders. They identify a pattern of immigrant optimism about the future and about schooling opportunities open to children in the new land. Yet, because the foreign-born youth are disadvantaged by their limited English skills, they argue that the second-generation U.S.-born children of immigrant parents are most likely to maximize the opportunities afforded to them by the new society.

In Chapter 19, Carola Suárez-Orozco and Desirée Baolian Qin examine gender dynamics in the experiences of schooling among immigrant youth with a particular focus on the immigrant boy experience in school contexts. They examine the similarities and differences in schooling experiences for boys and girls. Findings from this study suggest that immigrant boys tend to perform more poorly academically than do their female counterparts. In the chapter, Suárez-Orozco and Desirée Baolian Qin discuss potential contributing factors such as network of relations, negative "social mirroring," perceived racism, peer pressures, academic identities, and parental controls.

This volume examines the new immigration in interdisciplinary and comparative perspective. Taken together, these articles and chapters represent the most influential and, in many cases, original scholarship on the new immigration. In selecting the individual contributions, we privileged articles that influenced a domain by generating debate and further scholarship. Rather than gloss over controversies, disagreements, and contradictory findings, we have chosen to include a range of perspectives. The perceptive reader will be able to tease out the various heated controversies as well as areas of consensus and analytic convergence.

The research for this volume was made possible by generous grants from the National Science Foundation, W. T. Grant Foundation, the Spencer Foundation, and the Ross Institute. We thank Robin Harutunian for her expert editorial suggestions.

PART I

Conceptual and Theoretical Considerations

Chapter 1

Right Moves? Immigration, Globalization, Utopia, and Dystopia

MARCELO M. SUÁREZ-OROZCO

Over the past decade, globalization has intensified worldwide economic, social, and cultural transformations. Globalization is structured by three powerful, interrelated formations: (1) the postnationalization of production and distribution of goods and services, fueled by growing levels of international trade, foreign direct investment, and capital market flows; (2) the emergence of new information and communication technologies that place a premium on knowledge-intensive work; and (3) unprecedented levels of worldwide migration that generate significant demographic and cultural changes in most regions of the world.

Globalization's puzzle is that although many applaud it as the royal road for development (for example, Friedman 2000; Micklethwait and Wooldrige 2000; Rubin 2002), it is generating strong currents of discontent. In large regions of the world, globalization has become a deeply disorienting and threatening process of change (Bauman 1998; Soros 2002; Stiglitz 2002). Globalization has generated the most hostilities where it has placed local cultural identities—including local meaning systems, religious identities, and systems of livelihood—under siege. Argentina is a case in point. After a decade of cutting-edge free-market policies, the economy of the country that was once the darling of such embodiments of globalization as the International Monetary Fund and World Bank imploded. At the beginning of the twentieth century, Argentina was one of the ten wealthiest countries in the world, yet it ended the century in default, with more than 40 percent of the population at poverty level. By early 2003, an estimated 50,000 *cartoneros* were living off the cartons they gathered every night from trash cans in Buenos Aires, one of the world's most elegant cities.

First and foremost, globalization is about movement. Its emerging regime—mobile capital, mobile production and distribution, mobile populations, and mobile cultures—is generating deep paradoxes. Regions of the world such as East Asia seem to have prospered immensely under globalization's regime (see Table 1, World Bank 2001). Yet, in the Argentinas of the world, the forces of globalization have conspired to intensify patterns of inequality and human suffering (Dussel 2000; Mittelman 2000; Nader 1993). The last decade of the twentieth century witnessed vast economic growth in the rich nations, especially the United States, but roughly 25 percent of the population of the developing world continued to live in desperate poverty, on less than a dollar a day (see Table 1.1).

TABLE 1.1 Population Living below US$1 per Day in Developing Countries 1990 and 1998

	Number of People below US $1 a Day (Millions)		Poverty Rate (%)	
	1990	1998 (Estimate)	1990	1998 (Estimate)
East Asia	452.4	278.3	27.6	15.3
Excluding China	92.0	65.1	18.5	11.3
South Asia	495.1	522.0	44.0	40.0
Sub-Saharan Africa	242.3	290.9	47.7	46.3
Latin America	73.8	78.2	16.8	15.6
Middle East/North Africa	5.7	5.5	2.4	1.9
Europe and Central Asia	7.1	24.0	1.6	5.1
Total	1276.4	1198.9	29.0	24.0

Source: World Bank, Global Economic Prospects and the Developing Countries 2000.

China's meteoric integration into the global economy has significantly reduced poverty, but, as in much of Latin America, globalization has also increased inequality (World Bank 2001:1).

There is a strong and somewhat amorphous, eclectic anti-globalization ethos, ubiquitously named, articulated, and performed in varied contexts, from Seattle to Genoa and Buenos Aires. Its message seems structured by a common grammar: The global project is destabilizing, disorienting, and threatening to large numbers of people the world over.

Yet, even though many hate what they see in globalization, others are seduced by its promise. Here is another paradox of globalization: As it continues to penetrate the local, cultural imaginaries of poor, developing countries, even if it destabilizes local economies and livelihoods, globalization generates structures of desire and consumption fantasies that local economies cannot fulfill. These twin factors, globalization's uneven effects on the world economy and the emergence of a global imaginary of consumption, are behind the largest wave of immigration in human history. Globalization's paradoxical power lies in its manufacture of both despair and hope. Millions of people, though, must realize their hope elsewhere, as migrants.

Globalization's discontent also visits the "other half": the wealthy, advanced, postindustrial democracies, which have, arguably, benefited the most under its reign. In the advanced, postindustrial democracies, the unprecedented, growing, and seemingly uncontainable migratory flows generated by globalization over the past decade are, alas, experienced as threatening and disorienting to local cultural identities and sensibilities. This is the case in most of western Europe, the United States, and Australia, where anti-immigrant sentiment and xenophobia have emerged as potentially explosive political and social concerns. The general move to the political right in Europe over the past few years can be linked to the fears and anxieties generated by globalization, immigration, and crime. Somewhat monomaniacal, anti-immigrant parties in western Europe have gained momentum over the past decade: the Vlams Bloc in Belgium, the Freedom Party in Austria, the People's Party in Denmark, and, in May 2002, the Front National in France. Voters in California overwhelmingly approved Proposition 187, a new law that denies illegal immigrants a host of publicly funded services, which includes schooling for children. In mid-2001, Australia denied a ship in distress, carrying hundreds of asylum seekers, entry to its ports. To paraphrase Tolstoy, globalization is making all the families of the world unhappy in the same way.

In this chapter, I examine certain anthropological concerns related to large-scale immigration and the flow of labor within the paradigm of globalization—a paradigm that will continue to attract the attention of anthropologists and allied social scientists in the decades to come (Inda and Rosaldo 2002b; Suárez-Orozco, Suárez-Orozco, and Desirée Baolian Qin 2003). First, I explore the parameters of the phenomena called "globalization." Next, I turn to the topic of large-scale immigration and examine recent scholarly debates in a variety of social science disciplines, including (but not limited to) cultural anthropology. Last, I examine several cultural processes of change facing those who pursue their fortunes beyond their national boundaries—the area ripest for important anthropological theoretical and empirical work in the future.

GLOBAL ANXIETIES

The study of globalization is generating considerable academic interest in a variety of disciplines, including anthropology, economics, sociology, political science, law, and education—for example, Appadurai 1996; Bauman 1998; Baylis and Smith 1997; Castles and Davidson 2000; Giddens 2000; Hardt and Negri 2000; Inda and Rosaldo 2002b; Jameson and Miyoshi 1999; King 1997; Lechner and Boli 1999; O'Meara, Mehlinger, and Krain 2000; Sassen 1998.

The term *globalization* in its current usage is quite broad and lacks well-defined epistemological, theoretical, and empirical boundaries. Even though the idea of globalization has gained increased circulation in the social sciences and is pregnant with potential—especially for theorizing broad processes of social change, from Detroit to Delhi—we cannot fully mine its analytic use until we attend to basic definitional and theoretical matters. Anthropologists, for example, tend to approach the problem of globalization in relation to their long-term interest in social organization and culture. Globalization detaches social practices and cultural formations from their traditional moorings in bounded (often national) territories. Globalization decisively undermines the once-imagined neat fit of language, culture, and nation. One hundred years ago, European and Euro-American anthropologists took long journeys to remote locations to study exotic social institutions and cultural beliefs. Globalization now delivers the "exotic" to the anthropologist's own backyard. In plain sight, Turkish cultural formations—language, marriage, kinship, ritual practices—are as ubiquitous in parts of Frankfurt as they are in Istanbul. Likewise, Mexican culture is now thriving in New York City, while New York culture is alive in Puebla, Mexico, via the cash and social remittances—that is, the social practices and cultural models immigrants acquire in the new setting and send back home (Levitt 2001a). Hence, we have witnessed over the past decade the emergence of an anthropological taste for topics such as immigration (Chavez 1992; Foner 2000, 2001e and f; Pessar 1995b; Roosens 1989), transnationalism (Basch, Glick Schiller, and Szanton Blanc 1994; Gupta and Ferguson 1992; Mahler 1995a), cultural hybrids (Canclini 1995), delicious dualities (Zentella 2002), and unsettling cultural conflicts (Shweder 2000; Wikan 2000), all brought about by globalization.

Anthropological involvement with the study of cultural forms and dispersal across time and space has a long history. Much of the early literature privileged the study of "culture contact" and "cultural borrowing" via trading, migrations, invasions, or conquest. Franz Boas's (1911b and 1940) early efforts, which resulted in the firm establishment of American anthropology as a major scholarly discipline in the early decades of the twentieth century, centered on theoretical debates over the "diffusion" (versus "multiple invention") of cultural forms (such as a fishing hook, folktale motif, or kinship term) across distinct culture areas. This work was critical to the dismantling of earlier extravagant and racist theories of stages in the cultural evolution of societies. Today, few anthropologists focus their theoretical or empirical work on culture areas or patterns of cultural diffusion per se. However, there is a strong genealogical line of continuity of anthropological concerns with the movement of people, cultural facts, and artifacts over time.

Political theorists, including political anthropologists, are focusing on the emergence of international systems, such as human and civil rights, reaching beyond the confines of individual nation-states. An Argentine torturer accused of committing crimes against humanity in his own country can now be arrested in Mexico and tried in Spain, as happened in February 2001 (Robben n.d.). Political theorists have also begun to examine how new de-territorializing processes shape the course of political fortunes in many parts of the world. Peoples in diaspora—Mexicans in Los Angeles and Dominicans in New York, for example—are emerging as powerful agents across national boundaries. Dual-citizenship agreements—the ability to maintain citizenship rights in more than one nation-state—are complicating the politics of belonging and making them more interesting (Castles and Davidson 2000).

Dominican politicos, for instance, have long been cognizant that election campaigns in their country need to be waged as much in New York, where Dominicans are now the largest immigrant group, as in Santo Domingo. Mexican politicians are now joining the new global game. In late December 2000, newly elected President Vicente Fox spent a day at Mexico's busy northern border personally welcoming some of the 1.5 million immigrants returning home for Christmas—as well as performing and telecasting a new strategic approach to paisanos living in the U.S. Under the Fox administration, the more than eight million Mexican citizens living in the U.S. are no longer an afterthought (or an embarrassment) to Mexican national pride. Likewise, the Salvadorian political leadership carefully takes into consideration the needs and voices of the Salvadorian diaspora in the United States. As a rough formula, a million people in the diaspora translates to nearly a billion-dollars in remittances sent home every year. This might help explain the newfound interest among Salvadorian and Mexican politicians in cultivating ties with their brothers and sisters living in the United States. The old adage "all politics is local" is now anachronistic.

For the purposes of this chapter, I define *globalization* as processes of change simultaneously generating centrifugal (as the territory of the nation-state) and centripetal (as supranational nodes) forces that result in the deterritorialization of basic economic, social, and cultural practices from their traditional moorings in the nation-state. Because globalization involves a kind of "post-geography" (Bauman 1998), mapping it is futile. Different regions of the world are, at once, implicated in multiple, overlapping globalization processes. Although *globalization*, by definition, refers to economic, social, and cultural processes that are postnational, I do not mean to suggest that it augurs the demise of the state apparatus. It is, I think, subtler than that.

Nation-states seem to respond to processes of globalization by displaying new forms of hyper-presence and hyper-absence. Globalization challenges the workings of the nation-state in various ways, from undermining national economies to making anachronistic traditional ideas of citizenship and of cultural production (Castles and Davidson 2000; Sassen 1998). In important ways, states appear hyper-absent qua the forces of globalization, for example, when billions of dollars enter and exit national boundaries with the apparatus of the state having little say over the course of these flows. On the other hand, states are responding to globalization by hyper-displays and performances of power. Arguably one of the most globalized spots in the world today and, alas, one of the most heavily trafficked international borders in the world is the vast region that both unites and separates the United States and Mexico. It is also one of the most heavily guarded borders in history (Andreas 2000). The militarization of the border at a time of record border crossings suggests a process more complex than the simple erosion or demise of the nation-state. In the places that matter, where states bump into each other, hyper-presence seems to be in full force. This is the case in post-September 11 United States, in post-Schengen Europe, and in Japan. (Per the Schengen agreement, there are no longer internal border controls among European Union member states. Hence, a French citizen needs no passport or visa to travel to Spain, and vice-versa.) Even though, internally, Europe has become borderless, external controls—that is, keeping would-be migrants from outside Europe—have intensified (Andreas and Snyder 2000). To claim that the state is waning is to miss one of the more delicious paradoxes of state performance.

What, if anything, is new about globalization? Is globalization simply modernization on steroids? Is it Westernization in fast-forward? Is it imperialism now driven by the extraordinarily high octane of American hyper-power? Alternatively, is it a phenomenon or a set of phenomena of a completely different order? Prominent scholars have claimed that globalization is best conceptualized as part of a long process of change, perhaps centuries in the making (Coatsworth 2002; Mignolo 1998; Sen 2000; Taylor 2002; Williamson 2002).

Two of globalization's three main currents represent continuity with previous processes of economic, social, and cultural change, but the third suggests a new and heretofore unseen force. Globalization is the product of new information and communication technologies that connect people, organizations, and systems across vast distances. In addition to creating and instantaneously circulating vast amounts of information and data, these technologies hold the promise of freeing people from the tyranny of space and time. These new technologies are rapidly and irrevocably changing the nature of work, thought, and the interpersonal patterning of social relations (Turkle 1997).[1]

In other ways, though, globalization now seems to mimic previous cycles of integration. For example, the globalization of capital is nothing new. If anything, it was more impressive one hundred years ago than it is today (Coatsworth 2002; Taylor 2002; Williamson 2002). At the beginning of the new millennium, financial markets, direct foreign investment, capital flow, and the production and distribution of goods and services continue to be highly globalized.

According to the World Bank (2001:1), a "growing share of what countries produce is sold to other foreigners as exports. Among rich or developed countries, the share of international trade in total output (exports plus imports of goods relative to GDP) rose from 27 to 39 percent between 1987 and 1997. For the developing countries it rose from 10 to 17 percent." Likewise, foreign direct investment (that is, firms making investments in other countries) overall "more than tripled between 1988 and 1998 from US$192 billion to US$610 billion" (ibid). From the time you woke up this morning to the time you go to bed tonight, more than a trillion dollars will cross national boundaries (Friedman 2000). The archetypical American car, the Chevrolet Corvette, is now a thoroughly globalized product. It is built nowhere and everywhere; the capital, labor, and parts originate in multiple continents. It is a car "on the move," so to speak, from its very conception. The global market is also generating global tastes. McDonald's is now Brazil's largest employer (Schlosser 2001). Market forces seduce and manipulate in even the remotest parts of the world with stunning results.

Another feature of globalization that seems to continue an old story is large-scale immigration. Globalization is about deterritorialization not only of markets, information, symbols, and tastes but also of large and growing numbers of people. Large-scale immigration is a world phenomenon that is transforming Africa, Asia, Europe, and the Americas. Sweden, a country of nearly nine million people, now has roughly one million immigrants. Approximately 30 percent of Frankfurt's population is immigrant. Amsterdam, by the year 2015, will be 50-percent immigrant. Leicester, England, is about to become the first city in Europe where whites are no longer the majority. Long held as the exception to the North American and European rule that immigrant workers are needed to maintain economic vitality, Japan is now facing a future in which immigrants will play a significant role (Tsuda 1996, 2003). Asia and Africa have large numbers of asylum seekers, refugees, and displaced persons (UNHCR 2001).

Globalization is the general backdrop for any understanding of the anthropology of immigration. At the turn of the millennium, an estimated 175 million transnational immigrants and refugees were living beyond their homelands. Globalization has increased immigration in a variety of ways. First, transnational capital flows tend to stimulate migration; where capital flows, immigrants follow (see, inter alia, Sassen 1988). Second, the new information, communication, and media technologies at the heart of globalization tend to stimulate migration because they encourage new cultural expectations, tastes, consumption practices, and lifestyle choices. Would-be immigrants imagine better opportunities elsewhere and mobilize to achieve them. Third, deeply globalized economies are increasingly structured around a voracious appetite for foreign workers. Fourth, the affordability of mass transportation has put the migration option within the reach of millions who, heretofore, could not do so. (In the year 2000, approximately 1.5 billion airline tickets were sold.) Fifth, globalization has stimulated new migration because it has produced uneven results. In Zhou and Gatewood's (2000:10) excellent summary:

> Globalization perpetuates emigration from developing countries in two significant ways. First, ... capital investments into developing countries transform the economic and occupational structures in these countries by disproportionately targeting production for export and taking advantage of raw material and cheap labor. Such twisted development, characterized by the robust growth of low-skilled jobs in export manufacturing, draws a large number of rural, and particularly female, workers into the urban labor markets. ... Second, economic development following the American model in many developing countries stimulates consumerism and consumption and raises expectations regarding the standard of living. The widening gap between consumption expectations and the available standards of living within the structural constraints of the developing countries, combined with easy access to information and migration networks, in turn create tremendous pressure for emigration. ... Consequently, ... capital investments in developing countries have resulted in the paradox of rapid economic growth and high emigration from these countries to the United States.

Any anthropological consideration of globalization must reflect upon the pains it has generated in certain regions of the developing world, perpetuating unemployment and further depressing wages (Bauman 1998; Dussel 2000). On the winning side of the new globalization game, jobs have increased in certain regions of the world. These jobs include the knowledge-intensive sector of the new economy and more traditional jobs in service and agriculture. The growth in jobs in globalization's winning zones has acted as an unstoppable vacuum, pulling millions of immigrants—skilled and unskilled, legal and illegal—from the developing world into the wealthier centers of the Northern Hemisphere.

LIVES BEYOND NATIONAL BOUNDARIES

In recent years, there has been renewed interest in the study of human migration (Suárez-Orozco, Suárez-Orozco, and Desirée Baolian Qin 2001a). Anthropologists have made significant theoretical contributions to the study of immigration. For example, see George DeVos's work on immigration and minority status in comparative perspective (DeVos 1992; Kleinberg and DeVos 1973; Lee and DeVos 1981), Nina Glick Schiller's collaborative work on immigration and transnationalism (Basch, Glick Schiller, and Szanton Blanc 1994; Glick Schiller, Basch, and Szanton-Blanc 1992a; Glick Schiller and Fouron 2001a), and John Ogbu's work on immigration and anthropology of education (Ogbu 1974, 1978; Ogbu and Matute-Bianchi 1986). Sociologists, demographers, and labor economists are also conducting important new research on immigration in the social sciences. The next generation of anthropological studies of immigration will be increasingly required to reckon systematically with the approaches and findings of our colleagues in allied disciplines and to continue making a case for the unique perspectives emerging from the ethnographic process. Interdisciplinary collaborations between allied social scientists are likely to provide the increasingly sophisticated scholarly frames now needed to deal with the complexities of immigration in the global era.

During the last decades of the twentieth century, most major nation-states saw the topic of immigration emerge as a significant issue with important public-opinion, policy, and research implications. Migration, from the Latin *migrare*, meaning "to change residence," has been a defining feature in the making of humanity from our very emergence as a species in the African savanna. Social scientists have traditionally defined *migration* as the more or less permanent movement of people across space (Petersen 1968). In the language of the social sciences, people "emigrate" out of one location and become "immigrants" in a new setting.

The idea of migration as the permanent movement of people across space suggests several important concerns. First is the relative permanence of immigrants in a new setting. For many (perhaps most), immigration represents a final move; for others, it is a temporary state before eventually returning "home." A central feature of the great transatlantic immigration that took place between Europe and North and South America from the 1890s until the 1910s was the high proportion of people who returned to Europe. By some accounts, more than a third of the Europeans who came to the Americas went back "home" (Moya 1998).

Sojourners represent another pattern of labor flow in which temporality defines immigration. They are the many immigrants who move for well-defined periods of time, often following a seasonal cycle, and eventually return home. Large numbers of migrant workers have followed this pattern—from African workers in the sub-Saharan region to Mexican agricultural workers in California (Cornelius 1992).

A third type comprises the many new immigrants wordwide who constantly shuttle back and forth. In recent years, certain scholars of immigration have argued that new transnational and global forces structure the journeys of immigrants in more complex ways than previously seen. Anthropologists have been at the forefront of this conceptual and empirical work (for example, Basch, Glick Schiller, and Szanton Blanc 1994). This research suggests that many immigrants remain substantially engaged (economically, politically, and culturally) in their newly adopted lands and in their communities of origin, moving back and forth in ways seldom seen in previous eras of large-scale immigration (Suárez-Orozco 1998).

The idea of immigration as movement across space also requires elaboration. Viewed anthropologically, immigration involves a change in residency and a change in community. Over the years, scholars have concentrated on two major types of large-scale migration: *internal migration* (within the confines of a nation-state) and *international migration* (across international borders). Although many scholars would argue that the large-scale movement of people within a nation-state is a phenomenon of a separate order from the large-scale movement of people across international borders, the differences between these two broad types of migration are often quite blurred.

Frequently, internal migrants share many characteristics with international migrants. Many move from rural villages to urban centers; many experience linguistic and cultural discontinuities; and many face the same bureaucratic and legal restrictions and discriminations that international migrants do. Much attention has been focused on international migration. Today, though, most immigrants are internal migrants staying within the confines of their nation-states. (China, Egypt, and Brazil have experienced high levels of internal migration.) In fact, in spite of the impression that the majority of international migrants are heading to the developed world (that is, Europe and North America), most immigration today is an intra-continental (that is, within Asia, within Africa) phenomenon. China alone has an estimated 100 million internal migrants who, in many ways, experience circumstances similar to those that transnational migrants face when moving across countries (Eckholm 2001:10). Some of the most important anthropological contributions to the study of immigration have focused on internal migration (for example, Brandes 1975; Colson 1971; Kemper 1977; Morgan and Colson 1987; and Scudder and Colson 1982).

MOVING ON—THE CAUSES AND CONSEQUENCES OF LARGE-SCALE IMMIGRATION

Scholars of immigration have generally theorized patterns of migration flows in terms of economic forces, social processes, and cultural practices (Suárez-Orozco, Suárez-Orozco, and Desirée Baolian Qin 2001a). Social scientists who privilege the economic aspects of immigration have examined how variables such as unemployment, underemployment, lack of access to credit, and, especially, wage differentials are implicated in labor migration (Dussel 2000; Suárez-Orozco, Suárez-Orozco, and Desirée Baolian Qin 2001b). Anthropologist Jorgé Durand, working with an interdisciplinary team of colleagues (see Chapter 2), has argued that international migration emerges as a risk management and diversifying strategy deployed by families and communities hoping to place their eggs in various territorial baskets (Massey, Durand, and Malone 2002). Changing cultural models about social standards and economic expectations have also been implicated in why people migrate (Moya 1998). In many cases, people migrate to actualize new consumption and lifestyle standards.

In nearly all advanced, postindustrial economies, bifurcated labor markets have worked as a powerful gravitational field, attracting many immigrants to work in the low-wage, low-status, and low-skilled secondary sector. Anthropologist T. Tsuda (1996, 2003) has noted that in Japan immigrant workers are sometimes called "3 k workers"; *3 k* is for the Japanese words meaning "dirty, demanding, and dangerous." When certain sectors of the opportunity structure are culturally coded as "immigrant jobs," they become stigmatized, and native workers tend to shun them almost regardless of wage dynamics. What would it take, in terms of wages, to make backbreaking work such as strawberry picking in California *not* an immigrant occupation?

Anthropological scholars of immigration have long maintained that cultural and social practices can generate—and sustain—substantial migratory flows. In many regions of the world, such as Ireland and Mexico, migration has been an adulthood-defining rite of passage (Durand 1998; Massey, Durand, and Malone 2002). In some cases, people migrate because others—relatives, friends, and friends of friends—migrated before them. The best predictor of who will migrate is who has already migrated. Transnational family reunification continues to be a critical vector in immigration today. In the year 1996, 915,900 immigrants were formally admitted in the United States. Among them, 594,604 were family-sponsored immigrants (Suárez-Orozco 1999). Since the early 1970s, family reunification has been one of the few formal ways to migrate into Europe (Suárez-Orozco 1994).

A number of studies have examined how transnational migratory social chains, once established, can generate a powerful momentum of their own. As Patricia Pessar has argued, gender is deeply implicated in the making of these chains (Pessar 2004). Established immigrants lower the costs of subsequent immigration because they ease the transition of new arrivals by sharing crucial economic, linguistic, and cultural knowledge—about job openings, good wages, fair bosses, and dignified working conditions (Waldinger 1997).

Other recent research that is highly relevant to anthropological concerns engages the theoretical debate over the role of immigrant workers in the global, postindustrial economy. In the context of the increasingly advanced, knowledge-intensive economies of today, are low-skilled immigrant workers anachronistic? Are immigrant workers a leftover from an earlier era of production?[2]

The comparative research of anthropologist "Gaku" (T.) Tsuda and political scientist Wayne Cornelius on the use of immigrant labor in two paradigmatic postindustrial economic settings—San Diego County, California, United States, and Hamamatzu, Japan—suggests a remarkable convergence in patterns of growing reliance on immigrant labor, in spite of marked differences in national context (for example, see Cornelius 1998). These data reveal a pattern of an enduring, indeed voracious, postindustrial demand for immigrant labor. Cornelius (1998:128) concludes, "As immigrants become a preferred labor force, employers do more to retain them, even in a recessionary economy."

These data suggest that immigrant workers become desirable to a wide variety of employers for three basic reasons. First, immigrants are willing to do low-pay work with little or no prospects for upward mobility—work that is boring, dirty, or dangerous but critical, even in firms involving highly advanced technologies. Second, employers perceive immigrant workers quite favorably, as reliable, flexible, punctual, and willing to work overtime. Often, employers prefer them to native-born workers. Third, immigrant transnational labor-recruiting networks are a powerful method for "delivering eager new recruits to the employer's doorstep with little or no effort on his part" (Cornelius 1998:128).

We have a reasonable understanding of how love (family reunification) and work drive immigration. On the other hand, the role of war and its relations to large-scale migratory flows has been generally neglected. Yet throughout history war and international migration have been closely linked. The threat of labor shortages during World War II led to temporary labor-recruiting efforts to attract much-needed immigrant workers to the United States (Calavita 1992). The resultant "*bracero*" program became a powerful force in building—via family reunification—a Mexican migration momentum that eventually turned into the largest and most powerful immigration flow into the United States in the twentieth century (Suárez-Orozco 1998).

In the aftermath of World War II, many of the major northwestern European democracies, such as Germany and Belgium, developed "guest worker programs" to recruit foreign workers, initially in southern Europe and subsequently in the Maghreb region of North Africa and in Turkey (Suárez-Orozco 1994, 1996). These programs came to an end in the early 1970s, but family-reunification and chain migration continued to bring immigrants from North Africa into Europe for years.

The Cold War deterred immigration, because of strict Iron Curtain controls, yet generated large population displacements. The robust Cuban diaspora in the United States can be traced more or less directly to the Cold War (Molyneux 1999). The low-intensity warfare in Central America during the 1980s generated the largest wave of emigration in the region's history. As a result, there are now more than a million Central American immigrants in the United States (Suárez-Orozco 1989b). In the 1990s, the ongoing conflicts in Zimbabwe and Angola generated large-scale migratory flows, especially into South Africa. The recent war in Afghanistan resulted in major population displacements (nearly two million Afghans). As of mid-2003, the Iraq war seems not to have generated the huge population displacements that previous warfare has tended to create.

Natural disasters have also displaced populations and started new migratory flows. The 1999 hurricanes, which devastated much of Central America, initiated significant flows of emigrants into North America.

GLOBAL FLOWS AND THE STATE

Whether social scientists examine the case of internal or international migrants, there is a consensus that the apparatus of the nation-state is decidedly implicated in migratory processes: by what the state does and by what it cannot do. States are in the business of regulating the movement of people, internally and internationally. The right to leave a country, to emigrate, is a recent phenomenon (Moya 1998).

Nation-states regulate, monitor, and police the inflow of international immigrants across borders. Large-scale international immigration is, in significant ways, the product of nation building. Argentina, Australia, and Israel come to mind as archetypal examples. Likewise, the reconfigurations of national boundaries have historically and contemporaneously generated large-scale migratory flows. The partition of British India into Pakistan and India stimulated one of the "largest migrations in human history" (Petersen 1968:290). More recently, the disintegration of the former Yugoslavia led to massive, mostly involuntary migratory movements.

In the area of international migration, nation-states generate policies designed to establish who is a legal or an illegal immigrant as well as who is an asylum seeker, a refugee, and a temporary guest worker. States regulate how many immigrants are legally admitted every year. The United States, for example, has admitted an average of nearly a million legal immigrants annually since 1990. On the other hand, legal immigration into northwestern Europe was greatly curbed following the oil crisis of the early 1970s (Cornelius, Martin, and Hollifield 1994; Suárez-Orozco 1996).

States also regulate the flows of asylum seekers, those escaping a country because of a well-founded fear of persecution. Agents of the state decide who is formally admitted as a refugee. In the post-Cold War era, there has been an explosive growth in the numbers of asylum seekers worldwide. For example, some 369,000 foreigners requested asylum in Europe during the year 1998. Only a small portion of those seeking asylum are eventually granted formal refugee status.

In recent years, many postindustrial democracies—including the United States and throughout northwestern Europe—have developed new strategies to deal with increasing numbers of asylum seekers (Suárez-Orozco 1994). For example, the 13,000 Kosovars who arrived in Germany in mid-1999 were given a three-month, renewable Temporary Protective Status on the condition that they not apply for refugee status, in effect forfeiting all the rights and entitlements that come with formal refugee status. Similar arrangements were made for asylum seekers from Bosnia.

In the face of growing numbers of asylum seekers and a widespread public concern that many of them are economic refugees in search of a better life in wealthier countries, various governments have put into place new formal and informal strategies. Many of these new strategies seem to be designed to prevent asylum seekers from accessing safe countries, where, under Geneva Convention agreements, they would have the right to a fair hearing.

The high-seas interdiction program put into effect in the United States in the early 1990s is an example. The strategy was conceived to prevent large numbers of Caribbean (especially Haitian) asylum seekers from arriving in U.S. territory, or even within its territorial waters, where they could establish certain legal protections. Apprehension in international waters and a return to Haiti leave asylum seekers with little practical recourse under international law. In Europe, a similar strategy has deemed certain areas in international airports not part of the national territory. For example, parts of the Brussels International Airport are not technically Belgian territory but are considered to be international territory. Asylum seekers entering such airports have been turned back because they were said to remain in international territory and, therefore, did not come under the jurisprudence of the Geneva Convention (Suárez-Orozco 1994).

Although advanced, postindustrial democracies are likely to continue facing significant numbers of asylum seekers, the majority is in the developing world. For example, at the beginning of the millennium, there were more than three million asylum seekers in the African continent.

The state does wield substantial power regarding internal and international migration, but in certain areas it faces strict limitations in the management of human migratory flows. Nowhere are these limitations more obvious than in the state's inability to control illegal immigration. In many parts of the world, undocumented or illegal immigration has become a permanent problem that periodically emerges as an unsettling political issue.

In the United States, for example, it is estimated that by the turn of the millennium there were seven million illegal immigrants. In Europe, the number of illegal immigrants is a more carefully guarded secret because of its dangerous political connotations. Most hard-core, rightwing political parties in Europe, including France's Front National, Belgium's Vlams Bloc, and Austria's Freedom Party, revolve around (illegal) anti-immigration platforms. In the 1990s, these once marginal parties made substantial gains with electorates quite concerned about the problem of undocumented immigration.

The enduring problem of illegal immigration in many parts of the world suggests that immigration is now structured by powerful global economic factors, social forces, and cultural practices that seem impervious to state actions such as controls of international borders (Andreas 2000; Cornelius, Martin, and Hollifield 1994). Transnational labor-recruiting networks, enduring wage differentials between nation-states, changing standards of consumption, family reunification, and war generate a powerful migratory momentum not easily contained by unilateral, or even multilateral, state interventions to curb it.

THE VARIETIES OF THE IMMIGRANT EXPERIENCE

When settled in a new country, how do immigrants fare? The United States, as the ür-country of immigration, provides an interesting case study. It is the only advanced, postindustrial democracy where immigration is at once history and destiny. The intensification of globalization in the past decade—arguably responsible for the greatest peacetime expansion of the U.S. economy—coincided with the largest number of immigrants in history (U.S. Census Bureau 1999). By the year 2000, the foreign-stock (the foreign born plus the U.S.-born second generation) population of the United States was nearly 55 million people (Portes and Rumbaut 2001), more than 32.5 million of them foreign-born. Two dominant features characterize this most recent wave of immigration: its intensity (the immigrant population grew by more than 30 percent in the 1990s) and the radical shift in the sources of new immigration. Until 1950, nearly 90 percent of all immigrants were Europeans or Canadians. Today, more than 50 percent of all immigrants are Latin American, and more than 25 percent are Asian—from regions of the world where globalization has generated especially uneven results (see Figure 1.1).

Immigrants to the United States today compose a heterogeneous population defying easy generalizations (Suárez-Orozco and Suárez-Orozco 2001). They include highly educated, highly skilled individuals drawn by the explosive growth in the knowledge-intensive sectors of the economy. They are more likely to have advanced degrees than the native-born population (see Figure 1.2).

These immigrants come to the United States to thrive. These immigrants, especially those originating in Asia, are among the best educated and most skilled folk in the United States. They are over-represented in the category of people with doctorates. Fully half of all entering physics graduate

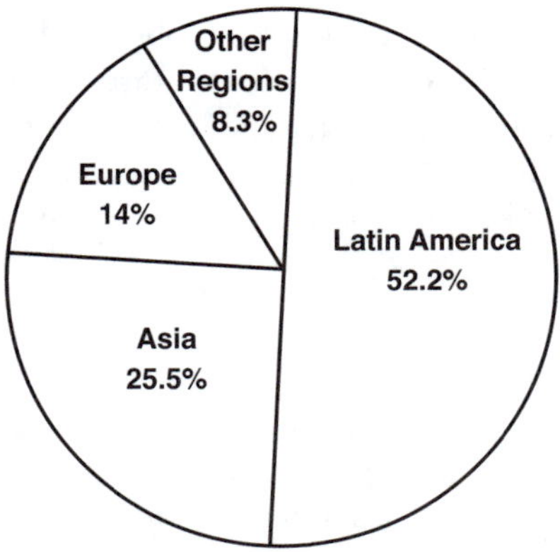

Fig. 1.1 Distribution of the foreign born by region of birth (2002).
Source: Current Population Survey 2002. PGP-3. U.S. Census Bureau.

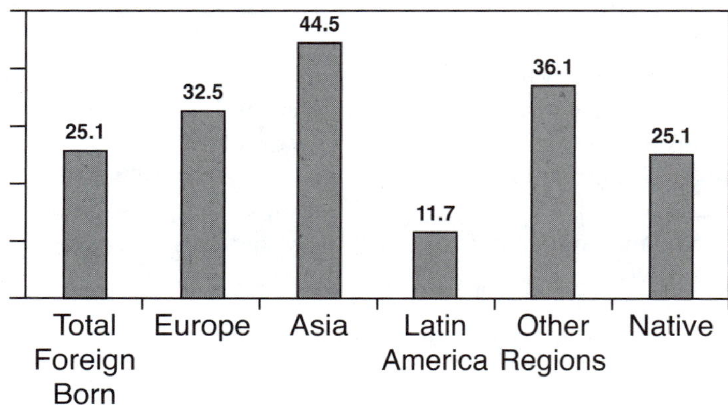

Fig. 1.2 Percentage of the immigrant population with a bachelor's degree or higher by origin (2000).
Source: Current Population Survey, March 2000. PGP-3. U.S. Census Bureau.

students in 1998 were foreign-born.[3] In California's Silicon Valley, 32 percent of all the scientists and engineers are immigrants (Saxenian 1999). Roughly a third of all Nobel Prize winners in the United States have been immigrants. In 1999, all (100 percent!) U.S. winners of the Nobel Prize were immigrants. With the exception, perhaps, of the highly educated immigrants and refugees escaping Nazi Europe, immigrants in the past tended to be poorly educated and more unskilled than today's immigrants (Borjas 1999). Never in the history of U.S. immigration have so many immigrants done so well so fast. Within a generation, these immigrants are bypassing the traditional transgenerational modes of status mobility and establishing themselves in the well-remunerated sectors of the U.S. economy.

At the same time, the new immigration group contains large numbers of poorly schooled, semi-skilled or unskilled workers, many of them in the United States without proper documentation (illegal immigrants). In the year 2000, more than 22 percent of all immigrants in the United States had less than a ninth-grade education (see Figure 1.3).

These are workers, many of them from Latin America and the Caribbean, drawn by the service sector of the U.S. economy, where there seems to be an insatiable appetite for foreign folk. They typically end up in poorly paid, low-prestige jobs often lacking insurance and basic safeties. Unlike the low-skilled factory jobs of yesterday, the kinds of jobs usually available to low-skilled immigrants today do not hold much realistic promise for upward mobility (Portes 1996: 1–15). These immigrants tend to settle in areas of deep poverty and racial segregation (Orfield 1998, 2002). Concentrated poverty is associated with the "disappearance of meaningful work opportunities" (Wilson 1997). When poverty is combined with racial segregation, the outcomes can be dim (Massey and Denton 1993:3).

CULTURE MATTERS

In all countries facing immigration, there have been major debates surrounding the cultural and socioeconomic consequences of large-scale population movements. In the United States, a palpable concern, not always fully articulated, relates to how the new immigrants—the majority of whom are non-English speaking, non-European people of color migrating in large numbers from the developing world—will culturally adapt to and transform their new country. In western Europe, there are similar concerns about the cultural adaptations of large numbers of immigrants coming

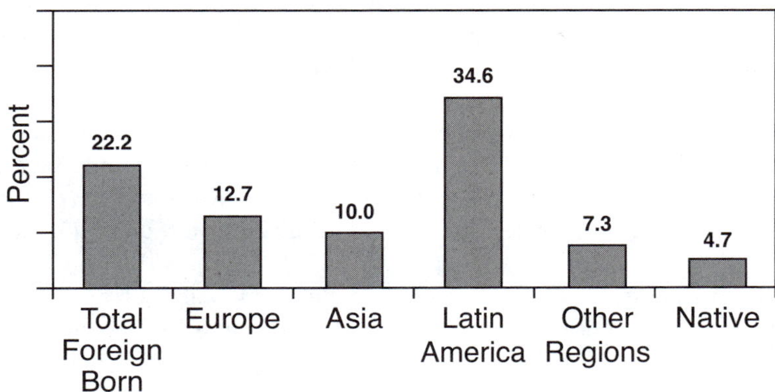

Fig. 1.3 Percentage of the immigrant population with less than the ninth grade completed by origin (2000).
Source: Current Population Survey, March 2000. PGP-3. U.S. Census Bureau.

into the Judeo-Christian continent from the Islamic world (Suárez-Orozco 1991b). The anxieties about the long-term vicissitudes of Islam in Europe have been greatly accentuated since September 11, 2001. Likewise, in Japan, a country where mythologies of racial and cultural homogeneity are deeply implicated in the construction of cultural identity, questions exist about the long-term consequences of increasing migration from Thailand, Korea, China, the Philippines, and South America (Tsuda 1996, 2003).

Some critics of immigration worry about the economic dimensions, and many others focus on the cultural implications. Analytically, it is sometimes useful to differentiate between two broad spheres of culture: instrumental culture and expressive culture. By *instrumental culture*, I refer to the skills, competencies, and social behaviors necessary to make a living and contribute to society. By *expressive culture*, I mean the values, worldviews, and patterning of interpersonal relations and sensibilities that give meaning and sustain the sense of self. Taken together, these qualities of culture generate shared meanings and understandings and a sense of belonging.

In the instrumental realm, globalization seems to be stimulating a worldwide convergence in the skills necessary to function in today's economy. In Los Angeles, Lima, or Lagos, the skills required to thrive in the global economy are fundamentally the same. These include communication skills and higher-order symbolic and cognitive skills, as well as habits of work and interpersonal talents common in any cosmopolitan setting. The ability to work with the culturally "other" is also a skill that will be increasingly remunerated, thanks to globalization.

Immigrant parents worldwide are very much aware that if their children are to thrive, they must acquire these skills. In math, children the world over will need the higher-order skills to master, at a minimum, fractions, decimals, line graphs, probabilities, and other basic statistics. In literacy, they will need the ability to read and understand complex instructions and manuals and to convey ideas in writing (in some cases, in more than one language). In logic, they will need problem-solving skills to address various possible outcomes by formulating and testing hypotheses, given certain antecedent conditions. Nearly everywhere, the ability to work with computers and with people from different linguistic, ethnic, and racial backgrounds will be essential for thriving in the workplace (see Murnane and Levy 1996, especially Chapter 2). Immigration for many parents represents nothing more, and nothing less, than the opportunity to offer children access to these skills.

THE ACCULTURATION DEBATE

Although immigrant parents encourage their children to cultivate the instrumental aspects of culture in the new setting, many are ambivalent about their children's exposure to some of the expressive cultural elements. During the course of our research with immigrant families in the United States, it has not been difficult to detect that many immigrant parents strongly resist a whole array of cultural models and social practices that they consider undesirable in American youth culture. These include cultural attitudes and behaviors they deem to be anti-education, anti-authority, and anti-family, such as sexually precocious behaviors and the glorification of violence. Many immigrant parents reject this form of acculturation (Suárez-Orozco and Suárez-Orozco 2001).

If *acculturation* is superficially defined as acquiring linguistic skills, job skills, and participation in the political process, the consensus on these shared goals is universal. If, on the other hand, we choose a broader, more ambitious definition of acculturation as also including the realm of values, worldviews, and interpersonal relations, a worthy debate ensues.

The first issue that needs airing is the basic question of "acculturating to what?" Taking the United States as a point of reference, we can observe that American society is no longer, if it ever was, a uniform or coherent system.[4] Because of immigrants' diverse origins, financial resources, and social networks, they end up gravitating to very different sectors of American society. Some are able to join integrated, well-to-do neighborhoods, but the majority experience American culture from the vantage point of poor urban settings. Limited economic opportunities, toxic schools, ethnic tensions, violence, drugs, and gangs characterize many of these environments. The structural inequalities in what some social theorists have called "American Apartheid" are implicated in the creation of a cultural ethos of ambivalence, pessimism, and despair (Massey and Denton 1993). Asking immigrant youth to give up their values, worldviews, and interpersonal relations to join this ethos is a formula for disaster.

For those immigrants who come into intimate contact with middle-class, mainstream culture, other trade-offs occur. New data suggest that many immigrant children perceive that mainstream Americans do not welcome them and, in fact, disparage them as undeserving to partake in the American dream (Suárez-Orozco 2000). Identifying wholeheartedly with a culture that rejects you has its psychological costs, usually paid with the currency of shame, doubt, and even self-hatred.

Even if middle-class, mainstream Americans wholeheartedly embraced new immigrants, it is far from clear that mimicking their behaviors would prove to be, in the long term, an adaptive strategy for immigrants of color. Mainstream, middle-class children are protected by webs of social safety nets that give them leeway to experiment with an array of dystopic behaviors, including drugs, sex, and alcohol. On the other hand, for many immigrant youth, without robust socioeconomic and cultural safety nets, engaging in such behaviors is a high-stakes proposition in which one mistake can have lifelong consequences. A white, middle-class youth caught in possession of drugs is likely to be referred to counseling and rehabilitation, but an immigrant youth convicted of the same offense is likely to be deported.

The current wave of immigration involves people from fantastically diverse and heterogeneous cultural backgrounds. Beneath surface differences, a common grammar can be identified among groups as culturally distinct from one another as Chinese, Haitian, and Mexican immigrants. The importance of the family in driving and sustaining immigration and the emphasis on hard work and optimism about the future are examples of shared immigrant values. (For an overview of recent research on immigration and family ties, see Falicov 1998; Rumbaut 1996; Suárez-Orozco and Paez 2002 [especially Chapters 12, 13, and 14]; Suárez-Orozco and Suárez-Orozco 1995; and Suárez-Orozco, Suárez-Orozco, and Desirée Baolian Qin 2001c. For an overview of immigrant optimism and achievement orientation, see Kao and Tienda 1995.)

These three aspects of culture come to the fore in the process of immigration. Consider, for example, the case of immigration and the family. Many immigrants come from cultures in which the family system is an integral part of the person's sense of self. Family ties also play a critical role in family reunification, a significant force driving the new immigration. Furthermore, after immigrants settle, many emotional and practical challenges force immigrants to turn to one another for support, accentuating family ties (Suárez-Orozco and Suárez-Orozco 2001).

Hard work and optimism about the future are also central to immigrants' raison d'être (Kao and Tienda 1995; National Research Council 1998; Rumbaut 1995; Steinberg, Bradford Brown, and Dornbusch 1996; Suárez-Orozco 1995). Their most fundamental motivation is to find a better life, and they tend to view hard work as essential to this. That many immigrants do the impossible jobs native workers refuse to consider is an indication of just how hard they are willing to work. Immigrant family ties, work ethic, and optimism about the future are unique assets that should be celebrated as contributions to the total cultural stock of the nation.

Countries unable or unwilling to tolerate or, indeed, thrive in the context of immigration-related changes need to carefully reconsider their dependence on immigrant labor. The one fundamental law of immigration is that it will change everyone involved: the immigrants and those among whom they settle. In the United States and Europe today, we eat, speak, and dance differently than we did thirty years ago, in part because of large-scale immigration. However, change is never easy. The changes brought about by the new immigration require mutual calibrations and negotiations.

Rather than advocate that immigrants, especially their children, abandon all elements of their culture as they embark on their uncertain assimilation journey, a more promising path is to cultivate and nurture the emergence of new hybrid identities and transcultural competencies.[5] These hybrid cultural styles creatively blend elements of the old culture with that of the new, unleashing fresh energies and potentials.[6]

The skills and work habits necessary to thrive in the new century are essential elements of acculturation. Immigrant children, like all children, must develop this repertoire of instrumental skills. At the same time, maintaining a sense of belonging and social cohesion with their immigrant roots is equally important. When immigrant children—be they Algerians in France, Mexicans in California, or Thais in Japan—lose their expressive culture, social cohesion is weakened, parental authority is undermined, and interpersonal relations suffer. The unthinking call for immigrant children to abandon their culture can result only in loss, anomie, and social disruption.

In the archetypical country of immigration, the United States, emerged the model of unilineal, or "straight line," assimilation. The bargain was straightforward: Please check all your cultural baggage before you pass through the Golden Gate. In that era, the young nation was eager to turn large numbers of European immigrants into loyal citizen workers and consumers. It was an era of nation building and bounded national projects.

Even then, however, accounts of immigrants rushing in unison to trade their culture for American culture were greatly exaggerated. German Americans, Italian Americans, and Irish Americans have all left deep cultural imprints in the molding of American culture. Even among fifth-generation descendants of the previous great wave of immigration, symbolic culture and ethnicity remain an emotional gravitational field (Glazer and Moynahan 1970).

Beyond the argument that maintaining the expressive elements of culture is symbolically important and strategic from the point of view of social cohesion, another argument is worth considering. In the global era, the tenets of unilineal assimilation are no longer relevant. Today there are clear and unequivocal advantages to being able to operate in multiple cultural codes, as anyone working in a major corporation knows. The ability to transverse cultural spaces has social, economic, cognitive, and aesthetic advantages. Dual consciousness has instrumental and expressive benefits. Immigrant children are poised to maximize their unique advantage. Although many view their cultural—including linguistic—skills as a threat, I see them as precious assets to be cultivated.

Large-scale immigration is both the cause and consequence of important cultural transformations. Immigration, I emphasize, inevitably leads to cultural changes and accommodations among both new arrivals and native citizens (Ainslie 1998). Immigration can be said to be the consequence of cultural change in that new cultural tastes and changing cultural conceptions of what is an acceptable standard of living have been implicated in large-scale migratory flows (Massey, Durand, and Malone 2002; Sassen 1988). Culturally, immigrants not only significantly reshape the ethos of their new communities (Ainslie 1998; Gutierrez 1998) but also are responsible for significant cultural transformations "back home" (Durand 1998). As certain immigration researchers (for example, Levitt 2001a) have argued, in many settings, immigrant "social remittances" profoundly affect the values, cultural models, and social practices of those left behind. Because of mass transportation and new communication technologies, immigration is no longer structured around the "sharp break" with the country of origin that once characterized the transoceanic experience (see Ainslie 1998; Suárez-Orozco and Páez 2002). Immigrants today are more likely to be at once "here" and "there," bridging increasingly unbounded national spaces (Basch, Glick Schiller, and Szanton Blanc 1994). In the process, they are transforming both home and host countries.

Increasingly transnational immigration will need to be framed in the context of powerful—and, as of yet, little understood—global formations. New patterns of capital flows, new information technologies, new patterns of communication, changing cultural expectations, and the ease and affordability of mass transportation are generating dynamics that transverse the traditional boundaries of the nation-state. Global capitalism is increasingly characterized by "borderless" economies predicated on transnational capital flows, newly opened markets, and immigrant-dependent economic niches. All these factors would suggest that immigration is certain to remain a vital social phenomenon in the new millennium.

Notes

1. Yet another paradox of globalization is that as it unites, it deeply divides the world between those who can access and manipulate the new technologies and those who are left behind—"stuck," so to speak—in local contexts (Bauman 1998).
2. Few topics have generated as much controversy as the economic consequences of large-scale labor migration. Do immigrants help or hurt the economies of their new countries? Do immigrants carry their own weight, or do they represent a burden to citizens and other established residents? Do complex, postindustrial economies need low-skilled immigrant workers, or have they become redundant? Much of the recent scholarship on immigration and the economy has tended to focus on concerns such as the fiscal implications of immigration, immigrant competition with native workers, and immigration and wages. Another important theme has been the economic integration and progress of immigrants over time (Borgas 1999; Espenshade 1997; National Research Council 1997; Suárez-Orozco, Suárez-Orozco, and Desirée Baolian Qin 2001b).
3. The research findings on the economic consequences of immigration are somewhat contradictory. Some economists claim that immigrants are a burden to taxpayers and an overall negative influence, especially on advanced, postindustrial economies (Huddle 1993). Others suggest that they continue to be an important asset (Simon 1989).
4. A recent study on the economic, demographic, and fiscal effects of immigration by the U.S. National Research Council (NRC) concludes that in the American setting, "immigration produces net economic gains for domestic residents" (National Research Council 1997:3). Not only do immigrants "increase the supply of labor and help produce new goods and services," but their presence also "allows domestic workers to be used more productively, specializing in producing goods at which they are relatively more efficient. Specialization in consumption also yields a gain" (National Research Council 1997:3–4). The NRC estimates that the immigration-related "domestic gain may run on the order of $1 billion to $10 billion a year" (National Research Council 1997:5). Given the size of the U.S. economy (about seven trillion dollars), it is clear that immigrants will neither "make it" nor "break it."
5. In fiscal terms, the NRC data suggest, "immigrants receive more in services than they pay in taxes" (National Research Council 1997:7). The panel estimates that "if the net fiscal impact of all U.S. immigrant-headed households were averaged across all native households the burden would be … on the order of $166 to $226 per native household."

6. The NRC study and other studies conclude that even though immigration is a plus in overall economic terms, low-skilled new immigrants have contributed to a modest drop in the minimum wage of low-skilled workers. They found that a 5-percent drop in wages since 1980 among high-school dropouts could be attributed to the new immigrants. However, no evidence exists to suggest that new immigration has "hurt" the economic condition of native minority workers, such as African-American (National Research Council 1997:5).
7. Other studies examine the issue of the socioeconomic progress made by immigrant workers. The research of Dowell Myers tracks, over time and across generations, various dimensions of the economic adaptations of immigrant-origin men in a region of the world heavily impacted by immigration: the state of California. His work explores three sequential outcomes: educational attainment, occupational mobility, and earnings. In fundamental ways, the recent Mexican immigrant experience in Southern California seems to replicate earlier patterns of immigrant adaptation. Yet, in other ways, Myers's finding suggests new—and disturbing—patterns.
8. Myers's research reveals that, upon arrival, Mexican immigrant men tend to be poorly educated, work in low-skilled occupations, and earn low incomes. Myers finds that over time immigrant men make modest improvements in their economic condition. However, he also suggests that important changes occur across younger cohorts within the first generation. These changes, according to Myers, are strongly related to the much higher educational attainment of immigrant children. In other words, Myers finds an old story with a new set of characters: Poorly educated immigrant men make modest gains over time, but their children are able to attain more education in the new country.
9. Still, Myers's data reveal a disturbing new pattern: Among the children of immigrants, higher education "does not appear to fully convert into higher occupational status or earnings; and higher occupational status translates even less well into higher earnings. These under-returns are most pronounced for the more recent arrivals from Mexico and for young cohorts, including native-born, both of whom newly entered the labor market in the 1970s and 1980s." Myers concludes, "The social implications of these falling returns to education and occupation are regrettable, because the declining reward system may discourage other" immigrant children from investing in schooling as the route for status mobility (Myers 1998:188).
10. See "Wanted: American Physicists," *New York Times*, July 23, 1999, p. A27. Of course, not all these foreign-born physics graduate students are immigrants. Some will return to their countries of birth, but others will surely go on to have productive scientific careers in the United States.
11. I concur with Alejandro Portes (1996:1) when he argues that we can no longer assume that new immigrants will assimilate into a coherent mainstream. He articulates a critical question that is now in the minds of many observers of immigration: "The question today is to what sector of American society will a particular immigrant group assimilate? Instead of a relatively uniform "mainstream" whose mores and prejudices dictate a common path of integration, we observe today several distinct forms of adaptation. One of them replicates the time-honored portrayal of growing acculturation and parallel integration into the white middle class. A second leads straight in the opposite direction to permanent poverty and assimilation to the underclass. Still a third associates rapid economic advancement with deliberate preservation of the immigrant community's values and tight solidarity."
12. I concur with Teresa LaFromboise and her colleagues (1998) on the need to reconceptualize what they call the "linear model of cultural acquisition."
13. Margaret Gibson (1988) articulates a theoretical argument on immigrant transculturation and a calculated strategy of "accommodation without assimilation" in her study of highly successful Sikh immigrants in California. For a theoretical statement on the psychology of ethnic identity and cultural pluralism, see Jean S. Phinney (1998).

References

Bauman, Z. 1998. *Globalization: The Human Consequences.* New York: Columbia University Press.

Borjas, G. 1999. *Heaven's Door: Immigration Policy and the American Economy.* Princeton, N.J.: Princeton University Press.

Espenshade, T., ed. 1997. *Keys to Successful Immigration: Implications of the New Jersey Experience.* Washington, D.C.: The Urban Institute Press.

National Research Council (NRC) 1997. *The New Americans: Economic, Demographic and Fiscal Effects of Immigration.* Washington, D.C.: National Academy Press.

Suárez-Orozco, M., C. Suárez-Orozco, and D. Qin-Hilliard, eds. 2001b. *The New Immigration: Interdisciplinary Perspectives Vol. 2.* New York: Routledge.

Huddle, D. 1993. The Costs of Immigration. Press release by Carrying Capacity Network, July.

Myers, D. 1998. Dimensions of Economic Adaption by Mexican-Origin Men. In *Crossings: Mexican Immigration in Interdisciplinary Perspectives*, edited by M. Suárez-Orozco, Cambridge, Mass.: David Rockfeller Center for Latin American Studies, Harvard University Press.

Simon, J. 1989. *The Economic Consequences of Immigration*, Oxford: Basil Blackwell.

New York Times 1999. Wanted: American Psysicists, July 23, A27.

Portes, A., and R. G. Rumbaut 1996. Immigrant America. 2d ed. Berkeley: University of California Press.

LaFromboise, F., H. Coleman, and J. gerton 1998. Psychological Impact of Biculturalism: Evidence and Theory. In *Readings in Ethnic Psychology*, edited by P. Organista, K. Chun, and G. Martin, New York: Routledge.

Gibson, M. 1987. The School Performance of Immigrant Minorities: A Comparative View. *Anthropology and Education Quarterly* 18(4): 262–275.

Chapter 2
Principles of Operation: Theories of International Migration

DOUGLAS S. MASSEY, JORGE DURAND, AND NOLAN J. MALONE

Most citizens and public officials *think* they understand the mechanics of international migration, of course, or they would not advocate such bold proposals or act with such assured abandon. In the North American case particularly, the reasons for Mexican immigration seem obvious. The prevailing wisdom begins with the commonsense observation that the United States is a rich country and Mexico, by comparison, is not. Although Mexico's 1997 GNP per capita of $3,700 places it in the upper tier of developing nations, it pales in comparison to the U.S. figure of $29,000., Nowhere else on Earth is there such a sharp contrast along a land border, much less one that is two thousand miles long.

As a result of this stark income differential, the standard of living is much higher north of the border. In per capita terms, Mexican private consumption is only 10 percent of that enjoyed in the United States. Obviously, simply by heading northward, crossing the border, and finding a job in the United States, the average Mexican can raise, often quite dramatically, his or her standard of living. Even at the current U.S. minimum wage, a migrant working full-time for a year would earn roughly three times the Mexican average income. Under these circumstances, what rational, self-interested Mexican would *not* want to emigrate to the United States? Simply by crossing a line, he or she would not only earn more income but gain access to better schooling, a richer infrastructure, improved social services, superior medical care, and a fuller array of consumer alternatives.

As far as most people are concerned, Mexican immigrants *choose* to come to the United States, making just such cost-benefit calculations. They believe that Mexicans rationally understand that the costs of migrating to the United States are more than offset by a variety of benefits. Even discounting for the costs of moving, crossing the border, looking for work, and adapting to a foreign culture, the material well-being of most Mexicans is substantially improved by relocating to the United States and pursuing work there, and each year hundreds of thousands of Mexicans seem to make precisely this decision. As long as the wage differential between Mexico and the United States is great, most people believe, workers south of the border have a strong incentive to move northward.

Although migration between Mexico and the United States goes back to the nineteenth century and has ebbed and flowed for more than a century, U.S. citizens and politicians have never been entirely comfortable with immigrants in general or Mexicans in particular (see Higham 1955; Espenshade and Calhoun 1993; Espenshade and Hempstead 1996). Public sentiment against immigrants has generally oscillated in tandem with expansionary and recessionary times and in conjunction with broader ideological currents (Meyers 1995). U.S. immigration policies have consequently swung back and forth between recruitment and restriction, acceptance and exclusion (Timmer and Williamson 1998).

For a variety of reasons, the late 1980s and early 1990s were a time of restrictive sentiment. The most obvious way to accomplish the assumed goal of reducing Mexican immigration, based on the understanding outlined earlier, was to lower the incentives by raising the costs and reducing the benefits of entry from Mexico. Unfortunately, the principal benefit—higher income—is not easily manipulable through policy mechanisms. No politician could ever vote to lower U.S. income as a means of reducing the incentives for immigration, and while U.S. political leaders might support efforts to raise incomes in Mexico, its economy is not under their direct control.

Given these constraints, U.S. policymakers focused on other, more malleable, costs and benefits. On the benefit side, the United States sought to reduce access to employment by criminalizing the hiring of undocumented workers and barring immigrants, undocumented and sometimes even documented, from receiving public services. On the cost side, the government hired more Border Patrol officers, increased their resources, and granted them new powers to detain, prosecute, and deport unauthorized aliens. By increasing the costs and lowering the benefits of undocumented migration, authorities hoped to deter Mexicans from entering and staying in the United States.

That something is seriously wrong with these policies and their underlying premises is suggested by the fact that they have not worked very well. As we document later, American attempts to raise the costs and lower the benefits of living and working in the United States have had little effect on the likelihood of undocumented migration, on increasing the odds of migrants returning home, on decreasing the odds of unauthorized employment, or on reducing the probability that migrants will undertake a successful border crossing. Other, more perverse consequences, however, have followed from these policies. The fundamental problem is that current policies are based on a rather narrow conceptualization of migration. The reality of contemporary immigration is considerably more complex than a simple calculus of costs and benefits.

A full understanding of international migration requires facing up to four basic questions: What are the forces in sending societies that promote out-migration, and how do they operate? What are the forces in receiving societies that create a demand for immigrant workers, and how do they function? What are the motivations, goals, and aspirations of the people who respond to these forces by migrating internationally? And what are the social and economic structures that arise in the course of migration to connect sending and receiving societies? The commonsense understanding of migration as a simple cost-benefit decision deals only with the third question, and it offers only one of several possible motivations for movement. In this chapter, we seek to develop a comprehensive explanation for international migration that addresses all four questions.

WHY PEOPLE MIGRATE

The conceptualization of Mexican immigration widely shared by legislators and the public as a cost-benefit decision corresponds to the theoretical apparatus of *neoclassical economics*. According to this theory and its extensions, international migration stems from geographic differences in the supply of and demand for labor (Ranis and Fei 1961). Countries with large endowments of labor relative to capital have low wages, while those with limited endowments of labor relative to capital have high wages. The resulting international differential causes workers from low-wage countries to move to high-wage countries. As a result of this movement, the supply of labor falls and wages rise in the former while they do the opposite in the latter, leading, at equilibrium, to an international wage differential reflecting the costs of international movement, pecuniary and psychic.

Associated with this macro theory is an accompanying microeconomic model of decision-making. Rational actors choose to migrate through a cost-benefit calculation that leads them to expect positive net returns, usually monetary, from international movement. Migration is analogous to investment in human capital (Sjaastad 1962), where human capital consists of personal traits and characteristics that increase a worker's productivity. Early in their lives, people invest in education to make themselves more productive and later reap benefits in the form of higher earnings.

Where one lives can be viewed as an individual trait that rational actors change by investing in a move. Migrants seek to go to places where, given their skills, they can be more productive and earn more money. Before they can reap this benefit, however, they must undertake certain investments: the material costs of traveling, the costs of sustenance while moving and looking for work, the effort involved in learning a new language and culture, the difficulty experienced in adapting to a new labor market, and the psychological burden of cutting old ties and forging new ones (Todaro and Maruszko 1987). According to neoclassical theory, migrants estimate the costs and benefits of moving to various international locations and then go to wherever the expected net returns are greatest (Borjas 1989, 1990).

In stylized terms, actors estimate expected net returns by taking the earnings anticipated in the destination country and multiplying them by the probability of obtaining and holding a job there, thus deriving an estimate of "expected destination earnings." These are then subtracted mentally from those projected for the community of origin (observed earnings multiplied by the probability of getting and holding a job there), and the difference is summed year by year over the individual's expected working life (with future years being discounted because money earned now carries more utility than money earned later). From this integrated difference the estimated costs of the move are subtracted to yield the total expected net return to international migration, and migrants go to wherever they expect that total return to be greatest (Todaro and Maruszko 1987; Massey and García España 1987).

A variety of anomalous observations suggest, however, that motivations for migration go beyond such cost-benefit calculations. Under neoclassical theory, migration should not occur in the absence of a wage differential, yet such flows are frequently observed. Moreover, if there are no legal barriers to movement, migration should continue until the wage differential between two areas is eliminated, yet migration streams commonly end well before wage gaps disappear. Widely observed patterns of circular migration are also difficult to explain from a strict neoclassical viewpoint; each year thousands of undocumented migrants and even many legal immigrants decide to return to Mexico (Warren and Kraly 1985; Jasso and Rosenzweig 1982, 1990; Lindstrom 1996; Reyes 2001). If the world really worked according to neoclassical principles, why would anyone migrate abroad temporarily to remit money back home in anticipation of an eventual *return?* A rational utility-maximizing actor logically should want to stay abroad permanently to enjoy forever the higher wages and consumption available in the United States, yet each year billions of dollars are remitted back to Mexico by migrants to improve their lives at home (Massey and Parrado 1994; Lozano Ascencio 1993, 1998).

These anomalies occur because the lifetime maximization of expected income is only one of several potential economic motivations for international migration, and not necessarily the most important. Neoclassical economics *begins* with the assumption that markets for goods and services exist, that they are complete and function well, that information and competition are perfect, and that rational individuals enter the market with exogenous tastes and preferences in order to maximize their utility (that is, they look out for number one). Given these assumptions, deductive logic is employed to discover what the world would look like if it indeed functioned according to neoclassical principles.

Yet reality is considerably more complex than the enabling assumptions of neoclassical economics. Markets for goods and services may not exist, they may be imperfect, and sometimes they may fail entirely, especially during the early phases of economic development. In addition, information is usually scarce and constrained by an individual's position in the social structure, and competition is far from perfect. Finally, even if individuals are rational and self-interested, they do not enter markets as atomized individuals but as members of families, households, and sometimes larger communities, social groupings that allow for *collective* strategies, which at times may dovetail with those of individuals and at other times be at odds with them.

If we imagine a world where families and households face the prospect of poorly functioning, missing, or failed markets, we come to a very different line of theoretical reasoning known as the *new economics of labor migration* (Stark and Bloom 1985). Unlike the neoclassical model, it does not assume that migration decisions are made by isolated actors, but that they are taken within larger units of interrelated people, typically families or households but sometimes entire communities. Within these units, people not only act individually to maximize expected income but also work collectively to overcome failures in capital, credit, and insurance markets (Taylor 1986, 1987; Stark 1991).

In most developed countries the risks to a household's material well-being are managed through private markets and government programs. Crop insurance and futures markets give farmers a means of protecting themselves against natural disasters and price fluctuations, and unemployment insurance and welfare programs protect workers against the vagaries of the business cycle and the dislocations of structural change. Private and government-sponsored pension systems allow citizens to minimize the risk of poverty in old age.

In relatively poor countries like Mexico, markets for futures and insurance are not well-developed, and the Mexican government is in no position to fill the gap by offering substitutes. As a result, Mexicans are not only poorer than other North Americans, they are also exposed to substantially greater *risk*. If society were indeed made up of atomized individuals acting solely in their immediate self-interest, then Mexicans probably would just have to suffer the risks quietly. However, most Mexicans do not live as solitary individuals but within households united by powerful family ties that precede the market (Vélez-Ibañez 1983; Lomnitz 1977; Adler-Lomnitz and Pérez Lizaur 1987; Camp 1989). Unlike atomized individuals, households can manage risk by diversifying their allocation of productive resources, one of which is labor.

Just as investors diversify risks by purchasing stocks across a range of firms, households diversify risks by sending out members to work in different labor markets. While some members (say, the wife and younger children) remain behind to work in the local economy, others (say, older sons and daughters) move to work elsewhere in Mexico, and still others (perhaps the household head and oldest son) migrate to work in the United States. As long as conditions in the various labor markets are negatively or weakly correlated, a household can manage risk through diversification. In the event that conditions at home deteriorate through rising unemployment, falling wages, failing crops, sagging prices, or high inflation, households can rely on migrant remittances as an alternative source of income.

In developing countries such as Mexico, markets for capital and credit are also weak or absent, preventing families from borrowing to smooth consumption or undertake productive activities (Taylor et al. 1996a, 1996b). In the absence of an efficient banking system, international migration becomes a reasonable strategy that poor families can use to accumulate cash in lieu of formal borrowing for consumption or investment. Households simply send one or more workers abroad to take advantage of higher wages to build up savings over a short time horizon.

CONTEXTS OF DECISION-MAKING

Individuals and households are almost always embedded within broader social systems that have their own organization and values, such as kinship networks, class hierarchies, ethnic and racial groupings, occupational sectors, and industrial or bureaucratic organizations. As social scientists have repeatedly shown, an individual's position within the social structure determines the context in which decisions are made. A person's structural position strongly influences his or her tastes, preferences, values, information, learning, resources, and, ultimately, the relative costs and benefits of any action being considered. By altering the context within which micro-level decisions are made, structural change in society can have rather pronounced effects in raising or lowering the probability of international migration.

Social and economic structures are commonly transformed through powerful macro-level forces that are *exogenous* to actors within any particular family or community, and social scientists have thus developed *structural theories* of international migration to acknowledge this fact. Building on the work of Immanuel Wallerstein (1974), a variety of theorists (Portes and Walton 1981; Petras 1981; Castells 1989; Sassen 1988, 1991; Morawska 1990) have linked the origins of international migration not so much to the decisions of individuals or households as to the changing scope and structure of global markets, a line of reasoning that is generally known as *world systems theory.* In this scheme, the expansion of markets into peripheral, nonmarket, or premarket societies creates mobile populations that are prone to migrate.

Driven by a desire for higher profits and greater wealth, owners and managers of large firms in developed nations enter poor countries on the periphery of the world economy in search of land, raw materials, labor, and markets. Migration is a natural outgrowth of the disruptions and dislocations that occur in this process of market expansion and penetration. As land, raw materials, and labor come under the control of markets, flows of migrants are generated. For example, when farmers shift from cultivating for subsistence to cultivation for markets, competition pushes them to consolidate land holdings, mechanize production, introduce cash crops, and apply industrially produced inputs. Land consolidation destroys traditional tenure systems based on common usufruct. Mechanization decreases the need for labor and makes unskilled agrarian workers redundant to production. The substitution of cash crops for staples undermines traditional social and economic relations, and the use of modern inputs, by producing high crop yields at low unit prices, drives out peasant farmers. All of these forces contribute to the creation of a mobile labor force: agricultural workers, displaced from the land, experience a weakened attachment to the community and become more prone to migrate internationally (Massey 1988; Hatton and Williamson 1998).

The extraction of raw materials for use in developed economies likewise requires new industrial methods reliant on paid labor. Offering wages to former peasants also serves to undermine traditional forms of social organization based on systems of reciprocity and fixed role relations, creating instead incipient labor markets based on new conceptions of individualism, private gain, change, and adaptation. Multinational firms enter poor nations to establish assembly plants and take advantage of their relatively low wages, often within special export-processing zones created by modernizing governments. The demand for factory workers strengthens local labor markets and further weakens traditional productive relations.

The insertion of foreign factories into peripheral regions undermines traditional economies in other ways: by producing goods that compete with those made locally, by feminizing the workforce without providing sufficient factory-based employment for men, and by socializing women for industrial work and modern consumption without providing a lifetime career capable of meeting these needs. The result once again is the creation of a population that is socially and economically uprooted and prone to migration, typically with international spillovers.

The same economic processes that operate globally to create migrants in peripheral areas simultaneously make it easier for them to migrate to the developed world (Sassen 1991). To ship goods, deliver machinery, extract and export raw materials, coordinate business operations, and manage foreign assembly plants, firms in core nations build and expand transportation and communication links to the peripheral countries where they have invested. These links not only facilitate the movement of goods, commodities, information, and capital but promote an opposing flow of people by reducing the costs of movement along reverse paths. Because global investment is inevitably accompanied by the creation of transportation and communication infrastructures, the international migration of labor generally parallels the international movement of goods and capital, only in reverse.

Economic globalization also creates cultural links between developed and developing nations. Sometimes the cultural links are longstanding, reflecting prior colonial relationships. Yet even in the absence of a colonial history, the cultural consequences of economic penetration can be profound. Although Mexico was colonized by Spain, Mexicans increasingly study at U.S. universities, speak English, and follow U.S. consumer styles, reflecting America's global economic hegemony. These cultural links naturally dispose them to migrate to the United States rather than other places, including Spain.

The world economy is managed from a relatively small number of urban centers in which banking, finance, administration, professional services, and research are concentrated (Castells 1989; Sassen 1991). In the United States these global cities include New York, Chicago, Los Angeles, and Miami; in Europe they include London, Paris, Frankfurt, and Milan; and qualifying for this status on the Pacific Rim are Tokyo, Singapore, and Sydney (Friedman 1986). Within these cities a wealth is concentrated to generate a strong demand for services from unskilled laborers (busboys, gardeners, waiters, hotel workers, domestic servants). At the same time the shifting of heavy industry overseas; the growth of high-tech manufacturing in electronics, computers, and telecommunications; and the expansion of services such as health and education all work to create a bifurcated labor market with strong demand for workers at both the top and the bottom of the occupational hierarchy, but with relatively weak demand in between.

THE DEMAND FOR IMMIGRANTS

The bifurcation of labor markets in global cities predicted by world systems theory dovetails with a larger line of theorizing known as *segmented labor market theory*, which grew out of institutional economics. Michael Piore (1979) has argued that international migration stems from a relatively permanent demand for unskilled labor that is built into the economic structure of developed nations. In his view, immigration is not caused by push factors in sending countries (such as low wages or high unemployment), but by pull factors in receiving societies (a chronic and unavoidable need for low-wage workers). The intrinsic demand for inexpensive labor stems from four fundamental problems faced by advanced industrial economies.

The first problem is *structural inflation*. Wages not only reflect conditions of supply and demand but confer status and prestige, social qualities inherent to specific jobs. In general, people believe that wages should reflect social status, and they have rather rigid notions about the correlation between occupational status and pay. As a result, wages offered by employers are not free to respond to changes in the supply of workers. A variety of informal social expectations and formal institutional mechanisms (such as union contracts, civil service rules, bureaucratic regulations, and human resource classifications) ensure that wages correspond to the hierarchies of prestige and status that people perceive.

If employers seek to attract workers for unskilled jobs at the bottom of an occupational hierarchy, they cannot simply raise wages for those jobs. Doing so would upset socially defined relationships between status and remuneration. If wages are increased at the bottom, employers will encounter strong pressure to raise wages at other levels of the job hierarchy. If the wages of busboys are raised in response to a labor shortage, for example, their wages may overlap with those of waitresses, thereby threatening the status of waitresses and prompting them to demand a corresponding wage increase, which threatens the position of cooks, who also pressure employers for a raise, and so on. As a result, the cost of raising wages to attract entry-level workers is typically more than the cost of those workers' wages alone. Thus, the prospect of structural inflation—the need to raise wages proportionately throughout the job hierarchy to maintain consistency with social expectations—provides employers with a strong incentive to seek easier and cheaper solutions, such as the importation of immigrants.

The demand for cheap, flexible labor is also augmented by the *social constraints on motivation* that are inherent to job hierarchies. Most people work not only to generate income but to accumulate social status. Acute motivational problems arise at the bottom of the job hierarchy because there is no status to be maintained and there are few avenues for upward mobility. The problem is inescapable because the bottom can never be eliminated from labor markets. Mechanization to eliminate the lowest and least desirable classes of jobs simply creates a new bottom tier composed of jobs that used to be just above the bottom rung. Since there always has to be a bottom of any hierarchy, motivational problems are inevitable. What employers need are workers who view bottom-level jobs simply as a means to the end of earning money and for whom employment is reduced solely to a matter of income, with no implications for status or prestige.

Immigrants satisfy this need on a variety of counts, at least at the beginning of their migratory careers. Migrants generally begin foreign labor as target earners: they are seeking to make money for a specific goal that will solve a problem or improve their status at home (such as building a new house, buying land, or acquiring consumer goods). Moreover, the disjuncture in living standards between developed and developing societies makes low wages abroad appear generous by the standards of the sending country. Finally, even though a migrant may realize that a foreign job carries low status, he does not view himself as a part of that society but as embedded within the status system of his home community, where hard-currency remittances buy considerable social status.

The demand for immigrant labor also stems from the *duality of labor and capital*. Capital is a fixed factor of production that can be idled by lower demand but not laid off; owners of capital bear the costs of its unemployment. Labor, in contrast, is a variable factor of production that can be released when demand falls, so that workers bear the costs of their own unemployment. Whenever possible, therefore, industrialists seek out the stable, permanent portion of demand and reserve it for the deployment of capital, leaving the variable portion of demand to be met by the addition and subtraction of labor, a dualism that creates distinctions among workers and leads to segmentation of the labor force.

Workers in the capital-intensive primary sector get stable, skilled jobs working with good tools and equipment. Employers are forced to invest in their human capital through training and education. Primary-sector jobs are complicated and require considerable knowledge and experience to perform, leading to the accumulation of firm- and job-specific knowledge. Primary-sector workers also tend to be unionized or highly professionalized, with contracts that require employers to bear a substantial share of the costs of layoffs (in the form of severance pay and unemployment benefits). Because of these costs and continuing obligations, workers in the primary sector become expensive to let go; they become more like capital.

The labor-intensive secondary sector, in contrast, is composed of poorly paid, unstable jobs from which workers may be laid off at any time with little or no cost to the employer. During down cycles an employer's first act is to shed such workers to cut the payroll. The resulting dualism thus yields a segmented labor market structure. Low wages, unstable conditions, and the lack of reasonable mobility prospects make it difficult to attract native workers into the secondary sector. They are instead drawn into the primary, capital-intensive sector, where wages are higher, jobs are more secure, and there is a possibility of occupational advancement. To fill the shortfall in demand within the secondary sector, employers turn to immigrants.

Taken together, motivation problems, structural inflation, and economic dualism create a demand for a particular kind of worker: one who is willing to labor under unpleasant conditions, at low wages, in jobs with great instability and little chance for advancement. In the past, this demand was met by women, teenagers, and rural-to-urban migrants. Historically women tended to participate in the labor force up to the time of their first birth, and to a lesser extent after their children had grown. They were not primary breadwinners, and their principal social identity was that of a daughter, wife, or mother. They were willing to put up with the low wages and instability because they viewed the work as transient and the earnings as supplemental; the positions they held were not threatening to their main social status, which was grounded in the family.

Likewise, teenagers historically moved into and out of the labor force with great frequency to earn extra money, gain experience, and try out different occupational roles. They did not view "dead-end" jobs as a problem because they expected to get better jobs in the future, after completing school, gaining experience, and settling down. Moreover, teenagers derive their primary social status from their parents, not their jobs. They view work instrumentally as a means of earning spending money, which they use to enhance their status among their peers by buying clothes, cars, and music; the job is just a means to an end.

Finally, rural areas of developed nations for many years provided industrial cities with a steady supply of low-wage workers. Movement from social and economic backwaters to dynamic cities created a sense of upward mobility regardless of the modesty of the circumstances at the place of destination. Even menial jobs in cities provided access to housing, food, and consumer goods that represented a step up in the world for impoverished migrants from the countryside.

In advanced industrial societies, however, these three sources of entry-level workers have drastically shrunk over time because of four fundamental demographic trends: the rise in female labor force participation, which has transformed women's work into a career pursued for social status as well as income; the rise in divorce rates, which has transformed women's employment into a source of primary support; the decline in birthrates and the extension of formal education, which have produced small cohorts of teenagers entering the labor force; and the urbanization of society, which has eliminated farms and rural communities as potential sources for new migrants to the city. The imbalance between the structural demand for entry-level workers and the limited domestic supply of such workers has generated an underlying, long-run demand for immigrants in developed countries.

WHY PEOPLE CONTINUE TO MIGRATE

Immigration may begin for a variety of reasons, but the forces that initiate international movement are quite different from those that perpetuate it. Although wage differentials, market failures, and structural change may motivate people to move in the first place, new conditions arise in the course of migration to make additional movement more likely, leading to the perpetuation of international migration across time and space. There has been a great deal of work on the perpetuation of international migration under the rubric of *social capital theory.* According to Pierre Bourdieu and Loic

Wacquant (1992:119), "social capital is the sum of the resources, actual or virtual, that accrue to an individual or a group by virtue of possessing a durable network of more or less institutionalized relationships of mutual acquaintance and recognition." The key characteristic of social capital is its convertibility: it can be translated into other social and economic benefits (Harker, Mahar, and Wilkes 1990).

People gain access to social capital through membership in interpersonal networks and social institutions and then convert it into other forms of capital to improve or maintain their position in society (Bourdieu 1986; Coleman 1990). Migrant networks are an important source of social capital for people contemplating a move abroad. They are sets of interpersonal ties that connect migrants, former migrants, and nonmigrants at places of origin and destination through reciprocal ties of kinship, friendship, and shared community origin. They increase the likelihood of international movement because they lower the costs and risks of movement and increase the expected net returns to migration.

In keeping with the dictum that "social capital…is created when the relations among persons change in ways that facilitate action" (Coleman 1990, 304), migration itself serves as the catalyst for change. Everyday ties of friendship and kinship provide few advantages, in and of themselves, to people seeking to migrate abroad. Once someone in a person's network has migrated, however, the ties are transformed into a resource that can be drawn upon to gain access to foreign employment and all that it brings. Each act of migration creates social capital among people to whom the migrant is related, thereby raising the odds of their migration (Massey, Goldring, and Durand 1994).

The first migrants who leave for a new destination have no social ties to draw upon, and for them migration is costly, particularly if it involves entering another country without documents. After the first migrants have left, however, the potential costs of migration are substantially lowered for the friends and relatives left behind. Because of the nature of kinship and friendship structures, each new migrant expands the set of people with social ties to the destination area. Migrants are inevitably linked to nonmigrants, and the latter draw upon the obligations implicit in relationships such as kinship, friendship, and even community to gain access to employment and assistance at the point of destination.

Once international migration has begun, private institutions and voluntary organizations also arise to satisfy the demand created by the growing imbalance between the large number of people who seek entry into capital-rich countries and the limited supply of visas they typically offer. This imbalance and the barriers that developed countries erect to keep people out create a lucrative niche for entrepreneurs dedicated to promoting international movement for profit, yielding a black market in migration services. As this underground market creates conditions conducive to exploitation and victimization, humanitarian organizations also arise to enforce the rights and improve the treatment of both legal and undocumented migrants (Hagan and Gonzalez Baker 1993; Christiansen 1996). Such organizations offer migrants another source of social capital (Goss and Lindquist 1995) by providing a range of services, such as border smuggling, clandestine transport, labor contracting, counterfeit documents, information and advice, and lodging, credit, and shelter at the points of destination (Prothero 1990).

The way in which social capital accumulates over time to perpetuate international migration represents a specific manifestation of a broader process that has been described as the *cumulative causation of migration* (first identified by Myrdal 1957). The causation of migration becomes cumulative because each act of migration alters the social context within which subsequent migration decisions are made, thus increasing the likelihood of additional movement. Once the number of network connections in a community reaches a critical threshold, migration becomes self-perpetuating because each act of migration creates the social structure needed to sustain it (Hugo 1981; Taylor 1986; Massey 1990; Massey, Goldring, and Durand 1994; Massey and Zenteno 1999).

In any bounded population, of course, processes of cumulative causation cannot continue ad infinitum. If migration continues long enough, networks eventually reach a point of saturation within any particular community. More and more community members reside in branch settlements overseas, and virtually all of those at home are connected to someone who lives abroad or has substantial foreign experience. When networks reach such a high level of elaboration, the costs of migration do not fall as sharply with each new migrant, and migration loses its dynamic momentum for growth. The prevalence of migration in the community approaches an upper limit, and migratory experience becomes so diffused that the stock of potential new migrants becomes very small and is increasingly composed of women, children, and the elderly.

If migration continues long enough, labor shortages and rising wages in the home community may further dampen the pressures for emigration (Gregory 1986), causing the rate of entry into the international migrant workforce to trail off (Hatton and Williamson 1994). When observed at the national level, this trend may be difficult to detect as new communities are continuously incorporated into the migratory stream. As the rate of out-migration decelerates in places with longer histories of migration, new areas are drawn into transnational circuits and their rates of migration begin to accelerate. As a result, the total outflow from the nation as a whole may continue to grow as migration spreads from place to place.

A SCHEMATIC DIAGRAM

Because the theories discussed in this chapter posit causal mechanisms operating at multiple levels of aggregation, the various explanations are not logically contradictory. It is entirely possible for individuals to engage in cost-benefit calculations; for households to seek to minimize risk and overcome barriers to capital and credit; for both individuals and households to draw upon social capital to facilitate international movement; and for the socioeconomic context within which migration decisions are made to be determined by structural forces operating at the national and international levels, often influenced by migration itself. Thus, a synthetic approach to theory construction is in order.

As we see it, international migration originates in the social, economic, and political transformations that accompany the expansion of markets. The entry of markets and capital-intensive production into nonmarket or premarket societies disrupts existing social and economic arrangements and brings about a displacement of people from customary livelihoods, thus creating a mobile population of workers who actively search for new means of sustenance. One means by which people displaced from traditional jobs seek to ensure their economic well-being is by selling their services overseas. However, higher foreign wages are not the only factor motivating people to emigrate. Households struggling to cope with the jarring transformations of economic development also use international migration as a means of overcoming frequent failures in markets for labor, insurance, capital, and credit.

The absence of unemployment insurance in developing nations creates an incentive for families to self-insure by sending one or more members overseas for work. By allocating workers to different geographic regions—rural, urban, and foreign—households diversify their labor portfolios to reduce risks to income. Moreover, as households plunge into the risky and unknown world of capitalist production, the absence of crop insurance and futures markets leaves them vulnerable to economic disaster, providing yet another incentive to self-insure through international migration. Families seeking to increase agricultural production or establish new business enterprises need capital, and the shift to a market economy creates new demands for expensive consumer items. The financing of both requires cash, and the inability of poorly developed banking systems to meet the demand for loans and credit gives households one final motivation for international movement. By sending a family member temporarily abroad for work, households can accumulate savings quickly to self-finance production or consumption.

While the early phases of economic development in poor nations create migrants, later phases of economic growth in wealthy nations yield segmented labor markets that attract them. Primary-sector jobs provide steady work and high pay for native workers, while jobs in the secondary sector offer low pay, little stability, and few opportunities for advancement, repelling natives and generating a strong demand for immigrant workers. The process of labor market segmentation is most acute in global cities, where a concentration of managerial, administrative, and technical expertise leads to a concentration of wealth and a strong ancillary demand for low-wage services. Unable to attract native workers, employers turn to immigrants and often initiate immigrant flows directly through formal recruitment.

Although often instrumental in initiating immigration, recruitment becomes less important over time because the same market processes that create flows of immigrants also create links of transportation and communication, as well as of politics and culture, to make international movement easier and cheaper. Immigration also stems from the actions that developed nations undertake to maintain international security, protect foreign investments, and guarantee access to raw materials overseas. Foreign entanglements create links and obligations that generate ancillary flows of refugees, asylum seekers, and military dependents.

Eventually labor recruitment becomes superfluous; once begun, immigration displays a strong tendency to continue through the growth and elaboration of migrant networks. Over time the process of network expansion becomes self-perpetuating because each act of migration creates social infrastructure to promote additional movement. As receiving countries implement restrictive policies to counter rising tides of immigrants, moreover, they only create a lucrative niche into which enterprising agents move to create migrant-supporting institutions, providing even more social capital for international migration.

During the initial phases of emigration from any sending country, the effects of capitalist penetration, market failure, network formation, and cumulative causation dominate in explaining the flows, but as out-migration reaches high levels, the costs and risks of international movement drop and movement is increasingly determined by international wage differentials and labor demand. As developing nations grow economically, international wage gaps diminish and well-functioning markets for capital, credit, insurance, and futures come into existence, reducing the incentives for emigration. If these trends continue, the country ultimately becomes integrated into the global economy as a developed, capitalist society, whereupon it undergoes a migration transition: net out-migration ceases, and the nation becomes an importer of labor. Historically, this process of development, emigration, and transition took European nations eight or nine decades, but by the late twentieth century the process seemed to have been compressed into just thirty or forty years.

References

Adler-Lomnitz, Larissa A., and Marisol Pérez-Lizaur. 1987. *A Mexican Elite Family*: 1820–1980. Princeton, N.J.: Princeton University Press.

Borjas, George J. 1989. "Economic Theory and International Migration." *International Migration Review* 23: 475–85.

——. 1990. *Friends or Strangers: The Impact of Immigrants on the U.S. Economy.* New York: Basic Books.

Bourdieu, Pierre. 1986. " The Forms of Capital." *In Handbook of Theory and Research for the Sociology of Education*, edited by John G. Richardson. New York: Greenwood Press.

Bourdieu, Pierre, and Loic Wacquant. 1992. *An Invitation to Reflexive Sociology.* Chicago: University of Chicago Press.

Camp, Roderic A. 1989. *Entrepreneurs and Politics in Twentieth-Century Mexico.* New York: Oxford University Press.

Castells, Manuel. 1989. *The Informational City: Information Technology, Economic Restructuring, and the Urban-Regional Process.* Oxford: Basil Blackwell.

Christiansen, Drew. 1996. "Movement, Asylum, Borders: Christian Perspectives." *International Migration Review* 30: 7–17.

Clune, Michael S. 1998. "The Fiscal Impacts of Immigrants: A California Case Study." In *The New Americans: Economic, Demographic, and Fiscal Effects of Immigration,* edited by James P. Smith and Barry Edmonston. Washington, D.C.: National Academy Press.

Coleman, James S. 1990. *Foundations of Social Theory.* Cambridge, Mass.: Harvard University Press.

Espenshade, Thomas J., and Charles A. Calhoun. 1993. "An Analysis of Public Opinion Toward Undocumented Immigration." *Population Research and Policy Review* 12: 189–224.

Espenshade, Thomas J. and katherine Hempstead. 1996. "Contemporary American Attitudes Toward U.S. immigration." *International Migration Review* 30: 535–70.

Friedman, John. 1986. "The World City Hypothesis." *Development and Change* 17: 69–83.

Goss, Jon D., and Bruce Lindquist. 1995. "Conceptualizing International Labor Migration: A Structuration Perspective." *International Migration Review* 29: 317–51.

Gregory, Peter. 1986. *The Myth of Market Failure: Employment and the Labor Market in Mexico.* Baltimore, Md.: Johns Hopkins University Press.

Hagan, Jacqueline M., and Susan Gonzalez Baker. 1993. "Implementing the U.S. Legalization Program: The Influence of Immigrant Communities and Local Agencies on Immigration Policy Reform." *International Migration Review* 27: 513–36.

Harker, Richard, Cheleen Mahar, and Chris Wilkes. 1990. *An introduction to the work of Pierre Bourdieu: The Practice of Theory.* London: Macmillan.

Hatton, Timothy J., and Jeffrey G. Williamson. 1994. "What Drove the Mass Migrations from Europe in the Late Nineteenth Century?" *Population and Development Review* 20: 533–60.

——. 1998. *The Age of Mass Migration: Causes and Economic Impact.* Oxford: Oxford University Press.

Higham, John. 1995. *Strangers in the Land: Patterns of American Nativism, 1860–1925.* New Brunswick, N.J.: Rutgers University Press.

Hugo, Graeme J. 1981. "Village-Community Ties, Village Norms, and Ethnic and Social Networks: A Review of Evidence from the Third World." In *Migration Decisionmaking: Multidisciplinary Approaches to Microlevel Studies in Developed and Developing Countries,* edited by Gordon F. DeJong and Robert W. Gardener. New York: Pergamon Press.

Jasso, Guillermina, and Mark R. Rosenzweig. 1982. "Estimating the Emigration Rates of Legal Immigrants Using Administrative and Survey Data: The 1971 Cohort of Immigrants to the United States." *Demography* 19: 279–90.

——. 1990. *The New Chosen People: Immigrants in the United States. New York:* Russell Sage Foundation.

Lindstrom, David P. 1996. "Economic Opportunity in Mexico and Return Migration from the United States." *Demography* 33: 357–74.

Lomnitz, Larissa. 1977. *Networks and Marginality: Life in a Mexican Shantytown.* New York: Academic press.

Lozano Ascencio, Fernando. 1993. *Bringing It Back Home : Remittances to Mexico from Migrant Workers in the United States.* La Jolla, Calif.: University of California at San Diego, Center for U.S.-Mexican Studies.

——. 1998. " Las Remesas de los Migrantes Mexicanos en Estados Unidos: Estimaciones para 1995." In *Migration Between Mexico and the United States: Binational Study, Vol.3, Research Repotrs and Background Materials.* Washington, D.C.: U.S. Commission on Immigration Reform.

Massey, Douglas S. 1988. "International Migration and Economic Development in Comparative Perspective." *Population and Development Review* 14: 383–414.

——. 1990. "Social Structure, Household Strategies, and the Cumulative Causation of Migration." *Population Index* 56: 3–26.

Massey, Douglas S., and Felipe García España. 1987. "The Social Process of International Migration." *Science* 237: 733—38.

Massey, Douglas S., Luin P. Goldring, and Jorge Durand. 1994. "Continuities in Transnational Migration: An Analysis of Nineteen Communities." *American Journal of Sociology* 99: 1492–1532.

Massey, Douglas S., and Emilio A. Parrado. 1994 "Migradollars: The Remittances and Savings of Mexican Migrants to the United States." *Population Research and Policy Review* 13: 3–30.

Massey, Douglas S., and René Zenteno. 1999. "The Dynamics of Mass Migration." *Proceedings of the National Academy of Sciences* 96(8): 5328–35.

Morawska, Ewa. 1990. "The Sociology and Historiography of Immigration." In *Immigration Reconsidered: History, Sociology, and Politics,* edited by Virgina Yans-McLaughlin. New York: Oxford University Press.

Meyers, Eytan. 1995. "The Political Economy of International Migration Policy: A Comparative and Quantitative Study." Ph.D. diss., University of Chicago, Department of Political Science.

Mydral, Gunnar. 1957. *Rich Lands and Poor.* New York: Harper and Row.

Petras, Elizabeth M. 1981. "The Global Labor Market in the Modern World-Economy." In *Global Trends in Migration: Theory and Research on International Population Movements,* edited by Mary M. Kritz, Charles B. Keely, and Silvano M. Tomasi. New York: Center for Migration Studies.

Piore, Michael J. 1979. *Birds of Passage: Migrant Labor in Industrial Societies.* New York: Cambridge University Press.

Portes, Alejandro, and John Walton. 1981. *Labor, Class, and the International System.* New York: Academic Press.

Prothero, R. Mansell. 1990. "Labor Recruiting Organizations in the Developing World: Introduction." *International Migration Review* 24: 221–28.

Reyes, Belinda I. 2001. "Immigrant Duration in the United States: The Case Study of Mexicans from Western Mexico." *International Migration Review* 35, forthcoming.

Sassen, Sasika. 1988. *The Mobility of Labor and Capital: A Study in International Investment and Labor Flow.* Cambridge University Press.
——. 1991. *The Global City: New York, London, Tokyo.* Princeton, N.J.: Princeton University Press.
Sjaastad, Larry A. 1962. "The Costs and Returns of Human Migration." *Journal of Political Economy* 70: S80–93.
Stark, Oded. 1991. *The Migration of Labor.* Cambridge, U.K.: Basil Blackwell.
Stark, Oded, and David E. Bloom. 1985. "The New Economics of Labor Migration." *American Economic Review* 75: 173–78.
Taylor, J. Edward. 1986. "Differential Migration, Networks, Information, and Risk." In *Migration Theory, Human Capital, and Development,* edited by Oded Stark. Greenwich, Conn.: JAI Press.
Taylor, J. Edward, Jaoquin Arango, Graeme Hugo, Ali Kouaouci, Douglas S. Massey, and Adela Pellegrino. 1996a. "International Migration and National Development." *Population Index* 62: 181–212.
——. 1996b. "International Migration and Community Development." *Population Index* 63: 397–418.
Timmer, Ashley S., and Jeffrey G. Williamson. 1998. " Immigration Policy Prior to the 1930s: Labor Markets, Policy Interactions, and Globalization Backlash." *Population and Development Review* 24: 739–72.
Todaro, Michael P., and Lydia Maruszko. 1987. "Illegal Migration and U.S. Immigration Reform: A Conceptual Framework." *Population and Development Review* 13: 101–14.
Vélez-Ibañez, Carlos G. 1983. *Rituals of Marginality: Politics, Process, and Culture Change in Central Urban Mexico, 1969–1974.* Berkeley, Calif.: University of California Press.
Wallerstein, Immanuel. 1974. *The Modern World System I: Capitalist Agriculture and the Origins of the European World Economy in the Sixteenth Century.* New York: Academic Press.
Warren, Robert, and Ellen P. Kraly. 1985. "The Elusive Exodus: Emigration from the United States." In *Population Trends and Public Policy* 8. Washington, D.C.: Population Reference Bureau.

Chapter 3
Rethinking Assimilation Theory for a New Era of Immigration[1]

RICHARD ALBA AND VICTOR NEE

Assimilation theory has been subject to intensive critique for decades. Yet no other framework has provided the social science community with as deep a corpus of cumulative findings concerning the incorporation of immigrants and their descendants. We argue that assimilation theory has not lost its utility for the study of contemporary immigration to the United States. In making our case, we review critically the canonical account of assimilation provided by Milton Gordon and others; we refer to Shibutani and Kwan's theory of ethnic stratification to suggest some directions to take in reformulating assimilation theory. We also examine some of the arguments frequently made to distinguish between the earlier mass immigration of Europeans and the immigration of the contemporary era and find them to be inconclusive. Finally, we sift through some of the evidence about the socioeconomic and residential assimilation of recent immigrant groups. Though the record is clearly mixed, we find evidence consistent with the view that assimilation is taking place, albeit unevenly.

Assimilation has fallen into disrepute. In an essay tellingly entitled "Is Assimilation Dead?" Nathan Glazer (1993:122) summarizes pithily the contemporary view: "Assimilation today is not a popular term." Glazer writes that he asked some Harvard students what they thought of the term and discovered that "the large majority had a negative reaction to it." The rejection of assimilation is not limited to students. While it was once the unquestioned organizing concept in sociological studies of ethnic relations, in recent decades assimilation has come to be viewed by social scientists as a worn-out theory that imposes ethnocentric and patronizing demands on minority peoples struggling to retain their cultural and ethnic integrity.

Without question, earlier social scientists in this field committed what are now regarded as intellectual sins. For instance, Warner and Srole (1945:285ff), in their classic account of assimilation among ethnic groups in New Haven, describe ethnic groups as "unlearning" their "inferior" cultural traits (inferior, that is, from the standpoint of the host society) in order to "successfully learn the new way of life necessary for full acceptance." Warner and Srole also correlated the potential for assimilation with a hierarchy of racial and cultural acceptability, ranging from English-speaking

Protestants at the top to "Negroes and all Negroid mixtures" at the bottom. The depiction of the ethnocentric tendency in classical American assimilation could hardly be clearer.

Yet whatever the deficiencies of earlier formulations and applications of assimilation, we hold that this social science concept offers the best way to understand and describe the integration into the mainstream experienced across generations by many individuals and ethnic groups, even if it cannot be regarded as a universal outcome of American life. In this essay, we attempt to redefine assimilation in order to render it useful in the study of the new immigration. (We are not alone in this attempt; see, for instance, Barkan 1995; Kazal 1995; Morowska 1994.) Our reformulation of assimilation emphasizes its utility for understanding the social dynamics of ethnicity in American society, as opposed to its past normative or ideological applications. As a state-imposed normative program aimed at eradicating minority cultures, assimilation has been justifiably repudiated. But as a social process that occurs spontaneously and often unintendedly in the course of interaction between majority and minority groups, assimilation remains a key concept for the study of inter-group relations. In what follows, we review the sociological literature on assimilation, with an eye to assessing its strengths and weaknesses; assay the validity of arguments for rejecting assimilation in understanding the new immigration; and sift through recent studies for clues concerning assimilation's course among the new immigrant groups.

THE CANONICAL ACCOUNT

Whatever the precise words, conceptions of assimilation have been central to understanding the American experience at least since colonial times. The centrality of assimilation for the scientific understanding of immigration is more recent, traceable to the Chicago School of the early twentieth century and especially to the work of Robert E. Park, W. I. Thomas, and their collaborators and students (McKee 1993). The social science use of assimilation thus emerged at the highpoint of a previous era of immigration and by means of observations in a city where the first and second generations then constituted the great majority of residents.

In 1921, Park and E. W. Burgess (1969:735) provided an early definition of assimilation: "a process of interpenetration and fusion in which persons and groups acquire the memories, sentiments, and attitudes of other persons and groups, and, by sharing their experience and history, are incorporated with them in a common cultural life." When read closely, this definition does not appear to require what many critics assume assimilation must: namely, the erasure of all signs of ethnic origins. Instead, it equates assimilation with the social processes that bring ethnic minorities into the mainstream of American life. The limited extent of the assimilation Park envisioned was made even more clear by another definition that he later created for the *Encyclopedia of the Social Sciences*, where "social" assimilation was "the name given to the process or processes by which peoples of diverse racial origins and different cultural heritages, occupying a common territory, achieve a cultural solidarity sufficient at least to sustain a national existence" (Park 1930:281).

Park's legacy is closely identified with the notion of assimilation as the end-stage of a "race-relations cycle" of "contact, competition, accommodation, and eventual assimilation," a sequence that, in the most famous statement of it, was viewed as "apparently progressive and irreversible" (Park 1950:138; see Barkan 1995:39–40; Lal 1990:41–45). In depicting the race-relations cycle, Park was rather deliberately painting with broad brush strokes on a large canvas, for the cycle refers obliquely to the processes in the modern world, including long-distance labor migration, that are bringing once separated peoples into closer contact. Competition is the initial, unstable consequence of contact as groups struggle to gain advantages over one another, and it eventuates in the more stable stage of accommodation, where a social structure of typically unequal relations among groups and a settled understanding of group position have come into being (Shibutani and Kwan

1965; Lal 1990:41–45). But no matter how stable, accommodation will eventually be undermined by the personal relationships that cross group boundaries, according to Park, who wrote that "in our estimates of race relations we have not reckoned with the effects of personal intercourse and the friendships that grow up out of them" (Park 1950:150).

Park has been faulted by many later writers for appearing to portray assimilation as an inevitable outcome in multiethnic societies (for example, Lyman 1973; Stone 1985). This is implied in Park's conception of stages. However, recent scholarship, as by Lal (1990), argues that the race-relations cycle played but a minor role in Park's sociology and that its fame rests more on his students' writings than on his own (see also McKee 1993:109–111). Park's students and associates did, in fact, make seminal contributions to the formulation of assimilation (for example, Burgess 1925; Wirth 1956; Warner and Srole 1945).

ASSIMILATION CONCEPTS: MILTON GORDON'S FRAMEWORK

The confusion among various formulations of assimilation in the early sociological literature has often been noted (Barkan 1995; Gordon 1964; for other general reviews of assimilation concepts, see Abramson 1980; Gleason 1980; Hirschman 1983). This problem was not solved until Milton Gordon's *Assimilation in American Life* (1964) provided a systematic dissection of the concept. His multidimensional formulation has proven attractive in part because it readily lends itself to operationalization and hypothesis formulation suitable for middle-range research. Although Gordon conceived of seven dimensions in all, the critical distinction in his conceptual scheme lay between acculturation and what he termed "structural" assimilation, by which he meant the entry of members of an ethnic minority into primary-group relationships with the majority group. This distinction, and its emphasis in particular on the character of an individual's primary-group affiliations, suggests one of the limitations of Gordon's scheme: it is oriented to a microsociological account of assimilation not conceptually integrated to larger social processes (see the dynamics of ethnic boundaries, Barth 1956). Nevertheless, Gordon's conceptual scheme proved to be useful to many students of ethnicity and has profoundly influenced scholarship on assimilation and ethnic change.

Acculturation, the minority group's adoption of the "cultural patterns" of the host society, typically comes first and is inevitable, Gordon argued. His discussion makes clear that these patterns extend beyond the acquisition of the English language to dress and outward emotional expression, and to personal values (Gordon 1964:79). He distinguished intrinsic cultural traits, those that are "vital ingredients of the group's cultural heritage," exemplified by religion and musical tastes, from extrinsic traits, which "tend to be products of the historical vicissitudes of the group's adjustment to the local environment" and thus are deemed less central to group identity (Gordon 1964:79). The distinction would seem to imply that extrinsic traits are readily surrendered by the group in making more or less necessary accommodations to the host society, but its implications are less clear about intrinsic ones. Certainly, Gordon had no expectation that fundamental religious identities are given up as a result of acculturation.

Gordon defined a cultural standard that represented the direction and eventual outcome of acculturation: the "middle-class cultural patterns of, largely, white Protestant, Anglo-Saxon origins," which he also described with Joshua Fishman's term as the "core culture" (Gordon 1964:72). In his view, acculturation was a largely one-way process; except in the domain of institutional religion, the minority group adopted the core culture, which remained in Gordon's view basically unchanged by this absorption. Gordon acknowledged only the possibility of change at the margins: "minor modifications in cuisine, recreational patterns, place names, speech, residential architecture, sources of artistic inspiration, and perhaps few other areas" (Gordon 1964:100).

In Gordon's account, acculturation could occur without being accompanied by other forms of assimilation, and the stage of acculturation only could last indefinitely. The catalyst for more complete assimilation instead is structural assimilation, which Gordon defined as "entrance of the minority group into the social cliques, clubs, and institutions of the core society at the primary group level." He hypothesized that "*once structural assimilation has occurred...all of the other types of assimilation will naturally follow*" (Gordon 1964:80–81, italics in original). This means in particular that prejudice and discrimination will decline (if not disappear), intermarriage will be common, and the minority's separate identity will wane.

On closer examination, Gordon's hypothesis is ambiguous as to whether it is meant to apply to individuals or groups. Even though the measurement of assimilation was put at the individual level, the hypothesis has been interpreted as applying literally to groups—a reading that becomes obvious when one recognizes that the hypothesized relationships among the different dimensions of assimilation need not hold in fact at the level of individuals. For example, individuals may be structurally assimilated, but prejudice and discrimination can still be widespread, as Gordon clearly understood. This ambiguity is important because of the desirability of formulating a concept of assimilation in which some independence between the individual and group levels is explicitly preserved (Barkan 1995). We will return to this point later.

Another limitation of Gordon's account was that it conceived of assimilation within a two-group framework of analysis (the "Sylvanians" and "Mundovians") and thus did not take into account the multi-group nature of American society. The language used by Gordon's definition ("social cliques, clubs, and institutions of the core society") implies that structural assimilation is to be equated with minority-group relationships to members of the majority group. The problem has been accentuated as American society has become more heterogeneous and the majority group smaller relative to the number of minority groups. Strictly speaking, Gordon's account does not extend to relationships between members of different ethnic minorities. Yet such situations are increasingly common. A broad rather than narrow two-group conception should be entertained if assimilation is to be faithful to the level of ethnic intermixing in American society (especially evident in terms of intermarriage and embodied in the Triple Melting Pot idea, Kennedy 1944).

Perhaps Gordon's structural-assimilation hypothesis should not be given the causal inflection his language implies. The strength of Gordon's conceptual scheme lies in its lucid articulation of some of the key dimensions of assimilation viewed as a composite concept. This leads to the recognition that, to some extent, the dimensions of assimilation can be arranged in terms of stages (Barkan 1995). When his hypothesis is read in this spirit, the core of the assertion is seen to be that structural assimilation signals the maturity of the assimilation process. Indeed, this has been the main use of the concept in the literature, as indicated by the frequent use of intermarriage data to measure assimilation's progress (Alba and Golden 1986; Lieberson and Waters 1988).

Identification assimilation, which represents a third dimension of Gordon's schema, has taken on importance in contemporary discussion of assimilation with respect to both the descendants of European immigrants and the new immigrant groups. Gordon (1964:71) defined this as the "development of [a] sense of peoplehood based exclusively on [the] host society." He recognized, too, that ethnic identity was not an undifferentiated concept and distinguished between "historical identification," which derived from a sense of the "interdependence of fate" (in Kurt Lewin's phrase) and typically extended to the ethnic group as a whole, and "participational identity," whose locus was the segment of the group most socially similar to the individual (the "ethclass," in Gordon's terminology, 1964:53). With the benefit of hindsight, Gordon's concept of identificational assimilation appears overly demanding, requiring the extinction of any form of ethnic identity in favor of an exclusively national, American identity. Consequently, it would seem to imply even the loss of family memories of extra-American origins, which seems not only an extraordinary expectation but one that flies in the face of the data demonstrating that the overwhelming majority of Americans still acknowledge some non-American ethnic ancestry (Lieberson 1985; Lieberson and Waters 1993). However, the knowledge that many individuals possess about their family histories should not be conflated with an ethnic identity that has practical consequences (Alba 1990; Gans 1979; Waters 1990).

An important part of Gordon's legacy is his delineation of alternative conceptions of the process and outcome of assimilation in the United States. Gordon described these as Anglo-Conformity and the Melting Pot. (He also identified a third model, Cultural Pluralism, which is less relevant to the canonical account.) These alternative conceptions are appropriately viewed as expressions of popular beliefs or ideologies about the constitution of civil society in America. The model of Anglo-Conformity, which corresponds in spirit with the campaign for rapid "pressure-cooker" Americanization during and after World War I, equated assimilation with acculturation in the Anglo-American mold and ignored other assimilation dimensions, being therefore indifferent to the occurrence or nonoccurrence of structural assimilation. The model of the Melting Pot has enjoyed several periods of popularity in American discussions of ethnicity, most recently in the immediate aftermath of World War II. It offered an idealistic vision of American society and identity as arising from the biological and cultural fusion of different peoples; and while its exponents usually emphasized the contributions of Europeans to the mixture, it allowed for a recognition of those from non-European groups as well. In terms of Gordon's scheme, the model operated along the dimensions of cultural and structural assimilation. This latter was invoked by the forecast of widespread intermarriage (Gordon 1964:125; Herberg 1960; Kennedy 1944, 1952). The cultural assimilation portion of the Melting Pot idea was rather ambiguous, however. Many early exponents spoke in ways that suggested a truly syncretic American culture that blended elements from many different groups, but later commentators were more consistent with Gordon's own conception: that acculturation is a mostly one-directional acceptance of Anglo-American patterns (Gordon 1964:127–128).

Gordon was an adherent of neither model. This may come as a surprise to many who know Gordon's views only in the context of the contemporary discussion of assimilation, for he has often been identified with a school that portrays assimilation as an almost inevitable outcome for immigrant groups. But this is not, in fact, a fair characterization. Although Gordon left little doubt that, in his view, acculturation was inevitable to a large degree, he did not see structural assimilation as similarly foreordained. His analysis of American society led to the conclusion that structural pluralism rather than cultural pluralism was the more accurate description. He envisioned the United States as constituted from ethnic subsocieties, in whose institutions and social networks most individuals spend the major portions of their social lives—literally from cradle to grave in many cases (Gordon 1964:159).

STRAIGHT-LINE ASSIMILATION

Another major piece of the canon is the notion of "straight-line assimilation," a phrase popularized by Gans (1973) and Sandberg (1973) to describe an idea stemming from Warner and Srole (1945). The straight-line notion adds a dynamic dimension to Gordon's somewhat static formulation in that it envisions a process unfolding in a sequence of generational steps. Each new generation represents on average a new stage of adjustment to the host society, that is, a further step away from ethnic "ground zero," the community and culture established by the immigrants, and a step closer to more complete assimilation (Lieberson 1973). Implied is the idea that generations are the motor for ethnic change, not just the time frame within which assimilation takes place. Each generation faces a distinctive set of issues in its relationship to the larger society and to the ethnic group, and their resolution brings about a distinctive pattern of accommodation. The idea of the generational inevitability of assimilation has been criticized, however, for assuming that all ethnic content is imported by immigrants and not recognizing that it can be created in response to conditions and out of cultural materials in the host society. Critics of the straight-line notion have argued that, instead, ethnicity may go through periods of re-creation, if not renaissance (Glazer and Moynihan 1970; Yancey, Ericksen, and Juliani 1976; Greeley 1977; Conzen et al. 1992). In recognition of this criticism, Gans (1992) has modified his description to the "bumpy-line theory of ethnicity," while still adhering to the core of the original concept: namely, that there is a generational dynamic behind ethnic change and that it moves, perhaps with tangents, in the general direction of assimilation.

The generational time frame assumes a view of ethnic change that is decidedly endogenous and that, perhaps ironically, tends to be ahistorical. By casting assimilation in terms of a dynamic internal to the group, the straight-line notion overlooks the impact of historically specific changes, such as the shifts in residential patterns resulting from the rapid expansion of suburbs in the post-World War II era. This, in combination with the hiatus of mass immigration in the 1920s, led to ethnic changes that corresponded closely with generational status—for example, in mother-tongue competence (Stevens 1985). Such generational effects may not be as pronounced in the current immigration where births in an ethnic group may be scattered across decades. Consequently, a common set of historical experiences is not likely to coincide with generational status, as was the case in the earlier mass immigration from Europe (and also Japan).

EXTENSIONS OF THE CONCEPTUAL CANON

Assimilation has been criticized over the decades, both from outside by those who reject it as a valid approach and by others who, operating within its conceptual frame, point out gaps or identify features that seem idiosyncratic to the experiences of some groups. Our concern here is to address criticism internal to the framework, leading us to consider some extensions of Gordon's contribution to the canon.

Gordon's concept of culture has been criticized for being static and overly homogeneous. As already noted, Gordon assumed that acculturation involved change on the part of an ethnic group in the direction of middle-class Anglo-American culture, which itself remained largely unaffected, except possibly for "minor modifications." An obvious problem with Gordon's view is that American culture varies greatly by locale and social class; acculturation hardly takes place in the shadow of a single, middle-class cultural standard. What is lacking in Gordon is a more differentiated and syncretic conception of culture as well as a recognition that American culture was and is more mixed, much more an amalgam of diverse influences, and that it continues to evolve.

It does not require a radical shift in perspective to recognize that assimilation and its expression in the form of acculturation are, at bottom, no more than the attenuation of an ethnic or racial distinction and the cultural and social differences that are associated with it.[2] Such processes can occur by changes in one group that make it more like another or by changes in two (or more) groups that shrink the differences and distance between them—group convergence, in other words. Moreover, acculturation need not be defined simply as the substitution of one cultural expression for its equivalent, whether the replacement comes from the majority or minority cultures, though such substitution certainly takes place. This narrow conception of acculturation is at the root of the frequently encountered view that one group "adopts" the cultural traits of another. The influence of minority ethnic cultures can occur also by an expansion of the range of what is considered normative behavior within the mainstream. Thus elements of minority cultures are absorbed alongside their Anglo-American equivalents or are fused with mainstream elements to create a hybrid cultural mix.

We suspect that ethnic influences on the mainstream American culture happen continuously—as the recent literature on the invention of ethnic and national traditions suggests (Conzen et al. 1992; Hobsbawm and Ranger 1983; Sollors 1989)—and that their occurrence is not limited to the domains where expansion and hybridization are most apparent, such as food and music. An obvious question is how one can recognize the incorporation into American culture of ethnic influences. The hallmark, we think, is that a cultural trait gradually loses its association with an ethnic group. In part, this happens because non-group members take it on, so that the empirical correlation between the trait and group membership is weakened. In part, it occurs as the trait is no longer labeled in an ethnic way. Over a longer time frame, the ethnic origins of a new element may be forgotten, and it becomes part of the mainstream repertoire, like the currently archetypal American recreational practices that, as Thomas Sowell (1996) notes, are derived from those brought by German immigrants. Similarly, the more intense family contacts that Greeley (1977) has documented for some groups, such as Irish and Italians, may have gradually influenced American conceptions of family life.

As noted earlier, Gordon's scheme did not recognize the distinction between individual and group levels of ethnic change. Thereby, it inadvertently sidestepped some of the most important lines of investigation within the assimilation framework: the reciprocal effects between group processes and individual attainment. The insight that a theory of assimilation must take the interaction between micro (individual) and mezzo (group or community) levels into account dates at least as far back as Breton's (1964) hypothesis that an ethnic community's "institutional completeness" influences its members' propensities to assimilate. In other words, the supply-side of ethnicity, the group and community context, may be decisive to the outcome at the individual level (Portes and Rumbaut 1996). If at the community level the opportunities to express ethnicity are meager or socially inappropriate, the intent to maintain ethnicity, assuming it exists, may be thwarted or transformed. The desire to find ethnic modes of behavior and expression, then, is likely to succeed where the supply-side of ethnicity is fairly rich in possibility. Where individuals assimilate in large numbers and are not replaced by a continuing immigration stream (a pattern characterizing many European-ancestry groups), the supply-side of ethnicity is diminished as a whole as well as narrowed in specific respects. Organizations dwindle in membership or find that their members belong to early generations or those with a more parochial outlook. Neighborhoods fail to retain the socially mobile sons and daughters of their residents, and their class character does not change to match the expanding class distribution of the group.

Some gaps in Gordon's account lend themselves to natural extensions by the addition of further dimensions of assimilation. (Odd though it seems, his multidimensional formulation overlooked important forms of assimilation.) Occupational mobility and economic assimilation, the key dimensions of socioeconomic assimilation, are not addressed in his discussion of assimilation. Yet this kind of assimilation is of paramount significance, both in itself, because parity of life chances with natives is a critical indicator of the decline of ethnic boundaries, and because entry into the occupational and economic mainstream has undoubtedly provided many ethnics with a motive for social (*structural*, in Gordon's sense) assimilation. Furthermore, socioeconomic mobility creates the social conditions conducive to other forms of assimilation since it likely results in equal status contact across ethnic lines in workplaces and neighborhoods.

Yet the concept of socioeconomic assimilation is not unambiguous, and two different usages need to be distinguished. In one, by far the more common in the literature on ethnicity and assimilation, socioeconomic assimilation is equated with attainment of average or above average socioeconomic standing, as measured by indicators such as education, occupation, and income (for example, Neidert and Farley 1985), a usage that can be traced to Warner and Srole (1945). Since many immigrant groups have entered the American social structure on its lower rungs, this meaning of socioeconomic assimilation is usually conflated with social mobility, leading to the frequently expressed expectation that assimilation and social mobility are inextricably linked. In the second usage, socioeconomic assimilation can be defined as minority participation in institutions such as the labor market and education on the basis of parity with native groups of similar backgrounds. If the emphasis in the first version falls on equality of attainment or position, the emphasis in the second is on equality of treatment; members of the immigrant minority and similarly situated members of native groups (which could be other minorities) have the same life chances in the pursuit of such scarce values as high-status jobs and higher education. The key question for the second version is: To what extent has an ethnic distinction lost its relevance for processes of socioeconomic attainment, except for initial conditions?

The distinction between the two types of socioeconomic assimilation is important because it pertains to whether the relationship between socioeconomic and other forms of assimilation is historically contingent. The descendants of European immigrants of the nineteenth and early twentieth centuries experienced a close link between social mobility and other forms of assimilation. But this may have reflected the opportunity structure available during a particular era in American history (Gans 1992; Portes and Zhou 1993). The question of whether the possible narrowing of opportunities in the contemporary United States will limit the prospects for socioeconomic assimilation of new immigrant groups or, instead, lead to a different pattern of assimilation must be kept open for the time being. The second kind of socioeconomic assimilation allows for "segmented" assimilation (Portes and Zhou 1993). According to this view, many labor migrants, with Mexicans as the preeminent example, may end up in the lower rungs of the stratification order, while human capital immigrants, common among Asian groups and Russian Jews in the current mass immigration, experience rapid social mobility.

Another dimension of assimilation that has received attention in recent years is residential or, following Massey (1985), spatial assimilation. Massey's formulation is the most systematic and has been used as a standard to assess the residential segregation of major racial/ethnic populations in the United States (Massey and Denton 1987, 1993). Spatial assimilation as a concept is linked to a model of incorporation that continues the Chicago School's ecological tradition and that views the spatial distribution of groups as a reflection of their human capital and the state of their assimilation, broadly construed. The basic tenets of the ecological model are that residential mobility follows from the acculturation and social mobility of individuals and that residential mobility is an intermediate step on the way to structural assimilation. As members of minority groups acculturate and establish themselves in American labor markets, they attempt to leave behind less successful members of their groups and to convert occupational mobility and economic assimilation into residential gain by "purchasing" residence in places with greater advantages and amenities. This process entails a tendency toward dispersion of minority group members, opening the way for increased contact with members of the ethnic majority and thus desegregation. According to the model, entry into relatively advantaged suburban communities that contain many whites is a key stage in the process (Massey and Denton 1988).

Like socioeconomic assimilation, residential assimilation has been given related but distinguishable interpretations in past discussion. Analogously, one is that the residential distribution of the minority approximates that of the majority—in other words, the group is found in the same locations and in similar concentrations as the majority. This is the condition of no segregation and is applicable only on the group level. A second meaning is that the residential opportunities of minority group members are equivalent to those of majority group members with similar resources. "Opportunities" here should be given a broad interpretation to include not just location (for example, access to desirable suburbs) but also housing (for example, home ownership and quality of dwelling). The question of whether minority group members can achieve residential situations as desirable as those of others with similar qualifications is one that can be posed at the individual level. A third and final meaning of residential assimilation refers to the existence of ethnic neighborhoods, which are generally viewed as housing social structures and cultural milieu supportive of ethnic distinctiveness (LaRuffa 1988; Alba, Logan, and Crowder 1997).

CREATING ASSIMILATION THEORY: SHIBUTANI AND KWAN'S ECOLOGICAL ANALYSIS

Even when extended as above, Gordon's analysis, the touchstone for all subsequent studies of assimilation, remains limited. Most important, it lacks a specification of the causal mechanisms giving rise to assimilation. Despite Gordon's reference to theories of assimilation, he did not formulate a theory in this sense. His contribution was to define a multidimensional framework whose descriptive concepts have proven highly useful, allowing analysts to measure the extent of the assimilation of racial and ethnic groups along various empirical dimensions. His linchpin hypothesis asserts that incorporation into primary groups of the dominant group precedes and stimulates other forms of assimilation. Yet the direction of causality could well be the opposite of what was claimed by the structural assimilation hypothesis, a question that cannot be resolved within Gordon's framework because there is no causal theory of assimilation.

At least one attempt to formulate a more complete theory of ethnic stratification and assimilation exists. Although it is not now a part of the assimilation canon, we include it in our discussion to suggest a direction in which the canon might fruitfully be expanded. The attempt we have in mind is that of Tomatsu Shibutani and Kian Kwan in *Ethnic Stratification* (1965). Whereas Gordon focused his study on assimilation in American society, Shibutani and Kwan elaborated a theory that expanded upon Park's race-relations cycle to focus broadly on explaining the dynamics of ethnic stratification around the globe. Despite this reach, their underlying aim was to gain new insights on the American experience of race relations through comparative historical analysis of systems of ethnic domination in diverse historical and societal settings, ranging widely to include Manchu rule over Han Chinese and ethnic stratification in the Roman Empire.

As Chicago School sociologists, Shibutani and Kwan employed Mead's symbolic interactionism as a core building block of their theory. Following Mead, they argued that how a person is treated in society depends "not on what he is," but on the "manner in which he is defined." Out of necessity, humans place people into categories, each associated with expected behavior and treatment, in order to deal in a routine and predictable manner with strangers and acquaintances outside of their primary groups. Differences giving rise to social distances are created and sustained symbolically through the practice of classifying and ranking. The social distances that arise thereby are the fundament of the color line that segregates minorities and impedes assimilation.

By social distance, Shibutani and Kwan (1965:263–271) mean the subjective state of nearness felt to certain individuals, not physical distance between groups. In their account, change in subjective states—reduction of social distance—precedes and stimulates structural assimilation, and not the reverse as implied in Gordon's hypothesis. When social distance is low, there is a feeling of common identity, closeness, and shared experiences. But when social distance is high, people perceive and treat the other as belonging to a different category; and even after long acquaintance, there are still feelings of apprehension and reserve. Social distance may be institutionalized, as it is in the case of the color line, where stereotypes, customs, social norms, and formal institutional arrangements maintain a system of stratification that employs ethnic markers to determine differential access to opportunity structures (Merton 1968). In Shibutani and Kwan's view of the American experience, social mobility through economic advancement, though not as common as it is perceived to be, allows for upward movement in class standing. But the system of ethnic stratification is more rigid. Ethnic identity for nonwhites is especially resilient to change. Although a member of a racial minority can improve his or her position in the opportunity structure, "ethnic identity, in those areas in which it makes a difference, places a ceiling upon the extent to which he can rise" (Shibutani and Kwan 1965:33).

Shibutani and Kwan intended their theory as an extension of Park's natural history of the race-relations cycle. Through a comparative historical approach, they examined case studies of contact, competition, accommodation, and assimilation stemming from migration. Their analysis uncovered many apparent exceptions to Park's optimistic conception of assimilation, for ethnic stratification orders tend to be long-lasting once established and institutionalized. Domination is initially gained through competitive advantages accruing to the group whose culture is best adapted to exploit the resources of the environment. Competition and natural selection push minorities into the least desirable residential locations and economic niches. A stable system of ethnic stratification is rooted in part in a moral order in which the dominant group is convinced that its advantages derive from natural differences and minorities come to believe in their inferiority and accept their lot at the bottom. But the dominant group also upholds its position and privileges through institutionalized power and outright coercion. Individual minority group members may achieve social mobility and gain economic parity, but as exceptions to the rule. Such upwardly mobile individuals, often of mixed race, acquire a marginal status that gives them a modicum of privilege and respect, but they are fully accepted neither by the dominant group nor by their own ethnic community. In a stable ethnic stratification order, individual assimilation can occur even while the system maintaining dominance remains intact.

Nevertheless, Shibutani and Kwan agree with Park that even stable ethnic stratification orders ultimately tend to become undone and that assimilation occurs at the final stage of the natural history of the race-relations cycle. Their use of ecological theory, which informs their analysis of ethnic stratification, plays a central role here, too, contributing a dynamic, macro-sociological dimension that is vital to their theoretical framework. It provides the crucial causal links between the micro-sociological part of the theory and much larger structures and processes.

The causal mechanisms that bring about the reduction of social distance stem from changes in "life conditions" that occur at the ecological level. In the absence of such changes, ethnic stratification orders tend towards stable equilibrium. In explaining the transformation of such orders, Shibutani and Kwan emphasize particularly the importance of technological innovation, which in turn induces alterations in the mode of production. As an illustration, they cite the invention of the automatic cotton picket, which diminished the demand for cheap labor in the south and sparked the migration of poor blacks and whites to the industrial north, altering the pattern of racial stratification throughout the United States. Changes in the economic system associated with technological shifts often introduce opportunities for minority groups to acquire new competitive advantages that make them indispensable to employers. These in turn lead employers to seek institutional changes favorable to the interests of minority groups—changes that, in a capitalist system, are relatively easy to institute when organizations and individuals pursuing profits find it in their economic interest to do so. As a contemporary example, one could point to the role of employers in supporting the immigration of workers, both skilled and unskilled, legal and undocumented, despite the public clamor for greater limits on legal immigration and a curtailing of illegal immigration. At one end of the economic spectrum, the interest of employers stems from the growing labor market demand for highly skilled workers (such as computer programmers) because of the postindustrial transformation of the American economy. At the other end, there is a continuing need for elastic sources of low-wage labor in the agricultural sector, in "degraded" manufacturing sectors such as the garment industry, and in personal service such as childcare (Sassen 1988).

Another ecological source of change stems from shifts in the often unstable demographic balance between majority and minority groups. As the relative size of minority groups increases, shifts in power become likely. For example, the increasing percentage of nonwhites in the United States contributes to the pressure on employers and schools to institute changes, such as policies promoting the value of diversity, to accommodate a more heterogeneous population. Similar changes can also be observed in other countries with large immigrant populations, such as Germany, where multiculturalist pressures have also arisen as an accommodative response to growing population diversity (Cohn-Bendit and Schmid 1992). Likewise, increases in population density, mainly in cities, alter ethnic relations by increasing the probability of chance meetings and, eventually, stable relationships between members of different ethnic groups.

The effects of ecological changes notwithstanding, Shibutani and Kwan assert that the most immediate source of a decline in social distance occurs when other changes stimulate the introduction of new ideas that challenge values and cultural beliefs previously taken for granted, as in the discrediting of white supremacist ideologies in the postcolonial world, and a "transformation of values" ensues.

Systems of ethnic stratification begin to break down when minority peoples develop new self-conceptions and refuse to accept subordinate roles. As they become more aware of their worth in comparison to members of the dominant group, what they had once accepted as natural becomes unbearable (Shibutani and Kwan 1965:350).

In Shibutani and Kwan's account, the context giving rise to higher rates of assimilation often follows the outbreak of protests and opposition. Social movements are the engine that sparks interest among dominant elites in instituting changes and reforms to alter the relationship between majority and minority in a manner that promotes assimilation.

We intend our brief discussion of Shibutani and Kwan's theory of ethnic stratification to sketch the outline of a missing component in the canon of assimilation, but not necessarily to provide the exact blueprint. Without a dynamic of the sort provided by this theory, Gordon's analysis of assimilation remains static, allowing for individual-level assimilation but not for more wholesale shifts in ethnic and racial boundaries. (As we noted earlier, Gordon remained a structural pluralist in his view of American society.) The link between micro-sociological changes in social distance, and thus interethnic relations and structural assimilation, and macro-sociological shifts points in the direction in which a theory of assimilation must move. Although the causal mechanisms that the Shibutani-Kwan theory posits may be revised in light of new research, clearly any analysis of the potential for assimilation in the United States, or anywhere else for that matter, cannot rely solely on confidence in processes of individual-level assimilation alone; it must pay attention to macroscopic processes rooted in population ecology and how these impinge on prospects for assimilation.

HOW RELEVANT ARE THE DIFFERENCES BETWEEN PAST AND PRESENT "ERAS OF IMMIGRATION"?

There is abundant evidence that assimilation has been the master trend among descendants of the immigrants of the previous era of mass immigration, who mainly came from Europe before 1930. This assimilation can be equated, above all, with long-term processes that have eroded the social foundations for ethnic distinctions and ultimately the distinctions themselves. These processes have brought about a rough parity of opportunities (among groups, not individuals) to obtain the desirable social goods of the society, such as prestigious and remunerative jobs, and loosened the ties between ethnicity and specific economic niches (Greeley 1976; Lieberson 1980; Lieberson and Waters 1988; Neidert and Farley 1985). Parity here refers to a broad convergence toward the life chances of the "average" white American, which has particularly affected the descendants of immigrants from peasant backgrounds (such as southern Italians) and does not exclude the exceptional achievements of a few small groups, such as Eastern European Jews. Assimilation has diminished cultural differences that once served to signal ethnic membership to others and to sustain ethnic solidarity; one result has been an implosion of European mother tongues (Alba 1988; Stevens 1992; Veltman 1983). Assimilation is also associated with a massive shift in residence during the postwar era—away from urban ethnic neighborhoods towards ethnically intermixed suburbs (Alba, Logan, and Crowder 1997; Gans 1967; Guest 1980)—and with relatively easy social intermixing across ethnic lines, resulting in high rates of ethnic intermarriage and ethnically mixed ancestry (Alba 1995; Alba and Golden 1986; Lieberson and Waters 1988). Finally, assimilation finds expression in the ethnic identities of many whites, which are "symbolic" in the sense defined by Herbert Gans and involve few commitments in everyday social life (Gans 1979; Alba 1990; Waters 1990).

Admittedly, the causes of this assimilation of European ancestry ethnic groups are much less well understood than is the result. But, at a minimum, the fact that this assimilation has involved groups with very different characteristics at time of immigration and varied histories in the United States suggests that the forces promoting it have been, and perhaps still are, deeply embedded in American society. Yet many scholars of contemporary immigration reject assimilation as a likely outcome on a mass scale for contemporary immigrant groups. One of the most compelling arguments they raise is that assimilation, as represented by the canonical account, is specific to a set of historical circumstances that characterized mass immigration from Europe but does not, and will not, apply to contemporary non-European immigrant groups (see Massey 1994; Portes and Rumbaut 1996).

THE ABSENCE OF A FORESEEABLE HIATUS IN THE IMMIGRATION STREAM

The decisive halt in the stream of mass immigration from Europe in the late 1920s, induced by restrictive immigration legislation followed by the Great Depression, is widely thought to have been fateful for ethnic groups. The ensuing four-decade interruption in steady, large-scale immigration virtually guaranteed that ethnic communities and cultures would be steadily weakened over time. The social mobility of individuals and families drained these communities, especially of native-born ethnics, and undermined the cultures they supported. There were few newcomers available as replacements. Over time, the modal generation shifted from the immigrant to the second and then from the second to the third.

Many students of post-1965 immigration believe that a similar hiatus in the contemporary immigration stream is unlikely. One reason is the apparent disinclination of the federal government to ratchet down the level of immigration, though this may be changing as the political climate generated by immigration issues heats up (Brimelow 1995). The legislation that set the main parameters for immigration during the 1990s, the Immigration Act of 1990, appears to have raised the level of legal immigration above the nearly record-setting pace of the 1980s (Heer 1996; Reimers 1992:262). Moreover, recent attempts to control the immigration flow, such as the 1986 IRCA law, have generally had unanticipated and even counterproductive consequences in the end, perhaps, many suggest, because the immigration-generating forces in the United States and in sending societies are so powerful that they thwart or bypass the attempts of the U.S. government to harness them (Donato, Durand, and Massey 1992; Heer 1996).

Movement across national borders appears to be an endemic feature of the contemporary international system, and this adds to the difficulty of substantially limiting contemporary immigration. United Nations projections suggest very large world population increases in the near future (by 2025); this will occur mostly outside the highly developed nations and thus add to the huge reservoir of people available to move (Heer 1996:137–145). Needless to say, emigration from less-developed countries is not just a product of population pressure but of the economic-development curve, which instills in broad segments of the population consumption tastes that cannot be satisfied by their native economies, and of the historical linkages that exists between less- and more-developed nations in the international system (Sassen 1988; Portes and Rumbaut 1996). Further, it is more difficult for national governments to control emigration than was the case a century ago. Such forces seem likely to engender large, difficult-to-control population movements far into the future, as exemplified by the large legal and illegal flows from Mexico to the United States.

If immigration to the United States continues indefinitely at its current level, population projections show that many of the ethnic groups arising from it will be dominated by the first and second generations well into the 21st century (Edmonston and Passel 1994). This will create a fundamentally different ethnic context from that faced by the descendants of European immigrants, for the new ethnic communities are highly likely to remain large, culturally vibrant, and institutionally rich. Ethnic community life, in combination with ethnic economies, according to this scenario, is likely to provide particularistic channels of mobility. In sum, there are likely to be strong incentives to keep ethnic affiliations alive even for the third generation, as long as the distance between the generations does not grow so great as to alienate them from one another.

Yet, if there is any proven rule in population projections, it is that the patterns of the present cannot be projected indefinitely into the future, for they will change in unforeseeable ways. The level of immigration could go up, to be sure, but it could also go down as a result of restrictive legislation backed up by tougher enforcement, a decline in the attractiveness of the United States to one or more of the main sources of current immigration, a weakening of the forces generating emigration from these countries, or some combination of these changes. Despite the current pessimism about efforts to control immigration flows to the United States, especially the undocumented immigration, control is not impossible, as is shown by the example of Germany, which has lengthy land borders with Eastern Europe, a potential source of many immigrants, but only a small residential population of undocumented immigrants in comparison with that of the United States.

Moreover, a decline in the attractiveness of the United States to potential immigrants could happen for any of a number of reasons, such as changes in the labor market that eliminate some of the niches exploited by immigrants, declines in the relative quality of life in the metropolitan areas that are the main receiving areas, or a rise in the relative attractiveness and accessibility of other countries as immigrant destinations.

Raising the prospect of a future decline in the general level of immigration is admittedly speculative. We are on firmer ground, we believe, in predicting that the immigration of some groups will decline and will not live up to the assumption of continued inflow far into the future. The assumption, in other words, will hold selectively, not uniformly. One reason for suspecting such declines is that the level of economic development of some sending nations may approach or even catch up to that of the United States, undermining a principal motive for immigration. This has happened in the case of Japan, which sent many immigrants around the turn of the 20th century, but currently is the source for few immigrants, other than managers in Japanese companies who are doing a tour of duty at U.S. branches. It could well happen in the cases of Korea and Taiwan. Indeed, there are signs of an incipient decline in Korean immigration: Between 1990 and 1994, the number of immigrant visas allocated to Koreans fell by 60 percent while the number returning home surged (Belluck 1995; Min 1996). For groups whose immigration abates, the prediction of ethnic communities continually revitalized by new immigration will prove inaccurate.

Finally, it perhaps should not be assumed that the cessation of mass immigration was essential to opening the way for assimilation for the descendants of late European immigration. In any case, we do not know whether and to what extent assimilation would have taken place. It is certainly a plausible hypothesis that assimilation would have proceeded, albeit at a slower pace. Similarly, in the new era of mass immigration, even if immigration continues at present levels, there is no reason to assume that the second and third generation will be locked into the same communal life and economic niches of the first generation. With the possible exception of Mexican immigration, which might be compared to the French-Canadian situation, the numbers of immigrants from each of the many immigrant streams are small relative to the overall U.S. population. Far from the closed ethnic boundaries common to situations of stable ethnic stratification often involving only a few ethnic groups, such heterogeneity increases the likelihood of chance meeting and associations across groups. Moreover, as long as ethnic economies are populated by small businesses with limited opportunities for advancement, the direction of job changes over time, even for the first generation, will be to secure jobs with better conditions of employment and returns to human capital in the mainstream economy (Nee, Sanders, and Sernau 1994).

THE RACIAL DISTINCTIVENESS OF MANY NEW IMMIGRANT GROUPS

A common argument holds that the descendants of earlier European immigrations, even those composed of peasants from economically backward parts of Europe, could eventually assimilate because their European origins made them culturally and racially similar to American ethnic core groups—specifically, those from the British Isles and some northern and western European countries. The option of assimilation will be less available to the second and later generations of most new immigrant groups because their non-European origins mean that they are more distinctive, with their distinctiveness of skin color especially fateful.

While we wish to avoid at all cost a Panglossian optimism about American racism, we find this argument less compelling than many do because we think that it treats perceptions of racial difference as more rigid than they have proven themselves historically. We grant that American treatment of non-Europeans has generally been characterized by racist discrimination of a more extreme cast than anything experienced by even the most disparaged of the European groups, as the well-known examples of the Chinese Exclusion Act of the late nineteenth century and the internment of Japanese Americans during World War II testify. Nevertheless, the view that the pathway to assimilation was smoothed for the descendants of European immigrants by their racial identification is an anachronism, inappropriately imposing contemporary racial perceptions on the past. There is ample evidence that native-born whites perceived some of the major European immigrant groups, such as the Irish, Jews, and Italians, as racially distinct from themselves and that such perceptions flowered into full-blown racist theorizing during the high-water period of mass immigration in the early decades of the twentieth century (Higham 1970). This is not just a matter of a language usage in which "race" was treated as a synonym for "nation" or "ethnic group." Many Americans believed that they could identify the members of some groups by their characteristic appearance (for example, "Jewish" facial features), and nineteenth-century caricatures of the Irish frequently gave them a distinctly simian cast.

Over time, racial perceptions of the most disparaged European groups shifted. The Irish, and perhaps other groups, initially struggled to put some racial and social distance between themselves and African Americans (Ignatiev 1995; Roediger 1991). But as these groups climbed the socioeconomic ladder and mixed residentially with other whites, their perceived distinctiveness from the majority faded. (World War II, a watershed in many ways for ethnic relations among whites, also had a powerful impact on attitudes towards European ethnics.) Intermarriage both marked this shift and accelerated it. We see no *a priori* reason why a similar shift could not take place for some contemporary immigrant groups and some segments of other groups. Here we think particularly of Asians and light-skinned Latinos. In the case of some Asian groups, the relatively high intermarriage rates of their U.S.-born members suggest their acceptability to many whites, the most frequent partners in intermarriage, and the absence of a deep racial divide (Lee and Yamanaka 1990; Qian 1997). Loewen's (1971) study of Chinese immigrants who migrated from the Western states to the South in the 1870s documents a transformation of racial attitudes that parallels that for the Irish.

When Chinese laborers first arrived in the Mississippi Delta, they joined free blacks as part of the "colored" agricultural labor force in a race-segregated society. Chinese immigrants and their descendants gradually "crossed-over" to gain acceptance in the white community by distancing themselves socially from blacks and acculturating to southern white culture. The post-1965 immigration of Asians to the United States takes place in a substantially different historical context of the post-Civil Rights Movement and in a new era of mass immigration. Although Loewen's case study of the Mississippi Chinese may not be applicable to the current immigration, it nonetheless shows that ethnic identity and boundaries are socially constructed and malleable.

The most intractable racial boundary remains that separating those deemed phenotypically black from whites. This boundary is likely to exert a powerful influence on the adaptation possibilities of immigrant groups, depending on where they are situated with respect to it. The evidence of this influence is already apparent; it is registered in the research observations about the identification dilemmas confronted by the children of black Caribbean parentage (Waters 1994; Woldemikael 1989) and recognized in the concept of "segmented assimilation" (Portes and Zhou 1993). But despite such evidence, there is also the countervailing experience of South Asian immigrants. Although South Asians have dark skin color, they are the highest income group in the United States and are predominantly suburban in their residence (Portes and Rumbaut 1996). Their experience suggests that it is not dark skin color per se but the appearance of connection to the African-American group that raises the most impassable racist barriers in the United States.

THE IMPACT OF ECONOMIC RESTRUCTURING ON IMMIGRANT OPPORTUNITY

The assimilation of European-ancestry Americans is linked to opportunities for social mobility that, within a brief historical period, brought about a tough parity of life chances across many ethnic groups—though not within them, as life chances remained structured by social class origins (Greeley 1976; Lieberson 1980). These opportunities were in turn linked to historically contingent, broad avenues of intergenerational movement that allowed immigrants of peasant origin with few work skills of relevance in an urban industrial economy nevertheless to gain a foothold through steady employment, often beginning in the manufacturing sectors (Bodnar 1985). According to a common view, similar openings are not to be found with the same frequency in the contemporary economy. This is due to economic restructuring, which has led to the elimination of many manufacturing jobs and the degradation of others and to their replacement in the spectrum of jobs open to immigrant workers with low-level service jobs that do not offer comparable wages, stability of employment, or mobility ladders (Sassen 1988). This result of economic restructuring is described by Portes and Zhou (1993) as an "hourglass economy," with a narrowed band of middle-level jobs and bulging strata at the bottom and the top. The presumption is that it will be more difficult for the descendants of contemporary immigrants, many of whom enter the labor force at or near the bottom, to make the gradual intergenerational transition upwards, because footholds in the middle of the occupational structure are relatively scarce (Portes and Zhou 1993). Movement into the top strata requires substantial human capital, particularly higher educational credentials, that is not likely to be within reach of all members of the second generation. A conclusion drawn by a number of scholars is that, to a degree not true of European ethnics, the current second generation is at risk of experiencing no, or even downward, mobility, unless the American economy becomes more dynamic than it has been since the early 1970s (Gans 1992).

Without question, economic opportunities are critical to the assimilation prospects of new immigrant groups. Because of the enormous variety among groups in the forms of capital—economic, cultural and social—they bring with them and in degree of support provided by the community contexts they enter, the restructuring of the economy does not have an equally negative impact on the opportunities of all groups (Light 1984; Portes and Rumbaut 1996; Waldinger 1986/87, 1996). Some groups, like the Cubans of Miami, have distinguished themselves by the development of ethnic sub-economies that are likely to afford the second generation better-than-average chances to succeed in the educational system and enter professional occupations. Others—several Asian groups spring readily to mind—enjoy, whether because of the professional occupations of their immigrant parents or the cultural capital they possess, high levels of educational attainment in the United States (Gibson 1988; Hirschman and Wong 1986; Model 1988; Nee and Sanders 1985; Light and Bonacich 1988). Moreover, the 1980s economic restructuring has stimulated economic growth in the 1990s, and this has brought about a sharp reduction of unemployment. As a result of tighter labor markets, even low-skilled manual laborers have experienced increases in hourly earnings.

The significance of economic restructuring for the second and subsequent generations would appear to be greatest for those groups described by Portes and Rumbaut (1996) as "labor migrant" groups, like the Mexicans. Even here, we caution that the distinction from the experiences of comparable European groups (southern Italians, for example) can be overdrawn, for they too did not enter an economy that was continuously generating a bountiful supply of opportunities for secure employment and upward mobility. A large portion of the second generation of the southern and eastern European groups came of age in the teeth of the Depression. Like the children of some contemporary immigrants, many in the earlier second generation responded to their perceived lack of opportunity and to their rejection at the hands of nativist whites by constructing what are now called "reactive identities," identities premised upon value schemes that invert those of the mainstream in important ways. We know for instance that, during the 1930s and perhaps afterwards, the children of southern Italian immigrants were widely perceived as posing problems in the educational system; they had high rates of dropout, truancy, and delinquency (Covello 1972), all signs that they were rejecting the conventions and values of a system that they perceived as rejecting them.

Yet the analyses of Lieberson (1980) demonstrate that the U.S.-born members of these groups experienced a fairly steady upgrading of educational and occupational attainment, even in the cohorts whose life chances would have been most affected by the Depression. This suggests to us that the emphasis on economic restructuring in the discussion of assimilation chances for contemporary immigrant groups may produce a too pessimistic reading of their prospects. Our additional remarks can only be suggestive at this point. But, since there is as yet no fully satisfactory explanation for the assimilation of the once disparaged southern and eastern European groups, it seems premature to judge the assimilation chances of contemporary immigrant groups as diminished because the socioeconomic structure of the United States has changed in the interim. As Perlmann and Waldinger (1997) note, to insist that assimilation is likely only if the situation of contemporary groups parallels that of earlier ones in precise ways seems to require something that history almost never does: repeat itself exactly. With respect to mobility, such an insistence loses sight of the ability of individuals and groups to adjust their strategies to the economic structures they find. We note in particular that the focus of the economic restructuring argument as applied to immigrants has been almost entirely on the labor market, and it has therefore ignored the educational system. However, not only has the association between social origins and educational attainment weakened over time (Hout et al. 1993), but postsecondary education is more available in some of the states where immigrants have concentrated (California and New York, especially) than elsewhere in the nation. Perhaps the pathways followed by earlier groups have been narrowed over time, but other pathways are likely to have opened up.

We are not denying that there are differences, and important ones, between the immigrations of the past and present and in the circumstances facing immigrant groups after arrival. Nor are we claiming that the parallels between the situations faced by the descendants of contemporary immigrants and those of earlier ones are so strong that patterns of assimilation among European Americans can be inferred as a likely outcome for new immigrant groups. But the distinctions between these situations are not as clear-cut as they are usually made out to be. None of them is, in our judgment, sufficiently compelling to rule out *a priori* the possibility of assimilation as a widespread outcome for some, or even most, contemporary immigrant groups. It is therefore imperative to examine with an open mind the cultural, residential, educational, and other patterns established by the new immigrants and their children for clues about the potential importance of assimilation.

EVIDENCE OF ASSIMILATION BY NEW IMMIGRANT GROUPS

The evidence bearing on the assimilation of new immigrant groups remains fragmentary in important respects, but it is nevertheless essential to review it for hints about the trajectory of these groups, especially across generations. It is critical at the outset, however, to emphasize the limited nature of the data available about the second generation and the virtual absence of any about the third or later generations. It is widely accepted that the immigrant generation does experience changes as it accommodates itself to life in a new society but that these changes are limited for individuals who come mostly as adults and have been socialized in another society, which is invariably quite different from that of the United States. Hence, the changes experienced by the immigrants themselves cannot be decisive for conclusions about assimilation. It is only with the U.S.-born, or at a minimum the foreign-born who immigrate at young ages and are raised mostly in the United States (usefully labeled by Rumbaut 1994 as the "1.5 generation"), that there is the possibility of assessing the limits of assimilation for new immigrant groups. But even in the case of the second generation, the literature on the assimilation of white ethnics offers reason to be cautious about inferences.

For most European groups, the assimilation of the second generation was partial. Indeed, the well-known studies of this generation depict in general individuals whose lives were profoundly affected by their ethnic origins, who mostly resided in ethnic communities and exhibited in a variety of ways thinking and behavior characteristic of the group as well as some degree of loyalty to it. (For the Italians, for example, there are the studies of Child 1943; Gans 1982; Whyte 1955.) It was only with the third and, in some cases, the fourth generations that the powerful undercurrent of assimilation came unmistakably to the surface. But for the new immigrant groups, the second generation is still young (Mexicans being the principal exception), and the studies that focus on it generally can track only its progress in school. The probative value of evidence about the second generation must be carefully examined.

Another critical limitation is the very limited time of exposure to American society for the subjects of many of the studies of new immigrant groups. Half of the Punjabi Sikh high school students on whom Gibson's (1988) study focuses arrived in the United States within the five years preceding the field-work; all of the subjects of Suárez-Orozco's (1989) study of Central American refugee school children had come within the preceding five years; and so on. Much of the data we possess about new immigrant groups can be characterized as pertinent to the earliest phases of their settlement in the United States, the phase that Park (1950) characterized as involving contact and competition. In the past histories of immigration and intergroup relations in the United States, the period of stable accommodation extended beyond the first and second generations. Thus, the observations that assimilation is far from complete or that immigrants and their children do not appear to want to assimilate should not be regarded as definitive for the longer-term changes that will occur to these groups. In what follows, we limit our review of the evidence for reasons of space. We have chosen, therefore, the two areas that we, as researchers, know best.

SOCIOECONOMIC ATTAINMENT

As many scholars have noted, a defining feature of the post-1965 immigration is the diversity of the socioeconomic backgrounds of contemporary immigrants. Rather than hailing primarily from rural communities, the new immigrants come from both rural and urban backgrounds, from underdeveloped regions of the Western Hemisphere, and from industrially developed areas of East Asia. Occupationally, the new immigration encompasses the full spectrum of jobs. Professional immigrants—engineers, mathematicians, computer scientists, natural scientists, teachers, and health workers—come mainly from Asian countries, and nearly a quarter come from other developing countries (Kanjanapan 1994). Hence, they are predominantly nonwhite. Many human-capital immigrants enter the labor market from professional and graduate schools in the United States. Their transition to jobs in the mainstream economy involves a school-to-job transition not dissimilar from that of the native-born. Most professional immigrants, however, enter the labor force through the occupational and family reunification categories of the 1965 immigration law (Jasso and Rosenzweig 1990). Human-capital immigrants educated abroad, after a period of downward adjustment, appear to shift into mainstream jobs as they acquire local work experience and acquire facility with the English language (Farley 1996), or they go into self-employment (Sanders and Nee 1996; Nee, Sanders, and Sernau 1994).

The economic assimilation of human-capital immigrants is less well-known, however, than are the experiences of immigrant entrepreneurs and workers in the ethnic economy and of traditional labor migrants. These are the groups that clump together into visible ethnic economies and communities. They are also the groups on which researchers have concentrated their attention because of theoretical and empirical differences centering on assimilation theory (Wilson and Portes 1980; Portes and Bach 1985) and because of growing concerns over the declining quality of immigrants (Chiswick 1986; Greenwood 1983) and its consequences for prospects for economic assimilation (Borjas 1990).

The Ethnic Economy. The early literature on ethnic economies focused on the experiences of Asian immigrant groups: the Chinese and Japanese (Light 1972; Bonacich and Modell 1980). These studies emphasized the importance of the ethnic economy in providing employment and profit for minorities facing harsh societal hostility. Despite institutional racism that excluded Asian ethnics from opportunities in the mainstream economy, these groups were able to sustain themselves through small-business economies that created alternative sources of opportunities under group control. This pattern gave rise to a stable accommodation that provided the economic basis for rearing and educating a second generation. The salient feature of the Chinese and Japanese ethnic economies was the extensive reliance on ethnic resources and solidarity in the accumulation of start-up capital and in competition with white firms.

In many respects, the ethnic economies of early Chinese and Japanese immigrants served a similar role in the subsequent assimilation of Asian ethnics as they did for the Jewish immigrant community. They provided a means for survival and modest economic gain when racial discrimination barred even the college-educated second generation from opportunities in the mainstream economy. The abatement of societal hostility and the assimilation of the American-born generations of Asian ethnics following World War II resulted in a secular decline of Chinatowns, which was not reversed until the start of the post-1965 immigration (Nee and Nee 1973). The Japanese ethnic economy was never fully reconstituted after the internment experience (Bonacich and Modell 1980). But once the color line broke down, the assimilated second generation abandoned parental small businesses to seek jobs in the mainstream. Implied in this choice is a perception of the limited nature of the economic mobility and opportunities provided by the ethnic economy, which is constituted by very small firms with limited capital and bounded markets (Nee and Nee 1973; Bonacich and Model 1980).

In the case of Chinese immigrant workers, Mar (1991) showed that jobs in the enclave provide even lower earnings than do those in the competitive secondary sector, which has been presumed to be associated with economic disadvantages for immigrants. Analyzing the job transitions of Asian immigrants, Nee, Sanders, and Sernau (1994) found that enclave workers received lower net earnings and lower returns to their human capital, but immigrants who previously worked for a co-ethnic employer were more likely to enter into self-employment. In Farley's analysis of the 1990 census, Chinese men earned the lowest net wages of male income earners in any immigrant group. Farley (1996) attributed this to the enclave economy effect on workers' wages:

> More so than other streams of current immigrants, it appears that the uneducated from China are concentrated in or trapped in a low-wage enclave economy, helping to explain why the Chinese are less effective than other immigrants in translating their characteristics into earnings. (p. 191)

One response to the enclave-economy debate has been to question the limits of the central concept (Sanders and Nee 1987). Light, Sabagh, Bozorgmehr, and Der-Martirosian (1994) argued that a broader concept of an ethnic economy better serves the needs of research. Defined as the self-employed and their co-ethnic employees, the ethnic economy can be readily measured (Bonacich and Modell 1980). By contrast, the enclave-economy concept is empirically unwieldy. Portes and Bach (1985) were unable to specify its boundaries with the precision needed for empirical study. Light and Karageorgis (1994) also point out that the debate over the enclave hypothesis overlooks a key datum: Ethnic enterprises in fact employ very few paid co-ethnic employees. Hence, the main object of study is not the co-ethnic employee in the ethnic economy, but the self-employed. Another limitation of the enclave concept is that relatively few ethnic economies have the spatial concentration and breadth of firms required to qualify as enclave economies (Logan, Alba, and McNulty 1994). This is not strictly speaking a limitation of the hypothesis, but of its relevance for groups other than Cubans in Miami, Koreans in Los Angeles, Japanese in Honolulu, and a few other cases.

A side effect of the enclave-economy debate, therefore, was to focus attention on the economic assimilation of immigrant entrepreneurs. Although researchers agree that self-employment constitutes an important aspect of the immigrant experience, they disagree about the relative advantages it confers. Borjas (1990) argues that the self-employed in the ethnic economy are not better off than immigrant workers with similar human capital. However, according to Portes and Zhou (1996), the analysis of earnings, when conducted with nominal income values rather than the logged form preferred by economists, reveals the "success stories" in the population of self-employed. In Los Angeles, for example, self-employed Asian immigrants earn $6.00 more per hour than other immigrants with comparable characteristics (Nee, Sanders, and Sernau 1994). Yet, as Portes and Zhou (1996) concede, if the average return for immigrant entrepreneurship is the main concern, then Borjas (1990) is right in arguing that entrepreneurs in the ethnic economy are not particularly successful.

Although the ethnic economy is an important institutional arrangement for immigrants, by no means does it provide the main route for their economic advancement. We agree with Borjas's assessment that "self-employment represents an important component of the immigrant experience in the U.S. labor market" (1986:505). However, in our view, the literature on the economic incorporation of contemporary immigrants risks overstating its significance (Aldrich and Waldinger 1990; Light and Karageorgis 1994). It is useful to keep in mind that just 14 percent of native-born non-Hispanic whites are self-employed and that only Korean immigrants show a higher concentration (28 percent) in self-employment. Despite the emphasis on immigrant entrepreneurship, in other words, all other immigrant groups report a lower level of involvement in the small-business sector than whites (Farley 1996). The modal labor market experience of immigrants is not in the ethnic economy nor in small-business ownership, but in the open economy. Immigrant workers may first establish a foothold in the immigrant labor market by working in the ethnic economy, but over time the direction of job changes is generally towards jobs with better remuneration and conditions of work, and these are mostly available in the mainstream labor market. Nee, Sanders, and Sernau (1994) show in their study of Asians in the Los Angeles immigrant labor market that ethnic boundaries and labor market sectors are much more permeable than they are assumed to be by the segmented labor market literature.

Immigrants in the Open Labor Market. In the analysis of economic assimilation of immigrant workers, labor economists have contributed important findings. Chiswick's (1977, 1978) pioneering studies of the earnings of immigrants indicated that after an initial period of income decline—which he interpreted as stemming from the "cost of immigration"—the earnings of immigrants gradually achieved parity within a 10-to-15 year time-line and then surpassed the earnings of native-born workers of the same ethnic background. However, this finding was subsequently challenged by Borjas (1985, 1987) as inconclusive because Chiswick relied on a cross-sectional research design, which conflated aging and immigration-cohort effects. By examining cohort changes, Borjas's analysis suggested that in the past five decades there was a major decline in the skills of immigrants. He pooled the 1970 and 1980 census data and found that the earnings growth of recent cohorts did not exceed the earnings levels of the native-born and were lower than the growth experienced by earlier cohorts of immigrants. He concluded that the third-world origin of many immigrants accounted for the decline in immigrant "quality," or human capital, compared with the earlier immigration from Europe. Like Chiswick's, Borjas's conclusions are vulnerable because of the use of census cross-sectional data. Even though he pooled data from two decennial censuses to examine cohort effects, he was nonetheless unable to study changes in earnings for the same workers while they acquired work experience and human capital in the United States (his data were not longitudinal, in other words). Moreover, the effect of the deep economic recession in the 1980s could not be taken into account in his analysis.

The debate stimulated by Borjas's criticism of Chiswick's optimistic forecast has been largely inconclusive, according to the assessment of Tienda and Liang (1994). To be sure, considerable variation exists in the quality of cohorts by national origin in the post-1965 immigration. The lower average skill of immigrants overall stems from the large relative size of the immigration from Mexico and some less-developed regions of Asia and Latin America. Other contingents of immigrants, such as those from India and Korea, bring levels of education considerably higher than that of the average American. Moreover, the effect of lower skill on economic mobility depends on the comparison group, as LaLonde and Topel (1991) have shown. If the comparison group consists of the U.S.-born members of the same ethnic group, then Chiswick's results are confirmed: Even recent cohorts of immigrants quickly achieve economic parity. This is not the case when native-born Americans in general make up the comparison group. But immigrants who came to the United States as children do achieve economic parity with the latter group of workers (Borjas and Freeman 1992). This finding is, of course, consistent with assimilation theory. Further, Kossoudji (1988) has argued that if English is learned promptly after arrival in the United States, "then language assimilation, as it is translated into a job-usable skill, may represent one vehicle of upward mobility."

A different order of problem with respect to economic assimilation is posed, however, by the large-scale migration of poorly educated and illegal aliens (Borjas 1994). One facet of the problem is that illegal immigrants concentrate in particular geographical locations (such as California) and then in enclaves within these. Spatial concentration of undocumented immigrants probably leads to substantial differences from other immigrants in the extent of economic disadvantage, which in turn is translated into a lower rate of economic assimilation for the children of illegal immigrants. Farley (1996), in examining the low educational background of both legal and illegal Hispanic immigrants, conjectures that the children of Hispanic immigrants in general may continue to suffer the consequences of their parents' low stock of human capital.

Overall, the economic literature on earnings assimilation suggests that post-1965 immigrants are handicapped not so much by race as by a lack of usable human capital (Borjas 1994). If earnings growth is slow, this is accounted for by the low stocks of human capital of recent cohorts of immigrants from developing economies. Their slower pace of economic assimilation can be attributed to the transformation of the American economy–that is, the general erosion of labor market demand for unskilled labor and the increasing demand for highly skilled workers (Katz 1994), though this affects natives and immigrants alike. In contrast, the sociological literature has highlighted the adverse labor market experience of racial minorities, with sociological analysts often conflating the cost of immigration with the cost of race. When the former is controlled for, however, the earnings gap between non-Hispanic whites and native-born children of immigrants narrows, so that Asian ethnics—mostly Chinese and Japanese among the U.S.-born who are old enough to be in the labor market—achieve substantive parity with whites in earnings growth (Nee and Sanders 1985; Farley 1996).

The relative openness of the American labor market stems from the regulatory environment facing large firms and bureaucracies. In the post-civil rights era, Title VII and other civil rights legislation make it more costly for firms (except possibly small businesses, due to the difficulty of monitoring and enforcement) to discriminate by gender and race. As a result, the workplace is more regulated today than it was at the time of the earlier immigrant waves to the United States. The principle of equality under the law has been definitively extended to legal immigrants and naturalized citizens. Even illegal immigrants are entitled to due process and have legal rights. As Liebman (1992) observed in a review of key court cases defining immigrant rights:

> The net effect … would seem to be that aliens are a protected class for purposes of constitutional adjudication, that state rules barring aliens from particular occupations will be scrutinized carefully by courts to see whether it is appropriate that a particular job be restricted to persons … even federal restrictions are constitutionally dubious unless enacted by Congress and justified by significant needs. (p. 372)

However, equality under the law does not extend to illegal immigrants, even though they are entitled to due process and possess limited rights of access to public services. This class of immigrants, estimated to be about 2.6 million at the time of the 1990 census (Fix and Passel 1994), is likely to concentrate in the underground informal ethnic and open labor markets in order to avoid deportation. Undocumented status restricts their labor market mobility since it effectively closes off opportunities to find jobs in the regulated portion of the urban labor market: large firms and government bureaucracies, where monitoring and enforcement of immigration laws are routine. The penalty for illegal status to human-capital immigrants is high, which in part explains why there are so few highly educated workers among the undocumented. Most illegal aliens have no more than an elementary school education, and a sizable number have no formal schooling. Tienda and Singer's (1994) analysis shows that the pattern of earnings growth of undocumented immigrants reflects "economywide shifts in the structure of wages as well as changing returns to different levels of schooling." In their view, the fact that "wages of undocumented immigrants increased at all is remarkable," given the general performance of the U.S. economy in the 1980s and the restrictions on labor mobility faced by illegal aliens.

The jobs that immigrants find in U.S. labor markets closely correspond to their level of education (Bean and Tienda 1987; Farley 1996). Human-capital immigrant streams—from India, China, Africa, Western Europe, and Canada—have a higher proportion of professionals and managers than the native-born American population. By contrast, immigrant groups with large numbers of workers who come with little formal education—from Cuba and other Carribean nations, El Salvador, Mexico, and other Central American countries—are disproportionately represented in low-wage blue-collar and service jobs. Consequently, there is a bimodal attainment pattern evident in the occupations and earnings of human-capital immigrants and labor migrants, roughly corresponding to the differences between Asian and Hispanic immigrants. Farley (1996) has compared the earnings of immigrants as reported in the 1990 census with the earnings of native-born workers in fourteen immigrant metropolises, including New York, Los Angeles, Miami, Washington, D.C., and Houston. He confirms the pattern, first discovered by Chiswick (1977), that the cost of immigration is most clearly felt in the years immediately following arrival in the United States, but that considerable economic mobility occurs over time. After 25 years of residence in the United States, immigrants reported earnings that are 93 percent of those of native-born non-Hispanic whites. The earnings gap between immigrants and the native born was smaller for women than for men.

However, taking the national origins of immigrants into account unveils a mixed picture of economic assimilation for non-European immigrants in the nation as a whole. Hispanic men—foreign and native-born—earn substantially less than Anglos, while Asian men—including the foreign-born—earn as much as men from the majority group. For women, the wage gap between Hispanic and Anglo workers is nearly as large as among men, but Asian women report higher wages than do Anglos. When Farley controlled for social and demographic characteristics—place of residence, education, reported English-speaking ability, work disability, and marital status—he found that Hispanic men earn 84 percent and foreign-born Asian men 87 percent as much as their Anglo counterparts. But native-born Asian men have achieved earnings parity with comparable Anglo males, and accordingly their position has improved since the 1980 census. The wage gap is less for women, with both native- and foreign-born Asian women and native-born Hispanic women earning more than comparable Anglo women. In sum, the early analyses of the 1990 census report results that are in line with expectations of assimilation theory. If anything, the economic assimilation of immigrants has progressed more rapidly for many post-1965 immigrants than it did for the earlier waves of immigrants from Europe due to the technological transformation of the American economy, which results in increased demand for high-skilled workers.

SPATIAL PATTERNS

One of the most noted features of the new immigration is its high degree of geographic concentration (Farley 1996; Portes and Rumbaut 1996; Waldinger 1989). Just a handful of states and metropolitan areas receive a majority of new immigrants and remain the primary areas of residence and work for the immigrants and their children. Of the immigrants who came during the late 1980s, more than 80 percent ended up in only six states, in order of share: California, New York, Florida, Texas, New Jersey, and Illinois (Farley 1996:169; see also Portes and Rumbaut 1996). Concentration within specific metropolitan areas is nearly as extreme: Los Angeles, San Francisco, New York City, Miami, Houston, and Chicago, taken in their broadest sense, as what the U.S. Census Bureau defines as "Consolidated Metropolitan Statistical Areas," were the places of settlement for more than half the immigrants who arrived between 1985 and 1990. In total, only fourteen metropolitan areas had above-average concentrations of the foreign-born in their populations as of 1990. But these fourteen, some of them among the largest metropolitan regions of the country, accounted for two-thirds of all immigrants (Farley 1996:185).

Some degree of geographic concentration is an inevitable by-product of immigration, which is guided by social networks and leads to settlement patterns determined partly by the need of new immigrants—who are unfamiliar with American society and frequently lacking proficiency in English—for assistance from kin and co-ethnics (Massey 1987). Even so, the impression is that the degree of geographic concentration among new immigrant groups exceeds that of older ones at a comparable stage of immigration (Massey 1994). Only immigrant groups with a heavy professional stratum, such as Indians, appear to be exceptions to contemporary concentration, since job considerations for professionals typically override the tendency to settle where large numbers of fellow ethnics have already done so. Places of settlement are also initially more dispersed for refugees whose original destinations in the United States are usually determined by government agencies and private sponsorship. Secondary migration, however, tends to bring about greater ethnic concentration, exemplified by the roles of Miami as a mecca for Cubans and Orange County, California, for Vietnamese (Gold 1992; Portes and Rumbaut 1996). The high degree of geographic concentration of the new immigrant groups is consistent with the notion that institutionally complete ethnic communities will support ethnicity for the second and subsequent generations as well as retard assimilation.

But the concentration of immigrant groups in a small number of metropolitan areas and of specific groups in an even smaller number appears incompatible with the rapid growth of ethnic populations that is projected to occur if immigration remains at its current level. The projections of the National Research Council (Smith and Edmonston 1997), for instance, suggest in its middle-of-the-road scenario that by 2020 Latinos and Asians, the two racial/ethnic populations receiving the bulk of the new immigration, will nearly double their combined share of the population, going from 12 percent (in 1990) up to 22 percent. It seems self-evident that these groups cannot remain as concentrated in a few states and metropolitan areas as they are today if growth occurs on this scale, although the implications of any dispersal can be debated. One possibility is the emergence of a much larger number of immigrant cultural centers, especially those associated with Spanish speakers, given their size in the immigrant stream (Massey 1994). Other areas of the country might begin to resemble the multicultural concentrations presently epitomized by Los Angeles, Miami, and New York. Yet the hypothesis that movement away from areas of original settlement tends to be associated with a ratcheting forward of assimilation seems generally borne out in the experiences of European-descent groups. This is also plausible when applied to new immigrant groups, in which case new areas of concentration may be more culturally and ethnically diverse than they were before but not as diverse as the original immigrant meccas. Much will depend on whether any dispersal is the result of a movement by native-born generations away from ethnic centers or of a fanning out of the immigration stream itself.

One form of spatial dispersal is less conjectural: Within the regions where they reside, new immigrants are on the whole but moderately segregated from the non-Latino white majority. In particular, research into metropolitan levels of residential segregation has established that, by the measure of standard segregation indices such as the index of dissimilarity, Asian and Hispanic segregation from the majority is considerably less than that of African Americans and within a range usually deemed as "moderate." Analyzing 1990 census data for all metropolitan areas with substantial black populations (*N*=232) (and at a small unit of aggregation), the census block group, which should raise segregation index values on average, Farley and Frey (1994) find that the average index of dissimilarity between Hispanics from non-Hispanics is 0.43, virtually unchanged from the 1980 index calculated in an equivalent way. That of Asians from non-Asians is also 0.43, representing in this case a slight increase from the 1980 value (0.41). By contrast, the average 1990 value for blacks is 0.64 (Massey and Denton 1987). Given that the Asian and Hispanic populations are growing rapidly through immigration and that newly arrived immigrants tend to enter communities where their group is already present in sizable numbers, an increase in the level of segregation is not unexpected and tells little about changes in the residential patterns of more long-standing Asian residents. In sum, the metropolitanwide studies suggest that the segregation of new immigrant populations is not extreme, just as was true of earlier European immigrants. A drawback of this research is that little attention has been paid to the residential patterns of specific groups within the Asian and Hispanic populations; obviously, such residential patterns can vary considerably. Also, there has not been sufficient attention given to the segregation of black immigrants, although an analysis of the impact of race on the residential situations of Hispanics strongly suggests that immigrants of black skin are likely to be channeled into black neighborhoods (Denton and Massey 1989; Kasinitz 1992).

Metropolitan-wide levels of segregation are aggregates that can disguise great individual variation in residential situation. Individual-level analyses are therefore warranted to determine how residential situation corresponds with personal and household characteristics, such as nativity and income. The model of spatial assimilation leads to the hypothesis that residential exposure to members of the racial/ethnic majority should increase in tandem with socioeconomic standing, acculturation as measured by proficiency in speaking the English language, and generational status. Alba and Logan have conducted a series of relevant studies for some of the main metropolitan regions of immigrant concentration, and by and large their findings uphold the spatial-assimilation hypothesis (Alba and Logan 1993; Alba, Logan, and Stults 1997; Logan and Alba 1993; Logan, Alba, and Leung 1996; Logan, Alba, and McNulty 1996; see also White, Biddlecom, and Guo 1993). For Asians and Latinos, the most powerful determinant of the racial and ethnic composition of their neighborhoods (that is, census tracts) is their own socioeconomic position; the greater their income and the higher their educational status, the larger the percentage of non-Latino whites in the population of the neighborhood where they reside. The ability to own a home also tends to increase residential exposure to the majority group, as does residence in the suburbs, which reflects socioeconomic status to an important degree. Linguistic acculturation is yet another determinant, but generational status (nativity) has little influence once these other variables are taken into account. The difference associated with linguistic assimilation is especially sizable among Latinos and is most pronounced between those who speak only English at home and those who do not speak English well. Bilinguals, who speak a mother tongue but are proficient at English too, are intermediate in terms of residing with non-Latino whites. The Alba-Logan analyses reveal again the important role played by skin color among Latinos. Light-skinned Latinos—those who describe themselves on census forms as "white" (about half of all Latinos in 1990)—find it easiest to enter neighborhoods with large numbers of non-Latino whites. Latinos who describe themselves racially as other than white or black reside on average in neighborhoods where the percentage of non-Latino whites is modestly lower, while those who self-describe as "black" (a small minority of all Latinos) live, as noted above, with far fewer members of the racial/ethnic majority.

The general consistency of these individual-level patterns with those predicted by the spatial-assimilation model suggests that the residential integration of immigrant and second-generation households with the majority population ought to increase over time. But a powerful countervailing trend is produced by the impact of continuing immigration into the metropolitan regions where immigrants and their children are concentrated. The immigration into these regions, combined with the apparent inclination of native groups to move away from them (Frey 1995), is altering the racial/ethnic composition of their neighborhoods in a way that reduces the availability of majority-group members as neighbors for upwardly mobile immigrant households. This impact is apparent when the Alba-Logan analyses are compared between 1980 and 1990, for the diversity of the neighborhoods where Asians and Latinos live increased noticeably during the 1980s (and, presumably, continues to increase). Still, even in the areas most heavily impacted by immigration, middle-income, linguistically assimilated Asian and Latino suburbanites tended as of 1990 to live in areas where non-Latino whites predominated. This statement is most in jeopardy in Los Angeles and Miami, the two regions with the highest proportions of foreign-born in their populations and where, therefore, the racial/ethnic shifts spurred by immigration are the farthest developed (Farley 1996:170). In other regions of immigrant settlement, such as San Francisco or New York, which have the third and fourth highest concentrations of new immigrant groups, the neighborhoods of even modestly affluent Asians and Latinos generally contain quite substantial non-Latino white majorities. Presumably the same would be even more true for most other metropolitan regions, where the concentrations of new immigrant groups are necessarily more modest.

From the standpoint of spatial-assimilation theory, the most intriguing feature of the residential patterns of new immigrants is frequent settlement in suburbs immediately upon, or soon after, arrival in the United States (Alba and Logan 1991; Alba et al. 1997; Waldinger 1989). This hallmark of the new immigration presents a remarkable contrast to the process of spatial assimilation as experienced by earlier European immigrant groups, whose members generally first established urban enclaves and subsequently migrated as individuals and families to the suburbs, typically after spending a generation or more in cities (Alba, Logan, and Crowder 1997; Glazer and Moynihan 1970; Massey 1985). However, according to 1990 census data; 43 percent of immigrants who arrived during the 1980s and were living in metropolitan areas already resided outside of central cities (that is, in areas commonly designated as "suburban"). The percentages of suburbanites were particularly high and growing among Asian groups. According to unpublished findings in Nee and Sanders's study of residential mobility of Asian immigrants in Los Angeles, within the first decade after their arrival many immigrant families "buy up" into ethnically mixed suburban neighborhoods. Thus, in 1990, 58 percent of Filipino households in metropolitan areas of the nation were located in suburbs, up from 49 percent in 1980 (Alba et al. 1997). The comparable 1990 figure for whites is only modestly higher: 67 percent. The lowest suburbanization percentage among Asian groups is found for the Chinese, who have long-standing urban enclaves (Nee and Nee 1973; Zhou 1992); but their 1990 rate, 46 percent, still represents a substantial increase from what it was a decade before (38 percent), despite the heavy immigration of ethnic Chinese during the 1980s. Rates of suburbanization are on average lower for Latino groups, although they are near 50 percent for two of the three largest: Mexicans (46 percent in 1990) and Cubans (51 percent).

The obvious question is whether suburbanization will have the same meaning for new immigrant groups that it held for older ones. There cannot be a definitive answer at this point in the history of the new immigration; the presently available indicators yield a mixed picture. In any event, one has to recognize that the term "suburbia" now covers such a vast range of residential contexts that a single, unqualified answer is ultimately unlikely. On one side of the ledger is the indisputable existence of extensive suburban ethnic enclaves, such as Monterey Park in Los Angeles (Horton 1995). The huge Los Angeles barrio is also for the most part outside the central city. While these are but two examples, and relatively extreme ones, evidence of a more general pattern comes from the Alba and Logan analyses of the predictors of suburban residence in the 1980 and 1990 censuses (Alba and Logan 1991; Alba et al. 1997). Specifically for Asian groups, they find that during the 1980s suburban residence became much less selective of the linguistically assimilated. This suggests that barriers to suburban entry have fallen for freshly arrived immigrants who may not speak English well. They can now reside in suburbia without detriment to their ability to function in daily life (for example, shop or participate in recreational activities), presumably because they find sufficient numbers of co-ethnics and an ethnic infrastructure in their vicinity. However, among Latino groups, linguistic assimilation is more consistently a predictor of suburban residence. It should also be noted that, among all immigrant groups, suburban residence is linked to higher socioeconomic position, as the spatial-assimilation model would predict.

On the other side of the ledger is the strong evidence that suburbanization means greater residential integration with non-Latino whites, the racial/ethnic majority. This finding emerges from the Alba-Logan analyses of who lives in which neighborhoods. After socioeconomic standing, residence in a suburb rather than a city is the strongest predictor of the percentage of non-Hispanic whites in the neighborhoods where Asians and Latinos live. Even in metropolitan regions most affected by the new immigration and where, therefore, many new immigrants are potential neighbors, this variable still typically adds about 20 percentage points to the share of the neighborhood constituted by the racial/ethnic majority. Perhaps this has little bearing for the immigrants themselves, who may find enough co-ethnics in their vicinity to maintain a life like the one they would have in a more traditional ethnic enclave, but it is likely to have a considerable impact on their children, who grow up in contexts that bring them frequently together with whites and members of other groups in schools and in play groups.

The evidence on residential patterns exhibits a contradictory quality that is probably inevitable at an early stage in the unfolding of the consequences of large-scale immigration. Immigrant groups are rather strongly concentrated in a small number of metropolitan regions, which continue to receive the bulk of the immigration stream. Within these regions, these groups are not strongly segregated from the majority population, and their exposure to non-Hispanic whites through their neighborhoods increases rather predictably with improvements in English-language proficiency, income, education, and with the purchase of a home or movement to the suburbs. While these seem like signs of incipient spatial assimilation, it is too early to draw such a conclusion, and much more research is needed on the impact of residential context. We are not yet able to say with any confidence whether residence in an area with many members of the majority is necessarily associated with greater and more socially intimate contact with it. There is also a dearth of data about forms of ethnic affiliation, such as ethnic churches, that might serve as agents of ethnic socialization for the children of suburbanized immigrants. Given the significance of suburbanization for many new immigrant groups, such questions demand more research attention than they have received.

CONCLUSION

Assimilation as a concept and as a theory has been subjected to withering criticism in recent decades. Much of this criticism rejects assimilation out of hand as hopelessly burdened with ethnocentric, ideological biases and as out of touch with contemporary multicultural realities. It has been common in this critique to portray assimilation as reliant upon simplistic conceptions of a static homogeneous American culture and to target the normative or ideological expression of assimilation: Anglo-conformity. While we think this criticism is frequently unfair in that it fails to consider, and properly discount, the intellectual and social context in which the canonical statements of assimilation were written, we recognize that it often enough hits the mark. But there is danger in the view of many critics that they have provided a strong rationale for rejecting assimilation, rather than for amending it. We believe that the latter is the appropriate course, for assimilation still has great power for an understanding of the contemporary ethnic scene in the United States. It must, in our view, remain part of the theoretical tool kit of students of ethnicity and race, especially those who are concerned with the new immigration.

One challenge that must be faced is whether the language of assimilation can bear this re-fashioning. If the terminology of assimilation is so freighted with bias and ambiguity, as many critics believe, then perhaps it must be abandoned and a new vocabulary invented, even if this merely redeploys some of assimilation's conceptual arsenal. We think a change in language would be unwise. Assimilation has had a central place in the American experience, and the issue of the continuity between the experiences of European Americans and those of new immigrant groups lies at the very heart of the doubts about the relevance of assimilation for the contemporary United States. To invent a new vocabulary is, in effect, to foreclose the examination of this issue with a terminological solution, separating contemporary realities from past ones with new words. The question of continuity must be left open.

In the most general terms, assimilation can be defined as the decline, and at its endpoint the disappearance, of an ethnic/racial distinction and the cultural and social differences that express it. This definition does not assume that one of these groups must be the ethnic majority; assimilation can involve minority groups only, in which case the ethnic boundary between the majority and the merged minority groups presumably remains intact. Assimilation of this sort is not a mere theoretical possibility, as the assimilation of many descendants of earlier Caribbean black immigration into the native African-American group indicates. Nevertheless, the type of assimilation that is of greatest interest does involve the majority group. The definition stated above avoids a pitfall frequently stumbled upon by conventional definitions, which focus exclusively on the minority ethnic group, assuming implicitly that only it changes. By intent, our definition is agnostic about whether the changes wrought by assimilation are one-sided or more mutual. Indeed, there should be no definitional prescription on this point, for it is likely that the unilaterality of the changes depends upon the minority group, the era, and the aspect of group difference under consideration. Language acculturation in the United States appears to be overwhelmingly one-sided, even if American English contains many borrowings from other tongues, indigenous and immigrant; we still understand the English of the British and they ours, indicating that our language has not strayed very far from its roots. Acculturation in some other areas—cuisine the most obvious, perhaps—is more mutual.

The above definition of assimilation is formulated at the group level, and the next question is how it is to be translated to the individual plane. Here there may be no alternative to defining assimilation in a more one-sided manner. It seems impossible to meaningfully discuss assimilation at the individual level as other than changes that make the individuals in one ethnic group more like, and more socially integrated with, the members of another. When assimilation implicates both majority and minority groups, the assimilation of individuals of minority origins involves changes that enable them to function in the mainstream society. From their point of view, acculturation, say, takes place in the direction of the mainstream culture, even if on another plane that culture is itself changing through the ingestion of elements from minority cultures. Over time, then, the cultural and social distance that minority-group individuals traverse while assimilating may narrow.

Though its definition of assimilation requires modification, the canonical account, especially as extended in the direction of manner suggested by Shibutani and Kwan (1965), has much to offer to the analysis of contemporary immigrant groups. Assimilation as a social process is in progress along a variety of indicators, as our review of the evidence indicates. The socioeconomic mobility of the new immigrants shows a distinct bimodal pattern. Human capital immigrants in particular appear to be experiencing substantial economic and residential mobility. By contrast, labor migrants have made slower progress, a finding that Borjas has attributed to the very low educational attainment of migrants from Central America and other underdeveloped regions of the world. Analyses of spatial assimilation show a mixed pattern of ethnic concentration and residential mobility. Labor migrants appear to concentrate in ethnic communities, while human capital immigrants show rapid transition to suburban residence and are less likely to congregate in dense settlement patterns. Not only does the early evidence attest to assimilation as a social process being experienced to greater or lesser extent by new immigrants, it is difficult even to discuss the new immigration without encountering the need to refer to the very substantial literature on assimilation. Only by contrasting differences and similarities between the old and new immigration will scholars gain a deeper understanding of the meaning of ethnicity in this new era of immigration.

Notes

1. Revised version of paper presented at the conference "Becoming American/America Becoming: International Migration to the United States," sponsored by the Social Science Research Council, Sanibel Island, Florida, January 18–21, 1996. We are grateful to the Social Science Research Council and to Josh DeWind for providing us with the opportunity and encouragement to work on this project. The participants at the conference gave us numerous helpful comments and suggestions, as well as the encouragement to see the project as worthy of continuing. In both respects, the comments of Phil Kasinitz, Rubén Rumbaut, Joel Perlmann, and Roger Waldinger deserve special acknowledgment. Victor Nee also acknowledges fellowship support from NSF grant No. SBR-9022192 as a Fellow of the Center for Advanced Study in the Behavioral Sciences.
2. We view "racial" distinctions as a type of "ethnic" distinction, one where physical characteristics constitute part of the way that a group is socially defined. (For a reasoned justification of this usage, see Waldinger and Bozorgmehr 1996.) In our usage, then, the term "racial" is implied in "ethnic." Because this usage is not universal, however, we sometimes use both terms to remind the reader that our discussion includes racial as well as nonracial ethnic groups.

References

Abramson, H. 1980. Assimilation and pluralism. In *Harvard Encyclopedia of American Ethnic Groups.* S. Thernstrom, A. Orlov, and O. Handlin, eds. Cambridge, MA: Harvard University Press.

Alba, R. 1995. Assimilation's quiet tide. *The Public Interest* 119:1–18.

—— 1990. *Ethnic Identity: The Transformation of White America.* New Haven, CT: Yale University Press.

—— 1988. Cohorts and the dynamics of ethnic change. In *Social Structures and Human Lives.* M. W. Riley, B. Huber, and B. Hess, eds. Newbury Park, CA: Sage.

Alba, R. and J. Logan. 1993. Minority proximity to whites in suburbs: An individual-level analysis of segregation. *American Journal of Sociology* 98:1388–1427.

—— 1991. Variations on two themes: Racial and ethnic patterns in the attainment of suburban residence. *Demography* 28:431–453.

Alba, R., J. Logan, and K. Crowder. 1997. White ethnic neighborhoods and assimilation: The Greater New York Region, 1980–1990. *Social Forces* 75:883–912.

Alba, R., J. Logan, G. Marzan, B. Stults, and W. Zhang. 1997. Immigrant groups and suburbs: A test of spatial assimilation theory. State University of New York–Albany. Unpublished paper.

Alba, R., J. Logan, and B. Stults. 1997. Making a place in the immigrant metropolis: The neighborhoods of racial and ethnic groups, 1990. State University of New York–Albany. Unpublished paper.

Aldrich, H. and R. Waldinger. 1990. Ethnicity and entrepreneurship *Annual Review of Sociology,* 16:111–135.

Barkan, E. 1995. Race, religion, and nationality in American society: A model of ethnicity—from contact to assimilation. *Journal of American Ethnic History* 14:38–101.

Barth, F. 1956. Ecologic relationships of ethnic groups in Swat, North Pakistan. *American Anthropologist* 58:1079–1089.

Bean, E. and M. Tienda. 1987. *The Hispanic population of the United States.* New York: Russell Sage Foundation.

Belluck, P. 1995. Healthy Korean economy draws immigrants home. *The New York Times.* Aug. 22. Pp. A1, B4.

Bodnar, J. 1985. *The Transplanted: The History of Immigrants in Urban America.* Bloomington: Indiana University Press.

Bonacich, E. and J. Modell. 1980. *The Economic Basis of Ethnic Solidarity: Small Business in the Japanese-American Community.* Berkeley: University of California Press.

Borjas, G. 1994. The economics of immigration. *Journal of Economic Literature* 32: 1667–1717.

—— 1990. *Friends or Strangers: the Impact of Immigrants in the U.S. Economy.* New York: Basic Books.

—— 1987. Self-selection and the earnings of immigrants. *American Economic Review.* 77:531–553.

—— 1986. The self-employment experience of immigrants. *The Journal of Human Resources* 21:485–506.

—— 1985. Assimilation, changes in cohort quality, and the earnings of immigrants. *Journal of Labor Economics* 3:463–489.

Borjas, G. and R. Freeman. 1992. Introduction and summary. In *Economic Consequences for the U.S. and Source Areas.* G. Borjas and R. Freeman, eds. Chicago: University of Chicago.

Breton, R. 1964. Institutional completeness of ethnic communities and the personal relations of immigrants. *American Journal of Sociology* 70:193–205.

Brimelow, P. 1995. *Alien Nation: Common Sense about America's Immigration Disaster.* New York: Random House.

Burgess, E. 1925. The growth of the city: An introduction to a research project. In *The City.* R. Park, E. Burgess, and R. McKenzie, eds. Chicago: University of Chicago.

Child, I. 1943. *Italian or American? The Second Generation in Conflict.* New Haven, CT: Yale University Press.

Chiswick, B. 1986. Is the new immigration less skilled than the old? *Journal of Labor Economics* 4:168–192.

—— 1978. The effect of Americanization on the earnings of foreign-born men. *Journal of Political Economy* 86:897–921.

—— 1977. Sons of immigrants: Are they at an earnings disadvantage? *American Economic Review* 67:376–380.

Cohn-Bendit, D. and T. Schmid. 1992. *Heimat Babylon: Das Wagnis der multikulturellen Demokratie.* Hamburg: Hoffmann und Campe.

Conzen, K., D. Gerber, E. Morawska, G. Pozzetta, and R. Vecoli. 1992. The invention of ethnicity: A perspective from the U.S.A. *Journal of American Ethnic History* 12:3–41.

Covello, L. 1972. *The Social Background of the Italo-American School Child.* Totowa, NJ: Rowman & Littlefield.

Denton, N. and D. Massey. 1989. Racial identity among Caribbean Hispanics: The effect of double minority status on residential segregation. *American Sociological Review* 54:790–808.

Donato, K., J. Durand, and D. Massey. 1992. Stemming the tide? Assessing the deterrent effects of the Immigration Reform and Control Act. *Demography* 29:139–157.

Edmonston, B. and J. Passel. 1994. The future immigrant population of the United States. In *Immigration and Ethnicity: The Integration of America's Newest Arrivals.* B. Edmonston and J. Passel, eds. Washington, DC: The Urban Institute Press.

Farley, R. 1996. *The New American Reality: Who We Are, How We Got Here, Where We Are Going.* New York: Russell Sage.

Farley, R. and W. Frey. 1994. Changes in the segregation of whites from blacks during the 1980s: Small steps towards a more integrated ociety. *American Sociological Review* 59:23–45.

Fix, M. and J. Passel. 1994. *Immigration and Immigrants: Setting the Record Straight.* Washington, DC: The Urban Institute.

Frey, W. 1995. Immigration and internal migration 'flight' from U.S. metropolitan areas: Toward a demographic Balkanization. *Urban Studies* 32:733–757.

Gans, H. 1992. Second generation decline: Scenarios for the economic and ethnic futures of post-1965 American immigrants. *Ethnic and Racial Studies* 15:173–192.

—— 1982. *The Urban Villagers: Group and Class in the Life of Italian-Americans.* 1962. Reprint. New York: The Free Press.

—— 1979. Symbolic ethnicity: The future of ethnic groups and cultures in America. *Ethnic and Racial Studies* 2:1–20.

—— 1973. Introduction. In *Ethnic Identity and Assimilation: The Polish Community.* N. Sandberg, ed. New York: Praeger.

—— 1967. *The Levittowners: Ways of Life and Politics in a New Suburban Community.* New York: Pantheon.

Gibson, M. 1988. *Accommodation without Assimilation: Sikh Immigrants in an American High School.* Ithaca, NY: Cornell University Press.

Glazer, N. 1993. Is assimilation dead? *The Annals of the American Academy of Social and Political Sciences* 530:122–136.

Glazer, N. and D. P. Moynihan. 1970. *Beyond the Melting Pot: The Negroes, Puerto Ricans, Jews, Italians, and Irish of New York City.* 1963. Reprint. Cambridge, MA: MIT Press.

Gleason, P. 1980. American identity and Americanization. In *Harvard Encyclopedia of American Ethnic Groups.* S. Thernstrom, A. Orlov, and O. Handlin, eds. Cambridge, MA: Harvard University Press.

Gold, S. 1992. *Refugee Communities: A Comparative Field Study.* Newbury Park, CA: Sage.

Gordon, M. 1964. *Assimilation in American Life.* New York: Oxford University Press.

Greeley, A. 1977. *The American Catholic: A Social Portrait.* New York: Basic Books.

—— 1976. *Ethnicity, Denomination, and Inequality.* Beverly Hills, CA: Sage.

Greenwood, M. J. 1983. The economics of mass migration from poor to rich countries: Leading issues of fact and theory. *American Economic Review* 73:173–177.

Guest, A. 1980. The suburbanization of ethnic groups. *Sociology and Social Research* 64:497–513.

Heer, D. 1996. *Immigration in America's Future: Social Science Findings and the Policy Debate.* Boulder, CO: Westview.

Herberg, W. 1960. *Protestant-Catholic-Jew.* New York: Anchor.

Higham, J. 1970. *Strangers in the Land: Patterns of American Nativism, 1860–1925.* New York: Atheneum.

Hirschman, C. 1983. America's melting pot reconsidered. *Annual Review of Sociology* 9:397–423.

Hirschman, C. and M. Wong. 1986. The extraordinary educational attainment of Asian Americans: A search for historical evidence and explanations. *Social Forces,* 65:1–27.

Hobsbawm, E. and T. Ranger. 1983. *The Invention of Tradition.* Cambridge: Cambridge University.

Horton, J. 1995. *The Politics of Diversity: Immigration, Resistance, and Change in Monterey Park, California.* Philadelphia, PA: Temple University Press.

Hout, M., A. Raftery, and E. Bell. 1993. Making the grade: Educational stratification in the United States, 1925–1989. In *Persistent Inequality: Changing Educational Attainment in Thirteen Countries.* Y. Shavit and H. P. Blossfeld, eds. Boulder, CO: Westview.

Ignatiev, N. 1995. *How the Irish Became White.* New York: Routledge.

Jasso, G. and M. Rosenzweig. 1990. *The New Chosen People: Immigrants in the United States.* New York: Russell Sage Foundation.

Kanjanapan, W. 1994. The immigration of Asian professionals to the United States: 1988–1990. *International Migration Review* 29:7–32.

Katz, L. 1994. Labor's past and future. *Challenge* 24:18–25.

Kasinitz, P. 1992. *Caribbean New York: Black Immigrants and the Politics of Race.* Ithaca, NY: Cornell University Press.

Kazal, R. 1995. Revisiting assimilation: The rise, fall, and reappraisal of a concept in American ethnic history. *American Historical Review* 100:437–472.

Kennedy, R. J. R. 1952. Single or triple melting pot? Intermarriage in New Haven, 1870–1950. *American Journal of Sociology* 58:56–59.

—— 1944. Single or triple melting pot? Intermarriage trends in New Haven, 1870–1940. *American Journal of Sociology* 49:331–339.

Kibria, N. 1993. *Family Tightrope: The Changing Lives of Vietnamese Americans.* Princeton: Princeton University Press.

Kim, I. 1981. *New Urban Immigrants: The Korean Community in New York.* Princeton, NJ: Princeton University Press.

Kim, K. C. 1985. Ethnic resources utilization of Korean immigrant entrepreneurs in the Chicago minority area. *International Migration Review* 19:82–111.

Kossoudji, S. 1988. English anguage ability and the labor market opportunities of Hispanic and East Asian immigrant men. *Journal of Labor Economics* 6:205–228.

Lal, B. B. 1990. *The Romance of Culture in an Urban Civilization: Robert E. Park on Race and Ethnic Relations in Cities.* London: Routledge.
LaLonde, R. and R. Topel. 1991. Labor market adjustments to increased immigration. In *Immigration, Trade, and the Labor Market.* J. Abowd and R. Freeman, eds. Chicago: University of Chicago Press.
LaRuffa, A. 1988. *Monte Carmelo: An Italian-American Community in the Bronx.* New York: Gordon and Breach.
Lee, S. and K. Yamanaka. 1990. Patterns of Asian American intermarriage and marital assimilation. *Journal of Comparative Family Studies* 21:287–305.
Lieberson, S. 1985. Unhyphenated whites in the United States. *Ethnic and Racial Studies* 8:159–180.
—— 1980. *A Piece of the Pie: Blacks and White Immigrants since 1880.* Berkeley: University of California Press.
—— 1973. Generational differences among blacks in the North. *American Journal of Sociology* 79:550–565.
Lieberson, S. and M. Waters. 1993. The ethnic responses of whites: What causes their instability, simplification, and inconsistency? *Social Forces* 72:421–450.
—— 1988. *From many strands: Ethnic and racial groups in contemporary America.* New York: Russell Sage Foundation.
Liebman, L. 1992. Immigration status and American law: The several versions of antidiscrimination doctrine. In *Immigrants in Two Democracies: French and American Experience.* D. L. Horowitz and G. Noiriel, eds. New York: New York University Press.
Light, I. 1984. Immigrant and ethnic enterprise in North America. *Ethnic and Racial Studies* 7:195–216.
—— 1972. *Ethnic Enterprise in America: Business and Welfare among Chinese, Japanese, and Black.* Berkeley: University of California.
Light, I. and E. Bonacich. 1988. *Immigrant Entrepreneurs: Koreans in Los Angeles, 1965–1982.* Berkeley: University of California.
Light, I. and S. Karageorgis. 1994. The ethnic economy. In *Handbook of Economic Sociology.* N. Smelser and R. Swedberg, eds. Princeton, NJ: Princeton University Press.
Light, I., G. Sabagh, M. Bozorgmehr, and C. Der-Martirosian. 1994. Beyond the ethnic enclave economy. *Social Problems* 41:65–79.
Lind, M. 1995. *The Next American Nation: The New Nationalism and the Fourth American Revolution.* New York: Basic.
Loewen, J. 1971. *The Mississippi Chinese: Between Black and White.* Cambridge, MA: Harvard University.
Logan, J. and R. Alba. 1993. Locational returns to human capital: Minority access to suburban community resources. *Demography* 30:243–268.
Logan, J., R. Alba, and S. Y. Leung. 1996. Minority access to white suburbs: A multi-region comparison. *Social Forces,* 74:851–881.
Logan, J., R. Alba, and T. McNulty. 1994. Ethnic economies in metropolitan regions: Miami and beyond. *Social Forces 72:691–724.*
Logan, J., R. Alba, T. McNulty, and B. Fisher. 1996. Making a place in the metropolis: Locational attainment in city and suburb. *Demography* 33:443–453.
Lyman, S. 1973. *The Black American in Sociological Thought: A Failure of Perspective.* New York: Capricorn.
Mar, D. 1991. Another look at the enclave economy thesis: Chinese immigrants in the ethnic labor market. *Amerasia* 17:5–21.
Massey, D. 1994. The new immigration and the meaning of ethnicity in the United States. Paper presented at the Albany Conference on American Diversity.
—— 1987. Understanding Mexican migration to the United States. *American Journal of Sociology* 92:1372–1403.
—— 1985. Ethnic residential segregation: A theoretical synthesis and empirical review. *Sociology and Social Research* 69:315–350.
Massey, D. and N. Denton. 1993. *American Apartheid: Segregation and the Making of the Underclass.* Cambridge, MA: Harvard University Press.
—— 1988. Suburbanization and segregation in U.S. metropolitan areas. *American Journal of Sociology* 94:592–626.
—— 1987. Trends in residential segregation of blacks, Hispanics, and Asians: 1970–1980. *American Sociological Review* 52:802–825.
McKee, J. 1993. *Sociology and the Race Problem: The Failure of a Perspective.* Urbana: University of Illinois.
Mencken, H. L. 1963. *The American Language.* Abridg. ed. New York: Knopf.
Merton, R. 1968. *Social Theory and Social Structure.* Glencoce: The Free Press.
Min, P. G. 1996. *Caught in the Middle: Korean Communities in New York and Los Angeles.* Berkeley: University of California.
—— 1984. From white-collar occupations to small business: Korean immigrants' occupational adjustment. *Sociological Quarterly* 25:333–352.
Model, S. 1988. The economic progress of European and East Asian Americans. *Annual Review of Sociology* 14:363–380.
Morawska, E. 1994. In defense of the assimilation model. *Journal of American Ethnic History* 13:76–87.
Nee, V. and B. Nee. 1973. *Longtime Californ: A Documentary Study of an American Chinatown.* Boston: Houghton Mifflin.
Nee, V. and J. Sanders. 1985. The road to parity: Determinants of the socioeconomic attainments of Asian Americans. *Ethnic and Racial Studies* 8:75–93.
Nee, V., J. Sanders, and S. Sernau. 1994. Job transitions in an immigrant metropolis: Ethnic boundaries and the mixed economy. *American Sociological Review* 59:849–872.
Neidert, L. and R. Farley. 1985. Assimilation in the United States: An analysis of ethnic and generation differences in status and achievement. *American Sociological Review* 50:840–850.
Park, R. E. 1950. *Race and Culture.* Glencoe: The Free Press.
—— 1930. Assimilation, social. In *Encyclopedia of the Social Sciences.* E. Seligman and A. Johnson, eds. New York: Macmillan.
Park, R. E. and E. Burgess. 1969. *Introduction to the Science of Sociology.* 1921. Reprint. Chicago: University of Chicago Press.

Perlmann, J. and R. Waldinger. 1997. Second generation decline? Children of immigrants, past and present—A reconsideration. *International Migration Review* 31(4).
Portes, A. and R. Bach. 1985. *Latin Journey: Cuban and Mexican Immigrants in the United States.* Berkeley: University of California Press.
Portes, A. and R. Rumbaut. 1996. *Immigrant America: A Portrait,* second ed. Berkeley: University of California Press.
Portes, A. and M. Zhou. 1996. Self-employment and the Earnings of Immigrants. *American Sociological Review* 61:219–230.
—— 1993. The new second generation: Segmented assimilation and its variants. *The Annals of the American Academy of Political and Social Sciences* 530:74–96.
—— 1992. Gaining the upper hand: Economic mobility among immigrant and domestic minorities. *Racial and Ethnic Studies* 15:491–522.
Qian, Z. 1997. Breaking the racial barriers: Variations in interracial marriages between 1980 and 1990. *Demography* 34:263–276.
Reimers, D. 1992. *Still the Golden Door: The Third World Comes to America.* New York: Columbia University Press.
Roediger, D. 1991. *The Wages of Whiteness: Race and the Making of the American Working Class.* New York: Verso.
Rumbaut, R. 1994. The crucible within: Ethnic identity, self-esteem and segmented assimilation among children of immigrants. *International Migration Review* 18:748–794.
Sanders, J. and V. Nee. 1996. Immigrant self-employment: The family as social capital and the value of human capital. *American Sociological Review* 61:231–249.
—— 1987. The limits of ethnic solidarity in the enclave economy. *American Sociological Review* 52:745–773.
Sandberg, N. 1973. *Ethnic Identity and Assimilation: The Polish Community.* New York: Praeger.
Sassen, S. 1988. *The Mobility of Capital and Labor.* Cambridge: Cambridge University Press.
Shibutani, T. and K. Kwan. 1965. *Ethnic Stratification.* New York: Macmillan.
Smith, J. and B. Edmonston. 1997. *The New Americans: Economic, Demographic, and Fiscal Effects of Immigration.* Washington, DC: National Research Council.
Sollors, W. 1989. *The Invention of Ethnicity.* New York: Oxford University.
Sowell, T. 1996. *Migrations and Cultures: A World View.* New York: Basic Books.
Steinberg, S. 1981. *The Ethnic Myth.* Boston: Beacon.
Stevens, G. 1992. The social and demographic context of language use in the United States. *American Sociological Review* 57:171–185.
—— 1985. Nativity, intermarriage, and mother-tongue shift. *American Sociological Review* 50:74–83.
Stone, J. 1985. *Racial Conflict in Contemporary Society.* London: Fontana Press/Collins.
Suárez-Orozco, M. 1989. *Central American Refugees and U.S. High Schools: A Psychological Study of Motivation and Achievement.* Stanford, CA: Stanford University Press.
Tienda, M. and Z. Liang. 1994. Poverty and immigration in policy perspective. In *Confronting Poverty: Prescriptions for Change.* S. H. Danzinger, G. D. Sandefur, and D. H. Weinberg, eds. New York: Russell Sage Foundation.
Tienda, M. and A. Singer. 1994. Wage mobility of undocumented workers in the United States. *International Migration Review* 29:112–138.
Veltman, C. 1983. *Language Shift in the United States.* Berlin: Mouton.
Waldinger, R. 1996. *Still the Promised City? African-Americans and New Immigrants in Post-Industrial New York.* Cambridge, MA: Harvard University.
—— 1989. Immigration and urban Change. *Annual Review of Sociology* 15:211–232.
—— 1986/87. Changing ladders and musical chairs: Ethnicity and opportunity in post-industrial New York. *Politics and Society* 15.
Waldinger, R. and M. Bozorgmehr. 1996. The making of a multicultural metropolis. In *Ethnic Los Angeles.* R. Waldinger and M. Bozorgmehr, eds. New York: Russell Sage.
Warner, W. L. and L. Srole. 1945. *The Social Systems of American Ethnic Groups.* New Haven, CT: Yale University Press.
Waters, M. 1994. Ethnic and racial identities of second-generation black immigrants in New York City. *International Migration Review* 28:795–820.
—— 1990. *Ethnic Options: Choosing Identities in America.* Berkeley: University of California Press.
White, M., A. Biddlecom, and S. Guo. 1993. Immigration, naturalization, and residential assimilation among Asian Americans. *Social Forces* 72:93–118.
Whyte, W. F. 1955. *Street Corner Society: The Social Structure of an Italian Slum.* 1943. Reprint. Chicago:
Wilson, K. and A. Portes. 1980. Immigrant enclaves: An analysis of the labor market experiences of Cubans in Miami. *American Journal of Sociology* 86:296–319.
Wirth, L. 1956. *The Ghetto,* 1928. Reprint. Chicago: University of Chicago.
Woldemikael, T. 1989. *Becoming Black American: Haitians and American Institutions in Evanston, Illinois.* New York: AMS Press.
Yancey, W., E. Ericksen, and R. Juliani. 1976. Emergent ethnicity: A review and a reformulation. *American Sociological Review* 41:391–403.
Yoon, I. J. 1996. *On My Own: Korean Immigration, Entrepreneurship, and Korean-Black Relations in Chicago and Los Angeles.* Chicago: University of Chicago Press.
—— 1991. The changing significance of ethnic and class resources in immigrant businesses: The case of Korean immigrant businesses in Chicago. *International Migration Review* 25:303–332.
Zhou, M. 1992. *Chinatown: The Socioeconomic Potential of an Urban Enclave.* Philadelphia, PA: Temple University Press.

Chapter 4
Everything You Ever Wanted to Know About Assimilation But Were Afraid To Ask

MARCELO M. SUÁREZ-OROZCO

As if by centennial design, the first and last decades of the twentieth century were eras of large-scale immigration (see Figures 4.1 and 4.2). During the first decade of the twentieth century, the United States saw the arrival of what was then the largest wave of immigration in history when a total of 8,795,386 immigrants, the vast majority of them European peasants, entered the country. By the 1990s, the wave of "new immigration" (which began in 1965) peaked when about a million new immigrants were arriving in the United States each year. By 1998 the United States had over 25 million immigrants, setting a new historic record.[1]

Two dominant features characterize this most recent wave of immigration: its intensity (the immigrant population grew by 30 percent between 1990 and 1997) and the somewhat radical shift in the sources of new immigration (up to 1950, nearly 90 percent of all immigrants were Europeans or Canadians). Today, more than 50 percent of all immigrants are from Latin America, and 27 percent are from Asia (see Table 4.1).

The recent U.S. experience is part of a broader—indeed, global—dynamic of intensified transnational immigration. Now, in the twenty-first century, the worldwide immigrant population is more than 100 million people—plus an estimated 20 to 30 million refugees. And these numbers reveal only the tip of a much larger immigration iceberg; by far the majority of immigrants and refugees remain within the confines of the "developing world" in individual nation-states. China, for example, has an estimated 100 million internal migrants.[2]

It is not surprising, then, that in recent years there has been renewed interest in basic research and policy in the field of immigration. While there is now robust scholarly activity on some aspects of immigration—for example, its economic causes and consequences—the scholarship on other important facets is somewhat anemic. For example, we know comparatively little about the long-term adaptations of immigrant children—the fastest-growing sector of the child population in the United States. Data and conceptual work on their health, schooling, and transition to the world of work are quite limited.[3] So is the work on the cultural processes of change generated by large-scale immigration. This is in part because labor economists, demographers, and sociologists have set the

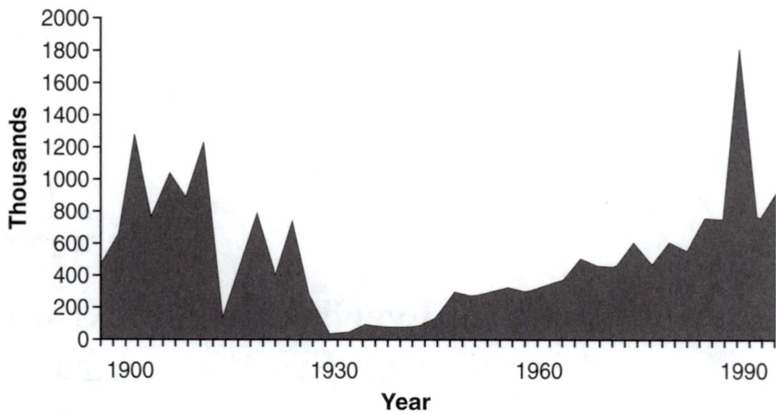

Fig. 4.1 Immigrants Admitted: Fiscal Years 1900–1996.
Source: Adapted from U.S. Department of Justice, Immigration and Naturalization Service, Statistical Yearbook of the Immigration and Naturalization Service (Washington, DC: G.P.O., 1998).

tone of the current research agenda—while anthropologists, psychologists, legal scholars, and scholars of the health sciences have played a more modest role.

Large-scale immigration is at once the cause and consequence of profound social, economic, and cultural transformations.[4] It is important to differentiate analytically between the two. While the claim has been made that there are powerful economic interests in having a large pool of foreign workers (a major cause of large-scale immigration), immigration nevertheless generates anxieties and at times even fans the fires of xenophobia (a major consequence of large-scale immigration). Two broad concerns have set the parameters of the debate over immigration scholarship and policy in the United States and Europe: the economic and the sociocultural consequences of large-scale immigration.

Recent economic arguments have largely focused on (1) the impact of large-scale immigration on the wages of native workers (Do immigrants depress the wages of native, especially minority, workers?), (2) the fiscal implications of large-scale immigration (Do immigrants "pay their way" taxwise, or are they a burden, consuming more in publicly funded services than they contribute?), and (3) the redundancy of immigrants, especially poorly educated and low-skilled workers, in new knowledge-intensive economies that are far less labor-intensive than the industrial economies of yesterday.[5]

Reducing the complexities of the new immigration to economic factors can, of course, be limiting. Indeed, there is an emerging consensus that the economic implications of large-scale immigration are somewhat ambiguous. Research shows that immigrants generate benefits in certain areas (including worker productivity) and costs in others (especially in fiscal terms). Furthermore, we must not lose sight of the fact that the U.S. economy is so large, powerful, and dynamic that, ideologies aside, immigration will neither make nor break it. The total size of the U.S. economy is on the order of $7 trillion; immigrant-related economic activities are a small portion of that total (an estimated domestic gain on the order of $1 to $10 billion a year, according to a National Research Council study).[6]

The fact that the most recent wave of immigration is comprised largely of non-European, non-English-speaking "people of color" arriving in unprecedented numbers from Asia, the Caribbean, and Latin America (see Table 4.2 and Figure 4.3) is at the heart of current arguments over the sociocultural consequences of immigration. While the debates over the economic consequences of

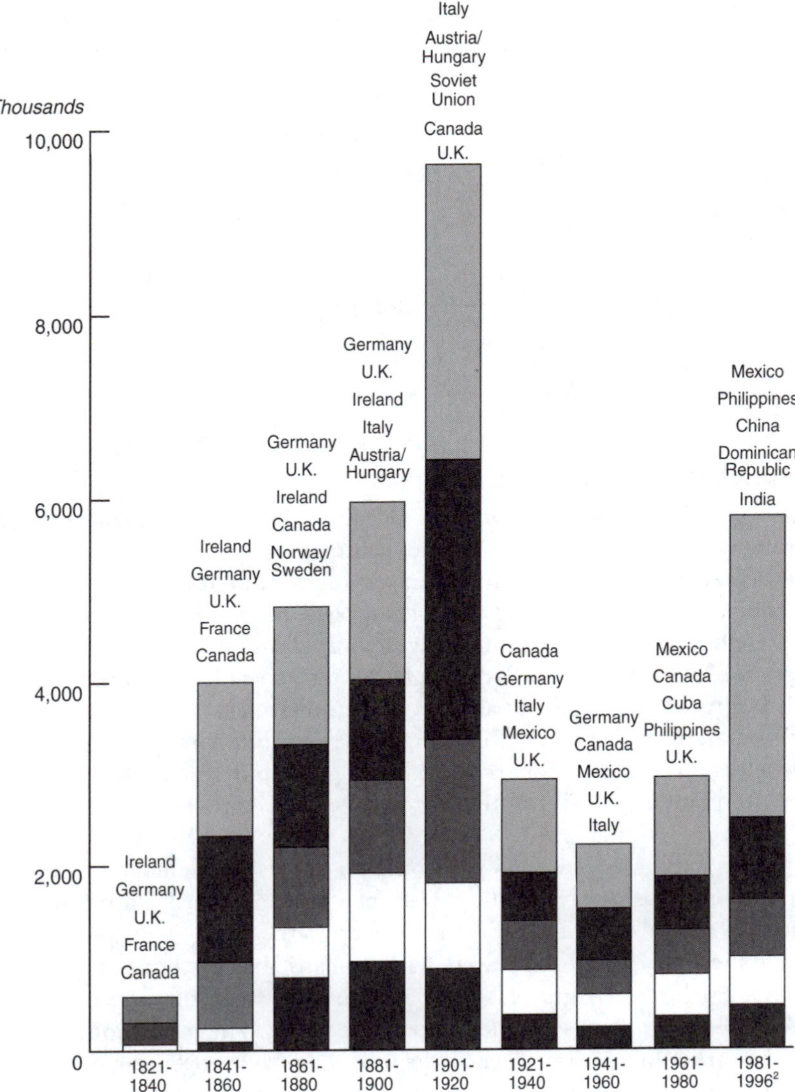

Fig. 4.2 Immigrants Admitted: Country of Origin, Top Five Countries.
[1] Includes People's Republic of China and Taiwan; [2] Sixteen-year period.
Source: Adapted from U.S. Department of Justice, Immigration and Naturalization Service, Statistical Yearbook of the Immigration and Naturalization Service (Washington, DC: G.P.O., 1998).

immigration are largely focused on the three areas of concern discussed above, the debate over the sociocultural implications is somewhat more diffused. Some scholars have focused on language issues, including bilingual education (Are they learning English?). Others examine the political consequences of large-scale immigration (Are they becoming American in letter and in spirit?). Still others focus on immigrant practices that are unpalatable in terms of the cultural models and social practices of the mainstream population (the eternal issues here are female genital cutting, arranged marriages, and, in Europe especially, the veil).

TABLE 4.1 Foreign-Born as a Percentage of the Total U.S. Population

	1880	1900	1920	1950	1960	1970	1980	1990	1997
Percentage of foreign-born	13.3	13.6	13.3	6.9	5.4	4.7	6.2	8.6	9.3*

* 1998 foreign-born population=25,208,000

Percentage of Foreign-Born by Region of Origin

	1880	1920	1950	1980	1997
Europeans	97%	93.6%	89.3%	49.6%	17%
Asians	1.6	1.7	2.65	18	27
Latin Americans	1.3	4.2	6.3	31	51

Source: Harvard Immigration Project, 2000.

RETHINKING ASSIMILATION

Old ideas about immigrant "assimilation" and "acculturation"—first articulated to make sense of the experiences of the transatlantic migrants of a century ago—have naturally been dusted off and tried out on the new arrivals. But in this case, applying the old to the new is not simply a reflex, a kind of intellectual laziness. Rather, I think it suggests that thinking about immigration in the United States is always, explicitly or implicitly, a comparative exercise: the here and now of the "new immigration" versus what, for lack of a better term, we might call the "mythico-historic" record.[7] This is a record in which equal parts of fact, myth, and fantasy combine to produce a powerful cultural narrative along the following lines: poor but hardworking European peasants, pulling themselves up by their bootstraps, willingly gave up their counterproductive old-world views, values, and languages—if not their accents!—to become prosperous, proud, and loyal Americans.[8]

Because the United States is arguably the only postindustrial democracy in the world where immigration is at once history and destiny, every new wave of immigration reactivates an eternal question: How do the "new" immigrants measure up to the "old"? This was asked one hundred years ago when the "new" immigrants were Irish, Italians, and Eastern Europeans and the "old" immigrants were English (see Figure 4.2). The recurring answer to that question is somewhat predictable. New immigrants always fail the comparative test by falling short of the mythico-historic standards set by earlier immigrants. Hence, the most basic rule governing public attitudes about immigration: We love immigrants at a safe historical distance but are much more ambivalent about those joining us now.[9]

It is hardly surprising, then, what questions many are asking today: Are the new immigrants of color recreating the structures of the foundational mythico-historic narrative—the grammar of which was articulated in Irish, Italian, and Eastern European accents on the streets and docks of the Lower East Side of Manhattan one hundred years ago? Or is today's unprecedented racial and cultural diversity—think of the more than one hundred languages now spoken by immigrant children in New York City schools—generating an entirely new script? Is what we hear today an incomprehensible Babelesque story, which is not only unlike anything we have heard before but is quite likely to contribute to our already polarized race relations and chronic "underclass" problems? Will today's new arrivals turn out to be like our mythical immigrant ancestors and assimilate, becoming loyal and proud Americans? Or, conversely, will they by the sheer force of their numbers redefine what it is to be an American?

TABLE 4.2 Region of Birth of Foreign-Born Population

Year	Total	Europe	Asia	Africa	Oceania	Latin America
1900	10,341,276	8,881,548	120,248	2,538	8,820	137,458
1960	9,738,091	7,256,311	490,996	35,355	34,730	908,309
1970	9,619,302	5,740,891	824,887	80,143	41,258	1,803,970
1980	14,079,906	5,149,572	2,539,777	199,723	77,577	4,372,487
1990	19,767,316	4,350,403	4,979,037	363,819	104,145	8,407,837

Source: Adapted from U.S. Census Bureau, Current Population Report. Series P23–195, Profile of the Foreign-Born Population in the United States: 1997 (Washington, DC: G.P.O., 1999).

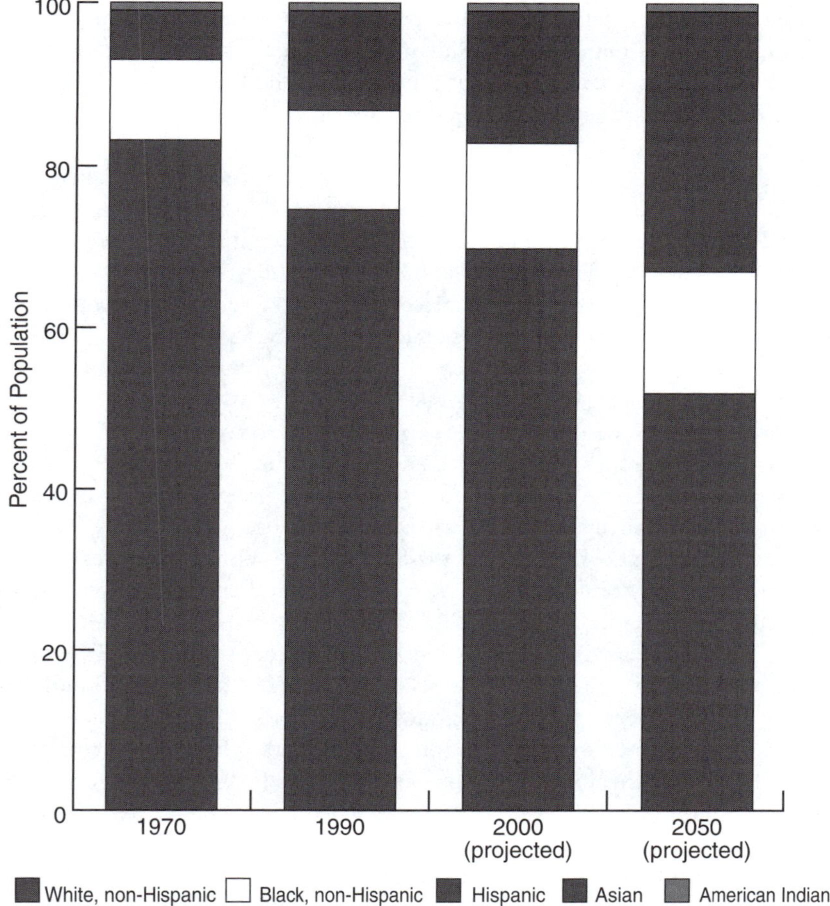

Fig. 4.3 Racial/Ethnic Composition of the Population.
Source: U.S. Census Bureau, Current Population Reports (Washington, DC: G.P.O., 1996).

Much of the analytic—as well as the emotional—framework for approaching the topic of immigration was developed as the then-young nation was in the process of metabolizing the great transatlantic European immigration wave of a century ago. Ideas about "assimilation" and "acculturation," terms often used interchangeably, were first introduced in the social sciences to examine the processes of social and cultural change set in motion as immigrants began their second journey: their insertion into mainstream American life.[10] The basic theme in the narratives of "assimilation" and "acculturation" theories that came to dominate the social sciences predicted that immigration sets in motion a process of change that is directional, indeed unilinear, nonreversible, and continuous.

The direction or aim of the process was said to be "structural assimilation" (typically operationalized in terms of social relations and participation in the opportunity structure) and "acculturation" (typically operationalized in terms of language, values, and cultural identifications) into what was, implicitly or explicitly, the prize at immigration's finish line: the middle-class, white, Protestant, European American framework of the dominant society.[11] The process as it was narrated in the social-science literature seemed to follow neatly the van Gennepian structural code: separation (from social relations and from participation in the opportunity-structure of the country or culture of origin), marginality (residential, linguistic, economic—especially during the earlier phases of immigration and especially acute among the first generation), and, finally, a generation or two after immigration, incorporation into the social structures and cultural codes of the mainstream.

The process of change was said to be nonreversible in that once an immigrant group achieved the goals of acculturation and structural assimilation, there was, so to speak, "no going back." This is in part because scholars of immigrant change conceptualized it as a dual process of gain (new culture, participation in new social structures) and loss (old culture, old social structures). The process was said to be continuous because it took place transgenerationally. The immigrant generation (outsiders looking for a way in), the second generation (Americanized insiders), the third and forth generations (the "Roots" generation in search of "symbolic ethnicity"), and so on all had their assigned roles in this telling of the immigrant saga.

The dominant narratives of immigrant assimilation were structured by three reasonable assumptions. I will call them the "clean break" assumption, the "homogeneity" assumption, and the "progress" assumption. These assumptions, I suggest, need reexamination in light of some of the distinct features characterizing the latest wave of immigration.

First, immigration was theorized to take place in clearly delineated waves (versus ongoing flows) between two relatively remote, bounded geopolitical and cultural spaces. Immigrants left country "A" to settle permanently in country "B." When immigrants chose to return to their country of origin, and large numbers did, it was again seen as a permanent move.[12] The norm, however, was that immigrants leaving Ireland or Eastern Europe were not supposed to look back. This is hardly surprising, since the very idea of immigration was to look forward to a new start and better opportunities in a new country. The renaming rituals at Ellis Island, when immigrants traded—some voluntarily, others involuntarily—exotic names for "Americanized" versions, signified the beginning of a new life. A "clean break" was needed before the process of Americanization could begin.

The second assumption was that immigrants would, in due course, over two or three generations, join the mainstream of a society dominated by a homogeneous middle-class, white, European American Protestant ethos.[13] While American society was never homogenous, "the color line" being a defining feature of its landscape, it was never assumed that the African American culture played a significant factor in the immigrant equation. When assimilation was debated it went without saying: Its very point was to join mainstream culture.

The third assumption dominating thinking about immigrant assimilation was structured by a powerful teleological reflex: Immigration is about uniform progress, about going from "good" (first generation) to "better" (second generation), to "best" (third and fourth generations). The immigrant's journey to success was the stuff of the American dream. *Ragtime*, the acclaimed Broadway musical, gives artistic form to this basic idea: The Russian family moves from the misery of the shtetl to glamorous Hollywood in one generation—assimilation in fast-forward, so to speak. Taken together with the two previous assumptions, a coherent narrative unfolds: As immigrants give up their old ways and they assimilate to middle-class, white European American Protestant culture, they find enormous rewards.

THE "CLEAN BREAK" ASSUMPTION: A CRITIQUE

It may no longer be useful to assume that immigration takes place between remote, neatly bounded geopolitical spaces, where a "clean break" is, even if not desired, inevitable. Indeed, in recent years, anthropologists and sociologists have claimed that what is novel about the "new immigrants" is that they are actors on a transnational stage.[14] The relative ease and accessibility of mass transportation (1.5 billion airline tickets were sold last year) and the new globalized communication and information technologies make possible a more massive back-and-forth movement of people, goods, information, and symbols than ever before.[15] Compared to Mexican or Dominican immigrants today, the Irish and Eastern European immigrants of last century—even if they had wanted to—simply could not have maintained the level and intensity of contact with the "old country" that we are now witnessing.[16] Furthermore, the new immigration from such places as Latin America and the Caribbean can be best characterized as an uninterrupted "flow" rather than neatly delineated "waves" typical of the earlier European transatlantic immigration. This ongoing, uninterrupted migratory flow is said to constantly "replenish" social practices and cultural models that would otherwise tend to be "lost" to assimilation.[17] Indeed, in certain areas of the Southwest, Latin American immigration is generating a powerful infrastructure dominated by a growing Spanish-speaking mass media (radio, television, and print), new market dynamics, and new cultural identities.[18]

Another relevant feature of the new transnational framework is that even as they enmesh themselves in the social, economic, and political life in their new lands, immigrants remain powerful protagonists in the economic, political, and cultural spheres back home.[19] With international remittances estimated at nearly $100 billion per annum, immigrant remittances and investments have become vital to the economies of most countries of emigration. A U.S.-Mexican Binational Study on Immigration estimates that remittances to Mexico were "equivalent to 57 percent of the foreign exchange available through direct investment in 1995, and 5 percent of the total income supplied by exports."[20]

Politically, immigrants are emerging as increasingly relevant actors with influence in political processes both "here" and "there." Some observers have noted that the outcome of the most recent Dominican presidential election was largely determined in New York City—where Dominicans are the largest group of new immigrants. Likewise, Mexican politicians—especially those of the opposition—have recently "discovered" the political value of the seven million Mexican immigrants living in the United States. The new Mexican dual-nationality initiative—whereby Mexican immigrants who become nationalized U.S. citizens would retain a host of political and other rights in Mexico—is also the product of this emerging transnational framework.[21]

Because of a new ease of mass transportation and new communication technologies, immigration is no longer structured around the "sharp break" with the country of origin that once characterized the transoceanic experience. Immigrants today are more likely to be at once "here" and "there," articulating dual consciousness and dual identities and, in the process, bridging increasingly unbounded national spaces.[22]

THE "HOMOGENEITY" ASSUMPTION: A CRITIQUE

It may no longer be useful to assume that immigrants today are joining a homogeneous society dominated by the middle-class, white, European American Protestant ethos.[23] The new immigrants are entering a country that is economically, socially, and culturally unlike the country that absorbed—however ambivalently—previous waves of immigrants. Economically, the previous large wave of immigrants arrived on the eve of the great industrial expansion in which immigrant workers and consumers played a key role.[24]

Immigrants now are actors in a thoroughly globalized restructured economy that is increasingly fragmented into discontinuous economic spheres. Some have characterized the new postindustrial economy in terms of the "hourglass" metaphor. On one end of the hourglass there is a well-remunerated, knowledge-intensive economic sphere that has recently experienced unprecedented growth. On the other end, there is a service economy where low-skilled and semiskilled workers continue to "lose ground" in terms of real wages, benefits, and security. Furthermore, in the new economy there are virtually no bridges for those at the bottom of the hourglass to move into the more desirable sectors. Some scholars have argued that unlike the low-skilled industry jobs of yesterday, the kinds of jobs typically available today to low-skilled new immigrants do not offer serious prospects of upward mobility.[25]

Another defining aspect of the new immigration is the intense social segregation between new immigrants of color and the middle-class, white, European American population. While immigrants have always concentrated in specific neighborhoods, we are witnessing today an extraordinary concentration of large numbers of immigrants in a handful of states in large urban areas polarized by racial tensions. Some 85 percent of all Mexican immigrants in the United States reside in three states (California, Texas, and Illinois). As a result of an increasing segmentation of the economy and society, large numbers of low-skilled immigrants "have become more, not less, likely to live and work in environments that have grown increasingly segregated from whites."[26] These immigrants have, by and large, no meaningful contact with the middle-class, white, European American culture. Rather, their point of reference is more likely to be co-nationals, co-ethnics, or the African American culture.

But perhaps the lethal blow to the homogeneity assumption comes from what I call a "culture of multiculturalism." Rather than face a "relatively uniform 'mainstream'" culture,[27] immigrants today must navigate more complex and varied currents. The cultural models and social practices that we have come to call multiculturalism shape the experiences, perceptions, and behavioral repertoires of immigrants in ways not seen in previous eras of large-scale immigration. A hundred years ago there certainly was no culture of multiculturalism celebrating—however superficially and ambivalently—ethnicity and communities of origin. Indeed, the defining ritual at Ellis Island was the mythic renaming ceremony when immigration officers—sometimes carelessly and sometimes purposefully—renamed new arrivals with more Anglicized names, a cultural baptism of sorts. Others chose to change their names to avoid racism or anti-Semitism, or simply to "blend in." Hence, Israel Ehrenberg was reborn as Ashley Montague, Meyer Schkolnick was reborn as Robert Merton, and Issur Danielovitch Demsky was reborn as Kirk Douglas.[28]

Immigrants today enter social spaces where racial and ethnic categories are important gravitational fields—often charged—with important political and economic implications. The largest wave of immigration into the United States took place largely after the great struggles of the civil rights movement.

In that ethos, racial and ethnic categories became powerful instrumental as well as expressive vectors. By "expressive ethnicity" I refer to the subjective feeling of common origin and a shared destiny with others. These feelings are typically constructed around such phenomena as historic travails and struggles (as in the case of the Serbian sense of peoplehood emerging from their defeat five centuries ago at the hands of the Ottomans in the Battle of Kosovo), a common ancestral language (as in the case of the Basques), or religion (as in the case of the Jews in the Diaspora).[29]

By "instrumental ethnicity," I mean the tactical use of ethnicity. In recent years, "identity politics" has become a mode of expressive self-affirmation as well as instrumental self-advancement. This is in part because ethnic categories have become a critical tool of the state apparatus. Nation-states create categories for various reasons, such as to count people for census, taxation, and apportionment for political representation. Ethnic categories as generated by state policy are relevant to a variety of civic and political matters; furthermore, they are appropriated and used by various groups for their own strategic needs.

Pan-ethnic categories such as "Asian American" and "Hispanic" are largely arbitrary constructions created by demographers and social scientists for purposes of data development, analysis, and policy. The term "Hispanic," for example, was introduced by demographers working for the U.S. Bureau of the Census in the 1980s as a way to categorize people who are either historically or culturally connected to the Spanish language. Note that "Hispanic," the precursor to the more *au courant* term Latino, is a category that has no precise meaning regarding racial or national origins. Indeed, Latinos are white, black, indigenous, and every possible combination thereof. They also originate in over twenty countries as varied from each other as Mexico, Argentina, and the Dominican Republic.[30]

For large numbers of new arrivals today, the point of reference seems to be the cultural sensibilities and social practices of their more established co-ethnics—that is, Latinos, Asians, Afro-Caribbeans—rather than the standards of the increasingly more remote middle-class, white, Protestant European Americans.

THE "PROGRESS" ASSUMPTION: A CRITIQUE

The foundational narratives of immigrant assimilation typically depicted an upwardly mobile journey. The story was elegant in its simplicity: The longer immigrants were in the United States, the better they would do in terms of schooling, health, and income. As Robert Bellah once noted, "The United States was planned for progress," and each wave of immigrants was said to recapitulate this national destiny. This assumption needs rethinking in light of new evidence. A number of scholars from different disciplines using a variety of methods have identified a somewhat disconcerting phenomenon. For many new immigrant groups, length of residency in the United States seems to be associated with declining health, school achievement, and aspirations.[31]

A recent large-scale National Research Council study considered a variety of measures of physical health and risk behaviors among children and adolescents from immigrant families, including general health, learning disabilities, obesity, and emotional difficulties. The NRC researchers found that immigrant youths tend to be healthier than their counterparts from non-immigrant families. These findings are "counterintuitive in light of the racial and ethnic minority status, lower overall socioeconomic status, and higher poverty rates of many immigrant children and families." The NRC study also found that the longer immigrant youths are in the United States, the poorer their overall physical and psychological health. Furthermore, the more "Americanized" they became, the more likely they were to engage in risky behaviors such as substance abuse, unprotected sex, and delinquency (see Figure 4.4). While the NRC data are limited, they nevertheless should be cause for reflection.[32]

In the area of education, sociologists Ruben Rúmbaut and Alejandro Portes surveyed more than five thousand high-school students in San Diego, California, and Dade County, Florida. Rúmbaut writes:

> [A]n important finding supporting our earlier reported research is the negative association of length of residence in the United States with both GPA and aspirations. Time in the United

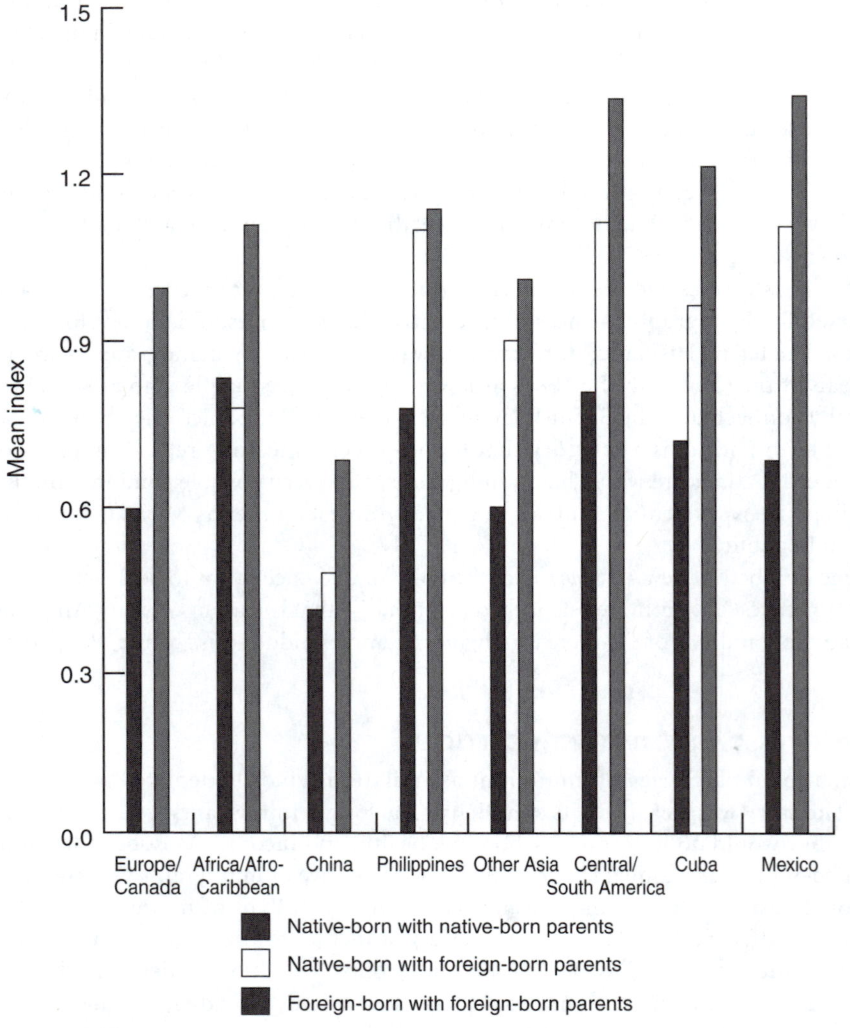

Fig. 4.4 Mean Risk Behavior by Ethnic Group and Immigrant Status.
Source: Adapted from National Research Council, *From Generation to Generation: The Health and Well-Being of Children in Immigrant Families* (Washington, DC: National Academy Press, 1998), 84. Copyright 1998 by the National Academy of Sciences. Courtesy of the National Academy Press, Washington, DC. Reprinted by permission.

> States is, as expected, strongly predictive of improved English reading skills; but despite that seeming advantage, longer residence in the United States and second-generation status [that is, being born in the United States] are connected to declining academic achievement and aspirations, net of other factors.[33]

In a different voice, Reverend Virgil Elizondo, rector of the San Fernando Cathedral in San Antonio, Texas, articulates this same problem: "I can tell by looking in their eyes how long they've been here. They come sparkling with hope, and the first generation finds hope rewarded. Their children's eyes no longer sparkle."[34]

A number of scholars are currently exploring the problem of decline in schooling performance, health, and social adaptation of immigrant children. Preliminary research suggests that several factors seem to be implicated. The various forms of "capital" that the immigrant families bring with them—including financial resources, social class and educational background, psychological and physical health, as well as social supports—have a clear influence on the immigrant experience. Legal status (documented versus undocumented immigrant), race, color, and language also mediate how children and families manage the upheavals of immigration. Economic opportunities and neighborhood characteristics—including the quality of schools where immigrants settle, racial and class segregation, neighborhood decay, and violence—all contribute significantly to the adaptation process. Anti-immigrant sentiment and racism also play a role. These factors combine in ways that seem to lead to very different long-term outcomes. Until better longitudinal data are available, it is no longer safe to assume that immigration inevitably leads to measurable progress.

Indeed, it may be wise to think about what is taking place today in the United States as two very distinct migratory formations—formations that have different causes and generate divergent outcomes. In the long term, these distinct dynamics may turn out to be quite different from what we have seen in the field of immigration before.

UTOPIA

One migratory formation is made up of highly educated, highly skilled workers drawn by the explosive growth in the knowledge-intensive sectors of the economy. These immigrants thrive. They are among the best-educated and most skilled people in the United States. Immigrants today are overrepresented in the category of people with doctorates. Fully half of all entering physics graduate students in 1998 were foreign-born.[35] Thirty-two percent of all scientists and engineers working in California's famed Silicon Valley are immigrants.[36] Roughly a third of all Nobel Prize winners in the United States have been immigrants. In 1999, all (100 percent!) U.S. winners of the Nobel Prize were immigrants. Perhaps with the exception of the highly educated immigrants and refugees escaping Nazi Europe, immigrants in the past tended to be more uniformly poorly educated and relatively unskilled than they are today.[37]

These immigrants are likely to settle in safe middle-class suburban neighborhoods—the kinds of neighborhoods that tend to have better schools. Their children, nor surprisingly, are outperforming native-born children in terms of grades, as winners of the nation's most prestigious science competitions, and as freshmen in the nation's most exclusive colleges—two of the three top Intel Science prizes in March 2000 went to immigrant youths. These highly educated and skilled immigrants are rapidly moving into the more desirable sectors of the U.S. economy, generally bypassing the traditional transgenerational modes of immigrant status mobility.[38] Never in the history of U.S. immigration have so many immigrants done so well so fast. For them, immigration means Utopia realized.

DYSTOPIA

The other migratory formation is made up of large numbers of poorly educated, unskilled workers—many of them in the United States without proper documentation (that is, as illegal aliens). These immigrants come to survive. Some are escaping economies that more or less "broke" during global restructuring; others are escaping violence or war. They are workers drawn by the service sector of the U.S. economy where there seems to be an insatiable appetite for foreign workers. They typically end up in poorly paid jobs that offer no insurance or basic safeties and no promise of upward mobility.

These immigrants tend to settle in areas of deep poverty and racial segregation. Concentrated poverty is associated with the "disappearance of meaningful work opportunities."[39] Youngsters in such neighborhoods are chronically underemployed or unemployed and must search for work elsewhere. In such neighborhoods, with few opportunities in the formal economy, underground or informal activities tend to flourish. These kinds of economies often involve the trade of illegal substances and are associated with gangs and neighborhood violence. This ethos is the primary point of reference for many poor immigrant children of color today.

When poverty is combined with racial segregation, the outcomes can be devastating. No matter what their personal traits or characteristics, people who grow up and live in environments of concentrated poverty and racial isolation are more likely to become teenage mothers, drop out of school, achieve only low levels of education, and earn lower adult incomes.[40]

One hundred years ago, low-skilled immigrant workers with very little formal schooling could, through floor-shop mobility, attain living wages and a comfortable lifestyle. Today's global economy is unforgiving of immigrants without skills and credentials. Furthermore, low-skill service jobs not only lead nowhere in the status hierarchy but also fail to provide for the basic needs of a family. Indeed, new research suggests that among new immigrants, a general pattern of declining returns on education means that with more schooling they will be getting fewer rewards in the post-educational opportunity structure than ever before in the history of U.S. immigration.[41] The high-school graduate who bypasses college and enters the workforce with no special skills has only a limited advantage over the high-school dropout.[42]

Poor, low-skilled immigrants of color have few options but to send their children to schools located in drug-, prostitution-, and gang-infested neighborhoods.[43] All too many immigrant schools can only be characterized as sites overwhelmed by a "culture of violence."[44] Many newly arrived immigrant youths find themselves deeply marginalized in toxic schools that offer inferior education.[45]

In the long term, many immigrant youths of color coming from low-skilled and poorly educated backgrounds will face serious odds. Intense segregation, inferior schools, violent neighborhoods, structural and interpersonal racism—all co-conspire to snuff the immigrants' most precious asset: hope and optimism about the future.[46]

CULTURE AND ASSIMILATION: CONCLUDING THOUGHTS

This latest wave of immigration has rekindled the eternal American debate about the long-term consequences of large-scale immigration. Some worry about the economic implications, while many others have focused on its cultural implications. I turn now to some of these cultural concerns because, I think, they rest on a somewhat flawed understanding of culture.

Analytically, it is sometimes useful to differentiate between two broad spheres of culture: "instrumental culture" and "expressive culture." By instrumental culture, I mean the skills, competencies, and social behaviors that are required successfully to make a living and contribute to society. By expressive culture, I mean the realm of values, worldviews, and the patterning of interpersonal relations that give meaning and sustain the sense of self. Taken together, these qualities of culture generate shared meanings and understandings, and a sense of belonging. In sum, the sense of who you are and where you belong is deeply patterned by these qualities of culture.

In the instrumental realm, there is arguably a worldwide convergence in the skills that are needed to function in today's global economy. Whether in Los Angeles, Lima, or Lagos, the skills that are needed to thrive in the global economy are in fundamental respects the same. These include communication, higher-order symbolic and technical skills as well as habits of work, and interpersonal talents that are common in any cosmopolitan setting.

Immigrant parents are very much aware that if their children are to thrive they must acquire these skills. Indeed, immigration for many parents represents nothing more, and nothing less, than the opportunity to offer children access to these skills. Indeed, we have yet to meet an immigrant parent who tells us that he does not want his daughter to learn English or to acquire the skills and work habits that will prepare her for a successful career whether in the United States or "back home."

While immigrant parents encourage their children to cultivate the "instrumental" aspects of culture in the new setting, they are decidedly more ambivalent about their children's exposure to some of the "expressive" elements of culture in the new land. During the course of our research, it has not been difficult to detect that many immigrant parents strongly resist a whole array of cultural models and social practices in American youth culture that they consider highly undesirable. These include cultural attitudes and behaviors that are anti-schooling ("school is boring") and anti-authority, the glorification of violence, and sexually precocious behaviors. Many immigrant parents reject and resist this form of acculturation.

Hence, I claim that the incantation of many observers—"acculturate, acculturate, acculturate"—needs rethinking. If acculturation is superficially defined as acquiring linguistic skills, job skills, and participation in the political process, then there is a universal consensus on these shared goals. If, on the other hand, we choose a broader definition of assimilation and acculturation as also including the realm of values, worldviews, and interpersonal relations, then a worthy debate ensues.

The first issue that needs airing is the basic question of "acculturating to what?" American society is no longer, if it ever was, a uniform or coherent system. Given their diverse origins, financial resources, and social networks, immigrants end up gravitating toward very different sectors of American society. While some are able to join integrated well-to-do neighborhoods, the majority of today's immigrants come to experience American culture from the vantage point of poor urban settings. Limited economic opportunities, toxic schools, ethnic tensions, violence, drugs, and gangs characterize many of these settings. The structural inequalities found in what some social theorists have called "American Apartheid" are implicated in the creation of a cultural ethos of ambivalence, pessimism, and despair. Asking immigrant youths to give up their values, worldviews, and interpersonal relations to join this ethos is a formula for disaster.[47]

For those immigrants who come into intimate contact with middle-class mainstream culture, other trade-offs will be required. As our data suggest, immigrant children of color perceive that mainstream Americans do not welcome them and, indeed, disparage them as not deserving to partake in the American dream.[48] Identifying wholeheartedly with a culture that rejects you has its psychological costs, usually paid in the currency of shame, doubt, and even self-hatred.

But even if the new immigrants were unambivalently embraced by middle-class mainstream Americans, it is far from clear that mimicking their behaviors would prove to be in the long term an adaptive strategy for immigrants of color. Mainstream middle-class children are protected by social safety nets that give them leeway to experiment with an array of dystopic behaviors that can include drugs, sex, and alcohol. On the other hand, for many immigrant youths, without robust socioeconomic and cultural safety nets, engaging in such behaviors is a high-stakes proposition in which one mistake can have lifelong consequences. While a white middle-class youth caught in possession of drugs is likely to be referred to counseling and rehabilitation, an immigrant youth convicted of the same offense is likely to be deported.

The current wave of immigration involves people from fantastically diverse and heterogeneous cultural backgrounds. Beneath surface differences, a common grammar can be identified among groups as culturally distinct from each other as Chinese, Haitian, and Mexican immigrants. The importance of family ties, the importance of hard work, and optimism about the future are examples of shared immigrant values.[49]

These three realms are aspects of culture that become highlighted and come to the fore in the process of immigration. Consider, for example, the case of strong family ties among immigrants. Many immigrants come from cultures in which the family system is an integral part of the person's sense of self. These family ties play a critical role in family reunification: an important force driving new immigration. Furthermore, once immigrants settle, family ties are accentuated because immigration poses many emotional and practical challenges that force immigrants to turn to one another for support.[50]

Hard work and optimism about the future are likewise central to the immigrant's raison d'être. The immigrant's most fundamental motivation is to find a better life. Immigrants tend to view hard work as essential to this project. The fact that many immigrants will do the impossible jobs that native workers simply refuse to consider is an indication of just how hard they are willing to work. Immigrant family ties, work ethic, and optimism about the future are unique assets that should be celebrated as adding to the total cultural stock of the nation.

Immigration generates change. The immigrants themselves undergo a variety of transformations. Likewise, the immigration process inevitably changes the members of the dominant culture. In the United States today we eat, speak, and dance differently from the way we did thirty years ago, in part because of large-scale immigration. But change is never easy. The changes brought about by the new immigration require mutual calibrations and negotiations.

Rather than advocating that immigrant children abandon all elements of their culture as they embark on their uncertain assimilation journey, a more promising path is to cultivate and nurture the emergence of new hybrid identities and bicultural competencies.[51] These hybrid cultural styles creatively blend elements of the old culture with that of the new, thereby unleashing new energies and potentials.[52]

The skills and work habits that are required to thrive in the new century are essential elements of assimilation. Immigrant children, like all children, must develop this repertoire of instrumental skills. At the same time, maintaining a sense of belonging and social cohesion with their immigrant roots is equally important. When immigrant children lose their expressive culture, social cohesion is weakened, parental authority is undermined, and interpersonal relations suffer. The unthinking call for immigrant children to abandon their culture can only result in loss, anomie, and social disruption.

The model of unilineal assimilation—in which the bargain was straightforward: Please check all your cultural baggage before you pass through the Golden Gate—emerged in another era.[53] The young nation then was eager to turn large numbers of European immigrants into loyal citizen workers and consumers. It was an era of nation-building and bounded national projects.[54]

But even then, accounts of immigrants rushing in unison to trade their culture for American culture were greatly exaggerated. German Americans, Italian Americans, and Irish Americans have all left deep cultural imprints in the molding of American culture. Even among fifth-generation descendants of the previous great wave of immigration, symbolic culture and ethnicity remain an emotional gravitational field.[55]

But beyond the argument that maintaining the expressive elements of culture is symbolically important and strategic from the point of view of social cohesion, there is another point worth considering. In the global era, the tenets of unilineal assimilation are no longer relevant. Today there are clear and unequivocal advantages to being able to operate in multiple cultural codes—as anyone working in a major (and now not-so-major) corporation knows. There are social, economic, cognitive, and aesthetic advantages to being able to move across cultural spaces. Dual consciousness has its instrumental and expressive advantages. Immigrant children are in a position to maximize that unique advantage. While many view their cultural—including linguistic—skills as a threat, I see them as precious assets to be cultivated.

A renowned historian once said the history of the United States is in fundamental respects the history of immigration.[56] Throughout history, U.S. citizens have ambivalently welcomed newcomers. The fear then, as now, focused on whether the immigrants would contribute to the American project. The gift of hindsight demonstrates just how essential immigration has proven to the making and remaking of the American fabric.

However, with diversity comes conflict and dissent. Working through frictions in the public sphere by reasoned debate and compromise is central to the idea and practice of democracy. Immigrant children are uniquely poised to play a significant role in the remaking of American democracy. In the era of multiculturalism and transnationalism, their bicultural experiences and skills prepare them well to be the cultural brokers able to find the common ground.

Notes

1. See, for example, Profile of the Foreign-Born Population in the United States: 1997 (Washington, DC: U.S. Census Bureau, Current Population Reports, 1999).
2. See, for example, Erik Eckholm, "For China's Rural Migrants, an Education Wall," *The New York Times*, December 12, 1999, A8.
3. See, for example, Carola Suárez-Orozco and Marcelo M. Suárez-Orozco, *Children of Immigration* (Cambridge, MA: Harvard University Press, 2000).
4. Theorists of immigration have argued that transnationalized labor-recruiting networks, family reunification, and changing cultural models and expectations about, for example, what is an acceptable standard of living are all powerfully implicated in generating and sustaining new migratory flows. Wars nearly always generate large-scale immigration: World War II gave birth to the Mexican bracero program, which started the largest wave of immigration to the United States in history. Without the Cold War, there would not be today over a million Cuban Americans in the United States. The Southeast Asian Diaspora is the product of the war in Indochina. The million or so Central Americans that now make the United States their home arrived following the intensification of the U.S.-backed counterinsurgency campaigns in El Salvador, Guatemala, and Nicaragua of the 1980s.
5. A great deal of energy has gone into assessing the economic consequences of immigration, and the research findings are somewhat ambiguous. Indeed, they are often contradictory. Some economists claim that the new immigrants are a burden to taxpayers and an overall negative influence on the U.S. economy; others suggest that they continue to be an important asset. A recent study on the economic, demographic, and fiscal effects of immigration by the National Research Council concludes that "immigration produces net economic gains for domestic residents." National Research Council, The New Americans: Economic, Demographic, and Fiscal Effects of Immigration (Washington, D.C.: National Academy Press, 1997), 3. For another overview of immigrants and the economy, see George Borjas, *Heaven's Door: Immigration Policy and the American Economy* (Princeton, NJ: Princeton University Press, 1999).
6. National Research Council, The New Americans, 5.
7. Suárez-Orozco and Suárez-Orozco, *Children of Immigration.*
8. For a recent exquisite treatment of this narrative, see Riv-Ellen Prell, *Fighting to Become Americans: Jews, Gender, and the Anxiety of Assimilation* (Boston: Beacon Press, 1999). Consider also the introductory paragraph on a *New York Times* story on the families of vice-presidential candidate Senator Joseph Lieberman and his immigrant wife, Hadassah Lieberman, a child of Holocaust survivors: "They came over on wobbling merchant marine ships, refugees with a few valises apiece that contained all they owned in the world. Rebuilding from scratch—they had, after all, lost their homes and most of their closest kin—they worked at low-paying jobs in dingy dress factories, luncheonettes, dry-goods stores. For many, it was too late for any grander aspirations. Their children would redeem their expectations." Joseph Berger, "Mrs. Lieberman's Story, and Others," *The New York Times*, August 13, 2000, A26.
9. Suárez-Orozco and Suárez-Orozco, *Children of Immigration.*
10. See Robert E. Park and Ernest W. Burgess, *Introduction to the Science of Sociology* (Chicago: University of Chicago Press, 1965); Milton M. Gordon, *Assimilation in American Life: The Role of Race, Religion, and National Origins* (New York: Oxford University Press, 1964); and Richard Alba and Victor Nee, "Rethinking Assimilation Theory for a New Era of Immigration," *International Migration Review* (31) (Winter 1997).
11. The process of change was said to be unilinear in that all new arrivals would be expected to undergo roughly the same process of change.
12. See, for example, Jose C. Moya, *Cousins and Strangers: Spanish Immigrants in Buenos Aires, 1850–1930* (Berkeley: University of California Press, 1998) and Michael Piore, *Birds of Passage: Migrant Labor and Industrial Societies* (New York: Cambridge University Press, 1971).
13. See, for example, Alejandro Portes, ed., *The New Second Generation* (New York: Russell Sage, 1996).
14. See Peggy Levitt, "Transnationalizing Civil and Political Change: The Case of Transnational Organizational Ties between Boston and the Dominican Republic," Ph.D. dissertation, Massachusetts Institute of Technology, 1996; "Commentary," in Marcelo M. Suárez-Orozco, ed., *Crossings: Mexican Immigration in Interdisciplinary Perspectives* (Cambridge, MA: David Rockefeller Center for Latin American Studies and Harvard University Press, 1998); Linda Basch, Nina Glick Schiller, and Cristina Szanton Blanc, *Nations Unbound: Transnational Projects, Postcolonial Predicaments and Deterritorialized Nation-States* (Basel, Switzerland: Gordon and Breach Science Publishers, 1994).
15. Borrowing the delicious words of Luís Rafael Sanchez, many new immigrants today live neither here nor there but rather in "la guagua aérea"—the air bus.
16. See Ricardo Ainslie, "Cultural Mourning, Immigration, and Engagement: Vignettes from the Mexican Experience," in Suárez-Orozco, ed., *Crossings: Mexican Immigration in Interdisciplinary Perspectives.*
17. See David G. Gutierrez, "Ethnic Mexicans and the Transformation of 'American' Social Space: Reflections on Recent History," in Suárez-Orozco, ed., *Crossings: Mexican Immigration in Interdisciplinary Perspectives.*

18. Since 1990, while the Hispanic population in the United States grew by more than 30 percent, its buying power has grown by more than 65 percent, to about $350 billion in 1997. This is changing the way business is conducted in many parts of the country.
19. Wayne Cornelius, "The Structural Embeddedness of Demand for Mexican Immigrant Labor," in Suárez-Orozco, ed., *Crossings: Mexican Immigration in Interdisciplinary Perspectives*; and Jorge Durand, "Migration and Integration," in ibid.
20. See Binational Study: Migration Between Mexico and the United States (Washington, DC: U.S. Commission on Immigration Reform, 1998). Cornelius, however, argues that over time Mexican immigrants in the United States are less likely to invest in capital improvements in the communities they emigrated from. In fact, he argues that a new feature of the Mexican experience in the United States is that as Mexican immigrants become increasingly rooted in the U.S. side of "the line," they mainly go back to these communities for rest and relaxation. See Cornelius, "The Structural Embeddedness."
21. Culturally, immigrants not only significantly reshape the ethos of their new communities but are also responsible for significant social transformations "back home." Peggy Levitt has argued that Dominican "social remittances" affect the values, cultural models, and social practices of those left behind. See Levitt, "Transnationalizing Civil and Political Change."
22. Basch, Schiller, and Blanc, *Nations Unbound.*
23. I concur with Alejandro Portes when he argues that we can no longer assume that new immigrants will assimilate into a coherent mainstream.
24. John Higham, *Send These To Me: Jews and Other Immigrants in Urban America* (New York: Atheneum, 1975).
25. Portes, *The New Second Generation.*
26. Roger Waldinger and Mehdi Bozorgmehr, eds., *Ethnic Los Angeles* (New York: Russell Sage Foundation, 1996).
27. Portes, *The New Second Generation.*
28. Lawrence J. Friedman, *Identity's Architect: A Biography of Erik H. Erickson* (New York: Scribner, 1999).
29. Lola Romanucci-Ross and George DeVos, *Ethnic Identity: Creation, Conflict, and Accommodation*, third ed. (Walnut Creek, CA: Alta Mira Press, 1995).
30. Nor do these categories address the sensibilities rooted in history and generation in the United States. A Latina can be a person who is the descendant of the original settlers in what is today New Mexico. Her ancestors spoke Spanish—well before English was ever heard in this continent. Her family has resided in this land before the United States appropriated the Southwest territories. She is considered a Latina as is a Mayan-speaking new arrival from Guatemala who crossed the border last week. Likewise, the term Asian brings together people of highly diverse cultural, linguistic, and religious backgrounds. A Chinese Buddhist and a Filipino Catholic are both considered Asian American though they may have very little in common in terms of language, cultural identity, and sense of self.
31. See Grace Kao and Marta Tienda, "Optimism and Achievement: The Educational Performance of Immigrant Youth," *Social Science Quarterly* 76 (1) (1995): 1–19, National Research Council, *From Generation to Generation: The Health and Well-Being of Children in Immigrant Families* (Washington, DC: National Academy Press, 1998); Ruben Rumbaut, "The New Californians: Comparative Research findings on the Educational Progress of Immigrant Children," in Ruben Rumbaut and Wayne Cornelius, eds., *California's Immigrant Children* (San Diego, CA.: Center for U.S.-Mexican Studies, University of California–San Diego, 1995); Laurence Steinberg, B. Bradford Brown, and Sanford M. Dornbusch, *Beyond the Classroom: Why School Reform Has Failed & What Parents Need to Do* (New York: Simon & Schuster, 1996); and Carola Suárez-Orozco and Marcelo Suárez-Orozco, *Transformations: Immigration, Family Life and Achievement Motivation Among Latino Adolescents* (Stanford, CA: Stanford University Press, 1995).
32. The data reported are largely cross-sectional panel data—some of it self-reported. Better-quality longitudinal data are now needed to develop a more clear sense of the factors leading to these worrisome trends. See National Research Council, *From Generation to Generation.* Quote from ibid., 159.
33. Rumbaut, "The New Californians."
34. Quoted in Roberto Suro, *Strangers Among Us: How Latino Immigration is Transforming America* (New York: Alfred Knopf, 1998), 13.
35. See "Wanted: American Physicists," *The New York Times*, July 23, 1999, A27. Of course, not all of these foreign-born physics graduate students are immigrants; some will indeed return to their countries of birth while others will surely go on to have productive scientific careers in the United States.
36. See AnnaLee Saxenian, *Silicon Valley's New Immigrant Entrepreneurs* (San Francisco, CA: Public Policy Institute of California, 1999). I am thankful to Professor Michael Jones-Correa of the department of government at Harvard University for alerting me to this important new study.
37. See, for example, George Borjas, "Assimilation in Cohort Quality Revisited: What Happened to Immigrant Earnings in the 1980s?" *Journal of Labor Economics* 13 (2) (1995): 211–245.
38. See Waldinger and Bozorgmehr, *Ethnic Los Angeles.*
39. William Wilson, *When Work Disappears: The World of the New Urban Poor* (New York: Vintage Books, 1997).
40. Douglas Massey and Nancy Denton, *American Apartheid* (Cambridge, MA: Harvard University Press, 1993).
41. See Dowell Myers, "Dimensions of Economic Adaptation by Mexican-Origin Men," in Suárez-Orozco, ed., *Crossings: Mexican Immigration in Interdisciplinary Perspectives*, 188.
42. See Richard Murnane, *Teaching the New Basic Skills: Principles for Educating Children to Thrive in a Changing Economy* (New York: Martin Kessler Books, Free Press, 1996).
43. In one such site, one of our research assistants found that boys sneak out of school at noon to watch pornographic films at a shop across the street from the school. Many of these schools are dilapidated and unkempt. Violence is pervasive. In an elementary school, a young girl was found raped and murdered on school premises. In another, an irate

parent stabbed a teacher in front of her students. In yet another school, just days after the Columbine incident, a cherry bomb was set off as one of our research assistants was conducting an interview. In many schools there is tremendous ethnic tension. In one of our sites, students regularly play a game they call "Rice and Beans" (Asian students versus Latino students) that frequently deteriorates into physical violence. In many sites immigrant students report living in constant fear; they dread lunch and class changes as the hallways are sites of confrontation and intimidation, including sexual violence.

44. An ethnographic study of a number of immigrant schools in Miami found that three factors were consistently present in schools with "cultures of violence." First, school officials tended to deny that the school had problems with violence or drugs. Second, many of the school staff members exhibited "non-caring" behaviors toward the students. Third, the schools took lax school-security measures. See Michael Collier, "Cultures of Violence in Miami-Dade Public Schools," working paper of the Immigration and Ethnicity Institute, Florida International University, November 1998.
45. These schools affect the opportunities and experiences of immigrant children in several immediate ways. They tend to have limited resources. Classrooms are typically overcrowded. Textbooks and curricula are outdated; computers are few and obsolete. Many of the teachers may not have credentials in the subjects they teach. Clearly defined tracks sentence students to non-college destinations. Lacking English skills, many immigrant students are often enrolled in the least demanding and competitive classes that eventually exclude them from courses needed for college. These schools generally offer few (if any) advanced-placement courses that are critical for entry in many of the more competitive colleges. The guidance counselor-student ratio is impossibly high. Because the settings are so undesirable, teachers and principals routinely transfer out in search of better assignments elsewhere. As a result, in many such schools there is little continuity or sense of community. Children and teachers are often preoccupied with ever-present violence, and morale is often very low.
46. For a superb but somewhat pessimistic study of how "persistent, blatant racial discrimination" along with inferior schools in high-crime neighborhoods are implicated in the transgenerational decline of West Indian immigrants in New York City, see Mary Waters, *Black Identities: West Indian Immigrants Dreams and American Realities* (Cambridge, MA: Harvard University Press, 1999).
47. Massey and Denton, *American Apartheid.*
48. See Carola Suárez-Orozco, "Identities Under Siege," in Antonius Robben and Marcelo M. Suárez-Orozco, eds., *Cultures Under Siege: Collective Violence and Trauma* (New York: Cambridge University Press, 2000).
49. For an overview of recent research on immigration and family ties, see Ruber Rúmbaut, "Ties that Bind: Immigration and Immigrant Families in the United States," in Alan Booth, Ann C. Crouter, and Nancy Landale, eds., *Immigration and the Family: Research and Policy on U.S. Immigrants* (Newport, NJ Lawrence Erlbaum, 1996). See also Suárez-Orozco and Suárez-Orozco *Transformations: Immigration, Family Life, and Achievement Motivation Among Latino Adolescents* and Celia Falicov, *Latino Families in Therapy: Guide to Multicultural Practice* (New York: Guilford, 1998). For an overview of immigrant optimism and achievement orientation, see Grace Kao and Marta Tienda, "Optimism and Achievement: The Educational Performance of Immigrant Youth," *Social Science Quarterly* 96 (1995): 1–19.
50. See Suárez-Orozco and Suárez-Orozco, *Children of Immigration.*
51. I concur with Teresa LaFromboise and her colleagues on the need to reconceptualize what they call the "linear model of cultural acquisition." See Teresa LaFromboise et al., "Psychological Impact of Biculturalism: Evidence and Theory," in Pamela Balls Organista, Kevin M. Chun, and Gerardo Marin, eds., *Readings in Ethnic Psychology* (New York: Routledge, 1998).
52. Margaret Gibson articulates a theoretical argument on immigrant transculturation and a calculated strategy of "accommodation without assimilation" in her study of highly successful Sikh immigrants in California. See Margaret Gibson, *Accommodation without Assimilation: Sikh Immigrants in an American High School* (Ithaca, NY: Cornell University Press, 1988). For a theoretical statement on the psychology of ethnic identity and cultural pluralism, see Jean S. Phinney, "Ethnic Identity in Adolescents and Adults: Review of Research," in Organista, Chun, and Marin, eds., *Readings in **[??28]** Psychology.*
53. By unilinear assimilation I mean the idea that various immigrant groups have followed roughly a single path of assimilation.
54. Bounded national projects are a counterpoint to the idea that today transnationalism means, among other things, that nations are becoming increasingly enmeshed or "unbounded," to borrow Linda Basch's word. Basch, Schiller, and Blanc, *Nations Unbound: Transnational Projects, Postcolonial Predicaments, and Deterritorialized Nation-States.*
55. See, for example, Nathan Glazer and Daniel Patrick Moynihan, *Beyond the Melting Pot* (Cambridge, MA: MIT Press, 1970).
56. Oscar Handlin, The Uprooted (Boston: Little, Brown, 1951).

Chapter 5
The New Second Generation: Segmented Assimilation and Its Variants

ALEJANDRO PORTES AND MIN ZHOU

> My name is Herb
> and I'm not poor;
> I'm the Herbie that you're looking for,
> like Pepsi,
> a new generation
> of Haitian determination—
> I'm the Herbie that you're looking for.

A beat tapped with bare hands, a few dance steps, and the Haitian kid was rapping. His song, titled "Straight Out of Haiti," was being performed at Edison High, a school that sits astride Little Haiti and Liberty City, the largest black area of Miami. The lyrics captured well the distinct outlook of his immigrant community. The panorama of Little Haiti contrasts sharply with the bleak inner city. In Miami's Little Haiti, the storefronts leap out at the passersby. Bright blues, reds, and oranges vibrate to Haitian merengue blaring from sidewalk speakers.[1] Yet, behind the gay Caribbean exteriors, a struggle goes on that will define the future of this community. As we will see later on, it involves the second generation (children like Herbie), which is subject to conflicting pressure from parents and peers and to pervasive outside discrimination.

Growing up in an immigrant family has always been difficult, as individuals are torn by conflicting social and cultural demands while they face the challenge of entry into an unfamiliar and frequently hostile world. And yet the difficulties are not always the same. The process of growing up American oscillates between smooth acceptance and traumatic confrontation depending on the characteristics that immigrants and their children bring along and the social context that receives them. In this article, we explore some of these factors and their bearing on the process of social adaptation of the immigrant second generation. We propose a conceptual framework for understanding this process and illustrate it with selected ethnographic material and survey data from a recent survey of children of immigrants.

Research on the new immigration—that which arose after the passage of the 1965 Immigration Act—has been focused almost exclusively on the first generation, that is, on adult men and women coming to the United States in search of work or to escape political persecution. Little noticed until recently is the fact that the foreign-born inflow has been rapidly evolving from single adult individuals to entire family groups, including infant children and those born to immigrants in the United States. By 1980, 10 percent of dependent children in households counted by the census were second-generation immigrants.[2] In the late 1980s, another study put the number of students in kindergarten through twelfth grade in American schools who spoke a language other than English at home at three to five million.[3]

The great deal of research and theorizing on post-1965 immigration offers only tentative guidance on the second generation's prospects and paths of adaptation because the outlook of this group can be very different from that of their immigrant parents. For example, it is generally accepted among immigration theorists that entry-level menial jobs are performed without hesitation by newly arrived immigrants but are commonly shunned by their U.S.-reared offspring. This disjuncture gives rise to a race between the social and economic progress of first-generation immigrants and the material conditions and career prospects that their American children grow to expect.[4]

Nor does the existing literature on second-generation adaptation, based as it is on the experience of descendants of pre-World War I immigrants, offer much guidance for the understanding of contemporary events. The last sociological study of children of immigrants was Irving Child's *Italian or American? The Second Generation in Conflict*, published fifty years ago.[5] Conditions at the time were quite different from those confronting settled immigrant groups today. Two such differences deserve special mention. First, descendants of European immigrants who confronted the dilemmas of conflicting cultures were uniformly white. Even if of a somewhat darker hue than the natives, their skin color reduced a major barrier to entry into the American mainstream. For this reason, the process of assimilation depended largely on individual decisions to leave the immigrant culture behind and embrace American ways. Such an advantage obviously does not exist for the black, Asian, and mestizo children of today's immigrants.

Second, the structure of economic opportunities has also changed. Fifty years ago, the United States was the premier industrial power in the world, and its diversified industrial labor requirements offered to the second generation the opportunity to move up gradually through better-paid occupations while remaining part of the working class. Such opportunities have increasingly disappeared in recent years following a rapid process of national de-industrialization and global industrial restructuring. This process has left entrants to the American labor force confronting a widening gap between the minimally paid menial jobs that immigrants commonly accept and the high-tech and professional occupations requiring college degrees that native elites occupy.[6] The gradual disappearance of intermediate opportunities also bears directly on the race between first-generation economic progress and second-generation expectations, noted previously.

THE NEW AMERICANS AT A GLANCE

Before examining this process in detail, it is important to learn a little more about today's second generation. In 1990, the foreign-born population of the United States reached an estimated 21.2 million. In absolute terms, this is the highest number in the history of the nation, although relative to the native-born population, the figure is lower than that at the turn of the twentieth century. In 1890, immigrants represented 14.8 percent of the total population, almost double today's figure of 8.6 percent. The foreign-stock population, composed of immigrants and their descendants, is, however, much higher. In 1990, roughly 46 million, or 18.5 percent of the total U.S. population, were estimated to be of foreign stock. This yields a net second-generation total of 24.8 million, or 10.9 percent of the American population.[7]

As an estimate of the new second generation, this figure is inflated by the presence of offspring of older immigrants. A team of demographers at the Urban Institute have estimated the contribution of post-1960 immigration, including immigrants and their children, to the total 1990 U.S. population. According to their estimate, if immigration had been cut off in 1960, the total population in 1990 would have been 223.4 million and not the 248.7 million actually counted. Hence post-1960 immigration contributed approximately 25.3 million. Subtracting estimates of net immigration for 1960–1990 provided by the same researchers, the new second generation, formed by children of post-1960 immigrants, represents 7.7 million, or 3.4 percent of the native-born population. This is a lower-bound estimate based on a demographic model and not on an actual count. It excludes children born to mixed foreign-native couples who are also normally counted as part of the second generation.[8]

More important, however, is the prospect for growth in future years. Given the record increase of immigration since 1960, the second generation as a whole is expected to grow rapidly, surpassing its former peak of roughly 28 million in 1940 sometime during the 1990s. As noted previously, however, the racial and ethnic composition of the second-generation's component attributable to post-1960 immigration is quite different from that which peaked just before World War II. More than 85 percent of children of immigrants in 1940 were born to Europeans, or, in current terminology, non-Hispanic whites. By contrast, approximately 77 percent of post-1960 immigrants are non-Europeans. Of the post-1960 immigrants, 22.4 percent are classified as Asians, 7.6 percent as blacks, and 47 percent as Hispanics. The latter group, which originates in Mexico and other Latin American countries, poses a problem in terms of phenotypical classification since Hispanics can be of any race.[9]

According to the 1990 census, 51.7 percent of the 22.3 million Hispanics counted were white, 3.4 percent black, and 42.7 percent of another race. The latter figure, possibly corresponding to the category of mixed race, or mestizos, was slightly larger among Mexicans, who constitute 60.4 percent of the total Hispanic population. Applying these figures with some adjustments to the post-1960 immigrant flow, it is reasonable to assume that approximately half of Hispanic immigrants would be classified as nonwhite. This phenotypical category would hence comprise a majority—roughly 54 percent—of the total inflow.[10]

Individual data from the 1990 census have not been released as of this writing. In an effort to learn more about the new second generation, Leif Jensen conducted an analysis of the one-in-a-thousand version of the Public Use Microdata Sample A (PUMS) from the 1980 census. He identified 3,425 children living in households with at least one foreign-born parent and who themselves were either native-born or had immigrated to the United States at a young age.[11] The number represented 5.1 percent of native-born, native-parentage children identified in the sample, a figure that is close to the estimated contribution of post-1960 immigration to the 1980 U.S. population: 5.8 percent.

The ethnic classification of Jensen's sample of new second-generation children in 1980 also corresponds closely with that of post-1965 immigrants reported previously. In Jensen's sample, 17.9 percent were classified as Asians, 6.8 percent as blacks, and 45.5 percent as Hispanics. The data does not provide a racial breakdown of Hispanics, but it does contain information on their national origin. Sixty-five percent of the 1,564 post-1965 Hispanic children were of Mexican origin; 7.5 percent were of Cuban origin; and the remaining 27.5 percent were from all other Latin American nationalities. Table 5.1 presents selected socio-demographic characteristics of this sample and compares them with those of native-born children of native parentage.

Not surprisingly, second-generation youths are far more likely to be bilingual than their native-parentage counterparts. Less than half of the children of immigrants speak English only, and two-thirds speak a language other than English at home in contrast with the overwhelming English

TABLE 5.1 Selected Characteristics Of Post-1965 Second-generation Youths And Native Youths Of Native Parentage, 1980 (Percentage unless noted)

Children's Characteristics	Post-1965 Immigrant Parent ($N = 3{,}425$)	Native-born Parents ($N = 67{,}193$)
Female	46.8	47.4
Mean age	7.5 years	11.9 years
Race or ethnicity		
White	27.4	78.9
Black	6.8	14.4
Hispanic	45.7	5.4
Mexican	29.7	3.3
Cuban	3.5	0.0
Other	12.5	2.1
Asian	19.5	0.5
Chinese	4.3	0.1
Filipino	5.1	0.1
Korean	2.6	0.0
Vietnamese	1.4	0.0
Other	6.1	0.3
English ability		
Speaks English only	47.7	95.5
Very well	26.5	2.7
Well	13.8	1.3
Not well or not at all	12.0	0.5
Language spoken at home		
English	33.6	94.9
Other	66.4	5.1
Household type		
Couple	89.7	79.0
Single male head	1.5	2.7
Single female head	8.8	18.3
Area of residence		
Central city	39.6	17.4
Non-central-city metropolitan area	48.4	49.8
Mixed	6.5	11.7
Non-metropolitan	5.5	21.1
State of residence*		
California	32.4	8.1
New York	12.8	7.2
Texas	9.9	6.1
Illinois	5.7	5.2
Florida	5.0	3.5
New Jersey	4.9	3.1
Mean family income	\$19,502	\$23,414
Poverty rate	20.8	13.8

TABLE 5.1 *(Continued)*

Mean education of family head	10.9 years	12.2 years
Mean education, self†	11.5 years	12.0 years
High school dropout†	22.8	22.9
School type		
Public	83.4	86.6
Private	16.6	13.4

Note: The youths in this sample reside in households with at least one parent present. This table is based on U.S. Census Public Use Microdata Sample A, as reported in Leif Jensen, *Children of the New Immigration: A Comparative Analysis of Today's Second Generation*, paper commissioned by the Children of Immigrants Research Project, Department of Sociology, Johns Hopkins University, reprinted as Institute for Policy Research and Evaluation Working Paper no. 1990–32 (University Park: Penn State University, Aug. 1990), tabs. 1–8.

* The six states with the largest concentrations of post-1965 immigrant parents.

† Restricted to those aged 20 or more and not enrolled in school.

exclusivity among native-parentage youth. However, linguistic assimilation is evident in the fact that only 12 percent of the second generation reports speaking English poorly. Households with immigrant parents are far more likely to be urban and to be found in central cities. Their geographic distribution by state also differs significantly from native-headed households. Just six states account for 71 percent of immigrant households, while the same states contain only 33 percent of the natives. Not surprisingly, immigrant parents tend to have more modest socioeconomic characteristics, as indicated by their lower family income, higher poverty rates, and lower education of the family head. However, they are about twice less likely to head single-parent households than are natives. Greater family cohesiveness may have something to do with second-generation educational outcomes. Figures in Table 5.1 indicate that children of immigrants are as likely to attend private schools, as unlikely to be dropouts, and as likely to graduate from high school as native-parentage youth.[12]

These comparisons are, of course, based on averages that conceal great diversity within each universe. Among second-generation youths in particular, preliminary field research indicates wide differences in educational, linguistic, and social psychological outcomes. None is more important than the forms that an inexorable process of cultural assimilation takes among different immigrant nationalities and its effects on their youths. We explore these differences and provide a theoretical explanation of their causes in the next sections.

ASSIMILATION AS A PROBLEM

The Haitian immigrant community of Miami is composed of some 75,000 legal and clandestine immigrants, many of whom sold everything they owned in order to buy passage to America. First-generation Haitians are strongly oriented toward preserving a strong national identity, which they associate both with community solidarity and with social networks promoting individual success.[13] In trying to instill national pride and an achievement orientation in their children, they clash, however, with the youngsters' everyday experiences in school. Little Haiti is adjacent to Liberty City, the main black inner-city area of Miami, and Haitian adolescents attend predominantly inner-city schools. Native-born youths stereotype Haitians as too docile and too subservient to whites and they make fun of French and Creole and of the Haitians' accent. As a result, second-generation Haitian children find themselves torn between conflicting ideas and values. To remain Haitian they would have to face social ostracism and continuing attacks in school; to become American—black American in this case—they would have to forgo their parents' dreams of making it in America on the basis of ethnic solidarity and preservation of traditional values.[14]

An adversarial stance toward the white mainstream is common among inner-city minority youths who, while attacking the newcomers' ways, instill in them a consciousness of American-style discrimination. A common message is the devaluation of education as a vehicle for advancement of all black youths, a message that directly contradicts the immigrant parents' expectations. Academically outstanding Haitian American students, Herbie among them, have consciously attempted to retain their ethnic identity by cloaking it in black American cultural forms, such as rap music. Many others, however, have followed the path of least effort and become thoroughly assimilated. Assimilation in this instance is not into mainstream culture but into the values and norms of the inner city. In the process, the resources of solidarity and mutual support within the immigrant community are dissipated.

An emerging paradox in the study of today's second generation is the peculiar forms that assimilation has adopted for its members. As the Haitian example illustrates, adopting the outlooks and cultural ways of the native-born does not represent, as in the past, the first step toward social and economic mobility but may lead to the exact opposite. At the other end, immigrant youths who remain firmly ensconced in their respective ethnic communities may, by virtue of this fact, have a better chance for educational and economic mobility through use of the material and social capital that their communities make available.[15]

This situation stands on its head the cultural blueprint for advancement of immigrant groups in American society. As presented in innumerable academic and journalistic writings, the expectation is that the foreign-born and their offspring will first acculturate and then seek entry and acceptance among the native-born as a prerequisite for their social and economic advancement. Otherwise, they remain confined to the ranks of the ethnic lower and lower-middle classes.[16] This portrayal of the requirements for mobility, so deeply embedded in the national consciousness, stands contradicted today by a growing number of empirical experiences.

A closer look at these experiences indicates, however, that the expected consequences of assimilation have not entirely reversed signs; rather, the process has become segmented. In other words, the question is into what sector of American society a particular immigrant group assimilates. Instead of a relatively uniform mainstream whose mores and prejudices dictate a common path of integration, we observe today several distinct forms of adaptation. One of them replicates the time-honored portrayal of growing acculturation and parallel integration into the white middle-class; a second leads straight in the opposite direction to permanent poverty and assimilation into the underclass; still a third associates rapid economic advancement with deliberate preservation of the immigrant community's values and tight solidarity. This pattern of segmented assimilation immediately raises the question of what makes some immigrant groups become susceptible to the downward route and what resources allow others to avoid this course. In the ultimate analysis, the same general process helps explain both outcomes. We advance next our hypotheses as to how this process takes place and how the contrasting outcomes of assimilation can be explained. This explanation is then illustrated with recent empirical material in the final section.

VULNERABILITY AND RESOURCES

Along with individual and family variables, the context that immigrants find upon arrival in their new country plays a decisive role in the course that their offspring's lives will follow. This context includes such broad variables as political relations between sending and receiving countries and the state of the economy in the latter and such specific ones as the size and structure of preexisting co-ethnic communities. The concept of modes of incorporation provides a useful theoretical tool to understand this diversity. As developed in prior publications, modes of incorporation consist of the complex formed by the policies of the host government; the values and prejudices of the receiving society; and the characteristics of the co-ethnic community. These factors can be arranged in a tree of contextual situations, illustrated by Figure 5.1. This figure provides a first approximation to our problem.[17]

To explain second-generation outcomes and their segmented character, however, we need to go into greater detail on the meaning of these various modes of incorporation from the standpoint of immigrant youths. There are three features of the social contexts encountered by today's newcomers that create vulnerability to downward assimilation. The first is color, the second is location, and the third is the absence of mobility ladders. As noted previously, the majority of contemporary immigrants are nonwhite. Although this feature may appear at first glance as an individual characteristic, in reality it is a trait belonging to the host society. Prejudice is not intrinsic to a particular skin color or racial type, and, indeed, many immigrants never experienced it in their native lands. It is by virtue of moving into a new social environment, marked by different values and prejudices, that physical features become redefined as a handicap.

The concentration of immigrant households in cities and particularly in central cities, as documented previously, gives rise to a second source of vulnerability because it puts new arrivals in close contact with concentrations of native-born minorities. This leads to the identification of the condition of both groups—immigrants and the native poor—as the same in the eyes of the majority. More important, it exposes second-generation children to the adversarial subculture developed by marginalized native youths to cope with their own difficult situation.[18] This process of socialization

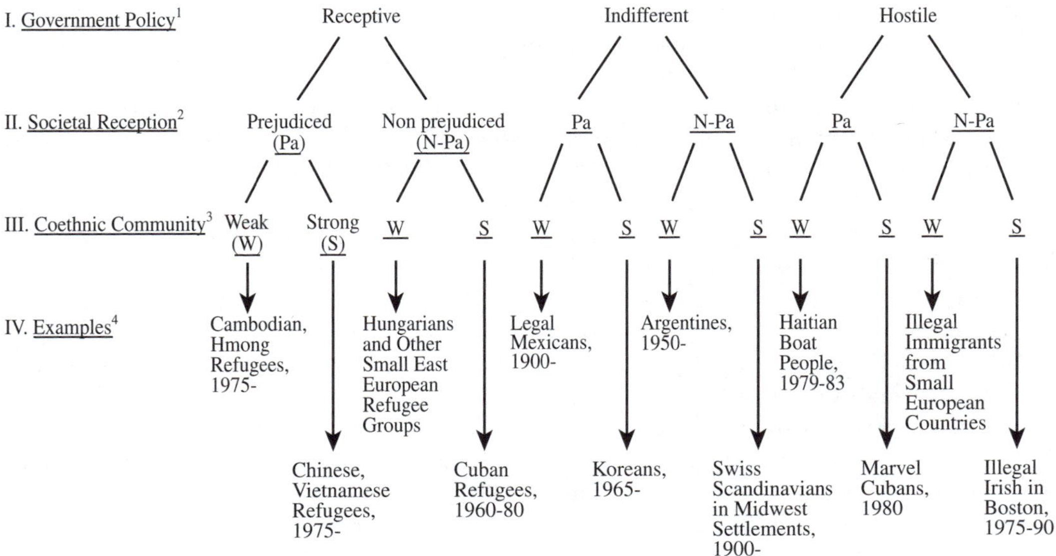

Fig. 5.1 Modes Of Incorporation: A Typology.

Source: Adapted from Alejandro Portes and Rubén G. Rumbaut, *Immigrant America: A Portrait* (Berkeley: University of California Press, 1990), p. 91. Copyright © 1990 by The Regents of the University of California.

1. Receptive policy is defined as legal entry with resettlement assistance, indifferent as legal entry without resettlement assistance, hostile as active opposition to a group's entry or permanence in the country.

2. Prejudiced reception is defined as that accorded to nonphenotypically white groups; nonprejudiced is that accorded to European and European-origin whites.

3. Weak co-ethnic communities are either small in numbers or composed primarily of manual workers; strong communities feature sizable numerical concentrations and a diversified occupational structure including entrepreneurs and professionals.

4. Examples include immigrant groups arriving from the start of the century to the present. Dates of migration are approximate. Groups reflect broadly but not perfectly the characteristics of each ideal type.

may take place even when first-generation parents are moving ahead economically and, hence, their children have no objective reasons for embracing a countercultural message. If successful, the process can effectively block parental plans for intergenerational mobility.

The third contextual source of vulnerability has to do with changes in the host economy that have led to the evaporation of occupational ladders for intergenerational mobility. As noted previously, new immigrants may form the backbone of what remains of labor-intensive manufacturing in the cities as well as in their growing personal services sector, but these are niches that seldom offer channels for upward mobility. The new hourglass economy, created by economic restructuring, means that children of immigrants must cross a narrow bottleneck to occupations requiring advanced training if their careers are to keep pace with their U.S.-acquired aspirations. This race against a narrowing middle demands that immigrant parents accumulate sufficient resources to allow their children to effect the passage and to simultaneously prove to them the viability of aspirations for upward mobility. Otherwise, assimilation may not be into mainstream values and expectations but into the adversarial stance of impoverished groups confined to the bottom of the new economic hourglass.

The picture is painted in such stark terms here for the sake of clarity, although in reality things have not yet become so polarized. Middle-level occupations requiring relatively modest educational achievements have not completely vanished. By 1980, skilled blue-collar jobs—classified by the U.S. census as "precision production, craft, and repair occupations"—had declined by 1.1 percent relative to a decade earlier but still represented 13 percent of the experienced civilian labor force, or 13.6 million workers. Mostly clerical administrative support occupations added another 16.9 percent, or 17.5 million jobs. In 1980, occupations requiring a college degree had increased by 6 percent in comparison with 1970, but they still employed less than a fifth—18.2 percent—of the American labor force.[19] Even in the largest cities, occupations requiring only a high school diploma were common by the late 1980s. In New York City, for example, persons with 12 years or less of schooling held just over one-half of the jobs in 1987. Clerical, service, and skilled blue-collar jobs not requiring a college degree represented 46 percent.[20] Despite these figures, there is little doubt that the trend toward occupational segmentation has increasingly reduced opportunities for incremental upward mobility through well-paid blue-collar positions. The trend forces immigrants today to bridge in only one generation the gap between entry-level jobs and professional positions that earlier groups took two or three generations to travel.

Different modes of incorporation also make available, however, three types of resources to confront the challenges of contemporary assimilation. First, certain groups, notably political refugees, are eligible for a variety of government programs including educational loans for their children. The Cuban Loan Program, implemented by the Kennedy administration in connection with its plan to resettle Cuban refugees away from South Florida, gave many impoverished first- and second-generation Cuban youths a chance to attend college. The high proportion of professionals and executives among Cuban American workers today, a figure on a par with that for native white workers, can be traced, at least in part, to the success of that program.[21] Passage of the 1980 Refugee Act gave to subsequent groups of refugees, in particular Southeast Asians and Eastern Europeans, access to a similarly generous benefits package.[22]

Second, certain foreign groups have been exempted from the traditional prejudice endured by most immigrants, thereby facilitating a smoother process of adaptation. Some political refugees, such as the early waves of exiles from Castro's Cuba, Hungarians and Czechs escaping the invasions of their respective countries, and Soviet Jews escaping religious persecution, provide examples. In other cases, it is the cultural and phenotypical affinity of newcomers to ample segments of the host population that ensures a welcome reception. The Irish who came to Boston during the 1980s is a case in point. Although many were illegal aliens, they came into an environment where generations of Irish Americans had established a secure foothold. Public sympathy effectively neutralized governmental hostility in this case, culminating in a change of the immigration law directly benefiting the newcomers.[23]

Third, and most important, are the resources made available through networks in the co-ethnic community. Immigrants who join well-established and diversified ethnic groups have access from the start to a range of moral and material resources well beyond those available through official assistance programs. Educational help for second-generation youths may include not only access to college grants and loans but also the existence of a private school system geared to the immigrant community's values. Attendance at these private ethnic schools insulates children from contact with native minority youths, while reinforcing the authority of parental views and plans.

In addition, the economic diversification of several immigrant communities creates niches of opportunity that members of the second generation can occupy, often without a need for an advanced education. Small-business apprenticeships, access to skilled building trades, and well-paid jobs in local government bureaucracies are some of the ethnic niches documented in the recent literature.[24] In 1987, average sales per firm of the smaller Chinese, East Indian, Korean, and Cuban enterprises exceeded $100,000 per year, and they jointly employed more than 200,000 workers. These figures omit medium-sized and large ethnic firms, whose sales and work forces are much larger.[25] Fieldwork in these communities indicates that up to half of recently arrived immigrants are employed by co-ethnic firms and that self-employment offers a prime avenue for mobility to second-generation youths.[26] Such community-mediated opportunities provide a solution to the race between material resources and second-generation aspirations not available through competition in the open labor market. Through creation of a capitalism of their own, some immigrant groups have thus been able to circumvent outside discrimination and the threat of vanishing mobility ladders.

In contrast to these favorable conditions are those foreign minorities who either lack a community already in place or whose co-ethnics are too poor to render assistance. The condition of Haitians in South Florida, cited earlier, provides an illustration of one of the most handicapped modes of incorporation encountered by contemporary immigrants, combining official hostility and widespread social prejudice with the absence of a strong receiving community.[27] From the standpoint of second-generation outcomes, the existence of a large but downtrodden co-ethnic community may be even less desirable than no community at all. This is because newly arrived youths enter into ready contact with the reactive subculture developed by earlier generations. Its influence is all the more powerful because it comes from individuals of the same national origin, "people like us" who can more effectively define the proper stance and attitudes of the newcomers. To the extent that they do so, the first-generation model of upward mobility through school achievement and attainment of professional occupations will be blocked.

THREE EXAMPLES

Mexicans and Mexican Americans

Field High School (the name is fictitious) is located in a small coastal community of central California whose economy has long been tied to agricultural production and immigrant farm labor. About 57 percent of the student population is of Mexican descent. An intensive ethnographic study of the class of 1985 at Field High began with school records that showed that the majority of U.S.-born Spanish-surname students who had entered the school in 1981 had dropped out by their senior year. However, only 35 percent of the Spanish-surname students who had been originally classified by the school as limited English proficient (LEP) had dropped out. The figure was even lower than the corresponding one for native white students, 40 percent. LEP status is commonly assigned to recently arrived Mexican immigrants.[28]

Intensive ethnographic fieldwork at the school identified several distinct categories in which the Mexican-origin population could be classified. Recent Mexican immigrants were at one extreme. They dressed differently and unstylishly. They claimed an identity as Mexican and considered Mexico their permanent home. The most academically successful of this group were those most proficient in Spanish, reflecting their prior levels of education in Mexico. Almost all were described by teachers and staff as courteous, serious about their schoolwork, respectful, and eager to please as well as naive and unsophisticated. They were commonly classified as LEP.

The next category comprised Mexican-oriented students. They spoke Spanish at home and were generally classified as fluent English proficient (FEP). They had strong bicultural ties with both Mexico and the United States, reflecting the fact that most were born in Mexico but had lived in the United States for more than five years. They were proud of their Mexican heritage but saw themselves as different from the first group, the *recién llegados* (recently arrived), as well as from the native-born Chicanos and cholos, who were derided as people who had lost their Mexican roots. Students from this group were active in soccer and the Sociedad Bilingue and in celebrations of May 5th, the anniversary of the Mexican defeat of French occupying forces. Virtually all of the Mexican-descent students who graduated in the top 10 percent of their class in 1981 were identified as members of this group.

Chicanos were by far the largest Mexican-descent group at Field High. They were mostly U.S.-born second- and third-generation students whose primary loyalty was to their in-group, which was seen as locked in conflict with white society. Chicanos referred derisively to successful Mexican students as "schoolboys" and "schoolgirls" or as "wannabes." According to M. G. Matute-Bianchi:

> To be a Chicano meant in practice to hang out by the science wing … *not* eating lunch in the quad where all the "gringos" and "schoolboys" hang out, cutting classes by faking a call slip so you can be with your friends at the 7–11 … sitting in the back of classes and not participating … *not* carrying your books to class … *not* taking the difficult classes … doing the minimum to get by.[29]

Chicanos merge imperceptibly into the last category, the cholos, who were commonly seen as "low riders" and gang members. They were also native-born Mexican Americans, easily identifiable by their deliberate manner of dress, walk, speech, and other cultural symbols. Chicanos and cholos were generally regarded by teachers as "irresponsible," "disrespectful," "mistrusting," "sullen," "apathetic," and "less motivated," and their poor school performance was attributed to these traits.[30] According to Matute-Bianchi, Chicanos and cholos were faced with what they saw as a forced-choice dilemma between doing well in school or being a Chicano. To act white was regarded as disloyalty to one's group.

The situation of these last two groups exemplifies losing the race between first-generation achievements and later generations' expectations. Seeing their parents and grandparents confined to humble menial jobs and increasingly aware of discrimination against them by the white mainstream, U.S.-born children of earlier Mexican immigrants readily join a reactive subculture as a means of protecting their sense of self-worth. Participation in this subculture then leads to serious barriers to their chances of upward mobility because school achievement is defined as antithetical to ethnic solidarity. Like Haitian students at Edison High, newly arrived Mexican students are at risk of being socialized into the same reactive stance, with the aggravating factor that it is other Mexicans, not native-born strangers, who convey the message. The principal protection of *Mexicanos* against this type of assimilation lies in their strong identification with home-country language and values, which brings them closer to their parents' cultural stance.

Punjabi Sikhs in California

Valleyside (a fictitious name) is a northern California community where the primary economic activity is orchard farming. Farm laborers in this area come often from India; they are mainly rural Sikhs from the Punjab. By the early 1980s, second-generation Punjabi students already accounted for 11 percent of the student body at Valleyside High. Their parents were no longer only farm laborers, since about a third had become orchard owners themselves and another third worked in factories in the nearby San Francisco area. An ethnographic study of Valleyside High School from 1980–1982 revealed a very difficult process of assimilation for Punjabi Sikh students. According to its author, M. A. Gibson, Valleyside is "redneck country," and white residents are extremely hostile to immigrants who look different and speak a different language: "Punjabi teenagers are told they stink ... told to go back to India ... physically abused by majority students who spit at them, refuse to sit by them in classes or in buses, throw food at them or worse."[31]

Despite these attacks and some evidence of discrimination by school staff, Punjabi students performed better academically than majority Anglo students. About 90 percent of the immigrant youths completed high school, compared to 70–75 percent of native whites. Punjabi boys surpassed the average grade point average, were more likely to take advanced science and math classes, and expressed aspirations for careers in science and engineering. Girls, on the other hand, tended to enroll in business classes, but they paid less attention to immediate career plans, reflecting parental wishes that they should marry first. This gender difference is indicative of the continuing strong influence exercised by the immigrant community over its second generation. According to Gibson, Punjabi parents pressured their children against too much contact with white peers who may "dishonor" the immigrants' families, and defined "becoming Americanized" as forgetting one's roots and adopting the most disparaged traits of the majority, such as leaving home at age 18, making decisions without parental consent, dating, and dancing. At the same time, parents urged children to abide by school rules, ignore racist remarks and avoid fights, and learn useful skills, including full proficiency in English.[32]

The overall success of this strategy of selective assimilation to American society is remarkable because Punjabi immigrants were generally poor on their arrival in the United States and confronted widespread discrimination from whites without the benefit of either governmental assistance or a well-established co-ethnic community. In terms of our typology of vulnerability and resources, the Punjabi Sikh second generation was very much at risk except for two crucial factors. First, immigrant parents did not settle in the inner city or in close proximity to any native-born minority whose offspring could provide an alternative model of adaptation to white-majority discrimination. In particular, the absence of a downtrodden Indian American community composed of children of previous immigrants allowed first-generation parents to influence decisively the outlook of their offspring, including their ways of fighting white prejudice. There was no equivalent of a cholo-like reactive subculture to offer an alternative blueprint of the stance that "people like us" should take.

Second, Punjabi immigrants managed to make considerable economic progress, as attested by the number who had become farm owners, while maintaining a tightly knit ethnic community. The material and social capital created by this first-generation community compensated for the absence of an older co-ethnic group and had decisive effects on second-generation outlooks. Punjabi teenagers were shown that their parents' ways paid off economically, and this fact, plus their community's cohesiveness, endowed them with a source of pride to counteract outside discrimination. Through this strategy of selective assimilation, Punjabi Sikhs appeared to be winning the race against the inevitable acculturation of their children to American-style aspirations.

Caribbean youths in South Florida

Miami is arguably the American city that has been most thoroughly transformed by post-1960 immigration. The Cuban Revolution had much to do with this transformation, as it sent the entire Cuban upper class out of the country, followed by thousands of refugees of more modest backgrounds. Over time, Cubans created a highly diversified and prosperous ethnic community that provided resources for the adaptation process of its second generation. Reflecting this situation are average Cuban family incomes that, by 1989, approximated those of the native-born population; the existence in 1987 of more than 30,000 Cuban-owned small businesses that formed the core of the Miami ethnic enclave; and the parallel rise of a private-school system oriented toward the values and political outlook of this community.[33] In terms of the typology of vulnerability and resources, well-sheltered Cuban American teenagers lack any extensive exposure to outside discrimination, they have little contact with youths from disadvantaged minorities, and the development of an enclave creates economic opportunities beyond the narrowing industrial and tourist sectors on which most other immigrant groups in the area depend. Across town, Haitian American teenagers face exactly the opposite set of conditions, as has been shown.

Among the other immigrant groups that form Miami's ethnic mosaic, two deserve mention because they represent intermediate situations between those of the Cubans and Haitians. One comprises Nicaraguans who escaped the Sandinista regime during the 1980s. They were not as welcomed in the United States as were the Cuban exiles, nor were they able to develop a large and diversified community. Yet they shared with Cubans their language and culture, as well as a militant anti-Communist discourse. This common political outlook led the Cuban American community to extend its resources in support of their Nicaraguan brethren, smoothing their process of adaptation.[34] For second-generation Nicaraguans, this means that the preexisting ethnic community that provides a model for their own assimilation is not a downtrodden group but rather one that has managed to establish a firm and positive presence in the city's economy and politics.

The second group comprises West Indians coming from Jamaica, Trinidad, and other English-speaking Caribbean republics. They generally arrive in Miami as legal immigrants, and many bring along professional and business credentials as well as the advantage of fluency in English. These individual advantages are discounted however, by a context of reception in which these mostly black immigrants are put in the same category as native-born blacks and discriminated against accordingly. The recency of West Indian migration and its small size have prevented the development of a diversified ethnic community in South Florida. Hence new arrivals experience the full force of white discrimination without the protection of a large co-ethnic group and with constant exposure to the situation and attitudes of the inner-city population. Despite considerable individual resources, these disadvantages put the West Indian second generation at risk of bypassing white or even native black middle-class models to assimilate into the culture of the underclass.

A recently completed survey of eighth- and ninth-graders in the Dade County (Miami) and Broward County (Ft. Lauderdale) schools includes sizable samples of Cuban, Haitian, Nicaraguan, and West Indian second-generation children. The study defined "second generation" as youths born in the United States who have at least one foreign-born parent or those born abroad who have lived in the United States for at least five years. All eligible students in the selected schools were included. The survey included both inner-city and suburban public schools, as well as private schools and those where particular foreign-origin groups were known to concentrate. The sample was evenly divided between boys and girls, and the students ranged in age from twelve to seventeen.[35]

Table 5.2 presents the responses of second-generation students from these nationalities to a battery of attitudinal and self-identification questions. The large Cuban-origin sample is divided between those attending public and private school. Large socioeconomic differences between the

TABLE 5.2 Second-Generation Eighth- and Ninth-Grade Students by National Origin, South Florida Schools, 1992 (Percentage unless noted)

	Cubans in Private School (*N* = 172)	Cubans in Public School (*N* = 968)	Haitians (*N* = 136)	Nicaraguans (*N* = 319)	West Indians (*N* = 191)	Total (*N* = 1,786)	p<	V^2 or Eta
Socioeconomic characteristics								
Father college graduate	50.0	21.4	11.0	38.6	18.8	26.1	.001	.27
Mother college graduate	39.0	17.5	11.0	28.2	26.2	21.9	.001	.15
Father occupation, mean prestige scores*	52.6	44.2	37.6	43.7	43.6	44.5	.001	.22
Mother occupation, mean prestige scores*	51.1	45.1	39.7	40.1	44.8	44.3	.001	.23
Family wealthy or upper-middle class†	57.0	42.7	37.5	35.4	49.2	43.1	.001	.10
Self-identification								
American	33.1	19.9	16.2	10.0	16.2	18.8	.001	.64
Black American	–	–	12.5	–	9.9	2.2	.001	.64
Hispanic American	3.5	7.6	1.5	39.5	0.5	11.7	.001	.64
Cuban‡	61.6	67.5	–	0.3	–	42.6	.001	.64
Haitian‡	–	–	53.7	–	3.1	4.4	.001	.64
Nicaraguan‡	–	0.6	–	44.8	–	8.3	.001	.64
Other nationality§	1.8	4.4	16.2	5.3	70.2	12.2	.001	.64
Aspirations								
College education or higher	97.1	82.6	86.7	79.0	84.8	83.9	.001	.11
Professional or business occupation	72.1	70.0	75.0	69.9	71.2	70.6	n.s.	.06
Perceptions of discrimination								
Has ever been discriminated against	29.1	38.2	67.6	50.8	64.4	44.6	.001	.23
Discriminated against by teachers	5.2	12.5	16.2	13.5	23.6	13.4	.001	.13

TABLE 5.2 *(Continued)*

Attitudes toward U.S. society								
There is racial discrimination in economic opportunities	91.3	79.2	84.6	81.5	89.5	82.3	.001	.11
Nonwhites have equal opportunites	30.8	53.6	44.9	52.4	41.9	49.3	.001	.14
The United States is the best country in the world	79.7	68.9	36.0	49.8	35.1	60.4	.001	.30
Friends								
Many or most friends have foreign-born parents	93.6	73.1	46.3	75.2	43.5	70.2	.001	.22
Friends' parents are								
Cuban	89.5	58.7	2.9	11.3	4.2	43.1	.001	.44
Haitian	–	1.2	30.1	1.3	12.6	4.5	.001	.44
Nicaraguan	7.6	24.8	2.9	69.0	2.1	26.9	.001	.44
West Indian	–	6.2	46.3	7.2	62.8	14.9	.001	.44
Other	2.9	9.1	17.7	11.2	18.3	10.6	.001	.44

Source: Alejandro Portes and Lisandro Parez, Children of Immigrants: The Adaptation Process of the Second Generation (Project conducted at the department of Sociology, Johns Hopkins University, in progress).
* Employed parents only; Treiman international prestige scale scores.
† Respondent's class self-classification.
‡ Includes hyphenated self-identifications of the same nationality, for example, Nicaraguan American.
§ West Indian self-identifications not classified individually by country.
Respondents' statements of the level of education that they realistically expect to attain.

four groups are highlighted in the first panel of Table 5.2. Cuban children in private schools have the best-educated parents and those with the highest-status occupations. Haitians in public schools have parents who rank lowest on both dimensions. Nicaraguans and West Indians occupy intermediate positions, with parents whose average education is often higher than that of the parents of public school Cubans but whose occupational levels are roughly the same. Reflecting these differences, more than half of private school Cuban respondents define their families as upper middle class or higher, while only a third of Haitians and Nicaraguans do so.[36]

The next panel of the table presents differences in ethnic self-identification. Less than one-fifth of these second-generation students identify themselves as non-hyphenated Americans. The proportion is highest among higher-status Cubans, but even among this group almost two-thirds see themselves as Cuban or Cuban American, a proportion close to their peers in public schools. Very few Cubans opt for the self-designation "Hispanic." Nicaraguan students, on the other hand, use this label almost as commonly as that of "Nicaraguan" itself. None of the Latin groups identify themselves as "black." Among Haitians and West Indians, however, roughly one-tenth already assume an identity as black American. Haitian self-identifications are similar to Nicaraguan in being less attached to the country of origin and in using pan-national labels more often than either Cubans or West Indians do. In total, about half of the Haitian children identified themselves as something other than "Haitian."[37]

Aspirations are very high in the entire sample, as indicated in the next panel of Table 5.2. Although significant differences in expectations of completing college do exist, at least four-fifths of every group expects to achieve this level of education. Similarly, roughly 70 percent of students from every nationality aspire to professional or business careers. These consistently high aspirations contrast with the reported wide differences in parental socioeconomic backgrounds and the differential effects of discrimination. The next panel of the table addresses the latter point, documenting the awareness that these teenagers have about the realities of American society. The two mostly black groups report discrimination against themselves two to three times more frequently than do Cubans. Majorities of both Haitian and West Indian youths reported having been discriminated against, and about 20 percent said that discrimination was by their teachers. In contrast, only 5 percent of Cubans in private school report such incidents. Nicaraguans occupy an intermediate position, with half reporting discrimination against themselves and 13 percent pointing to their teachers as the source.

Congruent with these personal experiences, Haitian and West Indian teenagers are more likely to agree that there is racial discrimination in economic opportunities in the United States and to disagree that nonwhites have equal opportunities. Interestingly, they are joined in these negative evaluations by private-school Cubans. This result may reflect the greater information and class awareness of the latter group relative to their less privileged Latin counterparts. However, all Cuban students part company with the rest of the sample in their positive evaluation of the United States. Roughly three-fourths of second-generation Cubans endorse the view that "the United States is the best country in the world"; only half of Nicaraguans do so, and the two mostly black groups take a distinctly less enthusiastic stance. These significant differences illustrate the contrasting levels of identification with their country and their local community by children of nationalities affected more or less by outside discrimination.

Introducing controls for native versus foreign birth of respondents attenuates these differences somewhat, but the overall pattern remains. Results of this survey illustrate the race between generalized career aspirations and the widely different vulnerabilities and resources created by first-generation modes of incorporation. Aspirations are very high for all groups, regardless of origin. However, parental socioeconomic backgrounds, resources of the co-ethnic community (as exemplified by the existence of a private school system), and experiences of discrimination are very different. They influence decisively the outlook of second-generation youths, even at a young age, and are likely to have strong effects on the course of their future assimilation. Illustrating these differences is the enthusiasm with which children of advantaged immigrants embrace their parents' adopted country and the much less sanguine views of those whose situation is more difficult.

CONCLUSION

The last panel of Table 5.2 highlights another intriguing fact about today's second generation. The best-positioned group—private-school Cubans—is the one least likely to step out of the ethnic circle in their interpersonal relationships, while the group in the most disadvantaged position—Haitians—is most likely to do so. Overall, the three Latin groups overwhelmingly select friends who are also children of immigrants, mostly from the same nationality. Less than half of the Haitians and West Indians do so, indicating much greater contact with native-parentage youths. Other Haitian American teenagers are not even the majority of foreign-parentage friends among our Haitian respondents.

Fifty years ago, the dilemma of Italian American youngsters studied by Irving Child consisted of assimilating into the American mainstream, sacrificing in the process their parents' cultural heritage in contrast to taking refuge in the ethnic community from the challenges of the outside world. In the contemporary context of segmented assimilation, the options have become less clear. Children of nonwhite immigrants may not even have the opportunity of gaining access to middle-class white society, no matter how acculturated they become. Joining those native circles to which they do have access may prove a ticket to permanent subordination and disadvantage. Under these circumstances, remaining securely ensconced in their co-ethnic community may be not a symptom of escapism but the best strategy for capitalizing on otherwise unavailable material and moral resources. As the experiences of Punjabi Sikh and Cuban American students suggest, a strategy of paced, selective assimilation may prove the best course for immigrant minorities. But the extent to which this strategy is possible also depends on the history of each group and its specific profile of vulnerabilities and resources. The present analysis represents a preliminary step toward understanding these realities.

Notes

1. Alejandro Portes and Alex Stepick, *City on the Edge: The Transformation of Miami* (Berkeley: University of California Press, 1993), chap. 8.
2. Defined as native-born children with at least one foreign-born parent or children born abroad who came to the United States before age twelve. See Leif Jensen, *Children of the New Immigration: A Comparative Analysis of Today's Second Generation*, paper commissioned by the Children of Immigrants Research Project, Department of Sociology, Johns Hopkins University, reprinted as Institute for Policy Research and Evaluation Working Paper no. 1990–32 (University Park: Pennsylvania State University, 1890).
3. Joan N. First and John W. Carrera, *New Voices: Immigrant Students in U.S. Public Schools* (Boston: National Coalition of Advocates for Students, 1988).
4. Michael Piore, *Birds of Passage* (New York: Cambridge University Press, 1979); Herbert Gans, "Second-Generation Decline: Scenarios for the Economic and Ethnic Futures of the Post-1965 American Immigrants," *Ethnic and Racial Studies* 15:173–92 (April 1992).
5. Irving L. Child, *Italian or American? The Second Generation in Conflict* (New Haven: Yale University Press, 1943).
6. See, for example, Saskia Sassen, "Changing Composition and Labor Market Location of Hispanic Immigrants in New York City, 1960–1980," in *Hispanics in the U.S. Economy*, ed. George J. Borjas and Marta Tienda (New York: Academic Press, 1985), pp. 299–322.
7. Jeffrey S. Passel and Barry Edmonston, "Immigration and Race: Recent Trends in Immigration to the United States" (Paper no. PRIP-UI-22, Urban Institute, May 1992), tab. 2.
8. The new immigration is defined as that which started after the 1965 Immigration Act. Inclusion of 1960–1965 immigrants in the totals just mentioned leads to only a slight over-count due to the relatively low numbers arriving before passage of the act. see Ibid., tab. 9.
9. Ibid.
10. U.S., Department of Commerce, Bureau of the Census, *Race by Hispanic Origin, 1990 Census of Population and Housing*, special tabulation prepared by the Ethnic and Hispanic Branch (Washington, DC: U.S. Department of Commerce. 1992).
11. In most cases, before age twelve. See Jensen, *Children of the New Immigration.*
12. Because of data limitations, comparisons of years of education completed and high school dropouts are limited to persons aged twenty or older still living with their parents. These results may not be representative of the respective universes of adult individuals. See ibid.
13. See Alex Stepick, "Haitian Refugees in the U.S." (Report no. 52, Minority Rights Group, London, 1982); Alex Stepick and Alejandro Portes, "Flight into Despair: A Profile of Recent Haitian Refugees in South Florida," *International Migration Review*, 20:329–50 (Summer 1986).
14. This account is based on fieldwork in Miami conducted in preparation for a survey of immigrant youths in public schools. The survey and preliminary results are described in the final section of this article.
15. On the issue of social capital, see James S. Coleman, "Social Capital in the Creation of Human Capital," *American Journal of Sociology*, supplement, 94:S95–121 (1988); Alejandro Portes and Min Zhou, "Gaining the Upper Hand: Economic Mobility among Immigrant and Domestic Minorities," *Ethnic and Racial Studies*, 15:491–522 (Oct. 1992). On ethnic entrepreneurship, see Ivan H. Light, *Ethnic Enterprise in America: Business and Welfare among Chinese, Japanese, and Blacks* (Berkeley: University of California Press, 1972); Kenneth Wilson and W. Allen Martin, "Ethnic Enclaves: A Comparison of the Cuban and Black Economies in Miami," *American Journal of Sociology*, 88:135–60 (1982).
16. See W. Lloyd Warner and Leo Srole, *The Social Systems of American Ethnic Groups* (New Haven, CT: Yale University Press, 1945); Thomas Sowell, *Ethnic America: A History* (New York: Basic Books, 1981).

17. See Alejandro Portes and Rubén G. Rumbaut, *Immigrant America: A Portrait* (Berkeley: University of California Press, 1990), chap. 3.
18. See Mercer L. Sullivan, *"Getting Paid": Youth, Grime, and Work in the Inner City* (Ithaca, NY: Cornell University Press, 1989), chaps. 1, 5.
19. U.S. Department of Commerce, Bureau of the Census, *Census of Population and Housing 1980. Public Use (1985) A (MRDF)* (Washington, DC: Department of Commerce, 1983).
20. Thomas Bailey and Roger Waldinger, "Primary, Secondary, and Enclave Labor Markets: A Training System Approach," *American Sociological Review,* 56: 432–45 (1991).
21. Professionals and executives represented 25.9 percent of Cuban-origin males age sixteen and over in 1989; the figure for the total adult male population was 26 percent. See Jesus M. García and Patricia A. Montgomery, *The Hispanic Population of the United States: March 1990,* Current Population Reports, ser. P-20, no. 449 (Washington, DC: Department of Commerce, 1991).
22. Portes and Rumbaut, *Immigrant America,* pp. 23–25; Robert L. Bach et al., "The Economic Adjustment of Southeast Asian Refugees in the United States," in *World Refugee Survey, 1983* (Geneva: United Nations High Commission for Refugees, 1984) pp. 51–55.
23. The 1990 Immigration Act contains tailor-made provisions to facilitate the legalization of Irish immigrants. Those taking advantage of the provisions are popularly dubbed "Kennedy Irish" in honor of the Massachusetts Senator who coauthored the act. On the 1990 act, see Michael Fix and Jeffrey S. Passel, "The Door Remains Open: Recent Immigration to the United States and a Preliminary Analysis of the Immigration Act of 1990" (Working paper, Urban Institute and RAND Corporation, 1991). On the Irish in Boston, see Karen Tumulty, "When Irish Eyes Are Hiding ...," *Los Angles Times,* 29 Jan. 1989.
24. Bailey and Waldinger, "Primary, Secondary, and Enclave Labor Markets"; Min Zhou, *New York's Chinatown: The Socioeconomic Potential of an Urban Enclave* (Philadelphia: Temple University Press, 1992); Wilson and Martin, "Ethnic Enclaves"; Suzanne Model, "The Ethnic Economy: Cubans and Chinese Reconsidered" (Manuscript, University of Massachusetts at Amherst, 1990).
25. U.S. Department of Commerce, Bureau of the Census, *Survey of Minority-Owned Business Enterprises, 1987,* MB-2 and MB-3 (Washington, DC: Department of Commerce, 1991).
26. Alejandro Portes and Alex Stepick, "Unwelcome Immigrants: The Labor Market Experiences of 1980 (Mariel) Cuban and Haitian Refugees in South Florida," *American Sociological Review,* 50:493–514 (Aug. 1985); Zhou, *New York's Chinatown*; Luis E. Guarnizo, "One Country in Two: Dominican-Owned Firms in New York and the Dominican Republic" (Ph.D. diss. Johns Hopkins University, 1992); Bailey and Waldinger, "Primary, Secondary, and Enclave Labor Markets."
27. Stepick, "Haitian Refugees in the U.S."; Jake C. Miller. *The Plight of Haitian*
28. M. G. Matute-Bianchi, "Ethnic Identities and Patterns of School Success and Failure among Mexican-Descent and Japanese-American Students in a California High School," *American Journal of Education,* 95:233–55 (Nov. 1986). This study is summarized in Rubén G. Rumbaut, "Immigrant Students in California Public Schools: A Summary of Current Knowledge" (Report no. 11, Center for Research on Effective Schooling for Disadvantaged Children, Johns Hopkins University, Aug. 1990).
29. Matute-Bianchi, "Ethnic Identities and Patterns," p. 253.
30. Rumbaut, "Immigrant Students" p. 25.
31. M. A. Gibson, *Accommodation without Assimilation: Sikh Immigrants in an American High School* (Ithaca, NY: Cornell University Press, 1989), p. 268.
32. Gibson, *Accommodation without Assimilation.* The study is summarized in Rumbaut, "Immigrant students," pp. 22–23.
33. García and Montgomery, *Hispanic Population*; U.S. Department of Commerce, Bureau of the Census, *Survey of Minority Owned Business,* Business Enterprises (1991).
34. Portes and Stepick *City on the Edge,* chap. 7.
35. Alejandro Portes and Lisaudro Perez, Children of Immigrants: The Adaptation Process of the Second Generation (Project conducted at the Department of Sociology, Johns Hopkins University, in progress).
36. Because of the large sample size, .001 is used as the criterion of statistical significance in these tabulations. Cramér's V^2 is used as the principal measure of strength of association. In comparison with other coefficients, it has the advantage of a constant range between 0 and 1. Higher values indicate stronger association. Eta is similarly defined but is used only for the continuous parental occupational status variables.
37. West Indian self-identification was not coded separately and hence is classified under "other nationality" in Table 2.

PART II

Psychological Aspects of Immigration: Families in Transition

Chapter 6
The Psychological Experience of Immigration: A Developmental Perspective

CYNTHIA GARCÍA COLL AND KATHERINE MAGNUSON

OVERVIEW OF RESEARCH

For the most part, past theories and research on international migration focus nearly exclusively on adults and tend to present children as appendages to their parents rather than as distinct subjects worthy of investigation (Sung 1985). The typical immigrant is conceptualized as a young adult who was socialized in his or her homeland and then relocated to another country. In contrast, immigrant children are often thought to be the first of their families to be socialized into the receiving community's culture. Thus, immigrant children are generally thought to have an easier time adapting than adults because they are younger, more malleable, and more exposed to the new culture through the native school system (Chud 1982).

Our inability to delineate comprehensive models and theories about the psychological and psychosocial impact of immigration on children has severely hampered our ability to work on this issue. To date, two models have been presented specifically for children, none have been supported by empirical research with children, and only one has attempted to account for the outcomes as well as the processes of international migration in all children. Chud's (1982) threshold model postulates that although the immigrant's home usually reverberates with the culture of the country of origin, there is a point at which there is "the beginning of something new" (p. 96). Chud referred to this point as the threshold. According to Chud, the threshold is wherever the host culture meets the immigrants' culture (for example, the front door). The importance placed on this meeting point is meant to highlight how the immigrant child interacts with two cultural systems in a dynamic fashion. Chud delineated three types of thresholds: unobstructed, problematic, and traumatic. The distinctions between the thresholds reflect the ease with which the child can move from one culture to another.

Laosa (1989) constructed a more specific model to explain how immigration affects Hispanic children, although it is relevant to non-Hispanic immigrant children. He utilized a metaphor of lenses and filters, which intensify or moderate the effect of events, to explain the interaction of the variables that mediate the stresses of migration and the child's adaptation, adjustment, and development over time. The variables that impact the child's development include the characteristics of the sending environment, the background of the family prior to migration, the characteristics of the receiving community, the cognitive structure and coping mechanisms of both the child and the family, the school context, and the dynamic and changing nature of psychosocial and developmental processes (see Laosa, 1989). Although Laosa's model seems useful and insightful, no empirical studies have been undertaken to support his work.

An additional model has introduced age as a variable to be included in analyses. Rumbaut (1991) created a general model to explain the relationship of migration, adaptation, and psychological distress among Indochinese refugees. The model suggests that a variety of variables will affect psychological outcomes over time. Of particular interest is the way in which Rumbaut emphasized the importance of the contextual variables in the adaptation process. In his model, the context of both exit and entry interact with the characteristics of an individual's migration process (that is, antecedent variables) and adaptation process (mediating variables) and lead to psychological distress measured by outcome variables. For example, variables that are thought to have an impact on the outcome of adaptation include an individual's motivation for migrating, socioeconomic status, social support network, sex, and age. The model was tested with longitudinal data on adult refugees collected by the Indochinese Health and Adaptation Research Project in San Diego, California. The model was able to explain a substantial amount of the variance in psychological distress outcomes. Much of the variance, however, remained unaccounted for (Rumbaut 1991).

The children who began to be socialized and educated in their homeland and then moved to the United States with the parents, members of the 1.5 generation, are often overlooked in the discussion of immigrants and particularly in generational comparisons (Hirschman 1994). However, the existence of such a cohort begs us to consider the impact of migration as a function not only of whether the immigrant is a child or an adult but also at what age they migrate and how long they have been in the United States. Although the literature on immigration is full of comments that a child's experience with migration depends on his or her development stage (Eisenbruch 1988; Hirschman 1994; Laosa 1989), this idea has yet to be fully articulated into the theories and principles that describe these children's experiences. This is critical because the role and importance of various factors involved in the migration process are mediated and differentiated by the age of the child (Hirschman 1994; Inbar 1977; Schrader 1978), a proxy variable for various developmental processes. This shift toward a developmental perspective requires the researcher to acknowledge the changing relationship between the person and the environment as well as the ongoing normative development of the child. As Laosa (1989) stated, "It is helpful to view the individual's characteristics (e.g., abilities, needs, behavioral style) and the environment (e.g., societal expectations, demands, opportunities)" (p. 27).

The research on immigrant adults is dominated by two different theories of adjustment: stress and selection. It is assumed that differences in adjustment are due either to the self-selection of migrants or to acculturative stress (that is, stress engendered by the migration process). Most studies of children deal specifically with the acculturative stress theory because children do not self-select their migration and in some instances neither understand nor accept the reasons they are given to justify their move to a new land (Ashworth 1982).

The emphasis placed on acculturative stress has led nearly all of the researchers concerned with immigrants to try to identify and document the negative impact of migration and acculturation through measurable indicators. Consequently, a large number of studies have focused on the comparative rates of maladjustment among young immigrants as presented in psychiatric or behavior disorders, rather than on the normative adjustment or development of these children. Ironically, studies have shown that the majority of immigrant children are not maladjusted. Rather, they are able to overcome the difficulties in immigration and acculturation and adapt readily to their surroundings, both at home and at school (Weinberg 1979). In a review of literature that considered the majority of studies that documented immigrant children's adjustment, Aronowitz (1984) concluded, "[S]tudies of a variety of kinds in disparate settings suggest that a cohort of immigrant children may adjust better, no differently, or less well than the native populations to which they migrate" (p. 243). However, Aronowitz also remarked that when disorders appear in immigrant children, they tend to be manifested in two distinct ways: as behavior disorders and as identity disorders in adolescence. Acute psychiatric disorders are less often presented in immigrant children (Sam 1994). Nevertheless, the way in which researchers have approached the study of immigrant children has led them to chart the adjustment of children based on measurable negative outcomes, and it has disposed them to overlook measurement of normative outcomes inclusive of the experiences and processes involved in acculturation and adjustment.

One reason this has happened is that many processes are involved in migration, and trying to disentangle the effects of the simultaneous and various processes is difficult. Relying on the native population to determine standards is misguided because of the sociocultural differences between immigrant children and the native population. However, different immigrant children have been exposed to all or many of the same processes; thus, determining comparison measures or standards with which to try to measure the effect of various processes is very complicated. Nicol (1971) suggested that, to reveal the effects of the process of migration, it would be helpful to compare children born to immigrant parents in the host country to those born in a foreign country who have undergone migration, but this has rarely been done. Most studies consider place of birth as an important variable indicator of one's degree of acculturation rather than as a core construct, which evokes different processes and engenders a different experience (for an exception, see Gil, Vega, andand Dimas 1994).

Furthermore, the lack of a developmental perspective combined with the emphasis of migration as a stressful experience has prevented researchers from trying to understand the ways in which immigration might serve as a growth-enhancing event. Little research or work has moved beyond discussing the ways in which children adjust or adapt and toward discussing the ways in which they might benefit psychologically from the event. Thus, what little is known about children and their rates of maladaptation leaves even less known about their subjective experiences as immigrant children, their abilities to cope and adapt, their ability to grow, and the impact that immigration has in their life (Rumbaut 1994; Sung 1985).

In general, most research on immigrant children not only lacks appropriate theoretical principles, but also lacks a consensus on methodological issues, such as how to choose samples and what constitutes appropriate comparison groups. The emphasis that theories have placed on the negative impact of migration and difficulties in obtaining access to informants have meant that many studies have drawn their samples from clinic-referred immigrant children rather than from the general population of immigrant children (for example, Burke 1980; Graham andand Meadows 1967; Lipson andand Meleis 1989). The variations in the rates of disorders found among different ethnic groups leads to the conclusion that it is erroneous to lump all immigrants together in one category for research purposes. Nevertheless, the small numbers of available subjects has led some researchers to study immigrant children as a unified group with similar behavior patterns (for example, Ekstrand 1976) or to combine ethnic or national groups that are considered similar (Cochrane 1979; Derbyshire 1970). Commenting on their own research, Touliatos and Lindholm (1980) suggested that "future studies of needs assessment should include a large enough sample so that all children of immigrants are not regarded as comprising one group or children in closely related ethnic groups are not combined" (p. 31).

Whereas some studies have not differentiated between ethnic groups, other studies have looked comparatively at the outcome of adaptation across groups of immigrant children and native children (for example, Cochrane 1979; Rumbaut 1994) or have looked very closely at one specific group without regard for any other groups (Kallarackal and Herbert 1976; Sung 1985). Very few studies have tried to look at how different ethnic groups have both similar and discrepant experiences (an exception is Rumbaut's work on the adjustment of Indochinese adolescent refugees, 1988, 1991, 1994). The way in which the sample groups have been constructed and the studies designed makes it hard to make generalizations about the psychological impact of migration and acculturation based on an aggregation of research findings on immigrant children.

Finally, research has indicated that emotions are expressed differently in different cultures; many cultural backgrounds discourage the direct expression of feelings and shape health beliefs to favor psychosomatic symptoms. However, little attention has been given to the incidence of these symptoms among immigrant children (Sam 1994; for an exception, see Rodriguez 1973). By not considering the effects of migration in psychosomatic outcomes we might be overlooking a very valuable source of information (Vega and Rumbaut 1991).

In summary, the extant literature presents studies that, for the most part, used conceptual models derived from research with immigrant adults and therefore lack a developmental perspective. Moreover, the emphasis has been on problematic outcomes rather than normative experiences or processes that lead to differential outcomes. Finally, methodological issues have included the composition of samples and the definition and measurement of constructs across different immigrant groups.

CHILDREN'S REACTIONS TO STRESS

Realizing that our knowledge and conceptualizations fall short in so many areas, what can we say about how immigration psychologically affects children? Migration and acculturation require the child to deal with stress. An individual's stress response is a transaction between the environment and the individual, with the meaning and appraisal of the event intrinsic to its definition. Whether the stress has a positive or negative impact and whether the stress has repercussions beyond the immediate context depend on a large number of factors.

Some characteristics of individual children are known to affect their stress response. The sex of a child has been associated with a variation in response to stress: Young boys show more stress than girls (Rutter 1983). It is unclear why this is, but it has been hypothesized that parents might be less supportive of boys' attempts to deal with stress.

The child's temperament also seems to be a likely factor in accounting for a child's stress response, although no direct evidence has pinpointed its specific contribution. In particular, an association has been found between the child's temperament and other people's—usually the parents'—reaction to the child. Therefore, the child's temperament may protect the child or put the child at risk by virtue of its effect on the parent-child interaction (Rutter 1983). Tradd and Greenblatt (1990) suggested that emotional flexibility, affective resources to express his or her experiences, and positive emotional outlook—all of which are considered parts of a child's temperament—are important in affecting the resilience of children. Finally, the individual's cognitive appraisal of the situation, attributional style, and locus of control all affect a child's response to stress (Rutter 1983; Tradd and Greenblatt 1990).

Relevant to the influence of cognitive appraisal are what Laosa (1989) termed "beliefs": general ideas about oneself and the environment that influence one's appraisal of events. This notion of beliefs is especially relevant for immigrant children because some of these beliefs may stem from shared historic or sociocultural premises of their homeland (that is, attitudes, beliefs, and values that are fundamental determinants or shared personality characteristics of a given culture).

One of the most important factors regarding children's reaction to stress is age. Maccoby (1983) pointed out that no linear increase or decrease in vulnerability to stress is associated with the development of children. However, the nature of the events and coping responses elicited changes as a child develops. Many factors that theoretically make young children more vulnerable to stress are balanced by factors that also make them less vulnerable. For instance, the unfamiliarity of a situation is an important element in an event's capacity to act as a stressor; and because a young child is essentially unfamiliar and inexperienced with the world, one would expect him or her to be susceptible to large amounts of stress. On the other hand, children do not experience stress from events whose power to harm is not understood. They are not humiliated by the failure to handle problems that are not their responsibility, and they are not upset by criticism when their ego is not developed and they are not invested in appearing strong (Maccoby 1983). Thus, although at first glance it might seem as if young children are more susceptible to stress, in many ways they are buffered by their age and their relationships with their caretakers.

Several other factors that have an impact on a child's stress response have been identified. Studies of children in institutional settings show that a stable relationship with an adult, not necessarily a parent, is associated with better social adjustment. Good relationships and family harmony also seem to be protective features. Kallarackal and Herbert (1976) attributed the low rate of deviance among immigrant Indian children in Britain to the quality of their family life, which the authors believed reduced the risk of developing disorders. The children in their sample were living with both parents, and their family relationships appeared to be warm and loving despite the parents' strict supervision and firm discipline. Likewise, Athey and Ahearn (1991) stated, "The ability of the family to provide a strong sense of safety and support to the child and to serve as a buffer against external threats plays a large role in how well the child functions and develops" (pp. 10–11). In addition, the impact of acute stress is also affected by the preexistence or concurrent background of chronic psychosocial adversity. The effect of a number of stressors is not merely cumulative. In fact, studies show that stresses potentiate each other; that is, the combined effect of the stressors can be far greater than the additive effect (Rutter 1979).

Finally, the manner in which the child comes to cope with the stress is an important factor in his stress response. In fact the child's response to the stress is often inextricable from coping mechanisms (Compas 1987). Coping refers to both intrapsychic processes and environmental manipulations that solve problems and regulate emotional distress. The coping process can include both effective and ineffective mechanisms. "A closer examination of studies of child and adolescent coping reveals that a strategy which might be adaptive for dealing with one stressor may be maladaptive when used in a different context or at a different point in time in response to the same stressor" (Compas 1987:399). Likewise, Laosa (1989) pointed out that although a child might possess a good repertoire of coping strategies and competencies in one cultural context, her coping skills might be ineffective, inappropriate, or even offensive after immigrating. Although it seems as if the coping process should have an outcome on the stressful event, the connection has yet to be recognized (Rutter 1983). The measurement of the effectiveness of coping processes and the concepts involved are rather elusive.

Very little research has studied how the perceived stressfulness of events and the coping mechanisms employed vary across cultures or across subcultures. An exception is El-Sheikh and Klaczynski's study (1993) of variations in the types of stress, coping responses, and control beliefs across three different subcultures of young girls in Egypt: middle class, inner city, and rural. The researchers explained:

> Various taxonomies have been developed to characterize the strategies that children use to cope with stress; but without acknowledging the different types of stressors children encounter in different subcultural environments, these taxonomies may not capture the full complexities of children's coping efforts.... The context effect becomes especially important

> across cultures. Not only may the resources available for successful coping differ but the cultural prescriptions for using available resources may vary, as may definitions of successful coping. (pp. 80–81)

The types of stressors and beliefs about control varied by subcultural group, although no differences were reported in coping strategies.

Not all children who are exposed to stressful situations are adversely affected by their experiences. The recognition of these children has led many to study resilience, "the ability to recover from or easily adjust to misfortune or sustained life stress" (Laosa 1989:6). However, Rutter (1979) pointed out that although children who suffer and come through their experiences unscathed have overcome adversity and are often referred to as invulnerable, this is a relative term. These children have not entirely escaped damage or been unaffected by their experiences. Furthermore, Seifer and Sameroff (1987) highlighted the difficulty of defining the central constructs of risk and invulnerability. They remarked that it is hard to distinguish between a risk factor or a protective factor and a factor that is merely influential in a child's development. Nevertheless, there is a large difference between those who become reasonably well-adjusted people in spite of chronic stress and disadvantage and those who become criminal, mentally ill, or educationally retarded (Rutter 1979).

Compas (1987), in his review of research on stress and coping in children, found that most of the studies focusing on resilient children and their environment do not look at how the invulnerable children cope with stress but instead try to identify enduring characteristics of the environment and the children "that distinguish them from others who respond maladaptively to stress" (p. 398). Three broad factors have consistently been found to characterize invulnerable children: dispositional and constitutional traits of the child, the presence of a supportive family environment, and a supportive individual or agency outside of the family. Rutter (1979) delineated a number of protective factors: temperament and sex, influences outside the home such as the school (which, given a positive atmosphere and quality as a social institution, can serve as a protective factor), the scope of opportunities, high self-esteem and scholastic attainment (the direction of association between self-esteem and scholastic attainment is unclear), cognitive structure and locus of control, one good stable relationship with an adult, and good coping skills (that is, learning how to deal with a variety of new situations as they grow up).

In summary, a child's response to stress is best understood as an interaction between his characteristics and the environmental demands. The individual characteristics of a child, such as temperament, developmental stage, sex, cognitive appraisal, and repertoire of coping skills, are important mediating factors. In addition, external factors such as parental reactions and the larger cultural context also have an impact on children's stress responses and the effectiveness of the responses. Finally, certain factors, or a combination of certain factors, may lead to unusual resilience in children or at least the ability to emerge relatively unscathed from particularly stressful life events.

STRESSORS OF THE MIGRATION EXPERIENCE

The process of migration and acculturation has its own unique set of stressors that is frequently termed acculturative stress. Berry (1990) described a set of stress behaviors in adult immigrants: lowered mental health, feelings of marginality and alienation, and heightened psychosomatic symptom levels. Berry, Kim, Minde, and Mok (1987) also identified several variables that moderated the relation between acculturation and stress: the nature of the larger society, the type of the acculturating group, the individual's attitude towards acculturation, the demographic and social characteristics of the individual, and the psychological characteristics of the individual. However, in many instances, immigrants are unaware of the stressful nature of the experience and its cumulative impact (Sluzki 1979).

Several specific circumstances inherent to the migration process are stressful. One source of stress is the loss of the homeland. Children mourn the loss of loved objects, even if those objects have failed to provide a reasonable and safe environment (Eisenbruch 1988). As Ashworth (1982) described, "Children can be deeply disturbed by the sudden loss of beloved relatives and friends; they may long for the familiar sights, sounds, and smells of the past" (p. 79). Baptiste (1987, 1993) argued that in the weeks immediately after the migration the family tends to obscure feelings of loss and longing but that frequently these feelings resurface months or even years later.

In addition to the more general loss of familiar surroundings, immigration frequently means the loss of significant individuals in the child's life. Graham and Meadows' (1967) study highlighted the impact of separation on a young child. The study focused on comparing West Indian children who were referred to a child guidance clinic with a control group of white British clinic-referred children. The West Indian children were found to have more antisocial disorders than the control group. Of the West Indian male children who had immigrated to England, not one had been brought to England with both parents. In the majority of instances, the children had been left in their native homeland with their maternal grandmothers before the age of three and were reunited with their parents in England after five or six years. Graham and Meadows attributed the higher rate of antisocial behavior exhibited by these boys to the separations that these children experienced. They explained that the children experienced two separations: one from their parents and one from their parental substitutes. Once reunited with their parents, the children denied recognizing their parents, professed a primary attachment to the parental substitutes, and expressed hostility at being taken away from their parent substitutes. Because the sample group consisted of clinic patients, the authors could not generalize their findings to the larger child immigrant population, but they concluded that migration that included an extended separation from parents affected children in an adverse manner.

Other studies have also pointed to the problems created when families are separated during international migration. Rodriguez (1973) found that children who had migrated with their mothers to Switzerland had adapted more easily than those who had remained behind with their maternal grandmothers and later rejoined their mothers. Burke (1980) identified what he termed the *rejected mother neurosis*, which occurred when an immigrant child reared by the maternal grandmother was reunited with the natural mother after a period of separation. Typically, the child withdrew from the mother and had problems confiding in the mother or treating the mother as a maternal figure. In response, the mothers had feelings of guilt and failure because of the children's negative reactions to the reunification.

Children's reactions to the loss of their familiar world and their significant attachments are shaped by developmental processes. For example, children have differing friendships and obedient stances toward others, depending on developmental age. A young child considers a friend someone with whom they play rather than a source of emotional support (Maccoby 1983). Consequently, young children have fewer problems leaving their peers. Likewise, young children who have an obedient stance toward their parents harbor less resentment about the decision to migrate than adolescents who question their parents' decisions. However, a separation from the primary caretaker during the migration process can be much more stressful for a young child between the ages of 6 months and 4 years than for a slightly older child, because during this period children are establishing selective attachments and beginning to maintain relationships during a period of separation. Rutter (1983) commented that children have milder and shorter grief reactions compared to adults, probably due to their cognitive level and varying ability to conceptualize death.

A change in the family's or parents' patterns of behavior after or during the migration can also produce stress for children. For example, role changes encountered during the migration can act as stressors. Sluzki (1979) noted that many families manifest a split between the instrumental and affective roles: One member, usually male, handles the activities that require engagement in the present or current environment while another member, usually female, centers on the present and past affective activities that sustain continuity with the previous environment. Although this coping mechanism is effective in the short term, it can be maladaptive if maintained too long, causing the isolation and retarded acculturation of the affective member and leading to the disruption of family life.

Although cultures have patterns that families utilize to manage members' developmental needs, migration frequently requires a family to adopt new patterns of interaction and coping that may conflict with the well-established patterns of the homeland (Cornille and Brotherton 1993). The normative internal pressures of developmental needs that result in modifications in the family structure and roles are confounded by the transition into the new culture. Problems arise when the transition is too slow or too fast. In other words, new problems of adjustment might be rooted in an old approach to developmental transitions, one that is no longer applicable to a new situation (Baptiste 1987, 1993; Cornille and Brotherton 1993).

Furthermore, the parents' individual responses to the immigration process has an effect on children's stress responses. Rutter (1983) noted that children who are entering the hospital react to the parents' anxiety, and Athey and Ahearn (1991) pointed out that parents' grieving and anxiety reactions "make it exceedingly difficult for parents to be as available and supportive to their children as they might otherwise be and as the child might need for optimum development" (p. 12).

Finally, for illegal immigrants, the fear of being deported can be extremely stressful and can interfere with a family's ability to provide emotional support for their children. Padilla, Cervantes, Maldonado, and Garcia (1988) found that undocumented status was the third most mentioned stressors of adult Mexican and Central American immigrants. Carlin (1990) pointed out that illegal immigrants' fear of being deported requires that they "endure frequent moving and hiding, little or no medical care, plus substandard housing, and no financial assistance" (p. 277). This fear of deportment is particularly stressful and salient given the recent attempts in California to limit social and educational services to illegal immigrants.

Migrating to a new country entails facing a large number of immediate stressors. Having left behind all that is familiar to them, children feel a sense of loss. For children who also face a separation from significant others, especially their parents, the feelings of loss and subsequent complications are particularly acute and are affected by their developmental age. Furthermore, the migration experience necessitates changes in family roles and patterns of interactions, which can be very stressful for both the family and the child. Likewise, the migration experience can cause stress and anxiety for parents, which can impact the child's reaction to the stress. Finally, living in the new country illegally can engender stress in immigrant families, youth, and children.

REFUGEE CHILDREN AND POST-TRAUMATIC STRESS DISORDER

Individuals' adaptations to the receiving community will be affected by the type of migrant they are (that is, voluntary or involuntary, Berry et al. 1987) and what circumstances surrounded their departure (Leslie 1993). This is most apparent in the study of refugees because, although all migrants encounter stress, refugees frequently encounter greater stress than voluntary migrants due to the nature of their pre-departure experiences (Rumbaut 1991). Leslie (1993) noted that for Central American refugees the most powerful predictor of immigrants' assessment of the stressfulness of life events was their exposure to war. Indeed, 50 percent of the participants in the study had left their country because of ongoing warfare, and all participants had experienced some war-related trauma. Consequently, refugee children are more likely to manifest severe stress reactions such as post-traumatic stress disorder (PTSD). However, the stress responses of refugee children may be overlooked, often children cannot speak for themselves, and the problems presented by older refugees overshadow those of children (Eisenbruch 1988).

A few studies have looked at trauma and traumatic responses in childhood, but it remains an under-researched area. Studies of traumatic stress primarily include either children in wars or children who have been the victims of devastating or violent episodes such as dam breaks and floods, terrorism, or the witness of a murder, rape, or suicide of their parents. All of these studies have found evidence of unresolved trauma. Children who are exposed to violence or live in violent environments generally show signs of PTSD (Osofsky 1995).

Refugee children experience a variety of traumatic events such as violence, loss, and severe deprivation, which puts them at risk for PTSD (Athey and Ahearn 1991; Rumbaut 1991). Rumbaut (1991) noted that refugees tend to face more undesirable life changes, a greater degree of danger, and a lesser degree of control than voluntary immigrants, largely because of their flight from war-torn countries. Espino (1991) concluded her study of Central American children with this thought:

> Families from war-torn areas arrive with the scars of traumas experienced in their country of origin as a result of exposure to violence and poverty. On their arrival they become part of the inner city working poor with the added anxiety of illegal status. The children, living in overcrowded, high-conflict homes, experience neglect and abuse. Marked educational delays further inhibit their capacity to adapt, resulting in lower self-esteem and depression. A large percentage of these children are further cognitively and emotionally handicapped and can be diagnosed as having PTSD. (p. 122)

When children are faced with a traumatic stress, their response depends on other developmental processes. Preschool children are particularly dependent on their parents and react with anxious attachment behavior. School-age children seem to change dramatically, becoming rude, irritable, argumentative, and complaining of somatic problems, and their school performance declines dramatically. Adolescents react more like adults; they engage in antisocial behavior or lose impulse control. They tend to fear being ostracized and are pessimistic about the future. (For diagnostic criteria of PTSD in children over age three, see Pynoos 1993.) In a study of Central American children, Arroyo (1985, cited in Espino 1991) found that young children also tended to withdraw and suffer from the loss of acquired skills and bedwetting, whereas school-age children suffered from learning inhibitions, and adolescents displayed antisocial behavior marked by delinquency. In addition, the manifestation and severity of children's reactions also appear to be related to the degree of violence, presence or absence of personal injury, and access to family support (Athey and Ahearn 1991).

The stress reaction and acculturation of a refugee child are mediated by several factors other than the severity of the traumatic events the child was exposed to before migrating and her developmental stage—for example, whether the refugee child remains with his or her biological family, an adoptive family, or a foster family has an impact on adjustment and adaptation (Carlin 1990; Rumbaut 1991). A child who remains with the biological family may retain a sense of security. Studies of refugee children who have remained with their parents show that families that stay together develop stronger bonds due to the shared crisis, and subsequently the children show fewer signs of psychological disturbance (for a review, see Ressler, Boothby, and Steinbock 1988). However, a child who remains with the biological family will probably not have access to adequate financial resources. Furthermore, the caregivers will most likely be experiencing their own problems with adjustment or depression. Because parental anxiety has a negative impact on children, children may experience additional problems. However, children placed in adoptive families and foster care families frequently face problems regarding their expectations, disenchantment, or cultural conflicts.

When refugee children are placed with foster families, the socio-demographic characteristics of the new family affect adjustment. Porte and Torney-Purta (1987) did a comparative study of unaccompanied Indochinese refugee minors in ethnic and nonethnic placements and found that children who lived in a home with an ethnic adult had substantially lower depressive scores than those who were placed in a nonethnic home. The benefits of the ethnic placement seemed to accrue beyond the depression scale. These children had higher GPAs, made more positive attributions about their academic performances, and were more likely to see their schoolwork as relatively more under their control. Likewise, they saw themselves as being successful at making friends and were more likely to turn to another person for help when feeling sad. Porte and Torney-Purta contended that the day-to-day contact with an adult who is similar to the refugee child is important because it facilitates social learning, provides a role model, and is a source of continuity in identification.

Similarly, Eisenbruch (1988) pointed out that although the Western concept remains of an uprooted individual, the concept of an *uprooted community* must also be considered to understand the acculturation of refugee children. He claimed that, often for refugees and immigrants, personal equilibrium rests on the receiving community's equilibrium and that social disintegration in this community can cause individual psychopathology. Eisenbruch's indices of community disintegration include economic inadequacy, cultural confusion, widespread secularization, high incidence of broken homes, few and weak associations, few patterns of recreations, high patterns of interpersonal hostility and crime, and a weak, fragmented network of communications. In addition to the condition of the receiving ethnic community, the condition of the nonethnic receiving community affects the transition of refugee families. Factors such as the labor market and governmental policies have an impact on the migration experiences of refugees.

However terrifying and difficult the transitional period is for the refugee, the experience can also be strengthening. Individuals may go on to be successful and contributing members of their receiving community. As Rumbaut and Rumbaut (1976) eloquently stated:

> Beyond the numerous casualties that this process inevitably produces, many of the survivors excel in their endeavors. All of their inner resources have been fully tested, their dormant qualities and potentials have been invoked, and their purposes and goals have been challenged. For those able to cope successfully with the exceptional demands, a more fulfilling and productive life may lie ahead. After all, a victory is rewarding in direct proportion to the amount of personal effort it requires.... The mass reception of refugees need not be a chaotic, counterproductive, or alienating experience. It can be enriching, creative, and an engaging opportunity to grow while learning a poignant lesson of universal history. (pp. 397–398)

In sum, for the immigrant child who is also a refugee, numerous other sources of stress add to the already enumerated stress of migration. The bulk of these new stresses are related to the experiences that surround the often involuntary departure from the native nation. In many cases the children witness traumatic events before arriving in a new land. A child's response to the traumatic events is mediated by age, and the adjustment to the new community is influenced by a number of factors, including separation from the family and the vitality of the ethnic community in the new nation. Although it may be easier to describe the deleterious effects of the refugee experience for children, it is still important for us to remember that many refugee children overcome their difficulties and become healthy and productive individuals with unique sets of strengths.

DEVELOPMENT OF A DUAL FRAME OF REFERENCE AND BICULTURALISM

After the initial stage of migration, a lifelong process of adaptation and acculturation begins. Thus, the psychological impact of immigration is not limited to the immediate sources of stress.

To understand the complexity and contradictions in the impact of immigration fully, it is necessary to focus on how migration can be simultaneously a stressful and a growth-enhancing experience. This reconceptualization is facilitated by seeing the process of migration in both a narrative and a temporal manner and considering the political, economic, sociological, and political context in which it occurs (Rumbaut 1991). By doing so, we move away from the underlying assumption that immigration has only negative psychological implications. What constitutes a stress in the initial period of immigration may or may not facilitate a longer-term benefit. As the immediate strains of the immigration experience subside, a more gradual process of acculturation and adaptation begins, and the individual child is faced with both greater challenges and greater rewards. Thus, research on immigrant children should inform how the process of immigration can increase an individual's repertoire of coping skills, facilitate the acquisition of new or different skills, and broaden opportunities as well as worldviews. For instance, the process of learning to speak English for a child whose parents only speak Chinese might be a large source of stress. However, having learned both languages, the child is bilingual, a valuable asset in an increasingly interdependent and multicultural world.

The process of acculturation requires immigrant children to navigate their way in both the culture of their parents and mainstream culture. A survey of immigrant parents conducted in Miami and Detroit (Lambert and Taylor 1990) showed that the respondents send a message to their children to become bicultural and bilingual. They want their children to maintain their cultural heritage and native language as well as to adopt measures that will make them more accepted and successful in their new home. This request is not without problems. As Cropley (1983) described, "[T]he crucial problem is being simultaneously exposed to two sets of norms—those of the homeland and those of the receiving society.... One set of socializing influences...attempts to pass on to the children the norms of the motherland, while another set of socializing influences transmits the norms of the receiving community" (pp. 110–111). He explained that native children are also exposed to two sets of socializing influences but that in their case there is a high level of agreement between the norms espoused by the family and those espoused by the wider society. In the case of immigrant children, there may be clear conflict or disagreement between the two forces (Cropley 1983). Immigrant children are therefore frequently metaphorically characterized as between two worlds or, as Zavala Martinez (1994a) described Puerto Ricans, "entremundos."

Baptiste's (1987) discussion of family therapy with Spanish-heritage immigrant families sheds further light on the difficulty that children face being between two worlds:

> The clash of values and styles places children in an impossible bind. A majority of these families migrated in search of a better life. Consequently, in order for the children to fulfill that dream and show their appreciation to their parents, they need to achieve in the new culture. In order to achieve, they need to let go of some of their native culture and make new friends, improve their English, and become acculturated. To do so, however, is to risk alienation from the family. On the other hand, rejection of the new culture assures that acculturation will not be achieved or at best will be delayed. (pp. 239–240)

Sung (1985) listed a number of areas in which young Chinese immigrants in the city of New York face bicultural conflicts. These areas included the expression of sexuality and aggressiveness, the assertion of independence and individualism, involvement in sports, and academics. Sung commented that these bicultural problems often go unrecognized by parents or teachers and that the children are censured for their behavior. The censure upsets the children and makes them feel as if they should choose between what is taught in the home and what is accepted by mainstream culture. "In his desire to be accepted and to be liked, he may want to throw off that which is second nature to him; this may cause anger and pain not only to himself but also to his parents and family" (Sung 1985:257).

One of the greatest difficulties involved in having a dual frame of reference is the transgenerational-transcultural problems it creates. Most children and their parents face generation conflicts, simply because the parents and the children are socialized into different worlds in a temporal sense. This generational conflict is even more pronounced in the children of immigrants because they are being socialized into different cultures as well. For example, Cropley (1983) saw one common source of conflict in Britain as the amount of freedom that immigrant adolescent girls are allowed to have. He noted that Pakistani parents do not consider higher education a strong priority for girls but that British society socializes girls to become more independent and strive for a higher level of self-development. Baptiste outlined several areas in which parent-child conflict is manifested in Spanish-heritage immigrant families, including the lessening of parental authority to discipline children or to select their children's mates. Another illustration offered by Sung (1985) is the difficulty that children of Chinese immigrant parents face when they believe that their parents do not love them because of the distance and formality that mark their relationships. The distant upbringing that they frequently receive stands in sharp contrast with the prevalent mainstream image of warm and affectionate parents.

The sense of being caught between two worlds is also an issue when the children of immigrants serve as a cultural bridge for their parents. School-age children usually acculturate faster and become fluent in the new language faster than their parents because of their exposure to the host society in their schooling (Baptiste 1993; Leslie 1993). Thus, in many families, the children serve as linguistic interpreters for their parents. In such a situation the child assumes a new role in the family, generational boundaries are crossed, and the child becomes privy to information that the child would otherwise not know. This change has the potential to cause significant stress for families that are accustomed to strict generational boundaries and parental authority and can cause distress for the child, making him or her feel like a yo-yo. Baptiste (1993) explained that when children serve as interpreters to complete a job application or during a visit to the doctor, they become involved in situations that children are usually excluded from. If the child asks questions about the situation at a later point, he or she is frequently reprimanded and reminded of his or her child status (Baptiste 1993; Koplow and Messinger 1990). Athey and Ahearn (1991) claimed that when a child serves as a cultural translator, the situation becomes one of "status inconsistency for the child—a situation in which a person occupies two or more distinct social statuses with incompatible social expectation leading to chronic stress" (p. 12). Furthermore, parents can come to resent their dependence and the children's involvement in adult business.

It has been suggested that, when a child takes on a role as an interpreter for the family, life events involving family members become particularly stressful. Zambrana and Silva-Palacios' (1989) study to assess how a group of Mexican American adolescents ranked stressful life events revealed that the highest-ranked perceived stresses were related to issues of family constancy or stability. Items such as parents getting sick or arrested generated high-stress responses. Zambrana and Silva-Palacios suggest that this is normative for adolescents and might be particularly relevant to these immigrant adolescents given their role in the family as negotiator with the external world. The researchers concluded that the adolescent's need to serve as an interpreter in a difficult situation might increase the perceived stressfulness of the situation. It is also possible that the emphasis that Mexican American culture places on family relationships contributes to this heightened perception of stress. The situation might be extremely stressful for the child not simply because he or she must serve as a translator, but because the family is undergoing a series of stressful situations.

Cropley (1983) also pointed out a special conflict between competing socializing forces regarding the education of immigrant children. In general, immigrants understand that education is highly valuable and is essential for achieving success in their new community. However, schools reflect the norms and values of the dominant society, which frequently includes prejudice against the immigrants. Therefore, schools are the single most powerful agent that threatens the norms of the homeland. To succeed in school, an immigrant child must accept norms that may conflict with the norms of the parents' country of origin. Cropley (1983) termed this the double bind; as children are encouraged to succeed, they are consequently encouraged to be alienated from the ways of the homeland.

Cropley's discussion of the double bind might be too narrow a perspective on the interaction of a child and the school context. Laosa (1989) took a more comprehensive look at how the school context has an impact on a Hispanic child's adjustment in the United States. He suggested a range of factors that influence a child's adjustment and adaptation, including ESL resources, the presence or absence of cultural minority students, the school climate, the ethno-linguistic composition of both the student body and the teaching staff, and the nature and frequency of teacher-parent interactions, parental involvement, and peer tutoring. Delgado-Gaitan's (1994) case study of Mexican-American and Mexican immigrant families documented the way in which the first-generation families handled cultural and linguistic alienation and cultural discontinuities. She found that first-generation American parents tried to remake their socialization roles in order to make the home more congruent with the school culture, while also trying to maintain an ethnic identity. She also found that parent and community organizations were pivotal in empowering the parents. Organizations provided effective means to intervene in the school system, taught the parents how to build learning environments that corresponded to the schools' expectations, and helped them maintain their culture and language. Delgado-Gaitan's work illustrates the importance of community-based organizations in a child's adaptation experience. Finally, Rumbaut (1991) found that the Vietnamese and Chinese adolescent refugees in the San Diego metropolitan area had high levels of education achievement in high school—higher even than native-born Anglo students. Higher grade point averages were associated with parents' sense of ethnic resilience and solidarity as well as their intention to stay in the United States and affirm their ethnic culture and social networks. Other factors that affected school achievement included socioeconomic status and parents' psycho-cultural status.

The notion of a dual frame of reference necessitates a further examination of what this term means in the lives of children and adolescent immigrants. Frequently, this notion leads scholars and researchers to focus on the idea that an immigrant child or adolescent is caught between two worlds—that is, that they belong to neither. More recently, the concept of biculturalism has emerged, which emphasizes that it is possible for an individual to function effectively in two or more cultures without any deleterious impact. The notion that an immigrant child, adolescent, or adult may come to be comfortable and capable interacting in both an ethnic culture and a mainstream culture is critical to a discussion of an immigrant's adjustment. It puts forth the suggestion that from an immigrant's dual frame of reference can emerge the capability to manage two cultural realities with comfort and efficacy. That is, an immigrant can come to belong to both the culture of the homeland and the culture of his or her receiving community. However, it is important to note that biculturalism does not mandate and is not contingent upon a bicultural self-identity (Rotherham-Borus 1993). We discuss the formation of ethnic identities and bicultural ethnic identities later in the chapter.

This ability to be bicultural does not necessarily mean that an individual switches between two cultural realms depending on the cultural context (that is, code switching), nor does it mean that an individual blends the two cultures. Instead, across domains such as values and language, the impact of biculturalism may be different. For instance, in the language domain, a bicultural individual may engage in code switching. However, because it is difficult to code switch in the realm of values, blending may occur. We argued elsewhere that the notion of biculturalism encompasses both affective and behavioral components and that a fully bicultural individual would "be competent in both cultures, engage in typical behaviors of both cultures, would prefer to remain involved in practices and lifestyles of both cultures, and would feel a sense of belonging toward both cultural communities" (Tropp, Ekrut, Alarcon, García Coll, and Vázquez 1994:8). Nevertheless, to be bicultural in all domains requires that an individual achieve functional competence in two cultures. However, this does not imply that biculturalism is dichotomous. There is a continuum of biculturalism, and an individual's position on this continuum can change as he or she grows more or less competent in another culture and as attitudes toward the individual's culture and the mainstream culture evolve (LaFromboise, Coleman, and Gerton 1993).

Bicultural competence has several dimensions, outlined by LaFromboise et al. (1993). Dimensions include knowledge of cultural beliefs and values, positive attitudes toward both majority and minority groups, a sense of efficacy in both cultures (that is, the belief that one has the ability to establish and maintain effective relationships in both cultures), communication ability, role repertoire (that is, a range of culturally appropriate behaviors), and a sense of being grounded (a well-developed social support system in or of both cultures). An individual must possess a competence in these arenas in order to manage the process of living in two cultures.

The ramifications of biculturalism are profound, especially in an increasingly multicultural society. The ability to be bicultural not only increases an individual's knowledge base (that is, cognitive content) but it encourages and fosters some important skills. Ramirez (1983) suggested that for those who embrace biculturalism, the greatest assets are adaptability and flexibility of coping and the ability to relate and empathize with a variety of people from different backgrounds. Furthermore, the bicultural individual is capable of learning from many cultures because he or she is more than just sensitive to many cultures—he or she is a part of and apart from many cultural realities. This has practical and behavioral implications. For example, Ramirez (1984) found that multicultural college students placed in leadership positions had more behavioral and perspective repertoires available than did leaders who were monocultural. They were more effective in communicating with all the members of their groups and made sure that everyone was able to express opinions and that the others understood. Similarly, Szapocznik, Kurtines, and Fernandez (1981) found the bicultural Cuban adolescents who had the ability to communicate and negotiate in two cultures were able to adjust better than adolescents who over-acculturated. For these adolescents, whose parents were immigrants from Cuba, "effective adjustment requires an acceptance of both worlds as well as skills to live among and interact with both cultures" (Szapocznik et al. 1981:354).

Although the notion of biculturalism is particularly salient for children who are born in one country and migrate to another, biculturalism will continue to be important for the second, third, and subsequent generations of immigrants in the United States (García Coll et al. in press). Many of the developmental processes that affect immigrant children will continue to affect their children as they grow up, not as immigrant children but as minority children (for a review of the literature on the development of minority infants and children, see García Coll 1990; García Coll et al. in press). Therefore, minority children share with immigrant children some important developmental processes and outcomes, such as biculturalism, that neither group shares with mainstream white children.

In sum, after a child arrives and the immediate stresses and strains of the migration process subside, a lifelong process of acculturation begins. The beginning of the acculturation process signifies an individual's endeavor to negotiate living in two cultures. In doing so, the two sets of socializing forces and norms to which the child is exposed may conflict, and problems may arise for families and their children. These problems may be particularly acute as immigrant parents and their children face not only a generational but also a transcultural gap. It has been suggested that the school may be an arena in which bicultural conflicts are manifested, but it is likely that the extent to which schooling creates bicultural conflicts is impacted by a large number of factors such as the ethnic composition of the student body and teaching staff, the availability of ESL resources, and the presence or absence of parent-teacher organizations. Although the notion of being between two worlds can create conflict, an individual can live effectively in more than one culture. Furthermore, by becoming bicultural an individual has gained valuable skills such as flexibility and adaptability in coping skills. Finally, acculturation and biculturalism are not just issues for recent immigrants but for all minority children.

BILINGUALISM

In order to become bicultural, the immigrant must acquire new skills in the new homeland. One of the main skills that immigrants acquire is the ability to speak the native community's language. Initially this can be stressful, because immigrants may be unfamiliar with the language or ridiculed about their accent by their peers (Zambrana and Silva-Palacios 1989. Sung (1985) determined in her study of Chinese immigrant students in New York that "the language barrier was the problem most commonly mentioned by the immigrant Chinese. Frequently, language looms largest because it is the conduit through which we interact with other people. It is the means by which we think, learn, and express ourselves" (p. 256). Immigrants must learn how to communicate with people in a nonverbal way; children must learn how to read expressions and gestures and to understand intonations of the new language (Westermeyer 1989).

For children of immigrants, the process of learning a new language is facilitated by enrollment in a mainstream school. Baptiste (1987, 1993) pointed out that children fearing the stigmatization of an accent are very invested in learning the language quickly. Hirschman's (1994) study of educational attainment for immigrants revealed that immigrant children had a high constant enrollment in schools regardless of the duration of their residence in the United States. He also noted an initial handicap for immigrants who had been here less than five years and a slightly higher rate for immigrants who had been here longer than five years. Some results indicated that a greater exposure to United States culture leads to poorer prospects and lower enrollment rates among Caribbean immigrants, who are more likely to be black and live in African American-dominated neighborhoods.

Although it is frequently assumed that social and emotional adjustment are related to language proficiency, Ekstrand (1976) found that among immigrant pupils in Sweden, social adjustment was only subtly associated with language proficiency. Therefore, although the acquisition of the host language may be necessary for an immigrant child's social adjustment, it is probably not sufficient. Similarly, Rumbaut (1994) found that a higher English proficiency and educational attainment as measured by the students' GPA were associated with immigrant children's positive self-esteem and depression score. "Knowledge of English in particular showed a strong positive association with self-esteem, underscoring the psychological importance of linguistic acculturation for children of immigrants in American social contexts" (Rumbaut 1994, pp. 783–784). However, these data did not demonstrate the direction of the associations or causality, and most likely, reciprocal effects are involved. Thus, although proficiency in the receiving community's language is associated with social adjustment, research has yet to clarify how a child's adjustment is related to language proficiency.

If children have not yet learned the language of their parents' homeland, it is important that they learn both the new language and their parents' language. Paulston (1978) concluded that children should have firm grounding in their mother language before trying to learn another language. Paulston found that children who migrated from Finland to Sweden at age ten succeeded in mastering two languages most easily. Children who migrated at age twelve learned Swedish well but somewhat slower than the ten-year-olds. The children who migrated prior to preschool or after one year of schooling had the hardest time mastering two languages; this was attributed to the absence of a sound linguistic base in their mother tongue. If children do not become bilingual, difficulties may arise in communicating with their parents, whose affective language is different than theirs (Koplow and Messinger 1990). Cropley (1983) noted that the mother tongue is a vital link with the norms of the immigrant's homeland, and an inadequate mastery of it represents a disruption of relationships with the original culture and parents. Accordingly, Rumbaut's (1994) survey of immigrant children revealed that children's preference for English and poor command of their parents' native language were positively associated with high levels of parent-child conflict.

Bilingualism is different from the promotion of the majority language at the loss of the minority language. Furthermore, bilingualism can be further differentiated, by the age at which an individual acquires the second language, into either successive or simultaneous bilingualism (Padilla and Lindholm 1984). Children who first learn one language and then acquire the second language are successive bilinguals. Children who are simultaneous or balanced bilinguals have age-appropriate abilities in two languages. The measurement of bilingualism and language proficiency has mostly been by standardized testing instruments. This tendency raises questions about how and whether instruments should be used to measure bilingualism in a naturalistic context (Padilla and Lindholm 1984).

It is clear that more is involved with becoming bilingual than simply acquiring more linguistic knowledge. Bilingualism at an early age may have profound effects upon the process of cognitive development. Early research into the impact of bilingualism on cognition found that bilingual children showed cognitive deficits (Lambert 1977; Padilla and Lindholm 1984). However, the research was methodologically flawed. In particular, the comparison groups were not matched in important sociocultural and economic variables. More recent research shows that balanced bilingualism can promote cognitive development or cognitive flexibility (Padilla and Lindholm 1984). Lambert (1977) reported that when he began his study of bilingual children in Canada, he expected to find bilingual children demonstrating cognitive deficits. However, balanced bilingual French-English children scored significantly higher than monolingual children on verbal and nonverbal measures, and the pattern of test results suggested that the children had a more diversified structure of intelligence and more flexibility in thought. Lambert's work is supported by similar research (for a review of research, see Diaz 1985; Padilla and Lindholm 1984) that also found a link between bilingualism and cognitive flexibility, creativity, or divergent thought. The ability of bilingual children to develop more flexible or divergent thinking may rest in part on the interrelation between language development and cognitive development. That is, children who are bilingual gain meta-linguistic awareness, an objective understanding of language. Consequently, their increased awareness of the cognitive functions of language leads to an increased use, understanding, and mastery of language for cognitive functions (Diaz and Klinger 1991).

However, the study of bilingualism and biculturalism needs to be further expanded. For example, there are varying levels of bilingualism. Research in the United States has been confounded by the fact that most educational opportunities for bilinguals do not promote a balanced knowledge of two languages but rather emphasize English at the expense of the native language. Most research outside the United States has tried to focus on balanced bilinguals. Consequently, it is unclear whether the benefits of becoming a balanced bilingual are shared by those who become successive bilinguals. Furthermore, the impact of bilingualism is hard to measure given the typically large range of other important factors that differ for bilingual and monolingual children in most study comparison groups. Whether one becomes bilingual depends on a large range of social variables, and even controlling for age, socioeconomic status, and years of schooling does not ensure that samples are equivalent on all relevant variables (Diaz 1985). This is particularly true given that within the United States, English is the sociolinguistically dominant language and its speakers benefit from higher prestige and greater communicative utility.

Discrepancies in social variables indicate that an analysis of bilingual individuals should consider contextual variables. Hakuta, Ferdman, and Diaz (1987) argued that the context in which bilingualism occurs should be included in research on the impact of bilingualism on cognition. In their framework, bilingualism is conceptualized as consisting of three levels of analysis. First, it is a characteristic of people who possess two language systems, which has implications for their cognitive development. Second, it is a psychosocial concept characteristic of people who organize the world into different groups that are associated with different languages, and it has implications for an individual's group affiliation or ethnic identity. Finally, bilingualism encompasses a societal concept that is characteristic of interactions between social groups and institutions and that corresponds to linguistic boundaries. This is the societal context in which a bilingual individual lives. These different levels take into consideration that individuals who acquire the ability to speak two languages are affected by the context of the community and society in which they reside.

Although our current knowledge base might be inadequate from which to draw any definitive answers about the effects of bilingualism and biculturalism on cognition, we know much about the effects of culture on cognition provided by cross-cultural studies of cognitive development in the past thirty years. Wagner's (1978, 1981) work on memory skills in northern Africa, Cole and Scribner's (1974) work among Liberian rice farmers, and the cross-cultural work done by many investigators on the universality of Piagetian stages (see Dasen and Heron 1981), for example, suggest that biculturalism has important consequences on developmental processes. A major lesson from this research, which might be particularly relevant for the study of immigrant children, is that the context of learning might be as important as the acquisition of the cognitive skill per se. Thus, Liberian rice farmers demonstrate better problem-solving skills for mathematical problems involving rice than abstract symbols; the opposite is true in the case of undergraduates in Michigan. The same can be said about rug sellers in Morocco or Guatemalan children doing conservation tasks. Cognitive development is not simply a matter of acquiring a particular skill that can be applied universally, because culture and context affect where, when, and how the skill is used. This needs to be studied if we hope to unravel the effects of biculturalism and acculturation on immigrant children.

In sum, it is important that immigrant children and adolescents learn the language of their new country as well as develop their knowledge of their parents' language. Although not knowing the new language may be stressful, the immigrant child is frequently invested in the learning process, and the learning process is facilitated through enrollment in native schools. Although earlier research showed that bilingual children demonstrated cognitive deficits, more recent work critiqued the methodologies of past studies and presented more promising results that suggest that balanced bilingual children develop more flexible or divergent cognitive skills than monolingual children. Unfortunately, research on bilingualism and cognition within the United States has been plagued by the facts that children are usually taught English at the expense of their native languages and that bilingual children within the United States usually differ from monolingual children on a wide range of relevant variables. Such discrepancies point to the need for a multilevel analysis of bilingualism. Finally, the knowledge that has been accumulated in the field of cross-cultural cognition suggests culture and context affect an individual's use of a particular cognitive skill; these findings may have particular bearing upon immigrant children. The impact of both bilingualism and biculturalism on cognitive development is an important avenue of research if we are to further understand the migration experience of adolescents and children.

IDENTITY AND SELF

Migration can have a major impact on a child or adolescent's self and identity processes. Although many adolescents have a difficult time during adolescence, immigrant children have a particularly difficult time because they are trying to forge an identity in a context that may be racially and culturally dissonant. Therefore, whereas many adolescents confront insecurities about themselves, immigrant adolescents frequently find these insecurities exacerbated by their membership in a minority group (Spencer, Swanson, and Cunningham 1991). Consequently, immigrant children and adolescents have the developmental task of constructing adequate ethnic identities as part of their more general identity development.

In the discussion of immigrants, an abundance of terms hint at the negative impact of migration on an individual's sense of self and identity: marginalized man, self-alienated, and uprooted. The underlying consensus is that arriving to settle in another culture can have negative implications for both an individual's sense of self and the way in which one understands and relates to others. Cropley (1983) argued that exposure to two sets of conflicting norms as a child can lead to self-alienation. He distinguishes between cultural identity and personal identity:

> Cultural identity involves acceptance of the norms of a particular society; personal identity, on the other hand, derives from a sense of belonging to a particular group. If the process of adoption of values, habits, attitudes, and the like of the receiving society is not accompanied by a feeling of belonging as an individual to some respected group, the result is self-alienation. Even more difficult is the situation in which the norms of the receiving society actually conflict with those factors which actually lead to a sense of belonging .... Even immigrants who have achieved good adaptation in the sense of cultural identity may experience enormous difficulties in the area of personal identity. The resulting identity conflict leads, nor infrequently ... to "a sense of masked inferiority." For example, West Indian pupils may describe themselves as speaking "bad" English or as coming from a "bad" family. (p. 121)

Brody (1966) echoed these thoughts: "This need to deal with multiple, conflicting and poorly perceived standards for behavior, the exclusion-produced defects on long-range planning for distant goals and the persistent reminders that one's personal worth is low, all contribute to an identity problem for the culturally excluded individual" (p. 855). Brody cited Erikson: "'Ego identity gains real strength only from wholehearted and constant recognition of...achievement that has meaning in the culture.' This kind of achievement appears to be out of reach for the bulk of the excluded, with a consequent lack of the rewards that assure a man of his personal worth, dignity, and importance to others" (Brody 1966:855). Mendelberg (1986) claimed that minority group members are unable to identify with the mainstream culture but that identifying with their ethnic group is "fraught with difficulties" (Mendelberg 1986:223).

What remains to be done is to move this discussion from a very vague and general discussion of the possible negative implications of migration on identity to a more concrete discussion that encompasses both the complexity of the processes and possible positive outcomes. This is necessary because it has yet to be shown that an ethnic self-identity—any particular ethnic self-identity—or minority status has a negative impact on self-concept (Rosenthal 1987; Rotherham-Borus 1993). Nonetheless, it would be just as misinformed to argue that immigration and minority status had no impact on identity processes. For immigrant children and adolescents, the development of ethnic identity appears to be a part of the process of forging an adequate personal identity.

To date, there is no widely agreed-on definition of ethnic identity, although most agree that ethnic identity formation is a complex, vital, and dynamic process (Zavala Martinez 1994b). Most children know their ethnic group and its obvious characteristics, but it remains unclear how a child's knowledge evolves into attitudes about and behaviors toward oneself and others. In a review of research and literature, Phinney (1990) found that as a construct, ethnic identity had been defined to encompass differing emphasis on self-concept derived from group membership, self-identification, feelings of belonging and commitment, shared values and attitudes, or attitudes toward one's own group. The different definitions and measures of ethnic identity utilized in research with adults and adolescents have generated findings that are inconsistent, contradictory, and hard to compare (Phinney 1990).

Examining identity formation in adolescents and children is confounded by the fact that identity formation is a dynamic process that continues over time and will likely be influenced by a variety of factors. Ethnic identification is usually considered achieved after a period of self-discovery and examination (Phinney 1993). However, most children and adolescents have not had such an experience; thus, discussions of immigrant children's and adolescents' self-identifications frequently focus not on self-identification but on the identification of reference groups (Rotherham-Borus 1993). Reference group identification or orientation reflects the youth's wish to be compared to a particular group (that is, ethnic group, mainstream, or bicultural) or held to the standards of this group. That is, it reflects what and who they admire and aspire to be. Young children usually do not verbally identify their chosen reference groups; choices are inferred from their behavioral responses on forced-choice tests (Rotherham-Borus 1993). However, as children grow they make self-determined choices that stem in part from their previous socialization patterns but also encompass greater variability and independence. The reference groups also become an organizing construct evident in self-labels, attitudes, values, social behaviors, and expectations (Rotherham-Borus 1993).

In the United States today a variety of ethnic identities or reference groups exist from which immigrant adolescents and children can choose: ethnic, pan-ethnic, bicultural, or mainstream (Rumbaut 1994). One identity is not more healthy or adaptive than another identity. As Rotherham-Borus (1990) explained, "[B]eing mainstream, bicultural, or ethnically identified are all associated with positive outcomes" (p. 1080). However, immigrants who have "explored ethnicity as a factor in their lives, and are clear about the meaning of their ethnicity are likely to show better overall adjustment" (Phinney 1993, p. 75). Emphasis should be placed on the process of an adolescent's identity development or choice of reference group rather than on the particular chosen identity.

The development of an ethnic identity and the choice of a reference group are both formed by and should be understood within the framework of the contexts in which an individual is developing. A large number of contextual factors appear to influence the reference group choice of immigrant adolescents. For example, research suggests that collective identity plays an important role in the process of reference group determination. As Fernández-Kelly and Schauffler (1994) observed, "Whether youngsters sink or soar frequently depends on how they see themselves, their families, and their communities. For that reason, the immigrant life is preeminently an examined life. Iterative processes of symbolic and factual association and detachment shape immigrants' self-definition" (p. 682).

Rumbaut (1994) conceptualized social identity and self-esteem as derivatives from self-comparisons with reference groups. Consequently, ethnic self-awareness is blurred or reinforced depending on the consonance or dissonance of the context. Rumbaut hypothesized that the process of identification is not a unidirectional process into the dominant group ethnicity. Rather, multiple ethnic identities may emerge corresponding to the distinct modes of immigrant adaptation and the social contexts of reception. Factors thought to have an impact on identity are experiences with racial discrimination, the location in which children live (for example, inner-city versus rural setting), and the ethnicity of the receiving community. Rumbaut suggests that a good combination of these factors can lead to a resilient ethnic identity and that a bad combination leads to an oppositional racial attitude.

The work of Rotherham-Borus (1989, cited in Rotherham-Borus, 1993) underscores the multi-deterministic nature of self-identification processes and the importance of the school and peer group context. They investigated the self-identification of adolescents in two ethnically and racially integrated high schools with balanced student bodies. In each school, about 45 percent of the black, Puerto Rican, and Filipino students self-identified as bicultural. The students from the integrated schools were compared with ethnic students from a school that had a less balanced student body (that is, more black and Puerto Rican students than white students) and greater cross-ethnic tensions. In this school, more than 70 percent of the Puerto Rican, black, and white students reported an ethnic identification. This study suggests that in contexts in which race and ethnicity are particularly salient, adolescents' self-identifications vary.

The choice of a bicultural identity is common among minority adolescents (Rotherham-Borus 1993). Rumbaut (1994), studying ethnic self-identification in children of immigrants in California and Florida, found that 27 percent identified with a national or ethnic origin, 40 percent identified as a hyphenated-American identity, 11 percent identified as Americans, and 21 percent chose pan-ethnic identifications. There were differences between the children who were native-born and those who were foreign-born: 43 percent of the foreign-born selected a national origin identity, whereas only 11 percent of the U.S.-born selected a national origin identity. Likewise, 32 percent of the foreign-born selected a hyphenated identity, and 49 percent of the U.S.-born selected a hyphenated identity. Only 3 percent of the foreign-born selected an American identity, whereas 20 percent of the U.S.-born selected such an identity. The use of pan-ethnic identity varied between ethnic groups. Less than 1 percent of the Asian youth surveyed identified with the Asian American pan-ethnic identity; however, 28 percent of Spanish-speaking children from Latin America chose the identity of Hispanic. The one exception was the Cuban children who were the least likely to choose a pan-ethnic identity.

Four contextual factors that affect a bicultural adolescent's choice of reference group have been distinguished: the freedom of contact, the attitudes of the majority group, the strength of the majority group, and the relationship of the family to the adolescent (Rosenthal 1987). These factors influence the adolescents' choice of labels and the relation between their self-labeling and their behavioral indices of adjustment. For example, when Rotherham-Borus (1989, cited in Rotherham-Borus, 1993) compared high schools with ethnic tensions to schools without tension, she found that the schools with less tension endorsed biculturalism more. In these schools, the students identified as bicultural had higher social competencies and performed better academically than the students identified as bicultural in the cross-ethnically tense schools (Rotherham-Borus 1993).

The ways in which these variables influence a child's or adolescent's developmental identity processes require careful and further investigation. Knight, Bernal, Garza, Cota, and Ocampo (1993) looked at the relation between ethnic identity and socialization among forty-five Mexican American children between six and ten years old. They proposed a model to explain how the characteristics of the family's social ecology influences the joint socialization experiences created by family and non-family agents, which then influence a child's ethnic identity and lead to ethnically based behavior. The model proposes that the more recently the family migrated to the United States, the more ethnically identified and less assimilated the adults are, the more the parents teach their children about their culture, and the more sense of ethnic identity and pride the children have. A study to confirm the model was carried out with Mexican American mothers and their children. Mothers who were comfortable with their Mexican culture taught their children more about their culture and had children who were more ethnically identified. Also of interest was that a mother's comfort with her culture was influenced by the immigrant generation of the father. In other words, if the father were a recent immigrant, the mother was more likely to teach her children about Mexican culture.

Finally, the work of Waters (in press) and Rumbaut (1994) reminds us not to lose sight of the individual characteristics of the immigrant adolescents and their influence on ethnic identity processes. Waters' interviews with West Indian adolescents found that the same number of girls and boys identified themselves as American rather than with an ethnic identification. However, the importance that the boys and girls attached to their self-identifications was different. The girls discussed being black American in terms of the freedom they desired from their parents and the restriction that their parents placed on them. They were critical of the strictness that their parents demonstrated. The boys discussed their black American identification in terms of racial solidarity, societal exclusion, and disapproval. They felt more racial harassment than their female counterparts and were less comfortable leaving their black neighborhoods.

Similarly, Rumbaut (1994) found that language use was closely linked to the formation and maintenance of an ethnic identity. Those who spoke English were more likely to identify as American. Those with a greater fluency in national language were more likely to pick a national identity, and bilinguals were more likely to pick hyphenated identities. The association of language use and choice of ethnic self-identity highlights the importance of individual acculturation rates and of interpersonal and social relationships. Thus, although we have emphasized the importance of contextual factors, we recognize that identity development is also strongly influenced by the characteristics of the individual.

Although the construct of ethnic identity has been conceptualized in several different ways, a consensus has emerged that immigration has an important impact on an individual's self and identity processes. Some authors have focused on the identity problems that children and adolescent immigrants face, employing such terms as "self-alienation" in their discussions. Other researchers have emphasized the multi-deterministic and dynamic nature of identity processes and reference group choices as well as the variety of ethnic labels and identities chosen by immigrant children and adolescents. A number of factors that affect an individual's choice of identity have been identified, yet it is still unclear how many of these factors affect self and identity processes. More research should be undertaken to understand the ways in which immigrant children develop their ethnic identities and how different contexts and variables influence this process.

COPING WITH DISCRIMINATION, RACISM, AND PREJUDICE

Another important developmental task for immigrant children and adolescents is that of coping with discrimination, racism, and prejudice. Discrimination against immigrants, and particularly immigrants of color, is widespread in America today, as evidenced by the introduction of Proposition 187 in California during the fall of 1994. However, the impact of discrimination on immigrant children is hard to measure and has not been subject to much investigation (García Coll et al. in press). This is increasingly true as overt racism becomes replaced by symbolic and subtle racism (Duckitt 1992). As racism evolves into a more complex and covert phenomenon, its effects become harder to document and measure in some instances.

Although adolescents of color may no longer face a legally segregated society, Waters (in press) found in her interviews with both immigrant and first-generation West Indian adolescents that these black adolescents, and particularly young males, felt that they were frequently the victims of racial harassment. Commonly reported situations included "being followed in stores because they were suspected of shoplifting, people recoiling in fear in public places—on the street, on the subway, in parks, and anywhere youngsters encountered whites" (Waters in press).

Padilla et al. (1988) reported that immigrant adults found discrimination a significant source of stress. The respondents indicated that they felt discriminated against and believed they were treated unfairly because they were Latino and that Americans had negative stereotypes of them. They also felt that they could not do much about being the victims of prejudice because they feared losing their jobs or residences if they confronted those who discriminated against them and because their command of English was not good enough to articulate their grievances effectively. Therefore, they endured the prejudice of native residents without taking any consequential action.

How the increasingly complex nature of discrimination and racism affects the adjustment of children immigrants in our society remains unclear. One possibility is that higher rates of behavioral disorders are seen in settings in which children experience discrimination. For example, Rutter, Yule, Berger, Yule, Morton, and Bagley (1974) studied immigrant school children in Britain and found that children who presented behavior disorders in school did not do so at home at the same rate. The authors were hesitant to pinpoint what it was about the school environment that led these children to have greater disturbances, but they suggested that the awareness of discrimination in the school setting may be a possible root of the disturbances. Although Graham and Meadow (1967) did not focus on the effect of discrimination in the immigrant child's life, they raised the issue: "[T]here is the question of color prejudice, and much less often, color discrimination, which many of the immigrant children attending the clinic put forward as one of the main reasons for their difficulties in school" (p. 114).

An interesting point of consideration was raised by Gil, Vega, and Dimas (1994) about variations in adolescent immigrants' perceptions of discrimination across generations. Their comparative analysis of the effects of acculturation and acculturative stress on the self-esteem of Hispanic and Latino adolescents showed that the process of adjustment was different for those who immigrated and those who were born in the United States. In particular they found that U.S.-born Hispanic adolescent males who had low acculturation levels were more likely to report perceived discrimination than foreign-born immigrant Hispanic adolescent males. They suggest that this was because foreign-born immigrants had different expectations about American society than U.S.-born immigrants. Rogler, Cortes, and Malgady (1991), in their review of studies on Hispanics' acculturation and mental health, suggested that because most migrations represent opportunity-seeking efforts, first-generation immigrants feel less deprived because immigration has improved their standards of living. However, subsequent generations have an increased sense of deprivation because of higher unmet aspirations. This is important because, according to Rogler et al. (1991), unmet expectations are a very likely contributor to psychological distress.

A further examination of immigrants' perceptions of discrimination suggests that differential experiences and expectations of discrimination can create generation gaps between first- and second-generation immigrants. Rumbaut (1994) found that parent-child conflict increased if the children experienced discrimination and believed that regardless of educational attainment the discrimination would continue. Rumbaut suggested:

> Perhaps the implicit outlook that sees discrimination as trumping education contradicts immigrant parents' folk theories of success .... That is, immigrant parents tend to define the situation in instrumental terms (extolling the virtues of hard work and good grades), whereas their children tend to seek to fit in socially and to experience in expressive terms the impact of disparagement within an ethnic minority status. (786–787)

Although immigrants might have different expectations and experiences, facing prejudice and discrimination on a regular basis requires that immigrant children and adolescents develop behavioral or psychosocial coping skills. Belonging to an ethnic enclave is one way in which immigrants cope with prejudice (Brody 1990; Fernández-Kelly and Schauffler 1994). Although the ethnic enclave is frequently thought of in stigmatizing terms, it is also a "staging ground" for the movement of migrants out into the larger society (Brody 1990). Moreover, for the immigrants who do not wish to move out into the larger society, the enclave may provide a social structure permitting success and leadership positions within a congenial cultural context. The ethnic enclave thus provides immigrants with opportunities outside of the receiving community's structure.

Rodriguez (1975) maintained that Puerto Ricans who lived in the "ghetto" were cushioned to some degree from discrimination; everyone who lived in the segregated neighborhood was like everyone else and was treated the same. Because the discrimination was not directed at individuals as much as it was directed at the entire group and was a fact of life, it seemed to be felt less. Similarly, Beiser (1988) found that the social support within an ethnic community was instrumental in reducing the depression and facilitating the adjustment of Southeast Asian refugees. Finally, we have argued elsewhere that an ethnic enclave can be a promoting environment for the development of minority children (García Coll et al. in press).

Although earlier theories about and studies of minority status and self-esteem suggested that minorities internalized the dominant group's negative evaluation and thus had lower self-esteem, more recent studies have shown that this is not necessarily true (Gil et al. 1994). It seems as if some individuals who face racism or discrimination are able to transform harmful messages and render them harmless (García Coll et al. in press). Minority children undergo a process of racial or ethnic socialization whereby they learn to cope with the demands of living in a society that might devalue their race, culture, and heritage (García Coll et al. in press; García Coll, Meyer, and Brillon 1995).

Jenson, White, and Galliher (1982) looked at negative self-evaluation of minorities in different sites in Arizona. They found that although African American and Chicano students perceived greater mistreatment than their white counterparts, they were no less likely to "think highly of themselves and their schoolmates as a result of the mistreatment" (p. 238). Phinney, Chavira, and Tate (1993) studied the effect of showing minority adolescents negative or threatening information about their ethnic group. The study found that the videotaped information had an effect on the subjects' overall rating of their group but not their ethnic self-identification. The group that saw a negative tape rated their group less favorably than the group that saw a neutral tape. However, the individuals were able to differentiate between themselves and the group, "recognizing that the negative traits in their group did not necessarily reflect on its members" (Phinney et al. 1993:476).

Fernández-Kelly and Schauffler (1994) discussed how the ability to shift ethnic identities often provides "a defense from a stigma and an incentive to defy the leveling pressures" (p. 684). Immigrants may shift between identifying themselves as Mexican, Hispanic, or Latino depending on with whom they are speaking. Moreover, the authors pointed out that Cubans who were members of a successful group resisted being brought into a broader classification of Hispanic. They also comment that one of the strongest antidotes to the downward pull of gangs is a sense of membership in a group with an undamaged collective identity. In this manner, an individual's self-identification as an immigrant can protect him or her from "negative stereotypes and incorporation into more popular but less motivated groups" (Fernández-Kelly and Schauffler 1994:683).

One possible result of discrimination is the formation of cultural mistrust or an oppositional identity. *Cultural mistrust* was a term created to describe the lack of trust that blacks exhibit toward whites. In the early 1980s, Terrell and Terrell (1981) developed the Cultural Mistrust Inventory, which measured specific characteristics of black individuals who reflected mistrust. It measured mistrust in four areas: educational and training settings, political and legal systems, work and business arenas, and the social and interpersonal contexts. The mistrust is thought to develop because of exposure to prejudicial or discriminatory practices of white dominant society. "Among adolescents the first elements of mistrust are thought to develop in the home, where parents and siblings provide some initial definitions, parameters, and cautions of being black in a predominantly white society" (Biafora, Taylor, Warheit, Zimmerman, and Vega 1993:269). The educational system is also thought to play a significant role in forming cultural mistrust. The importance of the school context was demonstrated by Rotenberg and Cerda (1994). They studied Native American and white children attending fourth or fifth grade in same-race and mixed-race schools and found that the groups demonstrated higher levels of trust in members of their own race. In a same-race school, Native American children expected a white child to be less likely to keep promises and secrets or to tell the truth. However, trust patterns were different in mixed-race schools, where Native American children only expressed that they did not think that white children were as likely to keep a secret.

As a reaction to discrimination, cultural mistrust can provide a positive psychological defense mechanism, despite the negative connotations of mistrust (Biafora et al. 1993). Cross (1995) suggested that a black oppositional identity can serve several protective functions for blacks. The protection function involves an awareness of racism as part of the American experience; the anticipation of racism regardless of one's social, educational, or economic status; ego defenses to be employed when one is faced with racism; a predisposition to find fault in one's circumstances rather than in oneself; and a religious orientation that prevents the development of bitterness or hatred of whites. The black identity helps the individual deal with the problems that being black creates on a daily basis. It mitigates "the pain, imposition, and stigma that come when one is treated with disrespect, rudeness, and insensitivity" (Cross 1995:197).

Most of the research on this issue has been based on African American blacks, and little research has determined whether the level of mistrust found in African Americans is also found in other minorities or in blacks from other ethnic and cultural backgrounds. Biafora et al. (1993) showed that one-third of the black students in their sample expressed mistrust of whites. Of particular interest is that the researchers found that Haitians, especially those born outside of the United States, expressed the highest levels of mistrust, with nearly 50 percent believing that blacks should be suspicious of "friendly whites." However, students of Caribbean Island backgrounds, especially those born in the United States, reported the lowest levels of mistrust. Similarly, Taylor, Biafora, and Warheit (1994) found no difference in mistrust levels among black middle-school boys of African American, Haitian, and other Caribbean Island origins.

Some evidence suggests that this mistrust of white society may be manifested to some degree in other minority populations who face discrimination. Athey and Ahearn (1991) commented that "racism in the settlement society is often an impediment to reestablishing a trustful and ordered community life. It stigmatizes and further isolates refugees" (p. 15). Rumbaut's (1994) respondents who faced discrimination were less likely to identify as Americans, and respondents who thought that people would discriminate against them no matter how well-educated they became were more likely to self-identify with their nation of origin. Attending a school where the majority of students were minorities increased the identification of pan-ethnic labels. Rumbaut concluded that experiences of rejection or exclusion, based on ascribed traits, clearly undercut the process of assimilation. However, because immigrants may use their ethnic identities to shield themselves from the negative impact of racism or discrimination and to differentiate themselves from other minority groups within the United States, the relation between immigrant status and cultural mistrust or oppositional identity is complex. Immigrants who view other minority groups as the victims of their own individual and collective liabilities (Fernández-Kelly and Schauffler 1994) might be less likely to develop cultural mistrust or an oppositional identity.

In sum, immigrant children and adolescents in the United States must learn to cope with racism, discrimination, and prejudice as it is manifested in both overt and subtle ways. Furthermore, the different expectations and experiences with discrimination that immigrants of different generations encounter can create conflict within families. The coping mechanisms that children develop include both behavioral and psychological skills. Behaviorally, immigrant families often learn to cope with discrimination by living in an ethnic enclave. Psychologically, immigrant children and adolescents do not internalize the mainstream society's negative evaluations, and some immigrants, especially black immigrants, might form cultural mistrust or an oppositional identity. However, more research needs to be done to unravel and document the various ways in which children learn to cope with prejudice, racism, and discrimination and the factors that influence their perceptions and reactions to mainstream society.

CONCLUSIONS

The initial focus of this chapter was the psychological effects of migration on children. In the past, the guiding frameworks and research have concentrated on the negative impact of migration. More recently, we and others (Delgado-Gaitan 1994; Diaz 1985; Gil, Vega, and Dimas 1994; LaFromboise, Coleman, and Gerton 1993; Laosa 1989; Rumbaut 1991, 1994; and others) are trying to present a more balanced and thorough view. That is, throughout this chapter we have tried to take into account the possible positive benefits of migration, the influence of the developmental stage on the adjustment process, the complexity of the involved processes, and the crucial influence of the present historical, political, economical, and educational contexts.

Rumbaut and Rumbaut's (1976) metaphor of migration as an experience of both death and rebirth is very suitable. Although created to describe refugees in particular, this metaphor suggests that all immigrants face a range of experiences in migration and subsequent adaptation. The metaphor recognizes a certain amount of loss involved in the migration experience; it also recognizes a certain amount of rebirth as well. Just as older ways of life and familiar people and places are often lost, new places, opportunities, people, and experiences are found.

As developmentalists we argue that the impact and process of migration and subsequent acculturation will be largely dependent on a person's developmental needs and issues. It has been suggested many times that children acculturate faster (thereby implying easier) than others, thus making the age of contact important. However, we propose that the relation between age and speed and ease of acculturation is in most cases curvilinear rather than linear. During the infancy, toddler, and preschool years, the rate of acculturation is actually more a function of the family's acculturation rate and attitude toward the new culture than the child's actual potential for acculturation. There is no question that children from very early on, because of their potential for learning and actual drive for mastery, are able to acculturate faster than adults. However, we have to consider the context for learning before school entry, which is mainly influenced by the primary caregivers (García Coll et al. 1995). Young children first learn and absorb their concepts of ethnic labels, attitudes, and behaviors from their adult caretakers (Rotherham-Borus 1993). Thus, we might expect that the acculturation rate might be slower before entering school, daycare, or preschool, then faster after entry into any one of these settings (if the settings demand acculturation), and then slower again after the formative years.

In the early years, the rate of acculturation will depend almost entirely on the level of the acculturation of the family, including the primary caregivers and significant others like substitute caregivers (for example, grandparents) and older siblings. We have argued elsewhere that acculturation levels impact parenting styles by influencing developmental expectations, mother-infant interactions, and feeding and caregiving practices (García Coll et al. 1995). Aside from their own level of acculturation, the primary caregivers' and significant others' attitudes toward the new culture is another important factor. This attitude can vary from acceptance and reception to rejection and avoidance. Depending on this attitude, for example, a mother may try—or not—to teach English to her toddler or may place her child in a primarily ethnically consonant setting. Rueschenberg and Buriel (1989) found that Mexican families' level of acculturation was positively associated with their utilization of external resources, even though the use of internal resources was not affected by their level of acculturation. Thus, a family who was very acculturated employed external resources to a higher degree than a less acculturated family, even if the two families maintained similar internal structures.

As a child grows and begins to be exposed to influences outside the family, the characteristics of these settings also affect the rate of acculturation (García Coll et al. 1995). With increasing age, there is a growing consistency between the children's understanding and the normative beliefs regarding ethnicity and society. Does the new setting affirm or celebrate diversity? Does it include instruction in the child's language and cultural background or demand complete acculturation? Are the available role models similar to those in the child's original culture or are there other attributes, values, and beliefs celebrated? What is the composition of the peer group, and, more important, what are the values of the group toward the two cultures and their interaction? As children grow into adolescents they actively determine their self-schema. Their choices, in part a reflection of their earlier socialization, are given to greater variation and independence (Rotherham-Borus, 1993). Consequently, during this period their choices are more reflective of their peer group and other institutions.

Finally, as developmentalists we are not willing to toss aside the many contexts that affect the child's development. We are aware that, as important as the individual's characteristics and developmental needs are, we must simultaneously seek an understanding of the contexts in which individuals grow and develop (Laosa 1989; Rumbaut 1994). These contexts include political, historical, economic, and educational circumstances of the sending and receiving communities, which play an active role in determining whether children accrue more positive or more negative outcomes from the experience of migration and the subsequent process of acculturation. For example, if unemployment is high in the receiving community, it will be difficult for the immigrant family to find work. They will suffer economically and will not feel as if they have gained a sense of mastery of their new environment. Similarly, if the receiving community's governmental policy is fiscally conservative, immigrant families might have less access to financial assistance or medical care, creating further obstacles to successful adaptation. Finally, migration in an era in which newcomers are considered a burden and therefore unwelcome by the receiving society, and in which racial and ethnic tensions are day-to-day occurrences, provides a different context for adaptation than an era in which newcomers are welcomed.

What we have yet to address is what determines whether the experience will be positive or negative, or what combination of positive and negative effects will be manifested for any one child. The answer seems to be that every child faces dialectical forces, challenges that can be positive or negative depending on the individual's characteristics, the family's characteristics, and the immediate and larger contextual forces that influence children, adolescents, and their families.

References

Aronowitz, M. 1984. The social and emotional adjustment of immigrant children: A review of the literature. *International Review of Migration* 18:237–257.

Ashworth, M. 1982. The cultural adjustment of immigrant children in English Canada. In R. C. Nann, ed. *Uprooting and Surviving*. Boston: D. Reidel.

Athey, J. L., and F. L. Ahearn. 1991. The mental health of refugee children: An overview. In J. L. Athey and F. L. Ahearn, eds. *Refugee Children: Theory, Research, and Services*. Baltimore, MD: Johns Hopkins University Press.

Baptiste, D. A. 1987. Family therapy with Spanish-heritage immigrant families in cultural transition. *Contemporary Family Therapy* 9:229–251.

Baptiste, D. A. 1993. Immigrant families, adolescents, and acculturation: Insights for therapists. *Marriage and Family Review* 19:341–363.

Beiser, M. 1988. Influences of time, ethnicity, and attachment on depression in Southeast Asian refugees. *American Journal of Psychiatry* 145:46–51.

Berry, J. 1990. Acculturation and adaptation: A general framework. In W. H. Holtzman and T. H. Borneman, eds. *The Mental Health of Immigrants and Refugees*. Austin, TX: Hogg Foundation for Mental Health, University of Texas.

Berry, J. W., Kim, U., Minde, T., and Mok, D. 1987. Comparative studies of acculturative stress. *International Migration Review* 21:491–511.

Biafora, F. A., Taylor, D. L., Warheit, G. J., Zimmerman, R. S., and Vega, W. A. 1993. Cultural mistrust and racial awareness among ethnically diverse black adolescent boys. *Journal of Black Psychology* 19:266–281.

Brody, E. B. 1966. Cultural exclusion, character, and illness. *American Journal of Psychiatry* 122:852–858.

Brody, E. B. 1990. Mental health and world citizenship: Sociocultural bases for advocacy. In W. H. Holtzman and T. H. Borneman, eds. *The Mental Health of Immigrants and Refugees.* Austin, TX: Hogg Foundation for Mental Health, University of Texas.

Burke, A. W. 1980. Family stress and the precipitation of psychiatric disorder: A comparative study among immigrant West Indian and British patients in Birmingham. *International Journal of Social Psychiatry* 26:35–40.

Carlin, J. 1990. Refugee and immigrant populations at special risk: Women, children and the elderly. In W. H. Holtzman and T. H. Borneman, eds. *The Mental Health of Immigrants and Refugees.* Austin, TX: Hogg Foundation for Mental Health, University of Texas.

Chud, B. 1982. The threshold model: A conceptual framework for understanding and assisting children of immigrants. In R. C. Nann, ed. *Uprooting and Surviving.* Boston: D. Reidel.

Cochrane, R. 1979. Psychological and behavioral disturbance in West Indians, Indians, and Pakistanis in Britain. *British Journal of Psychiatry* 134:201–210.

Cole, M., and Scribner, S. 1974. *Culture and Thought.* New York: Wiley.

Compas, B. E. 1987. Coping with stress during childhood and adolescence. *Psychological Bulletin* 101:393–403.

Cornille, T. A., and Brotherton, W. D. 1993. Applying the developmental family therapy model to issues of migrating families. *Marriage and Family Review* 19:325–340.

Cropley, A. J. 1983. *The education of immigrant children.* London: Croom Helm.

Cross, W. E. 1995. Oppositional identity and African American youth: Issues and prospects. In W. D. Hawley and A. W. Jackson, eds. *Toward a Common Destiny: Improving Race and Ethnic Relations in America.* San Francisco: Jossey-Bass.

Dasen, P. R., and Heron, A. 1981. Cross-cultural test of Piaget's theory. In H. C. Triandis and A. Heron, eds. *Handbook of Cross-Cultural Psychology: Volume 4. Developmental Psychology.* Boston: Allyn & Bacon.

Delgado-Gaitan, C. 1994. Socializing young children in Mexican-American families: An intergenerational perspective. In P. M. Greenfield and R. R. Cocking, eds. *Cross-Cultural Roots of Minority Child Development.* Hillsdale, NJ: Lawrence Erlbaum Associates.

Derbyshire, R. L. 1970. Adaptation of adolescent Mexican Americans to United States society. In E. B. Brody, ed. *Behavior in New Environments.* Beverly Hills, CA: Sage.

Diaz, R. M. 1985. Bilingual cognitive development: Addressing three gaps in current research. *Child Development* 56:1376–1388.

Diaz, R. M., and Klinger, C. 1991. Towards an explanatory model of interaction between bilingualism and cognitive development. In E. Bialystok, ed. *Language Processing in Bilingual Children.* New York: Cambridge University Press.

Duckitt, J. 1992. Psychology and prejudice. *American Psychologist* 47:1182–1193.

Eisenbruch, M. 1988. The mental health of refugee children and their cultural development. *International Migration Review* 22:282–300.

Ekstrand. L. H. 1976. Adjustment among immigrant pupils in Sweden. *International Review of Applied Psychology* 25:167–188.

El-Sheikh, M., and Klaczynski, P. A. 1993. Cultural variability in stress and control. *Journal of Cross-Cultural Psychology* 24:81–98.

Espino, C. M. 1991. Trauma and adaptation: The case of Central American children. In J. L. Athey and F. L. Ahearn, eds. *Refugee Children: Theory, Research, and Services.* Baltimore: Johns Hopkins University Press.

Fernández-Kelly, M. P., and Schauffler, R. 1994. Divided fates: Immigrant children in a restructured U.S. economy. *International Migration Review* 28:662–689.

García Coll, C. T. 1990. Developmental outcomes of minority infants: A process-oriented look into our beginnings. *Child Development* 61:270–289.

García Coll, C. T., Lambert, G., Jenkins, R., McAdoo, H. P., Crnic, K., Wasik, B. H., and Vázquez García, H. A. (in press). An integrative model for the study of developmental competencies in minority children. *Child Development.*

García Coll, C. T., Meyer, E. C., and Brillon, L. 1995. Ethnic and minority parenting. In M. Bornstein, ed. *Handbook of Parenting: Vol. 2. Biology and Ecology of Parenting.* Hillsdale, NJ: Lawrence Erlbaum Associates.

Gil, A., Vega, W. A., and Dimas, J. M. 1994. Acculturative stress and personal adjustment among Hispanic adolescent boys. *Journal of Community Psychology* 22:43–54.

Graham, P. J., and Meadows, C. E. 1967. Psychiatric disorder in the children of West Indian immigrants. *Journal of Child Psychology and Psychiatry* 8:105–116.

Hakuta, K., Ferdman, B., and Diaz, R. M. 1987. Bilingualism and cognitive development: Three perspectives. In S. Rosenberg, ed. *Advances in Applied Linguistics, Volume 2.* New York: Cambridge University Press.

Hirschman, C. 1994. Problems and prospects of studying immigrant adaptation from the 1990 Population Census: From generational comparisons to the process of becoming American." *International Migration Review* 28:690–713.

Inbar, M. 1977. Immigration and learning: The vulnerable age. *Canadian Review of Sociology and Anthropology* 14:218–234.

Jenson, G. F., White, C. S., and Galliher, J. M. 1982. "Ethnic status and adolescent self-evaluations: An extension of research on minority self-esteem. *Social Problems* 30:226–239.

Kallarackal, A. M., and Herbert, M. 1976, February 26. The happiness of immigrant children. *New Society* 422–424.

Knight, G. P., Bernal, M. E., Garza, C. A., Cota, M. K., and Ocampo, K. A. 1993. Family socialization and the ethnic identity of Mexican-American children. *Journal of Cross-Cultural Psychology 24*:99–114.

Koplow, L., and Messinger, E. 1990. Developmental dilemmas of young children of immigrant parents. *Child and Adolescent Social Work* 7:121–134.

LaFromboise, T., Coleman, H. L. K., and Gerton, J. 1993. Psychological impact of biculturalism: Evidence and theory. *Psychological Bulletin* 114:395–412.

Lambert, W. E. 1977. The effects of bilingualism on the individual: Cognitive and sociocultural consequences. In P. A. Hornby, ed. *Bilingualism: Psychological, Social, and Educational Implications.* New York: Academic Press.

Lambert, W. E., and Taylor, D. M. 1990. Language and culture in the lives of immigrants and refugees. In W. H. Holtzman and T. H. Borneman, eds. *The Mental Health of Immigrants and Refugees.* Austin, TX: Hogg Foundation for Mental Health, University of Texas.

Laosa, L. 1989. *Psychosocial Stress, Coping, and the Development of Hispanic Immigrant Children.* Princeton, NJ: Educational Testing Service.

Leslie, L. A. 1993. Families fleeing war: The case of Central Americans. *Marriage and Family Review* 19:193–205.

Lipson, J. G., and Meleis, A. I. 1989. Methodological issues in research with immigrants. *Medical Anthropology* 12:103–115.

Maccoby, E. E. 1983. Socio-emotional development and response to stressors. In N. Garmezy and M. Rutter, eds. *Stress, Coping, and Development in Children.* New York: McGraw-Hill.

Mendelberg. H. E. 1986. Identity conflict in Mexican American adolescents. *Adolescence* 21:215–224.

Nicol, A. R. 1971. Psychiatric disorder in the children of Caribbean immigrants. *Journal of Child Psychology and Psychiatry* 12:273–287.

Osofsky, J. D. 1995. The effect of exposure to violence on young children. *American Psychologist* 50:782–788.

Padilla, A. M., Cervantes, R. C., Maldonado, M., and Garcia, R. E. 1988. Coping responses to psychosocial stressors among Mexican and Central American immigrants. *Journal of Community Psychology* 16:418–427.

Padilla, A. M., and Lindholm, K. J. 1984. Child bilingualism: The same old issues revisited. In J. L. Martinez and R. H. Mendoza, eds. *Chicano Psychology.* New York: Academic Press.

Paulston, C. B. 1978. Education in a bi/multicultural setting. *International Review of Education* 24:302–328.

Phinney, J. S. 1990. Ethnic identity in adolescents and adults: Review of research. *Psychological Bulletin* 108:499–514.

Phinney, J. S. 1993. A three-stage model of ethnic identity development in adolescents. In M. E. Bernal and G. P. Knight, eds. *Ethnic Identity: Formation and Transmission among Hispanic and Other Minorities.* Albany, NY: State University of New York Press.

Phinney, J. S., Chavira, V., and Tate, J. D. 1993. The effect of ethnic threat on ethnic self concept and own-group ratings. *The Journal of Social Psychology* 133:469–478.

Porte, Z., and Torney-Purta, J. 1987. Depression and academic achievement among Indochinese refugee unaccompanied minors in ethnic and nonethnic placements. *American Journal of Orthopsychiatry* 57:536–547.

Pynoos, R. S. 1993. Traumatic stress and developmental psychopathology in children and adolescents. In J. M. Oldhams, M. B. Riba, and A. Tasman, eds. *American Psychiatric Press Review of Psychiatry (Vol. 12).* Washington, DC: American Psychiatric Press.

Ramirez, M. 1983. *Psychology of the Americas: Mestizo Perspectives on Personality and Mental Health.* Elmsford, NY: Pergamon.

Ramirez, M. 1984. Assessing and understanding biculturalism-multiculturalism in Mexican-American adults. In J. L. Martinez and R. H. Mendoza, Eds. *Chicano Psychology.* New York: Academic Press.

Ressler, E. M., Boothby, N., Steinbock, D. J. 1988. *Unaccompanied Children: Care and Protection in Wars, Natural Disasters, and Refugee Movements.* New York: Oxford University Press.

Rodriguez, C. 1975. A cost-benefit analysis of subjective factors affecting assimilation: Puerto Ricans. *Ethnicity* 2:66–80.

Rodriguez, R. 1973. Difficulties of adjustment in immigrant children in Geneva. In C. Zwingman and M. Pfister-Ammende, Eds. *Uprooting and After ….* New York: Springer-Verlag.

Rogler, L. H., Cortes, D. E., and Malgady, R. G. 1991. Acculturation and mental health status among Hispanics: Convergence and new directions for research. *American Psychologist* 46:585–597.

Rosenthal, D. 1987. Ethnic identity development in adolescents. In J. Phinney and M. Rotherham, eds. *Children's Ethnic Socialization: Pluralism and Development.* Beverly Hills, CA: Sage.

Rotenberg, K. J., and Cerda, C. 1994. Racially based trust expectancies of Native Americans and Caucasian children. *Journal of Social Psychology* 134:621–631.

Rotherham-Borus, M. J. 1989. The impact of ethnic identity in different school settings. Symposium on Ethnicity and Mental Health, Manhattan Children's Psychiatric Center, New York.

Rotherham-Borus, M. J. 1990. Adolescents' reference-group choices, self-esteem, and adjustment. *Journal of Personality and Social Psychology* 59:1075–1081.

Rotherham-Borus, M. J. 1993. Biculturalism among adolescents. In M. E. Bernal and G. P. Knight, eds. *Ethnic Identity: Formation and Transmission among Hispanic and Other Minorities.* Albany, NY: State University of New York Press.

Rueschenberg, E., and Buriel, R. 1989. Mexican American family functioning and acculturation: A family systems perspective. *Hispanic Journal of Behavioral Sciences* 11:232–244.

Rumbaut, R. G. 1988. The adaptation of Southeast Asian refugee youth: A comparative perspective. Paper presented at the thirteenth annual meeting of the Social Science History Association, Chicago, IL.

Rumbaut, R. G. 1991. The agony of exile: A study of the migration and adaptation of Indo-chinese refugee adults and children. In J. L. Athey and F. L. Ahearn, eds. *Refugee Children: Theory, Research, and Services.* Baltimore: Johns Hopkins University Press.

Rumbaut, R. G. 1994. The crucible within: Ethnic identity, self-esteem, and the segmented assimilation among children of immigrants. *International Migration Review* 28:748–794.

Rumbaut, R., and Rumbaut, R. 1976. The family in exile: Cuban expatriates in the United States. *American Journal of Psychiatry* 133:395–399.

Rutter, M. 1979. Protective factors in children's responses to stress and disadvantage. In M. W. Kent and J. E. Rolf, eds. *Primary Prevention of Psychopathology: Vol. III. Social Competence.* Hanover, NH: University Press of New England.

Rutter, M. 1983. Stress, coping, and development: Some issues and some questions. In N. Garmezy and M. Rutter, eds. *Stress, Coping, and Development in Children.* New York: McGraw-Hill.

Rutter, M., Yule, W., Berger, M., Yule, B., Morton, J., and Bagley, C. 1974. Children of West Indian immigrants-I. Rates of behavioral deviance and psychiatric disorder. *Journal of Child Psychiatry* 15:241–262.

Sam, D. L. 1994. The psychological adjustment of young immigrants in Norway. *Scandinavian Journal of Psychology* 35:240–253.

Schrader, A. 1978. The "vulnerable" age: Findings on foreign children in Germany. *Sociology of Education* 51:227–230.

Seifer, R., and Sameroff, A. J. 1987. Multiple determinants of risk and invulnerability. In E. J. Anthony and B. J. Cohler, eds. *The Invulnerable Child.* New York: Guilford.

Sluzki, C. E. 1979. Migration and family conflict. *Family Process* 18:379–390.

Spencer, M. B., Swanson, D. P., and Cunningham, M. 1991. Ethnicity, ethnic identity, and competence formation: Adolescent transition and cultural transformation. *Journal of Negro Education* 60:366–387.

Sung, B. L. 1985. Bicultural conflicts in Chinese immigrant children. *Journal of Comparative Family Studies* 26:255–269.

Szapocznik, J., Kurtines, W. M., and Fernandez, T. 1981. Bicultural involvement and adjustment in Hispanic-American youth. *International Journal of Intercultural Relations* 4:353–375.

Taylor, D. L., Biafora, F. A., Warheit, G. J. 1994. Racial mistrust and disposition to deviance among African American, Haitian, and other Caribbean Island adolescent boys. *Law and Human Behavior* 18:291–303.

Terrell, F. T., and Terrell, S. 1981. An inventory to measure cultural mistrust among blacks. *The Western Journal of Black Studies* 5:180–185.

Touhatos, J., and Lindholm, B. W. 1980. Behavioral disturbance in children of native-born and immigrant parents. *Journal of Community Psychology* 8:28–33.

Tradd, P. V., and Greenblatt, E. 1990. Psychological aspects of child stress: Development and the spectrum of coping responses. In E. Arnold, ed. *Childhood Stress.* New York: Wiley.

Tropp, L. R., Ekrut, S., Alarcon, O., García Coll, C., and Vázquez, H. A. 1994. Toward a theoretical model of psychological acculturation. *Working Paper Series,* No. 268. Wellesley, MA: Center for Research on Women.

Vega, W. A., and Rumbaut, R. G. 1991. Ethnic minorities and mental health. *Annual Review of Sociology* 17:351–383.

Wagner, D. A. 1978. Memories of Morocco: The influence of age, schooling, and environment on memory. *Cognitive Psychology* 10:1–28.

Wagner, D. 1981. Culture and memory development. In H. C. Triandis and A. Heron, eds. *Handbook of Cross-Cultural Psychology, Vol. 4: Developmental Psychology.* Boston: Allyn & Bacon.

Waters, M. C. in press. The intersection of gender, race, and ethnicity in identity development of Caribbean American teens. In B. Leadbetter and N. Way, eds. *Urban Adolescent Girls: Resisting Stereotypes.* New York: New York University Press.

Weinberg, A. 1979. Mental health aspects of voluntary migration. In C. Zwingman and M. Pfister-Ammende, eds. *Uprooting and After ....* New York: Springer-Verlag.

Westermeyer, J. 1989. *Mental Health for Refugees and other Migrants: Social and Preventive Approaches.* Springfield, IL: Thomas.

Zambrana, R. E., and Silva-Palacios, V. 1989. Gender differences in stress among Mexican immigrant adolescents in Los Angeles, California. *Journal of Adolescent Research* 4:426–442.

Zavala Martinez, I. 1994a. "Entremundos: Psychological processes of migration. In G. Lamberty and C. García Coll, eds. *Health and Development of Puerto Rican Women and Children in the United States.* New York: Plenum.

Zavala Martinez, I. 1994b. Quién soy? Who am I? Identity issues for Puerto Rican adolescents. In E. P. Salett and D. R. Koslow, eds. *Race, Ethnicity and Self.* Washington, DC: National Multicultural Institute.

Chapter 7

Identities Under Siege: Immigration Stress and Social Mirroring among the Children of Immigrants

CAROLA SUÀREZ-OROZCO

INTRODUCTION

Immigration is a phenomenon that involves more than 130 million people worldwide. In the United States, one out of every five children is the child of an immigrant. In New York City schools today, forty-eight percent of all students come from immigrant-headed households. This is not only an urban phenomenon: Schools across the country are encountering large numbers of children from immigrant families. It is increasingly clear that the adaptations of these children will be an important factor in the remaking of the American economy and society.

For many individuals, migration results in substantial gains. Some escape political, religious, or ethnic persecution while others migrate for economic reasons. Long-separated families may be reunited. Some immigrants are motivated by the opportunity for social mobility while others migrate in the spirit of adventure. Whatever their motives, immigration is considered worthwhile for many. Still, the gains of immigration come at considerable costs that could not have been anticipated at the moment of departure. The costs and pressures of migration are in particular felt by the children of immigrants.

The pressures of migration are profoundly felt by the children of immigrants. These children experience a particular constellation of changes and experiences that are likely to have an impact on their developing psyches. In this chapter, I examine how the stresses of immigration are complicated by both the structural barriers and the "social mirroring" of nativist responses and racism that many immigrant children encounter. When the inherent stresses of immigration are compounded by patterns of structural and psychological violence, immigration becomes traumatic.

Surprisingly little research has focused on the psychological experiences of immigrant children (Garcia-Coll and Magnuson 1998). Much of the work to date either has emphasized the adult immigrant experience or has examined the physical rather than the psychological health of these children. This chapter is a theoretical contribution to this emerging field based on analyses of the first wave of data from the Longitudinal Immigrant Student Adaptation Study (a large-scale interdisciplinary research project that I co-direct with Marcelo Suárez-Orozco). This project involved five groups of immigrant children from China, Central America, the Dominican Republic, Haiti, and Mexico. We followed 425 recently arrived immigrant children over the course of five years.[1] Using anthropological and psychological techniques, we assessed the children's adaptation to the new society, with particular emphasis on the schooling context.

STRESSES OF IMMIGRATION

Transitions of any kind have long been regarded by social scientists and mental health professionals to be stressful (Schlossberg 1984). Events such as moves, job changes, and ruptures in relationships are known to be highly disruptive, often triggering a variety of reactions including anxiety, anger, depression, somatic complaints, and illness (Dohrenwend 1986). Stress is particularly noxious when the individual is unable to cope in his or her usual manner. The stakes are even higher when he or she perceives that there are serious consequences to not adapting (House 1974). Both of these conditions are met in the process of immigration.

By any measure, immigration is one of the most stressful events a person can undergo. Most critically, immigration removes individuals from many of their relationships and predictable contexts: extended families and friends, community ties, jobs, living situations, customs, and (often) language. Immigrants are stripped of many of their sustaining social relationships as well as of their roles that provide them with culturally scripted notions of how they fit into the world. Without a sense of competence, control, and belonging, they may feel marginalized. These changes are highly disorienting and nearly inevitably lead to a keen sense of loss (Ainslie 1998; Grinberg and Grinberg 1989).

At the most dramatic end of the stress spectrum are the stresses that result in post-traumatic stress disorder (PTSD) symptomatology. Events such as experiencing or witnessing killing, rape, or torture often lead to transient as well as long-term symptomatology. Recent arrivals originating from the former Yugoslavia, Somalia, Indochina, Central America, and Haiti are examples of immigrants who come from regions where they may well have undergone trauma (Somach 1995). Symptom clusters resulting from PTSD include recurrent traumatic memories and a general numbing of responses, as well as a persistent sense of increased arousal leading to intense anxiety, irritability, and outbursts of anger, difficulty concentrating, and insomnia (Horowitz 1986; Smajkic and Weane 1995). Immigrants who experience trauma will often suffer recurring waves of these symptoms over a period of time; the severity of the symptoms will depend on the extent of the trauma and the psychological, social, and material resources available to the victims. These symptoms add significantly to the stresses of immigration.

Concern with violence is a recurring theme that we have found among many of our informants. An alarming number of immigrant children experience a variety of forms of stress, which may lead to post-traumatic symptomatology. In addition to the violence experienced prior to migration (in the cases where families are fleeing war or civil unrest), all too many immigrant children witness a disconcertingly high level of violence in their new neighborhood and school settings (see below). Furthermore, the actual border crossing is often a traumatic event for adults and children alike.

Scholars and human rights observers of the U.S.-Mexican border—the most heavily trafficked in the world—have noted that undocumented border crossers are subject to a variety of dangers, including exposure to environmental extremes (Eschbach et al. 1997) and violence at the hands of border agents, "coyotes" (paid crossing guides), and others (Amnesty International 1998:24). According to a recent Amnesty International report, "women are at particular risk of being physically abused, raped, robbed, or murdered on their journey" (1998:24). The number of women who are raped sometime during their crossing journey is reported to be very high.

Our own interviews with immigrant children reveal that many of them find the border crossing highly traumatic. Some report actual events that occur to them (such as being detained, deported, humiliated, or beaten). Others report perceptions of potential danger. A nine-year-old Mexican boy with clearly evident fear in his voice told us of his crossing: "I had to be careful of where I put my feet. My parents told me that the *migra* [slang term for agents of the Immigration and Naturalization Service] had put piranhas in the river to keep us away."[2]

Another form of stress specific to immigration has been termed acculturation (or acculturative) stress (Berry 1998; Flaskerud and Uman 1996; Smart and Smart 1995). Acculturation refers to the process whereby individuals learn and come to terms with the new cultural "rules of engagement." The individual's place of origin provides her with familiar and predictable contexts; these predictable contexts change in dramatic ways following immigration. As Polish immigrant Eva Hoffmann says in her exquisitely written memoirs, immigration results in falling "out of the net of meaning into the weightlessness of chaos" (Hoffmann 1989:151). Without a sense of competence, control, and belonging, migrants are often left with a keen sense of loss and marginality. A twenty-three-year-old Mexican informant insightfully summed up the experience: "I became an infant again. I had to learn all over again to eat, to speak, to dress, and what was expected of me."

RESPONSES TO THE STRESSES OF IMMIGRATION

While anticipating the migration and the initial period following the arrival, many immigrants experience a sense of euphoria (Sluzki 1979). Expectations are often high as the anticipated possibilities may seem boundless. Energies are focused on attending to the immediate needs of orienting themselves in the new environment, including finding work and a place to live. As the realities of the new situation are confronted, individuals normatively begin to experience a variety of psychological problems (Ainslie 1998; Arrendondo-Dowd 1981; Grinberg and Grinberg 1989; Rumbaut 1977; Sluzki 1979; Suárez-Orozco 1998). Most frequently, the cumulative losses of loved ones and familiar contexts lead to feelings along a spectrum of sadness to depression to "perpetual mourning" (Volkan 1993). The dissonances in cultural expectations and of predictable contexts lead many to experience an anxious disorientation (Grinberg and Grinberg 1989). Disappointed aspirations and dreams, when coupled with a hostile reception in the new environment, may lead to feelings of distrust, suspicion, anger, and even well-founded paranoia (Grinberg and Grinberg 1989).

The repercussions of the responses at the individual level are felt within the family. Sluzki (1979) argues that migration has destabilizing effects on the family. Indeed, migration creates particular pressures on the family system. It is not unusual for there to be an increase in conflict between family members following migration (particularly if there was preexisting marital tension). Migration often creates changes within the structure of the family: Former family leaders may be "demoted" (Shuval 1980) and the nature of the gender relationships may shift. Espin argues that "immigrant families may become entrenched in traditional social and sex role norms as a defense against the strong pressures to acculturate" (1987:493). In other cases, as immigrant women move into the workplace, their new role as family providers may at once provide them with new-found independence and create tensions within their relationships.

Many immigrant families incorporate extended family members and are more interdependent and hierarchical than traditional Anglo-American families (Smart and Smart 1995). Some of these characteristics may be in part culturally determined but others may be secondary to migration. Extended families will often live together to share both the financial and the childcare burdens. In the absence of other social support networks, they may rely on each other considerably more than most non-immigrant families.

Immigrant parents often have to make dramatic sacrifices for what they hope will be a better future for their children. Frequently they are fiercely protective of their children with deep-seated concerns about the perceived dangers of the new environment (including the potential of becoming too Americanized). Within the new context, they may set limits that are significantly more stringent than they would have had they stayed in their country of origin. At the same time, immigrant parents are often quite dependent upon their children. The children may develop language skills more quickly than their parents and consequently serve as interpreters and errand-runners for the family. Alternating between "parentifying" the children and, at the same time, severely constricting their activities and contacts, may create significant tensions within the family.

Many immigrant parents (particularly those coming from poorer families) work in several jobs. These multiple obligations lead them to be relatively unavailable to their children. For example, because their work schedules do not permit much flexibility, immigrant parents are often unable to attend school functions; as a result, educators lament the perceived lack of interest in their children's education. It is a mistake, however, to automatically interpret this as lack of interest or concern. Immigrant parents often tell us that they feel that working hard is the best way they can help their children; yet these long work hours leave the children unattended. This physical absence compounds the psychological unavailability that often accompanies parental anxiety and depression (Athey and Ahearn 1991). These two forms of absence all too frequently leave immigrant children to their own devices long before it is developmentally appropriate. While in some cases this leads to hyper-responsible internalized children, in other cases it leads to depressed children who are drawn to the lure of alternative family structures such as gangs (Vigil 1988).

The time frame for adaptation to the new culture is usually quite different for children than for adults. Children are quickly forced to contend with the host society more intensely than their parents. Schools represent an important first host-culture site encountered by the children. There they meet teachers (who are usually members of the dominant culture) as well as children from both the majority and other minority backgrounds. Hence, they are forced to contend more quickly and more intensely with the new culture than do their parents, who are likely to work in jobs that do not require much in the way of language skills or that may be largely populated by other members of the immigrant community (M. Suárez-Orozco 1998). The relative rapidity of the children's adaptation may create particular tensions. Parents may try to slow down the process by warning children not to act like other children in the new setting. Children may also have feelings ranging from vague to intense embarrassment in regard to aspects of their parents' "old-country" and "old-fashioned" ways.

The potential for miscommunication should not be overlooked or underestimated in immigrant families. As noted earlier, children often learn the new language more quickly than do their parents. Most children long to be like others; many will quickly show a preference for the language of the dominant culture (Portes and Hao 1998). Furthermore, even if the child continues to speak the home language, the level of fluency is likely to be influenced by the fact that after a number of years in the new culture, without a concerted effort, the vocabulary and literacy level of the language of origin usually lags far behind that of the host culture. Hence, while the child may easily communicate about basic needs in her language of origin, she is likely to have more difficulty communicating subtleties of thought and emotion in that language (Wong-Fillmore 1991). By the same token, often the opposite is true with the parents. Hence, one of the parties in the conversation is likely to be at a disadvantage in complicated communication sequences. Furthermore, in complex discussions, subtleties of meanings are likely to be missed and miscommunication may result. It is not uncommon to overhear discussions in which parents and children switch back and forth between languages and completely miss one another's intent. Children are also not above deliberately misleading their parents. A thirteen-year-old Mexican boy admitted to us that he had told his parents that the "F" on his report card stood for "fabulous"!

Our new research suggests that tensions between parents and children are particularly heightened in cases where the children have been separated from their parents for long periods of time. A number of the new immigrants are following a pattern whereby one or both parents go ahead to the host country and leave the children with relatives. These separations often last for several years. During this time, the child is likely to attach himself to a new caretaker, who may or may not have affectionately attended to his needs. If the child succeeds in attaching to the new caretaker, the separation from this caretaker in order to be reunited with the parent can be quite painful (compounding the mourning and loss that follows the immigration). If the separation was painful and the child was neglected or abused, this too will complicate the adjustment following migration. In any case, there is likely to be some fallout following these years of separation prior to migration (particularly within the Caribbean immigrant community as well as, increasingly, within the recent Central American community and from some areas in China).

A number of factors may significantly attenuate the severity of response to the transitions and stress of immigration (Garcia-Coll and Magnuson 1997; Laosa 1989; Rúmbaut 1996). These mediating variables can roughly be broken down into two categories: sending factors and receiving factors.

MEDIATING FACTORS

The sending context

Each individual brings with him characteristics, traits, and experiences that are referred to as sending (or antecedent) factors. The circumstances surrounding the migration can play a key role. Was the individual "pushed or pulled" out of his country of origin? If the immigrant is lured out of his homeland by the promise of opportunity and adventure, he is likely to be more positively disposed to the experience than if he is "pushed" out by ethnic, religious, or political conflict, chronic hardship, or famine in the homeland. By the same token, at least initially, the individual initiating the migration is likely to be more enthusiastic about the experience than a reluctant spouse, elderly parent, or child (Shuval 1980). We have found that children in particular often have little understanding of the reasons behind the motivation to migrate. As a result, they may not pass through a stage of looking forward in anticipation to the migration and may experience the move as an imposition upon them from which they have little to gain.

Pre-immigration stress and trauma may be critical to the subsequent adaptation of immigrants. Did he experience trauma that was directly linked to the decision to migrate? Individuals and families who flee conflict-torn areas may have witnessed traumatic events and may have been subjected to torture and other forms of physical and psychological violence (Suárez-Orozco 1989). This is almost always true of refugees, a special kind of migrant. In addition, as noted earlier, these traumas may be compounded by further violence during the actual process of migration.

Socioeconomic background has been found to be a consistent mediator of the stresses of the migration process (Flaskerud and Uman 1996). Higher levels of education as well as economic resources play a decisive role in minimizing structural impediments (C. Suárez-Orozco 1998). On the whole, upper-middle-class immigrants sustain the least loss. They may be able to retain much of their prestige and may be able to travel back and forth to maintain their social relationships. Individuals and families of middle and lower classes are less likely to have opportunities to visit and may particularly suffer from being cut off from their loved ones.

Immigrants of middle-class backgrounds often experience significant losses in prestige. They frequently find employment in positions far below their training and qualifications because of language difficulties, lack of connections, or lack of certification in certain professions. In addition, middle-class immigrants may suffer for the first time the painful experience of prejudice and discrimination in the new country. The poorest immigrants, who are largely members of the lower classes in their country of origin, often suffer tremendous adversity as a result of immigration. In spite of these difficulties—which may include xenophobia, racism, and fierce competition for the least desirable jobs—they often achieve relative improvements in their economic and social circumstances. In addition, while they certainly suffer from discrimination in the new country, social disparagement may not necessarily be a new experience. As members of the lower socioeconomic class, they are likely to have suffered such treatment in their country of origin.

Personality and temperamental factors are likely to play a significant role in how the individual will respond to the migration process (Garcia-Coll and Magnuson 1997; Shuval 1980). A healthy response to dramatic change requires the ability to be flexible and adaptable to new circumstances. Individuals who are particularly rigid, or who have a high need for predictability, are likely to suffer more than those who are more comfortable with change and new circumstances (Wheaton 1983). Those who are particularly shy, proud, or sensitive to outside opinions are also at higher risk as are those who are highly suspicious of the motivations of others. An effective arsenal of coping strategies, on the other hand, is a great asset (Lazarus and Folkman 1984; Pearlin and Schooler 1978).

By the same token, psychological and physical health prior to migration will also aid or impede the ease of the response to immigration. Individuals who are suffering from post-traumatic stress (as discussed earlier) are of course highly at risk. So, too, are individuals who suffer from depressive tendencies as well as any number of other psychiatric disorders. Physical health may also play a role, particularly if an illness or disability interferes with either maintaining gainful employment or with general quality of life.

A variety of other sending factors can also help to mediate the migration process. Possessing the language skills of the new country, clearly, is an asset. Religiosity and connection with a church may also play a positive role. The rural-to-urban shift (a not uncommon pattern for many immigrants) on the other hand may complicate the case of transition. Many immigrant children in our study report to us that they find it very difficult to adjust to the *encerramiento* (Spanish for being "shut-in"). While they may have had considerable freedom to play and roam their neighborhoods in their place of origin, they often lose such freedoms when they move to an urban environment.

The receiving context

Just as a number of factors related to the sending situation will ease or impede the adjustment to the new context, conditions in the new host milieu will also play a significant role. At the top of the list is the availability of a social support network. The relative absence of social support has been linked to the etiology of disease, mortality, slowed recovery, and mental illness. By the same token, the presence of a healthy social support network has long been regarded to be a key mediator to stress (Cobb 1988; Cohen and Syme 1985).

Interpersonal relationships provide a number of functions (Wills 1985). Instrumental social support includes the provision of tangible aid (such as running an errand or making a loan) as well as guidance and advice (including job and housing leads) that are so much needed by disoriented newcomers. Social companionship also serves to maintain and enhance self-esteem and provides much-needed acceptance and approval. A well-functioning social support network, quite predictably, is closely linked to better adjustment to the new environment. Of course, in part, the availability of an effective social support structure will be influenced by the individuals' preexisting social competence. Individuals with highly developed social skills are likely to be better able to establish and draw upon interpersonal relationships (Heller and Swindle 1983).

A number of other factors within the host environment play a role in the adaptation of the immigrants. Whether or not the immigrant is documented or undocumented will obviously impact the opportunity structure in which she is able to participate (Chavez 1992; Smart and Smart 1995) as well as the general quality of life. Feeling "hunted" by the Immigration and Naturalization Service (INS) is highly stressful (Padilla et al. 1988) and leads to anxiety and (well-founded) paranoia. For adults the availability of jobs will be key. Here, social networks will play a key role as employers often rely on migrant networks to provide them with a constant source of potential new employees (Waldinger 1997; Cornelius 1998). Ability to find work, questions of pay, seasonal availability, safety, and the unpleasantness of the job will also play a role in adjustment.

For children, the quality of their schools will play a key role in their transition. Unfortunately, many immigrant children find themselves in segregated, poverty-stricken, and conflict-ridden schools (Orfield 1998). Fear of violence is a central concern in the lives of many new immigrants. In our sample of schools, a number of administrators have reported high crime rates. In one of our participating middle schools, a student was recently raped and murdered; a high school principal told us of approximately thirty murders in the last year within the immediate neighborhood; and many other school officials and students complain of significant gang activity within the school environs. A middle school student told us that a security guard, who had supposedly been hired to protect the schools' students, was the main dealer of drugs on campus. During a focus group we conducted with Mexican immigrant students in a San Francisco Bay Area school, students revealed that only a few days earlier, an escaped prisoner had barricaded himself during school hours within the school grounds, leading to an exchange of gunshots between him and the police.

Obviously, neighborhood safety will do much to influence the quality of life for children and adults alike. Many immigrants move to inner-city areas in search of housing they can afford. Unfortunately, "affordable" urban housing is often located in areas that may be characterized as "war zones." An eleven-year-old Mexican girl told us: "There is a lot of violence here in the United States. They kill people in the streets." A thirteen-year-old Mexican girl said: "There I was freer. Here there are bad people who hurt children." A twelve-year-old Haitian girl recounted: "I don't like the neighborhood where I live. There is a lot of crime in the neighborhood. One day, we were sleeping and the police came and opened the door. There was a man in the apartment above us who had killed his wife.... I was scared because he could have come and killed us too." A ten-year-old Mexican boy reported a frightening incident: "I saw a man lying out in front of my house with blood on his legs and stomach. I think someone shot him." Another child, a thirteen-year-old Chinese girl, told us: "I have seen gang activities near my house.... I am afraid to go out. I don't feel safe."

Parents, too, fear for their children's safety. They often require them to stay within the confines of their (often cramped) living spaces, off the streets and out of harm's way. Many of our informants lamented the resulting loss of freedom following immigration. A thirteen-year-old Dominican boy said: "Back home, I had much more freedom. I didn't have to ask permission for every little thing. Here, our parents are much more protective of us. They are always after us telling us to be careful and not to come home late." When asked about what the most difficult thing about migration was for her, one twelve-year-old Mexican girl replied: "If you go out in the United States, you are always afraid of everything. In Mexico, you can go out with confidence." A fourteen-year-old Salvadorean girl said: "The most difficult thing about immigration is that I am always locked up in the house." A twelve-year-old girl who recently immigrated from Haiti recounted: "In Haiti I could go where I wanted. Here I cannot do that because there are bad kids." A fourteen-year-old Dominican boy said: "I don't like being closed in. You can't go out." A thirteen-year-old Chinese girl summed up the feeling of many of our informants: "It is very lonely in America having nobody to talk to and staying home all day long after school every day."

The general social climate of reception to the new immigrants plays a critical role in their adaptation. Garcia-Coll and Magnuson (1997:119) argue that "discrimination against immigrants today, and particularly immigrants of color, is widespread in America." Prejudice and exclusion are established forms of social traumata. "Prejudicial exclusion is, even if neglected, a potent psychosocial stressor impinging on the daily lives of many … interfering with their mental and social adaptation and adjustment" (Adams 1990:363). The exclusion can take a structural form (when individuals are excluded from the opportunity structure) as well as an attitudinal form (in the form of disparagement and public hostility).

In the following section, I illustrate some of the ways in which both structural and social exclusion are impacting the lives of immigrant children.

THE SOCIAL CLIMATE: HOSTILITY IN THE RECEIVING CONTEXT

Structural violence and exclusion

In recent years, there has been a growing concern about the large influx of new immigrants. A number of public opinion polls reveal negative attitudes towards immigrants. Over two-thirds of survey respondents indicated that they did not want to extend the invitation of the Statue of Liberty to new immigrants (Espenshade and Belanger 1998). In their thorough analysis of recent public opinion polls, Princeton scholars Espanshade and Belanger found that many respondents perceive that immigrants have a negative economic impact, drain the social service system, contribute to crime, and show little prospect of assimilation. These prevailing beliefs and sentiments led to several dramatic anti-immigrant initiatives (see M. Suárez-Orozco 1996).

California's Proposition 187 illustrates the explosive tensions generated by large-scale immigration in a state that had undergone a severe economic recession. In November 1994, California voters overwhelmingly approved this proposition, known as the "Save our State" initiative. This initiative was designed to "prevent illegal aliens in the United States from receiving benefits or public services in the State of California" (Proposition 187 1994:91), including emergency medical services and education for children.

This controversial initiative generated a great deal of legal action, including several suits in federal and state courts. Currently, the law is not being fully implemented. However, if it were to be, it is estimated that some 300,000 undocumented immigrant children in California would be banned from enrolling in public schools. Many observers argue that this proposition would do nothing to prevent further unauthorized immigration to California and could in the long term cost the taxpayers of that state far beyond whatever short-term savings could be realized by not providing public schooling to these immigrant children (Suárez-Orozco and Suárez-Orozco 1995).

The draconian 1996 Illegal Immigration Reform and Responsibility Act is another example of structural exclusion, which some observers have argued will have a harmful effect on large sectors of society (Eschbach *et al.* 1997; Hagan 1998). In addition to a steep intensification of deportations, the internal security provision of this new act ushered in a nationwide increase of fingerprinting, wiretapping, INS linkages with local and state law enforcement, and other measures supposedly designed to combat links between immigration, the drug trade, and terrorism. The act has obvious implications for the civil rights of immigrants and citizens alike, particularly those of color (see Eschbach *et al.* 1997; M. Suárez-Orozco 1998). The new law also changes in significant ways the process by which citizens and permanent residents can bring family members to permanently reside in the United States.

In 1996, former President Clinton announced "the end of the era of big government." Ironically, that same year the INS experienced an explosive growth. In September 1996, Clinton signed the Illegal Immigration and Responsibility Act. The Act, among other things, doubled the size of the U.S. Border Patrol over five years. Likewise, U.S. military personnel were given a substantial role at the southern border; there they assisted the INS in various initiatives, including surveillance and the maintenance and operation of highly sophisticated military equipment (Andreas 1998). Alarmingly, since the implementation of these policies, there has been a significant increase in human rights violations at the border (see Amnesty International 1998:24; American Friends Service Committee 1992) as well as deaths at the border resulting from exposure and violence as migrants make more dangerous crossings (Hagan 1998). Although the massive new law enforcement effort has made the southern border of the United States harder to cross, scholar Peter Andreas concludes that "illegal entry is certainly more difficult and dangerous, but there is little evidence to suggest that migrants are giving up and heading home" (Andreas 1998:347).

A side effect of these policies is the increasing criminalization of the border region. Unauthorized crossings went from being mostly acts of self-smuggling to a process structured around widening circles of criminality. Undocumented immigrants must increasingly rely on the work of professional alien smugglers and document forgers: a high-profits growth industry on both sides of the border. Some scholars of immigration have noted that, while the new border control efforts make for dramatic symbolic politics, they largely fail to reduce illegal immigration flows through the southern sector (Andreas 1998). While in the past many undocumented migrants would shuttle back and forth across the border in steady transnational flows, increasingly, once they make the crossing into the United States, many of them are unlikely to risk a return home. Hence, ironically, they are more likely to stay within the United States rather than return to their point of origin. Though these initiatives generate a seductive imagery of state control that reinforces the myth that the problem of illegal immigration is to be found on the border, the problem of unauthorized immigration clearly requires more intelligent, long-term, binational responses than we have seen to date (M. Suárez-Orozco 1998).

These exclusionary policies are not limited to the border. In recent years, we have witnessed a range of policies aimed at excluding immigrants (especially undocumented immigrants) from accessing a variety of publicly funded services. Immigration controls have moved slowly over the years from the border to the classroom (Proposition 187), the hospital (see Brown et al. 1998), and the welfare agency (see Eschbach et al. 1997). Noticeably missing from these initiatives is a systematic attempt to punish or police the businesses that secure significant gains through immigrant labor—whether documented or undocumented. The employer-sanction laws have been anemically enforced due to lack of resources, personnel, and political will. Businesses therefore continue to achieve great gains and risk little sanctioning for widespread use of unauthorized immigrant labor (Cornelius 1998).

These policies and practices are generating a pattern of intense exclusion and segregation between large number of immigrants and the larger society. This intense segregation is evident in the work force (see Waldinger 1996), schools (see Orfield 1998), and residential patterns (see M. Suárez-Orozco 1998). Increasingly large numbers of immigrants of color are settling into highly segregated neighborhoods where deep poverty, violence, and substandard schools are the norm. In these neighborhoods, countercultural gangs are ever present and eager to recruit and "socialize" immigrant children into alternative economics where drug-dealing and drug-taking is an important feature of the social scene (Vigil 1988).

These patterns of deep segregation are further intensified by an increasing segmentation in the U.S. economy. While some immigrants, particularly those who are highly educated and highly skilled, are readily moving into the knowledge-intensive sectors of the economy, large numbers of low-skilled immigrants find themselves in low-skilled service sector jobs—a sector of the economy that shows no prospect for status mobility (see Portes and Zhou 1993). Among the children of immigrants, new research suggests another worrisome development. A recent study by Dowell Myers suggests that, while the children of Mexican immigrants have made important gains in terms of school attainment, those gains have not been rewarded proportionally in terms of wages in the marketplace. Particularly for the children of immigrants, there has been a disconcerting pattern of "declining returns" to education (Myers 1998).

Psychological violence and social exclusion

The structural exclusion suffered by immigrants and their children is detrimental to their ability to participate in the opportunity structure. The attitudinal social exclusion also plays a toxic role. How does a child incorporate the notion that she is "an alien" and "an illegal," unwanted and not warranting the most basic rights of education and health care? Even if they are not undocumented, the hostility prevalent in the current climate radiates to all children with accents and darker complexions.

A resident of southern California articulated the fears of many: "You find the huge gangs of illegal aliens that line the streets, shake down our school children, spread diseases like malaria, and roam our neighborhoods looking for work or homes to rob. We are under siege" (quoted in Chavez 1992). One of the leaders in the Proposition 187 effort was propelled to "do something" after a visit to an Orange County social service agency. She says: "I walked into this monstrous room full of people, babies, little children all over the place and I realized no one was speaking English .... I was overwhelmed with this feeling: Where am I? What has happened here?" (quoted in Suro 1994). In Flushing, New York, like in many other communities across the nation, there has been a dramatic increase in its immigrant population in the last ten years. For many longtime residents, the change is "proving painful, even traumatic" (Dugger 1997). One resident commented, "Everything is changing" while another said, "It's very discombobulating, very upsetting. We all recognize that change is necessary but it just doesn't sit well." Though the new immigrants have brought resources to Flushing that have revitalized declining neighborhoods, a Congresswoman said of the new immigrants: "[They are] more like colonizers than immigrants. They sure as hell have lots of money and they sure as hell know how to buy property and jack up rents of retail shops and drive people out" (quoted in Dugger 1997).

Adults are not the only members of American society who share such feelings. Non-immigrant, non-minority students in public high school in northern California had these thoughts to share with educational researcher Laurie Olsen: "[Immigrants] come to take our jobs, and are willing to break their backs for shit pay, and we can't compete." Another said: "These Chinese kids come over here and all they do is work and work and work and work, and all you have to do is look in the AP [Advanced Placement] classes and you'll see they are filling them up. No one can compete anymore." Still another summed up a prevailing fear: "They just want to take over" (quoted in Olsen 1998:68).

These quotes suggest several points. Most obviously, the hostility is undisguised and unambivalent. The immigrants embody the feeling of "uncanny" (Freud 1968): the horror of being lost in a changing world that appears to be menacing activates such primitive defenses as splitting and projection. In the anti-immigrant talk, "aliens" appear either as parasites who are siphoning away limited resources (such as jobs and social services) or conversely as powerful and sinister aliens who control vast resources, thus eliciting envy.

Of course, anti-immigrant sentiments are nothing new. During the 1920s a frequent contributor to the *Saturday Evening Post* contrasted the "old immigrants" (from northern Europe) with the "new immigrants" (those from southern and eastern Europe). The former, he maintained, were able to blend into the melting pot. The latter he accused of entering the country simply to earn money with the intention of returning to their homelands. Maintaining that many were illiterate, he argued that they would be difficult to assimilate: "If the United States is the melting pot, something is wrong with the heating system, for an inconveniently large portion of the new immigration floats around in unsightly indigestible lumps. Of recent years, the contents of the melting pot have stood badly in need of straining in order that the refuse might be removed and deposited in the customary receptacle for such things" (Simon 1985:83). Though this was written in the 1920s, the sentiment it expresses was shared by many in the 1990s. The fear (then as now) was that "America has largely become the dumping ground for the world's human riffraff, who couldn't make a living in their own countries" (Simon 1985:83). The new immigrants of the time were viewed as intellectually inferior, lazy, crime-prone, and altogether unassimilable.

Indeed, a consideration of the historical record strongly suggests that there is a remarkable consistency in the responses to immigrants. Historian Rita Simon conducted an exhaustive review of media representations of immigrants in the United States over the span of one hundred years (1880–1980) and examined fifty years' worth of public opinion polls from their beginnings in the late 1930s (Simon 1985). Her findings illustrate a classic pattern of response to new arrivals: American citizens have held consistently negative attitudes towards people wishing to enter the United States; the more recent the immigrant group, the more negative the opinion. On the whole, while the people who came in earlier waves are thought to have been "good folk," new immigrants are viewed as "pure scum" (Simon 1985:88).

Princeton University's Espanshade and Belanger (1998) undertook a comprehensive study of American public opinion polls on immigration. In their study of national surveys by twenty different organizations over a thirty-year period, they found that, historically, there has been a very strong correlation between anti-immigrant sentiment and economic anxiety, particularly around unemployment rates. Put simply, when unemployment rates are high, anti-immigrant feelings are also high. Likewise, when unemployment rates drop and there is optimism about the economy, negative attitudes towards immigration have tended to level off. It is no accident then that the high level of anti-immigration sentiment peaked during the economic slump of the late 1980s and early 1990s. In media accounts in the latter part of the 1990s, concerns with immigration dropped off somewhat though the anti-immigration rhetoric continues to be close to the surface. In general, more educated respondents tend to be more positively disposed towards immigrants than less educated respondents (Espanshade and Belanger 1998). Perhaps, in a world of "limited good" (Foster 1972), these respondents perceive that they have less to gain and more to lose from immigrants than do members of the more privileged classes. Therefore, although the overall economic situation improved in the latter part of the 1990s, at the lower end of the wage structure native workers already concerned with the segmented hourglass economy continued to perceive a grave threat from the twin pressures of globalization (jobs leaving for the developing world) and immigration (migrants from the developing world competing for jobs at the bottom of the hourglass).

Fear of the cultural dilution of the country's Anglo-Saxon institutions and values is an enduring preoccupation that feeds the anti-immigrant ethos (Espanshade and Belanger 1998). Citizens today feel more positive about immigrants from Europe than they do about immigrants from Latin America and the Caribbean. Immigrants who do not speak English and who "look" different from the dominant Anglo-European majority make many non-immigrants uncomfortable. The fact that 80 percent of the "new immigrants" (post-1965) are of color (coming from Asia, Latin America, and the Caribbean) is clearly a further complicating factor in our race-polarized society. When it comes to immigration, race and color indeed matter. Immigration is an enduring concern that lurks just below the surface of public consciousness in the United States. Opportunistic politicians have long found immigrants to be convenient scapegoats onto which to direct righteous anger about all sorts of chagrins (Jones-Correa 1998). At best they are viewed as competitors and at worst they are seen as sinister. As a result, a range of negative attributes can be easily projected onto them.

George DeVos and Marcelo Suárez-Orozco (1990) developed an interdisciplinary, psychocultural framework to explore the experience of self in cultures where patterned inequalities shape social interaction. In addition to the obvious structural inequalities they face, some minorities are also targeted for "psychological disparagement." They become the object of symbolic violence that stereotypes them as innately inferior (lazier, prone to crime, and so forth). These attributes make these disparaged minorities, in the eyes of the dominant society, less deserving of sharing in the society's dream and justifies their lot in life.

IDENTITY FORMATION UNDER SIEGE

Social mirroring

How do these charged attitudes and rampant hostilities affect the immigrant child's sense of self? A first point to consider is whether or not children are aware of these hostilities. As part of the data collection for the Longitudinal Immigrant Student Adaptation Study, we asked immigrant children what the hardest thing about immigration was. Discrimination and racism were recurring themes discussed by many of the children. The following statements are representative of the kinds of responses we received. A thirteen-year-old Chinese girl told us: "Americans discriminate. They treat you badly because you are Chinese or black. I hate this most." A fourteen-year-old Mexican boy responded: "The discrimination [is the hardest thing].... Here [in the United States] Latinos discriminate against African Americans, African Americans against Latinos. You see it in the streets, and on TV and you hear it on the radio." A twelve-year-old Central American girl said: "One of the most difficult things about immigrating is that people make fun of me here. People from the United States think that they are superior to you." The perceived discrimination can take a variety of forms. A fourteen-year-old Haitian girl reported: "I do not like the discrimination. For example, when you go to a store, whites follow you to see if you are going to take something." A twelve-year-old Haitian boy told us: "There are many teachers that treat us [the students] well, but there are many who do not. There are teachers who, even though they deny it, are racists." An eleven-year-old Haitian girl recounted that she hated it "when whites yell at Haitians." A fourteen-year-old Haitian boy summed it up by saying: "The racism is here. The Americans believe they are superior to other races."

We asked all the immigrant children in our study to complete the sentence "Most Americans think [people from my country] are...." Strikingly, for Latino and Haitian immigrants, the most common response was: "Most Americans think that we are bad." Overwhelmingly, the children perceived that Americans had negative perceptions about them. Below are other responses we received:

> "Most Americans don't think well of us." (fourteen-year-old Central American girl)
> "Most Americans think that we are poor people." (nine-year-old Chinese girl)
> "Most Americans think that we are ignorant." (fourteen-year-old Mexican girl)
> "Most Americans think that we are stupid." (ten-year-old Haitian girl)
> "Most Americans think that we are very impolite." (twelve-year-old Chinese girl)
> "Most Americans think that we don't know anything." (fourteen-year-old Mexican girl)
> "Most Americans think that we can't do the same things as them in school or at work." (ten-year-old Mexican girl)
> "Most Americans think that we are good for nothing." (fourteen-year-old Central American boy)

> "Most Americans think that we are useless." (fourteen-year-old Dominican girl)
> "Most Americans think that we are garbage." (fourteen-year-old Dominican boy)
> "Most Americans think that we are members of gangs." (nine-year-old Central American girl)
> "Most Americans think that we are thieves." (thirteen-year-old Haitian girl)
> "Most Americans think that we are lazy, gangsters, drug-addicts that only come to take their jobs away." (fourteen-year-old Mexican boy)
> "Most Americans think that we are bad like all Latinos." (twelve-year-old Central American boy)
> "Most Americans think that we don't exist." (twelve-year-old Mexican boy)

Clearly then, immigrant children are aware of the prevailing ethos of hostility of the dominant culture. Psychologically, what do children do with this reception? Are the attitudes of the host culture internalized, denied, or resisted? Object-relations theorist D.W. Winnicott can provide some insight into the processes at work. Winnicott focused much of his writing on the relationship between the mother and infant, adding much to our understanding of the significance of this relationship in the formation of identity and a "sense of self." In articulating his concept of "mirroring," he argued:

> [T]he mother functions as a mirror, providing the infant with a precise reflection of his own experience and gestures, despite their fragmented and formless qualities. "When I look I am seen, so I exist." (Winnicott 1971:134)

Imperfections in the reflected rendition mar and inhibit the child's capacity for self-experience and integration and interfere with the process of "personalization" (Greenberg and Mitchell 1983:192–3).

The infant is highly dependent upon the reflection of the experience she receives from her mothering figure. The mother provides clues about the environment. In determining whether she needs to be frightened by new stimuli, the infant will first look to her mother's expression and response. An expression of interest or calm will reassure the infant while an expression of concern will alarm her. Even more crucial is the mother's response to the infant's actions. Does the mother show delight when the infant reaches for an object or does she ignore it or show disapproval? No one response (or non-response) is likely to have much effect, but the accumulation of experiences is significant in the formation of the child's identities and sense of self-worth. A child whose accomplishments are mirrored favorably is likely to feel more valuable than the child whose accomplishments are either largely ignored or, worse still, denigrated.

Although mirroring (along with a number of his other concepts) is an important contribution to our understanding of the developing child, Winnicott—like many of his psychoanalytic colleagues—overlooks the powerful forces of social systems and culture in shaping self-other relationships. Particularly as the child develops, the mirroring function is by no means the exclusive domain of maternal figures. In fact, with the exception of individuals falling within the autistic spectrum, all human beings are dependent on the reflection of themselves mirrored back to them by others. "Others" include non-parental relatives, adult caretakers, siblings, teachers, peers, employers, people on the street, and even the media. When the reflected opinion is generally positive, the individual (adult or child) will be able to feel that she is worthwhile and competent. When the reflection is generally negative, it is extremely difficult to maintain an unblemished sense of self-worth for very long.

These reflections can be accurate or inaccurate. In some cases, the reflection can be a positive distortion or what I call a "false good": In such a situation the response to the individual may be out of proportion to his actual contribution or achievements. In the most benign case, positive expectations can be an asset. In the classic "Pygmalion in the Classroom" study (Rosenthal and Jacobson 1968), when teachers believed that certain children were brighter than others (based on the experimenter randomly assigning some children that designation, unsubstantiated in fact) they treated the children more positively and assigned them higher grades. It is possible that some immigrant students, such as Asians, benefit somewhat from positive expectations of their competence as a result of being members of a "model minority"—though no doubt at a cost (Takaki 1989). In a less benign example of "false good" mirroring, individuals who are surrounded by those who do not inform them of negative feedback and laud even minimal accomplishments may develop a distorted view of their own abilities and accomplishments. This would be the case with many political leaders or movie stars as well as others with power and influence. There is also recent evidence that some children are overpraised; the resulting inflated sense of self-worth coupled with low frustration tolerance may be partially linked to violent outbursts (Seligman 1998).

I am more concerned, however, with the negative distortion or "false bad" case. What happens to children who receive mirroring on the societal level that is predominantly negative and hostile? Such is the case with many immigrant and minority children. When the assumptions about them include expectations of sloth, irresponsibility, low intelligence, and even danger, the outcome can be toxic. When these reflections are received in a number of mirrors, including the media, the classroom, and the street, the outcome is devastating (Adams 1990).

Even when the parents provide positive mirroring, it is often insufficient to compensate for the distorted mirrors that children encounter in their daily lives. In some cases, the immigrant parent is considered out of touch with reality. Even when the parents' opinions are considered valid, they may not be enough to compensate for the intensity and frequency of the distortions of the House of Mirrors that immigrant children encounter in their everyday lives. The statements made by the children in our study demonstrate that they are intensely aware of the hostile reception that they are encountering.

What can a child do with these hostilities? There are several possible responses. The most positive possible outcome is to be goaded into "I'll show you. I'll make it in spite of what you think of me." This response, while theoretically possible, is relatively infrequent. More likely, the child responds with self-doubt and shame, setting low aspirations in a kind of self-fulfilling prophecy: "They are probably right. I'll never be able to do it." Yet another potential response is one of "You think I'm bad. Let me show you how bad I can be."

Segmented assimilation

A number of theoretical constructs have been developed over the years to explore the immigration experience in American society. Historically, models developed to examine immigration were largely based on the European experience. These studies described patterns of assimilation (Gordon 1964) following various paths on what was depicted as a generally upwardly mobile journey. The argument was quite simple: The longer immigrants were in the United States, the better they did in terms of schooling, health, and income.

A number of distinguished sociologists, such as Gans (1992), Portes and Zhou (1993), Rùmbaut (1996), Waters (1990, 1996), and others, have argued that a new "segmentation" in American society and economy has been shaping new patterns of immigrant insertion into American culture. This research suggests what might be broadly termed a "trimodal" pattern of adaptation. Some immigrants today are achieving extraordinary patterns of upward mobility; they are quickly moving into the well-remunerated, knowledge-intensive sectors of the economy in ways never seen before in the history of U.S. immigration. On the opposite side of our hourglass economy, large numbers of low-skilled immigrants find themselves in increasingly segregated sectors of the economy and society; there they are locked into low-skilled service sector jobs without much promise of status mobility (Portes and Zhou 1997).[3] In between these two patterns are yet other immigrant groups that seem to approximate the norms of the majority population: These "disappear" into American institutions and culture without much notice.

This trimodal socioeconomic pattern seems to be related to how the children of today's immigrants tend to do in school. In the last few years, there have been several studies on the performance of immigrant children in schools. The data suggest a complex picture. In broad strokes, we can say that the immigrant children of today also fit a trimodal pattern of school adaptation (a critical predictor of success in this society). Some immigrant children do extraordinarily well in school, surpassing native-born children in terms of a number of indicators, including grades, performance on standardized tests, and attitudes towards education (De Vos 1983; Kao and Tienda 1995). Other immigrants tend to overlap with native-born children (Rúmbaut 1995; Waters 1996). Yet other immigrants tend to achieve well below their native-born peers (Kao and Tienda 1995; Rumbaut 1995; Suárez-Orozco and Suárez-Orozco 1995).

In addition to this pattern of variability in overall performance between groups, another disconcerting pattern has consistently emerged from the data. For many immigrant groups, length of residency in the United States is associated with declining health, school achievement, and aspirations (Kao and Tienda 1995; NRC 1998; Rúmbaut 1995; Steinberg 1996; Suárez-Orozco and Suárez-Orozco 1995; Vernez et al. 1996).

A recent large-scale National Research Council (NRC) study considered a variety of measures of physical health and risk behaviors among children and adolescents from immigrant families, including general health, learning disabilities, obesity, emotional difficulties, and various risk-taking behaviors. The NRC researchers found that immigrant youth were healthier than their counterparts from non-immigrant families. The researchers pointed out that these finding are "counterintuitive" in light of the racial or ethnic minority status, overall lower socioeconomic status, and higher poverty rates that characterize many immigrant children and families that they studied. They also found that the longer youth were in the United States, the poorer their overall physical and psychological health. Furthermore, the more "Americanized" they became, the more likely they were to engage in risky behaviors such as substance abuse, violence, and delinquency (NRC 1998).

In the area of education, Ruben Rúmbaut (1997) surveyed more than five thousand high school students in San Diego, California, and Dade County, Florida. He wrote:

> [A]n important finding supporting our earlier reported research is the negative association of length of residence in the United States with both GPA [grade point average] and aspirations. Time in the United States is, as expected, strongly predictive of improved English reading skills; but despite that seeming advantage, longer residence in the U.S. and second-generation status [that is, being born in the United States] are connected to declining academic achievement and aspirations, net of other factors. (Rúmbaut 1997:46–8)

In a different voice, Reverend Virgil Elizondo, rector of the San Fernando Cathedral in San Antonio, Texas, articulates this same issue: "I can tell by looking in their eyes how long they've been here. They come sparkling with hope, and the first generation finds hope rewarded. Their children's eyes no longer sparkle" (quoted in Suro 1998:13).

Negotiating identities

At no time in the lifespan is the urge to define oneself vis-à-vis the society at large as great as during adolescence. According to Erickson (1964), the single greatest developmental task of adolescence is to forge a coherent sense of identity. He argued that for optimal development, there needs to be a certain amount of complementarity between the individual's sense of self and the varied social milieus he or she must traverse. This model made a great deal of analytical sense to explain the experiences of individuals living in more homogeneous worlds across their lifespan.

However, in an increasingly fractured, heterogeneous, transnational world, there is much less complementarity between social spaces. Hence, today we are less concerned with theorizing identity as a coherent, monolithic, and enduring construct than in understanding how identities are implicated in the ability to traverse increasingly discontinuous social, symbolic, and political spheres. The children of immigrants must construct identities that will, if successful, enable them to thrive in incommensurable social settings such as home, school, the world of peers, and the world of work.

In this complex world, most children are required to move across discontinuous social spaces. For the children of immigrants, however, these discontinuities can be dramatic. Immigrant children today may have their breakfast conversation in Farsi, listen to African American rap with their peers on the way to school, and learn in mainstream English about the New Deal from their social studies teacher. Therefore, the experience of the children of immigrants offers us a particularly powerful lens through which to view the workings of identity.

Given the multiple worlds in which immigrant children live, they face particular challenges in their identity formation (Aronowitz 1984; Grinberg and Grinberg 1989; Phinney 1998; Vigil 1988). When there is too much cultural dissonance, negative social mirroring, and role confusion, and when the cultural guides are inadequate, an adolescent will find it difficult to develop a flexible and adaptive sense of self. Many are torn between the attachment to the parental culture of origin, the lure of the often more intriguing adolescent peer culture, and aspirations to join the American mainstream culture (which may or may not welcome them).

Optimistic hopes for the future are often tempered by pessimism born of deprivation and disparagement. While immigrant and second-generation youth may believe that the "American Dream" should be attainable with sufficient effort, the many limits of this dream become increasingly evident with experience. High school graduation no longer guarantees earnings sufficient to lead a good life; college tuition is prohibitively expensive; and networks and connections—which their parents may not have—do indeed make a difference in the opportunity structure.

To further encumber the process of identity-formation, the children of immigrants are a dissonant combination of precocious worldliness and sheltered naiveté. They are often vested with responsibilities beyond their years. They may be called upon to act as interpreters, to care for siblings, and to attend to chores at home while their parents work. They may be able to manipulate two languages and have insight into two different worlds. At the same time, particularly for girls, forays into the New World are often over-restricted by their anxious parents, contributing to a relative naiveté. With a limited network of informed individuals to provide adequate information and advice, many immigrant children have difficulty navigating the turbulent waters of adolescence.

Given this multiplicity of factors, it is clear that immigrant adolescents face special struggles in the formation of identity. Each individual forges an identity, finding ways to adapt to the vicissitudes of being a stranger in a new land. In 1937, Stonequist astutely described the experiences of social dislocation. He aptly described cultural transitions, which leave the migrant "on the margin of each but a member of neither" (Stonequist 1937:4). He emphasized that the common traits of what he termed the "marginal man" (written in pre-feminist 1937 after all) evolved from the conflict of two cultures rather than from the "specific content" (Stonequist 1937:9) of any particular culture. Stonequist contended that cultural differences create the most difficulty in circumstances where there are sharp ethnic contrasts and hostile social attitudes. His observations on the psychological costs of marginal status are as useful today as when he first wrote them.

In our work with immigrant children (Suárez-Orozco and Suárez-Orozco 1995) we have noted that youth attempting to traverse discontinuous cultural, political, and economic spaces tended to gravitate towards one of three dominant styles of adaptation, which we have termed "ethnic flight," "adversarial," and "bicultural." A single child, depending upon her age at migration, race, socioeconomic background, legal status, and, very importantly, context of resettlement in the United States, may first gravitate to one style of adaptation. As she matures and develops, and as her contexts change, she may develop another style of adaptation. We did not see these styles as fixed or mutually exclusive. We hypothesized that contexts, opportunities, networks, and social mirroring act as powerful gravitational fields that shape the adaptation of immigrant children.

Youths clustering around the "ethnic flight" style often struggle to mimic the dominant group and may attempt to join them, leaving their own ethnic group behind. These are the youths who minimize or even deny the negative social mirroring they encounter. An earlier body of social science research examined the related issue of "passing" among members of some ethnic minority groups (see Tajfel 1978, for example). This line of inquiry argued that individuals who attempted to pass had unresolved issues of what Erickson called "shame and doubt" (1964:109–12) for which they may struggle to overcompensate. Many immigrant youth who deploy an "ethnic flight" style may feel more comfortable networking with peers from the dominant culture. For these youths, learning standard English may serve not only instrumental purposes but often may become an important symbolic act of identification with the dominant culture. Among these youth success in school may be seen as a route for instrumental mobility. It is also a way symbolically and psychologically to dissemble and gain distance from the family and ethnic group. These are immigrants who travel their journey with light affective baggage. The idiom "making it" for these youth tends to be independence and individualistic self-advancement.

Among these youth, typically the culturally constituted patterns of parental authority lose legitimacy. For these youths (as for many of their mainstream American peers), parents are "out of it," and their ways, moral codes, values, and expectations are rejected as anachronistic. While this style of adaptation might have been consciously and unconsciously deployed by earlier waves of immigrants (especially those from Europe for whom their physical appearance allowed them the option of passing), from the vantage point of the new millenium, we are witnessing "the passing of passing" (De Vos 1992). For many immigrants of color today, this option is simply not viable.

Youth clustering around "adversarial styles" of adaptation structure their identities around a process of rejection by the institutions of the dominant culture—including schools and the formal economy. These youths respond to negative social mirroring by developing a defensively oppositional attitude. As Luis Rodriguez, the child of Mexican immigrants in southern California, recalled in his memoirs:

> You were labeled from the start. I'd walk into the counselor's office for whatever reason and looks of disdain greeted me—one meant for a criminal, alien, to be feared. Already a thug. It was harder to defy this expectation than just accept it and fall into the trappings. It was a jacket I could try to take off, but they kept putting it back on. The first hint of trouble and preconceptions proved true. So why not be proud? Why not be an outlaw? Why not make it our own? (1993:84).

These are the children who are pushed out and drop out of school at a time when the U.S. economy is generating virtually no meaningful jobs for those without formal schooling (Orfield 1998). Among these youth, the culturally constituted parental authority functions are typically corroded. These youth, therefore, tend to have serious difficulty with their parents and relatives (see Vigil 1988) and typically gravitate towards those sharing their predicament: their peers. In many cases, the peer group, not the elders, is in charge of the lives of these children. These youths are likely to act out behaviorally (Aronowitz 1984: Garcia-Coll and Magnuson 1997). In these situations, youth often construct spaces of competence in the underground and alternative economies. At the margins of the dominant society, these young people develop an oppositional counterculture identity from which gangs may emerge. Anthropologist John Ogbu and his colleagues (1998) have argued that, for many youths, in contexts of severe inequality and ethnic antagonism, learning standard English and classroom success may elicit severe peer-group sanctioning when it is viewed as "acting white" or being a "coconut," an "Oreo," or a "banana."

Youth clustering around the "bicultural style" deploy what we have termed "transnational strategies." These children typically emerge as "cultural brokers" mediating the often conflicting cultural currents of home culture and host culture. The "work of culture" (to borrow the term of anthropologist Obeyesekere 1990) for these youths consists of crafting identities in the "hyphen, linking aspects of the discontinuous—and, at times incommensurable—cultural systems they find themselves inhabiting. Some of the youth will achieve bicultural and bilingual competencies, which become an integral part of their identity. These youth respond to negative social mirroring by identifying it, naming it, and resisting it. These are youth for which the culturally constructed social strictures and patterns of social control of immigrant parents and elders maintain a degree of legitimacy. They are able to network with equal ease among members of their own ethnic group as well as with others from different backgrounds. There is considerable evidence that those who develop bicultural efficacy (that is, social competence in both cultures) are at a significant advantage over those who are alienated with a part of their identity (La Fromboise, Coleman, and Gerton 1998).

Among those bicultural youth who "make it" in the idiom of the dominant society, issues of reparation often become important components of their life trajectories. In some such cases, when one's success appears in the context of the sacrifice of loved ones—who struggled to give them opportunities in the new land—feelings of compensatory guilt are quite common. Among many such youths, success in school will have not only the instrumental meaning (of achieving advancement, better-paying opportunities, and independence) but also the important expressive meaning of making the parental sacrifice worthwhile. To make it for these youth may involve reciprocating and giving back to parents, siblings, peers, and other members of the community (Suárez-Orozco 1989; Suárez-Orozco and Suárez-Orozco 1995).

The majority of immigrant children, coming from a variety of countries and social classes, arrive with extremely positive attitudes towards schooling and education. Three out of four of our 425 recent-arrival informants supplied "education" as the response to an open-ended sentence completion task: "In life the most important thing is …." Yet a number of studies have shown that the longer the children are in the new environment, the less positive they are about school and the more at risk they are to disengage from academic pursuits. Kohut (1971) theorized that loss, mourning, and the narcissistic injuries of humiliation are linked to destructive tendencies such as aggression and violence. I would argue that the losses and mourning resulting from immigration coupled with the narcissistic injuries of the host culture's reception are a dangerous combination that may in large part account for this disconcerting pattern of decline.

Given that one in five children in the United States is a child of immigrants, how these children adapt to their new country should be a crucial societal concern. The pathways they take and the identities they form are multiply determined. The resources, experiences, stresses, and trauma—as well as the coping strategies they bring with them—all play a key role. The structural environment (including neighborhood, employment opportunities, and schools) within which they find themselves must not be overlooked. I have also argued that the social mirroring that the children encounter is critical. Immigrant children suffer a variety of forms of stress and loss that is only compounded by corrosive social disparagement. We should not underestimate the toll that these experiences and shattered dreams take upon the souls of developing children. The positive attitudes of recent immigrant children are a remarkable resource; as a society we would be best served by harnessing rather than crushing those energies.

I would like to thank Marcelo Suárez-Orozco for his helpful comments. I am most grateful to June Erlick, Jennifer Hayes, and Mariela Paez for their careful reading and suggestions regarding an earlier version of the chapter. I would also like to thank the National Science Foundation, the W. T. Grant Foundation, and the Spencer Foundation for their generous support of our Longitudinal Immigrant Student Adaptation Study (jointly with Marcelo Suárez-Orozco).

Notes

1. The children attend forty-two schools in eight school districts in the Boston and San Francisco areas. Ethnographic observations are conducted by twenty-nine highly trained, bilingual, bicultural, graduate social science students.
2. Please note that all quotations from our informants are translations from their native languages.

References

Adams, P. L. 1990. Prejudice and Exclusion as Social Traumata. In J. D. Noshpitz and R. D. Coddington, eds., *Stressors and the Adjustment Disorders.* New York: John Wiley and Sons.

Ainslie, R. C. 1998. Cultural Mourning, Immigration, and Engagement: Vignettes from the Mexican Experience. In M. Suárez-Orozco ed., *Crossings: Mexican Immigration in Interdisciplinary Perspectives.* Cambridge, MA: Harvard University Press.

American Friends Services Committee, 1992. *Sealing Our Borders: The Human Toll. Third Report of the Immigration Law Enforcement Monitoring Project. A Project of the Mexico-U.S. Border Program.* Philadelphia: American Friends Services Committee.

Amnesty International, 1998. From San Diego to Brownsville: Human Rights Violation on the USA-Mexico Border. News Release, May 20, 1998. http:// www.amnesty.org.

Andreas, P. 1998. The U.S. Immigration Control Offensive: Constructing an Image of Order on the Southern Border. In M. Suárez-Orozco, ed., *Crossings: Mexican Immigration in Interdisciplinary Perspectives.* Cambridge, MA: Harvard University Press.

Aronowitz, M. 1984. The Social and Emotional Adjustment of Immigrant Children: A Review of the Literature. *International Review of Migration* 18:237–57.

Arrendondo-Dowd, P. 1981. Personal Loss and Grief as a Result of Immigration. *Personnel and Guidance Journal,* 59:376–8.

Athey, J. L. and F. L. Ahearn. 1991. *Refugee Children: Theory, Research, and Services.* Baltimore, MD: Johns Hopkins University Press.

Berry, J. 1998. Acculturative Stress. In P. Organista, K. Chun, and G. Marin. *Readings in Ethnic Psychology.* New York: Routledge.

Brown, E. R., R. Wyn, H. Yu, A. Valenzuela, and L. Dong. 1998. Access to Health Insurance and Health Care for Mexican American Children in Immigrant Families. In M. Suarez-Orozco, ed., *Crossings: Mexican Immigration in Interdisciplinary Perspectives.* Cambridge, MA: Harvard University Press.

Chavez, L. 1992. *Shadowed Lives: Undocumented Immigrants in American Society.* Fort Worth, TX: Harcourt Brace College Publishers.

Cobb, S. 1988. Social Support as Moderator of Life Stress. *Psychosomatic Medicine* 3(5):300–14.

Cohen, S. and S. L. Syme. 1985. Issues in the Study and Application of Social Support. In S. Cohen and S. L. Syme, eds., *Social Support and Health.* Orlando, FL: Academic Press.

Cornelius, Wayne. 1998. The Strutural Embeddedness of Demand for Mexican Immigrant Labor. In *Crossings: Mexican Immigration in Interdisciplinary Perspectives.* Marcelo M. Suárez-Orozco, ed. Cambridge, MA: David Rockefeller Center for Latin American Studies, Harvard University Press.

De Vos, G. 1973. *Socialization for Achievement: Essays on the Cultural Psychology of the Japanese.* Berkeley, CA: University of California Press, 1992. *The Passing of Passing in Contemporary Society. Cohesion and Alienation: Minorities in the United States and Japan.* Boulder, CO: Westview Press.

De Vos, G. and M. Suárez-Orozco. 1990. *Status Inequality: The Self in Culture.* Newbury Park, CA: Sage Press.

Dohrenwend B. P. 1986. Theoretical Formulation of Life Stress Variables. In A. Eichler, M. M. Silverman, and D. M. Pratt, eds., *How to Define and Research Stress.* Washington, DC: American Psychiatric Press.

Dugger, C. 1997. Queens Old-Timers Uneasy as Asian Influence Grows. *New York Times.* March 31.

Erickson, E. 1964. *Identity, Youth, Crisis.* New York: W. W. Norton.

Eschbach, K. J., Hagan, N., Rodriguez, S. Bailey, and R. Hernandez-Leon. 1997. *Death at the Border—June 1997.* http:// www.nnirr.org.

Espanshade, T. and M. Belanger. 1998. Immigration and Public Opinion. In M. Suárez-Orozco, ed., *Crossings: Mexican Immigration in Interdisciplinary Perspectives.* Cambridge, MA: Harvard University Press.

Espin, O. M. 1987. Psychological Impact of Migration on Latinas. *Psychology of Women Quarterly* 11:489–503.
Flaskerud, J. H. and R. Uman. 1996. Acculturation and its Effects on Self-Esteem Among Immigrant Latina Women. *Behavioral Medicine* 22:123–33.
Foster, G. 1972. The Anatomy of Envy: A Study of Symbolic Behavior. *Current Anthropology* 13(2):165–202.
Freud, S. 1968 [original 1919]. The Uncanny. In *The Standard Edition of the Complete Psychological Works of Sigmund Freud*, ed., J. Strachey. London: The Hogarth Press.
Furnham, A. and S. Bochner. 1986. *Culture Shock*. London: Methuen.
Gans, H. 1992. Second-Generation Decline: Scenarios for the Economic and Ethnic Futures of the Post-1965 Immigrants. *Ethnic and Racial Studies* 15 (April):173–92.
Garcia-Coll, C. and K. Magnuson. 1997. The Psychological Experience of Immigration: A Developmental Perspective. In A. Booth, A. Crouter, and N. Landale, eds., *Immigration and the Family: Research and Policy on U.S. Immigrants*. Mahwah, NJ: Lawrence Erlbaum Associates, Publishers.
Gordon, M. 1964. *Assimilation in American Life*. New York: Oxford University Press.
Greenberg, J. R. and S. A. Mitchell. 1983. *Object Relations in Psychoanalytic Theory*. Cambridge, MA: Harvard University Press.
Grinberg, L. and R. Grinberg. 1989. *Psychoanalytic Perspectives on Migration and Exile*. New Haven, CT: University Press.
Hagan, J. 1998. Commentary to the U.S. Immigration Control Offensive. In *Crossings: Mexican Immigration in Interdisciplinary Perspectives*. Marcelo M. Suárez-Orozco, ed. Cambridge, MA: David Rockefeller Center for Latin American Studies, Harvard University Press.
Heller, K. and R. W. Swindel. 1983. Social Networks, Perceived Social Support, and Coping with Stress. In R. D. Felner, ed., *Preventative Psychology: Theory, Research, and Practice in Community Intervention*. New York: Penguin Press.
Hoffmann, E. 1989. *Lost in Translation: A Life in a New Language*. New York: Penguin Books.
Horowitz, M. 1986. *Stress Response Syndromes*. 2nd edition. Northvale, NJ: Jason Aronson.
House, J. S. 1974. Occupational Stress and Coronary Heart Disease: A Review. *Journal of Health and Social Behavior* 15:12–27.
Jones-Correa, M. 1998. Commentary: Immigration and Public Opinion. In M. Suárez-Orozco, eds., *Crossings: Mexican Immigration in Interdisciplinary Perspectives*. Cambridge, MA: Harvard University Press.
Kanner, D. A., J. C. Coyne, C. Scaefer, and R. S. Lazarus. 1981. Comparison of Two Models of Stress Measurement: Daily Hassles and Uplifts Versus Major Life Events. *American Journal of Behavioral Medicine* 4:1–39.
Kao, G. and M. Tienda. 1995. Optimism and Achievement: The Educational Performance of Immigrant Youth. *Social Science Quarterly* 76(1):1–19.
Kohut, H. 1971. *The Analysis of Self: A Systematic Approach to the Psychoanalytic Treatment of Personality Disorders*. New York: International Universities Press.
La Fromboise, T., H. Coleman, and J. Gerton. 1998. Psychological Impact of Biculturalism. In P. Organista, K. Chun, and G. Marin, eds., *Readings in Ethnic Psychology*. New York: Routledge.
Laosa, L. 1989. *Psychological Stress, Coping, and the Development of the Hispanic Immigrant Child*. Princeton, NJ: Educational Testing Service.
Lazarus, R. S. and S. Folkman. 1984. *Stress, Appraisal and Coping*. New York: Springer Publishing Company.
Myers, D. 1998. Dimensions of Economic Adaptation by Mexican-Origin Men. In M. Suárez-Orozco, ed., *Crossings: Mexican Immigration in Interdisciplinary Perspectives*. Cambridge, MA: Harvard University Press.
National Research Council, 1998. *Children of Immigrants: Health Adjustment, and Public Assistance*. Washington, DC: National Research Council.
Noshpitz, J. D. and R. D. Coddington. 1990. *Stressors and the Adjustment Disorders*. Hoboken, NJ: Wiley and Sons.
Obeyesekere, G. 1990. *The Work of Culture: Symbolic Transformation in Psychoanalysis and Anthropology*. Chicago: University of Chicago Press.
Ogbu, J. and H. D. Simons. 1998. Voluntary and Involuntary Minorities: A Cultural-Ecological Theory of School Performance with Some Implications for Education. *Anthropology and Education Quarterly* 29(2):1155–88.
Olsen, L. 1998. *Made In America: Immigrant Students in Our Public Schools*. New York: The New Press.
Orfield, G. 1998. Commentary on the Education of Mexican Immigrant Children. In M. Suárez-Orozco, ed., *Crossings: Mexican Immigration in Interdisciplinary Perspectives*. Cambridge, MA: Harvard University Press.
Organista, P., K. Chun, and G. Marin, eds. 1998. *Readings in Ethnic Psychology*. New York: Routledge.
Padilla, A., R. Cervantes, M. Maldonado, and R. Garcia. 1988. Coping Responses to Psychosocial Stressors Among Mexican and Central American Immigrants. *Journal of Community Psychology* 16:418–27.
Pearlin, L. I. and C. Schooler. 1978. The Structure of Coping. *Journal of Health and Social Behavior* 19(3):2–21.
Phinney, J. 1998. Ethnic Identity in Adolescents and Adults. In P. Organista, K. Chun, and G. Marin, eds. *Readings in Ethnic Psychology*. New York: Routledge.
Portes, A. and R. Rumbaut. 1990. *Immigrant America: A Portrait*. Berkeley, CA: University of California Press.
Portes, A. and L. Hao. 1998. English First or English Only?: E Pluribus Unum: Bilingualism and Language Loss in the Second Generation. *Sociology of Education* 71(4):269–94.
Portes, A. and M. Zhou. 1993. The New Second Generation: Segmented Assimilation and Its Variants. *Annals of the American Academy* 530, November.
Proposition 187. 1994. *Illegal Aliens. Ineligibility for Public Services. Verification, and Reporting*. Initiative Statute. Sacramento, CA: State of California.
Roberts, R., C. Roberts, and Y. R. Chen. 1998. Ethnocultural Differences in Prevalence of Adolescent Depression. In P. Organista, K. Chun, and G. Marin, eds. *Readings in Ethnic Psychology*. New York: Routledge.
Rodriguez, Luis. 1993. *Always Running*. New York: Touchstone Books.

Rogler, L. 1998. Research on Mental Health Services for Hispanics: Targets of Convergence. P. Organista, K. Chun, and G. Marin, eds. *Readings in Ethnic Psychology.* New York: Routledge.

Rosenthal, R. and L. Jacobson. 1968. *Pygmalion in the Classroom: Teacher Expectations and Pupils' Intellectual Development.* New York: Holt, Rinehart and Winston.

Rumbaut, R. D. 1977. Life Events, Change, Migration, and Depression. In W. E. Fann, I. Karocan, A. D. Pokorny, and R. L. Williams, eds. *Phenomenology and Treatment of Depression.* New York: Spectrum 1995, The New Californians: Comparative Research Findings on the Educational Progress of Immigrant Children. In R. Rumbaut and W. Cornelius, eds. *California's Immigrant Children.* La Jolla, CA: Center for U.S.-Mexican Studies.

1996. *Becoming American: Acculturation, Achievement, and Aspirations Among Children of Immigrants.* Paper presented at the Annual Meeting of the American Association for the Advancement of Science, Baltimore, MD, Feb. 10.

1996. Ties That Bind: Immigration and Immigrant Families in the United States. In *Immigration and Family: Research and Policy on U.S. Immigrants.* A. Booth, A. C. Crouter and N. Landale, eds. Mahwah, NJ: Lawrence Erlbaum.

1997. Achievement and Ambition Among Children of Immigrants in Southern California. Paper presented to the Jerome Levy Economics Institute of Board College, Annandale-on-the-Hudson, NY.

Schlossberg, Nancy K. 1984. *Counseling Adults in Transition: Linking Practice with Theory.* New York: Springer.

Seligman, M. 1998. The American Way of Blame. *American Psychological Association Monitor* 29(7):2.

Shuval, J. 1980. Migration and Stress. In I. L. Kutasshm et al., eds. *Handbook on Stress and Anxiety: Contemporary Knowledge, Theory, and Treatment.* San Francisco: Jossery-Bass.

Simon, Rita J. 1985. *Public Opinion and the Immigrant: Print Media Coverage, 1880–1980.* Lexington, MA: Lexington Books.

Sluzki, Carlos. 1979. Migration and Family Conflict, *Family Process* 18(4):379–90.

Smajkic, Amer and S. Weane. 1995. Special Issues of Newly Arrived Refugee Groups. In Susan Somach, ed. *Issues of War Trauma and Working with Refugees: A Compilation of Resources.* Washington, DC: Center for Applied Linguistics Refugee Service Center.

Smart, J. F. and D. W. Smart. 1995. Acculturation Stress of Hispanics: Loss and Challenge. *Journal of Counseling and Development* 75:390–6.

Somach, Susan, ed. 1995. *Issues of War Trauma and Working with Refugees: A Compilation of Resources.* Washington, DC: Center for Applied Linguistics Refugee Service Center.

Steinberg, S. 1996. *Beyond the Classroom: Why School Reform Has Failed and What Parents Need to Do.* New York: Simon and Schuster.

Stonequist, E. V. 1937. *The Marginal Man: A Study in Personality and Cultural Conflict.* New York: Scribners.

Suárez-Orozco, Carola. 1998. The Transitions of Immigration: How Do Men and Women Differ? *DRCLAS News* Winter:6–7.

Suárez-Orozco, C. and M. Suárez-Orozco. 1995. *Transformations: Migration, Family Life, and Achievement Motivation Among Latino Adolescents.* Palo Alto, CA: Stanford University Press.

Suárez-Orozco, M. 1989. *Central American Refugees and U.S. High Schools: A Psychosocial Study of Motivation and Achievement.* Stanford, CA: Stanford University Press.

1996. California Dreaming: Proposition 187 and the Cultural Psychology of Ethnic and Racial Exclusion. *Anthropology and Education Quarterly* 27(2):151–67.

1998. *Crossings: Mexican Immigration in Interdisciplinary Perspectives.* Cambridge, MA: Harvard University Press.

Suro, R. 1994. California's SOS on Immigration. *The Washington Post,* Sept. 29.

1998. *Strangers Among Us: How Latino Immigration is Transforming America.* New York: Alfred Knopf.

Tajfel, H. 1978. *The Social Psychology of Minorities.* New York: Minority Rights Group.

Takaki, R. 1989. *Strangers from a Different Shore.* New York: Penguin.

Vernez, G., A. Abrahamse, and D. Quigley. 1996. *How Immigrants Fare in U.S. Education.* Santa Monica, CA: Rand.

Vigil, Diego. 1988. *Barrio Gangs: Street Life and Identity in Southern California.* Austin: University of Texas Press.

Volkan, V. D. 1993. Immigrants and Refugees: A Psychodynamic Perspective. *Mind and Human Interaction* 4(2):63–9.

Waters, M. 1990. *Ethnic Options: Choosing Identities in America.* Berkeley: University of California Press.

1996. *West Indian Family Resources and Adolescent Outcomes: Trajectories of the Second Generation.* Paper presented at the Annual Meeting of the American Association for the Advancement of Science, Baltimore, MD, Feb. 10.

Waldinger R. 1996. *Still the Promised City? African-Americans and New Immigrants in Postindustrial New York.* Cambridge, MA: Harvard University Press.

1997. *Social Capital or Social Closure?—Immigrant Networks in the Labor Market.* Los Angeles: Lewis Center for Regional Policy Studies, University of California, Los Angeles, Working Paper Series, No. 26.

Wheaton, B. 1983. Stress, Personal Coping Resources, and Psychiatric Symptoms: An Investigation of Interactive Models. *Journal of Health and Social Behavior* 24(9):208–29.

Wills, T. A. 1985. Supportive Functions of Interpersonal Relationships. In S. Cohen and S. L. Symee, eds., *Social Support and Health.* Orlando, FL: Academic Press, Inc.

Winnicott, D. W. 1971. *Playing and Reality.* Harmondsworth, England: Penguin.

Wong-Fillmore, L. 1991. When Learning a Second Language Means Losing the First. *Early Childhood Research Quarterly* 6:323–46.

Chapter 8
The Immigrant Family: Cultural Legacies and Cultural Changes[1]

NANCY FONER

This chapter examines the way family and kinship patterns change in the process of immigration—and why. Offering an interpretative synthesis, it emphasizes the way first-generation immigrants to the United States fuse together the old and new to create a new kind of family life. The family is seen as a place where there is a dynamic interplay between structure, culture, and agency. New immigrant family patterns are shaped by cultural meanings and social practices that immigrants bring with them from their home countries as well as by social, economic, and cultural forces in the United States.

Immigrants live out much of their lives in the context of families. A lot has been written about the way family networks stimulate and facilitate the migration process itself, the role of family ties and networks in helping immigrants get jobs when they arrive in the United States, and the role of families in developing strategies for survival and assisting immigrants in the process of adjustment, providing a place where newcomers can find solace and support in a strange land and can pool their resources as a way to advance. Along with the increasing interest in gender and generation, there is a growing literature on the position of women and children in immigrant families—and an awareness that the family is not just a haven in a heartless world but a place where conflict and negotiation also take place.

In this chapter, I take a different tack. My concern is with the way family and kinship patterns change in the process of immigration—and why. The focus, I want to emphasize, is on first-generation immigrants who come from one world to live in a new one and, in the process, fuse together the old and new to create a new kind of family life (see Kibria, 1993). In this account, the family is not simply a site where immigrants create and carry out agendas or strategies, nor are family relations and dynamics reducible to rational economic calculations. Rather, the family is seen as a place where there is a dynamic interplay between structure, culture, and agency—where creative culture-building takes place in the context of external social and economic forces as well as immigrants' pre-migration cultural frameworks.

Clearly, a host of structural constraints and conditions that immigrants confront in their new environment shape the kinds of family arrangements, roles, and orientations that emerge among them. So do the norms and values they encounter when they move to the United States. Moreover, immigrants are not passive individuals who are acted upon by external forces. They play an active role in reconstructing and redefining family life. Indeed, members of the family, by virtue of their gender and generation, have differing interests so that women (and men) and young people (and older people) often try to fashion family patterns in ways that improve their positions and further their aims (see Kibria, 1993; Oxfeld, 1993).

But something else is at work, too. The cultural understandings, meanings, and symbols that immigrants bring with them from their home societies are also critical in understanding immigrant family life. Obviously, immigrants do not exactly reproduce their old cultural patterns when they move to a new land; but these patterns continue to have a powerful influence in shaping family values and norms as well as actual patterns of behavior that develop in the new setting. Indeed, as Nazli Kibria (1993) observes, immigrants may walk a delicate tightrope as they challenge certain aspects of traditional family systems while they also try to retain others.

Attention to the role of immigrants' "cultural roots"[2] in shaping new family patterns bids us to look at the way these patterns differ from one group to another—despite common structural conditions they face and despite common social processes and dynamics of family life. Family patterns among Korean immigrants and Haitians in the United States, to name just two groups, diverge in many ways at least in part because of the cultural background of each group. The very meaning of the term family and other basic, taken-for-granted cultural aspects of kinship, like who is considered a relative, vary among different immigrant populations. Indeed, the particular groups that social scientists study may well influence the models they develop about family life and family change. It is not surprising that scholars who study Asian immigrants, whose family and kinship systems are markedly different from those of Americans, have tended to put more emphasis on the role of cultural continuity with the sending society than scholars who study Caribbean immigrants, whose family patterns are more like those in this country.

PRE-MIGRATION CULTURAL INFLUENCES

Several studies have pointed out ways that pre-migration cultural conceptions and social practices continue to have force in the United States. These conceptions and practices do not continue unchanged, of course. They are restructured, redefined, and renegotiated in the new setting. Yet immigrants continue to draw on pre-migration family experiences, norms, and cultural frameworks as they carve out new lives for themselves in the United States (see Hondagneu-Sotelo 1994).

To be sure, the cultures from which immigrants come are themselves the product of change, so it is misleading to assume a timeless past of family tradition there. Indeed, family patterns in the sending society may well have undergone significant transformations in the lifetimes of the immigrants or their parents. In her study of Japanese immigrants who came to the United States in the first decades of this century, Sylvia Yanagisako (1985:17–18) notes that the Japan in which they grew up in the late nineteenth century was as dynamic as the United States in which their children grew up in the twentieth century. At the end of the nineteenth century, Japan was characterized by great population growth, industrialization, a spreading market economy, and increasing urban migration. At the same time as ideas from the West were finding their way into Japan, the ideology of the ruling warrior class, including ideas about marriage and family practices—such as parentally arranged marriages and standards of primogenitural succession and inheritance—were spreading to the peasantry in a process of "samuraization." To take another example, recent Vietnamese refugees to the United States grew up in Vietnam in the period between the 1950s and 1970s when the upheavals of war and urbanization led to dramatic transformations in traditional kinship structures (Kibria 1993; see also Freeman 1995).

Although there is no such thing as a timeless tradition, immigrants may come to think of life in their home society in these terms. As Yanagisako puts it, they may construct their own versions of tradition as they reconceptualize the past to make sense of current experience and to speak to current dilemmas and issues. These "invented traditions" can have a life of their own in that immigrants may interpret and act upon the present in light of their models of the past (Yanagisako 1985:247).

Among the many factors that help to keep alive (albeit in modified form) cultural patterns from the home country are strong immigrant communities and institutions, dense ethnic networks, and continued, transnational ties to the sending society. In many cases, immigrants are part of what have been called multi-local binational families (Guarnizo 1997), with parents and children distributed in households across national borders. Whatever their living arrangements, those in the United States are able, through modern transportation, to visit back and forth, and through modern communications they are able to participate in family events and decisions from a distance (Basch, Glick-Schiller, and Szanton-Blanc 1994; Foner 1997; Rouse 1991). This continued, close contact with home communities—or, as Roger Rouse (1991) puts it, simultaneous engagement in places with different forms of experience—often strengthens immigrants' attachments to family values and orientations in the home society. Indeed, transnational connections may foster a complex cross-fertilization process, as immigrants bring new notions to their home communities while at the same time they continue to be influenced by values and practices there.

This said, consider some ways that the cultural elements that immigrants bring with them can have an impact on family life in the United States. In her study of Vietnamese families in Philadelphia, Nazli Kibria (1993) argues that the Vietnamese ideology of family collectivism promoted cooperative kin-based economic practices that helped families cope and survive in the immigrant setting. The notion that the kin group was of more significance than the individual drew strength from Confucian ideology, including the importance of ancestor worship. In the households she visited, family altars with photographs of deceased relatives were a common sight; the death anniversaries of important departed ancestors were almost always observed with the performance of rites to honor them. Ancestor worship, Kibria writes, "affirmed the sacredness and essential unity of the kin group as well as its permanence in comparison to the transience of the individual. … It highlighted obligation as a key feature of a member's relationship to the kin group … [and] familial obligation was defined by the idea that the needs and desires of the kin group took precedence over personal ones" (1993:100).

Partly because Vietnamese immigrants believe that kinship ties are an effective way to cope with uncertainty and economic scarcity, they engaged in what Kibria calls a process of kin-group reconstruction in the absence of close kin in Philadelphia. They elevated distant kin to the position of closer relatives, placed more importance than they used to on kinship ties forged by marriage, and redefined non-kin with whom they had close "kinship-like ties" as kin, using kinship terms (like brother) to refer to them and their relations. Among recent Hmong refugees in Wausau, Wisconsin, patrilineal clan and lineage ties continue to influence day-to-day relations. Socializing, anthropologist JoAnn Koltyk (1998) observes, is largely confined to patrilineal kin. Unless they are in the same kin group, Hmong next-door neighbors do not visit or sometimes even greet each other.

Another example of the continued impact of pre-migration cultural beliefs and social practices is arranged marriages among South Asian immigrants. In many South Asian immigrant families, parents formally arrange the marriage of their children. When young people reach marriageable age, usually after finishing college, an all-points bulletin is broadcast through the networks of family and friends (Lessinger 1995). Sometimes, immigrants return to India to find a spouse or rely on friends and relatives there to help in the search. Newspaper advertisements may be used to broaden the pool of candidates. A good number of classified advertisements in Indian newspapers relate to

American-born or American-raised people who are looking for spouses. One recent advertisement read, "U.S.-raised Ivy League graduate seeks U.S.-raised girl"; another said, "Match for beautiful, progressive, U.S.-born medical student. Looking for U.S.-born young man, handsome, and professional" (Jaleshgari 1995).

Long Island leaders in predominantly South Asian neighborhoods, according to a recent account in *The New York Times*, estimate that almost one-half of American-born or American-raised people of South Asian heritage agree to formally arranged marriages (Jaleshgari 1995). Some young people view arranged marriages positively, seeing them as a way to avoid the frightening American dating scene, involving premarital sex and potential rejection. More commonly, young people submit, if reluctantly, to arranged marriages in the face of parental pressure (Lessinger 1995). In the closely-knit Punjabi Sikh community in rural "Valleyside" California, gossip, shame, and guilt were sanctions that parents used to ensure that children (especially daughters) went along with parental marriage plans. Young people who married without their parents' blessings risked being cut off, although anthropologist Margaret Gibson (1988:126–127) notes that Punjabi youths' ties to family and community were so strong that this ultimate sanction was rarely needed. Other accounts indicate that new conflicts and tensions have developed around arranged marriages in the United States (see short stories of Divakaruni 1995) and that "courtship" and marriage patterns are changing in many ways (see Lessinger 1995).[3] Still, arranged marriages are alive and well in South Asian immigrant communities, and, for better or worse, they are an issue with which the younger generation are often forced to deal.

NEW FAMILY PATTERNS

If immigrants bring with them a "memory of things past" that operates as a filter through which they view and experience—and create—new lives in the United States, it is also clear that much changes here. Faced with new circumstances in the United States, many beliefs, values, and cultural symbols as well as behavior patterns undergo change. While some former beliefs and social institutions persist apparently intact, they may change, if only subtly, in form and function in the new environment.

To say that immigrants change, however, does not mean that they become fully assimilated into American culture. Indeed, the classic concept of assimilation glosses over many complexities in the way immigrants and their institutions change in this country. As many scholars have pointed out, the notion of assimilation, as commonly understood, is too simplistic to analyze immigrant change in a complex society like the United States where there is no undifferentiated, monolithic "American" culture. Indeed, the notion of segmented assimilation is an attempt to refine the assimilation concept. Segmented assimilation refers to the fact that immigrants assimilate to particular sectors of American society, with some becoming integrated into the majority white middle class and others assimilating into the inner-city underclass (Portes and Zhou 1993; Portes 1995).

Yet even if we find similar behavior patterns among immigrants and certain Americans, this is not necessarily an indication of assimilation in the sense of internalizing the new ways and values. Rather, these behavior patterns may be independent responses to similar social or economic conditions that immigrants and the American-born face. Moreover, as Yanagisako (1985) argues, immigrants and native-born Americans may have apparently similar norms regarding, for example, conjugal relations, but they may conceptualize these norms in light of different folk histories. These very conceptions and models of the past can influence the way people act and thus play a role in further shaping or modifying kinship norms and behavior. Immigrants "interpret their particular cultural histories in ways that generate issues of meaning and symbolic categories that in turn structure their kinship norms" (Yanagisako 1985:260).

A long line of scholars have recognized that the cultures of immigrant groups differ both from the culture left behind in the sending country and from American mainstream culture. In their 1918–1920 study of the Polish peasant in America, Thomas and Znaniecki wrote of the "creation of a [Polish-American] society which in structure and prevalent attitudes is neither Polish nor American but constitutes a specific new product whose raw materials have been partly drawn from Polish traditions, partly from the new conditions in which the immigrants live, and partly from American social values as the immigrant sees and interprets them" (1996:108). Some 40 years later, Glazer and Moynihan's critique of the melting pot notion tried to get at the way New York's immigrant groups became "something they had not been, but still something distinct and identifiable" (1963:14). Margaret Gibson argued that the end result of assimilation or acculturation among immigrants need not be the rejection of old traits and their replacement. Rather, "acculturation may be an additive process or one in which old and new traits are blended" (Gibson 1988:25).

In my work on Jamaican immigrants, I have found it useful to think of the process by which new cultural and social patterns emerge among them as a kind of "creolization" process. The term creolization has long been used in the Caribbean to describe the social system that developed in Jamaica and other West Indian societies. Neither African nor English, the locally developed system of social relations and cultural forms was something completely new—creole—that was created in the context of specific West Indian economic, social, and political circumstances (Smith 1967; Mintz and Price 1992). The population, Raymond Smith writes, became increasingly "creolized rather than Anglicized, a process which affected Englishmen as well as others" (1967:234).

Thinking in terms of a kind of creolization process occurring among late-twentieth-century immigrants in the United States suggests that we look at the blend of meanings, perceptions, and social patterns that emerges among the immigrants. This blend, needless to say, is different for each immigrant group, reflecting, among other things, its specific cultural, social, and demographic characteristics. At play are the complex processes of change as customs, values, and attitudes that immigrants bring from home begin to shift in the context of new hierarchies, cultural conceptions, and social institutions they confront in this country (Foner 1977, 1994). As I have argued elsewhere, Jamaican immigrants do not become exactly like Americans, black or white. Nor are they any longer just like Jamaicans in the home society. New meanings, ideologies, and patterns of behavior develop among them in response to conditions and circumstances they encounter here.

The Vietnamese case cited above is a good example of this kind of creolization process. Confucian family ideology lingers on in many ways, but there are new arrangements, too, as more distant kin, in-laws, and "fictive kin" have been drawn into the bosom of the family (Kibria 1993). As noted in my own research on Jamaican family life in New York, I also found a mix of old and new. As in Jamaica, the household was primarily women's domain. There seemed to be little change in attitudes to illegitimacy or common-law unions among most immigrants; these were still widely accepted practices with no stigma attached to them. Much to women's dismay, men continued in New York to have a propensity to wander and to divert resources away from the household. Yet, there were also changes. Jamaican women in New York were less tolerant of men's outside sexual exploits and more likely to demand that men help out and spend time at home. The reasons: Women had greater financial independence in New York; they were at work and did not have female relatives available to provide assistance; and they were influenced by dominant American values extolling the ideal of marital fidelity and "family togetherness" (Foner 1994, 1986). A number of studies of other groups have shown that though immigrants "bring their own versions of 'traditional' patriarchal codes to the United States" (Pessar 1996), their households become less patriarchal and more egalitarian here as women gain access to social and economic resources previously beyond their reach and as they participate more actively in public life (Espiritu 1997; Grasmuck and Pessar 1991; Hondagneu-Sotelo 1994; Kibria 1993; Pessar 1987).

To return, once more, to Yanagisako's (1985) detailed analysis of Japanese American kinship, her work provides a good illustration of the kind of culture creation or culture-building process I am talking about. As Japanese immigrants (and their children) constructed their family lives here, they drew on models of "Japanese" as well as "American" kinship, creating a "Japanese American" synthesis (1985:22). Japanese American kinship, she writes, is, at all levels of analysis, similar to and different from what has been described as the kinship system of white middle-class Americans. The composition of Japanese American family gatherings and life-cycle celebrations is larger and genealogically more extended than is generally reported for the white middle class. Concerning normative expectations, the filial responsibilities of second-generation (Nisei) sons and daughters appear more sharply defined and more differentiated by gender than the filial responsibilities articulated by middle-class whites. Moreover, the assignment of the role of representative of the sibling group to the elder brother in certain kinship and community affairs such as funerals is not common among other Americans (Yanagisako 1985:255).

What also holds Japanese kinship together, Yanagisako argues, and differentiates it from kinship among other Americans is "Japanese Americans' shared model of their cultural history. The model is at the same time a charter for what Japanese American social life should continue to be and how it might change. Other Americans do not share this charter even though they may share many of its provisions, for other Americans do not conceptualize their kinship relations in terms of their connections with an ancestral Japanese past and the experience of Japanese immigrants to America" (1985:258).

The maintenance of extensive transnational connections among certain groups, or certain sectors of groups, adds a further dynamic to the process of change as new family forms develop in the context of transnational communities or migration circuits. For example, in the "multi-local binational families" that are frequently found among Dominicans, one or both parents live in New York City with some or none of their children while other children live on the island in households headed by relatives or non-relatives (Guarnizo 1997). Among successful Korean professionals and businessmen, what Pyong Gap Min (1998) calls "international commuter marriages" arise when the husband returns to Korea for a better job while his wife and children remain in the United States to take advantage of educational opportunities here. They visit several times a year and talk on the phone at least once a week.

FACTORS SHAPING FAMILY CHANGE

Why do family and kinship patterns among immigrants change and develop the way they do? This is an enormously complicated question that would require detailed study of a wide range of groups to determine the combination of factors that produce certain kinds of changes in particular populations. As a way to begin building a framework for studying immigrant family change, I want to suggest some of the factors involved.

I have already discussed the role of pre-migration family, marriage, and kinship beliefs and practices in shaping family lives here. The demographic composition of the immigrant group also has an impact; sex and age ratios in each group affect marriage and family patterns. For example, a markedly unbalanced sex ratio will encourage marriage outside the group or consign many to singlehood or the search for spouses in the home country. Kibria argues that the scarcity of Vietnamese women in the United States enhanced unmarried women's value in the "marriage market," giving them greater bargaining power in their relationships with men. The women were able to use the threat of leaving a relationship to push partners to meet their demands (1993:112–121; see

Goodkind 1997). In other groups, a sizable proportion of old people may ease the childcare burdens of working women (for example, see Orleck 1987, on Russian Jews). In still other cases, the absence of immigrants' close kin in the new setting creates the need to improvise new arrangements, a reason why "fictive kin" are common in immigrant communities and why men sometimes find themselves filling in as helpmates to their wives in childcare and other household tasks.

Quite apart from cultural or socio-demographic features of the immigrant group, external forces in the new environment shape immigrant family lives as they provide new opportunities and constraints as well as new sets of values, beliefs, and standards. There are, for a start, economic conditions and opportunities. The immigration literature is filled with examples of immigrant women gaining authority in the household and increased leverage in relations with their spouses now that they have greater opportunities for wage employment and contribute a larger share of the family income in the United States. By the same token, declines in men's earning power can reduce their authority (see Kibria 1993:109–112). Among certain groups, old people have suffered a decline in status in the United States because, among other things, they no longer control valued resources such as land (see Chan 1994; Oxfeld 1993). Another scenario has been reported for New York's Korean elderly. Access to government welfare programs in the United States has allowed many to be more independent of their children—economically and residentially—than they would have been in Korea. According to Pyong Gap Min's account, the Korean elderly welcome these changes, pleased not to have to ask their children for money or to face restrictions and frequent conflicts that come with living with sons and daughters-in-law (1998).

Certain kinds of economic arrangements are more likely to support the continued importance of extended-kin ties than others. As an example from the period prior to World War II, the predominance of family businesses among the Japanese in Seattle (before the incarceration of the Japanese in internment camps) provided the Issei with an economic base for the stem family system of differentiated filial relations. First sons could be groomed to work in the family business, assume its management, and eventually support elderly parents with the proceeds from an enterprise that they had themselves worked to build. The wives of first sons could be incorporated into the household as useful, productive workers as well as reproducers of the next generation. Second sons and daughters could be "married out" of the household to create a ring of affinal ties with other households in the community (Yanagisako 1985:158).

Immigrants are also inevitably influenced by dominant American cultural beliefs and values concerning marriage, family, and kinship that are disseminated by the mass media, schools, and other institutions. (The term "influence" includes cases where immigrants enthusiastically embrace certain American beliefs and values or tentatively begin to accept or even angrily reject them.) Some family members are more enthusiastic about certain American values and norms than others. Typically, women are more eager than men to endorse values that enhance their position, just as young people generally support new norms that give them greater freedom that their parents may resist.

As I mentioned earlier, I found that Jamaicans were influenced by American notions about the desirability of nuclear family "togetherness" and joint husband-wife activities. Dominican women studied by Grasmuck and Pessar (1991) claimed to be patterning their more egalitarian relations with their spouses on what they believed to be the dominant American model. According to Kibria (1993), American notions about the equality of men and women and an acceptance of women who smoke, drink beer, and wear "clothes that show their bodies" challenged Vietnamese norms of feminine behavior and gender relations. In general, American ideas about what kinds of dating and premarital sexual behavior are appropriate, as well as about romantic love and free marriage choice, provide ammunition for immigrant children who want to reject arranged marriages and close supervision of their relations with the opposite sex. Indeed, parents may modify their demands in the face of the new American values for fear of alienating their children altogether and creating a legacy of resentment (Yanagisako 1985). Alternatively, serious conflicts may develop when young people (or women), spurred on by changed expectations and expanded economic opportunities, are more assertive in challenging parental (or spousal) authority (see, for example, Min 1998; Pessar 1995).

Finally, the legal system in the United States provides a further impetus to change, making certain pre-migration customs and practices illegal or giving legal support to challenges to these practices. One reason wife-beating is less common among Vietnamese immigrants in the United States than in Vietnam is that immigrants are highly conscious that such behavior is "illegal." Kibria tells of cases where women telephoned the police during physical confrontations with their partners (1993:121–125). In my research on Jamaicans, I found that children threatened to, and sometimes actually did, call the police to prevent or stop physical abuse from their parents. Parents bitterly resented this new infringement on their authority and ability to discipline their children through physical beatings, but many tempered their behavior as a result.

The United States legal system and government agencies can affect family relations by defining family membership and rules, like those pertaining to inheritance, in terms of American cultural assumptions. United States immigration laws themselves, based on American notions of the nuclear family, facilitate the immigration of parents, legitimate children, and legal spouses while often separating "illegitimate" children and "common-law" spouses as well as siblings and other close, cooperating kin (see Garrison and Weiss 1987). A study of the Laotian Hmong in California notes that social service agencies affect the Hmong's sense of what constitutes a "family" by using the nuclear (rather than extended) family as the unit of distribution for various kinds of assistance (Chan 1994). And the fact that women are frequently the intermediaries between their households and outside government agencies (including various kinds of public assistance programs) often expands the scope of their activities and plays a role in improving their status in this country (Hondagneu-Sotelo 1994; Kibria 1993).

CONCLUSION

In the wake of the enormous recent immigration to the United States, we are only just beginning to understand the complex ways that the new arrivals construct—and reconstruct—their family lives here. In this article, I have discussed some of the dynamics involved, including the cultural meanings and social practices immigrants bring with them from their home countries as well as structural, economic, and cultural forces in their new environments. As we search for common factors that impinge on and shape immigrants' family lives—or look for evidence of ways that immigrants are becoming more like "Americans"—we also need to bear in mind that each group puts a unique stamp on family and kinship relations that stems from its special cultural and social background.

Clearly, a lot more work needs to be done in this field. We need additional, careful cultural—as well as structural—analyses of immigrants' family lives to appreciate the new forms and patterns that develop among them here. Of late, there has been considerable analysis of the way that the status of immigrant women, men, and young people change in the United States, but we also need studies that investigate the meanings that immigrants attach to their kinship and family relations. Cultural analysis is important, not because culture constitutes a controlling code and thereby assumes causal priority in the understanding of social action, but because, as anthropologist Raymond Smith reminds us, "without adequacy at the level of meaning the other dimensions of the analysis are all too likely to be rooted in the unexamined assumptions of the observer's own culture" (1988:27; see also Schneider 1968).

The complex interplay between culture, structure, and agency—stressed throughout this article—is involved in other questions that call for further study. This article has focused on the first generation, but obviously it is crucial to explore how, and to what extent, their present family arrangements, roles, and orientations will leave a mark on the second generation who are born and raised in the United States. Among the immigrants themselves, there is the question of whether some of the changes in family relations I have mentioned here, such as women's increased power in dealings with their spouses, are simply a temporary phase and that if circumstances allow, premigration forms will be reconstituted. Alternatively, shifts in family and kinship relations in the United States may have a lasting effect, altering immigrants' expectations and notions about what is acceptable behavior and "the right thing to do" in the family and among kin. It seems highly likely that changes in actual social relations, however small, will leave a permanent mark and will ultimately impress themselves on normative patterns that guide action. Moreover, there is the intriguing possibility, noted by Richard Alba and Victor Nee (1996), that family patterns and values among some immigrant groups will affect notions of what is considered "normal" behavior in mainstream America and, over time, become part of the standard repertoire. Whether—and how—such processes will take place in the years ahead is just one of the many questions that pose a challenge for future research.

Notes

1. I would like to thank Josh DeWind, Charles Hirschman, Philip Kasinitz, and Mary Waters for their comments on an earlier version of this article.
2. There is no single definition of culture agreed upon by anthropologists. Here I use it to refer to the "taken-for-granted but powerfully influential understandings and codes that are learned and shared by members of a group" (Peacock 1986).
3. One way the arranged-marriage institution is shifting in the United States, according to Lessinger (1995), is that caste, language group, and religion are less important in mate selection if the young people are otherwise compatible in terms of education and profession. Also "semi-arranged marriages" are becoming increasingly common. Parents introduce suitable prescreened young men and women who are then allowed a brief courtship period during which to decide whether they like each other well enough to marry.

References

Alba, R. and V. Nee. 1996. The Assimilation of Immigrant Groups: Concept, Theory, and Evidence. Paper presented at the Social Science Research Council conference on Becoming American/America Becoming. Sanibel Island. February.

Basch, L., N. Glick-Shiller and C. Szanton-Blanc. 1994. *Nations Unbound: Transnational Projects and the Deterritorialized Nation-State.* Langhorne, PA: Gordon and Breach.

Chan, S. 1994. *Hmong Means Free.* Philadelphia, PA: Temple University Press.

Divakaruni, C. 1995. *Arranged Marriage.* New York: Doubleday.

Espiritu, Y. L. 1997. *Asian American Women and Men.* Thousand Oaks. CA: Sage.

Foner, N. 1997. What's New About Transnationalism? New York Immigrants Today and at the Turn of the Century. Paper presented at New School for Social Research, conference on "Transnational Communities and the Political Economy of New York in the 1990s." New York. February.

—— 1994. Ideology and Social Practice in the Jamaican Diaspora. Working Paper No. 65, Russell Sage Foundation. New York.

—— 1986. Sex Roles and Sensibilities: Jamaican Women in New York and London. In *International Migration: The Female Experience.* R. Simon and C. Brettell, eds. Totowa, NJ: Rowman and Allenheld.

—— 1977. The Jamaicans: Cultural and Social Change among Migrants in Britain. In *Between Two Cultures: Migrants and Minorities in Britain.* J. L. Watson, ed. Oxford: Basil Blackwell.

Freeman, J. 1995. *Changing Identities: Vietnamese Americans, 1975–1995.* Needham Heights, MA: Allyn and Bacon.

Garrison, V. and C. Weiss. 1987. Dominican Family Networks and United States Immigration Policy: A Case Study. In *Caribbean Life in New York City.* E. Chaney and C. Sutton, eds. New York: Center for Migration Studies.

Gibson, M. 1988. *Accommodation without Assimilation: Sikh Immigrants in an American High School.* Ithaca. NY: Cornell University Press.

Glazer, N. and D. Moynihan. 1963. *Beyond the Melting Pot.* Cambridge, MA: MIT Press.

Goodkind, D. 1997. "The Vietnamese Double Marriage Squeeze." *International Migration Review* 31(1):108–127.

Grasmuck, S. and P. Pessar. 1991. *Between Two Islands.* Berkeley: University of California Press.

Guarnizo, L. E. 1997. Going Home: Class, Gender, and Household Transformation among Dominican Immigrants. In *Caribbean Circuits.* P. Pessar, ed. New York: Center for Migration Studies.
Hondagneu-Sotelo, P. 1994. *Gendered Transitions: Mexican Experiences of Immigration.* Berkeley: University of California Press.
Jaleshgari, R. 1995. "Taking Life's Big Step: Marriage (Arranged)." *The New York Times* (*Long Island Weekly*). Aug. 13.
Kibria, N. 1993. *Family Tightrope: The Changing Lives of Vietnamese Americans.* Princeton, NJ: Princeton University Press.
Koltyk, J. 1998. *New Pioneers in the Heartland: Hmong Life in Wisconsin.* Needham Heights, MA: Allyn and Bacon.
Lessinger, J. 1995. *From the Ganges to the Hudson: Indian Immigrants in New York City.* Needham Heights, MA: Allyn and Bacon.
Min, P. G. 1998. *Traditions and Changes: Korean Immigrant Families in New York.* Needham Heights. MA: Allyn and Bacon.
Mintz, S. and R. Price. 1992. *The Birth of African-American Culture: An Anthropological Perspective.* Boston: Beacon Press.
Orleck, A. 1987. The Soviet Jews: Life in Brighton Beach, Brooklyn. In *New Immigrants in New York.* N. Foner, ed. New York: Columbia University Press.
Oxfeld, E. 1993. *Blood, Sweat and Mahjong: Family and Enterprise in an Overseas Chinese Community.* Ithaca, NY: Cornell University Press.
Peacock, J. 1986. *The Anthropological Lens.* Cambridge: Cambridge University Press.
Pessar, P. 1996. The Role of Gender, Households, and Social Networks in the Migration Process: A Review and Appraisal. Paper presented at the conference "Becoming American/America Becoming: International Migration to the United States, Social Science Research Council, Sanibel Island, FL. Jan. 18–21.
—— 1995. *A Visa for a Dream: Dominicans in the United States.* Needham Heights, MA: Allyn and Bacon.
—— 1987. The Dominicans: Women in the Household and the Garment Industry. In *New Immigrants in New York.* N. Foner, ed. New York: Columbia University Press.
Portes, A. 1995. Children of Immigrants: Segmented Assimilation. In *The Economic Sociology of Immigration.* A. Portes, ed. New York: Russell Sage Foundation.
Portes, A. and M. Zhou. 1993. The New Second Generation: Segmented Assimilation and its Variants. *The Annals of the American Academy of Political and Social Sciences* 530:74–96.
Rouse, R. 1991. Mexican Migration and the Social Space of Postmodernism, *Diaspora* 1:8–23.
Schneider, D. 1968. *American Kinship: A Cultural Account.* Englewood Cliffs, NJ: Prentice-Hall.
Smith, R. T. 1988. *Kinship and Class in the West Indies.* Cambridge: Cambridge University Press.
—— 1967. Social Stratification. Cultural Pluralism and Integration in West Indian Societies. In *Caribbean Integration: Papers on Social, Political, and Economic Integration.* S. Lewis and T. G. Mathews, eds. Rio Piedras: Institute of Caribbean Studies, University of Puerto Rico.
Thomas, W. I. and F. Znaniecki. 1996. *The Polish Peasant in Europe and America 1918–1920.* Reprint. E. Zaretsky, ed. Urbana: University of Illinois Press.
Yanagisako, S. 1985. *Transforming the Past: Tradition and Kinship among Japanese Americans.* Stanford, CA: Stanford University Press.

Chapter 9

Families on the Frontier: From Braceros in the Fields to Braceras in the Home

PIERRETTE HONDAGNEU-SOTELO

Why are thousands of Central American and Mexican immigrant women living and working in California and other parts of the United States while their children and other family members remain in their countries of origin? In this chapter, I argue that U.S. labor demand, immigration restrictions, and cultural transformations have encouraged the emergence of new transnational family forms among Central American and Mexican immigrant women. Postindustrial economies bring with them a labor demand for immigrant workers that is differently gendered from that typical of industrial or industrializing societies. In all postindustrial nations we see an increase in demand for jobs dedicated to social reproduction, jobs typically coded as "women's jobs." In many of these countries, such jobs are filled by immigrant women from developing nations. Many of these women, because of occupational constraints—and, in some cases, specific restrictionist contract-labor policies—must live and work apart from their families.

My discussion focuses on private paid domestic work, a job that in California is nearly always performed by Central American and Mexican immigrant women. Not formally negotiated labor contracts, but rather informal occupational constraints, as well as legal status, mandate the long-term spatial and temporal separation of these women from their families and children. For many Central American and Mexican women who work in the United States, new international divisions of social reproductive labor have brought about transnational family forms and new meanings of family and motherhood. In this respect, the United States has entered a new era of dependency on braceras. Consequently, many Mexican, Salvadoran, and Guatemalan immigrant families look quite different from the images suggested by Latino familism.

This chapter is informed by an occupational study I conducted of more than two hundred Mexican and Central American women who do paid domestic work in private homes in Los Angeles (Hondagneu-Sotelo 2001). Here, I focus not on the work but on the migration and family arrangements conditioned by the way paid domestic work is organized today in the United States. I begin by noting the ways in which demand for Mexican—and increasingly Central American—immigrant labor shifted in the twentieth century from a gendered labor demand favoring men to one characterized by robust labor demand for women in a diversity of jobs, including those devoted to commodified social reproduction. Commodified social reproduction refers to the purchase of all kinds of services needed for daily human upkeep, such as cleaning and caring work. The way these jobs are organized often mandates transnational family forms, and in the subsequent section, I (1) draw on a modest-size survey to suggest the prevalence of this pattern and (2) sketch trajectories leading to these outcomes.

I then note the parallels between family migration patterns prompted by the Bracero Program and long-term male sojourning, when many women sought to follow their husbands to the United States, and the situation today, in which many children and youths are apparently traveling north—unaccompanied by adults—hoping to be reunited with their mothers. In the earlier era, men were recruited and wives struggled to migrate; in a minority of cases, Mexican immigrant husbands working in the United States brought their wives against the women's will. Today, women are recruited for work, and, increasingly, their children migrate north some ten to fifteen years after their mothers. Just as Mexican immigrant husbands and wives did not necessarily agree on migration strategies in the earlier era, we see conflicts among today's immigrant mothers in the United States and the children with whom they are being reunited. In this regard, we might suggest that the contention of family power in migration has shifted from gender to generation. I conclude with some questions for a twenty-first-century research agenda.

GENDERED LABOR DEMAND AND SOCIAL REPRODUCTION

Throughout the United States, a plethora of occupations today increasingly rely on the work performed by Latina and Asian immigrant women. Among these are jobs in downgraded manufacturing, jobs in retail, and a broad spectrum of service jobs in hotels, restaurants, hospitals, convalescent homes, office buildings, and private residences. In some cases, such as in the janitorial industry and in light manufacturing, jobs have been re-gendered and re-racialized so that jobs previously held by U.S.-born white or black men are now increasingly held by Latina immigrant women. Jobs in nursing and paid domestic work have long been regarded as "women's jobs," seen as natural outgrowths of essential notions of women as care providers. In the late twentieth-century United States, however, these jobs entered the global marketplace, and immigrant women from developing nations around the globe were increasingly represented in them. In major metropolitan centers around the country, Filipina and Indian immigrant women make up a sizable proportion of HMO nursing staffs—a result due in no small part to deliberate recruitment efforts. Caribbean, Mexican, and Central American women increasingly predominate in low-wage service jobs, including paid domestic work.

This diverse gendered labor demand is quite a departure from patterns that prevailed in the western United States only a few decades ago. The relatively dramatic transition from the explicit demand for *male* Mexican and Asian immigrant workers to demand that today includes women has its roots in a changing political economy. From the late nineteenth century until 1964, the period during which various contract-labor programs were in place, the economies of the Southwest and the West relied on primary, extractive industries. As is well-known, Mexican, Chinese, Japanese, and Filipino immigrant workers, primarily men, were recruited for jobs in agriculture, mining, and railroads. These migrant workers were recruited and incorporated in ways that mandated their long-term separation from their families of origin.

As the twentieth century turned into the twenty-first, the United States was once again a nation of immigration. This time, however, immigrant labor is not involved in primary, extractive industry. Agribusiness continues to be a financial leader in the state of California, relying primarily on Mexican immigrant labor and increasingly on indigenous workers from Mexico, but only a fraction of Mexican immigrant workers are employed in agriculture. Labor demand is now extremely heterogeneous and is structurally embedded in the economy of California (Cornelius 1998). In the current period, which some commentators have termed postindustrial, business and financial services, computer and other high-technology firms, and trade and retail prevail alongside manufacturing, construction, hotels, restaurants, and agriculture as the principal sources of demand for immigrant labor in the western United States.

As the demand for immigrant women's labor has increased, more and more Mexican and (especially) Central American women have left their families and young children behind to seek employment in the United States. Women who work in the United States in order to maintain their families in their countries of origin constitute members of new transnational families. And because these arrangements are choices that the women make in the context of very limited options, they resemble apartheid-like exclusions. These women work in one nation-state but raise their children in another. Strikingly, no formalized, temporary contract-labor program mandates these separations. Rather, this pattern is related to the contemporary arrangements of social reproduction in the United States.

WHY THE EXPANSION IN PAID DOMESTIC WORK?

Who could have foreseen that as the twentieth century turned into the twenty-first, paid domestic work would become a growth occupation? Only a few decades ago, observers confidently predicted that this job would soon become obsolete, replaced by such labor-saving household devices as automatic dishwashers, disposable diapers, and microwave ovens and by consumer goods and services purchased outside the home, such as fast food and dry cleaning (Coser 1974). Instead, paid domestic work has expanded. Why?

The exponential growth in paid domestic work is due in large part to the increased employment of women, especially married women with children, to the underdeveloped nature of U.S. childcare centers, and to patterns of U.S. income inequality and global inequalities. National and global trends have fueled this growing demand for paid domestic services. Increasing global competition and new communications technologies have led to work speed-ups in all sorts of jobs, and the much-bemoaned "time bind" has hit professionals and managers particularly hard (Hochschild 1997). Meanwhile, normative middle-class ideals of child rearing have been elaborated (consider the proliferation of soccer, music lessons, and tutors). At the other end of the age spectrum, greater longevity among the elderly has prompted new demands for care work.

Several commentators, most notably Saskia Sassen, noted the expansion of jobs in personal services in the late twentieth century. Sassen located this trend in the rise of new "global cities"—cities that serve as business and managerial command points in a new system of intricately connected nodes of global corporations. Unlike New York City, Los Angeles is not home to a slew of Fortune 500 companies, but in the 1990s it exhibited remarkable economic dynamism. Entrepreneurial endeavors proliferated and continued to drive the creation of jobs in business services, such as insurance, real estate, public relations, and so on. These industries, together with the high-tech and entertainment industries in Los Angeles, spawned many high-income managerial and professional jobs, and the occupants of these high-income positions require many personal services that are performed by low-wage immigrant workers. Sassen provides the quintessentially New York examples of dog walkers and cooks who prepare gourmet take-out food for penthouse dwellers. Their Los Angeles counterparts might include gardeners and car valets, jobs filled primarily by Mexican and Central American immigrant men, and nannies and housecleaners, jobs filled by Mexican and Central American immigrant women. In fact, the number of domestic workers in private homes counted by the U.S. Census Bureau doubled from 1980 to 1990 (Waldinger 1996).

I favor an analysis that does not speak in terms of "personal services," which seems to imply services that are somehow private, individual rather than social, and that are superfluous to the way society is organized. A feminist concept that was originally introduced to valorize the non-remunerated household work of women, *social reproduction* or, alternately, *reproductive labor*, might be more usefully employed. Replacing *personal services* with *social reproduction* shifts the focus by underlining the objective of the work, the societal functions, and the impact on immigrant workers and their own families.

Social reproduction consists of those activities that are necessary to maintain human life, daily and intergenerationally. This includes how we take care of ourselves, our children and elderly, and our homes. Social reproduction encompasses the purchasing and preparation of food, shelter, and clothing; the routine daily upkeep of these, such as cooking, cleaning, and laundering; the emotional care and support of children and adults; and the maintenance of family and community ties. The way a society organizes social reproduction has far-reaching consequences not only for individuals and families, but also for macro-historical processes (Laslett and Brenner 1989).

Many components of social reproduction have become commodified and outsourced in all kinds of new ways. Today, for example, not only can you purchase fast-food meals, but you can also purchase, through the Internet, the home delivery of customized lists of grocery items. Whereas mothers were once available to buy and wrap Christmas presents, pick up dry cleaning, shop for groceries, and wait around for the plumber, today new businesses have sprung up to meet these demands—for a fee.

In this new milieu, private paid domestic work is just one example of the commodification of social reproduction. Of course, domestic workers and servants of all kinds have been cleaning and cooking for others and caring for other people's children for centuries, but there is today an increasing proliferation of these services among various class sectors and a new flexibility in how these services are purchased.

GLOBAL TRENDS IN PAID DOMESTIC WORK

Just as paid domestic work has expanded in the United States, so too it appears to have grown in many other postindustrial societies, in the "newly industrialized countries" of Asia, in the oil-rich nations of the Middle East, in Canada, and in parts of Europe. In paid domestic work around the globe, Caribbean, Mexican, Central American, Peruvian, Sri Lankan, Indonesian, Eastern European, and Filipina women—the latter in disproportionately large numbers—predominate. Worldwide, paid domestic work continues its long legacy as a racialized and gendered occupation, but today, divisions of nation and citizenship are increasingly salient.

The inequality of nations is a key factor in the globalization of contemporary paid domestic work. This has led to three outcomes. (1) Around the globe, paid domestic work is increasingly performed by women who leave their own nations, their communities, and often their families of origin to do the work. (2) The occupation draws not only women from the poor socioeconomic classes, but also women who hail from nations that colonialism has made much poorer than those countries where they go to do domestic work. This explains why it is not unusual to find college-educated women from the middle class working in other countries as private domestic workers. (3) Largely because of the long, uninterrupted schedules of service required, domestic workers are not allowed to migrate as members of families.

Nations that "import" domestic workers from other countries do so using vastly different methods. Some countries have developed highly regulated, government-operated, contract-labor programs that have institutionalized both the recruitment and the bonded servitude of migrant domestic workers. Canada and Hong Kong provide paradigmatic examples of this approach. Since 1981 the Canadian federal government has formally recruited thousands of women to work as live-in nannies/housekeepers for Canadian families. Most of these women came from Third World countries in the 1990s (the majority came from the Philippines, in the 1980s from the Caribbean), and once in Canada, they must remain in live-in domestic service for two years, until they obtain their landed immigrant status, the equivalent of the U.S. "green card." This reflects, as Bakan and Stasiulis (1997) have noted, a type of indentured servitude and a decline in the citizenship rights of foreign domestic workers, one that coincides with the racialization of the occupation. When Canadians recruited white British women for domestic work in the 1940s, they did so under far less controlling mechanisms than those applied to Caribbean and Filipina domestic workers. Today, foreign domestic workers in Canada may not quit their jobs or collectively organize to improve the conditions under which they work.

Similarly, since 1973 Hong Kong has relied on the formal recruitment of domestic workers, mostly Filipinas, to work on a full-time, live-in basis for Chinese families. Of the 150,000 foreign domestic workers in Hong Kong in 1995, 130,000 hailed from the Philippines, and smaller numbers were drawn from Thailand, Indonesia, India, Sri Lanka, and Nepal (Constable 1997:3). Just as it is now rare to find African American women employed in private domestic work in Los Angeles, so too have Chinese women vanished from the occupation in Hong Kong. As Nicole Constable reveals in her detailed study, Filipina domestic workers in Hong Kong are controlled and disciplined by official employment agencies, employers, and strict government policies. Filipinas and other foreign-born domestic workers recruited to Hong Kong find themselves working primarily in live-in jobs and bound by two-year contracts that stipulate lists of job rules, regulations for bodily display and discipline (no lipstick, nail polish, or long hair; submission to pregnancy tests; etc.), task timetables, and the policing of personal privacy. Taiwan has adopted a similarly formal and restrictive government policy to regulate the incorporation of Filipina domestic workers (Lan 2000).

In this global context, the United States remains distinctive, because it takes more of a laissez-faire approach to the incorporation of immigrant women into paid domestic work. No formal government system or policy exists to legally contract foreign domestic workers in the United States. Although in the past, private employers in the United States were able to "sponsor" individual immigrant women who were working as domestics for their green cards using labor certification (sometimes these employers personally recruited them while vacationing or working in foreign countries), this route is unusual in Los Angeles today. Obtaining legal status through labor certification requires documentation that there is a shortage of labor to perform a particular, specialized occupation. In Los Angeles and in many parts of the country today, a shortage of domestic workers is increasingly difficult to prove. And it is apparently unnecessary, because the significant demand for domestic workers in the United States is largely filled not through formal channels of foreign recruitment but through informal recruitment from the growing number of Caribbean and Latina immigrant women who are *already* legally or illegally living in the United States. The Immigration and Naturalization Service, the federal agency charged with enforcement of migration laws, has historically served the interests of domestic employers and winked at the employment of undocumented immigrant women in private homes.

As we compare the hyper-regulated employment systems in Hong Kong and Canada with the more laissez-faire system for domestic work in the United States, we find that although the methods of recruitment and hiring and the roles of the state in these processes are quite different, the consequences are similar. Both systems require the incorporation as workers of migrant women who can be separated from their families.

The requirements of live-in domestic jobs, in particular, virtually mandate this. Many immigrant women who work in live-in jobs find that they must be on call during all waking hours and often throughout the night, so there is no clear line between working and nonworking hours. The line between job space and private space is similarly blurred, and rules and regulations may extend around the clock. Some employers restrict the ability of their live-in employees to receive phone calls, entertain friends, attend evening ESL classes, or see boyfriends during the workweek. Other employers do not impose these sorts of restrictions, but because their homes are located in remote hillsides, suburban enclaves, or gated communities, live-in nannies/housekeepers are effectively restricted from participating in anything resembling social life, family life of their own, or public culture.

These domestic workers—the Filipinas working in Hong Kong or Taiwan, the Caribbean women working on the East Coast, and the Central American and Mexican immigrant women working in California—constitute the new braceras. They are literally "pairs of arms," disembodied and dislocated from their families and communities of origin, and yet they are not temporary sojourners. In the section that follows, I suggest some of the dimensions of this phenomenon and present several illustrative career trajectories.

THE NEW BRACERAS AND TRANSNATIONAL MOTHERHOOD

What are the dimensions of this phenomeon that I refer to as the new braceras and the new forms of transnational motherhood? Precise figures are not available. No one has counted the universe of everyone working in private paid domestic work, which continues to be an informal sector—an "under the table" occupation. Accurately estimating the numbers in immigrant groups that include those who are poor and lack legal work authorization is always difficult. Several indicators, however, suggest that the dimensions are quite significant. My nonrandom survey of 153 Latina immigrant domestic workers, which I conducted at bus stops, at ESL evening classes, and in public parks where Latina nannies take their young charges, revealed the following. Approximately 75 percent of the Latina domestic workers had children of their own, and a startling 40 percent of the women with children had at least one of their children "back home" in their country of origin.

The survey finding that 40 percent of Latina domestic workers with children of their own had at least one child living in their country of origin is substantiated by other anectodal indicators. In a study of immigrant children in Los Angeles' Pico-Union area, a largely Central American and Mexican immigrant neighborhood, sociologists Barrie Thorne and Marjorie Faulstich-Orellana found that half of the children in a first-grade class had siblings in El Salvador. Investigative journalist Sonia Nazarrio, who has researched immigration in Mexico, El Salvador, and newcomer schools in Los Angeles, told me that a high percentage of Central American children remain "back home" for lengthy periods while their parents are working in the United States. Similarly, sociologist Cecilia Menjivar (2000), in her study of Salvadorans in San Francisco, finds that many Salvadoran immigrant workers are supporting their children in El Salvador.

Given these various indicators, an estimated 40 to 50 percent of Central American and Mexican women leave their children in their countries of origin when they migrate to the United States. They believe the separation from their children will be temporary, but physical separation may endure for long, and sometimes undetermined, periods of time. Job constraints, legal-status barriers, and perceptions of the United States as a dangerous place to raise children explain these long-term separations. In the remainder of this section, I discuss how job constraints in live-in paid domestic work encourage this pattern, but first, I briefly discuss how legal status and perceptions of the United States play a role.

Private domestic workers who hail primarily from Mexico, Central America, and the Caribbean hold various legal statuses. Some, for example, are legal, permanent residents or naturalized U.S. citizens, many of them beneficiaries of the Immigration Reform and Control Act's amnesty-legalization program, which was enacted in 1986. Most Central American women, who prevail in the occupation, entered the United States after the 1982 cutoff date for amnesty-legalization, so they did not qualify for legalization. Throughout the 1990s, a substantial proportion of Central

Americans either remained undocumented or held a series of temporary work permits, granted to delay their return to war-ravaged countries.

Their precarious legal status as an "illegal" or "undocumented immigrant" discouraged many immigrant mothers from migrating with their children or bringing them to the United States. The ability of undocumented immigrant parents to bring children north was also complicated in the late 1990s by the militarization of the U.S.-Mexico border through the implementation of various border-control programs (such as Operation Gatekeeper). As Jacqueline Hagan and Nestor Rodriguez compellingly show, the U.S.-Mexico border has become a zone of danger, violence, and death. This not only made it difficult to migrate with children, it also made it difficult to travel back and forth to visit family members "back home." Bound by precarious legal status in the United States, which might expose them to the risk of deportation and denial of all kinds of benefits, and by the greater danger and expense in bringing children to the United States, many immigrant mothers opted not to travel with their children or send for them. Instead, they endure long separations.

Many immigrant parents of various nationalities also view the United States as a highly undesirable place to raise children. Immigrant parents fear the dangers of gangs, violence, drugs, and second-rate schools to which their children are likely to be exposed in poor, inner-city neighborhoods. They are also appalled by the way immigration often weakens generational authority. As one Salvadoran youth put it, "Here I do what I please, and no one can control me" (Menjivar 2000213).

Even mothers who enjoyed legal status and had successfully raised and educated their children through adolescence hesitated to bring them to this country. They saw the United States as a place where their children would suffer job discrimination and economic marginalization. As one Salvadoran domestic worker (who had raised her children on earnings predicated on her separation from them) exclaimed when I spoke with her at an employment agency: "I've been here for 19 years. I've got my legal papers and everything, but I'd have to be crazy to bring my children here. All of them have studied for a career, so why would I bring them here? To bus tables and earn minimum wage? So they won't have enough money for bus fare or food?" (Hondagneu-Sotelo and Avial 1997).

Although precarious legal status and perceptions of the United States as an undesirable place in which to raise children are important in shaping transnational family forms, the constraints of paid domestic work, particularly those that are typical in live-in work, virtually mandate family separations.

Live-in jobs serve as a port of entry for many Latina immigrant women, especially for those who lack access to rich social networks. According to the survey I conducted in Los Angeles, live-in domestic workers work an average of sixty-four hours per week. Work schedules typically consist of six very long workdays and may include overnight responsibilities with sleepless or sick children. This makes it virtually impossible for live-in workers to sustain daily contact with their own family members. As a consequence of the sub-minimum wages typical of live-in work and the blurred line around hourly parameters in their jobs, some women remain separated from their families and children while working as braceras for more years than they had originally anticipated. Two cases will illustrate some of these trajectories.

When I met her, Carmen Velasquez, a thirty-nine year-old Mexicana, was working as a live-in nanny-housekeeper, in charge of general housekeeping and the daily care of one toddler, in the hillside suburban home of an attorney and schoolteacher. Carmen, a single mother, had migrated alone to California ten years before, leaving behind her three children when they were four, five, and seven years old. Since then, she had seen them only in photographs. The children were now in their teens. She regularly sent money to the children and communicated by letters and phone calls with them and her three *comadres* (co-godmothers), who cared for one of the children each in Mexico.

Carmen had initially thought that it would be possible for her to maintain these arrangements for only a short while. She knew she could work hard and thought that working as a live-in domestic worker would enable her to save her earnings by not paying rent or room and board. But, as she somberly noted, "Sometimes your desires just aren't possible."

A series of traumatic events that included incest and domestic violence prompted her migration and had left her completely estranged from the father of her children, her parents, and her siblings. With only the support of her female comadres in Mexico, and assisted by the friend of a friend, she had come north "without papers," determined to pioneer a new life for herself and her children.

Her first two live-in jobs, in which she stayed for a total of seven years, included some of the worst arrangements I have had described to me. In both cases, she worked round-the-clock schedules in the homes of Mexican immigrant families, slept on living room couches or in hallways, and earned only $50 a week. Isolated, discouraged, and depressed, she stayed in those jobs out of desperation and lack of opportunity.

In comparison with what she had endured, she expressed relative satisfaction with her current live-in job. Her employers treated her with respect, paid $170 a week, gave her a separate bedroom and bathroom, and were not, she said, too demanding in terms of what they expected of her. Unlike the workdays of many other live-in nannies/housekeepers, her workday ended when the *señora* arrived home at 5 p.m. Still, when I asked whether she now had plans to bring her children to Los Angeles, she equivocated.

She remained vexed by the problem of how she could raise her children in Los Angeles and maintain a job at the same time. "The *señora* is kind and understanding," she said, "but she needs me here with the baby. And then how could I pay the rent, the bus fare to transport myself? And my children [voice quivering] are so big now. They can't have the same affection they once had, because they no longer know me...." As psychologist Celia Jaes Falicov underscores in Chapter 11, there are many losses incurred with migration and family reunification. Women such as Carmen sacrifice to provide a better life for their children, but in the process, they may lose family life with their children.

Some women *do* successfully bring and reintegrate their children with them in the United States, but there are often unforeseen costs and risks associated with this strategy. Erlinda Castro, a Guatemalan mother of five children, came to the United States in 1992. She left all five children behind in Guatemala, under the care of the eldest, supervised by a close neighbor, and joined her husband in Los Angeles. She initially endured live-in domestic jobs. These jobs were easy to acquire quickly, and they enabled her to save on rent. After two years, she moved into an apartment with her husband and her sister, and she moved out of live-in domestic work into housecleaning. By cleaning different houses on different days, she gained a more flexible work schedule, earning more with fewer hours of work. Eventually, she was able to send money for two of the children to come north.

The key to Erlinda's ability to bring two of her children to the United States was her shift in domestic employment from live-in work to housecleaning. According to my survey results, Latina immigrant mothers who work in live-in nanny/housekeeping jobs are the most likely to have their children back home (82 percent) than are women who work cleaning houses. And mothers who clean different houses on different days are the least likely to have their children in their countries of origin (24 percent).

Bringing children north after long periods of separation may entail unforeseen "costs of transnationalism," as Susan Gonzalez-Baker suggests. Just as migration often rearranges gender relations between spouses, so too, does migration prompt challenges to familiar generational relations between parents and offspring. In the following section, I draw some parallels between these rebellions of gender and generation.

BRACEROS AND THEIR WIVES, BRACERAS AND THEIR CHILDREN: REBELLIONS OF GENDER AND GENERATION

The Bracero Program, the institutionalized contract-labor program that authorized the granting of five million contracts to Mexican agricultural workers, most of them men, remained in place from 1942 to 1964. This program, like earlier contract-labor programs that recruited Mexican, Filipino, and Chinese men to work in the western and southwestern United States, incorporated men as pure workers, not as human beings enmeshed in family relationships. Mandated by formal regulations, but made possible by patriarchal family culture and male-dominated social networks, this pattern of male-selective migration remained in place for many years following the end of the Bracero Program (Hondagneu-Sotelo 1994). This pattern is still not uncommon.

In many families, however, this migration pattern prompted gender rebellion among the wives of braceros. Many wives of braceros and other Mexican immigrant men working in the United States after the end of the program sought to migrate to the United States, and many of them did so in the face of resistance from their husbands. Elsewhere, I have detailed some of these processes and have referred to this pattern as "family stage migration" (Hondagneu-Sotelo 1994). In many instances, Mexican women worked hard to persuade their husbands to help them migrate to the United States, and when this failed, many of them turned to their own social-network resources to accomplish migration. Although patriarchal practices and rules in families and social networks have persisted, labor demand has changed in ways previously outlined in this chapter, and now both women and men creatively reinterpret normative standards and manipulate the rules of gender. As they do, understandings about proper gendered behavior are reformulated, and new paths to migration are created.

Just as wives have followed their husbands north, so too are children today following their mothers to California and other states. *Los Angeles Times* investigative journalist Sonia Nazarrio told me that every year the INS captures approximately five thousand unaccompained minors traveling illegally across the U.S.-Mexico border. Because this figure does not include those who are apprehended and choose voluntary deportation within 72 hours, and those who are never apprehended, Nazarrio believes that the number of unaccompanied minors migrating to the United States from Central America and Mexico each year may be as high as forty to fifty thousand. She estimates that about half are coming to be reunited with their mothers.

In some cases, these are the children of mothers who, after having established themselves financially and occupationally, have sent money for the children's migration. These children and youths enter either accompanied by smugglers or through authorized legal entry. In other cases, these are children who have run away from their grandmothers, paid caregivers, or fathers. In both cases, the children and youths face tremendous dangers, and fatalities are not unheard of. Nazarrio reports that many of them travel north by hopping moving trains, risking life and limb as they embark and disembark, and that they are victimized, robbed, and raped by roving bandits and thugs and by delinquent gang members who are returning north after having been deported. After the 1996 immigration law imposed new restrictions on criminal aliens—even on legal immigrants falsely convicted of crimes (a common practice in Los Angeles, which was victimized by a corrupt police force in the 1990s)—many immigrants were deported. Members of tough Los Angeles street gangs, such as Mara Salvatrucha or the 18th Street Gang, have been deported to El Salvador, Guatemala, and Mexico, and they too are traveling on these northbound trains back to California. Meanwhile, children and other minors are trekking northward for the first time, in hopes of being reunited with their mothers and other family members.

What happens once these children are reunited with their mothers? A short honeymoon may occur upon reunification, but long periods of discord typically follow. Once in the United States, the children are apt to blame their mothers for the economic deprivation and the emotional uncertainty and turmoil they have experienced. They may express contempt and disrespect for their mothers. The emotional joy of reunification that they may have anticipated quickly sours when they realize their mothers are off working for hours, and they may feel betrayed when they discover that their mothers have new husbands and children. Competition with new half-siblings forms part of the backdrop through which they reintegrate. And finally, their mothers' long workdays leave them on their own for a good portion of their waking hours. In one case reported by Menjivar (2000:209), a Salvadoran mother brought her daughter to San Francisco, only to have Child Protective Services take her daughter and deem her an unfit mother for working seventy hours a week. Many of the children and youths miss their grandmothers, or whoever was their primary caregiver during their formative years, and feel neglected and rejected by family in the United States. Many, indeed, wish to return to their homeland.

CONCLUSION

What do these developments mean for a twenty-first-century research agenda on Latino families? Clearly, they force us to rethink monolithic understandings of Latino families, familism, and sentimentalized notions of motherhood. There are also many remaining empirical questions about the impact of these transnational processes on children and youth. How does the length of separation affect processes of adaptation? How does the age at which the children are reunited with their "bracera" mothers affect family social relations? How do these migration processes affect adolescent identity and school performance? Answering questions such as these will require incorporating children and youths into research as active agents in migration.

The trajectories described here pose an enormous challenge to those who would celebrate any and all instances of transnationalism. These migration patterns alert us to the fact that the continued privatization of social reproduction among the American professional and managerial class has broad repercussions for the social relations among new Latina immigrants and their families. Similarly, strong emotional ties between mothers and children, which we might dismiss as personal subjectivities, are fueling massive remittances to countries such as El Salvador and the Philippines. Our most fundamental question remains unanswered: Who will continue to pick up the cost of raising the next generation? Surely, we can hope for a society wherein Latina immigrant women and children are not the first to bear those costs.

References

Bakan, Abigail B., and Daiva Stasiulis. 1997. Foreign Domestic Worker Policy in Canada and the Social Boundaries of Modern Citizenship. In Abigail B. Bakan and Daiva Stasiulis, eds. *Not One of the Family: Foreign Domestic Workers in Canada*, Toronto: University of Toronto Press.

Constable, Nicole. 1997. *Maid to Order in Hong Kong: Stories of Filipina Workers*. Ithaca and London: Cornell University Press.

Cornelius, Wayne. 1998. The Structural Embeddedness of Demand for Mexican Immigrant Labor: New Evidence from California. In Marcelo M. Suárez-Orozco, ed. *Crossings: Mexican Immigration in Interdisciplinary Perspectives*. Cambridge, MA: Harvard University, David Rockefeller Center for Latin American Studies.

Coser, Lewis. 1974. Servants: The Obsolescence of an Occupational Role. *Social Forces* 52:31–40.

Hagan, Jacqueline and Mestor Rodriguez. 2002. Resurrecting Exclusion: The Effects of 1996 U.S. Immigration Reform on Communities and Families in Texas, Elsalvador, and Mexico. In *Latinos: Remaking America*. Marcelo M. Suárez-Orozco and M. Paez, eds. Berkeley: University of California Press.

Hochschild, Arlie. 1997. *The Time Bind: When Work Becomes Home and Home Becomes Work*. New York: Metropolitan Books, Henry Holt.

Hondagneu-Sotelo, Pierrette. 1994. *Gendered Transitions: Mexican Experiences of Immigration*. Berkeley: University of California Press.

Hondagneu-Sotelo, Pierrette. 2001. *Domestica: Immigrant Workers and Their Employers*. Berkeley: University of California Press.

Hondagneu-Sotelo, Pierrette, and Ernestine Avila. 1997. 'I'm Here, But I'm There': The Meanings of Latina Transnational Motherhood. *Gender & Society,* 11:548–571.

Lan, Pei-chia. 2000. Global Divisions, Local Identities: Filipina Migrant Domestic Workers and Taiwanese Employers. Dissertation, Northwestern University.

Laslett, Barbara, and Johanna Brenner. 1989. Gender and Social Reproduction: Historical Perspectives. *Annual Review of Sociology* 15:381–404.

Menjivar, Cecilia. 2000. *Fragmented Ties: Salvadoran Immigrant Networks in America.* Berkeley: University of California Press.

Waldinger, Roger, and Mehdi Bozorgmehr. 1996. The Making of a Multicultural Metropolis. In Roger Waldinger and Mehdi Bozorgmehr, eds. *Ethnic Los Angeles.* New York: Russell Sage Foundation.

Chapter 10
Making Up For Lost Time: The Experience of Separation and Reunification Among Immigrant Families

CAROLA SUÁREZ-OROZCO, IRINA L. G. TODOROVA, AND JOSEPHINE LOUIE

In the United States today, one-fifth of the nation's children are growing up in immigrant homes. In the process of migration, families undergo profound transformations that are often complicated by extended periods of separation between loved ones not only from extended family members, but also from the nuclear family. Though many families are involved in these transnational formulations, there has heretofore been little sense of the prevalence of these forms of family separations, nor of the effects on family relations. Further, such research has generally been conducted with clinical populations using Western theoretical frameworks and perspectives of families, limiting its applicability to immigrant families. The data presented in this article are derived from a bicoastal interdisciplinary study of 385 early adolescents originating from China, Central America, the Dominican Republic, Haiti, and Mexico. Findings from this study indicate that fully 85 percent of the participants had been separated from one or both parents for extended periods. While family separations are common to all country-of-origin groups, there are clear differences between groups in lengths of separations as well as people from whom the youth are separated. Descriptive statistics of country-of-origin preculence, patterns, and outcomes are presented. Results of analyses of variance indicate that children who were separated from their parents were more likely to report depressive symptoms than children who had not been separated. Further, qualitative data from youth, parent, and teacher perspectives of the experience of separation and reunification provide evidence that the circumstances and contexts of the separations lead to a variety of outcomes. We conclude with a discussion of attenuating and complicating factors that family therapists should consider in the assessment and treatment of immigrant families.

Globalization is transforming the shape of the family (Glick-Schiller 1992). With more than 130 million immigrants and refugees worldwide, the proportion of families involved in migrations is considerable. In the United States today, one-fifth of our nation's children are growing up in immigrant homes. In the process of migration, families undergo profound transformations that are often complicated by extended periods of separation between loved ones—not only from extended family members, but also from the nuclear family.

Families who migrate often do so in a "stepwise" fashion (Hondagneu-Sotelo 1992). Historically, the pattern was of the father going ahead, establishing himself while sending remittances home, and then sending for the wife and children as soon as it was financially possible. Today, the First World's demand for service workers draws mothers from a variety of developing countries often to care for "other people's children" (Hondagneu-Sotelo 1992). In cases where mothers initiate migrations, they leave the children in the care of extended family such as grandparents or aunts, along with the father if he is still part of the family. In many other cases, both parents go ahead, leaving the children in the care of extended family. When it is time for the children to arrive, they may be brought to the new land all together or in other instances. The children are brought in one at a time. Often the reunification of the entire family can take many years, especially when complicated by financial hurdles as well as immigration laws (Arnold 1991; Simpao, 1999). These migration separations usually result in two sets of disruptions in attachments: first from the parent, and then from the caretaker to whom the child has become attached during the parent/child separation.

IMMIGRANT FAMILY SEPARATIONS RESEARCH

Very little has been written about family separations arising out of the immigrant experience. Several clinical reports of Caribbean families in Canada and Great Britain note substantial negative family ramifications upon reunification (Bagley 1972; Burke 1980; Gordon 1961; Sewell-Coker Hamilton-Collins, and Fein 1985). Some of the literature points to negative sequelae for children both in the phase when the child is left with relatives as well as when reunification occurs. While apart from the parent, children may feel abandoned and may respond by detaching from the parent that left her (Glasgow and Ghouse-Shees 1995). Once reunified, children often miss those who have cared for them in their parent's absence as well as extended family members and friends (Arnold 1991; Seiarra 1999). Particularly when separations have been protracted, children and parents frequently report that they feel like strangers (Forman 1993).

Complications in family relations are also reported as a frequent outcome. Over the course of time, the family may have evolved in such a way that excludes the parent who has been away, making rejoining the family system difficult (Partida 1996). Parents tend to expect their children to be grateful for their sacrifices but instead often find them ambivalent about joining their parents in the migratory process (Arnold 1991; Boti and Bautista 1999; Chestham 1972; Seiarra 1999). Parents often report difficulties in reasserting control over their children (Arnold 1991; Boti and Bautista 1999; Sewell-Coker et al. 1985). Reestablishing this authority may be complicated by parental guilt, which may result in inconsistencies and overindulgence (Arnold 1991; Burke 1980). A "continual pattern of rejection and counter-rejection" may emerge, leading families to seek treatment (Glasgow and Gouse-Shees 1995).

Some have argued that the widespread cultural practice of "child fostering" or "child shifting" may normalize the process of the separation. Throughout the Caribbean, either because of family hardship or in order to provide the child with a better educational opportunity, children are often sent to live with extended family members (Bagley 1972; Burke 1980; Gordon 1964; Sewell-Coker et al. 1985; Soto 1987; Waters 1999). This widely accepted cultural practice occurs during the course of migrations abroad as well as within the native land and is not viewed as deviant. In communities where child fostering is widely practiced, no stigma is attached to its occurrence

(Burke 1980; Sewell-Coker et al. 1985; Soto 1987; Waters 1999). Some have gone so far as to argue that child fostering can be an enriching experience and can help to provide all those involved with a wider network of supportive social relations than would be available prior to the event (Soto 1987).

At the individual level, attachment difficulties have been noted (Wilkes 1992) because children often withdraw from the parents with whom they are reunited (Burke 1980). Depressive responses have also been reported in children (Rutter 1971) as well as mothers (Hohn 1996). Clinical reports indicate that some youth may respond by acting out in a variety of ways (Burke 1980; Wilkes 1992). It should be noted, however, that the clinical literature reporting on immigrant family separations and reunifications might not accurately represent the responses in families that do seek treatment. This clinical literature is likely to overestimate the pathological responses to separations, because only families experiencing difficulties are likely to present themselves for treatment.

For example, two dissertation studies not drawn from clinical populations found no clear link between separations and outcomes. A study of stress responses among Jamaican immigrant families found that while many mothers were depressed, the children who were separated from their mothers did not demonstrate higher levels of stress responses than children who had not been separated (Hohn 1996). Likewise, in a study of college-age students that compared immigrants who had been separated from their parents during early development to immigrants who had not been separated, no relation was found between the separation and either object relations or motivation for intimacy (Simpao 1999). While these studies may be limited by their use of standardized instruments, which had not been normed on the populations under consideration, they raise the possibility that the link between separations and negative outcomes may not be direct.

Theoretical frameworks

Several bodies of literature provide a potential framework for understanding aspects of the processes involved in family separations. Object-relations theorists would predict that ruptures in parental relationships would lead to significant developmental challenges. Winnicott argued that children develop into secure adults within the context of stable parental relationships (Winnicott 1958). Object-relations theorists generally maintain that early relationships are the foundation of the sense of self and the capacity for relationship with others (Greenberg and Mitchell 1983). Though many object-relations theorists place much emphasis on infancy and preschool attachments, others have argued that the capacity to develop object relations is not firmly established in preschool years but continues to develop into adolescence (Western 1989). Any disruptions in primary object relations are thought to create significant pathologies.

This theoretical framework may have limited applicability to immigrant families, however. Object-relations theory places emphasis on the mother-child dyad privileging a Western understanding of the nuclear family. Many immigrant families come from cultures that include a wide, supportive net of extended family members. In extended families, the "emotional eggs" may be more widely dispersed among several "emotional baskets." When there are multiple significant relationships, others besides parents can effectively attend to the emotional needs of developing children. Hence, when a parent leaves, while he or she may be missed, the temporary loss may not be traumatic.

Attachment theorists also maintain that disruptions in "affectional bonds" with parental figures have profound psychological and developmental implications (Amsworth 1989: Bowlby 1973: Lyons-Ruth 1996).

> An attachment figure is never wholly interchangeable or replaceable by another, even though there may be others to whom one is also attached. In attachments … there is a need to maintain proximity, distress upon inexplicable separation, pleasure or joy upon reunion, and grief at loss (Amsworth 1989:709).

Early-attachment theorists would generally predict that the attachment with the mother or primary caretaker is of particular significance. Again, this Western model may be overemphasizing the pathogenic potential of ruptures in the parent-child dyad. Amsworth has recognized that parent surrogates, siblings, and peers also may be extremely significant as attachment figures (Amsworth 1989). Hence, disruptions in these extended family relationships can also lead to feelings of sadness and loss.

The literature on the experience of loss provides another frame for broadening our understanding of the possible consequences of ruptures in family relationships (Boss 1999; Doka 1989; Feshbach and Feshbach 2001; Hepworth, Ryder, and Dreyer 1984; Neimeyer 2001; Payne, Horn, and Relf 1999; Shapiro 1994). Loss that can result from death as well as a variety of other "exits" is a transition that requires adaptation and may trigger a variety of physical, emotional, and behavioral responses. Some argue that it is the loss of the individual (or individuals) that triggers such responses, while others claim it is the secondary losses (loss of routines, emotional or financial security, and so forth) accompanying the initial loss that ultimately cause negative sequelae (Goldstein, Wampler, and Wise 1997; Payne et al. 1999). In immigrant family separations, these secondary losses are likely to play a significant role in adaptation.

The response to what Boss (1999) has termed "ambiguous loss" is particularly relevant to parent-child separations during the migratory process, Ambiguous losses—when a loved one is either physically present but psychologically unavailable, or when they are physically absent but psychologically present—may lead to complications in the resolution of grief. Since the parent is not dead but simply gone for what is often expected to be a short time, "permission" to grieve may not be granted. The child's loss may thus go unrecognized and lead to disenfranchised grief, whereby silence surrounds the loss (Doka 1989). Under such circumstances, the expected emotions of grieving- sadness guilt, anger, and hopelessness may be prolonged because there is no public arena in which to express these emotions. In immigrant family separations, because there is no clear-out finality in the relationship, responses may take the form of low-grade chronic symptomatology rather than intense, acute responses.

A broader systemic theoretical framework helps us to predict how losses and separations might affect families and children. It is critical to understand the way in which the adults in the child's circle as well as the wider culture react to the loss (Shapiro 1994; Silverman 2000). Grief triggers a crisis in family development that affects all members as they attempt to accommodate the absence of a "vital member of an interdependent family" (Shapiro 1994). Both the subjective individual experience—as well as the "systemic interweaving of grief reactions in the family, community, and culture"—are influential in family and individual development (Shapiro 1994). If the remaining caretaker is overcome with his or her own losses, he or she may not be available to help the child contain her emotions. Critical to well-being is the child's ability to keep the missing parent or caretaker psychologically present (Silverman 2000). This process may be best served when children are able to identify with a part of the loved one, thus maintaining an ongoing relationship even in her absence. If the child has continuity of care and someone who provides connection, research suggests that the child will be able to make meaning of the loss and accommodate to it in the Piagetian sense of the word (Silverman 2000).

Recent scholarship in the field of loss and trauma suggests that people are involved in a process of meaning-reconstruction after facing disruptive life events in which they lose the connection with someone they love (Neimeyer 2001; Payne et al. 1999). Meaning-making and meaning-finding approaches to loss do not de-emphasize the suffering that accompanies such events. Rather, they place the losses in a more complex web that also includes possibilities of finding value and new meaning with what remains after the loss. They also situate loss in a social and relational context, rather than viewing it as a private experience. As such, they emphasize the cross-cultural differences not only of the practices of grieving, but also in the meanings and meaning reconstruction of loss (Neimeyer 2001).

Attachment and object-relations theory, along with the clinical literature on parent-child separations and loss, would generally predict that separations resulting from immigration as well as concomitant reunifications are likely to be quite problematic. There is, however, no clear empirical indication of what proportion of migratory journeys involve separations and whether or not complications are as widespread as the literature would predict.

Prevalence

Though many families seem to be involved in these transnational formulations, there is little sense of the prevalence of these forms of family separations nor of the effects on family relations (Falicov 2002). There are also no available data providing evidence of cross-cultural patterns of immigrant family separations. What we know tends to be anecdotal and largely derived from clinical reports (Falicov 1998; Glasgow and Gouse-Shees 1995; Prince 1968; Seiarra 1999). While these reports are important in delineating the syndrome and its clinical ramifications, they do not shed light on the prevalence of family separations caused by migrations. These studies, because they are derived from clinical populations, only focus on families and youth that are in treatment. Thus, such findings may overly pathologize the outcome of separations. In this article, using data from a nonclinical population, we will report on the prevalence and nature of these separations. Using quantitative and qualitative data we will discuss how children experience immigrant separations. We will also reflect on the effect of separations, the possible negative consequences as well as the families' resilience, and delineate factors that may complicate or attenuate the separation.

METHOD

Data presented here are derived from part of the Longitudinal Immigrant Student Adaptation Study (LISA) conducted at Harvard University. This interdisciplinary and comparative study was designed to document the adaptations of recently arrived immigrant youth coming from a variety of sending countries. We will report and discuss the findings that emerged from parent and child interviews designed to elicit background information about the participants, as well as findings from a follow-up child interview in which we asked a series of questions about the separation and reunification.

Cross-cultural research with immigrant youth is inherently challenging. There is a growing consensus in the field that mixed-method designs, linking emic and etic perspectives, triangulating data, and embedding emerging findings into an ecological framework are essential to this kind of endeavor (Branch 1999; Bronfenbrenner 1988; Doucolle-Gates, Brooks-Gunn, and Chase-Lansdale 1998; Hughes, Seidman, and Edwards 1993; Sue and Sue 1987; Szapocnik and Krurtines 1993). An important theme of the methodological debates surrounding the philosophical assumptions of qualitative and quantitative methods is whether they are compatible given radically different epistemological grounds (Guba and Lincoln 1994). While these debates continue, there is a growing body of work proposing that research that builds upon the strengths of both types of approaches is necessary to achieve an understanding of complex phenomena (Ponteyotto and Greiger 1999; Tashakkori and Teddlie 1998; Tolman and Szalacha 1999).

The LISA study uses research anthropology strategies to gain perspective on immigrant cultural models and social practices relevant to adaptation in the new setting. Youth are observed and interviewed in their schools, their communities, and their homes. Research psychology strategies are carefully deployed in order to establish a data baseline on immigration histories, social and family relations, and academic attitudes and behaviors. An interdisciplinary, multicultural team of bilingual and bicultural researchers enables us to gain entry into immigrant communities, establish rapport and trust with our participants, develop culturally sensitive instruments, and provide an interpretive community for data interpretation and the contextualization of findings.

Participants

The 383 youth participants are recent immigrants from Central America, China, the Dominican Republic, Haiti, and Mexico. The youth, whom we are following longitudinally, were between the ages of nine and fourteen at the beginning of the study. The participants, stratified by gender and country of origin, were recruited from fifty-one schools in seven school districts in the Boston and San Francisco greater metropolitan areas.

We negotiated entrance into specific school sites with high densities of immigrant students. With the help of school authorities, youth who potentially met the inclusion criteria were identified: recently arrived immigrants whose parents were both from the country of origin. Research assistants requested potential participants' involvement, assured them of confidentiality, and obtained parental informed consent. This is a sample of convenience. Random sampling would have been ideal, but it is not possible with a study that requires specific inclusion criteria coupled with signed permission from school personnel and parents, as well as a commitment to three years of participation. This limits to some degree our ability to generalize from our sample. In comparing the results of our descriptive statistics (parental education, parental employment, household size, etc.) to census and other available information on the U.S. immigrant population, we are confident that this sample is representative of a nonclinical population of recently arrived immigrants currently entering public school systems.

Procedures

Student and parent-structured interviews were developed to gather data systematically on a variety of relevant topics, including migration and demographic history, schooling in the country of origin, initial impressions of U.S. society in general and U.S. schools in particular, aspirations, attitudes toward schooling, patterns of cognitive and behavioral academic engagement, kinship, family life, and networks of social relations. The student interviews employ a variety of question formats: some open-ended, others forced-choice, and still others narrative. The interviews are translated into Spanish, Haitian Kreyol, Mandarin, and Cantonese. Participants can choose the language in which they wish to be interviewed. Interviews conducted with all informants are piloted to establish age, cultural, and linguistic appropriateness. They are then taped, translated into English, and coded.

Pattern of Separation Analyses

A major function of the structured interviews was in collecting the data for the quantitative analyses. A coding system was devised for the questions appearing on the student and parent-structured interview. The initial coding system was devised using a priori categories. As we began to review these data, additional categories emerging from the data were added. The coding system was reworked until we were able to establish a high overall inter-rater reliability (.90 Cohen's kappa).

Once the data were coded, descriptive statistics were calculated to determine group differences in patterns and lengths of separations.

Psychological outcome data

As part of the psychosocial measures included in our study, our cross-cultural research team developed a psychological symptom scale, informed by the DSM-IV (American Psychiatric Association, 1994) and the SGL-90 questionnaire (Derogatis 1977) that included questions determined by our interdisciplinary research team to be developmentally appropriate and cross-culturally relevant. The questions were piloted on informants at the same developmental level as our participants, representing each of the country-of-origin groups under consideration. This twenty-six-item scale consisted of five subscales: depression, anxiety, cognitive functioning, interpersonal sensitivity, and hostility.[1]

Qualitative data

The qualitative analysis was conducted with data gathered from several sources. These included open-ended questions from the structured interviews conducted with the whole sample of the 385 children participating in the LISA study and separately with their parents. We have also developed in-depth case studies with 80 children in the LISA study, which include detailed longitudinal, ethnographic observations in which the experience of separation was one of the important dimensions. In addition, twelve semi-structured, in-depth interviews focused specifically on the experience of separation were conducted with youth who had undergone lengthy separations. The data were organized and analyzed using two soft-ware programs. Folio Views and ATLAS Ti. These programs facilitated the inductive and deductive development and application of codes across data sources, as well as the creation of conceptual models from our results.

RESULTS

Prevalence and patterns of separations

Strikingly, fully 85 percent of the youth in our sample were separated from one or both parents during the process of migration (see Table 10.1). Also, there are significant differences between the ethnic groups participating in the LISA study. Families from the Chinese group, most frequently, tend to migrate as a unit, while the circumstances of migration for the Haitian and Central American groups impose a family disruption during migration in nearly all cases (96 percent for both groups).

From whom were these children separated? As we can see in Table 10.1, nearly half of our sample were separated from both parents. Note that this includes separation as a direct result of immigration as well as separation for multiple factors, including immigration combined with divorce, or the death of a parent, and so forth. Again, there are significant group differences. Separation from both parents was most likely to occur among the Central American families (in 80 percent of the cases). This incidence is also high among Dominican and Haitian families. When the child is separated from only one parent, it is most likely to be from the father, occurring in 30 percent of our cases. This was the typical pattern for Chinese and Mexican children. Separation from only the mother occurs much less frequently within the whole sample.

Immigrant children today, just as they were historically, are most likely to be separated from their fathers. Seventy-nine percent of our sample were separated from their fathers at some point in the migratory process (see Table 10.2). This occurred in 96 percent of the Central American families and in more than 80percent of the Dominican, Haitian, and Mexican families. It was least likely to occur among the Chinese, but it still occurred in nearly half the cases. It is important to note that even though separation only from the mother (without separation from the father) is relatively uncommon, the total incidence of children separated from their mother during the course of the immigration is very high. Fifty-five percent of the children are separated from their mothers sometime during the course of migration. There are dramatic differences here between groups. The Chinese children are least likely to be separated from their mothers, while the majority of Central American, Dominican, and Haitian children lived apart from their mothers for a time. Nearly half the Mexican children are separated from their mothers at some time during the migration.

Additionally, it is important to note that 28 percent of the children have been separated from their siblings as a direct result of migration. The stepwise pattern of bringing the children to the United States is more common among the Dominican and Central American groups, occurring in approximately one-third of the families. Finally, we must not forget that in most cases in which the child has been left in the country of origin, whether with one parent or alone, a significant bond of attachment is likely to have been formed with another primary caregiver, such as an aunt, uncle, grandparent, etc. The impact of the separation is quite apparent in the qualitative data we present below.

Length of separations

Families often expect that the process of establishing a home in the host country will not take long and that the family will be reunited within a short period of time. This may not occur for a variety of reasons, including financial obstacles and difficulties with legalizing immigration status, as well

TABLE 10.1 From Whom Was Child Separated?

	Chinese	Dominican	Central American	Haitian	Mexican	Total Sample
N = 380%	*n* = 78%	*n* = 35%	*n* = 77%	*n* = 71%	*n* = 81%	
Family arrives together	37	11	1	4	15	15
Family separated during the immigration	63	80	96	96	83	83
Mother only	15	3	0	10	2	6
Father only	10	25	16	27	12	30
Both parents	8	61	80	39	10	19

TABLE 10.2 From Whom Was Child Separated: Mother or Father?

	Chinese	Dominican	Central American	Haitian	Mexican	Total Sample
n = 78%	*n* = 75%	*n* = 77%	*n* = 71%	*n* = 81%		
Mother at some time during the migration	23	61	80	69	12	55
Father at some time during the migration	18	86	96	86	82	79

as for personal reasons such as divorce and separation of parents, propelled by the tensions of the migration process. Thus, the length of separation from parents can turn out to be unexpectedly long, with individual cases in our sample reporting being separated from one or both parents for nearly their entire childhood.

The difference between the groups in length of time that children have been separated from their mothers is striking (see Table 10.3). The majority of the Mexican youth were separated from their mothers for less than two years. Chinese children rarely separate from their mothers, but when they do it is usually from one to two years. For the Central American children on the other hand, the separation is protracted, lasting more than three years in 49 percent of the cases.

When separation from the father occurs during migration, it is often a very lengthy or permanent one (see Table 10.1). For those families who were separated, 51 percent had separations from fathers that lasted more than five years. This was the case for more than half of the Dominican and Central American families and in nearly three-quarters of the Haitian families.

Sequelae

We conducted one-way analyses of variance using the different family separation and family constellation patterns as predictors and the psychological symptom scales as outcomes. Analyses of family constellations revealed that children currently living in intact families noted significantly fewer depressive symptoms than those in the other types of family arrangements: $F\,(1.392) = 7.72$, $p < 0.01$. There were no differences in the other psychological sub-scales for the various family constellations.

We also conducted analyses of variance to determine if psychological symptoms varied across different family separation patterns. Children who were separated from their parents were more likely to report depressive symptoms than children who were not separated from their parents during migration: $F\,(1.388) = 1.54$. $p < 0.05$. Children who were separated from both parents had a higher level of reported symptoms compared to children who were not separated: $F\,(3.372) = 2.84$. $p < 0.05$. Girls who were separated from their parents were particularly likely to report depressive symptoms: $F(1.333) = 6.22$ $p < 0.03$. Again however, there were no significant differences between

TABLE 10.3 Length of Child's Separation From Mother Due to Migration

	Chinese	Dominican	Central American	Haitian	Mexican	Total Sample
$n = 17\%$	$n = 11\%$	$n = 31\%$	$n = 32\%$	$n = 26\%$	$N = 170\%$	
Up to 2 years	11	36	20	13	77	31
2–4 years	33	39	31	53	23	18
4+ years	6	25	49	31	0	28

TABLE 10.4 Length of Child Separation From Father Due to Migration

	Chinese	Dominican	Central American	Haitian	Mexican	Total Sample
$n = 35\%$	$n = 11\%$	$n = 51\%$	$n = 11\%$	$n = 52\%$	$N = 233\%$	
Up to 2 years	31	41	12	20	43	25
2–4 years	11	30	31	10	33	24
4+ years	37	37	47	71	33	31

the separated and non-separated groups for either the composite psychological symptom scale or for the other psychological symptom sub-scales.

It should also be noted that the level of total reported psychological symptoms and specifically depressive symptoms for those children who have been separated from their parents during migration is significantly different between ethnic groups. The Chinese children report the fewest, while the Haitian children report the highest psychological symptoms as a whole: $F(1.317) = 1.12$. $p < 0.01$, and depression in particular: $F(4.330) = 6.13$. $p < 0.001$.

Qualitative data

It was clear in our many interviews and conversations during the ethnographic process with immigrant youth, their parents, and their teachers that these separations were experienced as painful and complex by many of those affected. Below we briefly present the perspectives of children, parents, and teachers.

Children often spoke emotionally about separating from their loved ones. The children are asked: What was the hardest thing about coming to the United States? In the first-year interview, frequently the response reflected the painful nature of leaving behind a loved one. As one eleven-year-old Dominican girl said:

> The day I left my mother I felt like my heart was staying behind. Because she was the only person I trusted—she was my life. I felt as if a light had extinguished. I still have not been able to get used to living without her.[1]

For most children, the departure is a time of mixed feelings. There is an excitement about the prospect of reuniting with loved ones and a new life. On the other hand, migrating entails leaving behind caretakers, who for many years may have functioned as attachment figures for the child. Many spoke emotionally of the bittersweet nature of leaving. As an eleven-year-old Central American boy told us:

> Once I was in the plane they told me to be calm, not to be nervous, not to cry. I was crying because I was leaving my grandfather. I had conflicting feelings. On the one side I wanted to see my mother, but on the other I did not want to leave my grandfather.

While reunification is usually described with relief and joy, it is often interlaced with contradictory emotions. Feelings of disorientation are commonly expressed. At times, the children report not recognizing the parent and poignantly describe feeling like they are meeting a stranger. As a thirteen-year-old Haitian girl said:

> I didn't know who I was going to live with or how my life was going to be. I knew of my father but I did not know him.

In several cases, the children express fear of the parent who they have not seen in many years. When the family has evolved in the child's absence to include new parental figures and siblings, the reunification process is further complicated. A ten-year-old Chinese girl recalls:

> The first time I saw my father, I thought he was my uncle .... I was really afraid when I saw my father's face. He looked very strict. I was unhappy. My father was a stranger to me. I didn't expect to live with a stepmother.

Hence, reunification is often an ambivalent experience. The theme of forging a new relationship with a stranger is prevalent. This complicates the future development of the relationship, with the sense of distance and unfamiliarity persisting for different lengths of time.

Parents also spoke poignantly of the sadness of separating from their children. In many cases this happened when the children were infants and toddlers. Leaving the children can result from difficult economic conditions or dangerous circumstances in the country of origin. As the mother of a thirteen-year-old Central American boy explained:

> I was a single mother and there we were at war. I talked it over with my mother and she told me that maybe [things would be better] on "the other side." It was very hard above all to leave the children when they were so small. I would go into the bathroom of the gas station and milk my breasts that overflowed, crying for my babies. Every time I think of it, it makes me sad.

Parents and children maintain contact by phone, letters, and gifts, though long-distance communication can be difficult, especially in long-term separations, as the children grow up and the parent becomes an abstraction. The mother of a twelve-year-old Central American boy explained:

> They lived with my mother in El Salvador (I left when they were babies). I spoke to the eldest once a month by phone. As the little one grew, I spoke to him, too. But since he didn't know me, our communication was quite short. I really had to pull the words out of him.

It is very important for the parent that the child understands the reasons they left so that they can appreciate the sacrifice. This, of course, is not always the case. As the father of a 13-year-old Mexican boy confided:

> My son and my daughter are not warm toward me. They are still mad that I left them and was separated from them for years. Even when I explain to them that I came here for them, they don't hear, they don't understand. My daughter acted strangely when she first got here. She got jealous when I hugged my wife. She just wanted my attention for herself. Now that's changed and things are getting back to normal.

When the caretaker in the country of origin supports the relationship in the absence of the parent, easier reunification is reported. The mother of a thirteen-year-old Mexican girl told us:

> In spite of everything, we have a good relationship because my mother always spoke well of me. She always told her where I was and that some day I would come for her. So there's a certain respect.

Other parents point to the difficulties faced upon reunification and the building of the new relationship. As can be expected, such experiences are mostly evident for families in which the children have been separated from parents at a very young age and for long periods of time. The mother of a thirteen-year-old Central American girl admitted:

> Our relationship has not been that good. We were apart for eleven years and communicated by letters. We now have to deal with that separation. It's been difficult for her and for me. It's different for my son because I've been with him since he was born. If I scold him he understands where I'm coming from. He does not get angry or hurt because I discipline him, but if I discipline [my daughter] she takes a completely different attitude than he. I think this is a normal way to feel based on the circumstance.

Parents, like children, report that reunifications can be complicated for children who have to adapt to a new family constellation. Jealousy of new siblings or a new partner was frequently noted. These characteristics of the separation can lead to increased tension between the siblings and differential relationships of the parent toward the different children. The mother of a thirteen-year-old Central American boy disclosed: "We're getting used to each other. We are both beginning a different life together.... The kids are jealous of each other and my husband is jealous of them."

Parents also acknowledge the difficulties that children suffer when separated from other relatives that remain in the country of origin. The mother of a nine-year-old Mexican girl summed up the situation: "Before she came she missed us. Now she misses her grandparents."

Teachers echo the perspectives of the parents and children. In interviews we conducted with teachers asking about their views of the challenges that immigrant students face, several spontaneously offered observations about immigrant family separations. For example, a high school counselor informed us:

> Did you know we have kids who are here whose parents are not here? They live with relatives or friends like neighbors, old neighbors of the parents, and they work to support the parents back home. So some of the kids are coming to school and working as well. [In other cases] the family has been separated for many years ... so when they are reunited sometimes it's a mess in the literal sense of the word. The mother doesn't know the child; she left him and he grew up with grandmother .... The mother wasn't there and when he comes here the mother doesn't have the time to really build the relationship or maybe doesn't have the skills. Because she knows she's been working, sending money, caring for the child, and everything—she's been doing her part. But now it is the child's turn, you know, to show understanding, to show appreciation .... Sometimes you have the mother come first and the kids stay back home, and maybe father left home and has a new relationship, and the mother is in a new relationship. So that kids may be coming to a new family with other siblings and a stepparent.

A director of a high school's international center shared the following:

> I feel like I need to give [students] a great deal of personal and emotional support in the transition they are making. Talk with them, use our advising group to constantly talk about the problems of adjustment, adaptation, how are you feeling, what issues are coming up .... Almost universally they say things like, "I'm happy this year because I'm with my mother for the first time in five years, but I miss my grandmother who still lives in El Salvador." Or, "I don't see my dad anymore." You know the whole issue of family separations. There are a lot of emotional issues which come into this .... So many students come here because one parent has brought them and all of a sudden they are confronted with a parent they don't know very well. Maybe they have a whole other family they don't know .... We have people here from China, from Brazil, from Haiti, from Central America, and what is interesting is that they all [talk about] the same issues, "I don't know how to live with my parent."

DISCUSSION

Clinical implications

Here we have presented substantial evidence that separations between family members occur frequently during the journey of immigration. The vast majority of the immigrant children in our sample, arriving from five different countries of origin and recruited on two coasts, have been separated from one or both parents.[1] Given that 20 percent of children in the United States are growing up in immigrant homes, a substantial number of children are clearly affected by this phenomenon. The fact that such a large number of families are affected by separation has clear implications for clinicians treating immigrant families. While history-taking, clinicians should always ask whether family separations occurred. The evaluation should include inquiries about patterns of migration, length of separation, and family members' involvement. In cases of family disruptions, the family should not be viewed as deviant, as separations are normative to the migratory process.

Using a Western frame of attachment and object-relations theory along with a nuclear family framework would lead clinicians to predict that such separations would result in some degree of the psychological sequelae. Reports emerging from clinical contexts have corroborated a concern that family separations arising from the migratory experience lead to family friction and negative psychological outcomes (Arnold 1991; Brosse 1950; Burke 1980; CDI 1999). Our finding that children who arrived in the United States as a family unit involving no separations from their immediate family were less likely to report depressive symptoms than children whose families had separated during the migratory process partially substantiate this prediction.

Predictions based on the literature, however, would also lead us to expect that longer lengths of separation would be related to the reporting of greater psychological symptoms (Bowlby 1973; CDI 1999; Freud, Goldstein, and Solnil 1973). Our findings did not substantiate a relationship between length of separations and psychological symptoms. The fact that the total psychological symptom scale as well as the anxiety, cognitive functioning, interpersonal functioning, and hostility scales were not significantly different for separated and non-separated children lead us to conclude that the predicted outcomes may be less acute than might have been anticipated. These findings are in keeping with research on children undergoing the severe stress of war, which has demonstrated that behavioral disturbances often appear to be "less intense than anticipated" (Jensen and Shaw 1993).

While our data does illustrate a relationship between separation and increased levels of reported depressive symptoms, the statistical analyses do not allow us to make interpretations of direct causality. Other contributing factors may play a role in the report of these symptoms. For example, the level of reported depressive symptoms for those children who have been separated from their parents during migration is significantly different between ethnic groups.

Our findings may also be partially attributed to the ambiguous nature of the loss. Rather than viewing the loss as permanent, ideally the child views the loss as temporary, allowing her to keep the loved one psychologically present. Further, the extended nature of the immigrant family constellations may help to dissipate the loss.

Although the reporting of symptoms is generally less than we might have anticipated, our qualitative data, nonetheless, illustrate the poignancy of the separations from children's, parents,' and teachers' points of view. These findings are in keeping with research on children separated from their caretakers under circumstances other than migration, confirming that even in cases in which children do not manifest measurable psychological symptoms, most report missing their parents and caretakers (Charnley 2000; Totterman 1980). Separations from loved ones—extended family members as well as parents—seem to lead at least to transient feelings of loss and sadness in both adults and children.

Separations may also lead to temporary disruptions in family homeostasis when family members leave and are later reunited; it is to be expected that families would be temporarily destabilized. In most cases, the family will return to normal over time. In others, difficulties of clinical proportions may continue long after reunification. Future studies should systematically assess patterns and responses to family separations and reunifications. With better understanding of response patterns, clinicians would be able to distinguish between normal and temporary responses, as well as more pathogenic individual-level and family-level responses requiring clinical intervention.

We would emphasize that symptoms are not necessarily long-term and will undoubtedly be affected by the social contexts both in country of origin and in the receiving site. To understand immigrant children's responses to family separations, we must consider the complexity of the separation experience and the circumstances accompanying the separation. There is a wide range of variability in migratory patterns and circumstances. Further, it is quite likely that the psychological sequelae will not be manifested similarly across country of origin, groups, or developmental levels (Minuchin, Colapinto, and Minuchin 1998).

Complicating and attenuating factors

We postulate that a number of factors complicate the separation experience. Trauma arising from either a family tragedy (such as the death of a loved one) or from warfare or political, ethnic, or religious persecution, will dramatically alter the magnitude of the response. The sequelae may be more negative if the parent who goes away is the primary caretaker rather than the parent with whom the attachment is weaker. Associated losses may compound responses. Coming to terms with a parent leaving is more difficult if a child loses other critical supportive relationships concurrently. When predictable routines, so cherished by most children, are dramatically altered at the same time the parent leaves, the experience will be more disruptive (Boothby 1992). It may not be the separation alone but rather the accompanying "derailing events before, during, or after dislocation that lead to psychological distress of clinical proportions" (Perez-Foster 2001).

The demise of the marital relationship may occur in tandem with the migration (Boti and Bautista 1999; Simpao 1999). The anticipation of the immigration may cause relationships to rupture prior to immigration, and, in other cases, a break in the marital relationship may precipitate a parent's journey abroad in search of a stable income (Simpan 1999). At times, following protracted separations, once the family reunites the links in the marital dyad may be so weakened that the relationship comes apart in the new context; women may become significantly more independent, affairs may have occurred, or the more recently arrived partner may find the adjustment difficult (Boti and Bautista 1999). Hence, it is a challenge to ascertain which problems arise out of the immigration-related separation and which develop because of the marital separation.

The quality of several relationships will play a significant role in the nature of adjustment, including the child/parent(s) relationship bond prior to the migration (Arnold 1991) as well as the rapport between the caretaker(s) and child. Of critical importance is the relationship between the caretaking triangle: caretaker, child, and parent (Minuchin et al. 1998). Problems may emerge if the parent feels threatened by the caretaker (Falicov 2002) or if the caretaker is disparaging of the parent. When the parent and caretakers are able to work effectively as co-parents, disruptions are likely to be much less than when there is an ambivalent (or openly hostile) relationship. Below are two illustrations.

Mei is a twin born to a middle-class, urban Chinese family. She and her sister were largely raised by their paternal grandparents, who were openly hostile to their mother who is often away for her work. The family migrated when the sisters were ten years old. While the mother quickly found a job as a researcher, her father found the adjustment difficult. He returned to China with Mei, leaving her twin with the mother in the United States. After two years in China, they returned to the United States. There was tremendous marital discord. The mother and Mei's sister are openly hostile and disparaging of the father as well as Mei, whom they associate with him. Mei is withdrawn, depressed, and disengaged from school.

Joaquin is a fifteen-year-old raised in rural Nicaragua largely by his maternal grandparents. An extremely contentious relationship exists between the grandparents and Joaquin's father. They had only negative things to say about the father, who went to the United States early in Joaquin's childhood, taking the mother with him. At one point, Joaquin's father "kidnapped" (Joaquin's words) him from the grandparents, which culminated in a violent scene involving the brandishing of a machete. Four years after joining his parents in the United States, Joaquin names only his grandparents as significant people in his life. He is clearly socially isolated and longs desperately to return to Nicaragua.

On the other hand, a cooperative caretaking triangle can enrich the child's experience. The following situation exemplifies this.

Regine lived for five years with her single mother in Haiti's capital city until her mother migrated to the United States in search of regular income to support her daughter. Recognizing that she could not work long hours and suitably care for her daughter, she left Regine with her aunt, with whom she had a close relationship. Regine's mother maintained regular contact throughout the year with both her daughter and the caretaking aunt and went back every year to visit them. Regine also visited her mother several times during the summers. Once she joined her mother in the U.S. at age ten to stay permanently, Regine stayed in regular contact with her aunt, who remains an important psychological presence in her life. Her adjustment was smooth and she reports feeling lucky that she has two mothers—she refers to her biological mother as "maman" and to her aunt as "petite maman."

A caretaker's ambivalent relationship with the parent who has left may foreclose positive discussions about the missing parent (Shapiro 1994). If the caretaker is concurrently grieving the absence of the missing parent, the child is likely to hold back in talking about the loss, making it difficult to make meaning of the situation. Further, if the caretaker is also depressed by the separation from the parent, she will be less available psychologically to the child (Clarke-Stewart, McCartney, and Vandell et al. 2000; Falicov 1998; Hohn 1996; Lyons-Ruth, Wolfe, and Lyubchik 2000; Shapiro 1991; Suárez-Orozco and Suárez-Orozco 2001; Weissbourd 1996).

A variety of family characteristics may complicate or conversely act as a protective factor in the adjustment to this significant family transition. The remaining caretaker's ability to act as a holding environment that projects a sense of normalcy and high morale will be important (Boothby 1992; Perez-Foster 2001). Whether or not the family is able to maintain a sense of family coherence (Falicov 2002) will be critical. Are they able to expand the boundaries to include each point in the caretaking triangle? The ability to maintain authority as a parent is critical and may be compromised if the parent feels guilty about leaving the child (Arnold 1991; Burke 1980; Falicov 2002). Maintaining communication during the parents' absence is also linked to better outcomes, since inconsistent or minimal contact may be interpreted by the children as abandonment or not caring (Glasgow and Gouse-Shees 1995). Phone calls, letters, tapes, photographs, and gifts play critical symbolic roles in keeping the flame of the relationship alive (Robertson and Robertson 1971). Problems at the time of reunification may cause difficulties in the adjustment process. Often new unions have emerged—children may encounter new stepparents and siblings, and these transitions may be quite complicated (Arnold 1991).

In spite of these challenges, children often display remarkable resilience in the face of the adversities of family separation. Of critical importance to the adjustment process is how the child makes meaning of the situation of separation from parents and other loved ones. If the child is well-prepared for the separation, and if the separation is framed as temporary and necessary, undertaken for the good of the family, the separation will be much more manageable than if the child feels abandoned. Additionally, as our data suggest, separation followed by reunification, after an initial period of disorientation, may lead to an increased sense of closeness and intimacy in some families. Many of our participants viewed the relationship between parents and children as having increased in intensity because of the need to "make up for lost time."

Family therapists should be aware of the phenomenon of separation in their assessments and treatment of immigrant families because it creates a challenge to family relations and development.

For many children, the process is painful and leads to a sense of longing for missing parents. The "context and circumstances" of the separation will play a critical role in different outcomes (Wolkind and Rutter 1985). If the separation is cooperatively managed by parents and caretakers, and if the accompanying losses are minimized, the child, though changed, may not necessarily be damaged by the experience. Future research will be required to further unpack the short- and long-term effects of the separation as well as ways to attenuate the effects of separation.

The data for this research is part of the Harvard Longitudinal Immigrant Student Adaption study conducted by principal investigators Carola Suárez-Orozco and Miranda Suez-Orozco. This project has been made possible by findings provided by the National Foundation, the W. T. Grant Foundation, and the Spencer Foundation. The data presented, the statements made, and the views expressed are solely the responsibility of the authors.

Notes

1. The sub-scales of the symptom checklist we used included the following items: "Lately, do you …?":
   Depression: not have much energy, not feel like eating, cry easily, feel sad, feel not interested in much of anything, worry too much.
   Interpersonal sensitivity: feel critical of others, feel shy, feel others do not understand you, feel people do not like you, feel like you are not as good as other people.
   Cognitive functioning: have trouble remembering things, have trouble making decisions, have trouble concentrating.
   Anxiety: feel nervous, feel something terrible is going to happen, feel like your heart is racing, feel tense, keep remembering something frightening.
   Hostility: feel annoyed too easily, lose temper too easily, get into arguments too easily
   In addition to these items, the composite symptom scale also included the item "have stomach aches" for a total of 26 items.
2. We defined "parents" as biological or adoptive parents to whom the child had formed an attachment bond.
3. Note that for all tables in this article, chi-square analyses reached the significance level of $p < .01$. Also note that the percentages may not always add up to exactly 100 percent as all numbers were rounded.
4. All quotes have been translated from the respondent's native language.
5. We do not claim that this sample is representative of the entire immigrant population in the United States, because it was not randomly generated all across the country. While we have data on immigrant youth coming from five sending centers, immigrant families coming from other countries may have lower (or higher) rates of separations. Further, as participants were recruited from public schools, it would not be inclusive of middle- and upper-status families who send their children to private or schools. Therefore it may be somewhat of an overestimation of the for all immigrants across socioeconomic levels. We are confident, however, that it is representative of immigrant youth from these five sending regions attending public schools in the Boston and San Francisco areas. Although we cannot determine from this sample the exact proportion of immigrant youth affected, this study provides a strong indication of the magnitude of the phenomenon.
6. We include common-law arrangements in this category.

References

Ainsworth, M. 1989. Attachments beyond infancy. *American Psychologist 44*(4):709–716.
American Psychiatric Association. 1991. *Diagnostic and Statistical Manual of Mental Disorders,* fourth ed. Washington, DC: American Psychiatric Association.
Arnold, E. 1991. Issues of reunification of migrant West Indian children in the United Kingdom. In J. L. Roopnarine and J. Brown, Eds. *Caribbean Families' Diversity among Ethnic Groups.* Greenwich, CT: Ablex Publishing Corp.
Bagley, C. 1972. Deviant behavior in English and West Indian school children. *Research in Education* 8:47–55.
Boothby, N. 1992. Displaced children: Psychological theory and practice from the field. *Journal of Refugee Studies* 5(2):106–122.
Boss, P. 1999. *Ambiguous loss: Learning to live with unresolved grief.* Cambridge. MA: Harvard University Press.
Boti, M., and Bautista, F. 1999. *When Strangers Meet.* National Film Board of Canada. (Producer).
Bowlhy, J. 1973. *Separation, Anxiety and Anger.* New York: Basic Books.
Branch, C. W. 1999. Race and human development. *Racial and Ethnic Identity in School Practices: Aspects of Human Development.* Mahwah, NJ: Lawrence Erlbaum Associates.
Bronfenbrenner, U. 1988. Forward. In R. Pence, ed. *Ecological Research with Children and Families: Concepts to Methodology.* New York: Teachers College Press.
Brosse, T. 1950. *War-Handicapped Children.* Paris: UNESCO.

Burke, A. W. 1980. Family stress and precipitation of psychiatric disorder. A comparative study among immigrant West Indian and native British patients. In Birmingham. *International Journal of Social Psychiatry* 26(1):35–40.

CDI. 1999. *Families torn apart: Separation of Palestinian families in the occupied territories.* Jerusalem: Center for the Defense of the Individual.

Charnley, H. 2000. Children separated from their families in the Mozambique war. In C. Panter-Brick and M. T. Smith, eds. *Abandoned Children.* Cambridge, England: University Press.

Chestham, J. 1972. *Social Work with Immigrants.* London: Routledge and Regan Publishing.

Clarke-Stewart, K. A., McCartney, K., Vandell, D. I., Owen, M. T., and Booth, C. 2000. Effects of parental separation and divorce on very young children. *Journal of Family Psychology* 14(2):301–326.

Derogatis, L. R. 1977. The SCL-90. *Clinical Psychometric Research.*

Doka, K. J. 1989. *Disenfranchised Grief: Recognizing Hidden Sorrow.* New York: Lexington Books.

Doucette-Gates, A., Brooks-Gunn, J., and Chaso-Lansdale, L. P. 1998. The role of bias and equivalence in the study of race, class, and ethnicity. In V.C. McLoyd and L. Steomberg. *Studying Minority Adolescents: Conceptual, Methodological, and Theoretical Issues.* Mahwah. NJ: Lawrence Erlbaum.

Falicov, C. J. 1998. *Latino Families in Therapy: A Guide to Multicultural Practices.* New York: Guilford Press.

—— 2002. The family migration experience: Loss and resilience. In M. Suárez-Orozco and M. Paez, eds. *Latinos: Remaking America.* Berkeley, CA: University of California Press.

Feshbach, J., and Feshbach, S. 2001. *Psychology of Separation and Loss.* San Francisco: Jossey -Bass Publishers.

Forman, G. 1993. Women without their children: Immigrant women in the U.S. *Development* 4:51–55.

Freud, A., J. Goldstein, and A. Sulnit. 1973. *Beyond the Best Interests of the Child.* New York: Free Press.

Glasgow, G. F., and Gouse-Shees, J. 1995. Themes of rejection and abandonment in group work with Caribbean adolescents. *Social Work with Groups* 4:3–27.

Gliek-Schiller, N. 1992. Everywhere we go, we are in danger: Ti manno and the emergence of Haitian Transnational identity. *American Ethnologist,* 17(2):320–347.

Goldstein, R. D., Wampler, N. S., and Wise, P. H. 1997. War experiences and distress symptoms of Bosnian children. *Pediatrics* 100(5):873–878.

Gordon, M. 1961. *Assimilation and American life.* New York: Oxford University Press.

Greenberg, J. R., and Mitchell, S. A. 1983. *Object Relations in Psychoanalytic Theory,* Cambridge, MA: Harvard University Press.

Guba, E. G., and Lincoln, Y. S. 1994. Competing paradigms in qualitative research. In N. K. Denzin and Y. S. Lincoln, eds. *Handbook of Qualitative Research.* Thousand Oaks, CA: Sage.

Hepworth, J., Ryder, R. G., and Dreyer, A. S. 1981. The effects of parental loss on the formation of intimate relationships. *Journal of Marital and Family Therapy* 10:73–82.

Hondagneu-Sotelo, P. 1992. Overcoming patriarchal constraints: The reconstruction of gender relations among Mexican immigrant women and men. *Gender and Society* 6:393–415.

Huhn, G. E. 1996. *The effects of family functioning on the psychological and social adjustment of Jamaican immigrant children.* Unpublished doctoral dissertation. New York: Columbia University.

Hughes, D., Seidman, E., and Edwards, D. 1993. Cultural phenomena and the research enterprise: Toward a culturally anchored methodology. *American Journal of Community Psychology* 21(6):687–703.

Jensen, P. and J. Shaw 1993. Children as victims of war: Current knowledge and future research needs. *Journal of American Academy of Child Adolescent Psychiatry* 32(4):697–708.

Lyons-Ruth, K. 1996. Attachment relationships among children with aggressive behavior problems: The role of disorganized early attachment patterns. *Journal of Consulting Clinical Psychology* 64(1):64–73.

Lyons-Ruth, K., Wolfe, R., and Lyubehik, A. 2000. Depression and the parenting of young children: Making the case for early preventive mental health services. *Harvard Review of Psychiatry* 8(3):148–153.

Minuchin, P., Colapinto, J., and Minuchin, S. (1998). *Working with Families of the Poor.* New York: Guilford Press.

Neimeyer, R., ed. 2001. *Meaning Reconstruction and the Experience of Loss.* Washington, DC: American Psychological Association.

Partida, J. 1996. The effects of immigration on children in the Mexican-American community. *Child and Adolescent Social Work Journal* 13:211–254.

Payne, S., Horn, S., and Relf, M. 1999. *Loss and Bereavement.* Philadelphia: Open U Press.

Perez-Foster, R. 2001. When immigration is trauma: Guidelines for the individual and family clinician. *American Journal of Orthopsychiatry* 71(2):163–170.

Ponterotto, J., and Greiger, I. 1999. Merging qualitative and quantitative perspectives in a research identity. In M. Koppala and L. Suzuki, eds. *Using Qualitative Methods in Psychology.* Thousand Oaks, CA: Sage.

Prince, G. S. 1968. Emotional problems of children reunited with their migrant families in Britain. *Maternal and Child Care* 4:239–241.

Robertson, J., and Robertson, J. 1971. Young children in brief separation. *Psychoanalytic Study of the Child* 26:261–313.

Rutter, M. 1971. Parent-child separation: Psychological effects on the children. *Child Psychology and Psychiatry* 12:233–260.

Seiarra, D. T. 1999. Intrafamilial separation in the immigrant family. Implications for cross-cultural counseling. *Journal of Multicultural Counseling and Development* 27(18):30–41.

Sewell-Coker, B., Hamilton-Collins, J., and Foin, E. 1985. West Indian immigrants. *Social Casework* 60:363–368.

Shapiro, E. R. 1991. *Grief As a Family Process.* New York: Guilford Press.

Silverman, P. R. 2000. *Never Too Young to Know.* New York: Oxford University Press.

Simpao, E. B. 1999. *Parent-child separation and family cohesion amongst immigrants: Impact on object relations, intimacy, and story themes.* Unpublished doctoral dissertation, Long Island University.

Soto, I. M. 1987. West Indian child fostering: Its role in migrant exchanges. In C. Sutton and E. Chaney (Eds.), *Caribbean life in New York: City Sociocultural dimensions.* New York: Center for Migration Studies.

Suárez-Orozco, C. (2000). Identities under siege: Immigration stress and social mirroring among the children of immigrants. In A. Robben and M. Suárez-Orozco, eds. *Cultures Under Siege: Collective Violence and Trauma.* Cambridge, England: Cambridge University Press.

Suárez-Orozco, C., and Suárez-Orozco, M. 2001. *Children of Immigration.* Cambridge, MA: Harvard University Press.

Sue, D., and Sue, S. (1987). Cultural factors in the clinical assessment of Asian Americans. *Journal of Consulting and Clinical Psychology* 55:379–487.

Szapoenik, J., and Krurtines, W. M. 1993. Family psychology and cultural diversity. *American Psychologist* 21(6):687–703.

Tashakkorl, A., and Teddie, C. 1998. *Mixed Methodology: Combining Qualitative and Quantitative Approaches.* Thousand Oaks, CA: Sage.

Tolman, D., and Szalaeha, L. 1999. Dimensions of desire: Bridging qualitative and quantitative methods in a study of female adolescent sexuality. *Psychology of Women Quarterly* 23:7–39.

Totterman, N. 1989. *Intermittent father absence and the development of children.* Unpublished dissertation. Cambridge, England: University of Cambridge.

Waters, M. 1999. *Black Identities: West Indian Dreams and American Realities.* Cambridge, MA: Harvard University Press.

Weissbourd, R. 1996. *The Vulnerable Child.* Reading, MA: Perseus Books.

Western, D. (1989). Are "primitive" object relations really proedipal? *American Journal of Orthopsychiatry* 59:331–345.

Wilkes, J. R. 1992. Children in limbo: Working for the best outcome when children are taken into care. *Canada's Mental Health* 10:2–5.

Winnicott, D. W. 1968. *Through Pediatrics to Psycho- analysis.* London: Hogarth Press.

Wolkind, S. and Rutter, M. 1985. Separation, loss, and family relationships. In M. Rutter and L. Hersov, eds. *Child and Adolescent Psychiatry: Modern Approaches.* Oxford, England: Blackwell Scientific Publications.

Chapter 11
Ambiguous Loss: Risk and Resilience in Latino Immigrant Families

CELIA JAES FALICOV

> I wanted to bind Texas and Mexico together like a raft strong enough to float out onto the ocean of time, with our past trailing in the wake behind us like a comet trail of memories.
>
> John Phillip Santos, *Places ..., 1999, p. 5*

Latino immigrants, like many other immigrants, experience some degree of loss, grief and mourning. These experiences have been compared with the processes of grief and mourning precipitated by the death of loved ones (Shuval 1982; Warheit et al. 1985; Grinberg and Grinberg 1989; Volkan and Zintl 1993). Here I will argue, however, that migration loss has special characteristics that distinguish it from other kinds of losses. Compared with the clear-cut, inescapable fact of death, migration loss is both larger and smaller. It is larger because migration brings with it losses of all kinds. Gone are family members and friends who stay behind; gone is the native language, customs, and rituals; and gone is the land itself. The ripples of these losses touch the extended kin back home and reach into the future generations born in the new land.

Yet migration loss is also smaller than death, because despite the grief and mourning occasioned by physical, cultural, and social separation, the losses are not absolutely clear, complete, and irretrievable. Everything is still alive but is just not immediately reachable or present. Unlike the finality of death, after migration it is always possible to fantasize the eventual return or a forthcoming reunion. Furthermore, immigrants seldom migrate toward a social vacuum. A relative, friend, or acquaintance usually waits on the other side to help with work and housing and to provide guidelines for the new life. A social community and ethnic neighborhood reproduce, in pockets of remembrance, the sights, sounds, smells, and tastes of one's country. All of these elements create a mix of emotions—sadness and elation, loss and restitution, absence and presence—that makes grieving incomplete, postponed, ambiguous.

In this chapter, I attempt to integrate concepts from family-systems theory (ambiguous loss, boundary ambiguity, relational resilience) with concepts drawn from studies on migration, race, and ethnicity (familism, biculturalism, double consciousness) to deepen our understanding of the risks and resiliencies that accompany migration loss for Latinos. I propose that an inclusive "both/and" approach rather than an "either/or" approach to the dilemmas of cultural and family continuity and change increases family resilience in the face of multiple migration losses. As we will see, however, risks arise when the experience of ambiguous loss becomes unbearable and thwarts attempts at integrating continuity with change.

Although Latinos share many similarities in the aspects of family coping with loss that are addressed in this chapter, each family has a particular "ecological niche" created by combinations of nationality, ethnicity, class, education, religion, and occupation and by its individual history. Other variables that mediate the experience of migration are the degree of choice (voluntary or forced migration), proximity and accessibility to the country of origin, gender, age and generation, family form, and the degree and level of social acceptance encountered in the new environment (Falicov 1995, 1998).

AMBIGUOUS LOSS AND MIGRATION

The concept of ambiguous loss proposed by Pauline Boss (1991, 1999) describes situations in which loss is unclear, incomplete, or partial. Basing her thesis on stress theory, Boss describes two types of ambiguous loss. In one, people are physically absent but psychologically present (the family with a soldier missing in action, the noncustodial parent in divorce, the migrating relative). In the second, family members are physically present but psychologically absent (the family living with an Alzheimer's victim, the parent or spouse who is emotionally unavailable because of stress or depression).

Migration represents what Boss (1999) calls a "crossover" in that it has elements of both types of ambiguous loss. Beloved people and places are left behind, but they remain keenly present in the psyche of the immigrant. At the same time, homesickness and the stresses of adaptation may leave some family members emotionally unavailable to others. The very decision to migrate has at its core two ambiguous poles. Intense frustration with economic or political conditions compels the immigrant to move, but love of family and surroundings pulls in another direction.

Dealing with Ambiguous Loss

Many internal conflicts, moods, and behaviors of immigrants can be more easily understood when seen through the lens of "ambiguous loss."

Visits to the country of origin close the gap between the immigrant and that which is psychologically present but physically absent. Phone calls, money remittances, gifts, messages, and trips back home contribute to transnational lifestyles (Rouse 1992)—and to a psychologically complex experience of presence and absence.

Leaving family members behind has pragmatic and economic justifications, but it may also ensure a powerful psychological link. It may symbolize that migration is provisional and experimental rather than permanent. Leaving a young child with the immigrant's own parents may also assuage the immigrant's guilt about leaving and offer an emotional exchange for the help of shared parenting.

Encouraging relatives and friends to migrate eases the wrenching homesickness of migration. It is a way of saying "hello again" to some of the many to whom one has bid good-byes. It also means that social networks dismantled by migration may stand a chance of being partially reconstructed in the host country.

Latino immigrants also reconstruct urban landscapes of open markets and ethnic neighborhoods that provide experiences with familiar foods, music, and language. *Recreating cultural spaces* in this manner reestablishes links with the lost land while helping to transform the receiving cultures into more syntonic spaces (Ainslie 1998).

The long-lasting dream of returning home reinforces the gap between physical absence and psychological presence. A family may remain in a provisional limbo, unable to make settlement decisions or take full advantage of existing opportunities, paralyzed by a sort of frozen grief.

Family polarizations ensue when ambiguities overwhelm, as it were, the immigrant family's psyche. Spouses may come to represent each side of the conflict between leaving and staying, one idealizing and the other denigrating the country of origin or the "new" culture (Sluzki 1979). When such polarizations exist, they hint powerfully at denied or suppressed grief that may result in symptoms: depression or other emotional blocks to adaptation in adults, psychosomatic illness and selective mutism in children (Sluzki 1979, 1983; Grinberg and Grinberg 1989; Falicov 1998).

Generational legacies evolve when immigrant parents pass on their doubts, nostalgia, and sense of ambiguities to their children, who are sometimes recruited to one side or the other of the polarizations. Immigrant children may experience ambiguous loss themselves, but exposure to their parents' mixed emotions may significantly increase their stress.

The migration story itself can provide meaning and narrative coherence (Cohler 1991) to all life events. Experiences of success or of failure, the wife's new-found assertiveness, the ungrateful adult child—all can be readily explained: "It is because we came here." The question that will remain perennially unanswered is "How much is it migration, or is it just life challenges that would have appeared anywhere?" (Troya and Rosenberg 1999).

The construction of bicultural identities may result. The flow of people and information in a two-home, two-country lifestyle may give rise to a sense of "fitting in" in more than one place. Equally possible is the sense of not belonging in either place.

These behaviors of immigrants demonstrate the ambiguous, conflictual nature of migration losses. Yet they carry with them certain dynamic responses or "solutions" that demonstrate that people can learn to live with the ambiguity of never putting final closure to their loss. The adaptation depends on the contextual stresses that families encounter. Some are so excruciatingly oppressive that they prompt the family to repatriate. Under better circumstances, mixed feelings may be counteracted in part by building on family ties, social supports, and cultural strengths. Concepts from family systems theory and from acculturation studies can help us understand how ambiguous losses come to be tolerated and integrated in ways that strengthen families' resilience and empower their activism against social marginalization and injustice.

Dual Visions of Continuity and Change

From a family-systems viewpoint, for a family to be successful in coping with family transitions, flexible attitudes toward change and flexible efforts to preserve continuity need to coexist (Hansen and Johnson 1979; Melitto 1985; Falicov 1993). Most immigrant families manage to maintain contacts with their culture of origin and to reinvent old family themes while carving out new lives. New acculturation theories reflect this dynamic balance of continuity and change, rather than the traditional "either/or" linear theory of abandoning one culture to embrace the other. Terms such as *binationalism, bilingualism, biculturalism,* and *cultural bifocality* describe dual visions, ways of maintaining familiar cultural practices while making new spaces manageable, and ways of alternating language or cultural codes according to the requirements of the social context at hand (LaFramboise, Coleman, and Gerton 1993; Rouse 1992). Although there are compelling adaptational reasons for acquiring new language and cultural practices, there are equally compelling reasons for retaining cultural themes in the face of change, among them the attempt to preserve a sense of family coherence.

RELATIONAL RESILIENCE IN THE FACE OF LOSS

The concept of a "family sense of coherence," developed by Antonovsky and Sourani (1988), refers to the human struggle to perceive life as comprehensible, manageable, and meaningful. This striving for a sense of coherence (and hopefulness) is one of the key ingredients of *relational resilience*, those processes by which families cope and attempt to surmount persistent stress (Walsh 1998).

In this section, I explore immigrant families' attempts to restore meaning and purpose in their lives in the midst of multiple ambiguous losses. The aspects of relational resilience addressed in this discussion are family connectedness, family rituals, awareness of social marginalization, and belief or spiritual systems.

Family connectedness

Latinos' ethnic narratives almost invariably stress familism: inclusiveness and interdependence. In family-systems terms, family connectedness—the obligation to care for and support one another—is a defining feature of extended family life. This cultural tendency toward family connectedness seems to withstand migration and to persist in some form for at least one or two or more generations (Suárez-Orozco and Suárez-Orozco 1995; Sabogal et al. 1987). For immigrant families, familism may be manifest in the persistence of long-distance attachments and loyalties in the face of arduous social or economic conditions, in attempts to migrate as a unit and live close to one another, and in the desire to reunify when individuals have taken up the journey alone. The family members and the ideologies of these richly joined systems make their presence felt at a psychological and a physical level.

The Psychological Presence of Extended Familism. When extended family members are far away, *la familia* may become the emotional container that holds both dreams not yet realized and lost meanings that are no longer recoverable. At the most concrete level, immigrants send remittances back home in exchange for collective caretaking of remaining family members (children and/or elders), thus reinforcing a traditional system of emotional and economic interdependence. At a more abstract level, the idea itself of three-generational family can trigger other large existential meanings, such as one's lost national identity. A study of young adults (Troya and Rosenberg 1999) who had migrated to Mexico as children with parents seeking political refuge from South America demonstrates the powerful psychological presence of absent relatives. When asked for their spontaneous images formed in response to the words *patria* ("fatherland") and *tierra* ("land"), they associated these with the street or house where the grandmother or the aunt lived, reflecting (or perhaps creating anew) deep intergenerational bonds between country and family—a psychological familism.

Other studies show that as families acculturate (Rueschenberg and Buriel 1989; Sabogal et al. 1987; Suárez-Orozco and Suárez-Orozco 1995) they learn how to behave externally in a dominant culture that values assertiveness, independence, and achievement. Yet they do not abandon internally the connectedness and interpersonal controls of many collectivistic family systems.

The Physical Presence of Extended Family. When extended-family members are physically present, they play a significant role in shoring up the immigrant family. Their familism drives a concern for one another's lives, a pulling together to weather crises, a socio-centric child-rearing (Harwood, Miller, and Irizarry 1995), and a closeness among adult siblings (Chavez 1985).

Multigenerational dwellings, particularly the presence of grandmothers, can be influential in terms of transfers of knowledge, cultural exposures, nurturance, and instrumental help embedded in established sociocultural practices (Garcia-Coll et al. 1996) or even as a buffer against parental neglect or abuse (Gomez 1999). However, family life is not always as rosy as it seems. The description of Latino family connectedness is sometimes taken to such extremes that stereotypical images of picturesque family life dominate while tensions and disconnectedness among extended family members simmer below, ignored or discounted. Perhaps what matters, regardless of the particular positive or negative tone of the interactions, is the sense of being part of a family group, and that in itself affords a sense of continuity in the face of ruptured attachments and the disruptions of relocation.

Cultural family rituals

Another interesting avenue to study family resilience in the face of ambiguous losses is through the transmission of family rituals that reaffirm family and cultural identity. Family-systems theorists have long known about the power of rituals to restore continuity with a family's heritage while reinforcing family bonds and community pride (Bennett, Wolin, and McAvity 1988; Imber-Black, Roberts, and Whiting 1988). A good example is a clinical case of mine.

A poor, working-class Mexican-immigrant mother was very distressed over her daughter's refusal to have a *quinceañera* party. The intensity of the mother's emotion surprised me, because the party's ritual affirmation of the girl's virginity and future availability for dating hardly applied—everybody knew the girl was sexually involved with an older boyfriend. But for the mother, the *quinceañera* was the most unforgettable ("*inolvidable,* " she said) event in a woman's life and a memory that all parents dream of bestowing upon a daughter ever since the time of her birth. To abandon this valued ritual that lends coherence to a woman's life—even when its original contents had shifted or faded—represented too much cultural discontinuity for this mother.

The enactment of life-cycle rituals in the midst of cultural transformation can be construed as reflecting dual lifestyles, as being both ethnic and modern at the same time. Studies of immigrant families should include a close look at the persistence and the evolving new shapes of traditional family rituals—from routine family interactions (dinners or prayers) to celebrations of birthdays, holidays, and rites of passage or any gathering where a sense of family and national belonging is reaffirmed. Such study could help us understand not only the stable and shifting meanings of rituals but also their functions as metaphors for continuity and change.

Awareness of social marginalization

Although the notion of "dual vision" characterizes the incorporation of culture in the inner workings of many immigrant families, it also captures the nature of their interaction with larger external and institutional systems of the host country. The concept of "double consciousness," first described by Du Bois (1903) for African Americans, is useful here because it encompasses a perception of who one really is as a person within one's own group *and* a perception of who one is in the attributions of the larger society's story regarding the same group. Racial, ethnic, and class discriminations plague the individual stories of many Latino and Latina immigrant adults and children. One case of mine illustrates the painful awareness a Mexican family had of the gross, racist preconceptions of Latino immigrants by whites.

This family, a married couple with six children who had arrived from Oaxaca seven years ago, consulted me because a white, upper-class neighbor had accused their nine-year-old son of "molesting" her four-year-old daughter. As the Mexican boy's story unfolded, I learned that several children had been playing together in the fields when the little girl said she needed to urinate. The boy quickly pulled her panties down and held her in the upright position, but the girl ran crying home. Racism was undoubtedly part of the reaction to the boy's behavior. I recounted to the parents the alternative explanation to the "molestation," but the father responded, "I thank you, but we want you to tell [the white family that you think] our son is cured and this will never happen again." When asked why should I do this, he said, "Because, when they look at us, they think, 'These Mexicans are good people, *le hacen la lucha* [they struggle hard],' but if something goes wrong they suddenly see in us the faces of rapists and abusers. I promise you I will keep an eye on this boy, but please do not question their story. *No vale la pena* [It is not worth it]. It could cost us everything we worked for."

Here again is the ambiguity of gains, losses, and dual visions of immigrants. Striving for the dream of stability in a new land is riddled with pressures to subscribe to the dominant culture's story, which negatively judges dark-skinned, poor immigrants and deprives them of legal resources to fight unfair accusations. The social climate of structural exclusion and psychological violence suffered by immigrants and their children is not only detrimental to their participation in the opportunity structure but it also affects the immigrant children's sense of self, through a process of what Carola Suárez-Orozco (2000) aptly calls "social mirroring."

Indeed, most immigrants and their children are aware of the hostilities and prejudice with which they are regarded. From a psychological viewpoint, this awareness may be debilitating when internalized or denied, but it may be empowering when it helps stimulate strategic activism for social justice. Educators who stress the need for minority families' democratic participation in schools emphasize that awareness of one's own marginal status is the first step toward empowerment (Trueba 1999). Thus awareness of social injustices may create a measure of family resilience against assaults on identity.

Long-held beliefs and spiritual systems

People's *belief system*, or the meaning they make of their lives and experience, is a narrative construct that helps us understand a family's ability to deal with adversity (Walsh 1998; Wright, Watson, and Bell 1996). A family's tolerance for loss and ambiguity is related to its culture's tolerance for ambiguity; fatalistic and optimistic stances are likewise embedded in culturally based systems of meaning (Boss 1999).

Some Latino cultural narratives and spiritual beliefs promote acceptance of life's adversities, tempering the need to find answers and definitive solutions to losses (Falicov 1998). Roman Catholic beliefs value acceptance of suffering, destiny, and God's will. A belief that little in life is under one's control is also related to conditions of poverty and decreased agency (Garza and Ames 1972; Comas-Díaz 1989). These beliefs should not be misconstrued as passivity, however, but as a way of marshaling one's initiative to solve what can be solved while accepting what cannot be changed—a sort of mastery of the possible.

Like other cultural and ritual practices, the old religion often takes new forms and functions in the new land. Church participation may actually help inscribe various Latino groups in dual, evolving translational spaces. As Peggy Levitt (2002) so cogently describes, immigrants' church attendance can allow a double membership that crosses border arenas in the homeland while it grounds them locally through host country participation and even civic engagement. This balance of continuity and change may be at the core of resilient adaptations to ambiguous loss. Yet these dual visions are not always obtainable, nor is it always possible to make positive meaning out of the experience of migration. In the next sections, I describe situations where attempts to restore a sense of family coherence fail in the face of intense loss and irreparable ambiguity.

WHEN AMBIGUOUS LOSS BECOMES UNBEARABLE

Many circumstances surrounding migration can lead to overwhelmingly problematic physical and emotional disconnections among family members. Two of these circumstances are addressed here: (1) the overlap of the consequences of migration with the impact of other life-cycle transitions at any point in the life of an immigrant and (2) the short- and long-term effects of migration separations and reunifications among all family members. Both situations can be understood better by utilizing the concept of boundary ambiguity.

Boundary ambiguity

Ambiguous loss may become problematic when it generates confusion about who is in and who is out of the family. Boss (1991) labeled this phenomenon "boundary ambiguity," a concept that is increasingly being used in family research to describe effects of family-membership loss over time (Boss, Greenberg, and Pearce-McCall 1990) and that may be very helpful in illuminating migration losses. This construct encompasses the rules and definitions of family sub-systems (parental, marital, sibling, and other subgroups) and how they are perceived by each family group.

When ambiguous loss is compounded by life-cycle transitions

When nonambiguous, irretrievable losses—such as the death of a relative back home—occur in the life of an immigrant family, the uncertain, provisional, and ambiguous quality of the old good-byes accentuates that loss and creates confusion about where one belongs and exactly who constitutes one's family.

A thirty-six-year-old woman consulted me for depression after her father died suddenly in Argentina. Overwhelmed by sadness and guilt at not having made the effort to see him more often and by the unbearable loneliness of not being able to participate in communal grieving, this woman asked to have a separation from her white American husband. He was the one who had brought her to this country, and she felt him to be a much less loving man than her father. Asked about her adoring father's reaction to her leaving her country twelve years ago to get married, she promptly said, "Everybody told me that for him that day was like *el velorio del angelito* [the wake of his little angel]." Now she was experiencing a great deal of confusion about where she belonged. Her husband and children, who hardly knew her father, provided little comfort. She needed the support of her family of origin, but her own shared history with them had been truncated long ago. This case illustrates the rippling effects of ambiguous loss for the immigrant, for their children, and for the family of origin left behind. This woman's eight-year-old daughter was having behavior and school difficulties that paralleled the mother's depression.

Calling two women "Mami"

In addition to separations between extended and nuclear family, Latino immigrants increasingly experience separations between parents and children. A father or a mother frequently migrates first, leaving children behind and planning for later reunification. Such separations complicate experiences of loss, raise issues of inclusion/exclusion, and set the stage for boundary ambiguity.

When a father or a mother migrates first, leaving the family to be reunited later, the confusion may be mild and temporary or intense and prolonged. If sufficient time passes, a family in which the father migrated first may reorganize into a single-parent household, with mother as head and substitutes performing the parental functions of the absent father. Subsequent reunification is often stressful because family boundaries need to change yet again to allow for reentry of the absent member.

Increasingly today, mothers recruited for work make the journey north alone, leaving the children with other women in the family or social network. It is only after several years that these mothers are joined by their children, who often travel unaccompanied. In Chapter 9, sociologist Pierrette Hondagneu-Sotelo's incisive analysis of the changing labor demands driving these emergent transnational family forms, and of the possible new meanings of family and motherhood, provides a historical, economic, and social context for these complex and often traumatic separations and equally traumatic reunifications between mothers and children. Children are left behind with grandparents or other relatives so that an immigrant parent can face the dangers of illegal passage and the economic hardships of getting established in the new country without the added worry of having youngsters under their wing. Over time, the costs of these arrangements are significant.

The adjustments to parting and the adjustments at the time of a subsequent reunion place not only mother and child but also all the sub-systems of a three-generational family (including siblings who stayed in the sending culture and those born in the receiving country) at risk for developing boundary ambiguities and concomitant individual and relational problems. Psychotherapists and social workers often encounter immigrant children who call two women "Mami." We know very little about the meaning of this behavior. Does it point to an attempt to deal with ambiguous loss by accepting two mothers, one here and one there? Could it represent a fluid definition of family that reflects multiple attachments and wherein "Mami" is just a generic term for significant others? Of more concern, does it signify boundary ambiguity, the beginning of divided loyalties, and confusion about who is the real mother? What makes for a successful separation and reunion? What are the consequences of separation at different ages and for various lengths of time? What transforms ambiguous loss into conflict-laden boundary ambiguity?

An international furor over the fate of one young Cuban immigrant highlights an extreme case of boundary ambiguity. Custody of Elián González, a six-year-old Cuban shipwreck survivor, was fiercely contested by his deceased mother's relatives in Miami and by his father and grandmothers in Cuba, each side of the family (the immigrants and the non-immigrants) claiming the right to decide where Elián belonged (Cooper Ramo 2000). At the political level, the boundary ambiguity could not be resolved because it represented the long-standing tensions between Little Havana in Miami and Havana in Cuba. Yet the symbolism of belonging goes beyond the political. At the level of migration loss, the dispute struck deep in the hearts of immigrants who have remained in perpetual mourning for the total loss of the Cuba they once knew. It is tempting to speculate that it is precisely the prohibition to visit that makes it impossible for these immigrants to lead satisfactory dual lives, recharging their emotional batteries and becoming binational or bicultural. Their ambiguous losses instead solidify into a rigid migration narrative confined to an idealization of the island's past, recreated exclusively in the space of Little Havana. The conflict over Elián González's future was magnified by these historical factors, but it illustrates what may happen in families that polarize over their efforts to keep a child close to both sides of their existential predicament.

Clinicians encounter many families from Mexico, Central America, and the Caribbean who have undergone separation and reunion with children of all ages. After a period of time following reunification, mothers often request professional help with behavior problems and defiance of their authority. Many social and psychological factors contribute to mother-child disconnections and to the development of conflict. From a family-systems viewpoint, we can speculate on the family interactions that may contribute to—or help prevent—pernicious family-boundary ambiguities. One factor seems to be each family member's positive or negative perceptions of the decision to migrate—that is, how much approval or disapproval there is among the adults (the biological mother and the caretaker, for example) about the decision to separate temporarily. A related outcome is the quality of the relationship between the migrating parent(s) and the temporary caretakers and whether they all try to be cooperative and inclusive at long distance.

Ongoing studies will help us learn more about how to help families strengthen their resilience in the face of the many individual and relational risks inherent in these separations, yet the separations themselves, especially if prolonged, may pose nearly insurmountable obstacles to family cohesion. Studies of the nature of the ruptured attachments among family members, the loss of shared histories, and the effects of persistent economic stress on family life may yield greater understanding of the problematic "costs of transnationalism" for immigrant families.

DIRECTIONS FOR RESEARCH

Family-systems theorists and family therapists have become increasingly aware of the need to incorporate findings from studies of migration, race, and ethnicity in their efforts to develop culturally and socially responsible family-systems frameworks and approaches. Likewise, researchers investigating issues in migration, race, and ethnicity would enhance their work by expanding their studies of individuals to encompass three-generational immigrant family units as social systems in cultural transition.

The constructs of *ambiguous loss* and *boundary ambiguity* can be applied to studies of migration and to its intersection with life-cycle transitions, including the separations and reunions among all the generations and sub-systems of immigrant families. Integrating these concepts may contribute to a better theoretical understanding of risks and resilience for different families in the trajectory of migration. Likewise, exploring *family resilience* helps identify key relational processes that enable families to succeed and make some order and meaning out of the many stresses they encounter.

Narrative approaches and concepts, such as belief systems, incorporate a meaning-making lens that enables people to tell their stories and express their own insights into their unique experiences of loss, hardship and resilience. It is difficult to capture the rich texture of migration through quantitative work alone. The addition of other approaches—qualitative interviews, ethnographic texts, diaries, and case studies—may tap the nuances of multiple and unique outcomes. Small-scale comparative and longitudinal qualitative studies, such as following a small group of nuclear families who have undergone separations and reunifications and a similar group of families who have migrated as a nuclear unit, may greatly enrich our understanding of the many dimensions involved in these experiences.

Concepts that belong to the domain of family-systems studies have much potential to enhance the themes and findings generated in the domains of immigration research. Integrating the two streams of work would be mutually invigorating and would lead to greater understanding of the impact of migration on Latino families.

References

Ainslie, R. C. 1998. Cultural mourning, immigration, and engagement: vignettes from the Mexican experience. In M. Suárez-Orozco, ed. *Crossings.* Cambridge, MA: Harvard University Press.

Antonovsky, A., and Sourani, T. 1988. Family sense of coherence and family adaptation. *Journal of Marriage and the Family* 50:79–92.

Bennett, L. A., Wolin, S. J., and McAvity, K. J. 1988. Family identity, ritual, and myth: a cultural perspective on life cycle transitions. In C. J. Falicov, ed. *Family transitions: Continuity and Change Over the Life Cycle.* New York: Guilford Press.

Boss, P. 1991. Ambiguous loss. In F. Walsh and M. McGoldrick, eds. *Living Beyond Loss: Death in the Family.* New York: Norton.

Boss, P. 1999. *Ambiguous Loss: Learning to Live with Unresolved Grief.* Cambridge, MA: Harvard University Press.

Boss, P., Greenberg, J. R., and Pearce-McCall, D. 1990. Measurement of boundary ambiguity in families. *Minnesota Agricultural Experiment Station Bulletin* 593–1990:1–25.

Chavez, L. R. 1985. Households, migration, and labor market participation: The adaptation of Mexicans to life in the United States. *Urban Anthropology* 14:301–346.

Cohler, B. 1991. The life story and the study of resilience and response to adversity. *Journal of Narrative and Life History* 1:169–200.

Comas-Díaz, L. 1989. Culturally relevant issues and treatment implications for Hispanics. In D. R. Koslow and E. Salett, eds. *Crossing Cultures in Mental Health.* Washington, DC: Society for International Education, Training, and Research.

Cooper Ramo, J. 2000. A big battle over a little boy. *Time,* Jan. 17.

Du Bois, W. E. B. 1903. *The Souls of Black Folk.* Chicago: McClurg.

Falicov, C. J. 1993. Continuity and change: Lessons from immigrant families. *American Family Therapy Association Newsletter* Spring: 30–36.

Falicov, C. J. 1995. Training to think culturally: A multidimensional comparative framework. *Family Process* 34:373–388.
Falicov, C. J. 1998. *Latino Families in Therapy: A Guide to Multicultural Practice.* New York: Guilford Press.
Hansen, D., and Johnson, V. 1979. Rethinking family stress theory: Definitional aspects. In W. Burr, R. Hill, F. Nye, and I. Reiss, eds. *Contemporary Theories about the Family. Vol. I: Research-Based Theories.* New York: The Free Press.
García-Coll, C. Lamberty, G., Jenkins, R., McAdoo, H.P., Crnic, K., Wasik, B. H., and Vásquez García, H. 1996. An integrative model for the study of developmental competencies in minority children. *Child Development* 67:1891–1914.
Garza, R. T., and Ames, R. E. 1972. A comparison of Anglo and Mexican-American college students on locus of control. *Journal of Consulting and Clinical Psychology* 42:919–922.
Gomez, M. Y. 1999. The grandmother as an enlightened witness in the Hispanic culture. *Psycheline* 3(2):15–22.
Grinberg, L., and Grinberg, R. 1989. *Psychoanalytic Perspectives on Migration and Exile.* New Haven, CT: Yale University Press.
Harwood, R. L., Miller, J. G., and Irizarry, N. L. 1995. *Culture and Attachment: Perceptions of the Child in Context.* New York: Guilford Press.
Imber-Black, E., Roberts, J., and Whiting, R., eds. 1988. *Rituals in Families and Family Therapy.* New York: Norton.
LaFramboise, T., Coleman, H. L., and Gerton, J. 1993. Psychological impact of biculturalism: Evidence and theory. *Psychological Bulletin* 114(3):395–412.
Levitt, P. 2002. Two Nations Under God? Latino Religious Life in the U.S. in *Latinos: Remaking America.* Berkeley, CA: University of California Press.
Melitto, R. 1985. Adaptation in family systems: A developmental perspective. *Family Process* 24(1):89–100.
Rouse, R. 1992. Making sense of settlement: Class transformation, cultural struggle, and transnationalism among Mexican immigrants in the United States. In N. G. Schiller, L., Basch and C. Blanc-Szanton, eds. *Towards a Transnational Perspective on Migration.* New York: New York Academy of Sciences.
Rueschenberg, E. and Buriel, R. 1989. Mexican American family functioning and acculturation: A family systems perspective. *Hispanic Journal of Behavioral Sciences* 11(3):232–244.
Sabogal, F., Marín, G., Otero-Sabogal, R., Marín, B. V., and Perez-Stable, P. 1987. Hispanic familism and acculturation: What changes and what doesn't. *Hispanic Journal of Behavioral Sciences* 9(4):397–412.
Santos, J. P. 1999. *Places Left Unfinished at the Time of Creation.* New York: Viking.
Shuval, J. T. 1982. Migration and stress. In L. Goldberger and S. Breznitz, eds. *Handbook of Stress: Theoretical and Clinical Aspects,* second ed. New York: Free Press.
Sluzki, C. E. 1979. Migration and family conflict. *Family Process* 18(1):79–92.
—— 1983. The sounds of silence. In C. J. Falicov, ed. *Cultural Perspectives in Family Therapy.* Rockville, MD: Aspen.
Suárez-Orozco, C. E. 2000. Identities under siege: Immigration stress and social mirroring among the children of immigrants. In A. Robben and M. Suárez-Orozco, eds. *Cultures Under Siege: Violence and Trauma in Interdisciplinary Perspective.* Cambridge, MA: Cambridge University Press.
Suárez-Orozco, M. M., and Suárez-Orozco, C. E. 1995. *Transformations: Immigration, family life and achievement motivation among Latino adolescents.* Stanford, CA: Stanford University Press.
Troya, E., and Rosenberg, F. 1999. "Nos fueron a México: ¿Qué nos paso a los jóvenes exiliados consureños?" *Sistemas Familiares* 15(3):79–92.
Trueba, E. T. 1999. *Latinos Unidos: From cultural diversity to the politics of solidarity.* Lanham, MD: Rowman & Littlefield.
Volkan, V. D. and Zintl, E. 1993. *Living Beyond Loss: The Lessons of Grief.* New York: Charles Scribner's Sons.
Walsh, F. 1998. *Strengthening Family Resilience.* New York: Guilford Press.
Warheit, G., Vega, W., Auth, J., and Meinhardt, K. 1985. Mexican-American immigration and mental health: A comparative analysis of psychosocial stress and dysfunction. In W. Vega and M. Miranda, eds. *Stress and Hispanic Mental Health.* Rockville, MD: National Institutes of Health.
Wright, L. M., Watson, W. L., and Bell, J. M. 1996. *Beliefs: The Heart of Healing in Families and Illness.* New York: Basic Books.

Chapter 12
Cultural Mourning, Immigration, and Engagement: Vignettes from the Mexican Experience

RICARDO C. AINSLIE

In the spring of 1929 Freud wrote to the Swiss psychiatrist Ludwig Binswanger on the occasion of the death of the latter's favorite son:

> Although we know that after such a loss the acute state of mourning will subside, we also know we shall remain inconsolable and will never find a substitute. No matter what may fill the gap, even if it be filled completely, it nevertheless remains something else. And actually this is how it should be. It is the only way of perpetuating that love which we do not want to relinquish (Frankiel 1993:70).

Loss, Freud is clearly telling us, is inherently paradoxical, setting in motion psychological effort to resolve that which is inherently unresolvable. It is an experience that creates an emptiness that remains an emptiness despite efforts to fill it in. Perhaps the most important insight that Freud offers us, however, is that these irresolvable gaps become, again paradoxically, the very means through which we perpetuate our attachment to those whom we have lost. In its own way, mourning negates loss. The lost attachment remains emotionally alive so long as it is mourned.

The immigrant experience represents a special case of mourning in which mourning revolves around the loss of loved people and places occasioned by geographic dislocation.[1] This mourning is not necessarily of such a magnitude as to represent a clinical syndrome. Rather, it represents a psychological context that colors the immigrant's emotional world and that becomes represented at the level of motivation and engagement in ways that are both conscious and unconscious. Notwithstanding the preeminent economic motives that lie behind the decision to leave one's country and the fact that in many instances some measure of economic gain comes from that decision, immigrants are, as Volkan (1993) notes, "perpetual mourners" precisely because they must leave home to achieve those economic goals. In the character of their mourning, in the manner in which immigrants' mourning plays itself out in their individual and collective lives, powerful motivational forces are at work that shape how immigrants alter the worlds into which they have come to live. The immigrant's engagement with the processes of mourning plays an important role in the strategies deployed in managing grief, how the immigrant participates in the new social context, and the nature of his relationship with people and lands that have been left behind.

CULTURE, IDENTITY, AND CULTURAL MOURNING

Individual identity draws heavily from cultural, social, and familial elements that together become the foundation for intrapsychic experience (Erikson 1950). Elsewhere (Ainslie 1995) I have described culture as "both sustentative and suspensory," that is, as a series of socio-psychological enclosures that provide emotional nurturance while psychologically "holding" and organizing us. The subjective experience of culture can be understood, in developmental terms, as having its origins at the beginning of life, in the intimate engagements between parent and child, and increasingly becoming defined or structured by complex social signifiers such as language, ethnicity, and religion, which give culture its hue.

From the beginning of our emotional lives, the social experiences that govern our understanding of the known are seamlessly fused with cultural elements that only later can be reflected upon, becoming discernible to the individual as something "cultural." Neither the toddler in the papoose, nor the young child whose mother sings an "ethnic" lullaby, conceives of himself as immersed in a medium that we term "culture." Children simply experience. Yet from the start that experiencing is densely populated by all of the cultural elements that we come to love and that create for us a sense of the familiar, in both the experiencing and relational aspects of the word. For this reason, identity, in an intimate and psychological sense, is permanently soldered to those characteristics of our experience defined by the peculiarities of our individual parents and families as well as by the cultural elements that have given context to those lives. The link between culture and the deepest features of subjective experience is as ingrained as it is pervasive; this is why cultural dislocation has such profound psychological consequences for the individual.

It is the intimate connection between individual and collective experience that weds individual mourning to cultural mourning. When an immigrant leaves loved ones at home, he or she also leaves the cultural enclosures that have organized and sustained experience. The immigrant simultaneously must come to terms with the loss of family and friends on the one hand, and cultural forms (food, music, art, for example) that have given the immigrant's native world a distinct and highly personal character on the other hand. It is not only people who are mourned, but culture itself, which is inseparable from the loved ones whom it holds. This is the experience that I term cultural mourning. While the motives for migration (voluntary or involuntary) and the conditions left behind (economic, political) vary from person to person, all immigrants lose something essential to their lives in leaving their native homes. While these varied motives may structure the nature of the mourning that must be engaged (for example, the greater the ambivalence about leaving one's country, the more difficult mourning is likely to be), even those whose lives in their country of origin are characterized by conflict and deprivation will experience loss.

LOSS, MOURNING, AND RESTITUTIVE ATTEMPTS: THE PSYCHOLOGICAL "RETURN" AND THE CREATION OF POTENTIAL SPACE

Many have observed the parallel between the formation of the immigrant's new identity after moving to an adopted country and the mourning process that clinicians have come to recognize as characteristic of those who have lost a loved one (Garza-Guerrero 1974; Grinberg and Grinberg 1984; Volkan 1979; Volkan and Zintl 1993). When individuals experience a significant loss, the mourning process proceeds through an internal reworking of the mental representations of that relationship. Hans Loewald (1962), for example, notes that in mourning there is "the relinquishment of external objects and their internalization involves a process of separation, of loss, and restitution" (p. 125).

In uncomplicated grief, the mourner loosens ties to the representation of the dead through the work of mourning, gradually forming an identification with that person who promotes growth. Mourning facilitates the processes of internalization that ultimately lead to an experience of separation without psychic loss (Loewald 1962). In normal mourning, then, there is a gradual decathexis of elements of the relationship with the lost one, as well as a claiming of the full range of affect toward the lost one.

A common mechanism in mourning is the use of objects and fantasies that serve to dilute the impact of loss by virtue of maintaining a connection to the deceased. Volkan (1981) terms these activities "linking objects" or "linking phenomena" to indicate the function of such objects or fantasies in the management of grief—they are symbolic bridges to the representation of the dead person. These linking processes "provide a locus for externalized contact between aspects of the mourner's self-representation and aspects of the representation of the deceased. The mourner sees them as containing elements of himself and the one he has lost" (p. 20). These processes are also readily observed in the lives of immigrants who, having left loved ones and loved places behind, must absorb the consequences of that dislocation in order to be able to effectively manage the world into which they have come. In mourning these losses, immigrants keep the people and cultures they have left alive, psychologically, via the use of the linking objects and linking processes described by Volkan.

D.W. Winnicott, the eccentric but at times brilliant psychoanalytic theorist, offers us another vantage for understanding the processes of mourning and adaptive efforts to manage them. His theorizing is especially useful in understanding the concept of cultural mourning in that Winnicott weds a child's developing sense of people and the unfolding experience of culture into an indissolvable matrix of experience. Winnicott observed that culture is created out of that realm of experience situated between the infant's desire and the mother's response, in what he termed "the potential space" (1971). The potential space is an intermediate area of experiencing that lies between fantasy and reality, that is, between inner psychic reality and actual or external reality (Ogden 1990). Winnicott's use of the concept was initially intended to capture the psychological experience and struggle of the young child grappling with the need to feel emotionally fused with the mother while simultaneously forced to acknowledge the fact of her separateness. This tension, Winnicott proposed, is resolved via the creation of a domain of psychological experiencing that he termed the potential space. The function of the potential space for the child, and its evolution over the course of development, are not central to the present considerations. However, Winnicott's description of the potential space as pivotal in the management of experiences of separation and dislocation is important. Equally essential is Winnicott's description of the potential space as the area of cultural experience and the area of creative engagement with the world in which we live. These two definitions overlap in cultural mourning.

Winnicott (1951, 1967) theorized that, for the infant, the reality of an internal and an external world—the reality that parent and child are different people with distinct experiences—creates a challenge of momentous proportions. In this sense, children, too, are perpetual mourners. The potential space is the arena within which the child engages and attempts to resolve the tensions created by separateness; it is a domain of experience whose ambiguous status as simultaneously "me" and "not me" allows for the illusion of continuity between self and other while concurrently lending itself to the solution of this spatial and, more important, *experiential* distance. Modell (1968) emphasizes that the potential space is actively constructed, rather than passively received—that is, an illusion created out of what is interior and what is exterior:

> [T]he transitional inanimate object of the child ... stands midway between what is created by the inner world and that which exists in the environment .... It is something other than the

> self, but the separateness from the self is only partially acknowledged, since the object is given life by the subject. It is a created environment—created in the sense that the properties attributed to the object reflect the inner life of the subject (p. 35).

Whether as children or adults, we manage the ubiquity of dislocation, separation, and loss in our lives through the use of potential space; we construct arenas of experiencing in which we creatively dissolve those tensions, finding within them solutions that bridge the emotional gaps and spaces secondary to separation. For the infant, this might involve an object, say a favorite blanket that has rested between infant and mother in nursing, that becomes a constant comforter to be invoked at those junctures where contact is threatened or vulnerability is experienced. For adults, the manifestations of the potential space are considerably more subtle, insinuated into the worlds we construct, masked by social conventions, but no less amenable to creative engagement and the illusion of restoration of what is lost, as will be illustrated below.

A common feature of the immigrant's mourning is the attempt to deny or dilute the reality of dislocation. There are classic examples: the "new" designations for those communities established by immigrants from places called York, Jersey, or Hampshire; or the Little Italys and the Chinatowns, places within which immigrants have sought to recreate lost worlds. These efforts are transparent in their design. They attempt to mask the reality of loss via the creation of a psychological space, a version of Winnicott's potential space, within which the illusion that they are both "here" and "there," both "now" and "then," is made possible. In this manner, the immigrant mourner is soothed and comforted. Within these enclaves, individual and cultural mourning can be managed and absorbed through the illusion of blurred distances—intrapsychic, territorial, and cultural.

It is important to emphasize that in Winnicott's depiction, the potential space is only partially, and perhaps least interestingly, a retreat from the reality of separation. Most important, in Winnicott's framework the potential space is a form of creative engagement with the problematics of separation and loss, put in the service of constructively, if never perfectly, transcending them. The immigrant, like all mourners, uses the potential space to help resolve the unbearable tensions and contradictions of an existence in which separation brings significant anguish, which may be the case even when separations are chosen and desired. Such resolution facilitates the effective engagement with the new environment.

LA PULGA: AN ILLUSTRATIVE POTENTIAL SPACE

By midday on any given Sunday, the Austin Country Flea Market, on the eastern margin of the city of Austin, Texas,[2] is bustling. The price of admission is one dollar per carload, and the parking lot is full. Seventy to 80 percent of the fifteen- to eighteen-thousand people who come to the flea market on any given weekend are Hispanic (Gandara 1996), which in Texas means overwhelmingly Mexican or Mexican American. Most of these visitors call the Austin Country Flea Market "La Pulga" ("the flea" in Spanish), reflective of the fact that these immigrants have made the flea market their own. La Pulga has become the quintessential potential space for Mexican immigrants, with or without legal documents, who live and work in and around Austin. La Pulga is very reminiscent of the plazas typical of the towns and villages these immigrants have left. A stage and dance floor are located in the very heart of the square that is formed by the arrangement of vendor's stalls. In front of the stage are metal tables and chairs, and concessions sell food, beer, and soft drinks. Originally, the music ranged from blues and rock and roll to country and Mexican Norteño and Tejano music. However, accurately reading the tastes of their predominant clientele, the operators of the flea market now book Norteño and Tejano music almost exclusively. These conjuntos play Spanish-language music characteristic of northern Mexico and Texas, but the lyrics closely parallel the motifs typical of American country music: lost love, ill fate, and large doses of melancholy.

The men sit drinking Mexican beer, eating roasted corn, tacos, gorditas, and other Mexican foods, while watching couples on the dance floor. Many of the women are dressed in their Sunday finest.

La Pulga is concretely the reconstructed world these immigrants have left. Vendor stands sell Mexican videos, classic Mexican movies such as the famous comic Mario Moreno Cantinflas' El Padrecito (The Little Priest), Mexico's version of "Funniest Home Videos," and countless Mexican Rodeo movies, an especially popular genre for those from the Mexican provinces. The numerous produce stands are indistinguishable from their Mexican counterparts in terms of their selection of fruit and produce (papayas, mangos, tamarind, sugar cane stalks, and nopales abound) as well as in their atmosphere, with vendors actively beckoning passersby and promising the very lowest prices.

However, La Pulga is not only a setting that creates a temporary visual/sensory illusion that one is back home in Mexico, thereby replenishing these immigrants via a reimmersion in the lost familiar, but it is also a space full of the icons of the new culture in which he or she is trying to survive. Many stands reflect this crossroads. Vendors sell T-shirts that declare "Me vale Madre" alongside those with the Texas version: "Don't mess with me." Shirts and caps with the logos of professional American football teams are especially popular. Goods that are identified with the accoutrements of the American middle class, such as dining room sets, Avon skin care products, car care products, and used household appliances—all emblematic of success in the United States—are everywhere to be found. In what we might understand as a bilingual fusion of the somatics of contemporary American life, a sign over a stall selling healthcare products announces that they are excellent for "Weight loss/Dieta, Stress/Tensión, and Energy/Energía."

The indications are everywhere that La Pulga is a space where one may participate in the cultural forms definitional of American Life. One sees Mexican immigrants dressed in Dallas Cowboys' (Editor's note: now with the Arizona Cardinals) star Emmitt Smith sweatshirts or Guess jeans, eating hot dogs, their children speaking English, carrying bags full of Avon products. A large advertisement for Miller Lite beer seems to capture an important part of the La Pulga spirit. It reads, in English, "Lite Beer: Great Taste, Less Filling," along with the following caption in Spanish: "Que vida Tan Buena, Vivimos en Texas" ("What a good life, We live in Texas").

It is just as evident that La Pulga plays an important function in facilitating the immigrants' adaptation to the new culture with respect to the world of work. One readily finds materials to learn English, for example, on tape or in book and comic book formats. One can also purchase ID cards, an essential item for establishing a life in the United States. Many stalls sell new or used work tools for use in landscaping, construction, carpentry, and automotive repair. New and used clothing that will transform the Mexican immigrant's appearance from rural Mexican to urban, football-jerseyed American are sold at deeply discounted prices. "Connie's Money Den," with a sign indicating that she specializes in "Visa/Mastercard, Notary, Income Tax, Checks, & Immigration"—a kind of fiscal and legal jack-of-all-trades—caters to the needs of the undocumented worker lacking in English skills and sufficiently on the social and economic margins not to have access to these services via more conventional means.

Within La Pulga the Mexican and North American worlds become represented in the ways that cultures always manifest what is distinctly theirs: food, entertainment, and aesthetics, among other social rituals. La Pulga serves as a potential space where Mexican immigrants simultaneously live in the old country and the new, a kind of "as if" world wherein they can momentarily be home again, in the plazas of their villages and towns, while, at the same time, "playing" with the materials of the new culture. Articles catering to the nostalgic are found alongside cultural artifacts that reflect the necessities of work as well as the allure of the new culture. Via the illusion of return, La Pulga provides a restorative function that renews energies, rekindles hopes, and makes it possible to face the next week's hardships of labor, tensions, and discriminations. Simultaneously, La Pulga facilitates the procurement of what is essential for survival in this new environment, be it new cultural identifications (becoming a Dallas Cowboys fan) or purchasing tools needed for work. Winnicott's description of the potential space as a domain of experiencing that is both "me" and "not me," facilitating the transition between known and familiar and unknown psychological terrain, is an apt description of La Pulga—an intermediate zone, culturally, a creative mix of North American and Mexican cultures serving both aesthetic functions as well as comforting, entertaining, and utilitarian functions.

It is in this sense that these immigrant mourners have also altered the American cultural landscape. La Pulga is an illustration of immigrants transforming public space such that Mexicans can now live in the United States as if it were an extension of Mexico. However, in emphasizing the transitional function, the aspects of La Pulga that serve as potential space, I am suggesting more. The particular manner in which immigrants transform this and other public spaces is not merely linked to the recreation within the United States of the culture one has left. In addition, it is a transformation that makes that space usable as a resource so that the immigrant may more effectively engage the challenges posed by an unfamiliar culture. These immigrants have seized the flea market and made it their own. In vehicle for effective engagement in the new one. This is precisely what immigrants have always done, thereby shaping the receiving culture, altering its configurations, and all too often provoking deep anxieties among those being changed.[3]

TIME, DISTANCE, AND THE CHARACTER OF CULTURAL MOURNING

Important variables governing the vicissitudes of cultural mourning are the time one has been away from one's native country and the accessibility or ease of return. In the latter respect, Mexican immigrants comprise a unique group in the history of American immigration. The proximity of the two countries and the relative fluidity of their border can alter the character of cultural mourning. One is tempted to add a third variable as well: the emergence of modern communications technologies.[4]

To the extent that the immigrant's ties to the native country are maintained and continuously replenished, mourning is comparatively less necessary. In turn, the maintenance of such links is likely to affect the extent to which the immigrant relinquishes or alters ties to the culture of origin.[5] Accessibility allows immigrants to remain intimately connected to the world they have left, thereby actively sustaining its intrapsychic representations and the fantasy of return. In this context, emotional ties remain rich and potent long after immigrants from other, more distant, countries have been forced (by time, distance, and cultural tensions) to dilute or relinquish them altogether. Mourning does not really take place in the same sense because the link to the native soil remains immediate and is subject to relatively continuous cultural replenishing. One might speculate that such proximity is likely to eventuate in immigrant communities that remain insulated from mainstream American culture for internal reasons rather than those imposed by the host culture. Simply put, they have relatively less to mourn.

The residents of Tehuixtla, Puebla, are one such example.

THE MIRACLE OF TEHUIXTLA

Tehuixtla is a small village high in the mountains of the state of Puebla with a population of approximately two hundred inhabitants, its census decimated by rural Mexico's pervasive economic problems.[6] Materially, Tehuixtla simply does not provide enough for its people. As a result, the residents of Tehuixtla have left for the United States in a steady exodus. The character of this migration reflects sociologists' theorizing about the function of immigrant networks in relation to the activation of migration streams (Waldinger 1997). For the residents of Tehuixtla, migration patterns have resulted in three main groupings in this country living in New York, Los Angeles, and Houston. Each of these three clusters is tightly knit, with a great deal of communication within and between groups, as illustrated below. Many of the Tehuixtla expatriots have succeeded in obtaining legal immigrant status by marriage or at the time of the Immigration and Naturalization Service's (INS) amnesty program of the late 1980s.

Despite their legal status, the immigrants from Tehuixtla retain a vibrant and intense connection to the town from which they migrated. Most of the year, Tehuixtla is a ghost town. In December, however, the "miracle of Tehuixtla" (The New York Times, Dec. 25, 1996) takes place as those who have emigrated return and the town's population swells to several thousand during the Posada season (December 16–25) and New Year celebrations. They arrive in caravans of cars, vans, and pickup trucks, bringing their families home in a yearly pilgrimage that reunites them with the dwindling number of town elders, as well as the friends and relatives who have found their destinies in various American cities.

I interviewed two of some fifty Tehuixtla immigrants presently living in the Houston area. One, a twenty-seven-year-old man employed as a mechanic, has been in the United States since age sixteen. The other is a woman of twenty-five employed as a beautician. Both had obtained their legal papers during the INS amnesty.

The families in Houston, Los Angeles, and New York have a deep and enduring tie to Tehuixtla. In each of these communities, for example, the Tehuixtla immigrants organize annual events (dances, car washes, fund drives) to raise money for the town.[7] These efforts have rebuilt the town's church and the walls of the cemetery, among other community projects. However, the most daunting problem facing the community is the severe shortage of water, potable or otherwise. The town's emigrants have worked hard to find a solution to the water problem. For example, last year they funded efforts to dig a well, but the water from the new well is undrinkable because of its high salt content and the well produces too little. "We can't even shower there like we do here," the mechanic told me. The beautician underscored her concerns with a telling illustration: "We have to bring our own water because the children get sick if they drink the town's water." Increasingly desperate, the Tehuixtla residents living in the United States recently sought the services of a water witch from a nearby village in the hope that his magic will locate water where more conventional means have failed. These efforts also reflect the high level of collaboration among the three expatriate groups, who must agree on goals, raise funds, and coordinate their Tehuixtla projects from their respective communities in the United States.

Tehuixtla's water predicament reflects, both metaphorically and materially, the circumstances that drove its families to seek lives in the United States. The community cannot provide for its members' essential needs—natural resources and economic opportunities that are necessary for their collective survival. But such dire realities have done little to alter the conviction among most of those immigrants that Tehuixtla remains their home, that they are only temporarily living in the United States, and that it is only a matter of time before they return to take up their lives more or less where they left off.[8] Psychologically speaking, for these immigrants Tehuixtla remains part of the psychic present, not a lost past.

For example, both the mechanic and the beautician whom I interviewed spoke of their Houston Tehuixtla compatriots' intent to return. They told of shared plans that included opening a hotel, a shop for automotive repairs, a restaurant, and hardware stores, as well as chicken and hog farms. Many immigrants from the three North American communities have built or are building homes in Tehuixtla, where for most of the year the two-story, cinderblock homes with satellite dishes must seem odd in a town with such a small population, mostly the parents and grandparents of those who have left. In every sense, the immigrants from Tehuixtla are trying to keep their community alive.

The earnestness of these return fantasies, as well as their intensity, is impressive. The proximity of Mexico fuels these hopes. In the lives of these immigrants, Tehuixtla remains a powerful emotional beacon, orienting them toward their homeland. They remain, relative to the experience of many other immigrants, more tightly connected and identified with that community because Tehuixtla is so close and readily accessible. This emotional proximity has implications for the character of their cultural mourning. Their loss is not so complete. Indeed, many believe it to be only transient.

Every Christmas, when the "miracle of Tehuixtla" occurs and the lost children return by the busload and carload from the great urban centers of the United States, that hope is replenished and kept alive. The houses continue to be built, the grandparents renew their acquaintance with grandchildren who show up in Nike shoes and Houston Oilers T-shirts, speaking as much (or more) English as they do Spanish. And everyone hopes that the water witch will resolve the one clear obstacle to their permanent return by finding "sweet water" in sufficient quantities to sustain the thousands who would need it, the thousands who because they retain hope of return, cannot fully mourn the fact that they have had to leave in the first place.

CONCLUSION

While the reasons for leaving their homelands vary immensely, all immigrants are mourners. This spectrum of motivations may mediate, but it cannot alter, the fundamental reality that one has left a world that once was home for another that is not. That irreducible fact has psychological implications for the emotional life of every immigrant.

Epidemiological studies of the immigrant experience indicate that immigration takes a psychological toll. A positive relationship has consistently been found between immigrant status and such mental health indicators as level of depressive symptomatology (for example, Raymond, Rhoads, and Raymond 1980; Salgado de Snyder and Padilla 1987; Vega et al. 1984). Warheit et al. (1985) report that persons born in Mexico who have immigrated to the United States have more symptoms and psychosocial dysfunction than do Mexican Americans born in the United States, even when such variables as sex, age, marital status, and educational attainment are taken into account. Thus, immigration appears to be a double-edged sword. On the one hand it provides economic opportunities, a potential solution to the poverty that typically motivates immigrants to leave home; on the other hand, the experience of dislocation, coupled with significant acculturative stress attendant to negotiating an unknown culture, results in the noted symptoms.

These issues may be even more complex when one takes gender into account.[9] Salgado de Snyder (1987a, 1987b) reports a strong association between acculturative stress and level of depressive symptomatology among young Mexican immigrant women, who may experience greater levels of acculturative stress when compared with immigrant men. Similarly, immigrant females have been reported to score significantly higher than males on measures of cultural and family conflict (Salgado de Snyder and Padilla 1987), while women with higher ethnic loyalty (maintaining values, maintaining closer links to friends and family back in the country of origin) are reported to have lower levels of self-esteem, social support, and satisfaction, and higher levels of acculturative stress (Salgado de Snyder 1987a). On the other hand, in this same study Salgado de Snyder found that women who were occupied as full-time housewives had significantly higher depressive symptomatology than respondents who were employed outside of the home. It is certainly likely, as some (Baca Zinn 1980; Hondagneu-Sotelo 1992) have argued, that the immigration experience has a profound effect on the structure of roles and values in Mexican immigrant families, shifts that move these families in the direction of more egalitarian gender relations. These shifts suggest that there may be important gender differences in what I have termed cultural mourning.

In normal mourning, the person lost is gradually relinquished via an internalization of that relationship and all that it has meant. With this internalization, the significant features of that relationship become part of the ego. The ego is transformed by the loss, but more so by the reintegration of the lost object through the mourning process, as the mourner revisits the memories and feelings that bound them to the one who has left. In cultural mourning, in addition to mourning lost loved ones, one must mourn the loss of the cultural enclosures that have defined life and given it meaning. The immigrant must resolve both of these losses while simultaneously attempting to construct a new life where essential skills (in terms of language, education, etc.) may be lacking and where one may or may not be welcomed by the residents of the host country. In doing so, immigrants make use of linking objects and linking processes to help sustain the sense of connection to the lost worlds, a connection that is essential to the maintenance of one's psychological equilibrium. Specifically, immigrants construct transitional areas of experiencing, the potential space, within which they can reduce the feeling of loss and dislocation, if only transiently, while at the same time creatively engage the not-me world of the new culture in which they now live. It is by recreating themselves and simultaneously creating usable, intermediate spaces within their receiving country that immigrants, in their mourning, alter the contours of their new communities.

Notes

1. The experience of being in a new culture where roles and a variety of organizing assumptions are altered may also represent opportunities that are strongly desired and willingly embraced. The immigrant woman may relish a shift toward egalitarian family relations, for example, or the immigrant man may feel grateful for economic opportunities that allow him to purchase land in his village or to support extended family back home. Mourning is not the only experience of the immigrant, and it exists alongside other experiences that structure the immigrant's emotional life.
2. Interestingly, the Austin Country Flea Market is located in neutral territory, ethnically speaking.
3. Candidate Pat Buchanan's border stance in the 1996 presidential election is illustrative of these anxieties. Buchanan became a self-appointed spokesperson for the segment of the American population most threatened by the influx of immigrants from Mexico. Paradoxically, one might argue that a host country's anxieties about being transformed by immigrants taps the same psychological processes at work in the immigrants' mourning: the anxieties mobilized by the loss of the familiar.
4. For example, in one of my visits to La Pulga I interviewed a man selling satellite cable systems from which his clients could receive sixteen different Spanish-language stations, ten of them direct from Mexico. Virtually all of his business is Mexican. Technology has shortened the cultural distance, making it possible to continue inhabiting, psychologically, the world one has left behind. As an immigrant watches a favorite program broadcast from Mexico, his cultural space might be temporarily indistinguishable from that of the relatives he has left in that country.
5. An additional consideration is the degree to which the host culture fosters or inhibits the immigrant's integration—ethnic biases being an obvious example, economic marginalization being another. Jorge Durand notes that, historically, Mexican immigrants have very low naturalization rates. One might argue that the proximity between Mexico and the United States has made cultural replenishing easier for Mexican immigrants, thus diluting the motivations for becoming naturalized citizens.
6. See Enrique Dussel Peters' discussion (this volume) of the relationship between recent changes in Mexico's economy and immigration patterns to the United States.
7. Interestingly, these efforts sometimes take place under the dictates of North American cultural norms. The Tehuixtla immigrants often get together on the Fourth of July and Thanksgiving, American holidays that they celebrate and gatherings at which they examine the needs of their community in Mexico.
8. This is in contrast to other Mexican immigrants who report an intention to stay in this country.
9. I am indebted to Susan González Baker for her remarks on gender and immigration.

References

Ainslie, R. 1995. No Dancin' in Anson: An American Story of Race and Social Change. Northvale, NJ: Jason Aronson, Inc.

Baca Zinn, M. 1980. Employment and education of Mexican American women: The interplay of modernity and ethnicity in eight families. Harvard Educational Review 50: 47–62.

Durand, J. 1998. Migration and Integration: Intermarriages Among Mexicans and non-Mexicans in the U.S. In *Crossings: Mexican Immigration in Interdisciplinary Perspective.* Marcelo M. Suárez-Orozco, ed. Cambridge, MA: David Rockefeller Center for Latin American Studies.

Erikson, E. 1950. Childhood and Society. New York: W. W. Norton.

Frankiel, R. V., ed. 1994. Essential Papers on Object Loss. New York: New York University Press.

Gandara, Ricardo. 1996. Boots, vegetables, phones, tools and more. Austin American Statesman, Oct. 15.

Garza-Guerrero, A. C. 1974. Culture shock: Its mourning and vicissitudes of identity. Journal of the American Psychoanalytic Association 22(2): 400–429.

Grinberg, L., and R. Grinberg. 1984. A psychoanalytic study of migration: Its normal and pathological aspects. Journal of the American Psychoanalytic Association 32(1): 13–38.

Hondagneu-Sotelo, Pierrette. 1992. Overcoming patriarchal constraints: The reconstruction of gender relations among Mexican immigrant women and men. Gender & Society 6: 393–413.

Loewald, Hans. 1962. Internalization, separation, mourning, and the superego. In Essential Papers on Object Loss, ed. R. V. Frankiel. New York: New York University Press.

Ogden, T. H. 1990. The Matrix of the Mind: Object Relations and the Psychoanalytic Dialogue. Northvale, NJ: Jason Aronson, Inc.

Raymond, J., D. Rhoads, and R. Raymond. 1980. The relative impact of family and social involvement on Chicano mental health. American Journal of Community Psychology 8: 557–569.

Salgado de Snyder, V. 1987a. Mexican immigrant women: The relationship of ethnic loyalty and social support to acculturative stress and depressive symptomatology. Spanish Speaking Mental Health Research Center, Occasional Paper no. 22: 1–46.

—— 1987b. Factors associated with acculturative stress and depressive symptomatology among married Mexican immigrant women. Psychology of Women Quarterly 11: 475–488.

Salgado de Snyder, V., and A. Padilla. 1987. Social support networks: Their availability and effectiveness. In Health and Behavior: Research Agenda for Hispanics, ed. M. Gaviria and J. Arana. Chicago: University of Illinois, Simon Bolivar Hispanic-American Psychiatric Research and Training Program.

Vega, W., G. Warheit, J. Auth, and K. Meindhart. 1984. The prevalence of depressive symptoms among Mexicans and Anglos. American Journal of Epidemiology 120: 592–607.

Volkan, V. D. 1979. Cyprus—War and Adaptation: A Psychoanalytic History of Two Ethnic Groups in Conflict. Charlottesville, VA: University Press of Virginia.

Volkan, V. D. 1981. Linking Objects and Linking Phenomena: A Study of the Forms, Symptoms, Metapsychology, and Therapy of Complicated Mourning. New York: International Universities Press.

Volkan, V. D. 1993. Immigrants and refugees: A psychodynamic perspective. Mind and Human Interaction 4(2): 63–69.

Volkan, V. D., and E. Zintl. 1993. Life After Loss: The Lessons of Grief. New York: Charles Scribner's Sons.

Waldinger, R. 1997. Social capital or social closure? Immigrant networks in the labor market. Paper presented at the Conference on Immigration and the Socio-Cultural Remaking of the North American Space, 11–12 April, at Harvard University, David Rockefeller Center for Latin American Studies, Cambridge, MA.

Warheit, G. J., W. A. Vega, J. B. Auth, and K. Meinhardt. 1985. Psychiatric symptoms and dysfunctions among Anglos and Mexican Americans: An epidemiological study. Research in Community Mental Health 5: 3–32.

Winnicott, D. W. 1971. Transitional objects and transitional phenomena. Playing and Reality. New York: Basic Books.

—— 1971. The location of cultural experience. Playing and Reality. New York: Basic Books.

—— 1971. Dreaming, fantasying, and living. Playing and Reality. New York: Basic Books.

PART III

Immigration, Language, and Education

Chapter 13
Learning English in California: Guideposts for the Nation

PATRICIA GÁNDARA

Political events in California often have repercussions for the rest of the nation. Recently, California has been the site of intense legal battles over the education of its English learners, and events in the state have already affected a number of other states with large populations of English learners. This chapter offers a history of the politics and policies that have governed the education of English learners in the state over the last several decades. It reviews the effects of the most recent legal skirmish over limited-English-proficient students and predicts short- and longer-term outcomes that may result both for California and for the nation. Finally, the chapter looks to the future of education for English learners and suggests critical areas of research that may aid in constructing more enlightened educational policies for these students.

A BRIEF HISTORY OF BILINGUAL EDUCATION POLICY IN CALIFORNIA

California, through its initiative process, has been at the forefront of several national political movements in the last few decades. The passage of Proposition 13[1] in 1978 launched the famous tax revolt that swept the country during the early 1980s. Proposition 209,[2] passed by California voters in 1996, began a national backlash against affirmative action that continues unabated today. Most recently, Proposition 227, the anti-bilingual initiative that was passed in 1998, has set the stage for a showdown on bilingual education in a number of other states, including Colorado, Arizona, and possibly Massachusetts.

California has, on occasion, also been the site of progressive politics. It was one of the first states in the nation to enact a comprehensive bilingual-education bill: the Chacon-Moscone Bilingual-Bicultural Education Act of 1976, which gave schools detailed instructions about the type of language support that should be provided for English learners. California's legislation was stimulated by the 1974 Supreme Court ruling in *Lau v. Nichols*, which required schools to give limited-English-proficient students access to the same instruction that all other children received. The legislation recognized that limited-English-proficient students do "not have the English language skills necessary to benefit from instruction only in English at a level substantially equivalent to pupils whose primary language is English." Thus, "[t]he Legislature ... declare[d] that the primary goal of all programs under this article [was], as effectively and efficiently as possible, to develop in each child fluency in English" (California Education Code, 1976, Section 52161). The preferred means for doing so was through early use of the primary language, with a planned transition into English-only instruction. Although the act did not specify when this transition should occur, the expectation was that students would be mainstreamed into an English-only classroom by the fourth grade.

Although this 1976 legislation was clearly progressive in its time, it also framed the challenge facing English learners as primarily a *language problem*, and it framed the solution to this problem as transitional bilingual education. From a theoretical perspective, there are at least three possible goals of bilingual education: (1) the teaching of language, (2) the fostering of positive intercultural relations, and (3) the enhancing of academic or cognitive development. Each of these goals can also be represented on a continuum. For example, the teaching of language can be conceptualized as simply transitioning an individual from her native language into a second language as efficiently as possible. This represents the far-left end of a continuum. At the other end of the continuum is the possibility of the individual's becoming fully bilingual and biliterate and therefore having the ability to communicate in two languages. (See Figure 13.1)

In terms of intercultural relations, the far-left end of the continuum simply represents knowledge of one's own culture in the context of the mainstream culture; this is thought to support higher self-esteem (Spencer and Markstrom-Adams 1990). At the other end of the continuum is a fully bicultural or multicultural orientation, in which both members of the mainstream culture and members of the minority culture are taught to value and appreciate each other's culture and language and are encouraged to incorporate features of both into multicultural social identities (Rotherham-Borus 1994; Cazabon, Lambert, and Hall 1993). It has been argued that this orientation can reduce prejudice and ethnic stereotyping and enhance intergroup relations (Lindholm 1994; Freeman 1998; Genesee and Gándara 1999). (See Figure 13.2)

Finally, with respect to academic or cognitive competence, bilingual education can, at the far-left end of the continuum, simply help to prevent learning losses by providing instruction in the primary language in some or all subjects while the individual is transitioning into the second language. At the other end of the continuum, bilingual education can offer true cognitive advantages to students who are fully bilingual and biliterate, resulting in certain types of academic superiority over monolinguals (August and Hakuta 1997; Reynolds, 1991). (See Figure 13.3)

The California legislation, much like legislation in other states, provided for a program that could generally be located at the left end of the continuum in all three goal areas. All transitional bilingual-education programs, no matter how effective they are in helping students to join the

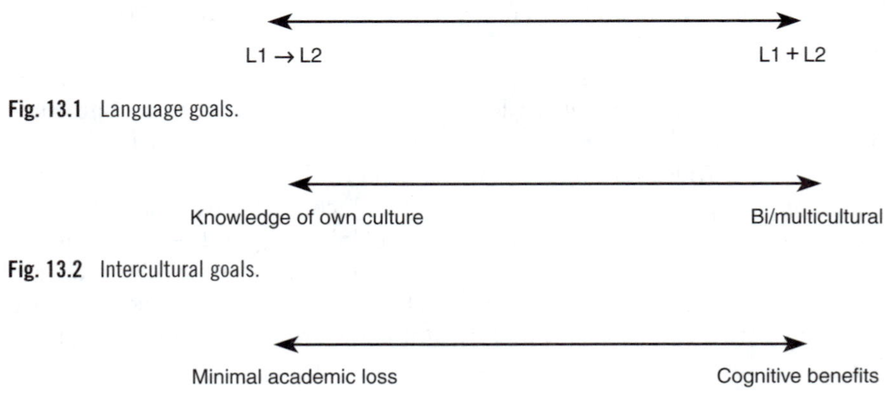

Fig. 13.1 Language goals.

Fig. 13.2 Intercultural goals.

Fig. 13.3 Cognitive and academic goals.

academic mainstream, implicitly foster prejudice against non-English languages because transitional programs are based on the "language as problem" model (Ruiz 1984). The children's non-English language is something to be dispensed with, and transitioned out of, as quickly as possible. Alternative conceptualizations of language difference include "languages as a resource" (Ruiz 1984) models that build on students' native languages as an avenue to enhanced academic competencies. Dual-language programs, for example, adopt the position that non-English languages are a resource for English learners and an enrichment for English speakers. By valuing the non-English language in the curriculum, such programs give that language—and its speakers—greater prestige, thus simultaneously addressing issues of intergroup relations.

California's legislation, like most legislation nationwide, was largely silent on issues of intercultural relations and academic development. Included were specific provisions for instruction in the "development of an understanding of the history and culture of California and the United States, as well as an understanding of customs and values of the cultures associated with the languages being taught" (California Education Code, 1976, Section 52163). However, nowhere in the legislation were there specific provisions for the cultural components of instruction, nor did the act provide any objectives for such cross-cultural instruction. Certainly there was no mention of a goal to reduce intercultural conflict through these programs, although it might be inferred from the program's inclusion of instruction in both the U.S. culture and the culture of the students. Nonetheless, because the program targeted the instruction of English learners, it appears that cross-cultural understanding was meant to apply, for the most part, to English learners, not to English speakers.

The act also specified that, to the greatest extent possible, no less than one-third of the students in a bilingual-education classroom should be fluent English-speaking students (California Education Code 1976, Section 52167). The law did *not* specify that these children should be of the dominant cultural group, although this was clearly inferred by many school personnel. It was thought that the presence of such students would provide important English models for the English learners. Unlike the Canadian experiments with immersion education, to which U.S. bilingual education is often compared, California's program did not have a goal of furthering more positive attitudes toward minority-language speakers (Genesee and Gándara 1999). In fact, the law did not specify any benefits that should accrue to the English speakers in these classrooms; and in the absence of any intent to provide for the *development* of the primary language (in this case nearly always Spanish), there was little reason for the parents of English speakers to want their children to be in such a classroom. In most cases, English speakers would not be exposed to sufficient Spanish to develop any true facility in the language, and Spanish speakers were encouraged to transition to English as quickly as possible. In this context, many parents of English speakers complained that learning was slowed down to accommodate the children who did not speak English and that their children derived no benefit from being in these classes. It became difficult to find sufficient numbers of English-speaking students to fulfill the one-third rule. For this reason, and, because resources were usually inadequate to meet even the needs of the English-learner population, most programs simply did not adhere to that rule. Thus, not only did these programs, as they were conceived, offer no clear means of enhancing intercultural communication, but in some cases they actually contributed to intercultural strife, pitting the needs of English speakers against those of English learners. Moreover, they sometimes increased tensions between African Americans and Latinos because of the perception that bilingual education, by clustering English learners into separate programs, undermined desegregation efforts (Donato 1997).

The focus on language as *the* problem that needed to be remedied, with the goal of transitioning students to English "as efficiently as possible," also meant that academic achievement was not articulated as an important goal for these programs. Therefore, a minimum threshold of academic competence was established for students to exit from the programs. This was often far below the median academic performance of all students in the district or state.[3] Although the arguments for incorporating the primary language into students' instruction were predicated on a belief that doing so made access to the standard curriculum possible during the time students were learning English, bilingual education, as conceived of in California law and regulations, was not designed to focus on academic achievement. Its main purpose was always simply to transition students into English.

Not surprisingly, this instructional policy was never without controversy. Bilingual advocates believed the program did too little to promote either academic competence or dual-language facility, and English-only proponents decried any use of the primary language, believing that it delayed students' entry into the mainstream of schooling. By 1986 the existing California bilingual-education legislation had "sunsetted" (was not reauthorized), so these programs continued under the authority of Department of Education regulations, which were shaped largely by federal requirements. Over the years there were numerous attempts to modify the law and to abandon the practice of primary-language instruction, but none of these attempts was ultimately successful.

In part because of the controversy generated by bilingual education, no policy was ever adopted to provide certified bilingual teachers for all English learners. Moreover, although a few school districts provided small financial bonuses for teachers with bilingual credentials, no statewide incentive policy was ever adopted to recruit sufficient numbers of bilingual teachers. Thus, by the time the Chacon-Moscone Act sunsetted, only about one-third of the students who were eligible for a bilingual program were able to be placed with a bilingual teacher.

CALIFORNIA'S PROPOSITION 227

It was in this context that Proposition 227 came onto the California political scene. Proponents of Proposition 227 contended that bilingual education had failed and therefore should be abandoned as a pedagogical strategy. As evidence for its failure, they cited the continuing underachievement of English learners and the failure of programs to reclassify more than 5 percent of limited-English-proficient students to fluent-English-proficient status annually. Bilingual-education advocates countered that, in addition to being inaccurate, the 5 percent figure was calculated from an ever-growing base of students, because the population of English learners in California had been mushrooming for two decades. More important, however, they noted that because of the lack of sufficient numbers of qualified teachers, most English learners were not enrolled in bilingual programs, so their academic underachievement could not be attributed to any failure of these programs. Nonetheless, Proposition 227 was passed by the voters of California in June 1998. It became law immediately, requiring that schools implement its provisions in the 1998–1999 school year.

Proposition 227 required that "all children in California public schools shall be taught English by being taught in English." The mandated pedagogical strategy was to place English learners for a period not normally to exceed one year in "sheltered English-immersion" classes. These are defined in the law as multi-age classrooms with students at the same level of English proficiency in which the focus of instruction is the development of English-language skills. The only exception to the English-only mandate was to be in cases in which parents sought a specific waiver of the English-only program for their children. According to Proposition 227, waivers could be allowed on the basis of one of three conditions: (1) the child already knew English; (2) the child was over ten years of age, and school staff believed that another approach might be better suited to the student; or (3) school staff determined that the child had special needs that could be better met in an alternative program.

Proposition 227 took a unique approach to ensuring implementation, an approach that had serious implications for schools and teachers. It provided that any educator who willfully and repeatedly refused to implement the law could be personally sued in court. Thus, in order to avoid legal liability, it was critical that teachers and administrators understand completely the provisions and restrictions of the law. However, the language of Proposition 227 left much to interpretation. For example, it was not clear what the course of action should be if students needed more than one year of specialized instruction (which virtually all of the research on language acquisition contends would be the case[4]); how much primary language might be acceptable under the law in the "sheltered English-immersion" classroom; or how much discretion schools or districts had in granting or denying parental-exception waivers. The State Board of Education issued regulations clarifying some of these matters in October 1998. However, because schools had to implement the law in September, when most began the new school year, these clarifications came too late to provide guidance in the early stages of implementation.

The context of Proposition 227: Reform run amok

A major theme in the implementation of Proposition 227 is the extent to which it has been affected by other school reform efforts. Proposition 227 was enacted in what has been the most active period of education reform in California in recent times. During the same period, class-size reduction, which began in 1996 with two grades, was expanded to include all of the primary grades (thus creating an enormous demand for new teachers); new curricular standards were introduced into the schools; a high-stakes testing program was implemented; and new restrictions against social promotion were enacted that could result in the retention of large numbers of students who do not meet grade-level standards. Teachers have had to respond to all of these mandates, often without adequate training themselves to address the needs of English learners.

The plethora of reforms has the potential to work at cross-purposes, for children in general, but especially for English learners. For example, imposing strict new curricular standards at the same time that statewide testing is implemented, without devoting any attention to the curriculum provided for English learners, has left many teachers wondering how best to prepare these students to meet the challenges that the testing imposes. Expanding class-size reduction to more grades increased the demand for teachers and required school districts to hire many new, untrained, and inexperienced teachers who were often assigned to classrooms serving English learners. Trying without any specific training to juggle new standards, a high-stakes test, and a roomful of students who do not speak English has proved to be a daunting—and sometimes demoralizing—task for many teachers.

How Proposition 227 has affected California schools

The extent to which Proposition 227 has influenced the schooling of English learners, who constitute one-fourth of all the state's public school children, is difficult to measure precisely because school and classroom practices have been affected by so many recent mandates. Some facts, however, are indisputable. Fewer children are receiving instruction from bilingual teachers than before the enactment of Proposition 227, and fewer are assigned to classrooms in which the primary language is used for academic instruction (see Figure 13.4).

It is notable that the percentage of students assigned to bilingual classrooms dropped by more than half—from 29 to just 12 percent. However, the percentage of students receiving only English instruction grew from 33 to 39 percent. Thus the category that expanded the most to accommodate the change in policy was that of English-language development (ELD) with primary-language support.[5] In other words, many classrooms utilize some primary language with students, although the manner in which this happens and its extent vary greatly from classroom to classroom. It is sometimes difficult to interpret the change in the numbers of students officially assigned to one program

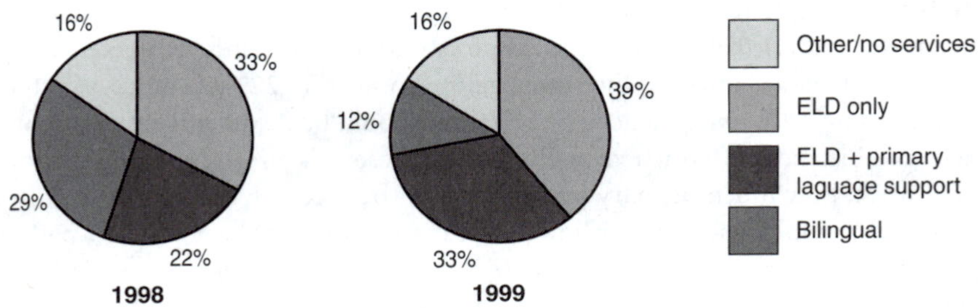

Fig. 13.4 Instructional services for English-language learners before and after Proposition 227.
Source: Rumberger and Gándara 2000

or another, because those numbers may obscure more than they reveal. For example, some schools and districts complied with Proposition 227 by creating their own interpretations of phrases such as *overwhelmingly in English*. Thus they might have been provided students "in structured English-immersion" classrooms with 52 percent of their instruction in English, meeting their own definition of *overwhelming*. Another strategy was to provide "preinstructional activities" and "review sessions" in the primary language, reserving the actual instructional time for English only. An administrator in one large district described the challenge of defining *overwhelmingly in English* in a way that met legal, though not necessarily instructional, objectives:

> [T]he state board of education has allowed districts in California to interpret that based on their own criteria as long as it's overwhelmingly in English. And so the district has determined that 60 percent of the time you have to teach in English, and 40 percent in Spanish or whatever it is. 60:40, 70:30, 80:20, 90:10, I've heard it all. And it all adds up to the point now that districts in California are forced to come up with a working definition based on the legal interpretations, not based on the instructional needs of the child. (Gándara et al. 2000)

A second change that we have noted is the pervasive concern about helping children to get ready for English testing no matter what type of classroom they are in. In separate studies in California schools that have been coordinated by the Linguistic Minority Research Institute,[6] we found a consistent pattern of erosion of strong literacy practices in favor of "bottom line" instruction aimed at yielding short-term gains on statewide tests in English. Often teachers commented that they did not feel good about what they were doing: leapfrogging much of the normal literacy instruction to go directly to English word recognition or phonics bereft of meaning or context. However, they worried greatly that if they spent time orienting the children to broader literacy activities, they risked jeopardizing students' English test scores. One teacher described her situation in the following words:

> I feel like the children are forced into silence. Really … they're really not getting the opportunity to express themselves as they normally would were they in a bilingual classroom. And I, I feel sorry for them … I really do. I think that it's very unfair. I don't think they're receiving an equal opportunity, equal education in the sense that they're really not learning to read …. They're learning to decode. [And] their decoding skills are coming along nicely, but the problem is that second-language acquisition, it takes time. And you know the district expects us to move these children from ELD level 1 to ELD level 4 in a matter of one year; with ELD level 4 then you can begin to present instruction of all the subjects in English (Gándara et al. 2000).

The impact of Proposition 227 that will probably have the longest-term policy consequences is its effect on utilization of the teaching force. Figure 13.5 shows the number of teachers serving as bilingual teachers and the numbers of those in training for bilingual positions, prior to Proposition 227 and in its aftermath.

In 1998, before the passage of Proposition 227, almost sixteen thousand certificated bilingual teachers were providing instruction to English learners. After the passage of Proposition 227, this number was reduced by one-third, to 10,690. Perhaps even more important, there were 10,894 teachers in the pipeline for bilingual credentials working in California schools in 1998, whereas in 1999, after the passage of Proposition 227, that number was reduced by nearly half to 5,670. Some portion of those teachers may still be pursuing their bilingual credentials, but without the perception that there is a demand for their services, it is not clear what incentive they have to continue to devote the additional time and effort necessary to acquire these specialized credentials.

Both the October 1998 memorandum from the state board of education and a fact sheet released by the Commission on Teacher Credentialing in the same month restated the importance of maintaining bilingual teachers in classrooms serving English learners. And this same commission reported that in a survey of districts after the passage of Proposition 227, all intended to continue hiring "as many as they can find."[7] Nonetheless, this is not the message articulated in some of the districts that chose to abandon primary-language instruction. One rural administrator explained the position of his district as follows:

> One thing I didn't mention earlier, and this may apply to several different questions, I'll just tell what it is: We no longer have to worry about that B-CLAD [bilingual credential]. That, you know, writing that annual staffing plan was just, it was futile! Because there's just no way you're going to get people to get their B-CLAD and that's what the law requires, that these people, if they have any students, which, in our district, is all over the place, they gotta be working towards their B-CLAD. It's not going to happen! And so, what's nice is, we don't have to play with that anymore (Gándara et al. 2000).

We think it quite possible that administrators in school districts that were not supportive of primary-language instruction before Proposition 227, and who used passage of the initiative as a reason to dismantle their programs immediately, may respond to official surveys with what they consider to be a bureaucratically correct answer. However, what they do and what they say may differ considerably.

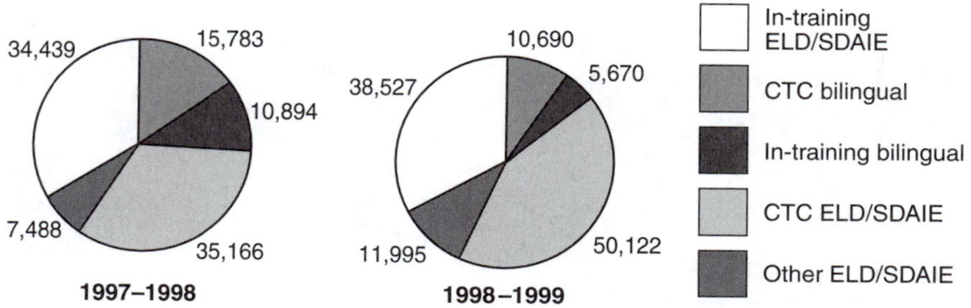

Fig. 13.5 Number of teachers providing instructional services for English learners, by certification, before and after Proposition 227.
Source: Gándara et al. 2000

Proposition 227 in the context of the California teacher crisis

Two major reports have recently called attention to the crisis that California faces in providing a qualified teacher for every student in the state, largely as a result of the class-size-reduction initiatives (Shields et al. 1999; Betts, Rueben, and Danenberg 2000). Current estimates are that 10 percent of teachers in California are teaching without proper authorization—they are not credentialed to teach. However, the distribution of these teachers is far from even. In fact, schools in high-income areas are likely to have no teachers in the classroom who lack teaching credentials, whereas in schools in low-income and minority areas, as many as 25 or 30 percent of the teachers may be without credentials. Not only are these teachers uncredentialed, but most are without any experience in the classroom. The students most likely to be taught by uncredentialed teachers are English learners. Figure 13.6 shows the distribution of uncredentialed teachers in the year prior to the onset of class-size reduction and in the year after, by percentage of English learners in the school.

Before the passage of Proposition 227, major inequities were noted in different students' access to credentialed teachers in California. English learners were then, and are now, the most likely to be taught by a teacher without any credentials. The difference now, however, is that much more is being asked of teachers, including the implementation of a new law that mandates a type of instruction about which there is considerable confusion, few related resource materials, and little help in interpretation.

Initial academic outcomes

More than two years after the passage of Proposition 227, the pundits and the policymakers made anxious pronouncements about its effects on California's English learners. Ron Unz, the author of the initiative, and his colleagues have declared it a success on the basis that the redesignation rates from limited-English-proficient (LEP) to fluent-English-proficiency (FEP) increased from 7 to 7.6 percent in the year following implementation. They have also noted that standardized test scores

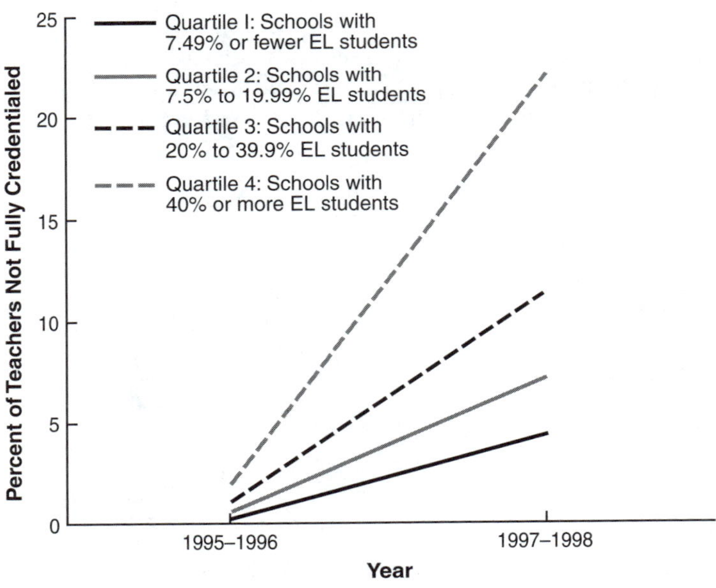

Fig. 13.6 Percentage of teachers without credentials by percent EL, before and after class-size reduction.
Source: Rumberger and Gándara 2000

are up for LEP students across the state. However, this is scant evidence on which to claim success. Proposition 227 was based on its author's contention that LEP students normally should need no more than one year of English instruction in order to join the mainstream, which claim suggests that all but a few students would be redesignated to FEP status at the end of one year. An increase of less than one percentage point would appear to fall far short of this goal. Moreover, although test scores did indeed increase for LEP students, they increased for students in bilingual classrooms as well as for those in English-only classrooms, and there was no consistently discernible difference between the two (Orr et al. 2000). Moreover, they also increased for English-only speakers. An increase in test scores for all students was predictable under any circumstances; simple familiarity with the standardized test normally confers small year-to-year gains (Hakuta 1999). And given the large increases in expenditures on education and the multiple reform efforts, a failure to raise test scores would have been very difficult to explain.

In spite of the test-score gains, however, gaps between the scores of English speakers and English learners remain very large: English speakers score three times as high as English learners in reading and more than twice as high in mathematics, averaged across all grades. And, in mathematics, where the test is least language-dependent, the *gains* for English-speaking students outstrip the gains for English learners, a result that raises the prospect that the test-score gap will only become wider with time (Gándara 2000).

HOW DID WE GET HERE?

It could be argued that California's present situation was highly predictable, given the decisions that it made more than two decades ago. It built a bilingual program founded on the notion that for English learners, language is *the problem*. The bilingual program, therefore, was constructed to solve that problem by transitioning these students "as efficiently as possible" into an English-only curriculum. The famed Swiss psychologist Jean Piaget, who studied the cognitive development of children, characterized American psychology as being obsessed with one question: *Can it (development) be speeded up?* He dubbed this "the American question." It is not surprising, then, that once there was consensus that language was the problem, the logical next question would be how quickly the problem could be resolved.

Every major evaluation of bilingual education has been asked to answer the same question: Which program most efficiently moves English learners into the mainstream of English instruction? Achievement has been measured only in the context of the amount of time it was presumed that children should take to complete the transition to English. Thus the most carefully conducted and comprehensive study of bilingual education was given only four years to establish whether there were achievement differences among children in different program types. Although Ramirez, Yuen, and Ramey (1991) found that the learning slope was steeper for the children in primary-language instruction, it was never possible to test the long-term effects of the instruction, in good part because the underlying assumption was that there should *be* no "long term" for bilingual instruction. Achievement was of interest only within the framework of an "efficient" program that produced English-only speakers.

Because the commitment to instruction in two languages has been weak, and because the mark of program success has been the rapidity with which programs are able to dispense with primary-language instruction, development of a corps of teachers with strong skills in the science and methods of learning and using two languages has never been a truly serious objective in California. Bilingual teachers have been viewed as expedient—useful up to a point, but not essential. Millions of dollars have been spent on evaluating the effectiveness of *programs* rather than the effectiveness of *teaching strategies* (August and Hakuta 1997). The assumption has been that teacher competencies are not critical if we can just identify the silver-bullet program. Of course, decades of research on classroom learning have pointed to one conclusion: Nothing matters more in school than the quality of the teacher (Shields et al. 1999; Haycock 1998). One wonders why it is not obvious that the same would hold true in a bilingual classroom.

The present circumstances can also be traced to the fact that most bilingual programs were not designed to focus on intercultural relations or academic achievement. California's bilingual-education law indicated that English learners were to learn something of their own culture, ostensibly to enhance their self-concept, but nothing in the law suggested that native-English speakers should know anything about the English-learners' culture. It is difficult to feel proud of one's cultural heritage when everyone else is ignorant of it. A primary reason for Canada's success with French-immersion programs is that they are geared toward helping the children of the dominant culture appreciate the language and culture *of the minority group* (Genesee and Gándara 1999).

It is telling as well that while the country wrung its hands over the low academic achievement of America's students, little was said about the much lower achievement of English learners. In fact, most testing programs have been reluctant even to measure it. The assumption has been that because the problem is language, once that is "fixed," the students' achievement will rise to meet that of their English-speaking peers. In fact, this does not happen. A recent study examined the influence of language background and other factors on the 1998 SAT-9 test performance of 26,126 second-, third-, and fourth-grade California students.[8] The study first examined the independent effects of language background and poverty on student achievement (see Figure 13.7, left panel).

The researchers found that poverty affects the achievement of all students, regardless of their language background, but because the majority of English learners are poor, they are at a particular disadvantage in school. The study next examined the impact of language background and ethnicity on student achievement (see Figure 13.7, right panel). Even Hispanic students from English-speaking backgrounds had significantly lower test scores than white students from English-speaking backgrounds. This suggests that because something other than English proficiency must be

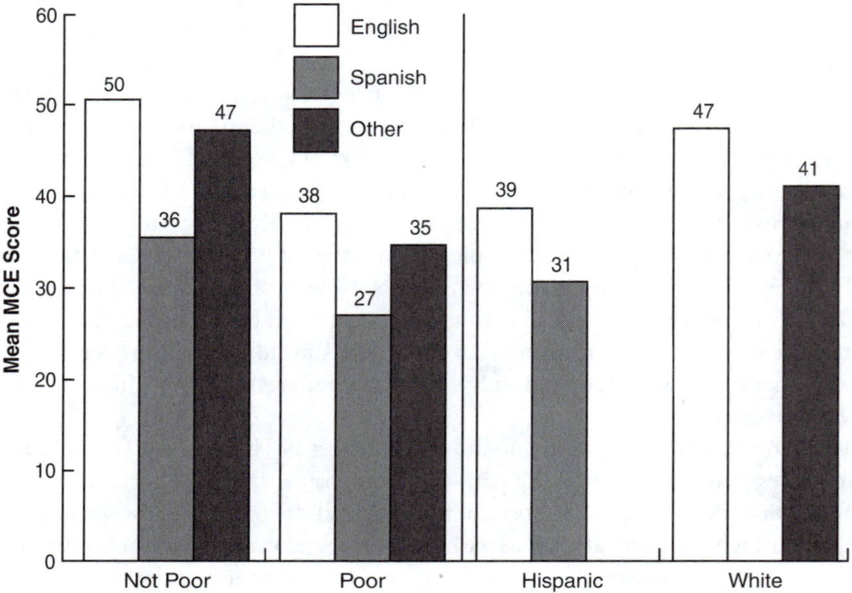

Fig. 13.7 1999 SAT-9 reading scores by language background and poverty, Hispanics and whites.
Source: Mitchell and Mitchell 1999

accounting for the differences, merely improving students' English proficiency is unlikely to raise their achievement to the levels of white, native-English speakers. Similarly, in a review of studies of high-quality programs of various types, we could identify none that showed that English learners ever achieved the same level of English-reading proficiency as their more advantaged native-English-speaking peers (Gándara 1997).

WHERE WE ARE GOING

California's social policy has been, for good or for ill, a harbinger of things to come in other states. Arizona, Colorado, and Massachusetts, in particular, are now poised to reexamine their instructional policies for English learners. California's bilingual programs have not differed greatly from the programs offered in these states, and it is probably safe to assume that similar political issues will be visited by these other states as well. It may therefore be instructive to assess the policy dimensions of recent events in California as a means of initiating a national conversation on the education of English learners.

The extraordinary impact of testing on instructional policy

High standards can be a very good thing, and they can be used as a policy tool to level the playing field for Latino students. The more transparent the standards are, the greater the likelihood that the Latino community can exert pressure to ensure that equal educational opportunities are provided in their schools. Furthermore, tests that are tied to these standards are an important means of holding schools accountable for giving students an opportunity to meet these standards. However, when testing does not take into account the curricular needs of English learners, it can have a very negative impact on instructional practice. We have seen that the blanket policy of testing all students in English (except those who have been in U.S. schools for less than one year), and tying the test results to sanctions and rewards for schools and students, has had the effect of distorting pedagogy in the classroom. Because teachers know that students who do not perform well on the tests *in English* can suffer penalties (for example, they can be held back a grade), we have seen a dilution of good literacy instruction in favor of an exclusive focus on phonics, decoding, and English vocabulary. We have seen bilingual teachers set aside broader literacy activities—storytelling, story-sequencing activities, reading for meaning, journal writing, and vocabulary development in the primary language—to focus exclusively on skills that would be tested on the standardized English test. Past research suggests that this may well produce short-term gains on test scores at the expense of deeper comprehension—a skill that will be tested in later grades, and one that is fundamental to more complex learning.

To the extent that standardized testing focuses solely on English skills, this is what teachers will endeavor to cultivate. Unfortunately, this may not be in the best interests of many English learners in the first several years of their schooling. It also sends the strongest possible message to schools that the only thing that counts is skills that are assessable in English. Deep and complex understandings of subject matter, framed in another language, are not valued. This is particularly worrisome because it may overlook some of our academically strongest students—those who come to American schools with a good academic foundation in their primary language and whose families have prepared them in important ways in the language of the home.

The impact of language policy on the preparation of bilingual teachers

One of the great ironies of the success of Proposition 227 is that its implementation relies to a great extent on the availability of teachers with good knowledge of the learning needs of English learners, and this generally means bilingual teachers. The meager research on "structured immersion" or "sheltered English" approaches concludes that teachers should be able to reinforce and help explain lessons and to check for understanding in the primary language, even if this is done minimally (Gersten and Woodward 1985; Krashen 1991). Sheltered English is, in fact, a strategy recommended for use by bilingual teachers who are able to shape instruction in terms of the linguistic needs of the child (Walqui-van Lier 1992). In the absence of a well-developed pedagogy, which structured English immersion does not have, bilingual teachers are best equipped with the training necessary to provide responsive instruction for English learners. However, the success of Proposition 227 has seriously undermined the market incentives for teachers to pursue bilingual credentials. All the evidence suggests that the most immediate impact of the initiative has been to reduce the supply of such teachers for the present and into the future. If this proves to be the case, the state will have lowered the bar on teacher standards for English learners at the same time that it is attempting to raise the bar for all other teachers. The very students who are likely to perform at the lowest levels, and who are therefore the most in need of excellent teaching, will continue to be the least likely to receive it. Thus the proposition's negative impact on the teacher corps may be its most profound and lasting legacy. Moreover, the erosion of the infrastructure of bilingual personnel—both in the classroom and in administrative positions—may make it very difficult to respond to alternative pedagogies.

A hopeful sign

Taking their cue from the Canadian experience, many researchers and policymakers have believed for some time that the most effective strategy for meeting the needs of English learners may well be through dual-immersion or two-way bilingual programs. These programs have the advantage that they incorporate the three core theoretical goals of bilingual instruction: academic enrichment, enhanced intercultural relations, and competence in two languages. They do this by combining English speakers and English learners in the same classroom with a curriculum that is taught in both languages but in proportions that balance issues of social power and linguistic hegemony. The goal of such programs is to produce students who are culturally and academically competent in two languages and who value cultural diversity.

When the current superintendent of public instruction in California came into office in 1994, she articulated a goal of providing the opportunity for all children to learn two languages; and polls of parent attitudes show strong support for such curricular innovation in the public schools (Huddy and Sears 1990; Krashen 1996). However, the din of political rhetoric assailing bilingual education drowned out the voices raised in defense of a more progressive education agenda that viewed language as an asset rather than a liability. In March 2000, then U.S. Secretary of Education Richard Riley went on record as supporting a major initiative to increase fourfold the number of dual-language programs nationwide over the next five years; he also pledged to provide the financial support to make this a reality. Riley was quoted as saying, "I think it is high time we begin to treat language skills as the asset they are, particularly in this global economy" (Cooper 2000). According to the Center for Applied Linguistics, California, in spite of Proposition 227, is the state with the largest number of dual-language programs: eighty-three. However, with California set on a course to dismantle its bilingual-education infrastructure, the question at hand is whether it is already too late for this state to respond to the call for a language policy that makes educational, social, and economic sense.

TOWARD A NEW RESEARCH AGENDA

Perhaps unwittingly, or perhaps because of the narrow visions and political constraints of the times, past research has largely played into a political agenda that was never intended to treat multilingualism as a real possible outcome for English learners. Thus, studies have tried diligently to answer questions such as "Which program most efficiently moves English learners out of their primary language and into the English-only mainstream?" and "How can we attract more 'good' (no mention of linguistically or culturally competent) teachers for English learners?" However, if we are to heed the concerns of Gene García, who asserts that teachers must pay attention to both the roots and the wings of our English learners, as well as the concerns of Luis Moll and Richard Ruiz who admonish educators to build on the cultural resources in students' communities, then we must shift the dominant research paradigm in the education of English learners. Among the questions that must be explored are:

1. In what ways does multilingualism contribute to greater academic and cultural competence in children from all backgrounds?
2. In what ways does multilingualism contribute to the social and economic benefit of the state and nation?
3. How do multilingual teachers who share knowledge of their students' cultural backgrounds and experiences differ in their instructional effectiveness from teachers who lack these attributes?
4. How can we build educational programs that enhance the possibility of true multilingualism for all students?

Notes

1. Proposition 13 limited the property tax in California to 1 percent of assessed value for both residential and commercial properties. Proposition 13 gradually eroded the property tax base and resulted in the state's having to take over the major funding of many local public services, including education. After the passage of Proposition 13 in California, a number of other states passed similar legislation reducing property taxes.
2. Proposition 209 was backed by the University of California regent Ward Connerly, who the year before had successfully engineered a majority vote of the University of California regents in favor of barring the use of race, ethnicity, or gender in consideration of candidates for admission to the university. Proposition 209 extended this bar to state employment and contracting, as well as enacting the prohibition against the use of affirmative action for admission to all state-supported educational institutions.
3. Multiple criteria are used to classify students from limited-English to English-proficient status. These multiple criteria, at the discretion of local districts, commonly consist of passing an English-proficiency test, being recommended by a teacher, and scoring at or near the 36th percentile on an academic achievement test in English.
4. See, for example, K. Hakuta. *How Long Does It Take to Learn English?* (Santa Barbara: University of California Linguistic Minority Research Institute, 1999).
5. The designation ELD, "English-language development," is used by the state department of education to include all programs that focus on the use of English for the purposes of instruction. It incorporates the "structured English immersion" program cited in the Proposition 227 initiative, as well as similar programs that go by other names, such as "sheltered English" and SDAIE (specially designed academic instruction in English).
6. The UG LMRI coordinated data collection and analysis of the effects of Proposition 227 in sixteen school districts and twenty-two schools in California during 1998–1999. Researchers from the UC–Berkeley, UCLA, and UC–Davis campuses were involved in the study, which has been released as Gándara et al. (2000).
7. *Proposition 227: A Fact Sheet That Focuses on CLAD/B-CLAD Teacher Preparation.* Office of Policy and Programs, California Commission on Teacher Credentialing, October 1998
8. Douglas E. Mitchell and Ross Mitchell. *The Impact of California's Class-size Reduction Initiative on Student Achievement: Detailed Findings from Eight School Districts* (Riverside: California Educational Research Cooperative, 1999). Available at http://cerc.ucr.edu/publications.

References

August, D., and Hakuta, K. 1997. *Improving the Schooling of Language Minority Students.* Washington, DC: National Research Council, National Academy Press.

Betts, J., Rueben, K., and Danenberg, A. 2000. *Equal Resources, Equal Outcomes? The Distribution of School Resources and Student Achievement in California.* San Francisco: The Public Policy Institute of California.

Cazabon, M., Lambert, W., and Hall, G. 1993. *Two-Way Bilingual Education: A Progress Report on the Los Amigos Program.* Santa Cruz, CA: National Center for Research on Cultural Diversity and Second Language Learning.

Cooper, K. 2000. Riley endorses two-way bilingual education. *Washington Post*, March 16:A2.
Donato, R. 1997. *The Other Struggle for Equality: Mexican Americans during the Civil Rights Era.* Albany: SUNY Press.
Freeman, R. 1998. *Bilingual Education and Social Change.* Clevedon, England: Multilingual Matters.
Gándara, P. 1997. *Review of the Research on the Instruction of Limited English Proficient Students.* Santa Barbara, CA: Linguistic Minority Research Institute.
Gándara, P. 2000. In the aftermath of the storm: English learners in the post-227 era. *Bilingual Research Journal* 24:1–13.
Gándara, P., Maxwell-Jolly, J., García, E., Asato, J., Gutiérrez, K., Stritikus, T., and Curry, J. 2000. *The Effects of Proposition 227 on the Instruction of English Learners. A Policy Brief.* Santa Barbara and Davis, CA: The Linguistic Minority Research Institute, Education Policy Center.
Genesee, F., and Gándara, P. 1999. Bilingual education programs: A cross-national perspective. *Journal of Social Issues* 55:665–685.
Gersten, R., and Woodward, J. 1985. A case for structured immersion. *Educational Leadership* 75:24–9.
Hakuta, K. 1999. *What Legitimate Inferences Can Be Made from the 1999 Release of SAT-9 Scores with Respect to the Impact of Proposition 227 on the Performance of LEP Students?* Available at http://www.stanford.edu/~hakuta/SAT9/index.htm.
Haycock, K. 1998. *Good Teachers Matter … A Lot.* Santa Cruz, CA: Center for the Future of Teaching and Learning.
Huddy, L., and Sears, D. 1990. Qualified public support for bilingual education: Some policy implications. *Annals of the American Academy of Political and Social Science* 508:119–134.
Krashen, S. 1991. Bilingual education: A focus on current research. *Occasional Papers in Bilingual Education 3* (Spring).
—— 1996. Surveys of opinions on bilingual education: Some current issues. *Bilingual Research Journal* 20:411–431.
Lindholm, K. 1994. Promoting positive cross-cultural attitudes and perceived competence in culturally and linguistically diverse classrooms. In *Cultural Diversity in Schools*, R. DeVillar, C. Faltis, and J. Cummins, eds. Albany: SUNY Press.
Mitchell, D., and Mitchell R. 1999. *The Impact of California's Class-size Reduction Initiative on Student Achievement: Detailed Findings from Eight School Districts.* Riverside: California Educational Research Center, University of California.
Orr, J., Butler, Y., Bousquet, M., and Hakuta, K. 2000. What Can We Learn about the Impact of Proposition 227 from SAT-9 Scores? An Analysis of Results from 2000. Available at http://www.stanford.edu/~hakuta /SAT9/SAT9_2000.
Ramirez, J. D., Yuen, S. D., and Ramey, D. R. 1991. Longitudinal study of structured English immersion strategy, early-exit and late-exit transitional bilingual education programs for language-minority children. *Final Report to the U.S. Department of Education.* Executive Summary and Vols. I and II. San Mateo, CA: Aguirre International.
Reynolds, A. 1991. *Bilingualism, Multiculturalism, and Second Language Learning.* Hillsdale, NJ: Erlbaum.
Rotherham-Borus, M. 1994. Bicultural reference group orientations and adjustment. In *Ethnic Identity*, M. Bernal and G. Knight, eds. Albany: SUNY Press.
Ruiz, R. 1984. Orientations in language planning. *Journal of the National Association of Bilingual Education* 2:15–34.
Rumberger, R., and Gándara, P. 2000. The schooling of English learners. In *Crucial Issues in California Education 2000: Are the Reform Pieces Fitting Together?* G. Hayward and E. Burr, eds. Berkeley and Palo Alto, CA: Policy Analysis for California Education (PACE).
Shields, P., Esch, C., Humphrey, D., Young, V., Gaston, M., and Hunt, H. 1999. *The Status of the Teaching Profession: Research Findings and Policy Recommendations.* Santa Cruz, CA: The Center for the Future of Teaching and Learning.
Spencer, M., and Markstrom-Adams, C. 1990. Identity processes among racial and ethnic minority children in America. *Child Development* 61:290–310.
Walqui-van Lier, A. 1992. *Doing Sheltered English Right.* Palo Alto, CA: Stanford University.

Chapter 14
Bilingualism and Second-Language Learning[1]

DIANE AUGUST AND KENJI HAKUTA

STATE OF KNOWLEDGE

The following review of the state of knowledge in bilingualism and second-language learning begins by distinguishing the various types of bilingualism. It then briefly examines the consequences of bilingualism. The third section looks at linguistic aspects of acquiring a second language, while the fourth addresses individual differences in second-language acquisition. The phenomenon of language shift—in which ethnic minority groups shift their primary language to that of the dominant majority—is then examined. The final section reviews findings on educational conditions for second-language learning.

Types of bilingualism

Bilingualism is pervasive throughout the world, but it varies according to (1) the conditions under which people become bilingual, (2) the uses they have for their various languages, and (3) the societal status of the languages. For example, in post-colonial Africa, students may be educated in English or French while another language is spoken in the home, and yet another (for example, Swahili in eastern Africa) may be used in public encounters and institutional settings, such as the courts (Fishman 1978). In officially bilingual countries such as Switzerland, children use one language at home and for most schooling. But, if they are middle class, they're expected to acquire competence in at least one other official language; French and German are of equivalent social status and importance to success. Yet another set of conditions is created in bilingual households, where parents who are native speakers of two different languages choose to use both in the home. Finally, bilingualism is often the product of migration. Immigrants frequently continue to use their native language—which may be of low status and not institutionally supported—at home and learn the dominant language of their new society only as required for work, public encounters, or schooling. The children of such families, for whom school is the primary social context, may end up fully bilingual, bilingual with the new language dominant, or having little knowledge of the parental language. They are the children of particular interest in this report.

A number of typologies of bilingualism have been offered. A major distinction among these typologies is that some focus their explanation at the individual and others at the societal level.

Individual level

Weinreich (1953) distinguishes among compound, coordinate, and subordinate bilinguals, who differ in the way words in their languages relate to underlying concepts. In the compound form, the two languages represent the same concept, whereas in the coordinate form, the concepts themselves are independent and parallel. In the subordinate form, the weaker language is represented through the stronger language. These different forms are clearly related to the social circumstances in which the two languages are learned, but the distinction also reflects an individual's mental makeup. Weinreich's distinction led to a number of studies seeking behavioral differences reflecting this typology (for example, Lambert et al. 1958). Though such attempts were essentially abandoned because of the difficulty of operationalizing the distinction, speculation that different bilingual experiences result in different cognitive and neural organization persisted. The emergence of procedures for seeing what prior stimuli facilitate the recognition of words presented later (called "lexical priming") has renewed interest in the possibility that we can tap the differential mental processes of the different types of bilinguals (Larsen et al. 1974).

A basic distinction at the individual level is that between simultaneous and sequential bilingualism: The former begins from the onset of language acquisition, while the latter begins after about age five, when the basic components of first-language knowledge are in place (McLaughlin 1984a). In the sequential type, a distinction is made between early and late bilinguals, according to the age at which second-language acquisition occurred (Genesee et al. 1978).

In general, research on distinctions among different types of bilingual individuals has failed to find consistent differences in task performance or processing variables. Much recent information-processing work has focused on the question of whether bilinguals process information in their two languages independently or interdependently—the findings not being related to any particular bilingual typology.

The above findings are important for discussion later in this report that addresses whether the linguistic outcomes of different types of education programs might result in qualitatively different types of individual bilinguals. They suggest, by and large, that bilingualism attained through different conditions of exposure will not be different in its fundamental cognitive organization.

Social level

Typologies of bilingualism based on societal variables have focused mainly on the prestige and status of the languages involved. Fishman et al. (1966) draw a distinction between "folk" and "elite" bilingualism, referring to the social status of the bilingual group. The "folk" are immigrants and linguistic minorities who exist within the milieu of a dominant language and whose own language is not held in high esteem within the society. The "elite" are those who speak the dominant language and whose societal status is enhanced through the mastery of additional languages. As Fishman observes, "Many Americans have long been of the opinion that bilingualism is 'a good thing' if it was acquired via travel (preferably to Paris) or via formal education (preferably at Harvard) but that it is a 'bad thing' if it was acquired from one's immigrant parents or grandparents" (pp. 122–123).

Similarly, Lambert (1975) distinguishes "additive" from "subtractive" bilingualism. This distinction focuses on the effect of learning a second language on the retention of the native language. In additive bilingualism, the native language is secure, and the second language serves as an enrichment. Canadian French immersion programs for the English-speaking majority are a prime example of additive bilingualism. In subtractive bilingualism, the native language is less robust; society assumes that it will be used only temporarily until replaced by the dominant language as the group assimilates. Most immigrants to the United States, Canada, and Australia experience this latter form of bilingualism.

These broader social distinctions can help us understand how differences in individual-level bilingualism relate to cultural setting. As macro-level descriptions, they are difficult to test, but they help explain why programs that seem quite similar can have such divergent effects in different social settings. For example, why does an immersion program in Canada succeed in teaching French to English-speaking students who continue to maintain full proficiency in English and to function at a high academic level, while an immersion program to teach English to Spanish-speaking immigrants in the United States often results in both a shift to monolingualism in English and academic failure? (Immersion programs in both cases are sensitive to the fact that the students are all non-native speakers of the language; however, they differ considerably with respect to the populations they serve and their ultimate goals regarding the development of the native language.)

Consequences of bilingualism

A commonly expressed fear about childhood bilingualism is that it could confuse the child, both linguistically and cognitively. This fear is rooted in an extensive literature on intelligence testing from the early 1900s (for a review, see Diaz 1983), when psychometricians compared the performance of bilingual immigrant children and U.S.-born children on various measures of intelligence and found that the monolinguals outperformed the bilinguals. Two explanations for this discrepancy were offered: the bilinguals (who at that time were predominantly from southern and eastern European countries) were genetically inferior to the western European monolinguals or the attempt to learn two languages caused mental confusion. This narrowly construed set of negative interpretations was captured well by noted psychologist Goodenough (1926). Observing a highly negative correlation between the extent to which different language groups used their native language in the home and the mean IQ scores for these groups, she concluded: "This might be considered evidence that the use of a foreign language in the home is one of the chief factors producing mental retardation as measured by intelligence tests. A more probable explanation is that those nationality groups whose average intellectual ability is inferior do not readily learn the new language" (p. 393).

The above literature has been largely discredited because of its failure to control for important variables, such as socioeconomic status, as well as the criteria used to select the bilingual samples (some studies, for example, used the students' last names as the basis for deciding whether they were bilingual). When such factors were controlled for, the results were reversed in favor of bilinguals. Indeed, Peal and Lambert (1962), widely credited for introducing important controls in monolingual-bilingual comparisons, describe a bilingual child as "a youngster whose wider experiences in two cultures have given him advantages which a monolingual does not enjoy. Intellectually his experience with two language systems seems to have left him with a mental flexibility, a superiority in concept formation, a more diversified set of mental abilities" (p. 20). Peal and Lambert's study gave rise to a large number of studies that selected bilinguals on a more considered basis. Generally, the results of these studies showed the bilingual groups to be superior on a variety of measures of cognitive skill, in particular, metalinguistic abilities (for a review, see Reynolds 1991). Much research in this tradition employs between-group comparisons. To control for confounding factors in such comparisons, other studies have used within-group variation in the degree of bilingualism and looked at the predictive value of this variation for cognitive outcomes (Duncan and DeAvila 1979; Galambos and Hakuta 1988; Hakuta 1987). Such studies continue to show positive relationships between degree of bilingualism and outcome measures.

Another tradition of research comes from case studies of individual children exposed to two languages at home. The earliest among these can be credited to the French linguist Ronjat (1913), but the seminal work even to this date is by Werner Leopold, who published a four-volume study of his German-English bilingual daughter Hildegard (1939, 1947, 1949a, 1949b). Ronjat's and Leopold's detailed studies of their own children gave rise to a rich tradition of linguists following their children around with notebooks (and later, tape recorders and video recorders). This literature has been reviewed most recently by Romaine (1995). Generally, the studies suggest that children can become productive bilinguals in a variety of language-use settings, though exposure to a language for less than twenty hours a week does not seem sufficient for a child to produce words in that language, at least up to age three (Pearson et al. 1977). Very few cases of what might be considered language confusion are reported.

Linguistic aspects of second-language Acquisition

The theoretical and empirical work in second-language acquisition serves as the basis for defining what one means by "proficiency" in a second language. Some researchers have defined it narrowly around the control of grammatical rules, others around the ability to use language in accomplishing cognitive tasks, and still others around the social and communicative aspects of language. This section describes how such broad definitions of language have influenced work on second-language acquisition. The theoretical assumptions underlying the construct of language proficiency have direct implications for the assessment of language proficiency, a topic addressed in Chapter 5.

Much of the research on second-language acquisition borrows heavily from the dominant paradigm in first-language acquisition and thus has focused on the problem of how linguistic structures are acquired. Many studies, for example, have examined the acquisition of morphological and syntactic features of language that are fully in place in native speakers by the age of five or six. Among these features are the grammatical aspects of language identified by Brown (1973) in his classic study of Adam, Eve, and Sarah, called Stage I through V speech: They include function words, sentence modalities, sentence embedding, and sentence coordination.

One important characterization of research on second-language acquisition relates to the researcher's definition of language. A narrow definition comes from formal linguistics, in particular from Chomsky's (1965) characterization of the logical problem of first-language acquisition as resolved by a "Language-Acquisition Device " that enables the learner to derive abstract linguistic knowledge from limited linguistic input. By showing the end-state knowledge to be deep and abstract and demonstrating that this knowledge is not accessible through induction (that is, observation of "surface data") or extrapolation from more general cognitive principles, one arrives at the logical conclusion that linguistic knowledge must be innate and highly specific to the task of language acquisition. This approach is typically taken by researchers with a background in formal linguistics (for example, White 1989; Schachter 1990) or psychologists who subscribe strongly to linguistic nativism (for example, Pinker 1994). A broader view, typically taken by cognitive psychologists such as Bates (1976), Bialystok (Bialystok and Hakuta 1994), and McLaughlin (1985), defines language to include vocabulary as well as pragmatic and communicative skills—aspects of language that are not considered by formal linguistics—and seeks explanations for language acquisition in general principles of learning and cognition. An even broader view emphasizes the social and interpersonal aspects of language and suggests that these aspects constrain language acquisition. Subscribers to this view include anthropologists (for example, Gumperz 1982) and sociolinguists (Preston, 1989). A view that combines the latter two perspectives is found in the literature on communicative, as opposed to linguistic, competence (Harley et al. 1990).

The literature generated by the above questions might be characterized as follows: Each position has managed to find a domain of inquiry that legitimizes it, but the relationship among the various positions is far from specified. Thus, research in Universal Grammar (a formal linguistics perspective) has shown that even adults display the ability to learn aspects of language that are abstract and presumably unlearnable from general cognitive or social principles (Epstein et al. in press). This would suggest that a complete theory of second-language acquisition must account for induction of abstract rules from inadequate surface data. Research by those taking the cognitive and functionalist position has shown that on sentence-processing tasks, second-language learners are sensitive to cognitively salient factors, such as the animacy of the subject of a sentence (in English, most subjects of sentences tend to be animate rather than inanimate). Thus, this view would argue that second-language learning can be regarded as a cognitive accomplishment. Those with a sociolinguistic orientation, on the other hand, have pointed to examples where social variables affect language use and structure, that is, where socially useful phrases are learned first (Hatch 1978), and bilinguals learn rules for code switching (Zentella 1981) and for adjusting their language use to social circumstances (for example, Bayley 1991; Preston 1989).

Thus we must conclude that second-language acquisition is a complex process requiring a diverse set of explanatory factors (Bialystok and Hakuta 1994). Developing an inclusive theory of how a second language is acquired therefore necessitates moving beyond the description of plausible acquisition mechanisms for specific domains to an explanation of how those mechanisms work together to produce the integrated knowledge of a language that enables its use for communication.

A second important dimension of second-language acquisition is the extent of involvement of the native language in the acquisition process. Are native speakers of Spanish different from native speakers of Vietnamese in their acquisition of English? In the early 1960s, the answer would have been a definitive "yes," based on contrastive analysis theory (Lado 1964). The 1970s saw an almost total rejection of the contrastive analysis approach and emergence of the view that second-language acquisition is accomplished through direct access to the language-acquisition device, without mediation by the native language. This change was supported empirically by studies that examined the types of errors made by second-language learners and found that many errors could not be attributed to language transfer, and that many errors predicted by a simple transfer theory were absent. Also, a number of studies focusing on the acquisition of English morphology by learners from different language backgrounds demonstrated remarkable similarities in order of acquisition—suggesting that the target language has more effect than the first language on the course of acquisition (Bailey et al. 1974). The paradigm shift away from a focus on transfer was marked by the emergence of the notion of "interlanguage" (Sclinker 1972), conceived of as a linguistic system unique to each learner who has not yet achieved full competence in the second language.

Nonetheless, language-transfer errors are frequent and have continued to fascinate researchers (Bialystok and Hakuta 1994; Odlin 1989). Even within the Chomsky-inspired Universal Grammar framework, language transfer, interpreted as "maintenance of first-language parameter settings," has gained momentum as an area of research. Finally, there is some interest in the possibility that language transfer would be more evident in the quantitative (speed of acquisition) rather than qualitative (for example, types of errors and patterns of acquisition) aspects of second-language acquisition (Odlin 1989)—that is, it takes longer to learn a language that is typologically very different from the native language than one that is relatively similar. For example, it would be easier for a native English speaker to learn French than Chinese.

A third dimension of importance is the age and concomitant cognitive skills of the second-language learner. The dominant first-language-acquisition research paradigms equated first- and second-language learners, thus minimizing attention to those aspects of second-language acquisition that are unique to the more cognitively developed learner. In the early literature, for example, Hakuta (1976) noted that Uguisu, a five-year old Japanese girl learning English, used connectives (*and, but, because*, etc.) much earlier in her English development than first-language learners do; furthermore, she was less constrained by memory factors than first-language learners. Lightbown (1977) similarly attested to a lack of semantic constraints among second-language learners, presumably owing to their more advanced cognitive level. Such observations help explain why older children acquire a second language so much more quickly than younger children (Snow and Hoefnagel-Höhle 1978).

Older language learners need to learn more complex linguistic structures in order to respond age-appropriately to the tasks for which they must use their second language. Snow (1987) suggests that older learners are more often faced with tasks in which various sorts of contextual support (such as helpful conversational partners, practice in talk about the topic) are unavailable. For example, adolescent immigrants in a submersion situation where they have no help in understanding the non-native language must produce language performances about complex or abstract topics with no conversational support at a much earlier stage of acquisition than preschool-aged immigrants. Furthermore, Snow's findings suggest that performance on highly supported or conversational tasks will not necessarily predict performance on less contextualized tasks. In one study of bilingual children, she showed that within either language, performance on contextualized tasks (such as face-to-face communication) was poorly related to that on less contextualized tasks (such as defining the meaning of a word) (Snow 1987, 1990). Experience on a particular type of task within a specific language was more important than overall language proficiency in predicting performance on that task (see also Malakoff 1988).

Cummins (1979, 1991) proposes a related task analysis that distinguishes two dimensions: degree of contextual support and degree of cognitive challenge. He argues that for a second-language speaker, performance on more conversationally supported and less challenging tasks (such as a chat with the English as a second language [ESL] teacher) will not predict performance on more challenging and autonomous tasks, test taking in particular, since the conversational abilities emerge first (Cummins and Swain 1986). While both Cummins and Snow agree that language task analysis is crucial to prediction of academic performance from language proficiency, they disagree about whether second-language learning necessarily starts with conversational skills. In fact, a frequent feature of immigrant bilingualism is that seemingly more difficult tasks may be performed better in the second than in the first language. These views of language share the important claim that academic language is different from language use in other contexts, a claim related to an underlying view of language as an ability with many components, rather than a single accomplishment that cannot be analyzed. Both suggest that second-language abilities should be assessed in relation to the uses of language the learner will require, rather than in isolation as an abstract competence.

Individual differences in second-language acquisition

The most striking fact about second-language learning, especially as compared with first-language learning, is the variability in outcomes. Many individual and group variables have been examined in attempts to explain success or failure in second-language acquisition. This section reviews the literature on various individual differences in second-language acquisition. In looking at this literature, it is important to appreciate that the definition of the outcome of the second-language-acquisition process has itself been variable, as discussed in the previous section.

Age of learning

One frequently cited factor is the age of the learner, with the assumption that younger learners acquire a second language more quickly and with a higher level of proficiency. Periodic reviews of this literature (Bialystok and Hakuta 1994; Collier 1987: Epstein et al. 1996; Harley and Wang 1997; Krashen et al. 1982; Long 1990; Snow 1987) have not supported this claim very well. Even though there is a critical period in the learning of a first language, this does not imply there is one for second-language learning. The following observations might be made:

- More mature learners generally make faster initial progress in acquiring morphological, syntactic, and lexical aspects of a second language.
- An increasing age of onset for second-language acquisition is correlated with declining ultimate attainment in the control of phonological, morphological, and syntactic aspects of language across age groups, beginning typically by ages six to seven and continuing into adulthood. In adult learners, this association between onset age and declining outcomes is most strongly manifested in oral aspects of second-language proficiency (maintenance of an accent).
- Some adult learners are nonetheless capable of near-native, if not native-like, performance in a second language, while some children are unsuccessful in achieving native-like performance.
- There is a general lack of evidence that acquisition processes differ across age groups, that is, that radically different types of errors are made or that there is a different sequence to the acquisition of structures for learners of different ages (Harley and Wang 1997).

Many researchers have assumed that the best explanation for the age-related decline in oral ability with a second language is a biological one, based on a critical or sensitive period in brain development (Johnson and Newport 1989, 1991; Oyama 1976; Patkowski 1980). However, the behavioral evidence is not consistent with evidence about periods of brain growth, and serious methodological problems have dogged even the most sound of existing studies (see Snow's 1987 review of critical period theory as well as Bialystok and Hakuta's 1994 review of Johnson and Newport's study). For example, proficiency assessments often focus on tasks such as judgments about grammatical or morphological correctness—matters in which younger learners have likely received formal instruction. Also, younger immigrants are typically younger at testing; younger subjects have an advantage in any test that involves auditory attention. Studies in which the conditions of acquisition were as comparable as possible for younger and older learners (for example, Genesee's 1981 study of early- versus late-immersion students) are less likely to show poorer ultimate performance for older learners.

Studies of age as a factor in the acquisition of English appropriate for academic use are consistent with the studies cited above in that children who start learning English in kindergarten in English-only educational settings take longer to achieve age-appropriate levels of performance on academic tasks than children who start in grades two through six (Collier 1987). This age difference may simply reflect the general finding that initial acquisition is faster for older learners with more cognitive skills, but it has also been interpreted as supporting the claim that second-language acquisition is faster and easier if continued development in the first language is supported through mastery of the basic grammar in the first language, around age six. Cummins (1979) has interpreted such findings as validating the importance of continued development of first-language grammar, although other researchers disagree (Rossell and Baker 1996; Porter 1990).

Intelligence

Another factor in second-language acquisition may be general intelligence. This factor has been addressed mainly in the arena of foreign-language learning in the classroom (Carroll 1986; Gardner 1983; Oller 1981). For immigrant learners and those in immersion settings, second-language learning is evidently not impeded by learning disabilities or low intelligence to the extent it would be in formal learning settings (Bruck 1982, 1984; for a review, see Genesee 1992). In the field of bilingual education, second-language acquisition has not been tied to questions of general aptitude, although educational practitioners commonly observe that second-language acquisition is easier for students with a history of formal education and higher socioeconomic backgrounds. Furthermore, correlational studies that examine relative proficiencies in the two languages of bilingual children show that native-language proficiency is a strong predictor of second-language development (Cummins 1984: Hakuta 1987).

It should be noted that assessing the intelligence of second-language learners is a risky process. Whenever possible, such assessments should be conducted in the native language—though if the assessment is closely tied to school tasks, the child may display better performance in the school language. Koopmans (1991) showed that native Spanish-speaking third to fifth graders in bilingual programs—children who had lived in the United States for an average of eleven years—performed better in Spanish on a logical reasoning task of a type rarely encountered in either home or classroom discourse. Malakoff (1988), on the other hand, showed that children at an international school performed better in the curricular than the home language on an analogies task, even at a very low level of general skill in the curricular language.

Attitudes

Studies investigating the predictive power of language attitudes and motivation for second-language acquisition have been limited, by and large, to students who study a foreign language that is generally used only in the classroom (Gardner and Lambert 1972). Such studies have shown that a positive attitude and motivation are significant factors in predicting oral communicative skills in a second language, whereas language aptitude predicts proficiency in knowledge of grammar and vocabulary. It is therefore clear that attitude and motivation are important factors in second-language learning in some contexts. Yet the few studies that have looked at the importance of these factors in the acquisition of English among immigrants to the United States have had largely negative findings. For example, Hakuta and D'Andrea (1992) studied Mexican-American attitudes toward English and Spanish and administered tests of English and Spanish proficiency. Attitude had no predictive power for English-proficiency, whereas a positive attitude toward Spanish predicted whether students continued to use that language as part of their sociolinguistic repertoire. In sociolinguistic settings such as the United States, it is likely that any variation in the attitudes of immigrant populations toward English will be largely overridden by the overwhelming importance of English to getting ahead in the society.

Personality

Many studies have attempted to isolate factors related to individual predisposition, over and above basic intelligence, toward second-language acquisition. Most of this work is focused on learning a foreign language rather than on learning a language in the society where it is used. A review of this literature shows a serious failure to address issues of construct validity (Bialystok and Hakuta 1994). Given the inordinate difficulty of validly measuring personality constructs cross-culturally, this is probably not a very fruitful area for future research, although it will continue to be a source of speculation because of its intrinsic interest.

Language shift

Language shift refers to the sociolinguistic phenomenon in which an ethnic group gradually moves its preference and use of language from its original ethnic language to the sociologically dominant language. Attempts to explain language shift range from macro-level population perspectives to micro-level analyses of language change within individual members of those communities.

Demographers and sociologists have tried to identify determinants of the vitality or imminent death of ethnic languages. Fishman et al. (1966), using an impressive variety of sources on language vitality in the United States, found rapid decline between 1940 and 1960 in the numbers of speakers of different languages. The only factor that consistently contributed to increasing those numbers was new immigration. In comparing data on language diversity in thirty-five nations, Lieberson et al. (1975) found that the amount of language loss occurring in the United States in a single generation would have taken about 350 years in other nations investigated. Analyzing data from the Survey on Income and Education, Veltman (1983, 1988) also found a consistent picture of rapid language shift in the United States. Most remarkably, even Spanish, the language for which geographical proximity and numbers of speakers favor maintenance, shows rapid loss, leading Veltman to conclude that in the absence of new immigration, the Spanish language will undergo rapid decline and extinction in the United States.

The shift from non-English to English that occurs may be both *intra-individual* and *intergenerational* in nature. That is, during the course of their lifetime, individuals shift their primary language preference from their native language to English, and ethno-linguistic communities in successive generations will likewise shift their linguistic preference. Ethnographic studies, as well as large-scale demographic information (Fishman et al. 1966; Lopez 1978; Veltman 1983), suggest that bilinguals in the United States show a strong preference for English in many conversational situations and that this preference is translated into a monolingual English upbringing for their offspring. In addition, though, consistent choice of English can lead to increased proficiency in English and decreased proficiency in the native language, even for an adult speaker (Seliger and Vago 1991).

Studies of children provide evidence that there can be intra-individual loss of skills in the native language as gauged through academic-achievement measures (Laosa 1995; Merino 1983), and cases of total loss of a first or dominant language by young children who do not persist in using it regularly are frequent (Burling 1959). Every bilingual can document decreased case and fluency in a long-neglected language, particularly with regard to vocabulary and complex grammar (for example, Grosjean 1982). However, studies that look at basic language proficiency identify highly robust aspects of the native-language grammar for students who have had the opportunity to develop the native language at home (Hakuta and D'Andrea 1992; Hakuta and Pease-Alvarez 1994), with the clearest evidence of shift occurring in the domain of language choice, not proficiency. It is less clear what happens to children who are exposed to English and become dominant in it before their native language is fully established. Parental reports based on an informal sample suggest the native language can be stunted or lost (Wong Fillmore 1991).

An understanding of basic questions about language maintenance and shift could well provide input needed to address practical issues such as the degree to which heritage languages can serve as a reservoir of bilingualism for the United States, the kinds of language instruction that would be useful to second-generation minority language speakers, and whether there are risks associated with the loss of familial languages by young children.

Educational conditions for second-language learning

Often, interactions with peers and teachers provide the primary source of input to child second-language learners. For some children, this experience begins in preschool and child care environments; for all others, their first real exposure to English is in kindergarten. The nature of these linguistic environments and their possible influences on English acquisition or on native-language maintenance or development have typically not been the focus of the basic research studies described thus far in this chapter. However, as theories of second-language acquisition have expanded to incorporate the social conditions under which learning takes place, there has been increased interest—over and above the concerns of program evaluation—in understanding the linguistic environment of the classroom setting and how it might relate to linguistic outcomes.

Some researchers have examined classrooms in trying to understand the opportunities they provide (or fail to provide) for students to contribute to conversational exchanges involving their fellow students, as well as their teachers (Ellis 1984). Proper accounting of what goes on linguistically in the classroom is important for a number of reasons. For example, such work would begin clarifying what might be meant by comprehensible input, a nation widely used by second-language acquisition researchers (Krashen 1982; Long 1983; Pica 1987). The relevant classroom features include adjustments similar to those that parents make when talking with young children, such as organizing talk around visible referents, using simple syntax, producing many repetitions and paraphrases, speaking slowly and clearly, checking often for comprehension, and expanding on and extending topics introduced by the learner. While researchers have examined recurring features of classroom interaction hypothesized to be relevant to students' development of language (see van Lier 1988), few studies have tried to link classroom communication and the learning of linguistic features, and those that have done so have not been successful (Ellis 1995).

Other researchers have begun to offer detailed pictures of the relative uses of the student's two languages in elementary-grade bilingual classrooms (Enright 1982; Milk 1990; Shultz 1975). Although these studies generally do not report outcome data with respect to English acquisition or native-language development, they have shown that English tends to predominate in terms of messages conveyed and frequency of use. For example, in her ethnographic study of mathematics teaching in five bilingual classrooms, Khisty (1995) found that teachers tended to use the students' native language, Spanish, as an "instrument to discipline, to call students' attention to the subject of the lesson, or to punctuate a statement" (p. 288). When providing mathematical explanations, teachers tended to revert to English, using only a scattering of Spanish words. However, Khisty found that these same teachers used Spanish consistently during reading and language arts instruction. Research on whether these conditions of use contribute optimally to the acquisition of English and/or maintenance of Spanish remains to be done.

A concern for documenting and understanding the factors that contribute to the diminished role of native languages in schools and classrooms has also framed classroom studies conducted in bilingual settings. Ethnographic research investigating bilingual programs has shown how social, cultural, and even political conditions may mediate the language-development goal and outcomes of the programs. For example, Pease-Alvarez and Winsler (1994) found that attitudes and beliefs favoring Spanish operate relatively independently from patterns of language choice in some classroom settings. Several other studies have shown how difficult it is to achieve the goal of dual language development and native-language maintenance in societies where assimilation toward the dominant group is the prevailing ideology. For example, Escamilla (1994) found that school-wide practices (for example, language choice among faculty members and the language used for public displays and presentations in the school) contrasted with the school's official commitment to the development and support of both languages. Similarly, McCollum (1993) found that in a middle school two-way bilingual program, Spanish-background students used primarily English at school by choice. She interpreted her findings in terms of "cultural capital," arguing that students perceived English, not Spanish, as the language of power and responded accordingly.

Other studies have looked more generally at the effects of English-only and bilingual school environments on the overall language and cognitive development of English-language learners. Paul and Jarvis (1992), for example, compared English-language learners in bilingual and monolingual pre-kindergarten classrooms, and found positive outcomes for the children in the former classrooms on a criterion-referenced test, the Chicago Early Assessment and Remediation Laboratory (EARLY). An evaluation study of the California Preschool Program, in which classroom activities were carried out exclusively in Spanish, shows similarly positive effects of first-language use on second-language acquisition (Campos 1995). Even though their preschool program was conducted entirely in Spanish, by first grade almost half of the Carpinteria children were at level 5 (fluent English) on the Bilingual Syntax Measure, as compared with fewer than 10 percent of English-language learners from daycare and other programs. Campos concluded that "there was no evident delay in the rate of English acquisition by the Carpinteria Preschool students, and they demonstrated competency in applying their English language skills. When compared with the language-minority comparison preschool group, they acquired English language fluency faster, transitioned out of bilingual education classrooms sooner, and achieved in English-language classrooms and on English-language standardized tests better. Clearly, first-language development in their preschool program did not interfere or delay their second-language learning. Instead, the results suggest that they were better prepared to understand and utilize opportunities in their learning environment" (p. 46). Further, the investigators reported that these students had apparently maintained their bilingual skills and that almost all were expected to graduate from high school.

Such studies point to the importance of understanding the linguistic environments of institutional settings that serve as the primary base for second-language acquisition. These environments are best thought of as both dependent variables that are outcomes of larger social and cultural processes and independent variables that affect the linguistic attainment of the children. A wide variety of methodologies must be brought to bear on this problem, ranging from interpretive, ethnographic studies on the social and cultural ecology within which such programs exist to more hypothesis-testing approaches that look at specific relationships between the linguistic environments and the linguistic attainments of English-language learners.

It is critically important to understand preschool environments for two major reasons. First, during the preschool years, language development itself is a major outcome of interest. The few studies reviewed suggest that the development of the native language and of English are interdependent, but additional work is needed in this area, particularly because the issue of native-language development through these programs promises to be just as controversial as what we have witnessed in the K-12 programs to date. Second, there are increasing calls for the expansion of high-quality preschool opportunities for all children (for example, Carnegie Corporation 1996). A critical ingredient in defining quality is the linguistic environment of these programs. This represents a window of opportunity where research can make a difference for a large number of programs and children.

RESEARCH NEEDS

2–1. Research is needed on the factors that account for variation in second-language acquisition. Variability in the degree of English acquisition can be attributable to variation in individual and group characteristics. More work is needed in particular on the latter factors.

Research on individual factors in second-language acquisition, including age of the learner, intelligence, and attitudes and motivation, has already yielded many answers. On the other hand, less is known about group effects, such as whether some groups of immigrants are more likely to acquire English rapidly or to higher levels than others, or whether certain sociolinguistic or educational conditions lead to more rapid acquisition of English than others. There has been insufficient research systematically relating rich information about the settings for learning English—such as how much direct instruction is provided, the order in which structures are taught, and the use of written versus oral modes for provision of input—to information about the rate and process of acquisition for individual learners. Furthermore, the individual factors that have been investigated may interact with group effects in ways that can yield new theoretical insights.

2–2. An important contribution to understanding variability in second-language acquisition would be an enhanced understanding of the components of English proficiency and how these components interact. Also important is the question of how proficiencies in the two languages of bilinguals are interrelated.
The above questions have a direct bearing on the appropriate assessment of English-language proficiency with respect to socially and academically valued outcomes (see also Chapter 5).

2–3. Assessment of second-language learners should involve analysis of unstructured, spontaneous speech in addition to more structured instruments. An important research goal is thus to create a common pool of spontaneous speech data for use by researchers.
The analysis of spontaneous speech could become systematized and routinely incorporated into the research culture if data sets were made widely available through the Internet. Such a system already exists in the field of child first-language acquisition through the Child Language Data Exchange System (MacWhinney 1991). Expansion of this system to include data on second-language acquisition and bilingual children would greatly increase the vitality and productivity of the field.

2–4. It is essential to understand the interaction between language and other domains of human functioning.
Research reviewed here on the consequences of bilingualism has concluded that there are no negative consequences of learning two languages in childhood and that there are some positive correlations between bilingualism and general cognitive ability. This research should move beyond seeking macro-level effects and begin looking for more detailed and specific relationships between linguistic representations on the one hand and cognitive and social representations on the other. This recommendation is revisited in the discussion of content-area learning and the recommendations in Chapter 3.

2–5. Macro-level questions about language shift in the United States have amply demonstrated the short-lived nature of non-English languages. Research is needed to help in understanding the dynamics of language shift.
Such research would include examining how messages concerning the value of native languages are conveyed, how children and youth understand such messages, what the effects are on the children's identities and their school achievement, and what the likelihood is of maintaining the native language while learning English. We need also to develop a more specific understanding of what is meant by language attrition, such as the relationship between language choice (choosing not to use one's native language) and the loss of language proficiency. Moreover, compared with current knowledge on the types of educational services provided to English-language learners to meet their needs in English, there is very little systematic information available on language programs for native-language development (such as courses in Spanish for Spanish speakers that are available in some high schools and universities). Finally, large-scale survey research is needed to determine Americans' attitudes toward both languages other than English and their speakers, and whether those attitudes are shared by the minority-language speakers themselves.

Notes

1. This chapter provides a broad overview of the findings of research on bilingualism and second-language learning and analyzes how theories in these areas have been reflected in thinking about the education of language-minority children in the United States. The literatures associated with these traditions are diverse in their methodologies and epistemologies and have undergone dynamic changes over the course of their history, extending back well over a century. They have developed largely independently from the educational and programmatic concerns that are the focus of this study, but they provide the fundamental science for the linguistic aspects of our inquiry. By necessity, a broad

overview of these rich traditions involves a high level of synthesis. This review draws liberally from several existing general syntheses, which should be consulted for further details (Baetens-Beardsmore 1986; Bialystok and Hakuta 1994; Grosjean 1982; Hakuta 1986; Hamers and Blanc 1989; Klein 1986; Larsen-Freeman and Long 1990; McLaughlin 1984a, 1985; and Romaine 1995).

References

Bactens-Beardsmore, H. 1986. *Bilingualism: Basic Principles,* second ed. Clevedon, England: Tieto.

Bailey, N., C. Madden, and S. D. Krashen. 1974. Is there a "natural sequence" in adult second language learning? *Language Learning* 24:235–243.

Bates, E. 1976. *Language and Context.* New York: Academic Press.

Bayley, R. J. 1991. Variation theory and second-language learning. Unpublished Ph.D. Dissertation. School of Education. Stanford University.

Bialystok, E., and K. Hakuta. 1994. *In Other Words.* New York: Basic Books.

Brown, R. 1973. *A First Language: The Early Stage.* Cambridge, MA: Harvard University Press.

Bruck, M. 1982. Language-disabled children's performance in an additive bilingual education programs. *Applied Psycholinguistics* 3:45–60.

—— 1984. Feasibility of an additive bilingual program for the language-impaired child. In Y. LeBrun and M. Paradis, eds. *Early Bilingualism and Child Development.* Amsterdam: Swets & Zeitlinger.

Burling, R. 1959. The language development of a Garo and English-speaking child. *Word* 15:45–68.

Campos, S. J. 1995. The Carpinteria Preschool Program: A long-term effects study. In E. Garcia and B. McLaughlin, eds. *Meeting the Challenge of Linguistic and Cultural Diversity in Early Childhood Education.* New York: Teacher's College.

Carnegie Corporation. 1996. *Years of Promise. A Comprehensive Learning Strategy for America's Children.* New York: Carnegie Corporation.

Carroll, John B. 1986. Second language. R. F. Dillon and R. J. Sternbery, eds. *Cognition and Instruction.* Orlando. FL: Academic Press.

Chomsky, N. 1965. *Aspects of the Theory of Syntax.* Cambridge, MA: MIT Press.

Collier, Virginia P. 1987. Age and rate acquisition of second language for academic purposes. *TESOL Quarterly* 21(4):617–641.

Cummins, J. 1979. Cognitive/academic language proficiency, linguistic interdependence, the optimum age question, and some other matters. *Working Papers on Bilingualism* 19:197–205.

—— 1984. *Bilingualism and Special Education.* San Diego, CA: College Hill Press.

—— 1991. Language development and academic learning. In L.M. Malavé and G. Duquette, eds. *Language, Culture and Cognition.* Clevedon, England: Multilingual Matters.

Cummins, J., and M. Swain. 1986. *Bilingualism in Education.* New York: Longman.

Diaz, R. M. 1983. Thought and two languages: The impact of bilingualism on cognitive development. *Review of Research in Education* 10:23–54.

Duncan, S., and E. DeAvila. 1979. Bilingualism and cognition: Some recent findings. *NABE Journal* 4:15–50.

Ellis, Nick C. 1995. Psychology of foreign language vocabulary acquisition: Implications for CALL. *Computer Assisted Language Learning* 8(2):103–128.

Ellis, Rod. 1984. Communication strategies and the evaluation of communicative performance. *ELT Journal* 38(1):39–44.

Enright, Brian E. 1982. Criterion-referenced Tests: A Guide to Separate Useful from Useless. Paper presented at the Annual International Convention of the Council for Exceptional Children. Houston, TX. April 11–16; Session T-27. University of North Carolina–Charlotte.

Epstein, S. D., D. Flynn, and G. Martohardjono. 1996. Second-language acquisition: Theoretical and experimental issues in contemporary research. *Behavior and Brain Sciences* 19(4):677–758.

Escamilla, Kathy. 1994. The sociolinguistic environment of a bilingual school: A case study introduction. *Bilingual Research Journal* 18(1–2): 21–47.

Fishman, J. A. 1978. *Advances in the Study of Societal Multilingualism.* The Hague, Netherlands, and New York: Mouton.

Fishman, J. A., V. Nahiray, J. Hofman, and R. Hayden. 1966. *Language Loyalty in the United States: The Maintenance and Perpetuation of Non-English Mother Tongues by American Ethnic and Religious Groups.* The Hague: Mouton.

Galambos, Sylvia Joseph, and Kenji Hakuta. 1988. Subject-specific and task-specific characteristics of metalinguistic awareness in bilingual children. *Applied Psycholinguistics* 9(2):141–62.

Gardner, R. C. 1983. Learning another language: A true social psychological experiment. *Journal of Language and Social Psychology* 2:219–239.

—— 1985. *Social Psychology and Second-Language Learning: The Role of Attitudes and Motivation.* London and Baltimore, MD: E. Arnold.

Gardner, R. C., and W. C. Lambert. 1972. *Attitudes and Motivation in Second-Language Learning.* Rowley, MA: Newbury House.

Gardner, R. C., R. N. Lalonde, and J. MacPherson. 1985. Social factors in second-language attrition. *Language Learning* 5:519–540.

Genesee, F., J. Hamers, W. Lambert, L. Mononen, M. Scitz, and R. Starck. 1978. Language processing in bilinguals. *Brain and Language* 5:1–12.

Genesse, F. 1981. A comparison of early and late second-language learning. *Canadian Journal of Behavioral Sciences* 13:115–128.

—— 1992. Second/foreign language immersion and at-risk English-speaking children. *Foreign Language Annals* 25:199–213.

Goodenough, F. 1926. Racial differences in the intelligence of school children. *Journal of Experimental Psychology* 9:388–397.
Grosjean, F. 1982. *Life with Two Languages.* Cambridge, MA: Harvard University Press.
Gumperz, J. 1982. *Discourse Strategies.* Cambridge, England: Cambridge University Press.
Hakuta, K. 1976. A case study of a Japanese child learning English. *Language Learning* 26:321–351.
—— 1986. *Mirror of Language: The Debate on Bilingualism.* New York: Basic Books.
—— 1987. Degree of bilingualism and cognitive ability in mainland Puerto Rican children. *Child Development* 58(5): 1372–1388.
Hakuta, K., and D. D'Andrea. 1992. Some properties of bilingual maintenance and loss in Mexican background high-school students. *Applied Linguistics* 13(1):72–99.
Hakuta, K., and L. Pease-Alvarez. 1994. Proficiency, choice, and attitudes in bilingual Mexican-American children. In G: Extra and L. Verhoeven, eds. *The Cross-Linguistic Study of Bilingual Development.* Amsterdam, Netherlands: Academy of Arts and Sciences.
Hamers, J., and M. Blanc. 1989. *Bilingualism and Bilinguality.* Cambridge, England, and New York: Cambridge University Press.
Harley, B., and W. Wang. 1997. The critical period hypothesis: Where are we now? In A. M. B. de Groot and J. F. Kroll. eds. *Tutorials in Bilingualism: Psycholinguistic Perspectives.* Hillsdale, NJ: Erlbaum.
Harley, B., J. Cummins, and M. Swain. 1990. *The Development of Second-Language Proficiency.* Cambridge, England, and New York: Cambridge University Press.
Hatch, E. 1978. Discourse analysis and second-language acquisition. In E. Hatch, ed., *Second Language Acquisition: A Book of Readings.* Rowley, MA: Newbury House.
Johnson, J. S., and E. L. Newport. 1989. Critical period effects in second-language learning: The influence of maturational state on the acquisition of English as a second language. *Cognitive Psychology* 21:60–99.
—— 1991. Critical-period effects on universal properties of language: The status of subjacency in the acquisition of a second language. *Cognition* 39:215–258.
Khisty, Lena Licón. 1995. Making inequality: Issues of language and meanings in mathematics teaching with Hispanic students. In W. G. Secada, E. Fennema, and L. B. Adajian, eds., *New Directions for Equity in Mathematics Education.* New York: Cambridge University Press.
Klein, W. 1986. *Second-Language Acquisition.* Cambridge, England: Cambridge University Press.
Koopmans, Matthijs. 1991. Reasoning in two languages: An assessment of the reasoning ability of Puerto Rican elementary school children. *Linguistics and Education* 3:345–358.
Krashen, S. 1982. *Principles and Practice in Second-Language Acquisition.* Oxford, England: Pergamon.
Krashen, S., R. Scarcella, and M. Long, eds. 1982. *Child-Adult Differences in Second-Language Acquisition.* Rowley, MA: Newbury House.
Lado, Robert 1964 *Language Teaching. A Scientific Approach.* New York: McGraw Hill.
Lambert. W. E. 1975. Culture and language as factors in learning and education. In A. Wolfgang, ed. *Education of Immigrant Students.* Toronto: Ontario Institute for Studies in Education.
Lambert, W., J. Havelka, and D. Crosby. 1958. The influence of language-acquisition contexts on bilingualism. *Journal of Abnormal and Social Psychology* 66:239–243.
Laosa, L. M. 1995. *Longitudinal Measurements of English-language Proficiency Acquisition by Children Who Migrate to the United States from Puerto Rico.* Princeton, NJ: Educational Testing Service.
Larsen, J., T. Fritsch, and S. Grava. 1974. A semantic priming test of bilingual language storage and compound vs. coordinate bilingual distinction with Latvian-English bilinguals. *Perceptual & Motor Skills* 79:459–466.
Larsen-Freeman, D., and M. Long. 1990. *An Introduction to Second-Language-Acquisition Research.* London and New York: Longman.
Leopold, W. 1939. *Speech Development of a Bilingual Child: A Linguist's Record. Vol. 1: Vocabulary Growth in the First Two Years.* Evanston, IL: Northwestern University.
—— 1947. *Speech Development of a Bilingual Child: A Linguist's Record. Vol. 2: Sound Learning in the First Two Years.* Evanston, IL: Northwestern University.
—— 1949a. *Speech Development of a Bilingual Child: A Linguist's Record. Vol. 3: Grammar and General Problems in the First Two Years.* Evanston, IL: Northwestern University.
—— 1949b. *Speech Development of a Bilingual Child: A Linguist's Record. Vol. 4: Diary From Age Two.* Evanston, IL: Northwestern University.
Lieberson, S., G. Dalto, and M. Johnston. 1975. The course of mother-tongue diversity in nations. *American Journal of Sociology* 81:34–61.
Lightbown, Patsy M. 1977. French L2 learners: What they're talking about. *Language Learning* 27(2):371–381.
Long, Michael H. 1983. Linguistic and conversational adjustments to non-native speakers. *Studies in Second-Language Acquisition* 5(2): 177–193.
—— 1990. The least a second-language acquisition theory needs to explain. *TESOL Quarterly* 24(4):649–666.
Lopez, D. E. 1978. Chicano language loyalty in an urban setting. *Sociology and Social Research* 62:267–278.
MacWhinney, B. 1991. *The CHILDES Project: Tools for Analyzing Talk.* Hillsdale, NJ: Erlbaum.
Malakoff, Marguerite E. 1988. The effect of language of instruction on reasoning in bilingual children. *Applied Psycholinguistics* 9(1):17–38.
McCollum, Pamela. 1993. Learning to Value English: Cultural Capital in a Two-Way Bilingual Program. Paper presented at the annual meeting of AERA. Atlanta, GA.
McLaughlin, Barry. 1984. *Second-language Acquisition in Childhood: Volume 1. Preschool Children.* Hillsdale, NJ: Erlbaum.
—— 1985. *Second-language Acquisition in Childhood: Volume 2. Schoolage Children.* Hillsdale, NJ: Erlbaum.

Merino, B. J. 1983. Language loss in bilingual Chicago children. *Journal of Applied Developmental Psychology* 4:277–294.
Milk, R. 1990. Preparing ESL and bilingual teachers for changing roles: Immersion for teachers of LEP children. *TESOL Quarterly* 24(3):407–426.
Odlin, T. 1989. *Language Transfer: Cross-linguistic Influence in Language Learning.* Cambridge U.K.: Cambridge University Press.
Oller, J. W. Jr. 1981. Language as intelligence. *Language Learning* 31:465–492.
Oyama, S. 1976. A sensitive period for the acquisition of a non-native phonological system. *Journal of Psycholinguistic Research* 5:261–285.
Patkowski, M. 1980. The sensitive period for the acquisition of syntax in a second language. *Language Learning* 30:449–472.
Paul, B., and C. Jarvis. 1992. The effects of native language use in New York City pre-kindergarten classes. Paper presented at the 1992 Annual Meeting of the American Educational Research Association. San Francisco, CA. ERIC Document ED351874.
Peal, E., and W. E. Lambert. 1962. The relation of bilingualism to intelligence. *Psychological Monographs: General and Applied* 76(546):1–23.
Pearson, B., S. Fernández, V. Lewedeg, and D. Oller. Input features in lexical learning of bilingual infants (ages 10–30 months). *Applied Psycholinguistics* 1997, 18, 41–58.
Pease-Alvarez, Lucinda, and A. Winsler. 1994. Cuando el maestro no habla espanol: Children's bilingual language practices in the classroom. *TESOL Quarterly* 28(3):507–535.
Pica, Teresa. 1987. Second-language acquisition, social interaction, and the classroom. *Applied Linguistics* 8(1):3–21.
Pinker, S. 1994. *The Language Instinct.* New York: Morrow.
Porter, R. P. 1990. *Forked Tongue: The Politics of Bilingual Education.* New York: Basic Books.
Preston, D. R. 1989. *Sociolinguistics and Second-Language Acquisition.* New York: Basil Blackwell.
Reynolds, A. 1991. *Bilingualism, Multiculturalism, and Second-Language Learning.* Hillsdale, NJ: Erlbaum.
Romaine, J. 1995. *Bilingualism*, second ed. Oxford, England: Blackwell.
Ronjat, J. 1913. *Le développement du language observé chez un enfant biliugue.* Paris: Champion.
Rossell, Christine, and Keith Baker. 1996. The educational effectiveness of bilingual education. *Research in the Teaching of English* 30(1):385–419.
Schachter, J. 1990. On the issue of completeness in second-language acquisition. *Second Language Research* 6:93–124.
Seliger. H., and R. Vago, eds. 1991. *First-Language Attrition: Structural and Theoretical Perspectives.* Cambridge and New York: Cambridge University Press.
Selinker, L. 1972. Interlanguage. *International Review of Applied Linguistics* 10:209–230.
Shultz, N. W. Jr. 1975. *On the autonomy and comparability of linguistic and ethnographic description.* Lisse, Netherlands: Peter de Ridder.
Snow, C. E. 1987. Relevance of the notion of a critical period to language acquisition. In M. Bornstein, ed. *Sensitive Periods in Development.* Hillsdale, NJ: Erlbaum.
—— 1990. The development of definitional skill. *Journal of Child Language* 17:697–710.
Snow, C. E. and M. Hoefnagel-Höhle. 1978. The Critical period for language acquisition. *Child Development* 4:1114–1128.
van Lier, L. 1988. *The Classroom and the Language Learner.* London: Longman.
Veltman, C. 1983. *Language Shift in the United States.* New York: Mouton.
—— 1988. *The Future of the Spanish Language in the United States.* New York and Washington, DC: Hispanic Policy Development Project.
Weinreich, U. 1953. *Languages in Contact.* The Hague: Mouton.
White, L. 1989. *Universal Grammar and Second-Language Acquisition.* Philadelphia, PA: Benjamins.
Wong Fillmore, L. 1991. When learning a second language means losing the first. *Early Childhood Research Quarterly* 6(3):323–346.
Zentella, A. C. 1981. Language variety among Puerto Ricans. In C. A. Ferguson and S. B. Heath, eds. *Language in the USA.* New York: Cambridge University Press.

Chapter 15
A Meta-Analysis of Selected Studies on the Effectiveness of Bilingual Education

ANN C. WILLIG

A meta-analysis of selected studies on the efficacy of bilingual education was conducted and the results were compared with a traditional review of the same literature. When statistical controls for methodological inadequacies were employed, participation in bilingual education programs consistently produced small to moderate differences favoring bilingual education for tests of reading, language skills, mathematics, and total achievement when the tests were in English, and for reading, language, mathematics, writing, social studies, listening comprehension, and attitudes toward school or self when tests were in other languages. The magnitude of effect sizes was influenced by the types of programs compared, language of the criterion instruments, academic domain of the criterion instruments, random versus non-random assignment of students to programs, formula used to calculate effect sizes, and types of scores reported in the studies. Programs characterized by instability and/or hostile environment were associated with lower effect sizes. The synthesized studies contained a variety of methodological weaknesses which affected the magnitude of the effect sizes. Initial group differences—in language dominance, in environmental language exposure, in need for the bilingual program—were not uncommon. In some cases, comparison groups contained bilingual program "graduates." In others, experimental groups changed in composition during the study through the exiting of successful students and their replacement with newcomers subsequent to pretesting and prior to posttesting. Although the technique of meta-analysis allows for statistical control of methodological inadequacies, the methodological inadequacies in the synthesized studies render the results less than definitive and highlight the need for quality research in the area of bilingual education. Problems inherent in conducting research on bilingual programs are discussed in relation to the outcomes of this synthesis, and guidelines for future research are proposed.

In spite of the fact that federally supported bilingual education has been implemented in the public schools of this country for a decade and a half, there is still a great deal of controversy over both federal and state policies regarding these programs. Diverse conclusions from the few existing reviews of literature on the effectiveness of bilingual education have provided no ready answers for policymakers have mainly fueled the arguments both supporting and opposing bilingual education. The one large-scale national evaluation of the Title VII bilingual programs (Danoff, Coles, McLaughlin & Reynolds, 1977a, 1977b, 1978) also produced more controversy than answers. Among reviewers finding evidence in support of bilingual education are Troike (1978) and Dulay and Burt (1978). Troike (1978), who reviewed seven select studies, concluded, "*Quality* bilingual programs *can* meet the goal of providing equal educational opportunity for students from non-English-speaking backgrounds" (p. 15, emphasis in original). Dulay and Burt (1978) reviewed twelve studies and concluded that bilingual education was successful because it either improved or did not hinder academic achievement in school. Engle (1975) found evidence inconclusive in answer to the question of whether or not reading instruction introduced in the first language led subsequently to a more rapid acquisition of reading skills in the second language.

Baker and de Kanter (1981) reviewed twenty-eight studies and concluded that the case for bilingual education is extremely weak. This review, done under the auspices of the Office of Planning, Budget, and Evaluation (OPBE) of the U.S. Department of Education, was widely publicized in the mass media and has influenced policy-makers at both state and federal levels.

The most extensive primary study to date, a nationwide evaluation of the ESEA Title VII programs (Danoff et al. 1977a, 1977b, 1978), yielded mixed results and produced a great deal of heated controversy due to widespread criticism of the research design and methodology (see, for example, Cardenas 1977; Gray 1977; O'Malley 1978).

The differences in conclusions reached in the various literature reviews and primary studies can be accounted for by several factors. These include (a) differences in the quality of the primary research studies on which conclusions were based, (b) variations in the set of studies selected by each reviewer, and (c) differences in the goals and foci of the reviewers.

With regard to quality, the inadequacy of research on bilingual education is evidenced by the fact that in each major attempt to review the research evidence, reviewers rejected a majority of the studies on methodological grounds (Baker and de Kanter 1981; Dulay and Burt 1978; Engle 1975; Troike 1978). For example, Troike (1978) reports that only seven of 150 research and evaluation reports surveyed at the Center for Applied Linguistics were adequate for inclusion in a review. Dulay and Burt (1978) surveyed 180 studies and found only twelve to be acceptable for review. Likewise, Baker and de Kanter (1981) found that only twenty-eight of 300 studies met their criteria for methodological adequacy. Inadequacies of the research studies in general were reflected in research design, in the failure to document or describe the educational programs under scrutiny, in the statistical treatments of the data, and in the failure to equate the experimental and comparison groups on such characteristics as language proficiency and socioeconomic status.

Differences in the selection criteria of the various reviewers are reflected by the fact that some studies accepted as methodologically adequate by one reviewer were rejected by others. A major reason for the disparate selection of studies stems from differences in the intents and goals of each reviewer that, in turn, determined not only which studies would be selected for review but also what questions would serve as foci for the review.

The purpose of the Troike review was to determine what kinds of effects *can* be produced by bilingual education programs rather than to evaluate bilingual programs in general. Given this framework, Troike focused on those studies that provided evidence to indicate that bilingual education *can* have a significant impact on school achievement. In contrast, Baker and de Kanter (1981) were interested in evaluation of the total spectrum of programs that have been implemented, regardless of program quality per se. Examining the impact of bilingual education on achievement in two subject areas, math and English, these authors focused on whether bilingual education accelerates children's learning over that in traditional education programs.

The types of questions asked by each of the reviewers highlights still another influence on the types of conclusions reached in each review: differences in the interpretations of what constitutes success for a bilingual program. Some reviewers interpret bilingual education to be successful as long as it does not hinder children in the learning of English while it promotes learning of the non-language subjects. Dulay and Burt (1978) concluded that bilingual education was successful in the studies they reviewed because it either improved or did not impede achievement in school. Similarly, Canadian researchers who have studied the impact of total-immersion programs consider the programs to be successful if the children can be taught in the second language and still maintain grade level in non-language subjects (Swain 1979). Other reviewers, such as Baker and de Kanter (1981), consider bilingual education to be effective only if it accelerates children's learning of English over what it would have been without the program.

The problems inherent in unravelling the tangled mass of evidence from the large variety of programs that have been studied have been addressed by Swain (1979), who points out that it is necessary to take into consideration differences in the various programs, in the children attending the programs, in the communities in which the programs operate, and in the research strategies employed in the studies themselves. As Swain points out, that is a rather large order: "Attempting to come to grips with all the literature, and all the contradictory conclusions reached in the various research and evaluation studies, quite simply, boggles the mind!" (p. 23).

Given the difficulties encountered to date in synthesizing evidence related to the effectiveness of bilingual education, the intent of the current study was to conduct a statistical synthesis of the literature on bilingual education using the methods of meta-analysis as described by Glass (1978) and Glass, McGaw, and Smith (1981). For a number of reasons, it was decided to synthesize the same body of literature that had been reviewed narratively by Baker and de Kanter. First, according to its authors, the Baker and de Kanter report was the most comprehensive review in existence at the time this synthesis was begun. Second, the report generated a great deal of controversy among researchers (Hernandez-Chavez, Llanes, Alvarez, and Arvizu 1982; Littlejohn 1981; Rotberg 1983; Seidner 1982; Willig 1982; Yates and Ortiz 1983) and was afforded national publicity in the mass media—publicity that ultimately influenced the decisions of state and federal educational policy-makers. Third, in selecting the studies to be included in their review, Baker and de Kanter fortuitously used criteria that heightened the possibility that the studies would be amenable to meta-analysis. It was believed that a resynthesis of the same literature, using the techniques of meta-analysis, would (a) provide a check on the Baker and de Kanter conclusions by using a different review methodology, (b) yield a comparison of the two methodologies, (c) extract detailed and meaningful information from the data sources that might provide a better understanding of the dynamics and effects of bilingual programs, and (d) identify research issues needing further attention that concern both meta-analysis and bilingual education.

In order to extract information that would be most meaningful for bilingual education in the United States, two selection criteria were added to those employed by Baker and de Kanter. These required that the programs that were the object of any study be located in the United States and that the programs be regular school programs representing kindergarten, primary, or secondary grades. These added restrictions had the effect of excluding five studies from the pool of twenty-eight that were addressed in the Baker and de Kanter review. The excluded studies were three Canadian reports (Barik and Swain 1975; Barik, Swain, and Nwanunobi 1977; Lambert and Tucker 1972) on total- or structured-immersion programs (to be explained below), one review of bilingual education in the Philippines (Ramos, Aguilar, and Sibayan 1967), and one U.S. study (McConnell 1980). The rationale for each of these exclusions is outlined below.

STUDIES EXCLUDED FROM THE SYNTHESIS

Canadian immersion programs

The Canadian immersion programs were not considered to be relevant to bilingual programs in the United States due to a number of basic differences in program goals, designs, and contexts. These differences have been reviewed in considerable detail by Swain (1979). Whereas bilingual education in the United States includes the use of two languages as a medium of instruction, structured-immersion programs in Canada typically have been programs where middle- to upper-class English-speaking monolingual students are instructed *totally* in French until the third or fourth year of schooling. Once the second language is learned, children begin to study in two languages and continue to do so throughout their school years. The goal is to have students learn a second language with no decrease in academic performance or native language skills. Students who participate in the programs are volunteered by parents who want their children to learn two languages. In contrast, children entering bilingual programs in the United States usually are of lower socioeconomic status and have a heterogeneous mixture of abilities in each language and a heterogeneous mixture of patterns of language use. Although two languages are used as a medium of instruction, there is a great deal of program variation in the allocation and organization of the languages across time intervals and subject matter. Furthermore, as soon as oral communication skills in English are considered to be adequate, the children tend to be exited from the programs and receive instruction only in English from that point on. The switch from the use of two languages to the exclusive use of English characterizes what are known as *transitional* bilingual programs. The goal of these programs is to have children learn a second language and at the same time to increase academic performance. When English skills are not totally mastered in the first few years of the programs, results are often interpreted negatively, even when there has been no decrease in academic skills.

The *enrichment* nature of the Canadian programs presents a striking contrast to the *compensatory* nature of the U.S. programs when one considers the result of the programs. In the United States, where children are exited to the regular school program as soon as they learn oral English, the second language will gradually replace the home language, which is often denigrated by the students themselves and by others in the dominant culture. The result is *subtractive bilingualism* where the child's total language competence is reduced. In the high status Canadian programs, both languages are ultimately maintained throughout the school years and the result is *additive* bilingualism, where total language competence is expanded.

The nature of program development in the two countries and research on the effectiveness of the programs in meeting their goals also contributes to the fruitlessness of comparing U.S. and Canadian programs. The Canadian programs have been characterized by slow and steady growth that has been integrated with well-financed curriculum and materials development and with a comprehensive plan of formative evaluation. Research tends to be longitudinal, following children from kindergarten to sixth grade and beyond. Whenever aggregated research and evaluation results on Canadian programs are reported, they represent programs that are similar in design and that serve student groups with homogeneous language characteristics.

In contrast, program development in the United States has been characterized by a shotgun implementation of numerous programs prior to the development of materials and curriculum and before trained teachers became available. There has been no integrated plan for evaluation and aggregated research results represent many program variations where heterogeneous language patterns exist both within and across programs. Typically researchers have failed to control for these variations or to consider the interaction of program characteristics with student and community characteristics (Swain 1979).

Although it is well known among bilingual educators that the Canadian immersion programs have been quite successful in meeting their goals, the very basic differences between these programs and U.S. bilingual programs precludes meaningful comparisons of program effectiveness between the two countries.

Other excluded studies

Since meta-analysis is most appropriate for primary studies, a report by Ramos et al. (1967) was also excluded from this synthesis. The report was not a primary study but a review of twenty years of findings from various studies on bilingual education in the Philippines. Just as in the U.S. studies, there was diversity in the results of the Philippines studies. Ramos et al. concluded that variations in the effectiveness of teaching children in their vernacular depended on the quality of teacher training and curriculum materials, and that whenever quality programs were implemented with adequate curriculum materials and teacher training, results of bilingual programs were highly favorable.

The final study excluded from this synthesis was an apparently very successful bilingual program in the United States (McConnell 1980). However, most of the results from this program were based on preschool or after-school supplementary programs that had been compared to non-treatment conditions, and there was no way to determine whether the effects were due to the extra instructional time or to the fact that the instruction used the students' native language. Initially, the intention was to include this study in the synthesis but effect sizes were so overwhelming in magnitude, favoring the bilingual program groups (about 1.9), that they totally skewed the distribution of effect sizes in the direction favoring bilingual education. Further investigation into alternative explanations that could account for these extraordinary results revealed that the scores used in lieu of a comparison group may well have included the scores of the experimental children in such a way that the design probably included aspects of a pre-post design. McConnell's comparison scores were an over-the-years accumulation of pretest scores of children who had entered the program at various ages. However, these scores appear to have been grouped by age in years. If this is the case, children who were post-tested at the end of their third year of age and who had entered the program at the beginning of their third year would be compared to the accumulated scores of all three-year-olds obtained when they entered the program. The comparison scores, then, would include the pretest scores of these same experimental children who were pretested at the beginning of their third year of age. In view of this problem, as well as the dissimilarity of this program to any other program in the set of studies., McConnell's study was excluded from the synthesis.

The twenty-three studies finally used in the present synthesis, then, were the following: American Institutes for Research (AIR) (1975), Ames and Bicks (1978), Balasubramonian, Seelye, and De Weffer (1973), Carsrud and Curtis (1979), Cohen (1975), Cottrell (1971), Covey (1973), Danoff et al. (1977a, 1977b, 1978), Huzar (1973), Kaufman (1968), Legarreta (1979), Lum (1971), Matthews (1979), McSpadden (1979, 1980), Moore and Parr (1979), Olesini (1971), Pena-Hughes and Solis (1980), Plante (1976), Skoczylas (1972), Stebbins, St. Pierre, Proper, Anderson, and Cerva (1977), Stern (1975), and Zirkel (1972).

Specific issues guiding the synthesis included the following: (a) the effects of bilingual education on the learning of the second language, including all identifiable sub-areas or aspects of the language; (b) the effects of bilingual education on mathematics achievement and on all other school subjects for which information was available, such as science, social studies, and first-language arts; (c) the influence of bilingual education on school attendance or dropout rates, as well as attitudes and self-concept; (d) the mediating effects of substantive variables, such as program designs, characteristics of the program settings, of the students, teachers, and community; and (e) the mediating effects of the research designs and methodological characteristics of the individual studies.

METHOD

Coding of the studies

Variables coded for inclusion. The variables coded and included in this study can be organized roughly into seven categories. These include (a) information necessary for the calculation of effect sizes, (b) measurement variables, (c) characteristics of the primary research and research methodology, (d) characteristics of the students or samples in the primary studies, (e) characteristics of the teachers, (f) characteristics of the educational projects, and (g) characteristics of the actual programs. Detailed codes were developed for a total of 183 variables represented by these categories. Also included were a number of variables indicating that certain codes were based on coder assumptions rather than explicit information. This was necessary whenever, in the absence of explicit information, a reasonable assumption could be made on the basis of implicit information or other evidence reported in the study. Although the accuracy of information based on such assumptions is far from ideal, the documentation of assumptions did provide some degree of control and allowed for more information to be included than would have been possible otherwise.

Coding protocols. All coding was done from original versions of the studies. This introduces a difference from the Baker and de Kanter (1981) review, which sometimes based information on summaries or second-person reviews of studies. Whenever information necessary for coding was not included in the studies, every effort was made to obtain the information from the authors. Additional sources of information included copies of published tests that had been used in the studies as well as the manuals accompanying these tests. The test manuals provided information for coding test reliabilities, while perusal of an actual test often led to a more accurate coding of the domain of the test. For unpublished tests, such information was not available.

Not only were authors consulted and library resources used during the coding, but in one case (Kaufman, 1968), means and standard deviations from the primary study were recalculated in order to obtain statistics based on raw scores. This was necessary because the data reported were based on grade-equivalent scores that were considered to be inappropriate for use in statistical analyses. Although a few other studies also reported data based on grade equivalent scores, complete information necessary for the conversion back to raw scores was available only for the Kaufman study.

Coding reliability. The entire set of studies was precoded by the author during the preparation of the coding manual and again after completion of the manual. To check the reliability of the coding process, approximately one-third of the studies were coded a second time by research assistants. Coding reliabilities were calculated for each study in terms of the percentage or proportion of agreement between the coders across the total set of variables. These proportions ranged from .79 to .91 for the seven studies in the reliability check: specific proportions were .79, .81, .83, .85, .85, .89, and .91. Examination of coder agreement across the variables within each study revealed almost perfect agreement for the quantitative information, while agreement decreased with increases in the subjectivity of the coded information. The lowest agreement percentages represented those studies that included the least amount of information since a greater number of coder inferences had to be made in those cases.

Estimation of effect sizes

Variations of effect size formulas. The preferred formula for estimating effect sizes when integrating studies that use treatment and comparison groups is the simple difference between the mean of the treatment group and the comparison group on the final status scale, divided by the standard deviation of the comparison group (Glass et al. 1981). Other estimates of effect size are also possible when the reporting form of the data in the studies precludes a straightforward application of the basic formula (Glass et al. 1981; McGaw and Glass 1980).

The formulas suggested by these authors were used in this study, with the preferred choice always that which would enable the effect size to come closest to the utilization of raw scores on the final status scale in the numerator and a standard deviation based on the final status scale of the comparison group in the denominator. The choice of formula depended on the information supplied in the particular study for which effect sizes were being calculated. Even with the options described, not all studies provided sufficient information to enable the calculation of effect sizes.

Correcting for bias in effect sizes. Hedges (1981) devised a correction factor for effect sizes after demonstrating that estimates yield inflated effect sizes when samples are small. The correction factor was applied to all effect sizes calculated in this study using Hedge's formula:

$$c(m) = \frac{1 - 3}{4m - 1}$$

where $c(m)$ is the correction factor and m is the sample size of the comparison group.

Weighting of effect sizes. Many of the studies included in this synthesis contained multiple scores from the same students, such as a number of scores representing various tests and subtests. The simple tabulation of all effect sizes would mean that studies reporting many scores would weigh more heavily in the analyses than studies reporting only one or a few scores. Since averaging the total number of scores for each study would result in a loss of information, effect sizes were weighted by the reciprocal of the number of effect sizes from each independent sample. Thus sample, rather than study, was used as the independent unit. This procedure satisfied the independence requirements of inferential procedures while making it unnecessary to aggregate the findings above levels at which more interesting relationships could be studied (Steinkamp and Machr 1984). When variables related to specific academic domains were included in an analysis, weights were still based on independent samples, but they represented the reciprocal of the number of effect sizes for each independent sample *within* the various categories of test domain.

Statistical procedures

In all of the statistical analyses, the dependent variable was the estimated effect size corrected for bias with Hedge's correction factor. Independent variables were the characteristics of the research, participants, and educational programs. During the first stage of analysis, the contribution of each independent variable to the variance in effect sizes was examined with one-way analyses of variance or, in the case of continuous variables, bivariate linear regressions, using programs from Nie, Hull, Jenkins, Steinbrenner, and Bent (1975). The R^2 values from these analyses were plotted and those variables with values greater than .20, as well as all conceptually important variables, were retained for the second stage of analysis.

In the second stage of analysis, the retained independent variables were combined and entered into multifactor analyses using the Type III general linear model approach to the analysis of variance described in Freund and Littell (1981). This effects, including interactions. The procedure corresponds to Yate's weighted squares of means analysis, which is described in Steel and Torrie (1980) and Searle (1971). Although Hedges and Stock (1983) have suggested a slightly different model for the analysis of effect sizes, their re-analyses of data from Glass and Smith (1979) and Smith and Glass (1980) ultimately did not suggest substantial changes in the conclusions drawn in those studies. Consequently, the procedure described by Freund and Littell (1981) and programmed by the SAS Institute (1979) was used in the current analyses.

The most parsimonious combination of variables for explaining the variance of the effect sizes was determined by entering into these analyses those variables deemed essential for statistical control (for example, effect size formula, type of score, and language in which tests were administered), as well as the variable that indicated the types of programs compared in each individual study. The remaining variables were then tested until a model was determined that would account for the maximum proportion of the total variance of effect sizes and that, at the same time, would sacrifice the smallest number of effect sizes during the listwise deletion for missing data.

RESULTS

Overview

Three major types of findings emerged from the current synthesis. The first identified from a large group of variables those that conjointly accounted for the major portion of the variance of effect sizes across studies. These were (a) types of programs compared, (b) academic domain of the criterion instruments, (c) language of the criterion instruments, (d) random or nonrandom assignment of children to the experimental or comparison programs, (e) effect size formulas, (f) type of score, and (g) the interaction of domain of test by language of test.

Inspection of the adjusted means for these variables produced the second major finding: that there were overall significant, positive effects for bilingual education programs both for tests administered in English and tests administered in Spanish. When effect sizes were categorized by academic domain, significant effects favoring bilingual education when compared to submersion were found for (a) reading in English, (b) language in English, (c) mathematics in English, and (d) total achievement in English. For tests not administered in English, significant effects favoring bilingual education were found for (a) listening comprehension, (b) reading, (c) writing, (d) total language, (e) mathematics, (f) social studies, and (g) attitudes toward school or self. Supplementary analyses based on those studies that did not report sufficient information to permit the calculation of effect sizes also supported these results. These analyses were simple chi square tests for tallies of outcomes that did or did not favor bilingual education.

The third major finding was the fact that the quality of the research studies, as reflected by uncontrolled differences between experimental and comparison groups, contributed significantly to the results of the studies. Studies that failed to use random assignment of students to experimental and comparison groups produced inequitable comparisons between bilingual program students and students who differed in language dominance and/or their need for a bilingual program. Furthermore, some comparison groups contained students who had been successfully exited from bilingual programs and some experimental groups changed in composition in such a way that, subsequent to the pretest and prior to the post-test, the better students were exited and students in greater need of the program were added. Actual program variables that affected the results of the studies were the stability of the experimental program and the use of comparison programs that were similar to the bilingual programs.

Findings for each category of results are detailed in this section. Preceding the major findings, however, is a description of the final database and its comparison to the data yielded by the narrative review (Baker and de Kanter 1981) where outcomes were counted with simple tallies of statistical significance.

Effect sizes by individual studies

Coding of the twenty-three studies yielded a total of 714 instances where treatment groups were contrasted with comparison groups on a criterion instrument. Effect sizes were estimable for 513 of these contrasts and represented seventy-five independent samples from sixteen of the studies. Only positive and negative tallies (vote scores) could be recorded for the remaining seven studies due to insufficient information for the calculation of effect sizes. Since these tallies provide minimal information and merely indicate whether outcomes favor one group or another (regardless of statistical significance), results based on the analysis of effect sizes constitute the major findings.

Table 15.1 lists the studies that yielded effect sizes as well as the number of effect sizes, mean effect sizes, and standard deviations for each academic domain represented in each study. It is important to note that this group of studies, as well as those for which only vote scores were calculable, is characterized in general by a great deal of diversity in the types of programs studied, both bilingual and other. Furthermore, there is a general paucity of information concerning the nature of the programs in terms of program design, curriculum and curriculum materials, and characteristics of the staff. Thus the results of this synthesis are based on a conglomerate of programs, only a few of which offer detailed information on the characteristics of the experimental treatments.

To allow for a comparison of the kind of information supplied by meta-analysis and that obtained with the traditional method of synthesis, the effect sizes in Table 15.1 are further categorized according to the language in which tests were administered. This allows for the juxtaposition of effect sizes to the corresponding portions of the summary table found in Baker and de Kanter (1981). Since Baker and de Kanter summarized differences that were based on statistical significance only, the tallies in their table that indicate no differences refer to a lack of statistical significance.

On a study-by-study basis, there appears to be a fair amount of correspondence between the effect sizes for any given study and the tallies from the Baker and de Kanter table, especially when one notes the standard deviations of the various effect sizes. Inspection of effect sizes, however, provides the reader with a better feel for the direction and size of differences between groups even in the absence of statistical significance. For example, when there is not a statistically significant difference between experimental and comparison groups, the magnitude and direction of an effect size will still indicate which group actually fared better on a test even if the difference did not reach significance. *A positive effect size indicates that the experimental group fared better, while a negative effect size indicates that the comparison group fared better. The magnitude of an effect size indicates the difference between the groups in standard deviation units relative to the standard deviation of the control group.* For example, a positive effect size of .33 would indicate that the experimental group scored about one-third of a standard deviation higher than the comparison group, while an effect size of –.33 would indicate that the experimental group scored about one-third of a standard deviation below the comparison group. Assuming equal within-group variances and normal distributions, an effect size of .33 could also be interpreted to mean that the average student in the experimental group would be at the sixty-third percentile of the comparison group.

It is precisely the nature of the information contained in an effect size that accounts for differences between syntheses based on vote scores and meta-analyses. Whereas differences found in each study may have insufficient power to reach statistical significance, an accumulation of estimates of the magnitudes of differences from many studies increases both this power and the likelihood of detecting true differences between treatment conditions. As will be seen later in this section, such accumulations did indeed detect differences favoring bilingual education in a number of academic areas.

Major variables influencing effect sizes

Table 15.2 presents the analysis of variance that includes the most parsimonious combination of variables for explaining variation in the effect sizes. The variables in this model were extracted from a group of twelve variables identified during the first stage of analysis that were essential conceptually or that had R^2 values of sufficient magnitude to warrant their further study. Among the variables in the first stage of analysis that did *not* demonstrate sufficient systematic variation to be retained for further study were the grade level of the samples and sample size. Bivariate regressions

TABLE 15.1 A Study-by-Study Comparison of Effect Size Data With Vote Scores From the OPBE Report

Study	*N* of ESs	Mean ES	SD of ESs	Summary of vote scores from Baker and de Kanter
Carsrud & Curtis, 1980				
Five samples, grades 2–5				English: TBE better than submersion in one grade; TBE no different from submersion in one grade
Range of *n*'s[b]: 32–513				
Bilingual ed. vs. submersion				
Tests in English				
Total language	6	.10	.18	Math: TBE no different from submersion
Math	4	.12	.16	
Total achievement	5	.15	.11	
Tests in Spanish				
Reading/reading vocabulary	30	.39	.31	
Total language	12	.62	.48	
Total achievement	5	.16	.12	
Cohen 1975				
Three samples, grades K-3				English: TBE no different from submersion on 86 of 100 language skills; submersion better than TBE on 11; TBE better than submersion on three
Range of *n*'s[b]: 9–90				
Bilingual ed. vs. submersion				
Tests in English				
Oral production	54	−.35	.54	Math: TBE no different from submersion in two of three grades; TBE better than submersion in one grade
Listening comprehension	4	.05	.59	
Writing language	5	−.16	.40	
Total language	20	−.14	.52	
Math	3	.32	.86	
Tests in Spanish				
Oral production	54	−.11	.58	
Writing language	5	.81	.25	
Total language	21	.06	.62	
Total achievement	3	.43	.50	
Attitudes/self-concept	6	.39	.49	
Covey 1973				
One sample, grade 9				
Range of *n*'s[b]: 152–180				English: TBE better than submersion
Bilingual ed. vs. submersion				
Tests in English				Math: TBE no different from submersion
Reading/reading vocabulary	1	.74	.0	
Total language	1	.36	.0	
Math	1	.27	.0	
Attitudes/self-concept	4	.74	.31	
Danoff et al. 1977a, 1977b, 1978				
27 samples, grades 2–6				
Range of *n*'s[b]: 20–1,453				English: Submersion better than TBE

TABLE 15.1 (Continued)

Bilingual ed. vs. submersion				
Tests in English				Math: TBE no different from submersion
Reading/reading vocabulary	22	.01	.17	
Total language	22	–.06	.19	
Math	12	.03	.17	
Tests in Spanish				
Math	10	.21	.19	
Attitudes/self-concept	5	.10	.16	
Huzar 1973				
Three samples, grades 2–3				
Range of *n*'s[b]: 76–84				English: TBE no different from submersion
Bilingual ed. vs. submersion				
Tests in English				
Total language	4	.27	.36	
Kaufman 1968				
Two samples, junior high				
Range of *n*'s[b]: 45–50				English: TBE better than submersion on two component scores of a standardized achievement test and no different on seven component scores in one school; TBE no different from submersion on nine tests in another school
Bilingual ed. vs. submersion				
Tests in English				
Reading/reading vocabulary	3	.31	.34	
Writing language	1	.54	.0	
Total language	2	.41	.44	
Tests in Spanish				
Reading/reading vocabulary	4	1.34	.17	
Total language	2	1.39	.27	
Legarrela 1979				
Four samples, grade K				
Range of *n*'s[b]13–52				
Bilingual ed. vs. submersion				English: TBE better than submersion or TBE no different from submersion, depending on the test; TBE with ESL better than TBE without ESL component.[c]
Tests in English				
Listening comprehension	1	.66	.0	
Submersion/ESL plus bilingual/ESL vs. same combination, no ESL				
Tests in English				
Communicative competence	1	–.41	.0	
Listening comprehension	1	.82	.0	
Tests in Spanish				
Communicative competence	1	–.71	.0	

TABLE 15.1 (Continued)

Alternate immersion vs. concurrent translation				
Tests in English				
Communicative competence	1	.71	.0	
Listening comprehension	1	1.34	.0	
Tests in Spanish				
Communicative competence	2	2.17	.08	
Lum 1971				
Five samples, grade 1				English: ESL alone better than TBE on three tests; ESL alone no different from TBE on two tests
Total *n* of students[b]: 55				
Bilingual ed./ESL vs. submersion/ ESL				
Tests in English				
Oral production	3	–.82	.22	
Total language	2	–.15	.19	
McSpadden 1980				
Four samples, grades K-2				
Range of *n*'s[b]: 57–103				English: Submersion better than TBE in one of three grades; TBE no different from submersion in two grades
Bilingual ed. vs. submersion				
Tests in English				Math: Submersion better than TBE in one of two grades; TBE no different from submersion in two grades
Total achievement	10	.09	.39	
Total language	1	.47	.0	
Math	4	–.22	.79	
McSpadden 1979				
Two samples, grades K-1				English: TBE no different from submersion
Range of *n*'s[b]; 60–98				
Bilingual ed. vs. submersion				
Tests in English				Math: TBE no different from submersion
Listening comprehension	1	.42	.0	
Reading/reading vocabulary	4	.20	.20	
Math	2	.37	.36	
Tests in French				
Listening comprehension	2	3.04	.37	
Total language	2	1.67	.15	
Math	2	2.59	.84	
Social studies	2	1.67	.23	
Olesini 1971				
Range of *n*'s[b]: 25–60				English: TBE better than submersion in one of three components of a standardized test; TBE no different from submersion in one component

TABLE 15.1 (Continued)

Bilingual ed. vs. submersion				
Tests in English				
Reading/reading vocabulary	4	.97	.30	Math: TBE better than submersion on one component of a standardized test; TBE no different from submersion on one component
Total language	4	.37	.24	
Math	4	.56	.30	
Total achievement	3	.62	.08	
Pena-Hughes & Solis 1980				
One sample, grade K				English: Immersion[d] better than TBE
Total *n* of students[b]: 156				
Alternate immersion vs. concurrent translation				
Tests in English				
Total language	1	.64	.0	
Tests in Spanish				
Total language	1	.39	.0	
Stebbins et al. 1977				
Five samples, grades K-3				English: TBE no different from submersion
Range of *n*'s[b]; 164–219				
Bilingual ed. vs. submersion				Math: TBE no different from submersion
Tests in English				
Reading/reading vocabulary	10	–.06	.43	
Total language	25	.03	.39	
Math	20	.13	.32	
Total achievement	5	.15	.20	
Attitudes/self-concept	5	.05	.30	
Skoczylas 1972				
One sample, grade 1				English: TBE no different from submersion
Total *n* of students[b]: 47				
Bilingual ed./ESL vs. submersion/ESL				Math: Submersion better than TBE
Tests in English				
Oral production	1	.37	.0	
Listening comprehension	1	.13	.0	
Math	1	–.65	.0	
Tests in Spanish				
Oral production	1	.65	.0	
Listening comprehension	1	–.27	.0	
Total achievement	1	.21	.0	
Stern 1975				
Four samples, grades 4–6				English: Submersion better than TBE
Range of *n*'s[b]; 64–225				
Bilingual ed. vs. submersion				Math: Submersion better than TBE

TABLE 15.1 (Continued)

Tests in English				
Reading/reading vocabulary	8	−.48	.22	
Total language	8	−.42	.27	
Math	16	−.45	.13	
Total achievement	4	−.50	.15	
Zirkel 1972				
Five samples, grades 1–3				English: TBE better than submersion on one test: TBE no different from submersion on four tests
Range of *n*'s[b]: 18–104				
Bilingual ed. vs. submersion				
Tests in English				
Total achievement	2	.22	.20	
Tests in Spanish				
Total achievement	2	.17	.06	
Attitudes/self-concept	2	.03	.01	
Bilingual/ESL vs. submersion/ESL				
Tests in English				
Total achievement	2	1.17	.82	
Tests in Spanish				
Total achievement	2	.44	.31	
Attitudes/self-concept	2	.12	.36	
Support/ESL vs. submersion/ESL				
Tests in English				
Total achievement	1	−.01	.0	
Tests in Spanish				
Total achievement	1	−.33	.0	
Attitudes/self-concept	1	−.29	.0	

[a] Copied from Baker and de Kanter 1981, Table 1.
[b] Ranges or totals represent *n*'s associated with individual ESs.
[c] This comparison of TBE with ESL vs. TBE without ESL apparently refers to Legarreta's data from a submersion program with ESL that was combined with data from a bilingual program with ESL and then compared to combined data from submersion without ESL and bilingual education without ESL. In effect, this yielded an ESL vs. a non-ESL condition.
[d] Baker and de Kanter consider this program to be a total-immersion program, while Pena and Hughes describe it as an alternate immersion program and compare it to another bilingual program.

of effect size with grade level and with sample size yielded R^2 values of only .01 and .03, respectively, and p values of .38 and .12. Consequently, effect sizes were aggregated across grade levels and sample sizes for the remaining analyses.

In the model presented in Table 15.2, six variables were found to account conjointly for about 50 percent of the total variance of effect sizes. These include the types of programs compared, academic domain of the criterion instrument, language of the criterion instrument, assignment of students to programs (random versus matched groups and unknown types of assignment), and two variables that demonstrated sufficient systematic variation to necessitate their inclusion for statistical control—the formulas used to calculate effect sizes and the types of scores reported in the studies (for example, raw scores, percentiles, grade equivalents, or others). Each of the six variables accounted for a significant portion of the variance in effect sizes even with the variance of the remaining variables held constant.

In examining more detailed information concerning the variables in Table 15.2, it was noted that 466 of the 495 effect sizes came from comparisons of bilingual programs to submersion programs. The thin spread of data over the remaining types of comparisons precluded the examination in this model of the interaction of domain of test by language of test, a variable that would add too many categories to the analysis. To examine this interaction variable, an additional multifactor analysis of variance, shown in Table 15.3, was carried out on data representing only comparisons of bilingual versus submersion programs. This made it possible to include the interaction of the language of the criterion tests with the academic domain of the tests.

The six variables in Table 15.3 account conjointly for 63 percent of the total variance of effect sizes when bilingual education is compared only to submersion programs. Each of the six variables, including the interaction of test language by test domain, accounts for a significant portion of the variance in effect sizes when the variance of the remaining variables is held constant.

Patterns of variation in the major variables

Table 15.4 reveals in more detail the patterns of variation that are reflected by the independent variables in the above analyses by showing the adjusted means for effect sizes and their standard errors for each category of the individual variables. The adjusted means may be interpreted as indicating the best possible estimate of the mean effect size when the effects of the five other major variables are held constant. Although the adjusted means are the most relevant due to the fact that they control for the effects of the remaining variables, there is always the possibility of over- or under-adjustments in analyses of this type; thus unadjusted means are also presented for the reader's

TABLE 15.2 Analysis of Variance of Effect Sizes for Bilingual vs. Submersion Programs Only With Language by Domain Interaction[a]

Variable	df	Sum of squares[b]	*F* value	PR F
Academic domain of criterion	8	2.05	2.75	.0057
Language of criterion	1	3.10	33.31	.0001
Assignment to programs	2	1.02	5.49	.0044
Effect size formula	6	4.66	8.34	.0001
Type of score	5	3.28	7.05	.0001
Language of test by domain	7	2.38	3.66	.0008

Note: SS model = 48.00: SS error = 40.60: df = 29/436: $F = 17.44$: $p = .0001$: multiple $R^2 = 63$.
[a] Effect sizes weighted by independent sample within domain of test.
[b] SS value takes into account the pesence of all variables in the model.

TABLE 15.3 Analysis of Variance of Effect Sizes With Multiple Independent Variables[a]

Variable	df	Sum of squares[b]	*F* value	PR F
Types of program compared	4	2.20	5.29	.0004
Academic domain of criterion	8	2.53	3.04	.0024
Language of criterion	1	6.72	64.70	.0001
Assignment to programs	2	2.54	12.20	.0001
Effect size formula	6	7.97	12.78	.0001
Type of score	5	3.33	6.40	.0001

Note: SS model = 48.85; SS error = 48.63; df = 26/468: $F = .0001$: multiple $R^2 = .50$.
[a] Effect sizes weighted by independent sample within domain of test.
[b] SS value takes into account the presence of all variables in the model.

interest. The means presented for all variables except the academic domain and the interaction of academic domain by language of test are those that accompany Table 15.2 and include all types of bilingual programs. Adjusted means were not obtainable across all types of programs for the test domain or interaction with language due to the thin spread of scores across programs as previously described. Adjusted means were obtainable for these two variables when the analysis was restricted to the 466 effect sizes representing comparisons of bilingual programs to traditional (submersion) programs. Thus the means and adjusted means for the academic domain of criterion instrument and the interaction of this variable with language of test represent the comparisons of bilingual education and submersion that accompany the analysis presented in Table 15.3.

An overall observation to be made about Table 15.4 is that almost every adjusted mean has a positive value, which indicates that test scores favor the experimental groups. These results will be described below in greater detail for each of the variables presented in the table, beginning with the types of programs that are represented by the experimental groups.

Means for types of programs compared. Examination of the mean effect sizes for the various types of programs demonstrates that a positive effect is produced by bilingual program participation once other important sources of variation are held constant. Categories 1 and 2 reflect the major comparisons between bilingual programs and submersion programs. For example, category 1 indicates an adjusted mean effect size of .63 for 466 comparisons between bilingual programs (with and without English as a Second Language [ESL] instruction) and traditional or submersion programs that did not include ESL instruction. The second comparison, with a mean of .60, yielded similar results when bilingual programs that included ESL were compared to submersion programs that also included ESL. Both of these means are significantly different from 0, indicating a positive effect when all test scores are aggregated across domain and language of test and means are adjusted for these aggregated variables. (Effect size means for the categories of both language and domain of test are presented in Table 15.4 and will be discussed in turn.)

Interpretation of the mean effect size is facilitated if it is recalled that the magnitude of the effect sizes, as calculated in this synthesis, are interpretable in terms of the standard deviation of the comparison group. This means that when compared to groups of students in traditional all-English (submersion) programs, the bilingual experimental groups scored almost two-thirds of a standard deviation higher on the criterion instruments than the comparisons groups when other major sources of variation were controlled. Cohen's (1969) interpretation of an effect size of .20 as small, .50 as medium, and .80 as large provides an additional point of reference for interpreting these effect sizes. Still another way of interpreting effect sizes is to assume that the effect sizes of the treatment and comparison groups are from normal distributions and to view them in terms of sets of overlapping normal distributions. Using this interpretation, an effect size of .63, such as that favoring bilingual over submersion programs, would indicate that the average student in the bilingual programs scored higher than 74 percent of the students in the traditional programs when all test scores were aggregated.

The remaining three categories under Types of Programs Compared reflect miscellaneous comparisons based on a limited number of effect sizes. For example, the third category compares programs with and without ESL by combining scores from a traditional program that included ESL and a bilingual program that included ESL, and comparing them to a similar combination of scores from programs that did not include ESL. The three comparisons came from the same study (Legarreta 1979), and the adjusted mean effect size of –.05 indicates little or no difference between the groups receiving ESL and those not receiving ESL. The p value for a test of the hypothesis that the mean does not differ from zero supports this interpretation. Although the nature of the data precludes the inclusion in the same analysis of Types of Programs and the interaction of domain and language of test, it is important to note that the aggregation of scores from different types of tests, even with

TABLE 15.4 Adjusted Means, Standard Error of the Adjusted Means, and Background Information on Independent Variables From the Multifactor Analyses of Variance

Variable	*N* of ESs[a]	Unadjusted mean[b]	Adjusted mean[b]	Std. error adj. mean	$p > T$[c]
Types of programs compared[d]					
Bilingual vs. submersion	466	.09	.63	.09	.0001
Bilingual/ESL. vs. submersion/ESL	17	.07	.60	.15	.0002
Submersion, bilingual/ESL vs. submersion, bilingual/no ESL	3	–.10	–.05	.33	.8788
Two bilingual models	6	1.24	1.19	.19	.0001
"Support"/ESL vs. submersion/ESL	3	–.21	.13	.26	.6216
Assignment to programs[d]					
True random assignment	27	.78	1.02	.19	.0001
Matched groups	85	.06	.20	.15	.1717
Unknown	383	.07	.26	.13	.0356
Language of criterion test[d]					
English	316	–.03	.26	.12	.0370
Non-English	179	.33	.74	.13	.0001
Academic domain of criterion[c]					
Listening comprehension	4	1.79	1.36	.23	.0001
Social studies	2	1.68	—[f]	—[f]	—[f]
General/total achievement	26	.11	.42	.16	.0070
Oral production	108	–.23	.25	.20	.2231
Total language	122	.15	.47	.08	.0001
Reading/reading vocabulary	96	.21	.53	.11	.0001
Math	75	.08	.38	.09	.0001
Writing language	11	.34	.68	.35	.0509
Attitudes/self-concept	22	.28	.42	.11	.0002
Interaction: language of test by domain of test[c]					
English					
Oral production	54	–.35	.13	.27	.6333
Listening comprehension	2	.54	.20	.32	.5422
Reading/reading vocabulary	62	.05	.20	.08	.0161
Writing language	6	–.05	.17	.35	.6332
Total language	85	.01	.21	.07	.0071
Math	63	–.02	.18	.08	.0427
Total achievement	19	.09	.33	.10	.0020
Attitudes/self-concept	9	.36	.26	.15	.0743
Non-English					
Oral production	54	–.11	.36	.27	.1745
Listening comprehension	2	3.05	2.52	.28	.0001
Reading/reading vocabulary	34	.50	.86	.18	.0001
Writing language	5	.81	1.18	.57	.0405
Total language	37	.50	.73	.11	.0001
Math	12	.61	.58	.12	.0001
Total achievement	7	.16	.51	.28	.0696

TABLE 15.4 *(Continued)*

Social studies	2	1.68	1.06	.25	.0001
Attitudes/self-concept	13	.22	.58	.15	.0002
Type of score from test[d]					
Raw scores	254	.25	.56	.11	.0001
Grade equivalents	18	.42	.67	.17	.0001
Percentiles	36	–.46	.16	.16	.3179
Standard scores	7	.62	.54	.21	.0108
Expanded standard scores	70	.03	.61	.15	.0001
Rating scales	110	–.09	.44	.15	.0029
Effect size formula[d]					
$x_c – x_c / S_c$	26	.52	.21	.15	.1659
Same as above using adjusted means	15	1.33	1.38	.19	.0001
$l \sqrt{1 / n_c + 1 / n_c}$	75	–.09	.26	.16	.1083
Same as above, but *t* obtained from adjusted *F* statistic	91	–.08	.14	.15	.3711
$϶_c – ϶_c / S_{Gc}$*	38	.44	.69	.16	.0001
$϶_c – ϶_c / S_{Gc}$*	185	.06	.31	.13	.0182
Adjusted difference between means, divided by S_c	65	.06	.49	.19	.0115

[a] After listwise deletion of cases with missing data.
[b] Based on data weighted by sample within academic domain of test.
[c] HO: adjusted mean = 0.
[d] These means are from multifactor analysis in Table 15.2.
[e] These means are from multifactor analysis in Table 15.3 and represent effect sizes from bilingual vs. submersion programs only.
[f] Nonestimable.
* $϶_c$ and $϶_c$ indicate mean gain scores of experimental and control groups, respectively; S_{Gc} indicates a standard deviation of the comparison group's gain scores, while S_c is the standard deviation based on raw scores of the control group on the final status scale.

statistical adjustments for this aggregation, masks important variation that is of conceptual significance. This is illustrated in this instance by the breakdown of the unadjusted means for the Legarrela study (in Table 15.1), which shows an effect size of –.41 for communicative competence and an effect size of .82 for listening comprehension.

Six effect sizes from kindergarten programs in two different studies form the basis for the fourth category under Types of Programs Compared. Here, a mean effect size of 1.19 was obtained when different types of bilingual programs were compared, indicating that under certain circumstances some models are more effective than others. These programs will be discussed more fully later in this chapter.

The final program comparison represents a situation where a submersion program that included ESL and had a bilingual aide was compared to another submersion program with ESL that did not have a bilingual aide. For the current synthesis, this treatment program was categorized as a "support" program, reflecting the fact that it was not actually a bilingual program and that its major distinguishing characteristic was the presence of a bilingual aide. The mean for the three effect sizes in this situation was .13 and was not significantly different from zero.

Language of test by academic domain of test. The adjusted mean effect sizes that are broken down according to the Academic Domain of Criterion and the Language of the Criterion Tests in Table IV are all positive and, with the exception of the domain of oral production, significantly different from 0. Since this group of means represents scores aggregated across the domains and the languages of the tests (for bilingual versus submersion programs only), the effect sizes in the latter part of Table 15.4 are more meaningful and will be considered next. These effect sizes represent the interaction of the domain of test by the language of the test. As noted, these means also are based solely on those comparisons of bilingual education programs to submersion programs.

When tests were administered in English, significant adjusted means ($p < .05$) favoring bilingual education were found for tests in reading (.20), total language (.21), math (.18), and total achievement (.33). Although the means for listening comprehension, writing, and attitudes were of similar magnitude (.20, .17, and .26, respectively), there were too few effect sizes and too great a spread in these categories to allow for statistical significance. The similarity in magnitude of these effect sizes suggests that with a larger database, significant positive effects might also be found for these subject areas.

Although the adjusted mean for tests of oral production in English was positive, it was not significant. The standard error of this mean suggests that there was considerable variation in the effect sizes in this category. It is interesting to note that there is a similar pattern for the adjusted mean effect size for oral production tests that were *not* in English, even though this mean was larger.

The adjusted mean effect sizes for tests administered in languages other than English were all positive and, with the exception of oral production and total achievement, all significant. The largest effect sizes, all greater than one standard deviation, were for listening comprehension, writing, and social studies. Reading, total language, math, and self-concept also yielded large to medium effect sizes of .86, .73, .58, and .58, respectively. The non-significant mean for total achievement (.51) represents only seven effect sizes.

In sum, the adjusted means for the various types of programs compared indicate a positive effect for bilingual education when other important variables are controlled. Although the absolute magnitude of such effects can only be estimated given the limitations of the present database, indications from the next variable to be described suggest that these estimates might be fairly accurate if research in bilingual education were to include more studies with rigorous research designs.

Random versus nonrandom assignment to programs. The aspect of research design most potent for the studies included in this synthesis is whether or not random assignment was used to determine which children would be in the experimental and control groups. The largest number of effect sizes came from studies that contained no information concerning the manner in which experimental and comparison groups were formed. Since these studies tended to contain little information describing methodology and appeared in general to be of poorer quality than those where explicit reporting procedures were used, the assignment to programs by unknown criteria is assumed to be nonrandom. The adjusted mean effect size for groups formed through true random assignment, with the variance of the five remaining variables held constant, is 1.02, while means for the groups formed through matching or by unknown criteria are .20 and .26, respectively. Interpretation of these effect sizes in terms of overlapping normal distributions, as described earlier, indicates that when the experimental design was based on random assignment, the average student in the randomized bilingual groups scored higher than 85 percent of the students in the comparison groups—an impressive difference indeed.

Variables reflecting artifacts of the meta-analysis. The two remaining variables in Table 15.4 were entered into the analyses for purposes of statistical control. Means for the Effect Size Formulas indicate that the highest effect sizes were based on calculations using the adjusted means that were reported in the primary studies. The high means from adjusted sources could reflect either more favorable results when factors within a study were controlled or higher means influenced by the formula used, or both. Additional variation, both for this variable and for Type of Score, probably reflects variations due to differences in the studies more than anything else. For example, the low effect sizes based on percentile scores all came from the same study (Stern 1975). As will be discussed later, there are numerous other explanations for the low effect sizes found in this study.

Additional influential variables

In addition to the set of variables entered into the multifactor analyses just discussed, other variables demonstrating high R^2 values from the initial one-way analyses of variance revealed a pattern that was remarkably consistent with the part of the factorial analysis that examined the effects of nonrandom assignment. These variables could not be included in the factorial analysis due to limited numbers of effect sizes, high intercorrelations, or the nesting of these variables within other major variables. However, the conceptual importance of the results from these one-way analyses warrants their presentation for illustrative purposes. These results are presented in Table 15.5 along with the unadjusted means (weighted by sample) and other background information. Superscripts attached to the mean values indicate which means belong to the same classification when subjected to a Scheffe Test with alpha set at .05.

The variables presented in Table 15.5 provide explanatory information concerning the importance of random assignment to research in bilingual education in that they reflect direct outcomes

TABLE 15.5 Results of One-Way Analyses of Variance for Relevant Variables

Variable	*N* of ESs	*N* of samples	Mean ES: weighted[a]	SD
Language dominance of students				
Both exp and comp groups Spanish-dominant	224	14	.43	.78
Both exp and comp groups English-dominant	70	18	.02	.19
Exp group is Spanish-dominant; comp group is English-dominant	40	11	.08	.32
($F = 2.95$; $df = 2/40$: $p = .0637$)				
Why comps not in bilingual program				
Eliminated thru random assignment	29	9	.67[b]	.64
Qualified, but in school with no program	204	5	–.17[b,c]	.63
Not qualified for bilingual program	36	4	–.46[c]	.21
($F = 6.54$; $df = 2/15$: $p = .0091$)				
Confounding of comp groups with students who had previously attended bilingual programs				
No	266	24	.38[b]	.70
Yes	112	31	–.03[c]	.26
($F = 9.04$; $df = 1/53$; $p = .0040$)				
Exit history, exp group				
Successful students exited from program and replaced with incoming students	36	4	–.46[b]	.21
No students exited, no replacements	407	31	.38[c]	.64
($F = 6.44$; $df = 1/33$; $p = .0161$)				
Comp program contains elements of bilingual program				
No	260	20	.32[b]	.73
Yes	117	32	–.05[c]	.28
($F = 6.60$; $df = 1/50$; $p = .0132$)				
Stability of exp program				
Frequent reorganization and high teacher turnover	36	4	–.46[b]	.21
Program seems stable	253	19	.45[c]	.80
($F = 4.83$; $df = 1/21$: $p = .0394$)				

[a] Weighted by independent sample.
[b,c] Means with different superscripts differ according to Scheffe Test with alpha set at .05.

of *non*random assignment by highlighting unwanted differences between the experimental and comparison groups. The first of these, language dominance, is discussed not because of its statistical significance, which was slightly greater than .05, but because of its conceptual value. (The dearth of reported information concerning language dominance probably accounts for this lack of significance.)

Language dominance. The means presented in Table 15.5 for language dominance of the experimental and comparison groups indicate that when both groups were Spanish-dominant there is an effect of almost one-half of a standard deviation (.43) favoring the experimental groups. On the other hand, when the experimental group was Spanish-dominant and the comparison group was English-dominant, the effect sizes show little or no difference between the groups on the criterion instruments. Similarly, when both groups were English-dominant, there is little difference between the groups, indicating that bilingual education has not hindered academic achievement for the English-dominant bilingual groups. Of interest, but not reflected directly in Table 15.5, is the fact that there were 219 effect sizes for which it was impossible to code language dominance. Of those that were coded, sixteen codes were based on coder assumptions due to the non-explicit nature of the available information. (Separate analyses indicated that the assumptions had virtually no impact on the variation in effect sizes.) It is important to note that even when language dominance was explicitly reported in studies, the basis for determination of dominance was often a simple overall judgment made by the researcher, school principal, or teacher. Formal determinations of language dominance were rare.

The available language dominance information from one particular study was not incorporated into the above analysis due to the questionable nature of the reported information. In this one study, both the experimental and comparison groups were reported to be Chinese-dominant (Lum 1971) and the mean effect size for language was –.55. As will be discussed, there are a number of explanations for this finding, one of which underscores the importance of equating groups on neighborhood language exposure as well as language dominance.

Non-language differences. Three additional variables in Table 15.5 illustrate further differences between experimental and comparison groups that result from nonrandom assignment. Although the first of these variables is somewhat redundant with that indicating whether there was random or nonrandom assignment, it incorporates additional information not found in the latter variable. The distinction made in this case is whether or not children in the comparison group would have been qualified for, or in need of, a bilingual program (that is, not deemed limited-English-proficient). The mean effect size when children in the comparison groups were not qualified for a bilingual program was substantially lower than when the comparison students qualified, but were not admitted to the program because of random assignment or because they attended a school where a bilingual program was not available. The effect size of –.46 indicates that the experimental groups scored almost one-half standard deviation lower than the comparison groups when the comparison groups were not limited-English-proficient and not qualified for the bilingual program. When this difference was controlled for through random assignment, the mean was .67. When comparison students qualified for the program but were in a school that offered no program, the effect size fell between these two extremes.

Another, and rather surprising, difference found between some experimental and comparison groups was that the comparison groups contained students who had been in bilingual programs prior to the onset of the research study. For these studies, the mean effect size reflected no differences between the groups (–.03). When comparison groups did not contain such students, the effect size favored the bilingual program groups by well over one-third of a standard deviation, or .38.

Exit history, which reflects another experimental-comparison group difference, indicates that some students were exited from the experimental groups when they became proficient in English and were replaced with incoming students in need of the program. This means that the composition of the experimental groups changed in a way that ensured a mean indicating no gain. When such a condition existed, the experimental groups scored almost one-half of a standard deviation below the comparison groups (–.46). When there was clearly no change in the composition of the experimental group, the effect size favored the bilingual program groups by more than one-third of a standard deviation (.38).

Summarizing the four analyses just discussed, it becomes clear that the lack of random assignment in bilingual education research and evaluation has allowed major uncontrolled differences between experimental and comparison groups to contaminate research findings. Whenever these inequalities were present, research results indicated no differences between the groups or they favored the comparison groups. In all instances where major inequalities were not present, substantial effect sizes favored the bilingual program groups.

Program characteristics. The fact that much of the variance in effect sizes stems from characteristics of the research rather than characteristics of the educational programs is reflected also in the general lack of information describing the programs in this set of studies. In spite of the paucity of information regarding the programs, information from just a few studies enabled the identification of two variables representing program characteristics that *were* associated with significant variation in effect sizes. These are the last two variables presented in Table 15.5.

The first of these program characteristics again represents faulty research design, although in this case it reflects unwanted similarities between the experimental and comparison programs. In these instances the comparison programs contained elements of bilingual programs, such as bilingual teachers or aides who had taught previously in bilingual programs, or who had even completed bilingual teacher-training programs. When bilingual programs were compared with programs of this type, there was little or no difference between the groups, as indicated by the effect size of –.05. In contrast, when the comparison programs did not contain similarities to the bilingual programs, the mean effect size favored the bilingual programs by almost one-third of a standard deviation (.32).

The remaining program variable reveals information about the effects of the stability of the bilingual program. As can be seen in Table 15.5, when the bilingual program is characterized by frequent reorganization and high teacher turnover, the mean effect size favors the comparison groups by almost one-half of a standard deviation (–.46). On the other hand, when the program appears to be stable, the effect size favors the bilingual program groups by almost one-half of a standard deviation (.45).

One overall observation regarding Table 15.5 is that the results of the individual analyses are quite consistent with those in Table 15.4. Although the means in Table 15.5 are not adjusted and reflect the raw means of variable categories, they are consistent with the adjusted means in Table 15.4 not only logically, but also in terms of their positive direction and magnitude. In all categories of the variables in Table 15.5 that reflect no major preexisting differences between experimental and comparison groups, and in those categories that reflect acceptable program conditions, the unadjusted mean effect sizes are positive and range from .32 to .67.

Results based on vote scores

Although the most meaningful results derived from the current synthesis were those based on effect sizes, examination of the vote scores from the seven studies for which effect sizes were not calculable yielded results consistent with the findings based on effect sizes. The "seven studies" for which effect sizes were not calculable were those by American Institutes for Research (1975), Ames and Bicks (1978), Balasubramonian et al. (1973), Cottrell (1971), Matthews (1979), Moore and Parr (1979), and Plante (1976). The vote scores from these seven studies were tallied and categorized by type of program compared and language of the test. For comparison of bilingual education and submersion, vote scores for tests administered in English totaled seventy-nine. Of these, fifty-three favored the bilingual program groups, ten were identical, and sixteen favored the comparison groups. A chi square statistic, using Yate's correction for one degree of freedom, was calculated to test the difference between the proportion of scores favoring the bilingual program groups or the comparison groups. The chi square statistic of 19.85 was statistically significant with $p < .001$. For tests administered in languages other than English, there were twenty vote scores, all favoring the bilingual program groups.

From this same group of studies, there were only six vote scores that compared bilingual education with ESL to submersion with ESL, and all of these favored the bilingual program groups. In sum, these results support the findings based on effect sizes that revealed positive effects for bilingual education programs both for tests administered in English and tests administered in Spanish.

DISCUSSION

Although the current synthesis revealed positive effects for bilingual programs, the overwhelming message derived from these data suggests that most research conclusions regarding the effectiveness of bilingual education reflect weaknesses of the research itself rather than effects of the actual programs. The positive effects of bilingual education, which were found for all major academic subjects whether tests were administered in English or in other languages, became apparent only when it was possible to use statistical controls for a number of major methodological weaknesses that were identified in the primary studies—weaknesses that were all substantially related to low effect sizes. Since these research problems must be remedied before it will be possible to obtain definitive information on the effectiveness of bilingual education, the weaknesses and their implications will be discussed in detail. A second area of the discussion will center on research factors at a different level—those that can influence the conclusions drawn by reviewers or synthesizers of primary studies. Conclusions reached through any one review or synthesis of literature (including meta-analysis) cannot provide definitive answers any more than individual studies since they are influenced by differences in methodologies as well as the types of interpretations made by reviewers themselves. Such influences will be illustrated by a comparison of this meta-analysis with the narrative review that was based on the same set of studies.

METHODOLOGICAL PROBLEMS IN THE PRIMARY STUDIES

Random assignment in bilingual research

Most of the methodological weaknesses identified in the primary studies involved the comparison of bilingual program students to students who differed from them in ways that made the comparisons unfair. These differences, which were related to lower effect sizes (indicating less effectiveness for the bilingual programs), included a failure to equate experimental and comparison groups on language dominance and other language-related variables, as well as the inclusion of students in the comparison groups who had previously been in bilingual programs. In some instances the ex-bilingual program students in the comparison groups had been exited successfully from the bilingual programs, while students in greater need of the program were added to the experimental groups. Also related to lower effect sizes were comparison programs that contained elements of bilingual programs, and were, therefore, undifferentiated in aspects of the treatment that was under study. The only actual program characteristic related to effect sizes was a lack of stability in the bilingual program. Less stable programs produced lower effect sizes.

The nature of the design problems identified in this study suggests the remedy: Research designs must provide means by which individual differences in the total pool of subjects can be distributed equally between the experimental and control groups. In well-controlled studies, this equal distribution of differences is attained through the use of random assignment. In fact, without random assignment, one always risks confounding study findings with undesirable, preexisting group differences. Campbell and Boruch (1975) have pointed out that studies of compensatory education are especially susceptible to these confounding differences. The current results suggest that research in bilingual education is perhaps more susceptible than any other kind of program to differences between experimental and comparison groups when random assignment is not employed.

Although the use of random designs to compare children in bilingual programs to children receiving no special program is precluded by legal considerations, there are ways to use random designs in bilingual research without jeopardizing opportunities for any child. This point will be elaborated upon in the last section of this chapter. In the current synthesis, effect sizes were available for only three studies using random assignment (Covey 1973; Huzar 1973; Kaufman 1968). The scarcity of well-controlled studies warrants some discussion on the importance of randomization in general, as well as a discussion of the specific problems in bilingual education research and evaluation that result from lack of randomization and that have been raised in this meta-analysis.

Campbell and his colleagues have argued extensively for the use of random assignment in studies on experimental educational programs (see, for example, Campbell and Boruch 1975; Campbell and Erlebacher 1970). These authors point out that in the absence of a true experimental design, a melange of parameters must be *identified* and *estimated* in order to assure the comparability of the groups or to allow for adjustment of the differences. Since the identification and estimation of all-important factors is usually impossible, they suggest the best recourse is to balance the unknown factors across the groups through random assignment. In addition, these authors believe that statistical procedures in quasi-experimental designs will usually under-adjust for group differences and, when the research concerns special educational services, such under-adjustments will make the programs look ineffective or harmful. In furthering their arguments, the authors posit that each statistical technique used to adjust for preexisting group differences must be based on assumptions that are often untenable and, even more frequently, unverifiable.

The problems associated with nonrandom assignment are illustrated quite convincingly in one of the studies included in the current synthesis. In a nationwide evaluation of the Follow Through Programs, Stebbins et al. (1977) evaluated many program models from different areas of the country. Three major types of analyses were carried out for each program model: (a) analyses comparing the experimental groups with non-Follow Through (NFT) children who were from the same locale as the experimental children; (b) analyses comparing the experimental children with a prediction model based on all NFT children from sponsors across the nation; and (c) analyses comparing each experimental group with a group considered to be its "best match," regardless of the area of the country in which the comparison group resided. In these latter comparisons, the best-matched comparison groups were those who were most perfectly equated to the experimental groups on ethnicity, family income, mother's education, preschool attendance, whether or not the mother was the head of the household, the first language, and the pretest score. The researchers found that results from the three analytical models differed dramatically for the same experimental groups, depending on which of the three comparisons was used. Stebbins et al. decided that the analyses using local comparison groups seemed to have the most reliable results, even when the "best matched" group was not the local group. In view of this, the researchers based their final reports on the local comparisons.

The fact that such discrepant results could occur, depending on whether a local comparison group was used or a group from a different area, even though the latter was a better match on 11 important covariates, illustrates the problems involved in trying to compensate for nonrandom assignment through attempts to match experimental and comparison groups. In the current synthesis, failure to compensate adequately for nonrandom assignment was revealed by the number of uncontrolled differences that had a substantial impact on the magnitude of the effect sizes. Many of the differentiating characteristics are peculiar only to research dealing with bilingual populations or to bilingual education. Among the most obvious of these are those variables that deal with language.

Equating groups on language variables

In bilingual education research, where the criteria for entry to and exit from bilingual programs have typically been based on the student's *relative* proficiency (that is, language dominance) in two languages (one of which, in the U.S., is English), and where the ability to benefit from educational programs is partly based on the ability to understand the language in which these programs are presented, it is apparent that the equating of experimental and comparison groups on *absolute* proficiency in *both* of the languages is imperative if one is to make fair comparisons for purposes of educational evaluation. When a more or less homogeneous group of students is assigned to the experimental and comparison groups through truly random procedures, variation in linguistic proficiency across the languages of concern should balance out rather evenly. When groups are formed through procedures that are not truly random, other ways must be found to equate the students in the two groups on their language proficiencies. These equating procedures would seem to require some sort of language assessment or the use of language tests. This is where the problems start.

The use of language tests for equating groups on language proficiency introduces a host of problems that might roughly be divided into two categories: (a) statistical considerations that stem from the use of test scores for matching experimental and comparison groups and (b) problems that stem from a number of issues in the realm of language assessment. The statistical considerations have been discussed rather thoroughly by Campbell and Boruch (1975) and include problems stemming from regression to the mean and the use of statistical adjustments.

Statistical problems in the equating of language groups

Regression to the mean. In research and evaluation on bilingual programs, regression to the mean is an unavoidable complication when bilingual program groups are matched with other groups on language tests for the purposes of equating groups. Groups slated to participate in bilingual programs in the United States usually are from a population whose distribution of language scores falls at the lower end of a scale (at least in English). On the other hand, the comparison groups, who for some reason have not been provided with a bilingual program, usually represent a population whose distribution of scores would fall in a higher range than the population of the experimental group. The matched students who are selected to compose the experimental and comparison groups, then, will be those whose language scores are comparable because they fall in an area where the two distributions overlap. Scores in this overlapping area will be the highest scores from the population slated for the bilingual program, while scores of the comparison group falling in the area of overlap will be the lowest scores from that particular population. If a post-test were administered without either group receiving a treatment or program, the language scores of the group slated for the bilingual program (even though it did not receive one) will have regressed to the mean of that population, downwards, while the scores of the comparison group will have regressed toward the mean of that population, or upwards, giving the appearance that something had caused the scores of those who had been slated for the bilingual program to deteriorate while scores of the other group had improved. Such an effect, which is simply a statistical artifact, will always occur when post-test scores are compared for groups whose pretest scores were matched but who came from populations that had different initial means. When one interjects a treatment or program between the pre- and post-tests, any true positive effects would not be detectable unless they were of sufficient magnitude to overcompensate for the effects of regression to the mean.

Statistical adjustments. One could argue that there may be ways to avoid the problems inherent in the matching of students based on language pretests by using various statistical techniques to adjust for the preexisting differences—techniques such as analysis of covariance or regression adjustments based on multiple covariates. Campbell and Boruch (1975) and Campbell and Erlebacher (1970) have pointed out that any such attempts to adjust statistically for preexisting group differences in the kinds of situations described above will often lead to systematic under-adjustments that will appear to be treatment effects. Furthermore, they point out that the under-adjustment always works against the group that was most in need of the program.

Concerning the possibility of using multiple covariates to adjust for group differences, such as, perhaps, a social advantage factor that includes the covariates of race, sex, father's occupation, income, and parents' years of schooling, Campbell and Boruch (1975) write:

> The only way in which a finite number of such covariates could provide adequate adjustment would be for one or more of them to be a perfect measure of the common factor, without irrelevant variance or error: Such covariates simply do not exist. (pp. 244–245)

In their discussion of the problems associated with covariance adjustments. Campbell and Boruch present a number of models for reliability-corrected covariance analyses, which, hypothetically, could yield unbiased adjustments. However, all of these models require the inclusion of coefficients of reliability for the tests involved. The less reliable the instruments, the less effective these methods will be. Thus any models that could possibly produce less biased adjustments for group differences in bilingual education research would depend on the reliability and validity of the language tests actually used. It is a known fact, however, that language tests in general, and the language tests in particular that are used to determine entry and exit into bilingual programs, have low reliability and low convergent validity (see, for example, Gilmore and Dickenson 1979; Hoepfner and Coniff 1974; Rivera and Simich 1981; Silverman, Noa, and Russell 1977; Troike 1982, 1983; Tucker 1974). In fact, some of the tests actually correlate negatively with each other (Ulibarri, Spencer, and Rivas 1981).

The lack of convergent validity in language testing suggests that the statistical concerns are only the tip of the iceberg when considering the problems of equating groups on language. An even more formidable set of problems surfaces when one considers the issues inherent in language assessment per se.

Problems in language assessment

The divergence in scores from various language tests ultimately stems from the fact that theory and practice in the area of language assessment are still in a state of confusion and instability (Baecher 1981). There have been several paradigm shifts in linguistics and psycholinguistics over the past twenty years (Bloomfield 1933; Chomsky 1957, 1965; Fillmore 1968; Labov 1970; Lado 1961; Shuy 1977), and each paradigm has led to tests that measure the aspects of language held to be most important by the theory predominating at the time. In defining language proficiency, differential emphasis has been placed on phonology, grammar, meaning and vocabulary, or the myriad skills necessary for communicative competence. The result has been a plethora of tests that demonstrate low convergent validity. The diversity in the various models of language proficiency is perhaps best illustrated by Cummins' (1981) description of models that range from one proposing sixty-four separate proficiencies to a model that proposes one global language proficiency factor.

The lack of reliability demonstrated by language tests is partly accounted for by the fact that each individual possesses a variety of language skills, and competence and performance will vary depending on the context or setting of language use, the interactants, their relationships and relative statuses, the domain of the communicative intent, and the topic. Although this is true of monolingual individuals, bilingual individuals have an even more varied repertoire of language uses that serves to complicate further any attempts to equate groups on language proficiency. For a child who lives in a dual-language environment, certain topics of conversation with certain types of individuals in certain kinds of settings may call forth one language, while very different topics with different individuals in different settings are usually dealt with in the other language. For example, topics that are commonly discussed in the home may be quite different from those discussed in school or in church, and each of these might normally be conducted in different languages. Thus language proficiency in the different domains will vary. Furthermore, in any dual-language community or neighborhood, this patterning of the languages involved will vary from individual to individual. The almost infinite variety of language use and the variations in reactions and motivations to language settings can only serve to ensure a lack of reliability in language tests. All of this leads back to the dilemma of equating groups for language proficiency—just what does one equate for? By now it must be apparent to the reader that before it becomes possible to even attempt to equate groups on language proficiency through matching or statistical adjustments, the problems of language assessment must be solved. The fact that many researchers in this synthesis gave no indication of the language dominance of their subjects and made no attempts to control for language differences simply attests to the overwhelming complexity of this issue.

Another language consideration that became apparent during coding of the study by Lum (1971) adds even more complexity to the language issue. This concerns the equating of experimental and comparison groups for language exposure in the neighborhood of residence and in the school setting. Although failure to equate for this variable was rather obvious in the Lum study, it was seldom obvious in other studies and the possibility of such a difference is seldom mentioned by researchers. The very absence of such information suggests the importance of discussing this variable.

Language exposure

Although information on language exposure was reported in very few of the studies examined in this synthesis, the direction of the results for group comparisons was similar to that of language dominance. When the language of the residential neighborhood was approximately the same for both the experimental and comparison groups, regardless of whether the language was English or non-English, effect sizes were positive for the bilingual program groups. On the other hand, when the neighborhood language of the comparison groups was English and that of the experimental groups Spanish, results showed little or no difference between the experimental and comparison groups. This could simply be another reflection of the fact that the experimental and comparison groups were not adequately equated for language dominance, or it could be the result of another process altogether—one that Campbell and Boruch (1975) have called "grouping feedback effects."

Grouping feedback effects occur when experimental and comparison groups come from different schools or neighborhoods and the distribution of measures on the criterion variables favors the comparison group's schools. An example of a feedback effect described by these authors concerns vocabulary. As the authors point out, vocabulary is a major component of intelligence and achievement tests and therefore of prime importance in educational programs. In bilingual education, vocabulary is of even greater importance given its relevance to the whole issue language proficiency and academic achievement (see, for example, Seville-Troike 1984) Campbell and Boruch's (1975) description of the feedback effect as it applies vocabulary development is quite germane to the findings regarding neighborhood language in this study:

Some of it (vocabulary) is certainly learned from classmates, so that children whose classmates have a lower level of vocabulary would learn less. Lower student vocabulary also lowers the vocabulary used by the teacher in classroom interaction and reading assignments. Neighborhoods and play groups have a similar effect. Thus, the feedback effects from the fact of social aggregation and segregation are almost certainly in the direction of increasing real group differences, and tend to reduce group overlap, both in relativistic scoring systems and on raw or absolute scores. (p. 273)

Although the feedback effect would tend to increase differences between the groups in the absence of any experimental treatment, the effect would be just to opposite when the group with the least amount of environmental feedback participates in an experimental program. For example, if the experimental and comparison groups in a study of bilingual education actually were similar in language dominance initially, yet the comparison group lived in a neighborhood that offered greater exposure to English, the feedback effect could provide advantages for the group that, in the presence of an experimental effect, would ultimately reduce group differences and obscure the treatment effects.

As before, Campbell and Boruch have suggested that the best way to control for the feedback effect is through random assignment. And, as before, it is necessary to emphasize that if controlling for the feedback effect is difficult in studies of monolingual programs, it is probably insurmountable in studies of bilingual education programs.

The complexity of controlling for language proficiencies, language exposure, and other language-related variables may perhaps be illustrated by Mackey's 1970 typology of bilingual programs, which is based on the language patterns used both in the bilingual programs and in the broader context of the programs. Mackey typology consists of a nine-by-ten matrix, where each of the ninety cells represents different combination of language patterns for the different types of bilingual programs and for the different community contexts in which the programs are found. The contextual variations indicate not only the specific patterns of language use for the languages used by the child, but also those used in the home, the bilingual program, the school, the neighborhood or area, and the nation as a whole. Furthermore, the relative status of each of the languages used in each setting influences the motivational factors in language learning. Each segment of the ever widening pattern of linguistic context ultimately impinges on the child. Experimental control for the innumerable language-related considerations seems possible only through true randomization. However, controlling for purely language-related variables is not the only problem faced by researchers and evaluators of bilingual programs. Other confounding variables were revealed in this synthesis that also were direct outcomes of nonrandom assignment.

Additional problems in equating groups

Formation of comparison groups. In addition to the language-based problems that seem to make random designs imperative for studies in bilingual research, there are other types of group differences that, if not controlled, can produce misleading results for program research and evaluation. One of the group differences having an impact on the effect sizes in this synthesis concerns the reasons the children in the comparison groups were not in the bilingual programs.

Although the variable for this factor is somewhat redundant with that indicating random or nonrandom assignment, the rationale for comparison group formation provided additional information not found in the latter variable. When children in the bilingual program group were compared to groups of children who were not in need of the bilingual program, the mean effect size was one of the lowest in the study and favored the comparison groups. When the comparison children *did* qualify for the program but were eliminated through the process of random assignment, the effect size favored the bilingual program group. On the other hand, when children who qualified for the bilingual program were in the comparison groups solely because they attended schools where no bilingual program was offered, the mean effect size favored the comparison groups to a much lesser degree than when the comparison children did not qualify for the program. Actually, this category of differences may simply be reflecting the same problems discussed above under grouping feedback effects. When the comparison children come from schools where there is no bilingual program, it is most likely that the lack of a bilingual program is due to an insufficient number of non-English-speaking children in the would be exposed to more English from peers, teachers, and probably people in the neighborhood of residence that children in schools where the school and neighborhood contain more non-English speakers.

Changes in group composition. Another methodological artifact related to effect sizes was a change in the composition of both the experimental and comparison groups over time, either during or prior to the study. Group composition changes in transitional bilingual programs because children are exited, or moved out of the bilingual program and into the traditional program as soon as they are thought to be sufficiently proficient in oral English. The slots vacated by these children then become available to new children who know less English and who are then added to the bilingual program. Through this process, the level of English proficiency in the experimental groups is constantly suppressed. On the other hand, the non-bilingual classes constantly receive the students who have been exited successfully from the bilingual programs. Since these non-bilingual classes often are those used for comparison groups, the level of English proficiency is guaranteed to be elevated above that of the experimental group.

The one researcher from the set of studies in this analysis who discussed her results in terms of this problem was Stern (1975), who studied the differential impact of transitional bilingual programs to those of submersion programs for grades one to six. Not only did the effect sizes from Stern's study represent the lowest in the whole set, but with the exception of the Lum (1971) study, it was the only study where every effect size favored the comparison groups. In Stern's conscientious exploration of factors having an impact on the programs she studied she points out that many of the children in the comparison groups had originally been in the bilingual programs. Furthermore, Stern noted that 56 percent of the Chicano children in the first grade, 62 percent in the second, 60 percent in the third, 41 percent in the fourth, 50 percent in the fifth, and 52 percent in the sixth had initial placement in the bilingual program *during the year of the evaluation.* Stern also found that the children who had been in the bilingual programs for the longest time were those who scored the lowest on the criterion tests. In discussing these results, she writes:

> We see that the children who have been longest in the program are consistently older than those who entered more recently. They are also much more regular in their attendance, hence their generally poorer achievement level cannot be attributed to lack of exposure or school motivation. The indications are that these are the slower learners who couldn't make it into the regular classroom. Ironically, the "regular" classroom is the one we have had to use as our control or contrast group. As we have reviewed the roster of children in that class we found many of the children who had originally been in the bilingual program. *They were among the highest scorers in the "control" group.* Over the years there has been a nonrandom skimming off of the most capable students in the bilingual classes. (p. 80, emphasis added)

Ironically, it appears that the presence of former bilingual education students in Stern's comparison groups may have increased the effect sizes in favor of these comparison groups. Only one other study from those included in this synthesis mentioned the fact that the comparison groups contained ex-bilingual program students (Danoff et al. 1977a). Just as in the Stern study, results for the Danoff et al. study were null or unfavorable to the bilingual programs. The extent of the confounding in the comparison groups in the AIR report is revealed by the fact that two-thirds or more of the non-Title VII Hispanic students (comparison group) had participated in bilingual programs for periods ranging up to a year prior to the AIR study (Danoff et al. 1977a, pp. VI-26). Furthermore, Danoff et al. point out that of the bilingual program children who composed the experimental groups, "72 percent or more of the students in grades two through six had two or more years of prior experience with bilingual education classes" (Danoff et al. 1977a, pp. VI-26).

Although Danoff and his colleagues offer no further information about the educational history of the children in the experimental and comparison groups, the situation they describe seems to resemble that described by Stern in her study: comparison groups composed of children who had been in bilingual programs prior to the study and children in the bilingual classes who were there either because they were new to the program or because they were the slower learners who stayed in the program for a longer time than those who had been exited. Thus the bilingual program "graduates" in the comparison groups may have raised the scores of these comparison groups just as they did in the Stern study. However, since Danoff et al. did not investigate why the comparison children were no longer in the bilingual programs, they could not be coded in this meta-analysis as having been officially exited.

Up to this point, results from this meta-analysis have been discussed in terms of their implications for that aspect of research design that ensures the comparability of experimental and control groups. In addition to findings relevant to this consideration, a limited amount of information in this meta-analysis reflected on another problem with research design—one that has to do with the nature of the treatments or programs that are the subject of study.

Issues concerning experimental treatments

An adequate treatment design in true experimental research means that the experimental treatment is well-documented and that this treatment plan is strictly adhered to in order to ensure replicability of the research by other scientists. Furthermore, the researcher ensures that the control condition contains none of the characteristics of the experimental condition unless the purpose of the research is to compare treatments characterized by various degrees of intensity. In either case, the differences and similarities between treatments must be precisely documented so that the same conditions can be treated in replication experiments. Although the situation is somewhat different in educational research, where frequently there is little or no control over the treatment conditions, it is even more important that the exact nature of the treatment or program be described and documented so that discrepant findings in similar studies can be examined in light of the program characteristics. Unfortunately, most research studies in bilingual education provide little or no description of the program characteristics. Without such information, little sense can be made of discrepant research findings.

Even less frequently does one find adequate descriptions of the comparison programs. Of those studies in this synthesis that provided information on the nature of the comparison programs, a few gave indications that bilingual programs may frequently be compared not to programs representing an absence of bilingual education, but to programs that contain some characteristics of the bilingual program. For example, Zirkel (1972) found the confounding of program characteristics to be a real problem in selecting the bilingual and comparison classes to be used in his study. He reports that some classes that had been labeled bilingual were indistinguishable from those that had been designated as comparison classes.

In the current analysis, when it was possible to document that comparison programs contained characteristics of the bilingual programs, the mean effect size indicated little or no difference between the groups. Where such confounding did not appear to exist, effect sizes favored the bilingual program groups.

Although it was possible to code the existence of such confounding for only four studies, one wonders how many other studies would have revealed the same type of problem had the information been documented and reported. Of the four studies reporting program similarities between the experimental and comparison groups, two intentionally compared different bilingual program models (Legarreta 1979; Pena-Hughes and Solis 1980). The remaining two studies, however, compared the effects of bilingual and non-bilingual programs, even though the non-bilingual programs contained aspects of the bilingual programs. For instance, in the AIR study (Danoff et al. 1977a), a substantial number of teachers and aides in the comparison programs had been involved in bilingual education to the extent that 22 percent of the comparison group teachers and 25 percent of the aides had taught bilingual education for two years or longer; 36 percent of the teachers and 23 percent of the aides had some course work in bilingual education; 59 percent and 50 percent, respectively, had attended bilingual in-service training programs; and 20 percent and 16 percent had attended state or national bilingual conferences. Furthermore, 79 percent of the non-bilingual program teachers were bilingual and used both Spanish and English with their bilingual friends. The characteristics and interests representing the comparison program staff certainly suggest that the comparison programs may have had many elements in common with the bilingual programs. Similarly, in the Lum (1971) study, where bilingual programs were compared to submersion programs with ESL components, Chinese and English were used in both the experimental and comparison programs, although to a much lesser extent in the comparison (ESL/submersion) programs. Teachers in both types of programs were English-Chinese bilingual. In sum, similarities in the experimental and comparison treatments confounded the results and preclude a clear attribution of results to differences in the treatments.

Quality of the programs

A final problem in the evaluation of bilingual programs concerns the nature and quality of the experimental program. Stern's (1975) careful documentation of the problems inherent in the classes she evaluated not only makes her study a prime source of examples for the problems that plague the evaluation of bilingual programs, it also suggests that these same problems have probably plagued other evaluations, even though they have not always been documented. Lack of documentation of problems that offer alternative explanations for research results only adds to the inconsistency and confusion surrounding the findings in bilingual program research and evaluation.

In addition to the points discussed earlier concerning Stern's study, Stern described two problems that affected the actual quality of the programs in her study. These were instability of the programs (exemplified by high teacher turnover rates), a great deal of disorganization, and hostile or uninterested attitudes of non-bilingual teachers and staff in the schools. Anecdotal information that depicts similar problems is known to many staff members and administrators of bilingual programs across the country. Among bilingual program personnel, typical tales describe bilingual programs that are hidden in basements or areas of their school where they are out of sight. Furthermore, bilingual teachers frequently relate tales of hostile, prejudicial comments or treatments by non-bilingual program teachers or administrators. In short, Stern's documentation of these problems, and the fact that the effect sizes for her programs were the lowest of all the studies included in this synthesis, serves to emphasize the importance of documenting program implementation problems whenever one attempts to evaluate the effectiveness of a program. Clearly these types of problems contribute to the ineffectiveness of programs, although with the current database it is impossible to ferret out the exact magnitude of this effect because of the confounding of many problems within the same studies.

At the time this meta-analysis was conceived, it was the hope of this researcher that the study would yield information concerning substantive issues related to bilingualism and bilingual education, such as the impact of variation in bilingual program models, characteristics of the students and staff, and contexts of bilingual programs. As it turned out, however, the variance of the effect sizes was dominated by factors reflecting the quality of the research studies themselves. Without research of an acceptable quality, it is impossible to extract information that addresses the more substantive issues. In spite of this predominance of methodological factors, a few bits of information did yield some suggestive evidence on more basic issues. The first of these concerns the concurrent use of two languages in bilingual programs versus the separation of languages into specific time blocks. The second emphasizes the importance of distinguishing between various aspects of language when evaluating programs and also provides tentative evidence in support of the distinctions that Cummins (1981, 1984) has made regarding the nature of language proficiency and the relation of these distinctions to school performance.

BEYOND METHODOLOGY: EVIDENCE RELATED TO SUBSTANTIVE ISSUES

Language patterns in bilingual models

One basic issue regarding the different patterns of language allocation possible in bilingual models is whether it is preferable to pattern the use of two languages so that they are used concurrently or whether they should be separated according to different time blocks or even different settings.

Two studies in this synthesis compared the effects of different bilingual models in kindergarten programs (Legarreta 1979; Pena-Hughes and Solis 1980). The comparisons in these cases produced adjusted mean effect sizes that were higher than those of any other type of comparison. Both studies compared models that used concurrent translation and alternate immersion.

It is important here to make a distinction between alternate immersion programs, which are a variety of bilingual education and structured- or total-immersion programs. In *alternate immersion*, both languages are used but separated into distinct time blocks or settings. Since children receive instruction in their first language for a separate portion of the day, the continued development of first-language skills and content learning is ensured. Any aspects of cognitive development that are dependent on language are able to evolve in a continuous fashion without the risk of a hiatus during the period of second-language learning. Thus the conceptual tools developed in conjunction with the first language continue to be available to a child. *Structured immersion*, on the other hand, is instruction offered in the second language only, and the continued development of first-language skills is typically excluded from the program for at least several years. As can be seen, alternate immersion is a bilingual program model, while structured immersion, at least for the first several years, is not.

Results of the Pena-Hughes and Legarreta studies provided evidence supporting the effectiveness of alternate immersion over concurrent translation for the kindergarten age group. The evidence is considered only suggestive, however, due to the confounding of differential program quality for some of the comparisons. Descriptions of the studies will clarify some of these points.

In the Pena-Hughes and Solis program (1980), an ongoing bilingual program that the researchers considered to be of questionable quality was compared to an experimental bilingual program in which morning kindergarten activities were conducted in English and afternoon activities in Spanish. The only information available describing the comparison program indicated that it was conducted primarily in Spanish, although the intent evidently was to have concurrent translation (E. Pena-Hughes, personal communication, Nov. 25, 1981). Furthermore, only the experimental program included special in-service teacher training sessions, which suggests that the Hawthorne effect, as well as differential teacher training, may have played a role in the results from this comparison. Students in both programs were from Spanish-speaking neighborhoods where even a large proportion of the television reception was in Spanish. Owing to the limited amount of information available on the comparison program, it is impossible to determine whether the very positive effects favoring the alternate immersion program were due to differences in program quality or differences in program models.

Legarreta (1979) studied several kindergarten program models and compared an alternate immersion program with a concurrent translation program. In the alternate immersion program, curriculum content and concepts were presented totally in Spanish for half of the day and in English for the other half. The comparison program used concurrent translation, with English used approximately 72 percent of the time and Spanish only 28 percent of the time. Test scores represented oral comprehension and communicative competence. As with Pena-Hughes' subjects, results favored the alternate immersion program.

The similarity of results for these two studies is interesting in that both experimental programs were alternate immersion programs and both comparison programs used concurrent translation, although Spanish predominated in the Pena-Hughes comparison program and English predominated in the Legarreta comparison program. Nevertheless, for both programs, alternate immersion proved to be superior to the comparison programs.

In spite of the fact that the variation in models may be confounded with variation in quality of the programs, the combined results of the two studies suggest that differences between program models *can* have an impact on the effectiveness of the programs and that research comparing various program models is an essential area for study. Furthermore, this minimal amount of evidence from two different areas of the country (the Mexican border and a large West Coast city) suggests that alternate immersion, where approximately a half-day is spent in each language, appears to be an effective approach for use with kindergarten children. More rigorous research must verify this suggestion as well as explore the effectiveness of this type of model at higher grade levels. Even if alternate immersion is found to be a superior model with younger children, the question must be addressed separately with older children who may be learning the second language after having achieved competency in the first language. If these older children use translations from their first language as a shortcut to learning the second language, concurrent presentation of the languages may be preferable.

In addition to the data from this meta-analysis that reflected on the language patterns in bilingual models, findings related to other aspects of language highlighted certain distinctions that are important in studying the impact of bilingual programs.

Differentiating aspects of language

In examining the adjusted means that were presented for the variable indicating the academic domain of the criterion instrument, it is interesting to note that there are differences between the various aspects of language. The most noticeable difference in the language-related tests administered in English is that between comprehension and production. In the studies included in this synthesis, where more than 65 percent of the effect sizes were based on periods of less than one year, the initial impact of the bilingual programs appears to be on language comprehension, both oral and written.

The precedence of comprehension over production for both the oral and written domains simply reinforces the importance of making such a distinction. Just as in the sequence of monolingual language development (see, e.g., Dale 1976) it appears that for second-language learning *in the context of bilingual programs*, comprehension precedes production. Troike (1969) has argued for the necessity of making this distinction in evaluating student performance. The need for, and at the same time the difficulty of distinguishing between the various aspects of language in research and evaluation in bilingual programs is exemplified by the fact that in coding the test domains for this synthesis. It was usually necessary to scrutinize actual copies of the tests in order to determine which aspects of language were being measured. For example, a researcher might indicate in a study that a test of vocabulary had been given, without distinguishing between vocabulary that was presented to the students orally (requiring responses such as pointing to pictures) and vocabulary that was presented in the written mode. If the various aspects of language are not differentiated in research and evaluation, not only will program diagnostics be less than optimal, but the intricacies of the language considerations in bilingual program settings may never be sorted out.

Although the distinction between oral and written language in English for the receptive and productive modes combined was not clear-cut in this study, the importance of this type of distinction has been emphasized by other researchers (for example, Bereiter and Sardamalia 1981; Cummins 1981, 1984; Donaldson 1978; Olson 1977). According to Cummins (1981, 1984), the skills required for face-to-face oral communication are unrelated to academic achievement, whereas those related to literacy, such as range of vocabulary and the ability to communicate or understand in the absence of any extralinguistic cues, are. He points out that monolingual children master many of the basic skills of context-embedded oral communication by approximately age six. Literacy-related skills, on the other hand, develop in the school context and expand throughout the school years. Cummins cites evidence suggesting that it takes children in bilingual programs about two years to master the oral language skills of the second language, while it takes about five to seven years to catch up to grade level for the literacy skills in the second language. The data of the current synthesis indicate that children in bilingual programs are definitely picking up reading skills in English at a faster rate than the comparison children. If this advantage were to continue over several years, the children in the bilingual programs would acquire grade-level reading skills in fewer years than similar children who have not been in bilingual programs.

An additional point of interest raised by the pattern of effect sizes for language variables is that the effect sizes for oral production, in both English and non-English, failed to reach significance, whereas those for reading did. This finding does not appear to support the views of Cummins (1981) as outlined above.

One possible explanation for this pattern, however, may be the nature of tests of oral production rather than the actual linguistic abilities of the children. All of the points discussed earlier in this paper concerning the lack of reliability of language tests in general are especially applicable to tests of oral production. Furthermore, the fact that scores in oral production failed to reach significance for both of the child's languages suggests that these test results may have been particularly influenced by the testing situation. Tests of oral production must be administered to each child individually—a characteristic that makes the results especially susceptible to the child's reactions to the test administrator and to other contextual factors. Children who are shy or reticent in one-to-one contacts with unfamiliar adults simply will not demonstrate their productive language abilities. This has been demonstrated convincingly by Labov (1970) in his classic example of situational effects on children's linguistic responses to adult testers or interviewers.

The dynamics of the situation described by Labov, wherein large linguistic differences were found when a child was interviewed by the same interviewer in both a formal, test-like situation and in an extremely casual setting in the company of the child's friends, seem especially applicable to the children who are represented in the current database, the majority of whom are Mexican American. Children from this cultural group tend to be especially reticent with unfamiliar adults due to the emphasis on respect for elders that is taught at home. Such reticence could well lead to the kinds of results found in this study for oral production in either of the child's languages.

Neglecting academic domains in bilingual program evaluation

One final observation concerning the results for the various tests used in these studies concerns subject areas where language is important as a vehicle of instruction but where language per se is not the focus of the subject. In this respect, it is interesting to note that effect sizes for social studies tests were among the highest. Although there are only two effect sizes for social studies, their presence and magnitude highlight the necessity of including non-language academic subjects in the research and evaluation on bilingual programs. The magnitude of these two effect sizes suggests that bilingual education may be succeeding in preventing academic lag in language-mediated academic subjects, but, unfortunately, these are seldom included in evaluation designs. As another example, the current emphasis on the importance of science education apparently has not been linked to bilingual education, even though the comprehension of scientific concepts is certainly dependent on comprehension of the language in which they are presented. However, not a single study in this set included scores for tests in science. Other areas that have been neglected in the evaluation of bilingual education effectiveness include attitudes and self-concept measures and information on school dropout levels and attendance rates. Although a few studies included information of this sort, the majority did not.

General quality of the research

The findings that have been discussed so far have been based on the data that were reported in the studies included in this synthesis. The overwhelming message of these findings reflects on the quality of research and evaluation in bilingual education. The unacceptable quality of the major portion of this research is substantiated not only by the information contained in the studies, but also by that *not* contained in the studies. Information crucial to understanding the research very often was not included in the reports. Documentation, of the nature and characteristics of the programs being studied, was frequently missing as was information on the characteristics of the students, teachers, and context of the programs. Even the kinds of information most basic for any reputable research report were frequently missing. This is exemplified by the number of comparisons for which effect sizes were not calculable due to failure to report means, standard deviations, and/or sample sizes. These study characteristics, together with the results of this meta-analysis, add up to one glaring message: It is imperative that the quality of research and evaluation in bilingual education be upgraded. How this is to be accomplished is a question that must be addressed not only by researchers in the field, but also by those individuals and agencies responsible for disbursing research monies and by editors and reviewers of journals that publish such research. The complexities inherent in providing optimal educational services to minority language groups will not be unraveled until quality research in bilingual education becomes a norm rather than a scarcity.

CONCLUSIONS

A major result of the current synthesis has been the relevation that bilingual education has been badly served by a predominance of research that is inadequate in design and that makes inappropriate comparisons of children in bilingual programs to children who are dissimilar in many crucial respects. In every instance where there did not appear to be crucial inequalities between experimental and comparison groups, children in the bilingual programs averaged higher than the comparison children on criterion instruments.

The remedy for this regrettable state of affairs in bilingual education research has been suggested throughout the discussion of these results. It has been pointed out that it is virtually impossible to truly equate groups of children from dual-language environments on all of the factors that constitute an adequate research design by attempting to match students or to employ statistical adjustments. It appears that the only plausible way to equate groups adequately is through the use of true randomized procedures.

The fact that true randomized designs are so scarce in bilingual research is partly due to federal and state legal mandates that require the provision of services to minority-language children whenever twenty or more are found in one attendance center. This, in effect, creates a situation where the only children who *could* constitute a comparison group will differ in important respects from the children in the bilingual programs.

The solution to this dilemma lies in carrying out research programs that compare the effectiveness of various types of program models. If research centers were established that are capable of carrying out at least two different program models or that have access to schools that will conduct such programs, well-planned research and evaluation could be integrated with the programs and random designs would be possible. Although research of this type could not answer the needs of program evaluation in schools or districts where there are insufficient students for such a design, it would certainly permit a sound determination of the effects of different kinds of models under different kinds of conditions. Program evaluation in non-research-based schools that duplicate these programs could then focus on questions concerning the quality of the programs they are offering and whether these programs are meeting specific criteria *that are not dependent on comparisons to non-program groups.* In fact, it seems that the only realistic approach to evaluation for school districts lies in a focus on program processes and a monitoring of these processes. School districts should not be put in the position of attempting to answer a question that is truly impossible to answer in non-research settings; that is, what are the effects of a bilingual program compared to the effects of no program at all?

The expense of research efforts that would establish programs and study program variations under sound, controlled conditions would probably be less than costly efforts at grandiose evaluations that ultimately yield useless information. For example, the cost of the national Title VII evaluation (AIR Report) could probably have financed several programs that included sound, integrated research in the design. Not only would such an endeavor have produced additional programs for a number of students, it would also have produced information useful for both evaluation and program planning. In discussing the necessity for smaller-scale, randomized experiments of educational programs, Campbell and Erlebacher (1970) write, "We are sure that data from 400 children in such an experiment would be far more informative than 4,000 tested by the best of quasi-experiments, to say nothing of an ex post facto study" (p. 207). The results of this synthesis have confirmed that observation.

Additional implications for research policy arise from the present comparison of the different synthesizing methodologies: meta-analysis and narrative review. In comparison to narrative review methods, meta-analysis has much greater power to detect true differences between groups due to the accumulation of estimated effect sizes over many studies and to make possible statistical controls for these effect sizes by aggregating specific methodological flaws across the group of studies. Furthermore, the omission of pertinent information is more easily identified through the coding process in meta-analysis. These advantages hold, however, only when the flaws of the primary studies are specifically addressed in the meta-analysis. That this is not usually done is a major contention in Slavin's (1984) discussion of the uses and misuses of meta-analysis. Slavin points out that it is too easy to regard meta-analysis as providing definitive answers to research questions. In this same light, it is also important to be aware that meta-analysis does not free one from subjectivity, even though the subjective influences are easier to keep track of in meta-analysis than in narrative reviews. During the process of conducting a meta-analysis, many decisions must be made, including (a) which studies to include in the synthesis, (b) what variables to code, (c) what kinds of codes will be devised, and (d) how to interpret the information in each study in accord with the codes. Numerous decisions are involved in each of these steps, and each decision admits additional subjectivity. There is a safeguard, however. Just as primary research studies require replication and verification, meta-analyses should be replicated and verified. The current meta-analysis was a partial replication of the Baker and de Kanter review where different methodologies were employed. The replication produced different results. In the same way, a replication of this meta-analysis would provide further verification or refutation of these results.

Note

1. This report is based on the author's doctoral dissertation, completed at the University of Illinois at Urbana-Champaign in the Department of Educational Psychology. I would like to thank my committee members, whose comments and guidance were invaluable: Martin Machr, Rudolph Troike, Marjorie Steinkamp, Robert Linn, Gary Cziko, Larry Braskamp, and Jesse Delia, all at the University of Illinois.

References

American Institutes for Research. 1975. Bilingual education program (Aprendemos en dos idiomas), Corpus Christi. Texas. In *Identification and description of exemplary bilingual education programs.* Palo Alto, CA: Author.

Ames, J. S., and Bicks, P. 1978. *An evaluation of Title VII bilingual/bicultural program, 1977–1978 school year, final report, community school district 22.* Brooklyn, NY: School District 22.

Baecher, R. E. 1981. Language proficiency assessment: Issues and definitions. In S. S. Seidner, ed. *Issues of language assessment: Foundations and research.* Springfield: Illinois State Board of Education.

Balasubramonian, K., Seclye, H. N., and De Weffer, R. E. 1973, May. *Do bilingual education programs inhibit English language achievement? A report on an Illinois experiment.* Paper presented at the Seventh Annual Convention of Teachers of English to Speakers of Other Languages, San Juan, Puerto Rico.

Baker, K. A., and de Kanter, A. A. 1981, Sept. 25. *Effectiveness of bilingual education: A review of the literature.* Washington, DC: Office of Planning, Budget and Evaluation, U.S. Department of Education.

Barik, H., and Swain, M. 1975. Three-year evaluation of a large-scale early grade French-immersion program: The Ottawa study. *Language Learning* 25(1):1–30.

Barik, H., Swain, M., and Nwanunobi, E. A. 1977. English-French bilingual education: The Elgin study through grade five. *Canadian Modern Language Review* 33(4):459–475.

Bereiter, C., and Scardamalia, M. 1981. From conversation to composition: The role of instruction in a developmental process. In R. Glaser, ed. *Advances in Instructional Psychology* (Vol. 2). Hillsdale, NJ: Lawrence Erlbaum Associates.

Bloomfield. L. 1933. *Language.* New York: Holt, Rinehart, and Winston.

Campbell, D. T., and Boruch, R. F. 1975. Making the case for randomized assignment to treatments by considering the alternatives: Six ways in which quasi-experimental evaluations in compensatory education tend to underestimate effects. In C. A. Bennett and A. A. Lumsdaine, eds. *Evaluation and Experiment: Some Critical Issues in Assessing Social Programs.* New York: Academic Press.

Campbell, D. T., and Erlebacher, A. E. 1970. How regression artifacts in quasi-experimental evaluations can mistakenly make compensatory education look harmful. In J. Hellmuth, ed. *Compensatory education: A national debate* (Vol. 3. *Disadvantaged Child*). New York: Brunner/Mazel.

Cardenas, J. A. 1977, June. AIR evaluation of bilingual education. *Intercultural Development Research Association Newsletter* (pp. 1–3). San Antonio, Texas.

Carsrud, K. E., and Curtis, J. 1979. *ESEA Title VII Bilingual Program: Final report.* Austin, TX: Austin Independent School District.

Chomsky, N. 1957. *Syntactic Structures.* The Hague, Netherlands: Mouton.

Chomsky, N. 1965. *Aspects of the Theory of Syntax.* Cambridge, MA: MIT Press.

Cohen, A. D. 1975. *A Sociolinguistic Approach to Bilingual Education.* Rowley, MA: Newbury House.

Cohen, H. 1969. *Statistical Power Analysis for the Behavioral Sciences.* New York: Academic Press.

Cottrell, M. C. February 1971. *Bilingual education in San Juan County, Utah: A cross-cultural emphasis.* Paper presented at the annual meeting of the American Educational Research Association, New York City.

Covey, D. D. 1973. *An analytical study of secondary freshmen bilingual education and its effect on academic achievement and attitude of Mexican-American students.* Unpublished doctoral dissertation. Arizona State University, Tempe.

Cummins, J. 1981. The role of primary language development in promoting educational success for language minority students. In California State Department of Education, ed. *Schooling and language minority students: A theoretical framework.* Los Angeles: National Dissemination and Assessment Center.

Cummins, J. 1984. *Bilingualism and Special Education: Issues in Assessment and Pedagogy.* Clevedon, England: Short Run Press.

Dale, P. S. 1976. *Language Development: Structure and Function* (second ed.). New York: Holt, Rinehart, and Winston.

Danoff, M. N., Coles, G. J., McLaughlin, D. H., and Reynolds, D. J. 1977a. *Evaluation of the impact of ESEA Title VII Spanish/English Bilingual Education Programs. Volume I: Study design and interim findings.* Palo Alto, CA: American Institutes for Research.

Danoff, M. N., Coles, G. J., McLaughlin, D. H., and Reynolds, D. J. 1977b. *Evaluation of the impact of ESEA Title VII Spanish/English Bilingual Education Programs. Volume II: Project descriptions.* Palo Alto, CA: American Institutes for Research.

Danoff, M. N., Coles, G. J., McLaughlin, D. H., and Reynolds, D. J. 1978. *Evaluation of the impact of ESEA Title VII Spanish/English Bilingual Education Programs. Volume III: Year two impact data, educational process, and in-depth analysis.* Palo Alto, CA: American Institutes for Research.

Donaldson, M. 1978. *Children's Minds.* Glasgow: Collins.

Dulay, H. C., and Burt, M. K. 1978. *Why Bilingual Education? A Summary of Research Findings* (second ed.). San Francisco: Bloomsbury West.

Engle, P. L. 1975. *The use of vernacular languages in education: Language medium in early school years for minority language groups. Bilingual education series #2.* Arlington, VA: Center for Applied Linguistics.

Fillmore, C. J. 1968. The case for case. In E. Bach and R. T. Harms, eds. *Universals in Linguistic Theory.* New York: Holt, Rinehart, and Winston.

Freund, R. J., and Littell, R. C. 1981. *SAS for linear models: A guide to the ANOVA and GLM procedures.* SAS Series in Statistical Applications. Cary, NC: SAS Institute.

Gilmore, G., and Dickenson, A. 1979. *The relationship between instruments used for identifying children of limited-English-speaking ability in Texas.* Houston: Region IV Education Service Center.

Glass, G. V. 1978. Integrating findings: The meta-analysis of research. In L. Shulman, ed. *Review of Research in Education* (Vol. 5). Itasca, IL: Peacock.

Glass, G. V., McGaw, B., and Smith, M. L. 1981. *Meta-Analysis in Social Research.* Beverly Hills, CA: Sage.

Glass, G. V., and Smith, M. L. 1979. Meta-analysis of research on class size and achievement. *Educational Evaluation and Policy Analysis* 1:2–16.

Gray, T. 1977, April. *Response to AIR study "Evaluation of the impact of ESEA Title VII Spanish/English Bilingual Education Program."* Arlington, VA: Center for Applied Linguistics.

Hedges, L. V. 1981. Distribution theory for Glass's estimator of effect size and related estimators. *Journal of Educational Statistics* 6(2):107–128.

Hedges, L. V., and Stock, W. 1983. The effects of class size: An examination of rival hypotheses. *American Educational Research Journal* 20(1):63–85.

Hernandez-Chavez, E., Llanes, J., Alvarez, R., and Arvizu, S. 1982. *A response to the DeKanter/Baker review* (Monograph No. 12). Sacramento: California State University, Cross-Cultural Research Center.

Hoepfner, R., and Conniff, W. Jr., eds. 1974. *CSF secondary school test evaluations: Grades 7 and 8.* Los Angeles: University of California, Center for the Study of Evaluation, Evaluation Technologies Program.

Huzar, H. 1973. *The effects of an English-Spanish primary grade reading program on second and third grade students.* Unpublished master's thesis. Rutgers University, New Brunswick, NJ.

Kaufman, M. 1968. Will instruction in reading Spanish affect ability in reading English? *Journal of Reading* 17 521–527.

Labov, W. 1970. *The Study of Nonstandard English.* Urbana, IL: National Council of Teachers of English.

Lado, R. 1961. *Language Testing.* London: Longmans, Green.

Lambert, W. E., and Tucker, G. R. 1972. *Bilingual Education of Children: The St. Lambert Experience.* Rowley, MA: Newbury House.

Legarreta, D. 1979. The effects of program models on language acquisition by Spanish speaking children. *TESOL Quarterly* 13(4):521–534.

Littlejohn, J. M. 1981, Oct. 10. *Comments on the final draft report of "The Effectiveness of Bilingual Education: A Review of the Literature"* (Memorandum). Washington, DC: U.S. Department of Education, Office for Civil Rights.

Lum, J. B. 1971. *An effectiveness study of English as a second language (ESL) and Chinese bilingual methods.* Unpublished doctoral dissertation. University of California–Berkeley.

Mackey, W. F. 1970. A typology of bilingual education. In T. Andersson and M. Boyer, eds. *Bilingual schooling in the United States* (Vol. 2). Austin, TX: Southwest Educational Development Laboratory.

Matthews, T. 1979. *An investigation of the effects of background characteristics and special language services on the reading achievement and English fluency of bilingual students.* Seattle: Seattle Public Schools, Department of Planning, Research, and Evaluation.

McConnell, B. 1980. *Individualized bilingual instruction. Final evaluation, 1978–1979 program.* Pullman, WA: Individualized Bilingual Instruction Evaluation Office.

McGaw, B., and Glass, G. V. 1980. Choice of the metric for effect size in meta-analysis. *American Educational Research Journal* 17(3):325–337.

McSpadden, J. R. 1979. *Acadiana bilingual bicultural education program. Interim evaluation report 1978–1979.* Lafayette, LA: Lafayette Parish School Board.

McSpadden, J. R. 1980. *Acadiana bilingual bicultural education program. Interim evaluation report 1979–1980.* Lafayette, LA: Lafayette Parish School Board.

Moore, F. B., and Parr, G. D. 1979. Models of bilingual education: Comparisons of effectiveness. *Elementary School Journal* 79(2):93–97.

Nie, N. H., Hull, C. H., Jenkins, J. G., Steinbrenner, K., and Bent, D. H. 1975. *Statistical Package for the Social Sciences* (second ed.). New York: McGraw-Hill.

Olesini, J. 1971. *The effect of bilingual instruction on the achievement of elementary pupils.* Unpublished doctoral dissertation, East Texas State University, Commerce.

O'Malley, J. M. 1978, Winter. Review of the evaluation of the impact of ESEA Title VII Spanish/English Bilingual Education Program. *Bilingual Resources* 1(2):6–10.

Olson, D. R. 1977. From utterance to text: The bias of language in speech and writing. *Harvard Educational Review* 47:257–281.

Pena-Hughes, E., and Solis, J. 1980. *abcs* (Unpublished report). McAllen, TX: McAllen Independent School District.

Plante, A. J. 1976. *A study of the effectiveness of the Connectient Pairing Model of Bilingual-Bicultural Education.* Hamden, CT: Connecticut Staff Development Cooperative.

Ramos, M., Aguilar, J. V., and Sibayan, B. F. 1967. *The determination of language policy.* Philippine Center for Language Study Monograph Series 2. Quizon City, Philippines: Alemor/Phoenix.

Rivera, C., and Simich, C. 1981. Language proficiency assessment: Research findings and their application. In S. S. Scidner, ed. *Issues of Language Assessment: Foundations and Research.* Springfield, IL: Illinois State Board of Education.

Rotberg, I. C. 1983, February. A reply to Baker. *Harvard Educational Review* 53(1):106.

SAS Institute. 1979. *SAS User's Guide.* Cary, NC: Author.

Saville-Troike, M. 1984. What *really* matters in second-language learning for academic achievement? *TESOL Quarterly* 18(2)-199–219.

Searle, S. R. 1971. *Linear Models.* New York: John Wiley & Sons.

Seidner, S. S. (1982). Political expedience or educational research? An analysis of Baker and de Kanter's review of the literature of bilingual education. In S. S. Seidner, ed. *Issues of Language Assessment: Foundations and Research.* Springfield: Illinois State Board of Education.

Shuy, R. 1977. Quantitative language data: A case for and some warnings against. *Anthropology in Education Quarterly* 8(2):73–82.

Silverman, R. J., Noa, J. K., and Russell, R. H. 1977. *Oral language tests for bilingual students: An evaluation of language dominance and proficiency instruments.* Portland, OR: Northwest Regional Educational Laboratory.

Slavin, R. E. 1984. Meta-analysis in education: How has it been used? *Educational Researcher* 13(8):6–15.

Skoczylas, R. V. 1972. *An evaluation of some cognitive and affective aspects of a Spanish-English bilingual education program.* Unpublished doctoral dissertation. University of New Mexico, Albuquerque.

Smith, M. L., and Glass, G. V. 1980. Meta-analysis of research on class size and its relationship to attitudes and instruction. *American Educational Research Journal* 17:419–433.

Stebbins, L. B., St. Pierre, R. G., Proper, E. C., Anderson, R. B., and Cerva, T. R. 1977, April. *Education as Experimentation: A Planned Variation Model* (Vols. IVA-IVC). Cambridge, MA: ABT Associates.

Steel, R. G. B., and Torrie, J. H. 1980. *Principles and procedures of statistics* (second ed.). New York: McGraw-Hill.

Steinkamp, M., and Maehr, M. L. 1984. Gender differences in motivational orientations toward achievement in school science: A quantitative synthesis. *American Educational Research Journal* 21(1):39–59.

Stern, C. 1975. *Final report of the Compton Unified School District's Title VII bilingual-bicultural project: September 1969 through June 1975.* Compton City, CA: Compton City Schools.

Swain, M. 1979. Bilingual education: Research and its implications. In C. A. Yorio, K. Perkins, and J. Schacter, eds. *On TESOL 79: The Learner in focus.* Washington, DC: Teachers of English to Speakers of Other Languages.

Troike, R. C. 1969. Receptive competence, productive competence, and performance. In J. E. Alatis, ed. *Monograph Series on Languages and Linguistics* 22:63–73.

Troike, R. C. 1978. Research evidence for the effectiveness of bilingual education. *NABE Journal* 3(1):13–24.

Troike, R. C. 1982. Zeno's paradox and language assessment. In S. S. Seidner, ed. *Issues of Language Assessment: Foundations and Research.* Springfield: Illinois State Board of Education.

Troike, R. C. 1983. *Can language be tested?* Unpublished manuscript.

Tucker, G. R. 1974. The assessment of bilingual and bicultural factors of communication. In S. T. Carey, ed. *Bilingualism, Biculturalism, and Education.* Edmonton: University of Alberta Press.

Ulibarri, D. M., Spencer, M. L., and Rivas, G. A. 1981. Language proficiency and academic achievement: A study of language proficiency tests and their relationship to school ratings as predictors of academic achievement. *NABE Journal* 5(3):47–80.

Willig, A. C. 1982. The effectiveness of bilingual education: Review of a report. *NABE Journal* 6(2–3):1–19.

Yates, J. R., and Ortiz, A. A. 1983, Spring. Baker and de Kanter review: Inappropriate conclusions of the efficacy of bilingual education. *NABE Journal* 7(3):75–84.

Zirkel, P. A. 1972. *An evaluation of the effectiveness of selected experimental bilingual education programs in Connecticut.* Hartford, CT: Department of Education.

Author

ANN C. WILLIG, coordinator of Longitudinal Research, Handicapped Minorities Research Institute, Department of Special Education, University of Texas–Austin. *Specializations:* Bilingual/multicultural education, bilingual special education, achievement motivation.

Chapter 16
When Learning a Second Language Means Losing the First

LILY WONG FILLMORE

In societies like the United States with diverse populations, children from linguistic minority families must learn the language of the society in order to take full advantage of the educational opportunities offered by the society. The timing and the conditions under which they come into contact with English, however, can profoundly affect the retention and continued use of their primary languages as well as the development of their second language. This article discusses evidence and findings from a nationwide study of language shift among language-minority children in the United States. The findings suggest that the loss of a primary language, particularly when it is the only language spoken by parents, can be very costly to the children, their families, and to society as a whole. Immigrant and American Indian families were surveyed to determine the extent to which family language patterns were affected by their children's early learning of English in preschool programs. Families whose children had attended preschool programs conducted exclusively in Spanish served as a base of comparison for the families whose children attended English-only or bilingual preschools.

THE PROBLEM

In this chapter, I address a problem in second-language learning that has long been acknowledged but that has not received the attention it deserves from researchers.[1] Specifically, this chapter deals with the phenomenon of "subtractive bilingualism," the name given the problem by Wallace Lambert, who first discussed it in relation to French-Canadian and Canadian immigrant children whose acquisition of English in school resulted not in bilingualism, but in the erosion or loss of their primary languages (Lambert 1975, 1977, 1981). The phenomenon is a familiar one in the United States. It is the story of countless American immigrant and native children and adults who have lost their ethnic languages in the process of becoming linguistically assimilated into the English-speaking world of the school and society. Few American-born children of immigrant parents are fully proficient in the ethnic language, even if it was the only language they spoke when they first entered school. Once these children learn English, they tend not to maintain or to develop the language spoken at home, even if it is the only one their parents know. This has been the story of past immigrant groups, and it is the story of the present ones. The only difference is that the process appears to be taking place much more rapidly today.

Few among us realize what is really happening. Quite the contrary. Over the past several years, there has been an increasing concern among educators, policy-makers, and members of the public that the new immigrants are not assimilating fast enough. There is a widespread belief among people who should know better that the new immigrants are resisting the necessity of learning English, and the reason why so many of them seem to have difficulty making progress in school is that they refuse to learn English. Bilingual education is often blamed for their problems: It is seen as the primary reason why these new immigrants are not learning English and why they are not making the academic progress they should be making in school. Many people see bilingual education as a cop-out: By educating children even in part through their primary languages, we allow them to get away without having to learn English. Because of these largely erroneous beliefs, bilingual education has lost considerable public support over the last few years. California no longer has a legal mandate for bilingual education, the legislation requiring it having expired a few years ago.[2] This has been a matter of great concern for those of us who regard bilingual education as the most appropriate and pedagogically sound way to educate the many language-minority students in the society's schools. Bilingual education is provided for only a fraction of the students who need it, and even then most of the available programs place greater emphasis on the learning of English than they do on the use and retention of the students' primary languages.

EARLY EDUCATION POLICIES AND PRACTICES

Even more troubling are the recent moves throughout the country to solve the immigrant language problem through preschool education. Over the past five years or so, early education has been touted as the ideal solution to the academic problems of language-minority students, whether these students are immigrants, non-immigrants, or Native Americans. The state of Texas led the way some years ago by passing legislation that provided preschool programs for four-year-old children from minority backgrounds. The idea behind this legislation was that the younger children are, the faster and more completely they learn a new language. At age three or four, the children are in a language-learning mode: They learn whatever language or languages they hear, as long as the conditions for language learning are present. By the time they are five, the reasoning goes, they will be English speakers and they can get right on with school. This past year, Texas extended the legislation to cover three-year-olds.

Other states have followed suit, and late in 1990 Congress augmented its funding for Project Head Start by $500 million dollars, to provide more programs of a similar nature throughout the country for the children of the poor, many of whom are language minorities. Head Start is a benevolent program in that its main objective is to give poor children some of the background experiences, and skills needed for school, including English, before they get there. For language-minority children, any program that emphasizes English at the expense of the primary language is a potential disaster, however. And therein lies the problem that this chapter addresses.

Consider what happens when young children find themselves in the attractive new world of the American school. What do they do when they discover that the only language that is spoken there is one that they do not know? How do they respond when they realize that the only language they know has no function or value in that new social world and that, in fact, it constitutes a barrier to their participation in the social life of the school? They do just as the promoters of early education for language-minority students hope they will. They learn English, and, too often, they drop their primary languages as they do. In time, many of these children lost their first languages.

How likely is this? We will argue that the likelihood of children forfeiting and losing their primary languages as they learn English under the conditions just described is very great—great enough to pose a major problem to the school and society whose policies and practices created the problem in the first place.

Over the past few years, some of us have become increasingly concerned about the consequences of emphasizing English for children at younger and younger ages. My students and I, for example, have documented the process of school language learning and primary language loss through case studies (Benjamin 1990; Kreven 1989; Wong Fillmore 1991). Early in 1990, as Congress was considering the George H. W. Bush administration's proposal to expand preschool funding for the purpose of teaching language-minority children English so they would be "ready for school," the situation seemed dire enough for us to step up the effort to document the effects of this practice in the hope of exerting some influence on the educational policies that were being formulated and implemented.

THE NO-COST STUDY ON FAMILIES

Methodology

At a plenary session of the 1990 National Association for Bilingual Education (NABE) conference,[3] Jim Cummins, Alice Paul, Guadalupe Valdés, and I called for a national survey of language-minority families whose children have participated in preschool programs that were conducted partly or entirely in English to determine the extent to which these programs were affecting the children's language patterns. Because of the urgency of the situation, we could not wait until we had funds to conduct the study. It had to be done immediately. We appealed to the NABE membership to join us in conducting the study as volunteers. The study, because it was conducted without funding, was called "The No-Cost Study on Families."[4]

We prepared an interview form that was translated into many languages—among them, Spanish, Korean, Japanese, Chinese, Khmer, and Vietnamese—and we held two workshops at the conference in which we trained people to conduct the family interviews. The selection criteria for the families to be interviewed were that they be language minorities and have children who have attended preschool programs in the United States. We wanted to know what languages were spoken by the adults in the family, especially those who were primary and secondary caretakers of the children. We asked about the programs the children had been in: What kind were they? Which languages were used in class by teachers and students? What did the parents like or not like about the programs? We asked about language-usage patterns in the home: What language did the adults use to the children? What did the children use to the adults in the home and to siblings? We asked whether or not there had been changes in the use of language at home as a result of the children's being in school, and what those changes were. We asked the parents to judge their children's proficiency in the language of the home: Were they as proficient as children of their age and experience usually are in that language? Finally, we asked the parents about their concerns: Were they worried about their children losing the language of the home? Whose responsibility did they think it was to help them retain it? What did they want us to tell policy-makers and educators about their concerns as parents? The interview consisted of 45 questions; all but two were framed as forced-choice-response questions.

Hundreds of people attended the two training sessions, and many of them eventually conducted interviews of families. Some participants recruited friends and associates to help in the effort. These volunteers—teachers, school administrators, social workers, researchers, students, parents and community workers—interviewed some 1,100 families across the country.[5] The families interviewed included American Indians, Arabs, Latinos, East and Southeast Asians from a variety of backgrounds, and assorted others. Included in the study were 311 families—all of them Spanish speakers—whose children attended preschool programs conducted entirely in their primary language. These families served as a base of comparison for us in interpreting the data from the families whose children had attended English-only or bilingual preschool programs. NCRG members at the University of California–Santa Cruz (UCSC)[6] were the NCRG researchers who were responsible for preparing the quantifiable data for analysis. No-Costers at the University of California–Berkeley (UCB)[7] and at the Foundation Center for Phenomenological Research in Sacramento[8] were responsible for processing the data that had to be treated qualitatively.

In mid-December 1990, we called a two-day No-Cost meeting of researchers, educators, and children's advocates at Berkeley to examine and interpret the data, to try to agree on what the data allowed us to say, and to decide how we might say it most effectively and forcefully. The thirty-five participants at this meeting came from all over the country and represented a broad spectrum of ethnic groups, academic institutions and disciplines, and advocacy groups.[9] Several individuals who could not travel to Berkeley participated in the meeting by telephone. The participants made a good many recommendations, including ones for additional analyses to be carried out on the data, other studies to be done in following up on some of the hypotheses generated by this survey, and ones for the dissemination of the findings. In this chapter, I report only those preliminary findings that members of this group have already gone over. Needless to say, there will be a great many other things to report before we are done with this work.

Preliminary findings from the No-Cost Survey

It should be noted that although more than 1,100 interviews were returned to us, not all of them were received in time to be processed and included in this preliminary analysis of the data. The analyses reported here represent 1,001 families, 690 in the main sample and 311 in the comparison sample.[10] Table 16.1 shows the ethnic makeup of the families included in the two sub-samples. As noted earlier, the 311 families that comprise the comparison group were all Spanish speakers, although three are shown on Table 16.1 as being otherwise.[11] So were two thirds of the others, thus Spanish speakers added up to 776 families, 77.5 percent of the total sample. This is not surprising because Spanish speakers are the largest language-minority group in the country. In 1987, 73 percent of the limited-English speakers in California schools were Spanish speakers, so the proportion of Spanish-speaking families in our sample is fairly representative of their numbers, at least in the state of California. There were ninety-four East and Southeast Asian families, including Chinese, Japanese, Koreans, Cambodians, Vietnamese, and Hmong, comprising 13.6 percent of the families in the sample. American-Indian families, including Navahos, Yaquis, Apaches, Papago (Tohono O'odham), and Pascua, comprise the next largest group, with sixty-two families, or 9 percent of the main sample. There were also thirty-four Arab families (5 percent) in the main sample as well, and twenty-four families (3.5 percent) from a variety of backgrounds, including Africans and Europeans.

Family size as shown in Table 16.2 was quite comparable between the two samples—84.9 percent of the main sample and 82.4 percent of the comparison families had from one to four children; 14.8 percent of the main sample and 17.2 percent of the comparison families had five or more children. A significant difference between the comparison and main sample families was found in the frequency of families with children under age five—80.5 percent of the comparison families had one or more preschool-age children, whereas just 63.4 percent of the main sample families did. This is not surprising because the families in the comparison sample were ones who had children currently enrolled in a preschool program, whereas the main sample consisted of families whose children either were in, or had been in, preschool programs.

The families in the study were generally intact, with both parents present in the home, and traditional in structure, with fathers regarded as heads of households (see Table 16.3). The families were

TABLE 16.1 Characteristics of the Families

	Families with Children in Bilingual/English ECE Programs (Main Sample)		Families with Children in Home Language ECE Programs (Comparison)	
Ethnic Background	No.	(%)	No.	(%)
Latinos	468	(67.8)	308	(99)
East & Southeast Asians	94	(13.6)		
American Indians	62	(9)		
Arabs	34	(5)		
Others	24	(3.5)	3	(1)
Missing data	8	(1.1)		
Total	690	(100)	311	(100)

TABLE 16.2 Family Size

	Main Sample %	Comparison %	All Families %
1–2 children	43.4	42.5	43.2
3–4 children	41.5	39.9	40.0
5 or more children	17.2	14.8	15.7

traditional in another important way. In both groups, mothers were reported as having the primary responsibility for caring for the children (82.7 percent of the main sample, and 84 percent of the comparison families). Fathers, grandparents, siblings, and other relatives were identified as primary caretakers in just a small number of families (see Table 16.4). The majority of families in both samples had been in the United States for more than ten years (67.6 percent in the main sample, and 54.5 percent for the comparison sample; see Table 16.5). There was a somewhat larger percentage of immigrant families in the main sample who had been in the United States for fewer than five years than in the comparison sample (13.5 percent versus 9.4 percent) and a higher percentage of comparison group families who had been in the United States between five to ten years (35.9 percent versus 19 percent).

Table 16.6, which shows length of residence in the communities where the families presently live, indicates a few notable differences between the two samples. There was a higher percentage of families in the main sample than in the comparison sample that had been in their present communities fewer than five years (44.4 percent versus 15.1 percent, or three times as many). The percentages

TABLE 16.3 Head of Household

	Main Sample %	Comparison %	All Families %
Father or Stepfather	78.9	68.9	75.5
Mother or Stepmother	18.4	26.9	28.1
Both	.1	2.2	.8
Grandparent/Aunt/Uncle	3.5	.9	3.4

TABLE 16.4 Primary Caretaker of Children

	Main Sample %	Comparison %	All Families %
Father or Stepfather	7.0	3.2	5.8
Mother or Stepmother	82.7	84.0	83.2
Grandparent	7.1	4.9	6.4
Aunt/Uncle	1.3	2.3	1.6
Sibling	1.0	4.2	4.2

TABLE 16.5 Length of Residence in United States

	Main Sample %	Comparison %
Less than 5 years	13.5	9.4
5–10 years	19.0	35.9
Over 10 years	67.6	54.5

TABLE 16.6 Length of Residence in Community

	Main Sample %	Comparison %	All Families %
Less than 5 years	44.4	15.1	30.9
5–10 years	23.1	38.8	28.1
Over 10 years	38.4	46.2	40.9

were commensurately greater for comparison families reporting residence both for periods of five to ten years, and for more than ten years than for the main sample. These differences may indicate that the families in the main sample were somewhat more upwardly mobile than the comparison families, but it may also be a reflection of the larger proportion of recently arrived families in the main sample. Despite these differences, the majority of families in both groups appear to be fairly stable in their places of residence. The differences in the patterns of language shift that we found do not seem to be easily relatable to residential patterns found among the families.

In some cases, the questions regarding language use in preschool programs proved to be difficult for parents to answer. We asked them to say whether the preschool programs their children had attended were conducted in English only or mostly, in the children's language only or mostly, or in both languages (i.e., bilingually). Not everyone could say, perhaps because they had not been in the preschool classrooms while they were in session, or because they could not tell. The problem may be that it is not always obvious to the casual observer what the instructional language of a preschool program is because teachers at that level seldom engage in whole-class or even group activities for which there is an obvious "language of instruction." In most preschool programs, teachers interact with children individually or in small groups, and parents may or may not know what language the teacher uses in speaking to the children, except where the teachers are clearly English or other language monolinguals. As noted earlier, the children in the 311 families that we are using as a basis of comparison for the families in the main sample attended preschool programs that we knew were being conducted exclusively in Spanish. As Table 16.7 shows, however, many of the parents even in this group were uncertain as to how to characterize the use of language in their children's classes, or they responded in ways that contradicted what we had already independently established to be the case for those programs. Similarly, there were families in the main sample who reported that their children had attended native-language-only preschools, although the selection criterion we had established was that the families be ones whose children had attended bilingual or English-only programs. We decided to accept their responses at face value, as we did all of the information provided by our interviewees, and to examine the effects in the data parents gave us on language usage against this information because there was no way that we might have confirmed or disconfirmed any of the other information independently.

Hence, as Table 16.7 shows, 30.6 percent of the main sample and 1.3 percent of the comparison families reported that their children were in preschools that used English predominantly or exclusively; 11 percent of the main sample and 74.6 percent of the comparison families had children in programs that were conducted in the language of the home; 46.7 percent of the main sample and 10.3 percent of the comparison families had children in bilingual programs, whereas 11.7 percent of the main and 13.8 percent of the comparison families were uncertain or could not say what languages were used in their children's programs. Clearly, the differences between the two groups were great enough to justify maintaining the categorical difference that we were drawing between the two.

Effects on language use in the home

First, a caveat: Given the data we have, it is not possible to determine whether or not there is a causal relationship between language use in preschool programs and changes in patterns of language use in the home. Many of the families we interviewed have children who have gone well beyond preschool, and the children in both our comparison and main sample families have learned a lot of English in the schools they have attended since they were in the preschools we asked about. Nonetheless, there were dramatic and highly significant differences to be seen in the data provided by the main sample families versus the comparison sample with regard to patterns of language use and maintenance in their homes. Let us consider their responses to our question concerning any changes parents might have noticed in language use at home once their children began attending preschool. The following analyses were based on responses from just those 609 families in the main sample and 268 families in the comparison sample for which parents provided information concerning language use in their children's preschool programs. The parents were asked to say whether or not there had been any kind of change in language use in the home, and if there were, what the change consisted of: greater or less use of English, and greater or less use of the home language (HL). Table 16.8 shows overall patterns of change reported in language use in the home for two

TABLE 16.7 Language Use Reported in Early Education Programs

	Main Sample		Comparison	
	No.	(%)	No.	(%)
English only or mostly	211	(30.6)	4	(1.3)
Language of home	76	(11)	232	(74.6)
Bilingual	322	(46.7)	32	(10.3)
Uncertain or don't know	81	(11.7)	43	(13.8)
Totals	690	(100)	311	(100)

samples. We can see that 30.9 percent of the families in the main sample reported no change in language patterns connected to their children's attendance in preschool programs, whereas just 18.3 percent of the comparison families said there had been no resulting change.

But change can be negative or positive. Because our concern in this study relates to language shift, we view the home language being displaced by English as a negative change especially in homes where the adults speak little or no English, whereas an increase in home language usage represents a positive change. We categorized "less English" as neutral, because it is unclear what kind of change it represents. When we grouped the responses in that manner, we found 50.6 percent of the main sample reporting a negative change in the language patterns in the home, that is, a shift from the home language to English versus 10.8 percent of the families reporting a negative change in the comparison sample. In other words, the families who had had their children in English-only and bilingual preschools were reporting negative changes 4.68 times more frequently than the comparison families were. The findings were even stronger when we analyzed the reports of language shift in relation to the kinds of programs the parents said their children had been in.

Table 16.9, which shows the changes in language patterns in relation to language use in early education programs for main sample families, reveals the importance of this factor. As we see, negative changes are reported in 64.4 percent of the families whose children attended English-only preschool, whereas they were reported in just 26.3 percent of those main sample families whose children attended primary language programs. Conversely, positive changes were reported by 42.1 percent of the primary language families, whereas they were reported in just 2.8 percent of the English-only families—or 15 times more frequently! Sad to say, bilingual education does not appear to offer children enough protection from language shift, as Table 16.9 shows: 47.2 percent of the main sample families with children in bilingual preschool programs reported a negative change in family language patterns, whereas just 18.6 percent reported a positive change. It is difficult to know just how bilingual these programs were, but it would be reasonable to guess that English was used more frequently than the children's home language in many of them, given the pattern of responses shown in Table 16.9. Table 16.10 relates reports of changes in comparison family language patterns after their children attended preschool programs. Here we see that the 72.8 percent of the families who knew that their children were in primary-language-only preschools reported positive changes in their family language patterns, whereas 10.3 percent reported negative changes—or 7 times more frequently. Families who thought their children were in bilingual schools did, in fact, report positive changes less frequently (46.9 percent) than did those who knew that the native language was used exclusively in the preschool, but they did not report negative changes much more frequently than did the others (12.5 percent versus 10.3 percent). They did report "no change" twice as frequently as did the other parents, however (34.4 percent versus 16 percent).

TABLE 16.8 Changes in Language Use at Home After Children Attended Early Education Programs

	Main Sample		Comparison	
	No.	(%)	No.	(%)
No noticeable change	188	(30.9)	49	(18.3)
Negative change (Less HL, More E)	308	(50.6)	29	(10.8)
Positive change (More HL)	98	(16.1)	185	(69)
Neutral (Less E)	15	(2.4)	5	(1.9)
Totals	609	(100)	268	(100)

Are the negative changes reported here really negative? One might argue that a shift to a greater use of English and less primary language use may not only be inevitable but desirable for these families in the long run. That question can be answered only in relation to facts about the families in our samples.

The first language in 97.7 percent of the main sample and 99 percent of the comparison sample families was reportedly a language other than English. Nevertheless, the families were clearly responding to the assimilative forces that work against the retention of ethnic languages in the society. Linguistic change almost always begins with the children in language-minority families. The children speak little or no English when they enter school, but they soon learn enough to get by. In that world, they quickly discover that the key to acceptance is English, and they learn it so they can take part in the social life of the classroom. And they take home what they have learned in school. All too often, English becomes their language of choice long before they know it well enough to express themselves fully in that language, and they use it both in school and at home. The parents in these families are considerably less proficient in English than they are in their primary languages, that is, assuming they know English at all. The assimilative forces that impel the children to learn English at school also operate on the adults when they come into contact with the world outside the home, of course. Without much English, the only jobs immigrants or refugees can hope to get in this society are ones at the lowest rungs of job ladders in any field of endeavor. Some attend adult school English classes, and others try to pick up what they can on their own. Neither of these measures will provide them with the exposure and help they need to learn the language for the most part. Adults seldom find themselves in the kinds of situations that allow them to learn a language as fully as children eventually do. It is not that they are incapable of learning; in fact, there is evidence suggesting that when the conditions are right, adults may be better language learners than children are (Krashen, Long, and Scarcella 1979; Snow and Hoefnagel-Höhle 1977). The conditions, however, are seldom right for adult immigrants. They rarely have the time or means to take advantage of the type of language study that might lead to proficiency in English.[12] In any event, it is more difficult

TABLE 16.9 Changes in Language Patterns in Main Sample Homes by Language of Early Education Program

	English Only		Bilingual		HL Only		Total	
	No.	(%)	No.	(%)	No.	(%)	No.	(%)
No change	66	(31.3)	98	(30.4)	24	(31.6)	188	(30.9)
Negative change	136	(64.4)	152	(47.2)	20	(26.3)	308	(50.6)
Positive change	6	(2.8)	60	(18.6)	32	(42.1)	98	(16.1)
Neutral change	3	(1.4)	12	(3.7)			15	(2.4)
Totals	211	(99.9)	322	(99.9)	76	(100)	609	(100)

TABLE 16.10 Changes in Language Patterns in Comparison Sample Homes by Language of Early Education Program

	English Only		Bilingual		HL Only		Total	
	No.	(%)	No.	(%)	No.	(%)	No.	(%)
No change	1	(25)	11	(34.4)	37	(16)	49	(18.3)
Negative change	1	(25)	4	(12.5)	24	(10.3)	29	(10.8)
Positive change	1	(25)	15	(46.9)	169	(72.8)	185	(69)
Neutral change	1	(25)	2	(6.2)	2	(.8)	5	(1.9)
Totals	4	(100)	32	(100)	232	(99.9)	268	(100)

for the adults than for the children to learn English. In families such as the ones in our two samples, the adults simply do not learn English as quickly or as well as the children. But English nevertheless enters the home. Evidence of this can be seen in the responses parents gave to our questions concerning the language their children used at home.

Because age and relative position in the family appear to be important variables in primary language maintenance among immigrant children, we asked respondents to our interviews to divide the children in the family into three groups: older children, middle children, and younger children. If the family's children did not divide up sensibly into three groups, then they were asked to do a two-way grouping: older versus younger. If all of the children were younger than five or six, the respondent was asked to describe them all as younger children. Thus, there were more families with younger children than older children, and few families with middle children. We then asked what language the older children used in speaking to the adults in the family and what they used when speaking to their siblings. We asked the same of the middle children and the younger.

What we found across the board were highly significant differences between our main and comparison samples in all age groupings of children. In every case, the children in the main sample were reported as using the home language less frequently than were the children in the comparison sample, and English more frequently. Tables 16.11 through 16.16 show that not only were the children using English more frequently and the native language less with their siblings, they were doing so as well with the adults in the home who, from all evidence, did not know English well. We see this across age groups in nearly a third of all main sample families (30.8 percent of the older children, 30.5 percent of the middle, and 27.1 percent of the younger), but in the comparison families this was reported far less frequently (5.6 percent of the older children, 5 percent of the middle, and just 1.7 percent of the younger ones). All groups of children in both samples used English even more frequently with siblings, as previously noted. For the main sample, 40.1 percent of the older children were reported as using English exclusively or mostly with siblings, as were 41.1 percent of the middle children and 33.6 percent of the younger children. Again, the children in the comparison families were doing so significantly less frequently in all groups (11 percent of the older children, 9.3 percent of the middle and 4.6 percent of the younger ones). When the children in our samples

TABLE 16.11 Language of Older Children to Adults

	Main Sample		Comparison	
	No.	(%)	No.	(%)
HL only or mostly	281	(55.1)	202	(87.1)
HL and English equally	72	(14.1)	17	(7.3)
English only or mostly	157	(30.8)	13	(5.6)
Total	510	(100)	232	(100)

TABLE 16.12 Language of Middle Children to Adults

	Main Sample		Comparison	
	No.	(%)	No.	(%)
HL only or mostly	216	(54)	191	(86.8)
HL and English equally	62	(15.5)	18	(8.2)
English only or mostly	122	(30.5)	11	(5)
Total	400	(100)	220	(100)

TABLE 16.13 Language of Younger Children to Adults

	Main Sample		Comparison	
	No.	(%)	No.	(%)
HL only or mostly	395	(61.1)	286	(94.7)
HL and English equally	76	(11.7)	11	(3.6)
English only or mostly	175	(27.1)	5	(1.7)
Total	646	(99.9)	302	(100)

TABLE 16.14 Language of Older Children to Siblings

	Main Sample		Comparison	
	No.	(%)	No.	(%)
HL only or mostly	206	(40.3)	180	(75.9)
HL and English equally	100	(19.6)	31	(13.1)
English only or mostly	205	(40.1)	26	(11)
Total	511	(100)	237	(100)

TABLE 16.15 Language of Middle Children to Siblings

	Main Sample		Comparison	
	No.	(%)	No.	(%)
HL only or mostly	161	(40.1)	176	(78.6)
HL and English equally	75	(18.7)	27	(12.1)
English only or mostly	165	(41.1)	21	(9.3)
Total	401	(99.9)	224	(100)

TABLE 16.16 Language of Younger Children to Siblings

	Main Sample		Comparison	
	No.	(%)	No.	(%)
HL only or mostly	289	(52.3)	227	(87)
HL and English equally	78	(14.1)	22	(8.4)
English only or mostly	186	(33.6)	12	(4.6)
Total	553	(100)	261	(100)

(who were reportedly using English and the home language about equally) are added to those who were using English mostly or exclusively, we see that English is clearly becoming the language of choice in well over 50 percent of the main sample homes. Clearly, this inclination is one of the forces for change in family language patterns. In contrast, although English was being used by the children in more than 20 percent of the comparison families, they tended to use it less in talking to their parents.

The effects of the children's use of English in the home can be seen both in what happens to their retention of the primary language as well as on their parents' language patterns. What do parents do when their children speak mostly English at home, a language the parents themselves do not know? There is evidence that these changes were affecting all of the family members. Many parents in the main sample reported that although English was not a language they were able to express themselves in easily, they were using it in speaking to their children. In contrast with the comparison families, where 93.9 percent of the parents used their own languages exclusively or mostly at home with family members, only 78 percent of the main sample parents did. That may simply mean that these families are becoming assimilated more rapidly and that these changes in language behavior are a natural part of the process. In families where the adults are bilingual, this would indeed be the case. As the children learn English and use it at home, the parents also switch over to it, at least in speaking with the children. But the families in this study were in most cases not bilingual: They were largely non-English-speaking monolinguals in other languages. As noted earlier, the primary language of the home was a language other than English in 99 percent of the comparison families and in 97.7 percent of the main sample families. Some of the parents knew English as well as they did their primary languages, but the overwhelming majority did not. In many homes where children lead the way in changing family language patterns, parents can barely speak English. But in self-defense they eventually learn enough to deal with—if not communicate with—the children. There is little genuine parent-child communication in such situations.

Consider, for example, this excerpt from an interview with a parent who was telling us about the problems she and her friends and relatives were having because of changes in family communication patterns. The interviewer (*Int.*) is describing the situation in a close friend's family in which the children stopped speaking Vietnamese after they learned English. The adults in the household have learned English, as the interviewee (*Mrs. P.*) has, in order to talk to their children:

Int. How about your other friends, do they have young children?

Mrs. P. Yeah, young childoon, ena frien'? Ena my frien' have ena three childoon. Born ena Vietnam. Uh, li-do! [*She gestures to indicate the height of the children she is talking about—around 30 inches tall (0.8 m)*]

Int. Oh, they came here when they were very little.

Mrs. P. Yeah, li-do. Ena three year ena four, fi' year. My father ena childoon, he doctor. He talk ena Engli'—no good! Yeah, ev'y ena family, talk Engli' ena childoon. Childoon no—ena don' know ena Vietnam. [i.e., 'Yeah, little. They were three, four, and five years old. The children's father is a doctor. He speaks English poorly. Yeah, everyone in the family—talk English to the children. The children don't know Vietnamese.']

Int. Oh, they don't speak any Vietnamese?

Mrs. P. No, no, no, don't know.

Int. The children were how old when they came here?

Mrs. P. Ena three year ena four year ena fi' year.

Int. Uh huh. And those children speak no Vietnamese?

Mrs. P. No, no Vietnamese.

Int. So the father can't talk with them.

Mrs. P. Yeah. Uh huh. S'e can't talk, s'e talk ena ena Engli'—ena no good Engli'. [i.e., 'He can't talk with them (in Vietnamese so) he talks with them in English, in poor English.']

Int. Oh, so in bad English.

Mrs. P. Yeah, yeah, no very good ena talk.

Int. So he doesn't talk to them in Vietnamese because they don't understand.

Mrs. P. Yeah, no, yeah, uh huh.

Int. They don't understand anything at all?

Mrs. P. No talk ena Vietnam.

Int. They don't understand? When their father talks in Vietnamese, do they understand? Like when your nephew and niece tell their children, 'bring me the shoe, get me something to eat,' you said they understand. Do your friend's children understand their father? [Mrs. P. had told the interviewer that her nephew's and niece's children couldn't speak Vietnamese, but they understood simple directives such as "Take me shoe" or "take me food."]

Mrs. P. No, no, don't understand. Friend ena childoon Engli' understand, Vietnam no. A li-do! uh, uh, Eat food, he understand. No. [i.e., 'No they understand nothing. The children understand only English, they don't understand Vietnamese. Oh, maybe they understand a little—things like "Eat dinner".']

Mrs. P. reports that in her own family, the older of her two children are still able to speak Vietnamese fluently. They were nine and eleven when the family came over to the United States in 1978. The youngest child, however, was just five then, and he entered school shortly after the family arrived in San Francisco. This son is able to understand a little Vietnamese, but not well, and he has difficulty speaking it. Mrs. P. described her son's difficulties with the language as follows:

Mrs. P. S'e sound ena ena ol' Vietnam. S'e s'e fo'got!
Int. He's forgotten his Vietnamese words?
Mrs. P. Yeah!
Int. When he speaks Vietnamese, what does he do, what does he say?
Mrs. P. Uh, s'e talk ena Engli' wor'—he ena "uh, uh, uh, f-fo-fo-fo'go'! Oh, ena mom, wha' wha' what' uh fo' go'!
Int. I see! So he can't remember the words.
Mrs. P. Yeah.

Mrs. P. reports that although she communicates with her older children entirely in Vietnamese, she uses both English and Vietnamese when she is with the youngest child. She says she has to use English because he does not know Vietnamese well enough to carry on a conversation with her, and besides, she knows English better than he knows Vietnamese.

We can find plenty of evidence of language erosion and language loss in the parents' judgment of their children's proficiency in the primary language. We asked the parents to say whether they thought their children were able to speak the home language as well as children their age should. We asked them to think about children the age of theirs who really could speak the language well, and to use them as a standard against which to judge their own children's skills. Native speakers are generally able to judge whether children are able to speak a language well or not, given their age. What they told us confirmed our suspicion that early exposure to English leads to language loss. Children in the main group were described as very deficient or completely unable to speak the home language six to eight times more frequently than were children in the comparison group. The children in the comparison group—children who had been in early education programs conducted entirely in the language of the home—were judged as being able to speak the primary language well considerably more frequently than were the children in the main sample. They were by no means safe, however, as we can see from the data presented in Tables 16.17 to 16.19. They leave their primary language preschool programs at age five or six and enter elementary school while they are still vulnerable to the assimilative forces operating on children. Their primary languages can and apparently do begin to erode once they encounter English in school, as these tables show. Children in the comparison sample are characterized as speaking the home language inadequately for their age a little less frequently than are children in the main sample, but not by much (in older children, 16.8 percent versus 23.2 percent; in middle children, 19 percent versus 26.3 percent; and in younger children, 23.6 percent versus. 28.6 percent). When the reports of language loss are added to those of language erosion, the figures are substantial, especially for the main sample: for older children, 35.6 percent; for middle children, 42.1 percent; and for younger children 44.8 percent.

TABLE 16.17 Older Children's Proficiency in Home Language

	Main Sample		Comparison	
	No.	(%)	No.	(%)
Speaks HL well, adequate for age	352	(64.3)	204	(81.6)
Speaks HL inadequately for age	127	(23.2)	42	(16.8)
Speaks HL poorly or not at all	68	(12.4)	4	(1.6)
Total	547	(99.9)	250	(100)

TABLE 16.18 Middle Children's Proficiency in Home Language

	Main Sample		Comparison	
	No.	(%)	No.	(%)
Speaks HL well, adequate for age	224	(57.9)	178	(78.8)
Speaks HL inadequately for age	102	(26.3)	43	(19)
Speaks HL poorly or not at all	61	(15.8)	5	(2.2)
Total	387	(100)	226	(100)

TABLE 16.19 Younger Children's Proficiency in Home Language

	Main Sample		Comparison	
	No.	(%)	No.	(%)
Speaks HL well, adequate for age	328	(52)	226	(74.1)
Speaks HL inadequately for age	180	(28.6)	72	(23.6)
Speaks HL poorly or not at all	102	(16.2)	7	(2.3)
Too young to talk	20	(3.2)		
Total	630	(100)	305	(100)

As shown in Tables 16.17, 16.18, and 16.19, the younger children both in the main and comparison samples show greater loss than do the older ones in the families. This has to do with the fact that where there are older and younger children in a family, the younger ones are exposed to English earlier because older siblings bring it into the home once they learn it at school. Another reason is no doubt that the children who are characterized as "older" can be quite a bit older than the younger children in the household, and they may not, in fact, have had to deal with English until their first language was beyond the slippery stage.

DISCUSSION

So what does all this mean? This examination of the data we have collected from families across the country suggests that as immigrant children learn English, the patterns of language use change in their homes, and the younger they are when they learn English, the greater the effect. The evidence would suggest that these children are losing their primary languages as they learn English. But why should they? What kind of explanation can we offer for this kind of loss? What theory of language learning would predict this kind of outcome? Should educators of language-minority children be concerned with issues like this? Can children really lose their native languages? What are the mechanisms and consequences of language loss, and what relevance does this problem have in a discussion of educational policies and practices? These problems would intrigue any researcher who wants to understand how people learn new languages. In order to really understand what the process of learning a second language involves in all of its cognitive and social dimensions, one really has to deal with the question of why it sometimes results in bilingualism—and why it sometimes does not. The situation described in this chapter is one that must be looked at more closely by other researchers, but it demands action beyond research. As educators and advocates for children and families, it is crucial that we understand what is happening and that we do something about the problem that our educational policies and practices are creating.

Why are so many children dropping their home languages as they learn English? This question can be answered only in reference to the societal context in which the children are learning English. Second-language learning does not result in the loss of the primary language everywhere. But it does often enough in societies like the United States and Canada, where linguistic or ethnic diversity are not especially valued. Despite our considerable pride in our diverse multicultural origins, Americans are not comfortable with either kind of diversity in our society. The U.S. English movement is just one sign of that discomfort. Language-minority children encounter powerful forces for assimilation as soon as they enter the English-speaking world of the classroom in the society's schools. Young children are extremely vulnerable to the social pressures exerted by people in their social worlds. But the social pressures they experience are not entirely external. Internal pressures are at work as well. Language-minority children are aware that they are different the moment they step out of their homes and into the world of school. They do not even have to step out of the house. They have only to turn on the television and they can see that they are different in language, in appearance, and in behavior, and they come to regard these differences as undesirable. They discover quickly that if they are to participate in the world outside the home, something has to change. Children do not apparently have to be in an all-English environment to discover that one of the things that stands between them and easy participation in their new world is language. They can tell by the way people interact with them that the only language that counts for much is English: the language they do not as yet speak. If they want to be accepted, they have to learn English, because the others are not going to learn their language. Children come to this conclusion whether they are in all-English classes or bilingual classes. And so they are motivated to learn English. At the same time, they are motivated to stop using their primary languages—all too often long before they have mastered the second language. As we have said, there are both internal and external pressures at work.

The younger children are when they encounter these assimilative forces, the greater the effect on their primary languages. It is especially problematic for children in the preschool period, that is, under the age of five. At this age, children have simply not reached a stable enough command of their native language not to be affected by contact with a language that is promoted as heavily as English is in this society. English is the high-status language; it is the societal language. Although young children neither know nor care about prestige and status, they do care about belonging and acceptance. They quickly sense that without English they will not be able to participate in the English-speaking world of the school, and so they learn it, and they give up their primary language.

And here we see a serious problem for these children and for those of us whose interest in language-minority children goes beyond an academic one in how they manage the linguistic adjustments they must inevitably make if they are to live in this society. We believe that the consequences of losing a primary language are far-reaching, and it does affect the social, emotional, cognitive, and educational development of language-minority children, as well as the integrity of their families and the society they live in.

What are the cognitive and educational consequences of losing one's primary language? What happens to familial relations when the language that children give up happens to be the only language that the parents speak? What is lost when children and parents cannot communicate easily with one another?

What is lost is no less than the means by which parents socialize their children: When parents are unable to talk to their children, they cannot easily convey to them their values, beliefs, understandings, or wisdom about how to cope with their experiences. They cannot teach them about the meaning of work, or about personal responsibility, or what it means to be a moral or ethical person in a world with too many choices and too few guideposts to follow. What is lost are the bits of advice, the *consejos* parents should be able to offer children in their everyday interactions with them. Talk is a crucial link between parents and children: It is how parents impart their cultures to their children and enable them to become the kind of men and women they want them to be. When parents lose the means for socializing and influencing their children, rifts develop and families lose the intimacy that comes from shared beliefs and understandings.

There is evidence, albeit anecdotal, to be gleaned from our interviews that these changes in the communication patterns in the home can have serious consequences for parent-child relationships. We included a couple of open-ended questions in the interview in which we asked the parents what they wanted us to tell policy-makers about their concerns and desires as parents. Many parents were worried about their children losing the language of the home. Many, but not all, did. Sad to say, there seems to be a barn-door principle at work here. The parents who expressed the greatest worry were the ones whose children had already begun to lose the language, and who were having trouble communicating with them. What we learned was that this loss can be highly disruptive on family relations.

Some of the saddest stories came from the people who conducted the interviews for this study. One of them told the story of a family that had been referred to county social services after the father was accused of abusing his children. Someone at school had noticed bruises on the children. When the children were questioned, they admitted that their father had beaten them with a stick. The children were taken into protective custody, and the father was brought in for questioning. The story that unfolded was tragic. The family is Korean, and its language is one that requires the marking of many levels of deference in ordinary speech. One cannot speak Korean without considering one's own social position and age relative to the position and age of one's addressee because a host of lexical and grammatical choices depend on such matters. It seems that the children in this family had stopped speaking Korean, although the parents spoke little else. Everything was under control at home, however, even if parents and children did not communicate easily with one another. Then one day the children's grandfather came from Korea for a stay with the family. Because the grandfather did not speak English, the father ordered the children to speak to him in Korean. They tried. They used the Korean they could remember, but it was rusty. It had been a long while since the children had spoken the language and they had forgotten little things, like the intricacies of the deferential system. They used none of the forms that children must use when speaking to an honored relative like their grandfather. The grandfather was shocked at the apparent disrespect the children were displaying towards him. He did what the situation called for: He scolded his son—the children's father—for not having trained his children properly. The father did what the situation required of him: He punished the children—with a stick—for their rudeness and disrespect. What was sad was that no one seemed to realize the role language played in this family drama.

It may take years before the harm done to families can be fully assessed. When the children are young, the parents feel hindered but not necessarily defeated if they cannot communicate easily with them. One family that has been in the United States for nearly 20 years revealed the extent to which breakdown in family communication can lead to the alienation of children from their parents. The four children, who are now teenagers, have completely lost their ability to speak or understand Spanish. The children are ashamed of Spanish, it was reported. They do not acknowledge it when their parents speak it, even though it is the only language the parents know. The mother reported that her 17-year-old son is having problems in school. He is often truant and is in danger of dropping out. She has tried to influence him but can't because he doesn't understand her. A recent attempt at discussion ended in physical violence, with mother and son coming to blows when words failed them.

The stories of families in which language and cultural shifts have resulted in the breakdown of parental authority and of the children's respect for their parents are often tragic. For the Southeast Asian refugee families especially, the breakdown of family can mean a loss of everything. Many of them left behind all of their possessions when they fled their native lands. They came to the United States with the hope of keeping their families intact. They do not understand what is happening to them as they see their families falling apart. They do not see how the language their children are learning in school figures in this process. They want their children to learn English. They know how critical it is to their economic survival in this country. They believe that they can maintain Hmong or Khmer or Lao or Vietnamese without help because these languages are spoken in the home. They ask, "How can children lose their language?" But they do. And by the time the parents realize what is happening, it is usually too late to do anything about it.

Let us consider some possible cognitive and educational consequences of primary language loss. We are convinced that there is a connection between native language loss and the educational difficulties experienced by many language-minority-background students. As noted earlier, children frequently give up their native languages long before they have mastered English. But what happens if their efforts to learn English are not altogether successful?

It is not hard for children to learn a second language, but we are all familiar with instances of second-language learning that fall short of the language being learned. Researchers have examined cases of language learning that may not have gone beyond the interlanguage stages documented in their studies (for example, Schumann 1974; Selinker, Swain, and Dumas 1975; Wong Fillmore 1992). In Selinker's (1972) terms, they ended up with "fossilized versions of interlanguages" rather than with fully realized versions of the target languages. What leads to this kind of outcome rather than the more complete mastery expected in second-language learning? Social and psychological factors have been implicated in the case of adult language learners, whereas situational factors have been critical in the case of children. Fossilized interlanguages are very likely to develop in the language-learning situations that we find in many schools with big enrollments of immigrant and refugee students. In the classrooms of such schools, non-English speakers frequently outnumber English speakers. In fact, except for their teachers, the learners may have little contact with people who know the language well enough to help them learn it. In any event, the language learners spend a lot more time talking with one another than they do with their teachers, and the English they hear most often is the imperfect varieties spoken by classmates rather than the more standard varieties spoken by their teachers. That being the case, the input they base their language learning on being the speech of learners like themselves is not altogether representative of the target language. Not surprisingly, language learning based on such input is neither perfect nor complete.

What happens when students do not learn well a second language after they have already decided to give up their first language? Can children who develop neither their first nor their second language fully take full advantage of the educational opportunities their parents and their teachers have to offer? These are questions that need to be examined closely in the light of what we have learned in this study.

So where does all this leave us? Does this suggest that we should abandon English in programs for language-minority children? Not at all. The problem is timing, not English. The children have to learn English, but they should not be required to do so until their native languages are stable enough to handle the inevitable encounter with English and all it means. Even then, teachers and parents must work together to try to mitigate the harm that can be done to children when they discover that differences are not welcome in the social world represented by the school. Parents need to be warned of the consequences of not insisting that their children speak to them in the language of the home. Teachers should be aware of the harm they can do when they tell parents that they should encourage their children to speak English at home, and that they themselves should try to use English when they talk to their children.

The researchers who have been working on this project realize that our work has just begun. The No-Cost study is far from finished, but already it has raised many questions that can only be addressed through further research. This chapter discusses some of the issues that need to be examined in greater detail. We hope other researchers will be motivated to do some of this research by the same concerns that got us involved—that is, by the very high cost we see language-minority children and their families paying for their participation in the society.

This article was written on behalf of the No-Cost Research Group (NCRG), consisting of the 300-plus individuals across the United States who participated in this study, preparing research materials, recruiting and training interviewers, interviewing families, processing and analyzing data, and interpreting findings. It includes many members of the National Association for Bilingual Education (NABE), and the No-Cost Research Group acknowledges the support of NABE's national leadership in this effort.

Correspondence and requests for reprints should be sent to Lily Wong Fillmore, Professor of Education, Graduate School of Education, University of California, Berkeley, CA 94720.

Notes

1. Merino (1983) and Pan and Berko-Gleason (1986) are notable exceptions.
2. The Bilingual-Bicultural Education Act was "sunsetted" in 1987, after several attempts to renew it failed. The legislature twice voted in favor of renewing bilingual education, but former Governor Deukmajian failed to sign either bill passed by the state legislature.
3. The conference was held in Tucson, Arizona, in March 1990.
4. This was actually a misnomer because, although there were no funds to support it, the study was not exactly without cost.
5. This was by no means a "representative sample" of the language-minority families in the United States. The selection of the families was linked to the participation of the individuals who were willing to conduct interviews for the study. A convenience sample like the one we have can nevertheless tell us a lot about what is going on in other families.
6. UCSC No-Costers were Barry McLaughlin, Eugene Garcia, and students associated with the Bilingual Research Group.
7. UCB No-Costers were Lily Wong Fillmore, Guadalupe Valdés, Susan Ervin-Trip, Leanne Hinton, and students in the Graduate School of Education's Language and Literacy Division.
8. Foundation Center No-Costers were Marilyn Prosser, Antonia López, Maria Auxiliadora Garibi Dorais, Dennis Rose, and the late Gloria F. Montejano.
9. Dean Ernesto Bernal (University of Texas–Pan American), *Denise De La Rosa (National Council for La Raza), Susan Ervin-Tripp (UCB), *Rosie Feinberg (University of Miami), Gene Garcia (UCSC), Leann Hinton, (UCB), Kenji Ima (CSU-SD), Victoria Jew (CSU-S), Hayes Lewis (Zuni Public Schools), Antonia Lopez (Foundation Center), Jim Lyons (NABE), Lois Meyer, (CSU-SF), George Miller (U.S. House of Representatives), Barry McLaughlin (UCSC), Laurie Olson (California Tomorrow), Alice Paul (University of Arizona), Delia Pompa (Children's Defense Fund), Marilyn Prosser (Foundation Center), Jon Reyhner (E-Montana College), Flora Rodriguez Brown (University of Illinois), William Rohwer (UCB), Migdalia Romero (Hunter College), Peter Roos (META), *Walter Secada (University of Wisconsin), *Lourdes Soto-Diaz (Penn State University), Hai Tran (BEMRC-U of Oklahoma), Guadalupe Valdés (UCB), Lily Wong Fillmore (UCB), Susan Larson (UCB), Hee Won Kang (UCB), Guillermina Nunes Wright (UCB), John Sierra (UCB), Craig Wilson (UCB), Jann Geyer (UCB), and Janice Patch (UCB). The asterisked individuals participated by phone.
10. The data on the other families will be included in future analyses, but we do not anticipate that they will alter the findings reported here in any notable way.
11. Three respondents gave noninterpretable answers to our questions about ethnic origins, so we categorized them as "others."

12. The intensive language programs offered by the Foreign Service Institute or the Defense Language Institute are examples of adult language programs that do lead to high levels of second- or foreign-language proficiency. Neither is open to the general public, however. But few adult immigrants could take advantage of programs like them even if they existed because they require full-time study and a special aptitude to handle the pressure-cooker methods used in such intensive programs. The ESL courses generally available to immigrant adults at night school seldom offer students more than survival-level English instruction.

References

Benjamin, R. 1990. *Explorations in language attitudes and maintenance efforts in a Mexican immigrant family.* Unpublished prequalifying paper for the Ph.D., Graduate School of Education, University of California, Berkeley.

Krashen, S., Long, M., and Scarcella, R. 1979. Age, rate and eventual attainment in second-language acquisition. *TESOL Quarterly* 13:573–582.

Kreven, H. 1989. *Erosion of a language in bilingual development.* Unpublished master's thesis, San Francisco State University.

Lambert, W. E. 1975. Culture and language as factors in learning and education. In A. Wolfgang, ed. *Education of Immigrant Students.* Toronto: Ontario Institute for Studies in Education.

Lambert, W. E. 1977. The effects of bilingualism on the individual: Cognitive and sociocultural consequences. In P. A. Hornby, ed. *Bilingualism: Psychological, Social, and Educational Implications.* New York: Academic.

Lambert, W. E. 1981. Bilingualism and language acquisition. In H. Winitz, ed. *Native Language and Foreign Language Acquisition.* New York: New York Academy of Science.

Merino, B. J. 1983. Language loss in bilingual Chicano children. *Journal of Applied Developmental Psychology* 4:277–294.

Pan, B. A., and Berko-Gleason, J. 1986. The study of language loss: Models and hypotheses for an emerging discipline. *Applied Psycholinguistics* 7:193–206.

Schumann, J. H. 1974. The implications of interlanguage, pidginization, and creolization for the study of adult second language acquisition. *TESOL Quarterly* 8:142–152.

Selinker, L. 1972. Interlanguage. *International Review of Applied Linguistics* 10:209–231.

Selinker, L., Swain, M., and Dumas, G. 1975. The interlanguage hypothesis extended to children. *Language Learning* 25:139–152.

Snow, C., and Hoefnagel-Höhle, M. 1977. Age differences in the pronunciation of foreign sounds. *Language and Speech* 20:357–365.

Snow, C., and Hoefnagel-Höhle, M. 1978. Age differences in second language acquisition. In E. Hatch, ed. *Second Language Acquisition.* Rowley, MA: Newbury House.

Wong Fillmore, L. 1991. Language and cultural issues in early education. In S. L. Kagan, ed. *The Care and Education of America's Young Children: Obstacles and Opportunities, The 90th Yearbook of the National Society for the Study of Education.* Chicago: University of Chicago Press.

Wong Fillmore, L. 1992. Learning a language from learners. In C. Kramsch and S. McConnell-Ginet, eds. *Text and Context: Cross-Disciplinary Perspectives on Language Studies.* Lexington, MA: Heath.

Chapter 17
Educational Progress of Children of Immigrants: The Roles of Class, Ethnicity, and School Context

ALEJANDRO PORTES AND DAG MACLEOD

Recent immigration to the United States has spawned a rapidly growing second generation, most of whom are of school age. This article reports the findings of a study of 5,266 second-generation high school students in Florida and California, who were children of Cuban and Vietnamese immigrants (representative of relatively advantaged groups) and of Haitian and Mexican immigrants (representative of relatively disadvantaged groups). The study found that parents' socioeconomic status (SES), length of U.S. residence, and hours spent on homework significantly affected the students' academic performance, but did not eliminate the effects of ethnic community. Attendance at higher-SES schools increased the average academic performance and the positive effect of parents' SES, whereas attendance at inner-city schools flattened the negative effect of ethnic disadvantage. However, school context had no appreciable effect on children from advantaged ethnic backgrounds.

The increasing number of children of recent immigrants, spawned by the growing waves of immigration since the mid-1960s, have been a neglected segment of the school population. The study of today's children of immigrants not only reveals new information about this increasingly important segment of the country's school-age youths, but bears on theoretical issues of broader import concerning the role of family status and ethnic community on individual performance. In this chapter, we examine how both parental status and the distinct characteristics of immigrant communities impinge on the educational attainment of the second generation.

Since the passage of the Immigration Act of 1965, which repealed discriminatory national quotas, hundreds of thousands of immigrants have come to the United States each year. Unlike the earlier wave of immigration at the beginning of the 20th century, post-1965 immigrants come primarily from Asia and Latin America. By 1990, the foreign-born population had reached almost twenty million, the highest absolute number in the 20th century, representing 8 percent of the national total. Without post-1960 immigrants and their descendants, the U.S. population in 1990 would have been approximately 223.4 million, rather than the 248.7 million actually counted (U.S. Census Bureau, 1993). Immigration accounted for a full 39 percent of the growth in the U.S. population between 1980 and 1990 (Fix and Passel 1991; Rumbaut 1994).

Sociological research on this new wave of immigration has focused on the first generation, composed of adult immigrants, refugees, and asylees. Although it has produced a wealth of new insights, it has neglected the parallel emergence of the children of these immigrants. The growth of the second generation has been fueled by the twin processes of family resettlement and the high fertility of immigrants. Early waves of immigrants are composed mainly of young men in search of economic opportunity; over time, however, the early arrivals tend to settle down and bring other family members. Within a few years, family migration becomes the norm, driven both by kin networks and by the family reunification provisions of U.S. law (Massey and Garcia España 1987; Portes and Rumbaut 1990).

As a result of these processes, the number of new children of immigrants will, in a few years, surpass the former peak of twenty-eight million children of immigrants reached in the 1940s (Passel and Edmonston 1992). The visibility and importance of this young population is heightened because of its concentration in a few states and major metropolitan areas. In 1990, just five states (California, Florida, New York, New Jersey, and Texas) accounted for 68 percent of the U.S. foreign-born population, and five cities absorbed 35 percent of the total (Rumbaut 1994; U.S. Census Bureau 1993). These are, of course, the same areas in which the new second generation has grown.

Apart from their tendency to concentrate in a few large cities, contemporary immigrants are an exceptionally diverse population. Sociological research on adult immigrants has documented a plurality of situations, ranging from the swift move into middle-class status of immigrant professionals and the building of vibrant entrepreneurial enclaves by certain immigrant groups to widespread poverty and dependence on low-paid menial jobs for others (Jensen 1989; Massey, Alarcón, Durand, and González 1987; Portes and Bach 1985; Stepick 1989). To a certain extent, these divergent outcomes have depended on the skills and resources of the first-generation immigrants; however, they have also depended on the political and social context in which the immigrants have settled.

For our purposes, the key issue is the extent to which these first-generation patterns of advantage or disadvantage are reproduced in the second generation. Most of today's children of immigrants are of school age. Fully 44 percent of foreign-born persons in the United States arrived during the 1980s, and one in every four arrived after 1985 (U.S. Census Bureau 1993). Accordingly, Jensen and Chitose (1994) estimated that the large majority of the new second generation is composed of children under age eighteen. For this reason, educational rather than labor market outcomes represent the best measure of the progress of the second generation as it seeks to adapt to American society. This article presents data on the educational performance of children of immigrants and examines its variation as affected by family, community, and school contextual factors.

THEORETICAL BACKGROUND

Research on educational attainment among native-born American youths has identified a number of key variables that are reliable predictors of levels of attainment in addition to innate ability, such as gender and age. One of the most powerful predictors of educational attainment is family socioeconomic status, which contributes directly and indirectly through its effects on intervening variables like hours spent on homework and children's aspirations (Eccles et al. 1993; Haller and Portes 1973; Spenner and Featherman 1978). A great deal of research in the sociology of education has focused on the extent to which the effects of family SES on educational attainment are mediated, enhanced, or neutralized by the school contexts in which children find themselves (Griffin and Alexander 1978; Ianni 1989; Raudenbush and Bryk 1989). By and large, such studies have concluded that the effect of family SES is resilient across different school contexts, although school context can affect the strength of its relationship with specific educational outcomes.

Studies have also emphasized the significance of family and community networks and the role of social capital in children's adaptation to school. Coleman (1988, 1990), for example, found that cohesive communities facilitate the role of parenting because adults reinforce each other's normative control of their children. The "closure" of such communities represents a form of social capital because it helps parents instill work discipline and achievement values in their young. Coleman cited several immigrant communities as examples of such tightly knit groups.

Contemporary research on the sociology of immigration recognizes that outcomes for foreign-born minorities are significantly influenced by the groups' "modes of incorporation" (Portes and Rumbaut 1990). That is, the context that receives immigrants plays a decisive role in their process of adaptation, regardless of the human capital the immigrants may possess (Guarnizo 1992; Rumbaut 1992; Zhou 1992). Thus, immigrants who are granted legal status, receive resettlement assistance, and are not subject to widespread discrimination are expected to experience both faster economic progress and a smoother process of social and psychological integration.

This argument immediately raises the question of the extent to which the contextual advantages or disadvantages experienced by first-generation immigrants are transmitted to the second generation. According to the literature on educational research, if a favorable reception results in more rapid occupational and economic advancement and, hence, higher parental SES, children's school performance should be superior. If this was the whole story, there should be no net ethnic effect associated with particular immigrant communities, since the influence of modes of incorporation on second-generation children would be mediated entirely by their families' SES.

It is also possible that a favorable context of reception allows an immigrant community to rebuild its social networks and maintain its internal solidarity and thus facilitates its members' accumulation of greater social capital. In this case, one would observe a significant ethnic effect associated with particular immigrant groups even after parental SES was controlled. A third possibility, of course, is that early modes of incorporation exercise no effect on either parents' SES or on the internal solidarity of the immigrant community and hence that their gross and net effects on children's educational attainment will be zero.

From these three possibilities, the literature on immigration suggests that the second is the most likely. There is evidence that a favorable governmental and societal reception leads to faster socioeconomic mobility, a more positive self-image, and better-integrated immigrant communities (Bailey and Waldinger 1991; Light 1984; Portes and Stepick 1993; Zhou 1992). As Coleman (1988) indicated, the greater social capital available in these situations should have positive effects on children's attainment even after parents' SES is controlled. Conversely, offspring of disadvantaged immigrants would be caught in the double bind of slower socioeconomic mobility and weaker and more unstable community bonds (Fernández-Kelly and Schauffler 1994; Zhou and Bankston 1994). Following this argument, we hypothesized that both parental SES and ethnic community will have significant independent effects on the second generation's academic performance. In the analysis presented here, we did not test directly the relationship between early modes of incorporation and first-generation outcomes, but assumed it on the basis of information on the experience of specific immigrant groups. In turn, this evidence provided the basis on which we examined the relationship between immigrant parents' SES and ethnicity and children's school achievement.

A second theoretical question pertains to the effect of school context on overall educational performance and its interactions with parental SES and ethnicity. In agreement with past studies of the educational attainment of children of native-born parents, we tested two hypotheses:

1. The test scores of second-generation children will be higher in schools with higher average SES that are not near inner-city areas.

2. Parents' SES will interact positively with average school SES. In other words, the positive effect of families' SES on children's academic attainment should be still stronger in schools in which other children also are from higher-status backgrounds (Coleman 1990; Raudenbush and Bryk 1986). Conversely, poorer children attending lower-status schools will be subject to a double handicap.

A similar prediction cannot be made about the relationships between schools and the hypothesized ethnic effects. It is possible that children from advantaged ethnic communities will do even better in more favorable school environments, along the lines of the predicted interaction of family SES and school SES. It is also possible, however, that the ethnic effect will actually be more visible in less privileged schools, an alternative given some credence by ethnographic and psychological research on recent immigrant children (Suárez-Orozco 1987; Zhou and Bankston 1994). The current state of knowledge provides no solid ground for predictions of possible joint effects of ethnic community and school context. On this point, we must let our results speak for themselves.

DATA AND METHOD

The data for our study came from a survey of 5,266 children of immigrants who were interviewed in the school systems of Miami and Fort Lauderdale in South Florida and San Diego, California, during the spring and fall of 1992. The sample was limited to eighth- and ninth graders to eliminate the well-known censoring bias created by school dropouts in later grades.[1] In line with the common usage in the literature on immigration, the *second generation* was defined as native-born children with at least one foreign-born parent or foreign-born children who were brought to the United States at an early age and have resided here ever since. Operationally, foreign-born children were included in the sample only if they had lived continuously in this country for at least five years. Differences between the length of U.S. residence of native-born and foreign-born children entered the analysis as predictors of the dependent variables.

School systems do not collect data on parents' nationality that could be used as a sampling framework. Therefore, the sample design was based on a selection of schools in each area that were representative of different socioeconomic levels, ethnic compositions, and geographic locations. In total, forty-two schools in the two metropolitan areas took part in the study. The sample was representative of the major immigrant nationalities in each area, but, in addition, a sampling stratum approximating 25 percent of the total sample was reserved for the smaller immigrant nationalities; in all, seventy-seven nationalities were represented in the sample.

South Florida and southern California were selected for the study because of the different compositions of their immigrant populations. South Florida is home to large concentrations of people from the Caribbean and South America—including Cubans, Nicaraguans, Haitians, West Indians, and Colombians. Southern California has large clusters of Mexicans, Central Americans, Vietnamese, Cambodians, and East Asians. In both areas, the aim of the sampling design was to include children attending schools in areas with a high concentration of immigrants, as well as those dispersed among the native-born population. The San Diego School District is sufficiently large to include both types of schools. In South Florida, however, it was necessary to expand the original Miami sample with a sample of schools in adjacent Broward County (Fort Lauderdale) because most Miami schools have a large number of first- and second-generation immigrants.

The student questionnaires gathered data on a large array of variables, including national origin, parents' education and occupation, family structure, length of U.S. residence, aspirations, and psychosocial dimensions related to the process of adaptation. These data were supplemented with records from the respective school systems on such factors as the students' grade-point averages, scores on standardized mathematics and reading tests, English as a Second Language (ESL) status (for children whose home language is not English), "primary exceptionality" (students' assignment to special programs, such as those for the gifted and talented, retarded children, and others with particular handicaps), and other variables. The school systems also furnished data on aggregate school characteristics, such as geographic location, ethnic composition, and percentage of students enrolled in the free school-lunch program. To our knowledge, these data are the only major source of information bearing on today's second generation and the only ones containing the variables required to test the preceding hypotheses.

The statistical analysis proceeded in two stages. First, ordinary least-squares (OLS) models of indicators of educational attainment were run to test the effects of individual-level predictors. Standardized scores on the mathematics and reading subtests of the Stanford Achievement Test for grades eight and nine were used as indicators of the dependent variable. Second, the interactions of school context with individual-level variables were examined through hierarchical linear models (HLMs). HLM is useful for determining how average differences in performance, represented by within-school intercepts, vary with the contextual characteristics of schools. It also tests whether individual-level regression slopes are affected by school variables. The method uses empirical Bayes estimators of within-school effects to take into account their differential reliability (Bryk and Raudenbush 1992:76–79).

Parental SES, used as a predictor in individual-level regressions, is an index constructed as the unit-weighted sum of scores on five variables: father's and mother's education, coded along a five-point scale of years completed; parental home ownership, coded as a dichotomy; and father's and mother's occupation, coded in Duncan's Socio-economic Index (SEI) prestige scores. The index is standardized to a mean of 0 and a standard deviation *(SD)* of 1. To test for ethnic effects, we selected immigrant nationalities in the two metropolitan areas for which sufficient evidence exists to categorize them as representatives of advantaged or disadvantaged contexts. The origins of these communities and their respective patterns of settlement are summarized next.

IMMIGRANT COMMUNITIES

Analytic difficulties

The choice of immigrant groups as representatives of ethnic advantage or disadvantage poses several analytic difficulties that must be overcome for the ensuing results to be meaningful. First, enough information must be available about each group in its local context to formulate predictions about the second generation's patterns of adaptation. Since the incorporation of immigrants varies with locality, it is not enough to know about, say, Chinese or Mexican immigrants in general; rather, one must have information about their reception in particular areas of settlement (Portes and Rumbaut 1990).

Second, it is not enough to have sufficient cases from each target nationality; these cases must be distributed over a number of schools to test hypotheses about the influence of school contexts. A sizable immigrant group whose children all attend the same school would make it impossible to examine the interaction effects of school context with parental SES and ethnic background. Third, first-generation advantage or disadvantage is not absolute, but relative to some standard. The most appropriate standard in this situation is the average for all immigrants; therefore, the total sample must be sufficiently large and diversified to provide a suitable standard of comparison.

If these conditions were met, we would be in a position to formulate *a priori* predictions about ethnic effects on educational performance. Indeed, we were able to identify four nationalities in the sample that met the preceding conditions: Their modes of incorporation in each target area were well known, they were well represented in the sample and spread over several schools, and the residual *N* after these groups were subtracted was large enough (2,681 cases encompassing seventy-three nationalities) to provide a suitable analytic standard.[2] Children of Cuban and Haitian immigrants in South Florida and those of Mexican and Vietnamese origin in southern California are such groups. In the following sections, we summarize their histories, which leads to predictions about their children's patterns of adaptation.

Cuban and Vietnamese communities

The Cuban and Vietnamese communities are products of communist takeovers in their respective countries, and most of their original members were political refugees. Both groups were received sympathetically by the U.S. government and were granted numerous forms of federal assistance. The bulk of these refugees arrived during the 1960s and 1970s, when strong anti-immigrant prejudice had not yet surfaced and when their plight as political refugees was conducive to a more favorable public reception (Boswell and Curtis 1984; Montero 1979).

Cuban and Vietnamese refugees made use of the considerable resources granted by the federal government and private organizations to create solidary and dynamic entrepreneurial communities. Although federal resettlement programs attempted to disperse them throughout the country, both groups gradually regrouped in certain localities: Cubans in the Miami metropolitan area and the Vietnamese in Orange and San Diego counties in California (Bach, Gordon, Haines, and Howell 1984; Boswell and Curtis 1984; Portes and Bach 1985; Rumbaut and Ima 1988).

Both groups have made significant strides toward occupational and economic integration. According to the 1990 census, more than half the adult Cubans and Vietnamese are now U.S. citizens and own their own homes. About one-fifth are employed in professional and executive occupations, and their unemployment rates are fairly low. Although they still trail native whites on these and other indicators, their conditions compare favorably with those of the total foreign-born population. At $35,600, the median annual household income of Cubans is roughly on par with the figure for all immigrant-headed households although still below that of non-Hispanic whites ($38,600); the median household income of Vietnamese is even higher, exceeding the foreign-born figure by more than $1,000 (U.S. Census Bureau 1990).

A great deal has been written about the development of the Cuban enclave in Miami (Alba, Logan, and McNulty 1994; Portes and Stepick 1993; Wilson and Martin 1982). Among other things, these studies have pointed to the bifurcation of this community between earlier waves of exiles, who came from the upper layers of Cuban society and were the beneficiaries of generous governmental assistance, and subsequent arrivals. The 1980 Mariel exodus marks the most important cleavage, since refugees who arrived at that time and later came from more modest origins and had a more negative reception in the United States (Bach, Bach, and Triplett 1981). The data at hand do not allow a direct test of the causal relation between these different modes of incorporation and outcomes for first-generation Cuban immigrants. However, the internal fragmentation of the Cuban community permits and indirect test: The predicted positive effect of ethnicity should be stronger among children of the earlier Cuban refugees who built the Miami enclave and weaker among the offspring of less advantaged and subsequent arrivals.

In contrast, the literature on the Vietnamese in southern California points to the recency of this group's arrival and its relatively uniform process of incorporation, marked by generous governmental assistance (Rumbaut and Ima 1988). During the past decade or so, this community has made significant strides toward entrepreneurship, despite the modest occupational and educational backgrounds of many of its members (Gold 1992; U.S. Census Bureau 1991). The combination of governmental support and strong ethnic ties seems to be responsible for this development.

Haitian and Mexican communities

The conditions of Haitians in south Florida and Mexicans in southern California are quite different from those of the Cubans and Vietnamese. Both communities contain large numbers of unauthorized immigrants, whom the Immigration and Naturalization Service (INS) has made vigorous efforts to apprehend and deport. Most Haitians who came during the 1980s requested political asylum, but their claims were routinely denied on the grounds that they were illegal economic immigrants. Those who remained in the United States were deprived of federal resettlement assistance, and many continued to be subject to deportation (Miller 1984; Stepick 1982). Similarly, Mexican immigrants in southern California are often unauthorized and subject to the same kinds of hostile actions by the INS. Even those who arrived legally experience pervasive discrimination and, as regular immigrants, are ineligible for the package of federal assistance benefits granted to refugees (Bach 1986; Barrera 1980; Massey 1987; Nelson and Tienda 1985).

The unfavorable incorporation of Haitian and Mexican immigrants, combined with their relatively low levels of human capital, has led to predictable outcomes. In 1990, less than a third of each group had become U.S. citizens, and less than half owned their own homes—figures that are both well below the mean for foreign-born persons. The proportion of working adults in professional or executive occupations was 11.3 percent for Haitians and 6.3 percent for Mexicans, both of which are a fraction of the foreign-born average of 23.3 percent. At $26,142, the median income of Mexican households trailed the median for non-Hispanic white households by more than $12,000; the Haitian income gap was smaller, but still a sizable $8,600 (U.S. Census Bureau 1990).

The conditions of these immigrant communities reflect their disadvantaged reception and subsequent slow progress. In South Florida, Haitian immigrants cluster in a neighborhood adjacent to Liberty City, the largest inner-city ghetto of Miami. Haitian churches, restaurants, and businesses have emerged in this area, which was inevitably dubbed Little Haiti. However, the institutional development of the community has been stunted by poverty, the tenuous legal status of many inhabitants, and outside discrimination. White Miamians tend to regard this area as just another addition to the inner city (Portes and Stepick 1993).

Mexican immigrants are a much older presence in southern California than are the Haitians in South Florida, but the unauthorized status of many and the menial jobs to which they have been confined for generations conspire against the emergence of a stable and economically self-reliant community. The fluidity of the movement back and forth across the border and the continuous arrival of new migrants give Mexican neighborhoods an unsettled, transient character that weakens the development of resilient community ties (Barrera 1980; Matute-Bianchi 1986; Roberts 1995; Samora 1971).

Differences in the modes of incorporation of these four immigrant groups are well known. Following our initial hypothesis, we expected that the educational performance of second-generation youths would vary significantly and that these national differences would not disappear even after SES and other individual predictors were controlled. We also expected that these ethnic effects would vary across school contexts, although, as we mentioned earlier, the direction of that interaction is uncertain.

RESULTS

Bivariate differences

Table 17.1 presents the breakdown of relevant variables in relation to the four target groups and the total sample. The first result of note is the large differences in average scores on academic tests. The median scores for the Cuban American and Vietnamese American children in mathematics significantly exceeded the average for the sample and surpassed those of their respective school systems (50 for Miami-Fort Lauderdale and 55 for San Diego).[3] The opposite was true for Haitian- and, especially, Mexican-origin students, whose scores were quite low relative to both the total sample and the median scores for their respective school systems.

With regard to standardized reading scores, the entire sample fell below the national median.[4] The Cuban American students' scores were only slightly lower than the national median and surpassed the average for the total sample by 6 percentage points. The Vietnamese American students' scores were below that standard, indicating only a modest English ability, but their scores were still above those of the Haitian- and Mexican American students.

These differences are roughly in agreement with our predictions. However, intergroup differences can be spurious, a product of family SES, region, recency of arrival, and other individual characteristics. As Table 17.1 also shows, there were significant differences among the groups in several of these potential predictors of school achievement. Among them, three deserve mention: parents' SES, hours spent on homework, and length of U.S. residence.

Parental SES. As was expected, the SES of the Cuban American parents exceeded the mean for the sample by a significant margin, whereas the other target groups, including the Vietnamese, fell below that norm. This finding indicates that any ethnic advantage that Vietnamese American students derive from membership in that community is not due to socioeconomic background.

Hours spent daily on homework. This variable has been used in the past as a predictor of academic achievement, partially explaining the effect of parental SES (Wigfield and Asher 1984). In this sample,

TABLE 17.1 Selected Characteristics of Second-generation Students in South Florida and Southern California, 1992

	Group					
Variable	Cuban	Haitian	Mexican	Vietnamese	Total	p[a]
Mathematics scores[b]						
Mean	58.50*	45.03*	31.87*	60.31*	53.76	.001
Median	62.00	41.00	25.00	65.00	55.00	
Reading scores[b]						
Mean	47.47*	30.40*	26.52*	37.45	41.55	.001
Median	46.00	27.00	18.00	31.00	40.00	
Parental SES[c]	0.15*	−0.17	−0.63*	−0.33*	0.00	.001
Daily homework hours	2.21*	2.82*	2.15*	3.00*	2.48	.001
Percentage native born	64.4*	50.3	54.3	16.2*	45.9	.001
Percentage less than 9 years in the United States	9.8*	30.1	29.2	43.6*	27.7	.001
Percentage California resident	0.5*	0.7*	96.6*	98.0*	46.0	.001
Percentage Florida resident	99.5*	99.3*	3.4*	2.0*	54.0	.001
Age	14.1*	14.4	14.2	14.3	14.2	N.S.[d]
Percentage female	47.4	52.4*	48.5	47.6	51.0	N.S.[d]
Percentage who expect to graduate from college	83.4*	82.5	51.1*	76.3	77.7	.001
N	1.227	178	758	372	5,266	

[a] Statistical significance of differences among the four nationalities.
[b] Total percentile scores on Stanford achievement test, 8th edition.
[c] Composite index standardized to mean 0, *SD* 1.
[d] N.S. = not significant.
* Group-to-total sample differences significant at the .001 level.

the hours that students spent on homework each day differed widely. Differences among the four nationalities and between each nationality and the total sample are significant at the .01 level or higher. According to these figures, the hardest-working students were the Vietnamese, which suggests a possible reason for their superior performance on the mathematics test.

Length of residence in the United States. The length of residence of the four groups also varied widely. Immigrant communities differ in their time of arrival and hence the proportion of their offspring who are native-born. Two-thirds of the Cuban American students were born in the United States, whereas the Mexican- and Haitian-origin children fell close to the sample mean of 46 percent. At the other extreme, more than two-fifths of the Vietnamese were born abroad and, at the time of the survey, had spent fewer than ten years in the United States. All these differences can be expected to have significant effects on academic performance.

Effects of parents' SES and ethnicity

This section presents multivariate results bearing on the predicted relationships among parental SES, ethnicity, and students' test scores. Each ethnic-group effect was computed relative to the total sample—the most suitable standard of comparison because the sample was large and representative of the entire second-generation universe in the target grades in each area.[5] Table 17.2 presents these findings arranged in three panels that compare the effects of SES and ethnicity in the full sample and, separately, for the two regional sub-samples. In each panel, parental SES and ethnic background effects are presented, controlling for age and sex, hours spent daily on homework, length of U.S. residence, and (in the full sample) region of settlement.[6] In the full and South Florida panels, separate columns present the effects of Cuban ethnicity restricted to children whose parents arrived between 1959 and 1979, the years before the 1980 Mariel exodus. These results allowed us to test for differential effects of ethnicity within the Cuban community, along the theoretical lines explained earlier.

Regardless of the sample or model specification, parental SES had a strong effect on the academic performance of the students in this sample. In the full sample, each *SD* unit in the SEI increased mathematics scores by almost 10 percentage points. The effect of parents' SES on reading achievement was 11 percentage points, after other variables were controlled. Of these other variables, the length of U.S. residence had the strongest effect, reducing the SES gross coefficient by a full percentage point. Following the formula of Clogg, Petkova, and Haritou (1995) for the standard error of the difference, this reduction is significant at the .01 level.[7]

The case for ethnicity is more complicated. In the full sample regressions, we found that second-generation students from disadvantaged groups did, indeed, have lower-than-average mathematics and reading scores and that the gap persisted after parental SES, length of U.S. residence, and hours spent on homework were controlled. The difference was particularly startling in the case of Mexican American students, whose mathematics scores, with controls in place, were 15 points lower than the average. The difference in reading scores was also a sizable: 12 percentage points for both the Mexican American and the Haitian American students. In several models, the initial (zero-order) academic gap actually increased when controls were introduced. These findings indicate a resilient negative ethnic effect on school performance, which supports our initial hypothesis.

Such is not entirely the case, however, for ethnic advantage. The superiority of the Vietnamese American students' mathematics scores remained with controls in place. Given the modest SES of most Vietnamese families, this finding suggests that the internal character of the community plays a key role in encouraging students to achieve. However, that advantage did not carry over to reading scores, a result attributable to the recent arrival of Vietnamese immigrants. The analysis supports this interpretation by showing a decline in the negative effect of Vietnamese ethnicity on reading

TABLE 17.2 OLS Regressions of Stanford Mathematics and Reading Scores on Selected Predictors, Second-generation Students in South Florida and Southern California, 1992

	Mathematics Scores				
	1. Full Sample		2. Florida		3. California
Predictors	1[a]	2[b]	3[a]	4[b]	5
Age	– 4.12**(.50)	(.50)	– 4.47**(.66)	– 4.43**(.65)	– 3.79**(.76)
Sex[c]	1.34 (.83)	1.42* (.83)	.41(1.10)	.52 (1.09)	2.64* (1.26)
Parental SES	9.36** (.62)	9.35** (.62)	8.42** (.82)	8.32** (.82)	9.81** (.96)
Length of U.S. Residence	1.00* (.50)	.60 (.50)	.04 (.72)	–.71 (.70)	1.89* (.71)
Daily Homework Hours	2.50** (.32)	2.51** (.32)	3.13** (.43)	3.15** (.43)	1.81** (.49)
Region[d]	4.66** (1.10)	3.59** (1.00)	–	–	–
Ethnic Origin					
Cuban (total)	–.73 (1.17)	–	–.01 (1.19)	–	–
Cuban (1959–79)	–	6.38** (1.70)	–	7.36** (1.70)	–
Haitian	– 9.73** (2.56)	– 8.63** (2.52)	– 9.69** (2.54)	– 8.86** (2.48)	–
Mexican	– 5.13** (1.43)	– 14.96** (1.43)	–	–	– 16.77** (1.63)
Vietnamese	10.12** (1.88)	10.03** (1.88)	–	–	10.44** (1.96)
Intercept	100.44	100.80	112.78	113.56	93.28
R	.43	.43	.33	.35	.48
R^2	.18	.19	.11	.12	.23

	Reading Scores				
	1. Full Sample		2. Florida		3. California
	1[a]	2[b]	3[a]	4[b]	5
Age	– 2.91** (.45)	– 2.88** (.46)	– 2.38** (.59)	– 2.39** (.58)	– 3.65** (.72)
Sex[c]	2.69** (.76)	2.74** (.76)	.48 (.97)	.50(.97)	5.25** (1.19)
Parental SES	10.86** (.57)	10.85* (.57)	8.90** (.73)	8.78** (.73)	12.79** (.91)
Length of U.S. Residence	4.49** (.46)	4.25** (.46)	2.57** (.53)	2.30** (.62)	5.97** (.67)
Daily Homework Hours	1.74** (.29)	1.74** (.29)	2.16** (.38)	2.16** (.38)	1.39** (.46)
Region[d]	.03 (1.01)	–.53 (.93)	–	–	–
Ethnic Origin					
Cuban (total)	–.05 (1.08)	–	1.30 (1.05)	–	–
Cuban (1959–79)	–	4.47** (1.55)	–	6.08** (1.51)	–
Haitian	– 12.12** (2.36)	– 11.55** (2.32)	– 12.10** (2.24)	– 11.94** (2.20)	–
Mexican	– 11.55** (1.32)	– 11.56** (1.31)	–	–	– 11.80** (1.55)
Vietnamese	– 2.49 (1.73)	– 2.55 (1.73)	–	–	– 1.28 (1.86)

TABLE 17.2 *(Continued)*

Intercept	62.75	63.06	63.12	64.29	65.94
R	.45	.46	.36	.37	.52
R^2	.21	.21	.13	.14	.27

[a] Unstandardized regression coefficients; standard errors in parentheses. This column includes all Cuban-origin respondents.

[b] Unstandardized regression coefficients; standard errors in parentheses. This column includes Cuban-origin respondents whose parents arrived between 1959 and 1979.

[c] Girls coded 1, boys 0.

[d] South Florida (Miami and Fort Lauderdale) coded 1, southern California 0.

* $p < .05$.

** $p < .01$.

scores when we controlled for length of U.S. residence. In the southern California sub-sample, this negative effect dropped 1.2 percentage points, a difference that is significant at the .001 level, following the formula of Clogg et al. (1995).

The Cuban ethnic effect on both test scores disappeared when controls were introduced in the full and South Florida samples. This result suggests that the Cuban advantage is primarily a consequence of social class and birth in the United States. Successive model specifications (not shown) indicated that the Cuban effect on mathematics scores washed out as soon as parental SES was introduced into the equation; a lingering positive effect on English ability was reduced to zero when we controlled for length of U.S. residence. Yet the second columns in the full and South Florida panels indicate that a positive ethnic effect remained among Cuban-American students whose parents were among the earlier exile cohorts: Offspring of pre-1980 Cuban parents retained a significant net advantage on both indicators of achievement.

This last finding corresponds with the known differences in the characteristics and contexts of reception of pre- and post-1980 Cuban refugees that were described earlier. It lends indirect support to the assumed causal effect of early modes of incorporation by showing that a net ethnic advantage accrues only to children whose parents were among the early (and better received) cohorts of Cuban exiles. In additional regressions, we interacted ethnic background with parental SES to examine possible differences across groups in the transmission of status advantage. Most of these interactions proved insignificant. A notable exception was the effect for Haitian American students, for whom the interaction was both significant and negative. This effect, which was more than 10 points on both measures of achievement, indicates that members of this group experienced not only a net ethnic disadvantage but a reduction in the positive effect of parental SES on academic performance. Though not predicted originally, this Haitian-SES interaction is consistent with our theoretical argument concerning the importance of the ethnic community for the performance of second-generation children.[8]

Contextual effects

Possible school-level variables that can affect individual educational outcomes include the average SES of the school's student population, the proportion of this population that belongs to ethnic minorities, and the geographic location of the school. We do not have information on the average SES of the student body in each school, since only eligible second-generation students were interviewed. However, the three school systems provided information on the proportion of students eligible for the federally funded lunch program. We used the obverse of these figures for the three school systems as proxies for the average SES of the schools.

The variable inner city was coded *1* if the school was located in central-city areas of Miami, Fort Lauderdale, or San Diego and *0* otherwise. The third contextual variable, percent minority, was difficult to interpret. An earlier analysis indicated that these difficulties were due to the fact that this variable defined both poor black and Hispanic students and middle-class Cubans and other Latin American students in Miami as minorities, thus yielding contradictory results. When restricted to the common definition of minorities as underprivileged groups, the variable turned out to be collinear with the variable inner city, which prevented the estimation of contextual interaction models. For this reason, we modeled individual-level effects on three second-level predictors: the between-school average effect (intercept), the average school SES, and the school urban location. In the full sample regressions, metropolitan region was added. By redefining this variable as a second-level predictor in the analysis, we controlled for potential differences in contextual effects across the two target regions.

By recoding individual predictors as deviations from their respective means in within-school regressions, we had the intercepts represent the average score of sampled students in each school. As the first step in examining school contextual effects, we modeled within-school educational performance as follows:

$$(1)\ P_{ij} = \beta_{oj} + \beta_{1j}\,(\text{SEX}) + \beta_{2j}\,(\text{AGE}) + \beta_{3j}\,(\text{LENGTH}) - \beta_{4j}\,(\text{SES}) + \beta_{5j}\,(\text{ADV}) + \beta_{6j}\,(\text{DIS}) + \in_{ij} \qquad (17.1)$$

where

P_{ij} is the test score of student *i* in school *j*.

β_{oj} is the average test score in school *j*.

β_{nj} are regression coefficients for each school *j*.

$\in_{ij}$ is a residual term with assumed mean 0 and normal variance σ.

SES is the parental SEI and ADV and DIS are dummy variables representing the relative advantage or disadvantage of an ethnic community, respectively.

Daily homework hours was excluded because of its failure to account for the effects of parental SES or ethnicity, but controls were retained for age, sex, and length of U.S. residence (LENGTH). In the full sample, *ethnic advantage* was defined as Cuban or Vietnamese origin, and *ethnic disadvantage* as Mexican or Haitian origin. These definitions allowed us to make full use of the entire sample of schools. In addition, using region as a second-level predictor made it possible to isolate differential effects of specific immigrant nationalities because each target group is concentrated in only one of the selected regions. Since there was no net Vietnamese effect on reading scores, we restricted this analysis to mathematics scores. Comparable results for reading scores in South Florida (in which the effects of both ethnic advantage and disadvantage are observable) are described in the text, when relevant. The analysis for mathematics scores was also replicated in the two regional samples. For reasons of space, the results of this analysis are omitted, although they are mentioned when relevant.[9]

For our purposes, the parameters of interest are the intercept (the average school performance) and the SES and ethnicity (DIS and ADV) slopes. Each of these parameters is modeled in the following second-level equation:

$$(2)\ \beta_{nj} = \Phi_{n0} + \Phi_{n1}\,\text{AVSES}_j + \Phi_{n2}\,\text{INNER}_j + \Phi_{n3}\,\text{REGION}_j + \mu_{nj} \qquad (17.2)$$

Where

β_{nj} is the *n* intercept or slope for school *j*

Φ_{n0} is the grand mean intercept or slope for all schools.

Φ_{nm} are second-level regression coefficients.

μ_{nj} is the residual between-school variance.

$AVSES_j$ (average SES) is the obverse of the proportion of students eligible for free lunch in school *j*. $REGION_j$ was entered as a predictor in the full sample regressions, with schools in South Florida coded *1* and those in southern California coded *0*. Second-level predictors were also centered around their respective means, so that Φ_{n0} represents the intercept or slope for the "average" school in the sample.

HLM was used to estimate these equations with the HLM2L software package (Raudenbush and Bryk 1986). It first computed OLS coefficients for Equation 1 and subsequently adjusted them for within-school reliability. This method conditionally shrinks between-school variance around the grand mean by eliminating estimated unreliability.

Table 17.3 presents the results for the full sample. It includes random coefficient models in which each parameter in Equation 1 is modeled as an outcome of its respective grand mean plus residual variance, followed by the full model specified in Equation 2. A comparison of the two models allowed us to estimate an R^2 analog indicating how much between-school true variance is accounted for by second-level predictors. The first row of Table 17.3 presents the initial within-school OLS average coefficients. It is not surprising that the pattern is the same as that observed in Table 17.2, with strong positive effects of parental SES and ethnic advantage and strong negative effects of ethnic disadvantage. The coefficients are not identical to those presented in Table 17.2 because the latter are based on the entire student sample, while HLM computes mean within-school coefficients for all schools for which data are available.[10]

The analysis-of-variance model presented in the first panel of the table shows wide dispersion around the grand mean, as noted by the high chi-square value for the intercept β_{oj}. This result indicates that schools in the sample varied significantly in their students' performance on mathematics tests (similar results were obtained in the random-effects regression of reading scores). The corresponding chi-squares for the slopes show that the effects of parental SES and ethnic disadvantage are not uniform across schools either. The high values here led us to reject the null hypotheses—$\beta_{nj} = \Phi_{no}$—for these two coefficients. In contrast, the chi-square for ethnic advantage in the full sample and the two regional sub-samples is insignificant. This finding indicates that children of Cuban or Vietnamese parents tended to perform uniformly better, regardless of the school context.

Reliabilities of coefficients at the bottom of the first panel furnish the basis for empirical Bayes estimates of final effects. As was expected, OLS intercepts have greater reliabilities, since they depend exclusively on within-school sample sizes, whereas slopes are estimated with lesser reliability because they depend both on school sample size and differences among schools. The reliabilities of the control variables (age, sex, and length of U.S. residence) are low, indicating little between-school variation in their respective effects.

The third panel of Table 17.3 presents the results of regressing within-school slopes on Level-2 predictors. The model (Equation 2) does an acceptable job of accounting for school differences in mathematics scores. It explains 46 percent of the variance in the full sample and more than 50 percent in both regional samples (regional equations not shown). The coefficient ϕ_{00} indicates the average mathematics score in the typical school in the sample, and ϕ_{01} shows that schools with a higher mean student SES produce significantly higher scores. Similarly, ϕ_{02} indicates that inner-city schools, where minority students are concentrated, are at a significant disadvantage in academic performance. Both results are in agreement with past findings and with our own expectations and are replicated in the separate California and Florida regressions. The results show that higher status and attendance at suburban schools increase students' average academic performance, thus compounding the disadvantage of students from poorer families who are forced to attend less privileged inner-city schools.[11]

Figure 17.1 depicts this handicap through plots of predicted mathematics scores in the full sample in inner-city and suburban schools and across the range of average school SES. Since the

TABLE 17.3 HLMs of Predictors of Mathematics Scores, Full Sample

Models	β_{oj} (Mean Mathematics Score)	β_{1j} (female Slope)	β_{2j} (Age Slope)	β_{3j} (Length of Residence Slope)	β_{4j} (Parental SES Slope)	β_{5j}[a] (Ethnic ADV Slope)	β_{6j}[b] (Ethnic DIS Slope)
Level 1 Model:							
Mean OLS Coefficients	51.52	1.38	– 4.80	0.44	6.50	10.34	– 6.26
Level 2 Model:							
Analysis of Variance							
Φ_{n0} (intercepts)	50.96	2.69	– 3.74	– 0.10	5.50	11.55	– 8.95
t-ratio	26.67	3.04	4.96	0.12	5.02	5.27	3.64
	(.001)[c]	(.01)	(.001)	(N.S.)[d]	(.001)	(.001)	(.01)
μ_{nj} (residual variance)	128.34	2.74	9.43	13.32	25.35	91.24	111.71
Null hypothesis							
Chi-square: $\mu_{nj} = 0$	520.50	38.10	47.59	37.88	59.89	36.21	59.72
	(.001)	(N.S.)	(.05)	(N.S.)	(.01)	(N.S.)	(.01)
Average reliability	.94	.10	.40	.53	.55	.51	.52
Level 2 Model:							
Predictors of Intercept and Slopes							
Φ_{n0} (Intercept)	50.73				5.98	8.25	– 7.23
t-ratio	38.42				6.32	5.43	3.41
	(.001)[c]				(.001)	(.001)	(.003)
Φ_{n1} (AVSES)[e]	0.22				0.13	– 0.02	0.13
t-ratio	4.04				2.95	0.29	1.25
	(.001)				(.01)	(N.S.)[d]	(N.S.)[d]
Φ_{n2} (INNER)[f]	– 9.46				0.44	4.27	17.71
t-ratio	3.37				0.20	1.17	3.40
	(.005)				(n.s.)	(n.s.)	(.003)
Φ_{n3} (REGION)[g]	5.72				– 3.16	– 7.62	10.65
t-ratio	2.33				1.61	2.49	2.58
	(.05)				(N.S.)[d]	(.05)	(.02)
$\mu_{nj}\Phi_{nm}$ *(residual variance)*	56.91				13.52	15.41	56.96
Percentage of explained variance:	55.6				46.7	83.1	49.0
Null hypothesis							
Chi-square: $\mu_{nj}/\Phi_{nm} = 0$	178.16				49.17	24.17	46.78
	(.001)				(.003)	(n.s.)	(.005)

[a] Ethnic advantage.
[b] Ethnic disadvantage.
[c] Probability levels in parentheses.
[d] Not significant.
[e] Average school SES.
[f] School located in the inner city.
[g] South Florida coded 1, southern California, 0.

coefficient Φ_{03} in Table 17.3 shows that average mathematics scores were higher in South Florida, separate lines are graphed for both regions. In agreement with past research on national samples, our results indicate that schools do not help equalize family status and ethnic differences in educational attainment; rather, they exacerbate the individual-level effects of these variables (Raudenbush and Bryk 1989).

The second set of hypothesized contextual effects pertains to slope differences across school contexts. Here, we do not model the slopes of control variables but concentrate on those of theoretical interest, namely, the effects of parental SES, ethnic advantage, and ethnic disadvantage. The coefficient Φ_{40} indicates the effect of parental SES in the average school. As expected, this effect is positive and highly significant in the full sample, as well as in the separate regional regressions. Each *SD* unit in parental SES in the full sample increases mathematics scores by an average of almost six points, an effect that is significant at the .001 level.

In addition, however, the contextual variable AVSES$_j$ leads to a steeper slope, as indicated by the corresponding coefficient, Φ_{41}, which is significant and positive in both the full and the regional regressions. This result indicates that students from higher-status families perform even better if they attend schools where their peers also come from high-status families. The obverse is, of course, the case for lower-status students attending poorer schools. The contrast is graphically portrayed in Figure 17.2, which shows the effect of parental SES-mathematics score in schools that are 1 *SD*

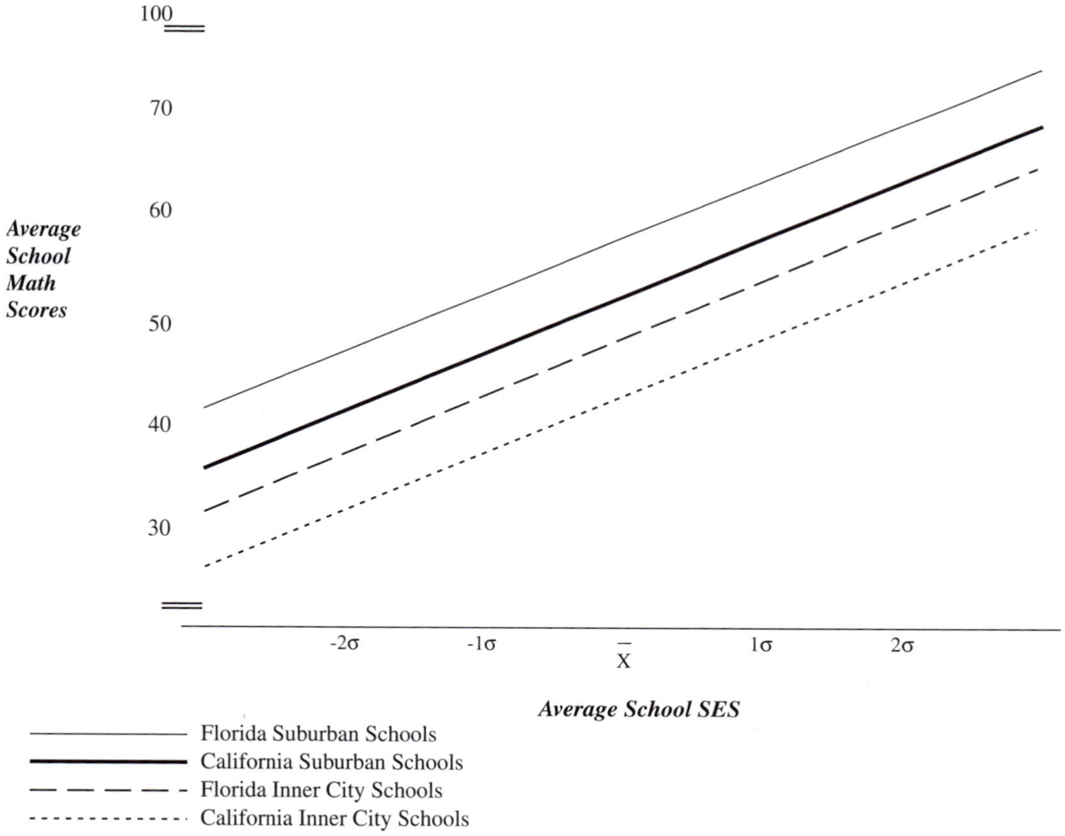

Fig. 17.1 Predicted Average Mathematics Scores of Second-generation Students in Different School Contexts.

above and 1 *SD* below the school SES grand mean. The steeper slope for high-SES schools is again in agreement with our theoretical expectations and past research. In essence, the figure shows that schools affect second-generation immigrant students no differently than they do those of native parents. In both cases, school contexts reinforce, rather than reduce, the original inequalities in achievement based on class privilege.

Differences in the effect of belonging to different immigrant communities are also revealing. As was mentioned previously, there was little between-school variation to explain the mean effect of ethnic advantage. The third panel of Table 17.3 shows that whatever variation remains is not explained by average school SES or school location, as indicated by the nonsignificant coefficients Φ_{51} and Φ_{52}. This result again indicates that the positive effects associated with advantaged immigrant groups are resilient across schools, being observable in both high-SES suburban and low-SES inner-city schools. Separate regional regressions of mathematics and reading scores in South Florida and southern California revealed an identical pattern for the individual effects of Cuban and Vietnamese ethnicity.[12] $REGION_j$ had a significant effect on this slope in the full sample regression. The negative sign of the coefficient means that, for mathematics scores at least, Vietnamese children in southern California display the stronger ethnic advantage.

In the typical school, coming from a disadvantaged immigrant background reduces mathematics scores by 7 percentage points, as indicated by the coefficient Φ_{60} in Table 17.3. The omitted regional regressions show that the gap remains about the same for Haitian-origin children in South Florida,

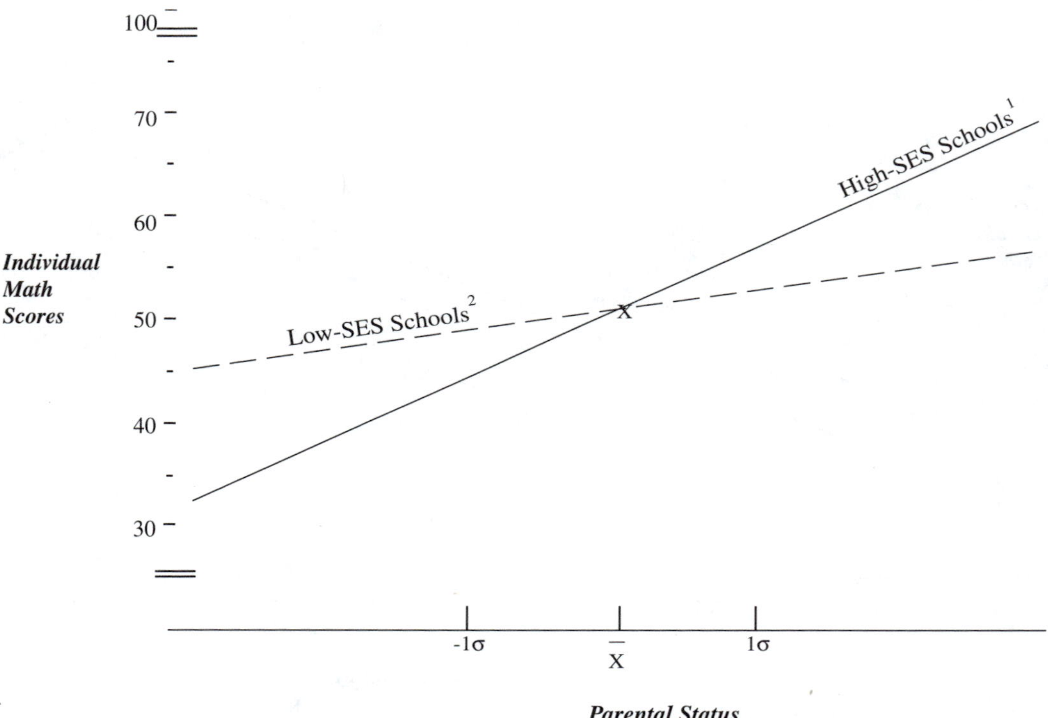

Fig. 17.2 Relationship of Parental SES and Individual Mathematics Scores in High- and Low-Status Schools, Second-generation Students.

1. One standard deviation above mean school SES.
2. One standard deviation below mean school SES.

but increases to 13 points among Mexican-origin students in southern California. The greater deficit associated with Mexican-immigrant origin is also captured by the coefficient for region, Φ_{63}, in the full sample, which is positive and significant, indicating greater relative disadvantage for children of that nationality. Yet, for both disadvantaged groups, school location has a significant effect. Inner-city schools tend to flatten this negative slope, indicating a partial reduction of ethnic disadvantage. Conversely, the ethnic disadvantage for Haitian- and Mexican-origin children attending suburban, non-minority schools is pronounced.

The partial disappearance of a negative ethnic effect in inner-city schools can be interpreted as a consequence of these schools' relatively lower academic levels. Put differently, in contexts of general disadvantage, second-generation Haitians or Mexicans do not perform much worse than average. Note finally that residual variances in the intercept, parental SES, and ethnic disadvantage slopes are not reduced to insignificance. This result indicates that while the model (Equation 2) performs acceptably, there are still unmeasured contextual effects on both: average within-school academic performance and its individual class and ethnic determinants. Again, this finding is replicated in the regional samples.

CONCLUSION

The onset of a new wave of immigration to the United States in the 1980s and the subsequent emergence and consolidation of new ethnic communities represent processes of prime importance for the future of American society. A strong case can be made that the decisive factor in this regard is not so much the fate of first-generation immigrants as that of their descendants. It is the children of immigrants who, as American citizens and full members of this society, will define the direction and outlook of their respective ethnic communities. At present, most of the new second generation is young, and, hence, many key adaptation outcomes are taking place in schools.

Our analysis indicates that second-generation students are no different from those of native parentage in being heavily influenced by their family's SES and by the average socioeconomic level of their schools. In addition, however, their national background plays a significant independent role. On the basis of past research, these resilient effects can be interpreted as a reflection of the individual characteristics and different modes of incorporation experienced by first-generation immigrants. The relative advantage or disadvantage associated with specific immigrant communities not only remains after family SES is controlled, but interacts in unexpected ways with the school contexts experienced by second-generation children. The gain attributable to relatively successful and well-integrated immigrant groups appears impervious to changes in school contexts: It is as strong in the impoverished inner-city schools as in suburban schools. On the other hand, the negative effects associated with disadvantaged ethnicity are most apparent when second-generation students face the stiffer academic competition of schools outside the central city.

To help the reader understand better what these differential effects mean, we shift methodological gears at this point to make use of ethnographic material collected as part of the same study. Random samples of approximately 120 foreign-born parents of the respondents were interviewed in Miami and San Diego. These interviews are revealing because they show the consistently different outlooks associated with specific nationalities. In them, the academic success or failure of the second-generation youths emerged as almost a self-fulfilling prophecy of their parents' collective attitudes and plans for the future. The Cuban immigrants in Miami tended to exude self-confidence and to view their children's college education not as a dream, but as a fait accompli—a perspective that was apparent even in working-class or poor parents. Thus, a Cuban mother, dependent on welfare because of a physical disability, still declared: "We Cubans are not used to failure ....

Many immigrants speak Spanish but there are differences. Cubans always had self-respect, a sense of duty toward their children, [and] a work ethnic."[13]

Across town, many Haitian parents saw themselves locked in combat with the surrounding inner city, whose influence on their children they vehemently denounced. To overcome this influence, they either tried to move to the suburbs or sent their children to Catholic or suburban "magnet" schools. Poverty and the powerlessness of their ethnic community thwarted most of these efforts. And, as we have shown, the effects of disadvantaged ethnicity follow Haitian children who manage to leave inner-city schools.

Three thousand miles to the west, the Mexican parents in San Diego reported a situation similar to that of the Haitian parents. The effects of precarious employment and weak social ties combined to weaken their control over their children. The Mexican parents also voiced high aspirations for their offspring, but their assessment of their own situation left little room for optimism. Their frequent complaints about the premature "Americanization" of second-generation teenagers were mixed with pessimistic comments about the lack of solidarity of their own ethnic community. Thus, a Mexican single mother reacted emotionally when asked about the extent of this support. Tears came to her eyes as she expressed disappointment that Mexicans as a group are not tight-knit and do not help each other "like the Vietnamese." In contrast, she cited jealousy and selfishness among her own people: "If they can't have it, they don't want anyone else to have it either."[14]

Forty blocks to the east in another working-class neighborhood in San Diego, a Vietnamese mother tried to explain why her daughter's grade-point average was "only" 3.8, rather than the perfect 4.0 of her older children. This woman lives on governmental assistance, to which her refugee status entitles her. She speaks little English, but seeks to maintain strict control of their children: "I raise them here as I did in Vietnam: to school and back home."[15] Her ability to do so is based on her family's close ties with other Vietnamese families. They live in an encapsulated world where adults tend to support each other's parenting rules. The situation parallels that described by Zhou and Bankston (1994:831) in their study of a Vietnamese community in New Orleans:

> [P]arents and children are constantly observed and judged by others as under a "Vietnamese microscope." If a child flunks or drops out of school, or if a boy falls into a gang or a girl becomes pregnant without getting married, he or she brings shame not only to himself or herself but also to the family.

These processes may help explain the notable finding that children from this low-status immigrant community retained a sizable academic edge, even after parental SES and the quality and location of the schools that they attended was controlled. The differences observed across these four nationalities may give rise to invidious comparisons based on the alleged superiority or inferiority of their respective cultures. Such a conclusion would be erroneous. In our view, the factors that account for the significant differences among these groups have to do with the human capital that immigrants bring with them from their countries of origin and the social context that receives them and shapes their adaptation in the United States.

Differences in modes of incorporation influence the subsequent development of immigrant communities. They are eventually reflected in the confident optimism with which some parents look at the future and point proudly to their group's achievements and the insecurity and collective despair of others. As the results of this study show, inequalities in the objective situations and subjective outlooks of parents converged with the observed academic performance of children, indicating that both class and ethnic privilege are transmitted from one generation to the next. It is too early to tell whether the fates of immigrant parents will continue to affect the lives of their children once the children move out of school and into adulthood. However, our findings clearly point to the ways in which early differences in the arrival and modes of incorporation of immigrants can have decisive consequences both for their own future and that of their American descendants.

Notes

1. As Berk (1983) showed, censored data affect not only the external generalizability of results but their internal validity, insofar as the actual shape of a relationship may be at variance with that found in a truncated sample. Data from South Florida indicate that 98 percent of children ages twelve to fifteen are in school, a finding that practically eliminates the censoring problem up to the ninth grade. Among sixteen and seventeen year olds (the tenth- and eleventh-grade cohorts), however, the proportion of children in school declines to 86 percent for Hispanics and 82 percent for blacks. During the following two years (the eleventh- and twelfth-grade cohorts), the figures drop further to 60 percent of Hispanics and just 43 percent of blacks (Perez 1989). Since a large proportion of children of immigrants are classified in these two ethnic categories, it was necessary to limit the sample to the lower high school grades to ensure that it was representative of the respective second-generation cohort.
2. Ethnic effects reported in the following section were computed relative to the entire sample—minus each specific target nationality.
3. Our estimates, based on data provided by the respective school systems.
4. The lower-than-average reading score for the entire sample is attributable to lingering difficulties with English by children from non-English-speaking homes, particularly those who are themselves foreign-born.
5. We also conducted a replication limited to the four target nationalities. The results (not shown) merely accentuate the empirical trends found in comparisons with the full sample.
6. Length of U.S. residence was introduced in the equation as a three-point variable, with native-born children coded the highest. Daily homework hours were the actual hours spent on homework, as reported by respondents, aggregated into six categories—from less than one to five or more.
7. Successive model specifications (not shown) indicated that length of U.S. residence, not other control variables, led to a significant reduction of the SES gross effect. The formula for the estimated variance of the difference between successive models is as follows:
   $S^2(d_k) = S^2(b_k) - S^2(b^*_k)\ \delta^2_v/\delta^2E$
   where
   $S^2(d_k)$ is the estimated variance of the difference between regression coefficients of exogenous variable K in the full and reduced models.
   $S^2(b_k)$ is the estimated variance of the K effect in the reduced model.
   $S^2(b^*_k)$ is the estimated variance of the K effect in the full model.
   δ^2_v/δ^2E is the ratio of residual variances in the full and reduced models.
8. The interaction effects were –10.77 on reading scores and –14.43 on mathematics scores, both significant at the .001 level.
9. A table with the full results of these second-level regressions in both regions is available from the authors.
10. Data are available for thirty-eight schools. Chi-square statistics may be based on a lesser number because of computational limitations arising from small numbers or limited variance in some schools.
11. Second-level effects on reading scores in the South Florida sample follow an identical pattern, with school SES increasing average test scores and central -city location reducing them. Both effects are statistically significant. The reduction in between-school variance accomplished by the model (Equation 2) is significantly less, however, than in the mathematics scores, suggesting that other contextual factors are at play.
12. All Cuban ethnic effects in these multilevel regressions are based on the sub-sample whose parents arrived in the United States between 1959 and 1979.
13. Unless otherwise specified, this and subsequent verbatim quotations are from the original interviews conducted as part of this project.
14. This quote is from a project interview in August 1995.
15. This quotation is from a project interview in December 1993, reported in Fernández-Kelly and Schauffler (1994:673–74).

References

Alba, Richard, John Logan, and Thomas L. McNulty. 1994. Ethnic economies in metropolitan regions: Miami and beyond. *Social Forces* 72:691–724.

Bach, Robert L. 1986. Immigration: Issues of ethnicity, class, and public policy in the United States. *Annals of the American Academy of Political and Social Sciences* 485:139–52.

Bach, Robert L., Jennifer B. Bach, and Timothy Triplett. 1981. The Flotilla ‘entrants’: Latest and most controversial. *Cuban Studies* 11:29–18.

Bach, Robert L., Linda W. Gordon, David W. Haines, and David R. Howell. 1984. The economic adjustment of Southeast Asian refugees in the United States. Pp. 51–55 in *World Refugee Survey, 1983*. Geneva: United Nations High Commission for Refugees.

Bailey, Thomas and Roger Waldinger. 1991. Primary, secondary, and enclave labor markets: A training system approach. *American Sociological Review* 56:432–45.
Barrera, Mario. 1980. *Race and Class in the Southwest: A Theory of Racial Inequality.* Notre Dame, IN: Notre Dame University Press.
Berk, Richard. 1983. An introduction to sample selection bias in sociological data. *American Sociological Review* 48:386–98.
Boswell, Thomas D. and James R. Curtis. 1984. *The Cuban-American Experience.* Totowa, NJ: Rowman & Allanheld.
Bryk, Anthony S. and Stephen W. Raudenbush. 1992. *Hierarchical Linear Models: Applications and Data Analysis Methods.* Newbury Park, CA.: Sage.
Clogg, Clifford C., Eva Petkova, and Adamantios Haritou. 1995. Statistical methods for comparing regression, coefficients between models. *American Journal of Sociology* 100:1261–93.
Coleman, James S. 1988. Social capital in the creation of human capital. *American Journal of Sociology* (Suppl.) 94:S95–S121.
——. 1990. *Foundations of Social Theory.* Cambridge, MA: Belknap Press of Harvard University Press.
Eccles, J. S., A. Arbreton, C. M. Buchanan, J. Jacobs, C. Flanagan, R. Harold, D. Mac Iver, C. Midgley, P. Reuman, and A. Wigfield. 1993. School and family effects on the ontogeny of children's interests, self-perceptions, and activity choice. *Nebraska Symposium. 1992.* Lincoln: University of Nebraska Press.
Fernández-Kelly, Patricia and Richard Schauffler. 1994. Divided fates: Immigrant children in a restructured U.S. economy. *International Migration Review* 28:662–89.
Fix, Michael and Jeffrey S. Passel. 1991. *The Door Remains Open: Recent Immigration to the United States and a Preliminary Analysis of the Immigration Act of 1990* (report of the Urban Institute and the Rand Corporation). Washington, DC: Urban Institute.
Gold, Steven J. 1992. *Refugee Communities: A Comparative Field Study.* Newbury Park, CA: Sage.
Griffin, Larry J. and Karl L. Alexander. 1978. Schooling and socio-economic attainments: High school and college influences. *American Journal of Sociology* 84:319–47.
Guarnizo, Luis E. 1992. One country in two: Dominican-owned firms in New York and the Dominican Republic. Unpublished doctoral dissertation. Department of Sociology, Johns Hopkins University.
Haller, Archibald D. and Alejandro Portes. 1973. Status attainment processes. *Sociology of Education* 46:51–91.
Ianni, Francis A. J. 1989. *The Search for Structure: A Report on American Youth Today.* New York: Free Press.
Jensen, Leif. 1989. *The New Immigration: Implications for Poverty and Public Assistance.* Westport, CT: Greenwood Press.
Jensen, Leif and Yoshimi Chitose. 1994. Today's second generation: Evidence from the 1990 U.S. Census. *International Migration Review,* 28:714–35.
Light, Ivan. 1984. Immigrant and ethnic enterprise in North America. *Ethnic and Racial Studies* 7:195–216.
Massey, Douglas S. 1987. Understanding Mexican migration to the United States. *American Journal of Sociology* 92:1372–1403.
Massey, Douglas, Rafael Alarcón, Jorge Durand, and Humberto González. 1987. *Return to Atzlán: The Social Process of International Migration from Western Mexico.* Berkeley: University of California Press.
Massey, Douglas S. and Felipe Garcia Españ. 1987. The social process of international migration. *Science* 237:733–38.
Matute-Bianchi, Maria Eugenia. 1986. Ethnic identities and patterns of school success and failure among Mexican-descent and Japanese-American tudents in a California high school. *American Journal of Education* 95:233–55.
Miller, Jake C. 1984. *The Plight of Haitian Refugees.* New York: Praeger.
Montero, D. 1979. *Vietnamese-Americans: Patterns of Resettlement and Socio-economic Adaptation in the United States.* Boulder, CO: Westview Press.
Nelson, Candace and Marta Tienda. 1985. The structuring of Hispanic ethnicity: Historical and contemporary perspectives. *Ethnic and Racial Studies* 8:49–74.
Passel, Jeffrey S. and Barry Edmonston. 1992. Immigration and race: Recent trends in immigration to the United States. Unpublished manuscript PRIP-UI-22, Urban Institute, Washington, DC.
Perez, Lisandro. 1989. Immigrant students in South Florida schools: A demographic profile and summary of current knowledge. Unpublished preliminary report of the Children of Immigrants Project, Department of Sociology; Florida International University, Miami.
Portes, Alejandro and Robert L. Bach. 1985. *Latin Journey: Cuban and Mexican Immigrants in the United States.* Berkeley: University of California Press.
Portes, Alejandro and Rubén G. Rumbaut. 1990. *Immigrant America: A Portrait.* Berkeley: University of California Press.
Portes, Alejandro and Alex Stepick. 1993. *City on the Edge: The Transformation of Miami.* Berkeley: University of California Press.
Raudenbush, Stephen and Anthony S. Bryk. 1986. A hierarchical model for studying school effects. *Sociology of Education* 59:1–17.
——. 1989. A multilevel model of the social distribution of high school achievement. *Sociology of Education* 62:172–92.
Roberts, Bryan R. 1995. Socially expected durations and the economic adjustment of immigrants. pp. 42–86 in *The Economic Sociology of Immigration,* Alejandro Portes, ed. New York: Russell Sage Foundation.
Rumbaut, Rubén G. 1992. The Americans: Latin American and Caribbean peoples in the United States. pp. 275–307 in *Americas, New Interpretive Essays,* A. Stepan, ed. New York: Oxford University Press.
——. 1994. Origins and destinies: Immigration to the United States since World War II. *Sociological Forum* 9:583–621.
Rumbaut, Rubén G. and Kenji Ima. 1988. *The Adaptation of Southeast Asian Refugee Youth: A Comparative Study.* Washington, DC: Office of Refugee Resettlement.
Samora, Julian. 1971. *Los Mojados: The Wetback Story.* Notre Dame, IN: Notre Dame University Press.
Spenner, Kenneth and David L. Featherman. 1978. "Achievement ambitions." *Annual Review of Sociology* 4:373–120.
Stepick, Alex, 1982. *Haitian Refugees in the U.S.* (Report No. 52). London: Minority Rights Group.

——. 1989. Miami's two informal sectors. Pp. 111–34 in *The Informal Economy: Studies in Advanced and Less Developed Countries*, A. Portes, M. Castells, and L. A. Benton, eds. Baltimore: Johns Hopkins University Press.

Suárez-Orozco, Marcelo M. 1987. Towards a psychosocial understanding of Hispanic adaptation to American schooling. pp. 156–68 in *Success or Failure? Learning and the Languages of Minority Students*, H. T. Trueba, ed. New York: Newbury House.

U.S. Census Bureau. 1990. *Census of Population and Housing, 1990*. Public Use Microdata, 5-percent sample.

——. 1991. *Survey of Minority-Owned Business Enterprises, 1987* (Publication No. MB 87–4). Washington, DC: U.S. Government Printing Office.

——. 1993. *The Foreign-Born Population of the United States, 1990* (Publication No. CPH-L-98). Washington. DC: U.S. Government Printing Office.

Wigfield, A. and S. R. Asher. 1984. Social and motivational influences on reading. In *Handbook of Reading Research*, P. D. Pearson, R. Barr, M. C. Kamil, and P. B. Mosenthal, eds. New York: Longman.

Wilson, Kenneth and W. Allen Martin. 1982. Ethnic enclaves: A comparison of the Cuban and black economies in Miami. *American Journal of Sociology* 88:135–60.

Zhou, Min. 1992. *New York's Chinatown: The Socioeconomic Potential of an Urban Enclave*. Philadelphia: Temple University Press.

Zhou, Min and Carl L. Bankston. 1994. Social capital and the adaptation of the second generation: The case of Vietnamese youth in New Orleans. *International Migration Review* 28:821–45.

Alejandro Portes, Ph.D., is John Dewey Professor of Sociology and International Relations, Department of Sociology, Johns Hopkins University, Baltimore. His main fields of interest are the sociology of immigration and ethnicity, economic sociology, sociology of education, and international development. He is presently studying children of immigrants: the adaptation of the second generation and transnational communities: their origin and effects among Cuban American immigrants in the United States.

Dag Macleod, MA, is Senior Research Assistant, Children of Immigrants project (under the direction of Dr. Portes), Department of Sociology, Johns Hopkins University, Baltimore. His main fields of interest are economic sociology, international development, and the sociology of immigration and ethnicity. His current work is on children of immigrants: the adaptation of the second generation and the construction of markets and embeddedness in the privatization of Mexico's telecommunications sector.

The data on which this paper was based were collected by the project, Children of Immigrants: The Adaptation Process of the Second Generation, supported by the Spencer Foundation, the Andrew W. Mellon Foundation, the National Science Foundation (Grant No. SES-9022555), and the Russell Sage Foundation. The authors appreciate the collaboration and comments of Min Zhou, Rubén G. Rumbaut, and Douglas MacIver. However, exclusive responsibility for the contents remains that of the authors. *Address all correspondence to Dr. Alejandro Portes, Department of Sociology, John Hopkins University, 3400 North Charles Street, Baltimore, MD 21218.*

Chapter 18
Optimism and Achievement: The Educational Performance of Immigrant Youth

GRACE KAO AND MARTA TIENDA

Objective. The rise in the volume and diversity of immigrants to the United States since 1960 has increased concerns about whether assimilation benefits educational achievement. This issue is addressed by evaluating the relative merits of three hypotheses regarding generational status and scholastic performance: (1) straight-line assimilation, (2) accommodation without assimilation, and (3) immigrant optimism. *Methods.* The National Education Longitudinal Study of 1988 is used to examine the impact of generational status on three indicators of educational achievement: grades, achievement test scores, and college aspirations of eighth graders. *Results.* Overall, the results are consistent with hypotheses (2) and (3) and suggest that behavioral differences between immigrant and native parents are essential ingredients in explaining the differential performance of immigrant and native youth. However, the effects of generational status on scholastic outcomes differ by race and ethnic group, such that parental nativity is most crucial for Asians and less so for Hispanics, while child's birthplace is more decisive for educational achievement among blacks. *Conclusions.* Because foreign-born youth are at a slight disadvantage due to their limited English skills and because immigrant parents promote academic achievement, second-generation youth (that is, native-born children of foreign-born parents) are best positioned to achieve scholastically.

The rise in the volume and diversity of U.S. immigrants since 1960 has spawned a spate of studies about the economic consequences and adaptation experiences of new arrivals. With few exceptions, most studies have focused on the integration experiences of adults, to the relative neglect of youth (Portes and Zhou 1993). Yet recent trends in international migration also have contributed to the ethnic diversification of the school-age population. The Population Reference Bureau (1989) reported that more than half of all students from forty-nine of the largest one hundred school districts are black, Hispanic, or Asian.

Taking note of the educational implications of recent demographic trends, researchers have identified several shortcomings of past and current research about immigrant youth. First, early studies focused primarily on Europeans who arrived at the turn of the century, thus limiting their applicability to Asian and Latino immigrant youth who dominate contemporary flows (Portes and Schauffler 1996; Portes and Zhou 1993). Second, most of the empirical work on the adaptation of immigrant children has focused on English acquisition or the effects of bilingualism on scholastic performance (Fernandez and Nielsen 1986; Portes and Schauffler 1996). Third, recent ethnographic studies of immigrant youth offer richly textured descriptions in specific school settings but are less informative about immigrant youth nationally (see Matute-Bianchi 1986; Ogbu 1991; Portes and Zhou 1993). Finally, there is disagreement about how educational achievement changes as immigrant youth and children of immigrants assimilate into U.S. society. Most analysts have argued that assimilation improves academic outcomes (for example, Matute-Bianchi 1986), but others have suggested that scholastic performance declines over successive generations. To explain this anomaly, some analysts have argued that foreign-born youth are especially motivated to succeed academically (Gibson 1993; Duran and Weffer 1992; Caplan, Choy, and Whitmore 1992; Rumbaut 1990). Others have attributed the scholastic success of recent immigrants to positive self-selection. However, few studies have considered specific mechanisms through which the association between immigrant stratification and educational performance emerges and evolves across generations.

Differences in family rules, family communication about school experiences, and parental participation in school activities are aspects of family life that may influence educational outcomes and differ across generational status groups. According to Caplan, Choy, and Whitmore (1992), immigrant households are more likely to have rules about grades and homework (rather than about household chores), which makes children aware that scholastic responsibilities assume primacy over other activities. Direct family communication about school has been shown to influence educational performance (Baker and Stevenson 1986), but the influence of communication on educational outcomes differs among race and ethnic groups (Schneider and Lee 1990; Kao, Tienda, and Schneider 1993). Similarly, we suspect that immigrant parents are less likely to speak directly to their children about school experiences, partly because they may communicate the importance of education in more abstract terms than their more acculturated counterparts and partly because the value of education assumes a normative priority in parental expectations of children. Finally, prior studies have found parental participation in scholastic activities to be positively correlated with high-achieving youth because such participation reflects parental interest in their children's academic life. If foreign-born parents feel uncomfortable participating in such activities due to cultural or language barriers, then the effect of parental immigrant status on their offspring's educational outcomes may operate through the lower rates of parental participation in school activities.

In this chapter we examine the educational performance of immigrant and second-generation youth relative to native-born youth whose parents also were born in the United States. Thus, we compare three generational groups who include (1) the first generation (immigrant children of immigrant parents); (2) the second generation (native-born children of immigrant parents); and (3) the native generation (native-born children of native-born parents) for black, Hispanic, Asian, and non-Hispanic white youth. Our general goal is to evaluate the association between immigrant status and academic achievement. Because there are well-known differences in educational attainments among black, Hispanic, and Asian youth (Mare and Winship 1988), in evaluating this association it is necessary to distill the influence of race and ancestry from that of parental or youth's birthplace. Specific objectives include (1) describing generational differences in academic performance and parental behavior toward academic pursuits among minority and non-minority youth, (2) assessing the impact of immigrant status on educational achievement, and (3) examining the effects of length of residence on the educational performance of foreign-born youth. We begin with a brief review of pertinent studies and theoretical approaches to understanding educational achievement and identify alternative hypotheses about how generational status influences scholastic performance.

THEORETICAL CONSIDERATIONS

Prior studies of how immigrant status influences educational achievement are of three general types. First, the *straight-line assimilation framework* predicts that, over time, ethnic and racial minorities will blend into the mainstream culture and become indistinguishable from native populations (Park 1914; Gordon 1964). Park argued that ethnic groups assimilate into American society in four stages. First, ethnic groups come into *contact* with one another, which is followed by a period of *conflict.* Eventually, the mainstream *accommodates* the minority group, and lastly, the minority group *assimilates* into the mainstream. Gordon (1964) extended Park's formulation by specifying the sub-processes of assimilation. Specifically, he theorized that cultural assimilation or acculturation is the first stage in an inevitable process of integration, which in turn is a prerequisite to the eradication of prejudice and discrimination by the majority group. Structural assimilation, the pivotal step in this process, is largely driven by increasing educational achievement of second and higher generational groups. Matute-Bianchi's (1986) study of a California high school lends support to the straight-line assimilation hypothesis because the most successful students within the Mexican population usually spoke English exclusively in school, and they participated in mainstream clubs rather than those geared toward Mexican students.

A more recent development in the literature has suggested that recent immigrant youth may be the highest academic achievers (Rumbaut 1990). For example, Gibson (1993) argued that Punjabi students in central California succeeded precisely because they *accommodated without assimilating.* In other words, these first-generation Punjabi youth adapted to their environment by learning English and following American customs at school, but their parents discouraged their primary interaction with American peers. She also found that teachers favored recent immigrants, but expected them to be "corrupted" as they assimilated with their native peers.

One interpretation of the academic success of immigrants has focused on the strength of values that promote educational achievement and family cohesiveness (Rumbaut 1990). For example, Caplan, Choy, and Whitmore (1992) showed that many Southeast Asian refugee youth devoted three hours nightly to homework, and that television watching was strictly limited. In addition, children worked together so that older siblings were required to tutor their younger siblings, with the result that older youth also benefited from reviewing school materials. Waters (1991), on the other hand, argued that the meaning attached to "assimilation" for foreign-born blacks is especially negative because native blacks are not viewed as being successful. In her words:

> The [black] immigrants do not face assimilation into an undifferentiated monolithic American culture which values being a native American more than a foreigner. In fact, if these immigrants assimilate they assimilate to being not just Americans but black Americans. It is generally believed by the immigrants at least and some would argue by American whites that it is *higher* social status to be an immigrant black than to be an American black. (p. 19)

Thus, the accommodation-without-assimilation perspective implies that academic achievement declines with time in the United States as immigrant youth assimilate with their native peers.

A final approach to understanding how immigration affects educational experiences has focused on the circumstances that produce geographic movement and the selectivity of migrants. Presumably, international migrants are self-selected and predisposed, if not outright anxious, to adapt to the host society (Chiswick 1979; Borjas 1990; Ogbu 1991). Although many find themselves at the bottom of the socioeconomic ladder initially, they generally expect that they or their offspring will eventually experience upward mobility. Ogbu (1991), for example, claimed that voluntary immigrants tend to overcome difficulties experienced in their host country because their cultural frame of reference is their home country, where they often faced harsher environments than in their destination (see Alvarez 1971). Also, because voluntary immigrants view their adjustment problems as temporary, they are more creative in inventing pragmatic solutions to their current predicaments. In contrast, many minorities who have lived in the United States for many generations are disillusioned with the prospects of upward mobility because of their real experiences with discrimination. If so, then native-born minority parents may pass on their leveled aspirations to their children. Alternatively, if immigrant parents are more optimistic about their children's chances of upward mobility than their own, conceivably the children of immigrants will outperform their native-born counterparts in scholastic endeavors (Caplan, Choy, and Whitmore 1992).

Korean and Chinese youth fit this ideal well because most have immigrant parents. Not surprisingly, prior research has attributed their academic success directly to parental valuation of education (Schneider and Lee 1990; Sue and Okazaki 1990; Kao 1995). Although recent immigrant youth may be at a disadvantage compared to their native-born counterparts with respect to English proficiency, they may still perform as well as their native-born counterparts because their parents' optimism about their socioeconomic prospects leads youth to behave in ways that promote educational success. But native-born youth of immigrant parents (second generation) should outperform both their foreign- and native-born peers because they enjoy both the optimism of parents *and* the advantage of English skills.

To recapitulate, the existing literature on the educational attainment of immigrant youth suggests three hypotheses. First, the *straight-line assimilation* hypothesis predicts that immigrant youth will have the lowest educational achievement but that achievement will increase with generational status. In contrast, the *accommodation-without-assimilation* hypothesis predicts that recent immigrant youth are best positioned to perform scholastically precisely because they have not been tainted by native peer culture, especially the oppositional forms (see Ogbu 1991). Finally, the *immigrant optimism* hypothesis posits that differences between immigrant and native *parents* are the essential ingredients to explaining generational differences in performance among youth. Because foreign-born youth may be at a slight disadvantage due to their lack of English skills, native-born children of foreign-born parents—the "second generation"—will outperform their peers. Our empirical analyses evaluated the merits of these alternative hypotheses.

DATA AND DEFINITIONS OF VARIABLES

We analyzed the first panel of the National Education Longitudinal Study of 1988 (NELS:88). This national survey utilized a two-stage probability sampling design that selected a nationally representative sample of 24,599 students from 1,052 randomly selected schools. NELS:88 began with a cohort of eighth graders in 1988 and followed them at two-year intervals through spring 1992, when most of the sample were twelfth graders. NELS:88 was especially suited to our analysis because Hispanics and Asians were over-sampled and both groups included large numbers of foreign-born youth and native-born youth of foreign-born parents. Finally, NELS:88 permitted an integration of information not only from students, but also their parents, teachers, and schools (National Center for Education Statistics 1990). Table 18.1 contains operational definitions of all variables.

Students were considered "first generation" if both they and their mothers were foreign-born. U.S.-born students whose mothers were born abroad were designated "second generation." All others were classified as members of the native population. We used mother's rather than father's immigrant status in determining students' generational status because mothers were more likely than fathers to respond to the parent questionnaires; because father's place of birth contained greater amounts of missing data; and most important, because previous research has suggested that mothers play a more critical role in managing their children's educational careers than fathers (Baker and Stevenson 1986).[1]

TABLE 18.1 Definitions of Variables

Variable	Definition
Generational Status	
First generation	Equals 1 if mother is foreign-born and eighth grader is foreign-born, 0 otherwise.
Second generation	Equals 1 if mother is foreign-born and eighth grader is U.S.-born, 0 otherwise.
Native generation	Equals 1 if respondent is not first or second generation, 0 otherwise.
Race and ethnicity	
Asian	Equals 1 if Asian, 0 otherwise (coded similarly for blacks, Hispanics, and whites).
Parental socioeconomic status	
Parent's education	Educational level of the parent with the highest level of education.
Family income	Midpoint value of the answer category for family income.
Family composition	
Mother and father	Equals 1 if respondent lives with both mother and father, 0 otherwise.
Student achievement	
LEP	Equals 1 if R classified by one of his/her teachers as limited English proficient (LEP), 0 otherwise.
Grades	Ranges from 0.5 to 4.0, with a 4.0 equaling an A average.
Math test scores	Standardized score for the mathematics test given to the eighth graders (similar measure for reading test scores).
Educational aspirations	
Aspire to graduate college	Equals 1 if respondent aspires to complete a four-year college degree, 0 otherwise.
R's educational aspirations	Ranges from 10 to 18, with 10 = less than high school and 18 = go beyond college.
Family rules (P's view)[a]	Dummy variables coded 1 to indicate existence of rules about maintaining a certain grade point average, homework, or household chores, 0 otherwise.
Family rules (R's view)[a]	Coded 0 = never, 1 = rarely, 2 = sometimes, and 3 = often regarding the frequency that parents check homework, require household chores done, limit TV watching, and limit going out with friends.
Family communication (P's view)	Coded 0 = not at all, 1 = rarely, 2 = occasionally, 3 = regularly to questions about the frequency parents talk to their children about school experiences, high school plans, and post-high school plans.
Family communication (R's view)	Coded 0 = not at all, 1 = once or twice, 2 = three or more times to questions about how often parents talk to their children about programs at school, school activities, and things studied in class.
Parental Participation (P's view)	Coded 1 if the parent belongs to parent-teacher organizations, go to parent-teacher meetings, participate in parent-teacher activities, or volunteer in school, 0 otherwise.
Parental Participation (R's view)	Coded 1 if the parent has ever attended a school meeting or attended a school event, 0 otherwise.

Source: The National Education Longitudinal Study of 1988 (NCES 1990).

[a] *P's view* refers to parent questionnaire items while *R's view* refers to student questionnaire items.

We examined multiple indicators of achievement, including middle-school grades, standardized math and reading test scores, and aspirations to graduate from college among eighth graders. Grades measured performance in school.[2] Standardized test scores from the math and reading portion of a cognitive test administered to each respondent provided a uniform assessment of mathematical and reading skill level of eighth graders. Finally, educational aspirations gauged the extent to which the youth were academically oriented. Parents' educational aspirations for their children's eventual educational attainment and children's perceptions of their mother's aspirations provided leverage in evaluating whether it was children's or parental immigration status that influenced educational performance and goals.

DESCRIPTIVE RESULTS

In tabulations not presented here, we examined a statistical profile of students and parents by generational status.[3] Consistent with recent immigration trends, most of the first-generation youth were of Hispanic or Asian origin, while most of the native-born youth were white. Foreign-born youth resided in families with lower incomes than second- or third-generation students, but their educational levels differed only from youth with native-born parents.

First-generation students had slightly higher grades than their third or higher generation counterparts, but they did not differ significantly from second-generation youth in this regard. However, there were no generational differences in math test scores. Neither did the educational aspirations of first and second-generation youth differ significantly, whether reported by students themselves or their parents. However, foreign-born parents had significantly higher educational aspirations for their children than did native-born parents. Thus, parental immigrant status appears to be a crucial factor shaping the educational aspirations of immigrant youth. We evaluate this possibility below as we assess more rigorously the association between generational status and scholastic performance.

MULTIVARIATE RESULTS

Table 18.2 presents regression estimates of background characteristics on four measures of performance: middle-school grades, eighth grade math and reading test scores, and aspirations to graduate from college. The dummy variables indicating first- and second-generational status are compared with native children of native-born parents (the omitted category). Overall, both first- and second-generation youth, that is the children of immigrants, earned higher grades and math scores and expressed higher educational aspirations than children of native-born parents. This generalization held even after the effects of race, ethnicity, and parental socioeconomic status were held constant. These results refute the straight-line assimilation hypothesis and lend support to the immigrant optimism hypothesis. Auxiliary analyses (not presented here) revealed that the effect of first generation did not differ from that of second generation and suggested one mechanism responsible for the educational success of first- and second-generation youth. Consistent with the descriptive tabulations, these results imply that parental immigrant status, with its attendant behavioral and normative implications, is pivotal in determining the scholastic performance of youth.

Like many prior studies, ours found significant race and ethnic effects on educational performance. Net of immigrant status, student and parental characteristics, Asians earned grades similar to their white counterparts. This finding qualifies prior comparisons indicating that Asians outperform whites. Consistent with other studies, black and Hispanic youth earned grades below those achieved by whites. However, and possibly because of difficulties with English, all minority groups achieved lower reading scores than their white counterparts. Black and Hispanic youth also earned lower math test scores. Despite the lower performance of minorities relative to whites, their

TABLE 18.2 Effects of Background Characteristics and Generational Status on Eighth Grade Performance Measures

	Grades	Math Scores	Reading Scores	College Aspirations[a]
Child's characteristics				
First generation	0.171***	1.590**	0.475	0.100***
	(0.047)	(0.595)	(0.603)	(0.029)
Second generation	0.118**	1.191**	1.003*	0.078***
	(0.036)	(0.451)	(0.458)	(0.022)
Asian	0.084	0.150	– 1.360*	– 0.017
	(0.051)	(0.636)	(0.645)	(0.032)
Hispanic	−0.075*	– 3.719***	– 3.355***	– 0.034
	(0.030)	(0.383)	(0.388)	(0.019)
Black	– 0.103***	– 6.040***	– 5.412***	0.054***
	(0.024)	(0.307)	(0.312)	(0.015)
Female	0.164***	– 0.131	2.278***	0.056***
	(0.016)	(0.197)	(0.200)	(0.010)
Parent's education				
Less than high school	– 0.173***	– 2.630***	– 2.734***	– 0.117***
	(0.032)	(0.403)	(0.409)	(0.020)
High school	–	–	–	–
Some college	0.103***	1.683***	1.992***	0.130***
	(0.021)	(0.266)	(0.270)	(0.013)
College graduate	0.357***	5.358***	5.148***	0.301***
	(0.028)	(0.353)	(0.359)	(0.017)
M.A.	0.457***	7.647***	7.453***	0.337***
	(0.034)	(0.423)	(0.430)	(0.021)
Ph.D., M.D.	0.428***	7.739***	7.450***	0.308***
	(0.048)	(0.598)	(0.608)	(0.030)
Family income (in $1.000's)	0.002***	0.037***	0.025***	0.002***
	(0.000)	(0.004)	(0.004)	(0.000)
Constant	2.611***	47.892***	47.085***	0.429***
	(0.022)	(0.271)	(0.275)	(0.013)
Adjusted R^2	.11	.22	.19	.13

Source: The National Education Longitudinal Study of 1988 (NCES 1990).
Note: Cell entries are weighted regression estimates. Standard errors are given in parentheses.
[a] Logistic regression estimates of the effects provide identical substantive results. We present OLS estimates for ease of interpretability and congruence to the other three models.
* $p < .05$.
** $p < .01$.
*** $p < .001$.

educational aspirations are equivalent to or higher than whites from comparable family backgrounds (Hauser and Anderson 1991; Kao and Tienda 1993).[4]

Results reported in Table 18.2 assume that the effects on scholastic performance of generational status are uniform across race and ethnic groups. However, studies based on specific minority and immigrant student populations have suggested that the influence on educational outcomes of generational status may differ among black, Hispanic, and Asian youth. Therefore, we evaluate the additivity and uniformity assumption in Table 18.3, which presents results of estimating separate models for Asian, black, Hispanic, and white students. For simplicity, only the effects of generational status are reported, but results of the full model are available upon request.

These results confirm that generational status does *not* influence educational achievement uniformly among race and ethnic groups. Asian first- and second-generation youth achieved higher grades and math and reading test scores, and they were more likely to aspire to graduate from college than third-generation (and beyond) Asian youth. We also estimated these models using the second generation as the baseline and found that first- and second-generation youth differed only in terms of their reading test scores. Second-generation Asians had the best reading test scores, followed by first-generation Asians, with third- and higher generation Asians having the worst reading

TABLE 18.3 Effects of Generational Status on Eighth Grade Performance Measures

	Grades	Math Test Scores	Reading Test Scores	College Aspirations
Asians				
First generation	0.491***	4.797***	2.506*	0.206***
	(0.094)	(1.317)	(1.219)	(0.054)
Second generation	0.443***	5.429***	5.358***	0.232***
	(0.104)	(1.476)	(1.367)	(0.061)
Adjusted R^2	.139	.198	.210	.106
Hispanics				
First generation	0.040	0.704	– 0.842	0.104*
	(0.075)	(0.884)	(0.921)	(0.049)
Second generation	0.085	0.778	– 0.180	0.078*
	(0.056)	(0.659)	(0.689)	(0.037)
Adjusted R^2	.028	.097	.083	.078
Blacks				
First generation	0.206*	2.507*	2.275	0.058
	(0.100)	(1.150)	(1.283)	(0.069)
Second generation	– 0.085	1.584	3.114*	0.096
	(0.095)	(1.088)	(1.212)	(0.066)
Adjusted R^2	.070	.106	.105	.056
Whites				
First generation	0.061	0.604	1.044	0.030
	(0.092)	(1.160)	(1.160)	(0.056)
Second generation	0.116*	0.435	0.267	0.054
	(0.052)	(0.656)	(0.659)	(0.031)
Adjusted R^2	.109	.148	.129	.143

Source: The National Education Longitudinal Study of 1988 (NCES 1990).

Note: Cell entries are weighted regression estimates. Standard errors are given in parentheses. These models are identical to those presented in Table 18.2 except that we analyze Asians, Hispanics, blacks, and whites separately. For ease of interpretation, we only present the estimates of the effects of generational status.

* $p < .05$.

*** $p < .001$.

test scores. For Asians, we reject the straight-line assimilation hypothesis. Yet these results cannot be used to adjudicate between the accommodation-without-assimilation hypothesis and the immigrant optimism hypothesis. That educational performance is relatively similar between first- and second-generation youth, however, underscores the pivotal influence of parental nativity status in fostering positive educational outcomes.

For Hispanics, generational status did not influence educational performance. However, there were significant generational differences in aspirations to graduate from college. Relative to U.S.-born Hispanic youth of native parents, first- and second-generation Hispanics were more likely to express aspirations to graduate from college. This result supports neither the straight-line hypothesis nor the accommodation hypothesis, but provides limited support for the immigrant optimism hypothesis.

Among blacks, our findings partly corroborate arguments of Waters (1991) inasmuch as first-generation blacks achieved the highest scholastic outcomes on two of the four achievement measures. Specifically, first-generation blacks earned higher grades and math test scores than all native-born blacks, while second-generation youth tended to have the highest reading scores. This is consistent with the argument that reading scores improve with English proficiency. Unlike the case among Hispanics, generational status does *not* account for any of the variation in educational aspirations among blacks. Unadjusted differences in math scores indicate that children of foreign-born parents were higher achievers. That this difference diminished little after controlling for family socioeconomic status lends support to the selectivity hypothesis for black immigrant youth, who may be more highly motivated to succeed scholastically.

Results for blacks are somewhat compatible with the immigrant optimism hypothesis, but this comparison illustrates the negative assimilation of black youth. That is, for blacks, unlike Asians, the presence of an immigrant parent may be insufficient to prevent regression of educational achievement toward that of U.S.-born blacks with native parents. For blacks, there appears to be no support for the straight-line hypothesis and limited support for the accommodation-without-assimilation and immigrant optimism hypotheses. However, this interpretation is tentative because the native (third or beyond) generation black youth in our sample were largely African Americans while the first- and second-generation immigrants were likely to be predominately Caribbean blacks. Thus, this comparison confounds nativity and ethnicity. Unfortunately, it is not possible to pursue this further with NELS:88.

In sum, for no group did we find support for the straight-line-assimilation hypothesis. In fact, all of our analyses suggest that Hispanic, black, and white students with immigrant parents performed as well as their native-born counterparts whose parents were U.S.-born, and that Asian students with foreign-born parents outperformed their counterparts whose parents were U.S.-born. For no group did we find a negative association between having immigrant parents and educational performance. This provides strong evidence against the straight-line hypothesis in favor of both the *accommodation-without-assimilation* and the *immigrant optimism* hypotheses.

To broaden our understandings of how immigrant parents differed from their native-born counterparts, we examined differences in parental behavior according to the generational status of children in Table 18.4. These measures address the frequency of parent-student discussion about academic experiences and differences in the nature of parental participation in their children's educational pursuits, which diagnostic analyses revealed are positively associated with grade performance.[5] Table 18.4 shows foreign- and U.S.-born parents differed in the extent to which they supervised their children's behavior. Although immigrant parents were no more likely to have rules about maintaining a specific grade point average or rules about homework than their native counterparts, they were slightly less likely to impose rules about household chores. Auxiliary tabulations revealed an inverse relationship between scholastic achievement (grades) and the imposition of rules about

TABLE 18.4 Parental Behavior by Student's Generational Status

	First Generation	Second Generation	Native Generation
Family rules (R's view)[a]			
How often parents check homework	2.016	2.032	2.099
	(0.990)	(1.024)	(0.990)
How often parents require chores to be done	2.430[b]	2.489[b]	2.564
	(0.787)	(0.788)	(0.724)
How often parents limit TV watching	1.565[b]	1.433[b]	1.106
	(1.093)	(1.139)	(1.053)
How often parents limit going out with friends	2.083	2.131[b]	2.036
	(1.016)	(0.989)	(1.017)
Family rules (P's view)[a]			
If rules regarding grades	0.721	0.741	0.725
If rules regarding homework	0.895	0.922	0.921
If rules regarding chores	0.837[b]	0.847	0.903
Family communication (P's view)			
How often talk about school experiences	2.476[ab]	2.611[b]	2.781
	(0.766)	(0.653)	(0.485)
How often talk about high school plans	2.251[b]	2.344	2.361
	(0.822)	(0.776)	(0.696)
How often talk about post-high school plans	2.098[b]	2.177	2.218
	(0.895)	(0.829)	(0.748)
Family communication (R's view)			
Discuss programs at school	1.160[b]	1.225	1.257
	(0.718)	(0.705)	(0.683)
How often discuss school activities	1.290[ab]	1.408[b]	1.500
	(0.702)	(0.671)	(0.648)
How often discuss things studied in class	1.323[b]	1.345[b]	1.412
	(0.722)	(0.699)	(0.722)
Parental participation (P's view)			
If belong to parent-teacher group	0.202[ab]	0.264[b]	0.328
If go to parent-teacher meetings	0.410[b]	0.449[b]	0.352
If go to parent-teacher activities	0.164[c]	0.232	0.262
If volunteer at school	0.128[ab]	0.191	0.192
Have place to study	0.509[b]	0.482[b]	0.399
Parental participation (R's view)			
If parent attend school meeting	0.538	0.596	0.559
If parent spoke to teacher	0.550[b]	0.621[b]	0.678
If parent visited R's classes	0.330	0.385[b]	0.292
If parent attend school event	0.478[ab]	0.571[b]	0.655
[*N*]	[1,277]	[1,714]	[18,831]

Source: The National Education Longitudinal Study of 1988 (NCES 1990).

Note: Means and proportions are weighted, *N*'s are unweighted. Standard deviations are given in parentheses. All variables beginning with "if" are dummy-coded. See Table 18.1 more a more detailed description.

[a] "*P*'s view" refers to variables taken from the parent questionnaire. "*R*'s view" refers to variables taken from the student questionnaire.

[b] Mean is different from that of the native generation at the 5-percent level.

[c] Mean is different from that of the second generation at the 5-percent level.

household chores. In fact, there is great consistency in parent and student reports of rules and household obligations, particularly for immigrant youth. This suggests that nonacademic responsibilities, such as household chores or required part-time work, compete with academic duties and foster a general orientation away from scholastic pursuits.

Immigrant parents also talked less to their children about current school experiences or their plans for high school and post-high school. Parents of first-generation children were even less likely than parents of second-generation children to talk about their school experiences. From the perspective of the eighth grader, generational status affects the frequency with which parents discuss school activities with their children.

Parental immigrant status also affected the extent to which parents participated in parent-teacher activities. Comparisons between parents of first- and second-generation youth indicate significant differences in propensities of their parents to join parent-teacher organizations, to volunteer at school, and to attend school events. Participation in these activities depended on the level of parental acculturation. However, immigrant parents of first- and second-generation children were more similar than they were different. They were just as likely to attend parent-teacher meetings, to provide a place to study, to talk to their children's teachers, or have visited their child's classes. In fact, all immigrant parents were more likely than their native-born counterparts to attend parent-teacher meetings.

Apparently, immigrant parents were more reluctant to participate in school activities that were diffusely linked to their own child's performance. Instead, they manifested their valuation of education by attending meetings that directly impacted on their child's achievement. In other words, immigrant parents were less likely to participate in school activities, but more likely to attend parent-teacher conferences than native-born parents. Overall, the behavioral patterns reported in Table 18.4 indicate that immigrant parents may be primarily concerned with the allocation of time and space to homework, while native-born parents are more concerned with talking to their children about the experience of school. These descriptive results lend support to the idea that immigrant status of parents rather than that of children is key in determining educational outcomes, although we found some evidence of the effects of acculturation on parental behavior.

Our results suggest that second-generation youth may be best positioned to achieve academically because they both benefit from the optimism of their immigrant parents and are more proficient in English. To pursue this question further, we examined the effect of mother's length of residence on educational achievement in analyses not presented here.[6] Overall, there was no discernible effect of mother's length of residence on youth's educational achievement, except on reading scores.[7] Thus, the nativity of the mother decisively influenced educational achievement of youth, but offspring's educational returns to length of time foreign-born parents spent in the United States were only apparent in reading test scores. This implies that immigrant parents are more successful at implementing their optimistic goals for their children after acquiring a minimum familiarity with the educational institutions and possibly also minimum proficiency in English.

DISCUSSION

To sum up, we found that students' immigrant or generational status has important consequences for scholastic performance, but that these effects intersect with race and Hispanic origin in shaping educational outcomes. Both our descriptive and empirical analyses indicate that parental immigrant status is more influential than the immigrant status of youth in determining scholastic performance. Multivariate results revealed little difference between the educational performance of first- and second-generation youth. Yet both groups tend to outperform their third-generation or higher counterparts on various scholastic outcomes. In addition, we found that racial and ethnic differentiation in scholastic performance is relatively absent among first-generation youth, but becomes increasingly salient with the family's length of residence in the United States. Our results show that immigration status of youth and parents accounts for much more of the variation in educational outcomes among Asian students than other minority or white students. Nonetheless, we found almost no evidence for the straight-line assimilation hypothesis because children of immigrant parents consistently performed scholastically at the level of or higher than their native counterparts. This generalization is obtained both within and between racial groups. Finally, we found no evidence that length of mother's U.S. residence influenced educational performance except for reading skills. Our results thus far support the hypothesis that native-born children of immigrant parents are best situated to perform academically due to both their mothers' higher aspirations for children and the children's English skills.

From our results one might infer that both cultural resources and immigrant parents' optimism about their children's prospects are decisive in the educational achievement of first- and second-generation youth. Hence, our findings provide some new clues about the development of racial and ethnic inequities in educational outcomes. For instance, we clearly show that the Asians who are high achievers have immigrant parents. Scholastic performance of third-generation or higher Asians is no better than that of white non-Hispanic youth. Our results also suggest that the educational achievement of black youth is affected primarily by their own experiences of acculturation. However, for Asians and (to a lesser extent) Hispanics, parental immigration status is highly influential in scholastic performance. Finally, our results suggest that immigrant status has almost no discernible educational consequence for white students. It appears that immigrant parents' optimism about their offspring's socioeconomic prospects decisively influences educational outcomes. Thus the second generation is best positioned for scholastic success by having foreign-born parents and the language fluency conferred by native birth in the United States.

These new insights about the relationship between educational achievement and immigrant generational status have policy implications. Most efforts to improve educational performance of immigrant and minority youth focus on the students themselves. Our results add to a growing number of studies emphasizing the need to involve parents in programs and policies aimed to "mainstream" minority youth. Diversity of the school-aged population need not be seen as a liability; indeed, the principal policy challenge is to generate the optimism of immigrant parents among U.S.-born parents.

Direct all correspondence to Grace Kao, Population Research Center, NORC and The University of Chicago, 1155 East 60th Street, Chicago, IL 60637. *A previous draft of this manuscript was presented at the 1994 annual meetings of the Population Association of America in Miami, Florida. We thank Karen Woodrow-Lafield, Barbara Schneider, and members of the Education Group at the University of Chicago for their comments. This research was supported by a grant from the Spencer Foundation.*

Notes

1. Diagnostic analyses revealed that substantive results based on father's birthplace are identical to those presented here.
2. Although we suspect these may be somewhat inflated, they should not affect our assessment of the relative position of each group.
3. This table is available upon request.
4. For a more detailed account of the paradox of high educational aspirations and low scholastic performance among minority youth, see Kao and Tienda (1993).
5. Only statistically significant differences are discussed.
6. These results are available upon request.

7. We also characterized the effect of time categorically with dummy variables as well as with both a linear and a squared term. The results are substantively similar to those presented here.

References

Alvarez, Adolfo. 1971. The unique psycho-historical experience of the Mexican-American people. *Social Science Quarterly* 52:15–29.

Baker, David P., and David L. Stevenson. 1986. Mothers' strategies for children's school achievement: Managing the transition to high school. *Sociology of Education* 59:156–66.

Borjas, George. 1990. *Friends or Strangers: The Impact of Immigration in the U.S. Economy.* New York: Basic Books.

Caplan, Nathan, Marcella H. Choy, and John K. Whitmore. 1992. *Children of the Boat People: A Study of Educational Success.* Ann Arbor: University of Michigan Press.

Chiswick, Barry. 1979. The economic progress of immigrants: Some apparently universal patterns. pp. 357–99 in William Fellner, ed. *Contemporary Economic Problems 1979.* Washington, DC: American Enterprise Institute.

Duran, Bernadine J. and Rafacla E. Weffer. 1992. Immigrants' aspirations, high school process, and academic outcomes. *American Educational Research Journal* 29:163–81.

Fernandez, Roberto M. and Francois Nielsen. 1986. Bilingualism and Hispanic scholastic achievement: Some baseline results. *Social Science Research* 15:43–70.

Gibson, Margaret. 1993. Accommodation without assimilation. Paper presented at the Conference on Immigrant Students in California. University of California, San Diego. Center for U.S.-Mexican Studies.

Gordon, Milton M. 1964. *Assimilation in American Life: The Role of Race, Religion, and National Origins.* New York: Oxford University Press.

Hauser, Robert M. and Douglas K. Anderson. 1991. Post-high school plans and aspirations of black and white high school seniors: 1976–86. *Sociology of Education* 64:263–77.

Kao, Grace. 1995. Asian-Americans as model minorities? A look at their academic performance. *American Journal of Education.* 103: 121–159.

Kao, Grace and Marta Tienda. 1993. Educational aspirations of minority youth. Paper presented at the 1993 annual meetings of the American Sociological Association.

Kao, Grace, Marta Tienda, and Barbara Schneider. 1993. Racial and ethnic variation in the educational pipeline. Paper presented at the 1993 annual meetings of the Population Association of America.

Mare, Robert D. and Christopher Winship. 1988. Ethnic and racial patterns of educational attainment and school enrollment. pp. 173–203 in Gary Sandefur and Marta Tienda, eds. *Divided Opportunities: Minorities, Poverty, and Social Policy.* New York: Plenum.

Matute-Bianchi, Maria Eugenia. 1986. Ethnic identities and patterns of school success and failure among Mexican-descent and Japanese-American students in a California high school: An ethnographic analysis. *American Journal of Education* 95:233–55.

National Center for Education Statistics (NCES). 1990. *National Education Longitudinal Study of 1988—Base Year: Student Component Data File User's Manual.* Washington, DC: U.S. Department of Education.

Ogbu, John U. 1991. Immigrant and involuntary minorities in comparative perspective. pp. 3–33 in Margaret A. Gibson and John U. Ogbu, eds. *Minority Status and Schooling: A Comparative Study of Immigrant and Involuntary Minorities.* New York: Garland.

Park, Robert E. 1914. Racial assimilation in secondary groups. *American Journal of Sociology* 19:606–23.

Population Reference Bureau. 1989. *America in the 21st Century: Human Resource Development.* Washington, DC: Population Reference Bureau.

Portes, Alejandro and Richard Schauffler 1996. Language Acquisition and Loss Among Children of Immigrants. pp. 432–443. In *Origins and Destinies: Immigration, place, and Ethnicity in America.* Silvia Pedraza and Ruben G. Rumbaut, eds. New York: Wadsworth.

Portes, Alejandro and Min Zhou. 1993. The second generation: Segmented assimilation and its variants. *Annals of the American Academy of Political and Social Sciences* 530(November):74–96.

Rumbaut, Ruben G. 1990. *Immigrant Students in California Public Schools: A Summary of Current Knowledge.* Report prepared for Johns Hopkins University, Center for Research on Effective Schooling for Disadvantaged Students.

Schneider, Barbara and Yongsook Lee. 1990. A model for academic success: The school and home environment of East Asian students. *Anthropology and Education Quarterly* 21:358–77.

Sue, Stanley and Sumie Okazaki. 1990. Asian-American educational achievements: A phenomenon in search of an explanation. *American Psychologist* 45:913–20.

Waters, Mary C. 1991. The intersection of race, ethnicity, and class: Second generation West Indians in the United States. Paper presented at the Race, Ethnicity, and Urban Poverty Workshop. Chicago: Northwestern University and the University of Chicago.

Chapter 19
Immigrant Boys' Experiences in U.S. Schools[1]

CAROLA SUÁREZ-OROZCO AND DESIRÉE BAOLIAN QIN

Currently the children of immigrants[2] comprise 20 percent of the U.S.'s youth population (Hernández and Charney 1998; Landale and Oropesa 1995). The majority of these children have Latino, Asian, or Caribbean origins, representing unprecedented cultural and linguistic diversity (Suárez-Orozco and Suárez-Orozco 2001). The last fifteen years have witnessed growing scholarly attention to their adaptation (Gibson 1988; Kao and Tienda 1995; Laosa 1989; Olsen 1997; Portes and Rumbaut 2001; Portes and Zhou 1993; Suárez-Orozco and Suárez-Orozco 2001; Sung 1987; Zhou and Bankston 1998). However, the issue of gender has been relatively unexplored in the literature on immigrant youth (Goodenow and Espin 1993; Valenzuela 1999). Several scholars have identified a general pattern that is consistent with the national trend: Immigrant girls tend to outperform boys in educational settings (Brandon 1991; Portes and Rumbaut 2001; Rong and Brown 2001). Yet, to date, very few studies have explored why this gendered pattern may exist. This chapter examines the experiences of schooling among immigrant youth, with a particular focus on the immigrant boy experience in school context.[2]

GENDERED TRENDS AMONG IMMIGRANT YOUTH

Gender appears to be a significant force in shaping patterns of adaptation among immigrant youth. Portes and Rumbaut contend that "gender enters the picture in an important way because of the different roles that boys and girls occupy during adolescence and the different ways in which they are socialized" (2001, 64). Although there has yet to be a large-scale, empirical comparative study that concentrates specifically on gender differences in immigrant children's academic engagement and achievement, a number of studies confirm the national trend that immigrant boys lag behind immigrant girls in academic settings across ethnic groups (Brandon 1991; Gibson 1988; Lee 2001; Portes and Rumbaut 2001; Desirée Baolian Qin 2001; C. Suárez-Orozco 2001; Waters 1996). Brandon's (1991) study of Asian American high school seniors shows that females reached higher levels of educational attainment faster than males. Rong and Brown (2001) find that immigrant African and Caribbean black females outperformed their male counterparts in schooling attainment. Waters' (1996) study of Caribbean American teens also suggests that it was far more likely for girls to graduate from high school than for boys. Similarly, Gibson (1993) finds that Mexican girls did better than boys in terms of grades and attitudes toward school.

Other researchers have found similar gender trends in academic engagement. In their recent report on second-generation youth with various Latino and Asian origins, Portes and Rumbaut (2001) find that, compared to girls, boys are less engaged, have significantly lower grades, have lower levels of interest and work effort, have lower career and educational goals, and are less likely to adhere to their parents' language. Similarly, in her work with Latino high school students, Lopez (in press) finds that, compared to their male counterparts, young women turn in homework more often, participate in more cultural activities, have better relationships with teachers, and have a more optimistic future outlook at school. In fact, Lopez describes young women's high school experience as "institutional engagement and oppression" and young men's as "institutional expulsion" (2004, 23).

In this chapter, we report preliminary findings from the Harvard Longitudinal Immigrant Student Adaptation (LISA) study. We will focus on the following two questions: Among immigrant students, what are the similarities and differences in schooling experiences for boys and girls? When differences occur, how might we account for them?

METHOD

Currently in its fifth year, LISA was designed to deepen our understanding of immigrant youth's academic engagement and schooling outcomes. A total of four hundred students, ages nine to fourteen, stratified by gender and country of origin—Central America, China, the Dominican Republic, Haiti, and Mexico—were recruited within the first few years of immigration. Youth were recruited from fifty-one schools in seven school districts in Massachusetts and northern California. Participating schools provided access to students, teachers, staff, and school records.

Our study takes an interdisciplinary, longitudinal, and comparative approach. This project utilizes a variety of methods, including structured student and parent interviews, ethnographic observations, projective and objective measures, reviews of school records, and teacher questionnaires and interviews. We adopt research strategies in the anthropological tradition to gain perspective on immigrant cultural models and social practices relevant to adaptation in the new setting. Youth are observed and interviewed in their schools, their communities, and their homes. These ethnographies allow us to gain the informants' points of view as well as identify locally relevant themes. Psychological methodologies, including structured interviews, sentence completions, and narrative tasks, are deployed to carefully establish a data baseline on immigration histories, social and family relations, and academic attitudes and behaviors. Using triangulated data is crucial when faced with the challenges of validity in conducting research with groups of diverse backgrounds. By sorting through self-reports, parent reports, teacher reports, and our own observations, we are able to establish both concurrence and disconnection in what youth say they do, what others say they do, and what we see them do. The longitudinal design also allows us to calibrate changes over time. An interdisciplinary, multicultural team of more than thirty bilingual and bicultural researchers enables us to gain entry into immigrant communities, establish rapport and trust with our participants, and develop culturally sensitive instruments. It also provides an interpretive community for understanding data and findings in context. In this chapter, we will report on preliminary findings that emerged from surveys, structured student and teacher interviews, field notes, and report cards.

RESULTS

Academic achievement

Findings from our study regarding academic achievement confirm the gender trend found for boys in general (Cornell 2000; U.S. Department of Education 1995; Grant and Rong 1999; Kleinfeld

1998; Pollack 1998) and Latino and black males in particular (Dunn 1988; Lopez forthcoming). Analyses of report-card data reveal that the immigrant boys in our sample who attend middle and high schools in seven school districts obtain, on average, lower grades than do girls ($F = 5.52$, $df = 1$, $p = .02$). Girls have a significantly higher GPA than boys in language arts. Boys also lag behind girls in math, science, and social studies. In fact, across every ethnic group in our sample—Chinese, Dominican, Central American, Mexican, and Haitian—boys have statistically lower grades than girls. Furthermore, girls were most likely to score in the highest grade range of B+ or better (24 percent of girls compared to 16 percent of boys), while boys were more likely to be represented in the lowest range of D- or lower (11 percent of boys compared to 8 percent of girls). Hence, girls tended to be the higher-achieving students and boys were more likely to be disengaged.

This trend of girls outperforming boys at school also emerged from the teacher interview data. As part of the study, we asked seventy-four middle- and high school teachers in seven school districts in urban areas on the East and West Coasts about their perspectives on teaching immigrant students. One of the questions they were asked was: "Have you noticed differences between how immigrant girls are doing and how immigrant boys are doing?" Forty percent of the teachers responded either that they had not noticed differences or that it depended on the issue or the student. Strikingly, however, 44 percent responded that boys did more poorly than girls either academically or socially. Only 13 percent thought that boys were doing better than girls on the whole. For example, a teacher working largely with Haitian students in the Boston area noted: "I would say that in general…the girls do better…because over the years that I have been here, most of the students who have gotten accepted to those Ivy League schools were girls for the most part." Immigrant-origin girls succeed in schools in less strictly academic ways as well. A counselor working with Latino students in California told us, "Student body presidents and officers are almost always girls."

Academic engagement

In recent years, a number of scholars have argued that academic achievement and adjustment are in large part a function of academic engagement (Jordan 1999; Pierson and Connell 1992; Steinberg, Lamborn, Dornbusch, and Darling 1992; Wick 1990). In order to perform optimally in the educational journey, the student must be engaged in learning. When a student is engaged, he is both intellectually and behaviorally involved in his schooling. He ponders the materials presented, participates in discussions, completes assignments with attention and effort, and optimally applies newfound knowledge in new contexts. Conversely, when academically disengaged, the student "simply go(es) through the motions" (Steinberg, Brown, and Dornbusch 1996, 15), putting forth minimum (and in extreme cases no) effort. Conceptually, we separate academic engagement into three dimensions: cognitive, behavioral, and relational. Cognitive and behavioral engagements are viewed as the manifestation of engagement, and relational engagement is viewed as mediator of these engagements. As part of the LISA study, we developed an interview protocol that examined these dimensions of academic engagement. Interviews were individually administered in the student's language of preference by bilingual researchers.

Cognitive engagement. Cognitive engagement was defined as the student's reported intellectual or cognitive engagement with schoolwork. This dimension includes both the elements of intellectual curiosity about new ideas and domains of learning, as well as the pleasure that is derived in the process of mastering new materials. In other words, do the students report that learning is inherently interesting to them? Cognitive engagement was assessed by asking students if they were currently interested in something, whether or not this interest was academically related, and whether they derived pleasure from learning new things. A composite score was assessed based on endorsing interest in math, science, language arts, and social studies courses. Our analyses show that the cognitive engagement scores for boys were not statistically different from those for girls and thus indicated no difference in cognitive engagement by gender.

Behavioral engagement (student self-report). Behavioral engagement refers to the degree to which students actually engage in the behaviors necessary to do well in school—attending classes, participating in class, completing assignments, and putting forth effort. We consider both general academic behaviors as well as subject-specific behaviors from both the student and teacher perspectives. Behavioral engagement was assessed by asking students to report expended effort in math, science, language arts, and social studies courses, attendance, lateness, and course-skipping frequency. They were also asked to rate a series of academic behaviors on a four-point Likert scale (for example, turning in homework, paying close attention in class, putting forth best efforts in class and on projects). Findings demonstrate no gender differences in self-reported behavioral engagement. The only exception is that boys admitted to skipping classes more often than girls.

Behavioral engagement (teacher report). Although boys did not report many differences in their own behaviors, analyses of the behavior checklists completed by teachers revealed another picture. Teachers were asked to rate a series of academic behaviors on a five-point Likert scale ranging from very poor to very good for each participant in our study. Teachers reported that boys were more likely than girls to demonstrate poor or very poor attention in class, whereas girls were more likely than boys to demonstrate good or very good attention (see Table 19.1).[3] Teachers also reported that boys were more likely than girls to demonstrate poor or very poor motivation and effort, whereas girls were more likely than boys to demonstrate good or very good motivation and effort. Similar patterns were reported for behaviors such as compliance with teacher requests: Thirteen percent of boys demonstrated very poor or poor behavior compared to 9 percent of girls, whereas 61 percent of boys compared to 77 percent of girls demonstrated good or very good behavior. Teachers also reported that girls were more likely than boys to demonstrate very good attendance and very good punctuality, and girls were more likely to complete homework. Boys, however, were more likely to fall in the very poor ratings for each of these manifestations of academic engagement. For the teacher reports, no significant gender differences emerged for the following academic behaviors: asking questions, teacher relations, peer relations, helping peers, or principal referrals. Interestingly,

TABLE 19.1 Teacher-Reported Levels of Behavioral Engagement by Gender (n=297)

		Boys	Girls	Chi-Square P value
Attention	Very Poor/Poor	24%	13%	
	Good/Very Good	47%	67%	.002
Motivation/ Efforts	Very Poor/Poor	30%	11%	
	Good/Very Good	44%	68%	.0001
Behavior	Very Poor/Poor	13%	9%	
	Good/Very Good	61%	77%	.002
Attendance	Very Poor/Poor	9%	8%	
	Good/Very Good	71%	79%	.02
Punctuality	Very Poor/Poor	8%	7%	
	Good/Very Good	68%	79%	.02
Homework	Never	7%	1%	
	Occasionally	21%	12%	
	Almost Always	27%	38%	.0001
	Always	19%	36%	

although teachers also did not report significant differences between boys and girls in English reading or English oral expression (or in native-language reading or oral and written language), they did report that girls demonstrated better understanding of English. Furthermore, teachers reported that boys were more likely to have very poor or poor written English skills (79 percent of boys compared to 42 percent of girls). Overall, the teachers perceived the girls in a much more positive light than the boys. One teacher's response summarizes well the general outlook of many of the teachers:

> Girls, in general ... tend to be more willing to buckle down, do their work, get all of their homework in. With boys, lots of times, there is more of a tendency to get distracted, to take as a role some antisocial types of behavior.

Relational engagement. Relational engagement is the degree to which students report meaningful and supportive relationships in school with adults as well as peers. We consider both the emotional and tangible functions of these relationships. Relational engagement was assessed by a composite score based on responses to a four-point Likert scale (from very true to very false) on thirteen items such as "Teachers care about me and what happens to me in class," "I can count on my friends to help me in school," and "If I have questions about school work, I can count on someone there to help me." Strikingly, we found that boys reported lower levels of relational engagement in school than girls ($F = 5.25$, $df = 1$, $p < .05$).

Relationships with teachers and administrators

Our structured student interview data indicated that boys tend to report more conflict with administrators and teachers at school than girls. Boys were also more likely than girls to report experiencing or witnessing their male friends' negative interactions with the school security guard. Boys were more likely than girls to perceive schools as a "prison." A boy from El Salvador told us:

> [At school] I don't like them taking electronic devices (pagers, cell phones) away, it's ridiculous. (Our school) is a closed campus; it doesn't get windows; (it is) too old. They want to put [up] cameras; we're going to be prisoners .... [It's] not good when security wants to catch you. They are rude and rough with the students. The security often throws you to the ground—not to me, but I have seen it.

In response to the question "How do teachers and administrators treat most students?" a Dominican boy stated:

> Bad. One time, a security guard threw my friend to the ground to search him because he saw my friend had a small knife in his pants' pocket. Another example is the teachers who always screaming, "Go to class!" and threatening you with suspending you from school. They say all these yelling at you. Everything is bad, if you talk, listen to music, etc.

Similarly, a Chinese boy who later dropped out of high school responded to the question "How do you feel about your school?" by saying: "Quite good. In terms of playing, [it's] quite fun to play. Easy to cut classes. I can walk out anytime I want. Things I don't like? Of course the security guards. They always stop me and ask me many things, probably because of my appearance." When asked, "How do teachers and administrators treat most students?" he responded: "Not much. Teaching is just a job. Teachers just try to get by, day by day, and get salary at the end of the month, whether you learn things or not, it's not their business."

The interview data also suggested that boys reported more racism at school than girls. For example, when asked his feelings about his school, one Dominican boy told us:

> The school environment is fine. The majority of the teachers are friendly, but some never, leave the racism against Hispanics. What I like most is to share with people and to learn. What I don't like the most is the teachers' racism, and that some teachers do not care about the students .... A teacher that I asked to speak slow because I didn't understand much English, told me that is what for I had come to the U.S. for and here English is spoken, and he told me to go back to Santo Domingo.

Similarly, another boy reported:

> Sometimes I didn't like some teachers. One teacher (Puerto Rican male) use to call me racial slurs in a joking manner. I used to hate those comments and told him so, but he continued doing so. I got picked on by a teacher so much that once I was going to hit him. I got suspended for eight days for it and he never got even reprimanded.

The immigrant boys in our study reflect on their lack of connection to, and their hostile and racist experiences with, their teachers and administrators. The boys appear to respond to these largely negative interactions with teachers by effectively "checking out" of the academic process.

Teacher expectations

Consistent with Lopez's (2004) insightful ethnographic observations, teachers in our study report having different expectations for the boys than for the girls. A teacher in the Boston area admitted:

> I find the girls are far more focused when it comes to their education. Also keep in mind, teacher perceptions play a key role. We tend to know that if a girl is very quiet she is a very good student, and we tend to nurture that type of individual far more. It may explain why a lot of girls tend to be successful.

Field notes taken by a researcher working with the LISA project in the San Francisco Bay area also reveal gender-based expectations from teachers:

> The teacher told me that before she started teaching she got "cultural awareness training" about the Mexican community in San Diego. She said: "They told me that Latino boys are aggressive and really, really, really macho and very hard to teach. And they taught me that the girls are pure sweetness." I asked her if she thinks these "insights" are true. "Well, yes," was her response.

Teachers in our study readily admitted to favoring girls:

> Girls ... are more hardworking, more than boys are. They are also neater with the work, more organized .... I usually favor girls more than boys; I also favor children that work diligently day after day, not necessarily the more intelligent ones .... Girls are more respectful than boys are.

Consistent with our survey findings regarding teachers' reports of behavioral engagement, the teachers told us in their interviews that they typically had more negative perceptions of the boys than the girls. These negative teacher expectations may well contribute to gender differences in academic outcomes.

DISCUSSION

Consistent with the literature, data from our study suggest that immigrant boys tend to demonstrate lower academic achievement and encounter more challenges in school than immigrant girls. From the student self-report data, we learn that boys do not report less cognitive or behavior engagement in school than girls. However, boys report being more disengaged relationally in the school than girls. They also tend to feel less support from teachers and staff and are more likely to perceive school as a negative, hostile, and racist environment. In addition, the teachers themselves report having more negative expectations of the boys than the girls. Thus, boys' poorer academic achievement and performance may not be due to less academic interest or capacity for learning (cognitive engagement) or from less effort applied in relation to schoolwork (behavior engagement). Rather, their poorer academic performance may be due to the combination of low social support (relational engagement), hostile experiences in school, and negative teacher expectations. In other words, negative social relations in school may be an important factor in explaining why immigrant boys are doing worse in school than their female peers.

Social relations. A critical difference between boys and girls is in the realm of social relationships. Social relationships serve a number of crucial functions, which include providing a sense of attachment and support within trusting relationships; inculcating aspirations, goals, and values; and conferring status and identity, among others (Stanton-Salazar 2001). In particular, relationships within schools provide several forms of support critical to academic outcomes, including access to knowledge about academic subjects, college, the labor market, and how bureaucracies operate; advocacy; role modeling; and advice (Stanton-Salazar 2001). In a series of elegant studies of Mexican American adolescent social networks within schools, Stanton-Salazar found that although boys were more likely to report family cohesiveness and supportive parental relationships, their school-based relationships were less supportive. Boys were less likely to be "engaged with teachers and counselors ... boys appeared to communicate less, which forced them to infer the meaning of an agent's words and actions, usually from a position of little trust" (Stanton-Salazar 2001, 203).

As part of the LISA study, a separate interview was administered specifically to assess networks of relationships. Participants were asked to name the most significant people in their lives and people that were important to them in the following categories: family members (including extended family), peers, adults in schools, adults in the community (such as mentors, neighbors, church members, community leaders), and individuals still in the country of origin. In addition, they were asked pertinent demographic data about these significant individuals, including racial and national background, language of communication, and frequency and place of contact. Finally, using a modified Q-sort strategy, the participants were asked to name which of these individuals served which functions (for example, who helps you with your homework? Who can you tell your troubles to? Who tells you what to do to prepare for college?).

Analyses of these data were quite revealing. Although there were no gender differences in the number of people spontaneously named in the initial list of "most important people" in their lives, there was a significant difference in the quality of these relations. Boys were more likely than girls to report that they had no one to turn to for specific functions, including no one to help with homework (24 percent of boys versus 15 percent of girls), no one to tell their problems to (17 percent of boys versus 5 percent of girls), no one they trust to keep their secrets (15 percent of boys versus 8 percent of girls), and no one to turn to if they needed to borrow money (7 percent of boys versus 2 percent of girls). In addition, we found that girls were more likely to name supportive relationships specifically with adults in their schools than were boys (49 percent of girls had at least one supportive adult relationship in school versus 37 percent of boys).

These findings support the other findings reported in this chapter. They suggest that gender differences in the quality of relationships in and out of school may help to explain the gender differences in academic outcomes. If boys are not receiving as much support (for example, for school-related as well as non-school-related difficulties) and guidance in and out of school, and are more likely to experience overt acts of hostility and low expectations from their teachers, they may find it much more difficult to achieve academically than girls. Research with non-immigrant youth has consistently found that teacher/student support as well as student/student support is critical for the academic achievement of both boys and girls (Roeser, Eccles, and Sameroff 1998).

Negative social mirroring. In addition to problems of support and expectations, there are other reasons, including negative social mirroring, that may help to explain why immigrant boys may perform more poorly in school than immigrant girls. Anthropological cross-cultural evidence from a variety of different regions suggests that the social context and ethos of reception plays an important role in immigrant adaptation. As John Ogbu (1978) and George DeVos (1980) have persuasively demonstrated, for youth coming from backgrounds that historically have been and continue to be depreciated and disparaged within the host society, academic outcomes are compromised. Boys from disparaged groups appear to be particularly at risk of poor academic outcomes. This is true, for example, for Afro-Caribbean youth in Britain, Canada, and in the United States; for North African males in Belgium; Koreans in Japan; and for Moroccans and Algerians in France (Suárez-Orozco and Suárez-Orozco 2001). These developing youth, like the children in our sample, are keenly aware of the prevailing ethos of hostility of the dominant culture (Suárez-Orozco 2000). We asked our sample of children to complete the sentence "Most Americans think that [Chinese, Dominicans, Haitians, Mexicans—depending on the child's country of origin] are …" Disturbingly, the modal response was the word "bad." Others, even more disconcerting, included "stupid," "useless," "garbage," "gang members," "lazy," and "we don't exist." When expectations of sloth, irresponsibility, low intelligence, and danger are reflected in a number of social mirrors, including the media, the classroom, and the street, the outcome can be devastating for immigrant children's adaptation (Adams 1990; Suárez-Orozco and Suárez-Orozco 2001). Psychologically, what do children do with this negative reception? Are the attitudes of the host culture internalized, denied, or resisted? The most positive possible outcome perhaps is to be goaded into "I'll show you. I'll make it in spite of what you think of me." More likely, however, the child responds with self-doubt and shame, setting low aspirations in a kind of self-fulfilling prophecy: "They are probably right. I'll never be able to do it." Yet another worrisome response is "You think I'm bad. Let me show you how bad I can be." Immigrant boys' less positive attitudes toward school may be attributable not only to their different experiences at school but also to how they are perceived within a larger social context (Lee 2001; Lopez 2004; Olsen 1997; Desirée Baolian Qin 2001; Sarroub 2001; Suárez-Orozco 2001; Waters 1996).

Peer pressure. Another factor that may help to explain boys' poorer school performance may be related to peer pressure. Many researchers have noted that peer pressure to reject school is quite strong among boys (Fordham 1996; Gibson 1988; Desirée Baolian Qin 2001; Smith 1999; Waters 1996). Furthermore, behaviors that gain respect with their peers often bring boys in conflict with their teachers. Some researchers point out that immigrant boys from certain ethnic backgrounds are more pressured by their peers to reject school when compared to immigrant girls (Gibson 1993; Suárez-Orozco 2001; Waters 1996). In her research with Punjabi youth, Gibson (1993) indicates that immigrant boys in general are more likely than their sisters to develop an "oppositional relationship" with the educational system or to see schooling as a "threat to their identity."

Field notes from the LISA study suggest that immigrant boys are more quickly recruited into the mores of their new social environments that are often in deeply impoverished inner-city schools that do not foster cultures of high-achievement orientation. Observing an English as a Second Language middle-school classroom, a researcher on our team noted, "I didn't see much interaction between recently arrived immigrant girls and the Chicana (young women of Mexican origin that have been in U.S. for two or more generations) students. In contrast, the immigrant boys seemed to be taken under the wing of the "backroom boys"—a term the researcher coined to describe disengaged boys who sat in the back of the classroom and often disrupted instruction. Another set of field notes revealed: "In contrast to the recently arrived immigrant boys, recently arrived immigrant girls sit to the front left of the classroom. They tend to huddle together and are very quiet. They don't participate in class but they follow along … as a strategy of survival."

Statements made by a number of teachers reveal similar patterns of boys' more rapid integration into their social settings. A teacher working in a largely Latino high school in the Boston area noted:

> In terms of the guys, one of the hardest things I see is they need to become tough. Dialogue becomes something of the past. You have to save face, you have to argue it out. The lack of tolerance is much more pronounced. The readiness to fist fight, to take it out …. It has a lot to do with the environment of our schools and cities.

Another teacher noted: "In Hispanic culture it's not too cool to be smart, carrying books …. [This affects boys more than girls] because they don't want to be harassed." A teacher working with a diverse group of immigrant-origin students told us:

> The males seem to have more leeway, more freedom to be with friends, and so they kind of become a little bit more, too—maybe I shouldn't let anyone here hear me say that—too Americanized …. The ones who still retain their customs from their country … actually do better academically …. [The problem of adopting] the clothing, speech, slang, and other mannerisms [of the new culture is] not really so much with the young ladies.

Hence, as Portes (1998) has noted, social relations can generate positive as well as negative social capital. Peer pressure to be cool, tough, and possible "American" may make it difficult for immigrant boys to do well in school.

Family responsibilities. Gender differences in family responsibilities at home may also play a role in explaining differences in academic outcomes between girls and boys. Research findings consistently suggest that compared with their brothers, immigrant girls have many more responsibilities at home (Lee 2001; Olsen 1997; Desirée Baolian Qin 2001; Sarroub 2001; Valenzuela 1999; Waters 1996). Valenzuela (1999) finds that compared with boys, immigrant girls participate more in tasks that require "greater responsibility" and "detailed explanations." Their roles include translating; advocating in financial, medical, and legal transactions; and acting as surrogate parents. Eldest children in particular are expected to assist with such tasks as babysitting, feeding younger siblings, getting siblings ready for school in the morning, and escorting them to school (Valenzuela 1999). Similarly, Lee (2001) finds that Hmong girls, in particular, are often expected to cook, clean, and take care of younger siblings. Olsen (1997) observes in her study that besides childcare and household chores like cleaning and washing, many immigrant girls, especially the oldest daughters, need to work to help the family.

Based on two waves of data collection, we found that although boys and girls did not report different levels of responsibility for translating, girls were significantly more likely to report responsibilities for cooking and childcare. Several teachers in our study expressed concern about excessive home expectations for immigrant girls. It is also possible, however, that developing a sense of responsibility at home may transfer to school settings. Jurkovic et al. (in press) found that while "filial responsibilities" sometime compete with schooling pursuits, performing caretaking tasks also provided youth with an increased sense of personal and interpersonal competence." Hence, these responsibilities may provide unanticipated benefits to girls who shoulder greater household responsibilities.

CONCLUSION

Our data present strong evidence not only of poorer academic performance among immigrant boys than among immigrant girls, but also the reasons why such gender differences may exist. Our data suggest that immigrant boys may not struggle in school because they have less internal motivation or are less able to achieve in school (that is, cognitive or behavioral engagement). Rather, they may struggle because of the social context that offers them little support, guidance, and encouragement to do well in school. The context of the school, home, and peers, as well as the larger culture, should be considered in any discussion of gender differences in academic outcomes among immigrant youth.

It is important to note, however, that there may be tremendous variation across and within immigrant groups that needs to be explored. Not all immigrant girls thrive in school and not all immigrant boys struggle in school. For example, Lee (2001) finds that although adolescent Hmong girls tend to have higher motivation and achievement, they were also more likely than boys to drop out of high school. Similarly, Gibson (1988) finds that Punjabi boys took more advanced courses, had higher rates of college attendance, and earned higher degrees than Punjabi girls. A recent article in *The New York Times* reports that although Latino boys have a higher high school dropout rate (28 percent) than Latina girls (26 percent), Latina girls are found to leave school earlier than boys and are less likely to return (Canedy 2001). This trend favoring boys seems to be particularly strong in cultures that are considered more traditional and have stricter gender role expectations and gender grading (Gibson 1988; Desirée Baolian Qin 2001; Sarroub 2001). These findings underscore the need to look within and across gender group variation in school outcomes among immigrant adolescents.

It is also important to note that although the focus of this chapter was on gender differences, there were many similarities detected between the immigrant boys and girls. For example, perceptions of school safety, attitudes toward Americans, beliefs about American attitudes toward their ethnic group, and responses on many projective narrative tasks revealed no gender differences. A number of common denominator experiences—including shared immigration stress, schooling and neighborhood contexts, and ethos of reception —may account for the similarities in the experiences of immigrant boys and girls (Suárez-Orozco and Suárez-Orozco 2001).

Future research should continue to consider gender differences in immigrant children's adaptation. We should also search for the commonalities, as well as the particular risks, challenges, and protective characteristics that are relevant to the lives of all immigrant youth. Interdisciplinary, multidisciplinary, triangulated research is essential to begin to understand the lived experiences, in and out of school, of the understudied population of immigrant youth. Given the high proportion of immigrant origin youth, their adaptations will have crucial implications for the nation we become.

Notes

1. The data for this research is part of the Harvard Longitudinal Immigrant Student Adaptation (LISA) study conducted by principal investigators Carola Suárez-Orozco and Marcelo Suárez-Orozco. Desirée Baolian Qin, a researcher with the study, collected data from Chinese informants and has been involved in instrument development

and analysis. We wish to thank Vivian Louie and Lisa Machoian for providing theoretical advice and to Robin Harutunian for helpful editorial suggestions. We also want to thank Terry Tivnan, Josephine Louie, Nora Thompson, and Quentin Dixon for their analytic work. This project has been made possible by generous funding provided by the National Science Foundation, the W. T. Grant Foundation, and the Spencer Foundation. The data presented, the statements made, and the views expressed are solely the responsibility of the authors.

2. In discussing immigrant youth, we will be referring to both the first generation (that is, children who are born abroad) as well as the second generation (children born in the United States of foreign-born parents).
3. All difference reported between boys and girls are tested with chi-square analyses. Only differences that reach statistical significance are reported in this chapter.

References

Adams, P. L. 1990. Prejudice and exclusion as social trauma. In Noshpitz, J. D. and R. D. Coddington, eds. *Stressors and Adjustment Disorders.* New York: John Wiley & Sons.

Aronowitz, M. 1984. The social and emotional adjustment of immigrant children: A review of the literature. *International Migration Review* 18:237–257.

Athey, J. L. and F. L. Ahearn. 1991. *Refugee Children: Theory, Research, and Services.* Baltimore, MD: Johns Hopkins University Press.

Brandon, P. 1991. Gender differences in young Asian Americans' educational attainment. *Sex Roles* 25:45–61.

Chavez, L. R. 1992. *Shadowed Lives: Undocumented Immigrants in American Society.* Fort Worth, TX: Harcourt Brace College Publishers.

Chu, J. 1998. *Relational Strengths in Adolescent Boys.* Paper presented at the American Psychological Association Annual Convention (106th), San Francisco, CA.

Cobb, S. 1988. Social support as a moderator of life stress. *Psychosomatic Medicine* 3:300–314.

Cohen, S. and S. L. Syme. 1985. Issues in the study and application of social support. In Cohen, S. and S. L. Syme, eds. *Social Support and Health.* Orlando, FL: Academic Press.

Cornell, R. W. 2000. *Men and Boys.* Berkeley, CA: University of California Press.

Das Dasgupta, S. 1998. Gender roles and cultural continuity in the Asian Indian immigrant community in the U.S. *Sex Roles* 38:953–974.

David, D. and R. Brannon. 1976. *The forty-nine percent majority: The male sex role.* Reading, MA: Addison-Wesley.

Desirée Baolian Qin, D. B. 2001. Understanding the adaptation and identity formation of Chinese immigrant adolescent girls: A critical review of the literature. Doctorate Qualifying Paper. Cambridge, MA: Harvard Graduate School of Education.

DeVos, G. A. 1980. Ethnic adaptation and minority status. *Journal of Cross-cultural Psychology* 11:101–124.

Dunn, J. 1988. The shortage of black male students in the college classroom: Consequences and causes. *The Western Journal of Black Studies* 12:73–76.

Espin, O. M. 1987. Psychological impact of migration on Latinas: implications for psychotherapeutic practice. *Psychology of Women Quarterly* 11:489–503.

Falicov, C. J. 1998. *Latino Families in Therapy: A Guide to Multicultural Practices.* New York: The Guilford Press.

Flaskerud, J. H. and R. Uman. 1996. Acculturation and its effects on self-esteem among immigrant Latina women. *Behavioral Medicine* 22:123–133.

Fordham, S. 1996. *Blacked Out: Dilemmas of Race, Identity, and Success at Capital High.* Chicago: University of Chicago Press.

Fuligini, A. 1997. The academic achievement of adolescents from immigrant families: The roles of family background, attitudes, and behavior. *Child Development* 69:351–363.

Garbarino, J. 2000. *Lost Boys: Why Our Sons Turn Violent and How Can We Save Them.* New York: Anchor Books.

Garcia Coll, C. and K. Magnuson. 1997. The Psychological experience of immigration: A developmental perspective. In Booth, A., A. C. Crouter, and N. Landale, eds. *Immigration and the Family: Research and Policy on U.S. Immigrants.* Mahwah, New Jersey, Lawrence Erlbaum Associates.

Gibson, M. A. (1988). *Accommodation without Assimilation: Sikh Immigrants in an American High School.* Ithaca, NY: Cornell University Press.

Gibson, M. A. 1993. Variability in immigrant students' school performance: The U. S. case. *Division G. Newsletter, American Educational Research Association.* Washington, D C.

Glasgow, G. F. and J. Gouse-Shees. 1995. Themes of rejection and abandonment in group work with Caribbean adolescents. *Social Work with Groups* 4:3–27.

Grant, L. and X. L. Rong. 1999. Gender, immigrant generation, ethnicity, and the schooling progress of youth. *Journal of Research & Development in Education* 33:15–26.

Griffin, S. T. 2000. *Successful African-American men: From childhood to adulthood.* New York: Kluwer Academic/Plenum Publishers.

Grinberg, L. and R. Grinberg. 1990. *Psychoanalytic Perspectives on Migration and Exile.* New Haven: Yale University Press.

Hernández, D. and E. Charney, eds. 1998. *From generation to generation: The health and well-being of children of immigrant families.* Washington DC: National Academy Press.

Hoffman, E. 1989. *Lost in Translation: A Life in a New Language.* New York: Penguin Books.

Hongdagneu-Sotelo, P. 1994. *Gendered transitions: Mexican experiences of immigration.* Berkeley, CA: University of California Press.

Hudson, R. J. 1991. Black male adolescent development deviating from the past: Challenges for the future. In Bowser, Benjamin P., ed. *Black male adolescents: Parenting and education in community context.* Lanham, MD: University Press of America.
Jordan, W. J. 1999. Black high school students' participation in school-sponsored sports activities: Effects on school engagement and achievement. *Journal of Negro Education* 68:54–71.
Jurkovic, G. J., G. Kuperminc, J. Perilla, A. Murphy, G. Ibanez, and S. Casey (in press). Ecological and ethical perspectives on filial responsibility: Implications for Primary Prevention with Latino Adolescents. *Journal of Primary Prevention.*
Kao, G. and M. Tienda. 1995. Optimism and achievement: The educational performance of immigrant youth. *Social Science Quarterly* 76:1–19.
Kleinfeld, J. 1998. The myth that schools shortchange girls: Social science in the service of deception. Washington, DC: The Women's Freedom Network.
Kruhlfeld, R. M. 1994. Buddhism, maintenance, and change: Reinterpreting gender in a Lao refugee community. In Camino, L. A. and R. M. Krulfeld, eds. *Reconstructing Lives.* Recapturing Meaning: Refugee Identity, Gender, and Culture Change. Amsterdam: Gordon and Breach.
Landale, N. S. and R. S. Oropesa. 1995. Immigrant children and the children of immigrants: Inter-and intra-ethnic group differences in the United States. *Institute for Public Policy and Social Research.* East Lansing: Michigan State University.
Laosa, L. 1989. *Psychological stress, coping, and the development of the Hispanic immigrant child.* Princeton, NJ: Educational Testing Service.
Leadbeater, B. J., G. P. Kupermine, C. Hertzog, and S. J. Blatt. 1999. A multivariate model of gender differences in adolescents' internalizing and externalizing problems. *Developmental Psychology* 35:1268–1282.
Lee, S. 2001. More than "model minorities" or "delinquents": A look at Hmong American high school students. *Harvard Educational Review* 71:505–528.
Loeber, R., D. P. Farrington, M. Stouthamer-Loeber, and W. B. Van Kammen. 1998. Multiple risk factors for multiproblem boys: Co-occurrence of delinquency, substance use, attention deficit, conduct problems, physical aggression, covert behavior, depressed mood, and shy/withdrawn behavior. In Jessor, Richard, Ed. *New perspectives on adolescent risk behavior.* New York: Cambridge University Press.
Lopez, N. 2004. Interrupting race(ing) and gender(ing) in high school: Second generation Caribbean youth in New York City. In Mollenkopt, J., P. Kasinitz, and M. Waters, eds. *The Second Generation in Metropolitan New York.* New York: Russell Sage Foundation.
Louie, V. 2001. Parents' aspirations and investment: The role of social class in the educational experiences of 1.5 and second-generation Chinese Americans. *Harvard Educational Review* 71:438–474.
Luthar, S. 1999. *Poverty and children's adjustment.* Thousand Oaks, CA: Sage Publications, Inc.
Mizell, C. A. 1999. Life course influences on African American men's depression: Adolescent parental composition, self-concept, and adult earnings. *Journal of Black Studies* 29:467–490.
National Center for Educational Statistics. 2001. *Drop-out rates in the United States: 2000.* Washington, DC: U.S. Department of Education.
Ogbu, J. U. 1978. *Minority Education and Caste: The American System in Cross-Cultural Perspective.* New York: Academic Press.
Olsen, L. 1997. *Made in America: Immigrant students in our public schools.* New York: The New Press.
Orfield, G. 1998. The education of Mexican immigrant children: A commentary. In Suárez-Orozco, Marcelo M., ed. *Crossings: Mexican Immigration in Interdisciplinary Perspective.* Cambridge, MA: David Rockefeller Center for Latin American Studies/Harvard University Press.
Phinney, J. and J. Landin. 1998. Research paradigms and studying ethnic minority families within and across groups. In McLoyd, Vonnie C. and Lawrence Steinberg, eds. *Studying Minority Adolescents: Conceptual, Methodological, and Theoretical Issues.* Mahwah, N.J.: Laurence Erlbaum Associates.
Pierson, L. H. and J. P. Connell. 1992. Effect of grade retention on self-system processes, school engagement, and academic performance. *Journal of Educational Psychology* 84:300–307.
Pollack, W. (1998). *Real Boys: Rescuing our sons from the myths of boyhood.* New York: Holt & Company.
Portes, A. 1998. Social capital: Its origins and applications in modern sociology. *Annual Review of Sociology* 24:1–24.
Portes, A. and R. G. Rumbaut. 2001. *Legacies: The story of the second generation.* Berkeley, CA: University of California Press.
Prince, G. S. 1968. Emotional problems of children reunited with their migrant families in Britain. *Maternal and Child Care* 4:239–241.
Rong, X. L. and F. Brown. 2001. The effects of immigrant generation and ethnicity on educational attainment among young African and Caribbean Blacks in the United States. *Harvard Educational Review* 71:536–565.
Rumbaut, R. 1977. Life events, change, migration and depression. In Fann, W. E., I. Karocan, A.D. Pokorny, and R.L., Williams, eds. *Phenomenology and treatment of depression.* New York: Spectrum.
Rumbaut, R. G. and W. A. Cornelius. 1995. *Becoming American: Acculturation, achievement, and aspirations among children of immigrants.* Annual Meeting of the American Association for the Advancement of Science, Baltimore, MD.
Sarroub, L. K. 2001. The sojourner experience of Yemeni American high school students: An ethnographic portrait. *Harvard Educational Review* 71:390–415.
Shuval, J. (1980). Migration and stress. In Kutasshm, I. L., ed. *Handbook of stress and anxiety: contemporary knowledge, theory, and treatment.* San Francisco, CA: Jossey-Bass.
Smart, J. F. and D. W. Smart. 1995. Acculturation stress of Hispanics: Loss and challenge. *Journal of Counseling and Development* 75:390–396.
Smith, R. 1999. *The education and work mobility of second generation Mexican Americans in New York City: Preliminary reflections on the role of gender, ethnicity, and school structure.* Eastern Sociological Society Meeting, Boston, MA.

Spencer, M. B., D. P. Swanson, and M. Cunningham. 1991. Ethnicity, ethnic identity, and competence formation: Adolescent transition and cultural transformation. *Journal of Negro Education* 60:366–387.

Stanton-Salazar, R. D. 2001. *Manufacturing Hope and Despair: The School and Kin Support Networks of U.S.-Mexican Youth.* New York: Teachers College Press.

Steinberg, L., S. D. Lamborn, S. M. Dornbusch. and N. Darling. 1992. Impact of parenting practices on adolescent achievement: authoritative parenting, school involvement, and encouragement to succeed. *Child Development* 63:1266–1281.

Steinberg, S., B. B. Brown, and S. M. Dornbusch. 1996. *Beyond the Classroom.* New York: Simon and Schuster.

Suárez-Orozco, C. 2000. Identities under siege: Immigration stress and social mirroring among the children of immigrants. In Robben, Anthony and Marcelo Suárez-Orozco, eds. *Cultures Under Siege: Social Violence & Trauma.* Cambridge, MA: University Press.

Suárez-Orozco, C. (2001). Psychocultural actors in the adaptation of immigrant youth: Gendered responses. In Agosín, Marjorie, ed. *Women and Human Rights: A Global Perspective.* Piscataway, NJ: Rutgers University Press.

Suárez-Orozco, C. (in press). Psychosocial factors in the adaptation of immigrant youth: Gendered responses. In Agostin, M., ed. *Women & human rights: A global perspective.* New Jersey: Rutgers University Press.

Suárez-Orozco, C., and M. Suárez-Orozco. 1995. *Transformations: Immigration, family life, and achievement motivation among Latino adolescents.* Stanford, CA: Stanford University Press.

Suárez-Orozco, C. and M. Suárez-Orozco. 2001. *Children of Immigration.* Cambridge, MA: Harvard University Press.

Suárez-Orozco, C., I. Todorova, and J. Louie. 2002. "Making up for lost time:" The experience of separation and reunification among immigrant families. *Family Process.*

Suárez-Orozco, M. 1998. *Crossings: Mexican immigration in interdisciplinary perspectives.* Cambridge, MA: David Rockefeller Center for Latin American Studies and Harvard University Press.

Sung, B. L. 1987. *The adjustment experience of Chinese immigrant children in New York City.* New York: Center for Migration Studies.

Tatum, B. 1997. *"Why Are All the Black Kids Sitting Together in the Cafeteria?" And Other Conversations About Race.* New York: Basic Books.

Thorne, B. 1997. Children and Gender: Construction of Difference. In Gergen, Mary M. and Sara N. Davis, eds. *Towards a new psychology of gender.* New York: Routledge.

U.S. Department of Education. 1995. *Conditions of education 1995.* Washington, DC: National Center for Educational Statistics.

Valenzuela, A. 1999. Gender roles and settlement activities among children and their immigrant families. *American Behavioral Scientist* 42:720–742.

Vernez, G., A. Abrahamse, and D. Quigley. 1996. *How Immigrants Fare in U.S. Education.* Santa Monica, CA: Rand.

Vigil, J. D. 1988. *Barrio Gangs: Street Life and Identity in Southern California.* Austin, TX: University of Texas Press.

Waters, M. 1996. The intersection of gender, race, and ethnicity in identity development of Caribbean American teens. In Leadbeater, B. J. R. and N. Way, eds. *Urban Girls: Resisting stereotypes, creating identities.* New York, New York University Press.

Weissbourd, R. 1996. *The Vulnerable Child.* Reading, MA: Perseus Books.

Wick, J. W. 1990. *Technical Manual and Names for School Attitude Measure.* Chicago: American Testronics.

Wills, T. A. 1985. Supportive functions of interpersonal relationships. In S. Cohen and S. L. Syme, eds. *Social Support and Health.* Orlando, FL: Academic Press.

Permissions

Suárez-Orozco, Marcelo M. 2002. "Right Moves? Immigration, Globalization, Utopia and Dystopia," in Nancy Foner (ed), *American Arrivals: Anthropology Engages the New Immigration.* Copyright © 2003 by the School of American Research, Santa Fe. Reprinted by permission of publisher.

Massey, Douglas S., Jorge Durand, and Nolan J. Malone. 2002. "Principles of Operation: Theories of International Migration," in *Beyond Smoke and Mirrors: Mexican Immigration in the Era of Economic Integration.* ©2002 Russell Sage Foundation, 112 East 64th Street, New York, NY 10021. Reprinted with permission.

Alba, Richard and Victor Nee. 1997. "Rethinking Assimilation Theory for a New Era of Immigration." *International Migration Review* 31(4):826-874.

Suárez-Orozco, Marcelo M. 2000. "Everything You Ever Wanted to Know About Assimilation But Were Afraid To Ask." In *Engaging Cultural Differences*, edited by Richard Shweder, Martha Minow, and Hazel Rose Markus. ©2002 Russell Sage Foundation, 112 East 64th Street, New York, NY 10021. Reprinted with permission.

Portes, Alejandro and Min Zhou. 1993. "The New Second Generation: Segmented Assimilation and Its Variants." *Annals of the American Academy of Political and Social Science* 530: 74-96, copyright ©1993 by American Academy of Political and Social Science. Reprinted by permission of Sage Publications, Inc.

García Coll, Cynthia and Katherine Magnuson. 1997. "The Psychological Experience of Immigration: A Developmental Perspective," in *Immigration and the Family: Research and Policy on U.S. Immigrants,* edited by A. Booth, A.C. Crouter, and N. Landale. Mahwah, NJ: Lawrence Erlbaum Associates, Inc. Reprinted by permission.

Suárez-Orozco, Carola. 2000. "Identities Under Siege: Immigration Stress and Social Mirroring Among the Children of Immigrants," in *Cultures Under Siege: Collective Violence and Trauma*, edited by Antonius C. G. M. Robben and Marcelo M. Suárez-Orozco. Cambridge, England: Cambridge University Press. Reprinted with the permission of Cambridge University Press.

Foner, Nancy. 1997. "The Immigrant Family: Cultural Legacies and Cultural Changes," *International Migration Review* 31(4):961-975.

Hondagneu-Sotelo, Pierrette. 2002. "Families on the Frontier: From Braceros in the Fields to Braceras in the Home," in *Latinos: Remaking America,* edited by Marcelo M. Suàrez-Orozco and Mariela Páez. Berkeley, CA and Cambridge, MA: University of California Press and David Rockefeller Center for Latin American Studies. ©2002 The Regents of the University of California. Reprinted by permission.

Suárez-Orozco, Carola, Irina L. G. Todorova, and Josephine Louie 2003. "Making Up For Lost Time: The Experience of Separation and Reunification Among Immigrant Families." *Family Process* 41(1):625-643. Reprinted by permission.

Falicov, Celia Jaes. 2002. "Ambiguous Loss: Risk and Resilience in Latino Immigrant Families," in *Latinos: Remaking America,* edited by Marcelo M. Suàrez-Orozco and Mariela Páez. Berkeley, CA and Cambridge, MA: University of California Press and David Rockefeller Center for Latin American Studies. ©2002 The Regents of the University of California. Reprinted by permission.

Ainslie, Ricardo 1998. "Cultural Mourning, Immigration, and Engagement: Vignettes from the Mexican Experience," in *Crossings: Mexican Immigration in Interdisciplinary Perspectives,* edited by Marcelo Suárez-Orozco. Cambridge, MA: The David Rockefeller Center for Latin American Studies and Harvard University Press. Reprinted by permission.

Gándara, Patricia. 2002. "Learning English in California: Guideposts for the Nation," in *Latinos: Remaking America,* edited by Marcelo M. Suàrez-Orozco and Mariela Páez. Berkeley, CA and Cambridge, MA: University of California Press and David Rockefeller Center for Latin American Studies. ©2002 The Regents of the University of California. Reprinted by permission.

August, Diane and Kenji Hakuta. 1997. "Bilingualism and Second-Language Learning," in *Improving Schooling for Language-Minority Children: A Research Agenda.* Washington, DC: National Academies Press. Reprinted by permission.

Willig, Ann C. 1985. "A Meta-Analysis of Selected Studies on the Effectiveness of Bilingual Education," *Review of Educational Research* 55(3):269-317. ©1985 by the American Educational Research Association. Reproduced with permission of the publisher.

Fillmore, Lily Wong. 1991. "When Learning a Second Language Means Losing the First." *Early Childhood Research Quarterly* 6:323-346. Reprinted by permission.

Portes, Alejandro and Dag MacLeod. 1996. "Educational Progress of Children of Immigrants: The Roles of Class, Ethnicity, and School Context," *Sociology of Education* 69: 255-275. ©1996 American Sociological Association. Reprinted by permission of the authors and publisher.

Kao, Grace and Marta Tienda. 1995. "Optimism and Achievement: The Educational Performance of Immigrant Youth." *Social Science Quarterly* 76(1):1-19.

Suárez-Orozco, Carola and Desirée B. Qin. 2002. "Immigrant Boys' Experiences in U.S. Schools," in *Adolescent Boys in Context*, edited by N. Way and Judy Chu. New York: New York University Press. Reprinted by permission.

Index

('n' indicates a note; 't' indicates a table)

C

D

E